447

+15·50

D1595780

Stress and Contradiction in Modern Capitalism

Public Policy and The Theory of the State

Edited by

Leon N. Lindberg
University of Wisconsin

Robert Alford
University of California-Santa Cruz

Colin Crouch
London School of Economics and
Political Science

Claus Offe
University of Bielefeld

Lexington Books
D.C. Heath and Company
Lexington, Massachusetts
Toronto   London

Library of Congress Cataloging in Publication Data

Main entry under title:

Stress and contradiction in modern capitalism.

    Papers from an international conference on "Patterns of Change in Advanced Industrial Society: Priorities for Social Science Research in the 1970's and 1980's", held in Nov., 1973 at Monterosso-al-Mare, Genoa: sponsored by the Council for European Studies and Giovanni Agnelli Foundation.
    Includes bibliographical references.
    1. Economic policy—Congresses. 2. Capitalism—Congresses. I. Lindberg, Leon N. II. Council for European Studies. III. Fondazione Giovanni Agnelli.

HD82.S8457	338.9	75-188
ISBN 0-669-99382-4		

Second printing October 1977.

Published simultaneously in Canada

Printed in the United States of America

International Standard Book Number: 0-669-99382-4

Library of Congress Catalog Card Number: 75-188

To the Memory of
Stephen Hymer

Contents

Preface   vii

General Introduction, *Leon N. Lindberg*   ix

Part I   **Planning Versus the Market**   1

            Introduction to Part I, *Robert R. Alford*   3

Chapter 1   Is Democratic Control of Capitalist Economies Possible?
Andrew Martin   13

Chapter 2   From Permacrisis to Real Crisis in French Social Security:
The Limits to Normal Politics, *Stephen S. Cohen and
Charles Goldfinger*   57

Chapter 3   The Economist and the Economic Roles of the Political
Authority in Advanced Industrial Societies, *Robert A. Solo*   99

Chapter 4   Toward a Politics of Economics: The State of Permanent
Receivership, *Theodore J. Lowi*   115

Chapter 5   The Theory of the Capitalist State and the Problem of
Policy Formation, *Claus Offe*   125

Chapter 6   Paradigms of Relations Between State and Society,
Robert R. Alford   145

Part II   **Inequality Versus Opportunity**   161

            Introduction to Part II, *Colin Crouch*   163

Chapter 7   Advanced Capitalism, Collective Consumption, and
Urban Contradictions: New Sources of Inequality and
New Models for Change, *Manuel Castells*   175

Chapter 8   Equality, Inflation, and Wage Control, *Martin Rein and
Peter Marris*   199

Chapter 9   The Drive for Equality: Experience of Incomes
              Policy in Britain, *Colin Crouch*   215

Part III   **Legitimacy Versus Efficiency**   243

              Introduction to Part III, *Claus Offe*   245

Chapter 10   Legitimacy and the Directive Capacity of the Political
              System, *Renate Mayntz*   261

Chapter 11   The Ideology of Intellectuals and Other People in the
              Development of Capitalism, *Michael Mann*   275

Chapter 12   Symbolism in Politics, *Murray Edelman*   309

Chapter 13   Politics as Sports: An Interpretation of the Political
              Ascendancy of the Sports Metaphor in America,
              Isaac Balbus   321

Part IV   **Dominance Versus Vulnerability**   337

              Introduction to Part IV, *Leon N. Lindberg*   339

Chapter 14   International Politics and International Economics: A
              Radical Approach, *Stephen Hymer*   355

Chapter 15   The International Politics of Postindustrial Societies: The
              Role of the Multinational Corporation, *James R. Kurth* 373

Chapter 16   Dominant States and Vulnerable Societies: The East-
              West Case, *Pierre Hassner*   393

Chapter 17   Multinational Corporations, National Economic Policies,
              and Labor Unions, *Alberto Martinelli*   425

              About the Contributors   445

              About the Editors   449

Preface

This book finds its origin in an international conference on "Patterns of Change in Advanced Industrial Society: Priorities for Social Science Research in the 1970s and 1980s," held in November 1973 at Monterosso-al-Mare on the Ligurian coast south of Genoa. The conference was sponsored by the Council for European Studies and the Giovanni Agnelli Foundation, and was the first in a series of activities initiated by the Council for European Studies and designed to mobilize resources, to focus research, and to encourage an interdisciplinary and European-American dialogue on the implications of contemporary changes in advanced societies and on the kind of future that may be emerging. Our concern was to focus on the institutional dilemmas, conflicts, or contradictions that seemed to be provoked by multifold social, economic and political changes and the interactions among them. We saw these as representing potential transformation processes, catalysts, or choice points for advanced industrial societies over several decades to come.

These same general programmatic concerns were continued and further elaborated in 1974 in three conferences: "Sources of Discontent and Institutional Innovation in Advanced Industrial Societies" (held jointly with the European Institute of Columbia University),[1] "Change and Public Policy" in May at Bellagio (conducted with the support of the Rockefeller Foundation and the Agnelli Foundation), and "Twentieth Century Capitalism: State, Economy and Society" held in Cambridge, Massachusetts in September.[2] In 1975 The Council for European Studies, in cooperation with the German Marshall Fund of the United States, initiated a program of Research Planning Groups in Comparative Public Policy Research, which shares many of the same preoccupations with contemporary policy problems of industrial society.[3]

Most of the chapters in this book come directly out of the Monterosso conference. The design for that conference and for this book was the work of a committee comprised of Robert Alford (Sociology, United States), Gianni Giannotti (Sociology, Italy), John Goldthorpe (Sociology, United Kingdom), Leon N. Lindberg (Political Science, United States), Claus Offe (Sociology, West Germany), and Jean-Jacques Salamon (Organization for Economic Cooperation and Development, Paris). It was our intention to stimulate discussion among researchers, from different disciplines and different nations, on the epistemological, methodological, substantive, and operational issues raised by macro-analyses of complex social systems. We wanted to clarify and make more explicit the assumptions that may underlie such work, and to stimulate a confrontation of rival approaches to the analysis of the contemporary dynamics of industrialized societies, in such a way that diverging ideas might become critical instances for each other that would help determine how to organize the research process.

The organization of this book follows in a general way the structure of the Monterosso conference. A few chapters appear here more or less in the form in which they were originally presented, but in most cases considerable revision was done or entirely new chapters were written. The discussions at Monterosso were extraordinarily lively and provocative, and some reflection of that atmosphere can be discerned in the pages that follow. The conference organizers, and the authors of these chapters, owe an inestimable debt to all those who participated[4] in that extended dialogue on the rocky shores of the Cinquaterre. Special thanks are due to the staff of the Hotel Porto Roca, who provided a perfect physical and gastronomic environment, and to the Giovanni Agnelli Foundation, which made it all possible.

L.N.L.

Notes

1. "Sources of Discontent and Institutional Innovation in Advanced Industrial Societies," held at the School of International Affairs, Columbia University, March 21-23, 1974. See summary in *European Studies Newsletter,* October 1974, vol. IV, no. 1, p. 3.
2. "Twentieth-Century Capitalism: State, Economy, and Society," held at the Harvard Faculty Club September 10-13, 1974, organized and chaired by Gerald Feldman (University of California, Berkeley) and Charles Maier (Harvard). See summary in *European Studies Newsletter,* January 1975, vol. IV, no. 4, pp. 4-6.
3. See description in Leon N. Lindberg, "CES Launches New Research-Related Activities in Public Policy," *European Studies Newsletter,* March 1975, vol. IV., no. 5, pp. 2-7.
4. Participants in the Monterosso Conference:

Robert A. Alford	Pierre Hassner	Renate Mayntz
Isaac Balbus	Volker Hauff	James O'Connor
Wendell Bell	Samuel P. Huntington	Claus Offe
Suzanne Berger	Stephen Hymer	Gianfranco Pasquino
Manuel Castells	Sten Johansson	Nicos Poulantzas
Bernard Cazes	Michael Kidron	Martin Rein
Colin Crouch	James Kurth	John G. Ruggie
Gianni Gianotti	Jacques Lautman	Robert Solo
Pier-Paolo Giglioli	Leon N. Lindberg	Michael Stewart
John Goldthorpe	Theodore J. Lowi	Aaron Wildavsky
Sverker Gustavsson	Alberto Martinelli	
Donald Hancock	Michael Mann	

General Introduction

Leon N. Lindberg

This book is intended to be a general call for comparative research on advanced capitalist societies, combining analysis of macro-societal change processes, a concern for critical political structures (notably the state), and a focus on public policy problems and the strategies of dominant and counter elites. The internal stability and external relationships of all of these societies are presently in flux, and for the first time since the 1940s, important transformations, indeed convulsions, in political arrangements seem in the offing. Advanced capitalist societies may be at a branching point in their overall development, and the policy choices made in the years to come are likely to be decisive. Great ideological debates are with us once again, recalling the 1920s and 1930s, and reminding us of the limitations of social science theories that only recently foresaw primary secular trends toward consensus, stability, and rationality, and enhanced control over the natural and social environment.

The editors and authors of this book are united in their conviction that the social sciences have an important role in describing these changes, explaining them, and providing some useful knowledge for policy analysis for those who seek to influence the scope and direction of the state and of public policies. At least four foci for research seem important:

1. Establishing or postulating those aspects of the contemporary situation that seem to threaten the viability and stability of existing structures and policies;
2. Specifying the linkages whereby these trends may induce structural change and policy failure or policy innovation;
3. Identifying the most salient issues, arenas, interactions, institutions, and processes in a period of crisis or "dissynchronization;"
4. Developing analytical tools appropriate both to the assessment of the long-term consequences of particular structural or policy changes, and to their normative valuation.

We focus our analyses of the dynamic interactions among societal, structural, and policy change upon four central topics. These are phrased in terms of four dilemmas or contradictions: planning versus the market, inequality versus opportunity, efficiency versus legitimacy, dominance versus vulnerability. Part I on *planning versus the market* examines various facets of the changes in the role of the state in the economy of Western capitalist societies since World

War II, and different rates of speed and direction from one country to another. The growth of the public sector in services, welfare, and even production, the regulation, taxation and subsidy of the private sector by the state, the fiscal crisis of the state faced with expanding demands but limited capabilities, and the spreading of incomes policies, are only a few of the many types of state action vis-à-vis the economy which have either been instituted or greatly increased in the last two decades. Part II on *inequality versus opportunity* examines the ways in which old and new sources of inequality of social condition restrict equalities of opportunity in Western capitalist societies. Special attention is given to those policy issues around which sustained contemporary debates about inequality are organized, viz. urban social services, incomes policies, etc. Part III on *efficiency versus legitimacy* focuses on the apparent disjunction between the increased load of tasks undertaken by modern capitalist governments and their diminishing capabilities to assure legitimation of such powers and tasks. For some, the central problem posed by this disjuncture is that an erosion of legitimacy does not imply any erosion of the power of ruling elites, but merely reinforces despair and encourages resort to repression. For others, the problem is how authority, which must be exercised more frequently and on a widening scale of time and space in unfamiliar issues of vital importance, can be organized and made acceptable. Part IV on *dominance versus vulnerability* shifts the analysis to how the international dimensions of advanced capitalist societies induce, impinge upon, or interact with, patterns of domestic, structural and policy change. Advanced capitalist nations have come to occupy positions of dominance in the international political economy, but their extensive international involvement has also produced new vulnerabilities, some of whose dimensions and destabilizing consequences have become clearer since the Yom Kippur War and the global petroleum crisis.

In approaching these complex topics we are guided by a strong sense of the partial and contingent nature of the several intellectual paradigms which organize social science inquiry. Social science—indeed all science—consists of both "discovered" and "invented" order. But in the social sciences, as Sir Geoffrey Vickers has argued,[1] the regularities we observe owe more to our efforts to impose mutually inconsistent "orders," which change over time and may only be confirmed or disconfirmed by events to which the analyst himself contributes. And this, suggests Vickers, weakens the confidence, or at least the single mindedness, with which we address ourselves to our most human function, that of imposing order on our experience and thus shaping our own future.

Consequently we seek to build into this book a diversity of analytical perspectives on contemporary capitalism. We try to assure a rough parity between American and European voices, and among three partially competing, partially overlapping paradigms of state-society relations: the pluralist, the elitist, and the Marxist (see Robert Alford's Introduction to Part I and his

Chapter 6). The dialogue/confrontation among Marxists and non-Marxists, whether they be labelled "liberal," "pluralist," or even "elitist," is, I think, particularly fruitful. The very title of this book, *Stress and Contradiction in Modern Capitalism: Public Policy and The Theory of the State,* symbolizes this interaction of ideological positions and analytical styles and paradigms. We began with the rather innocuous working title, "Patterns of Change in Advanced Industrial Societies: Priorities for Social Science Research in the 1970s and 1980s." It soon became clear, however, that our central preoccupation was capitalism and not industrialism, and that we shared a priority concern for the institutions, strategies, and policies of active intervention in change and transformation. In his introduction to Part III, Claus Offe notes the different roles and substantive implications of concepts and conceptual dichotomies in liberal social theory and in the Marxist theoretical tradition. Our title embodies two such contrasts: the one between the liberal concept of societal *stress* (or dilemma) and the Marxist concept of *contradiction;* the other between the current and fashionable liberal preoccupation with *public policy,* seen as political adaptation or "public learning" in the face of change, and the Marxist concern with *the theory of the state,* viewed in terms of a theory of social reproduction.

As I have noted above, all authors share a principal preoccupation with the state and with what the state does. Offe identifies this as the main area of convergence between liberal and Marxist theories. Both groups see the state as the major institutional system in advanced capitalist society that might perform the function of overcoming policy dilemmas or contradictions. Marxists differ, suggests Offe, in that they see the state's corrective and adaptive mechanisms for reconciling or repressing contradictions as themselves involved in the contradictions inherent in the capitalist mode of production. In any case, public policy and the theory of the state would seem to be an especially promising arena for an intellectual dialogue which we hope will stimulate empirical research and further theoretical development.

If this book, in which many flowers bloom in dazzling and often clashing combinations, has a principal message for future social science research, it is the following: Let the contemporary fashions of public policy research (theories of rational choice, systems analysis, PPBS, social indicators, evaluation research, preoccupation with quantification and methodological sophistication, etc.) and the preferences of governmental and foundation sponsors, not confine or constrain such inquiry to a narrowly conceived "policy science approach." I would urge that we heed Charles E. Lindbloom's warning that the policy sciences, and he takes economics to be the best example, are inherently conservative and superficial. Economics (and policy science) is conservative, says Lindbloom, because it does not ask radical questions about the social structure, and superficial because it considers only marginal changes within a given system of public policies. What is most needed in the social sciences is rather "the capacity to say something about sequences of social behavior and institutional organization."[2]

In my own view, the thrust of this book is that future comparative policy research should satisfy at least four broad criteria.

First, particular attention ought to be given to the complex problems of *measuring and conceptualizing policy content.* The kinds of data most readily at hand and most susceptible to quantification and therefore the most frequently used, (for example, data on governmental expenditures for welfare, warfare, or other purposes) may often produce misleading conclusions and ignore the most interesting issues. We need to develop policy conceptualizations that recognize hierarchies among policies, that can comprehend the extent to which particular policy areas are nested within, constrained by, or given meaning by actions in other policy areas. For example, Harold Wilensky's stimulating recent book on *The Welfare State and Inequality*[3] draws conclusions about the determinants of differences in welfare state effort on the basis of a conceptualization of "welfare output," meaning public expenditures for health, education, housing, pensions, etc., as a percent of GNP. Such a conceptualization fails to take into account the type of program, style of administration, varying distributive intent and distributive consequences of different types of programs, or whether policies are financed by means of progressive or regressive taxation. Most importantly, any sectoral or expenditure approach to public policy runs the risk of under-rating the parameter-setting role of macroeconomic policies pursued by the state in order to maintain that mix of full employment, price stability, investment, redistribution, growth, and balance of payments stability considered desirable or attainable by dominant elites. As Hugh Heclo[4] concluded from his survey of Swedish and British social policy in the 19th and 20th centuries: social policy develops "in the interstices allowed to it" by prevailing economic policies and economic orthodoxies. This suggests priority attention to how such policies are made and how such orthodoxies are sustained and "reproduced."

Second, policy research should be based on *in-depth longitudinal analysis* that views policy and change in policy as adaptation to changing conditions and changing elite and mass perceptions, attitudes, and values. Understanding the texture of policy in any given country, and relating environmental and growth factors to intermediate structural and political variables to ideological and systemic variables, requires historical analysis of the circumstances surrounding the emergence of particular programs and changes in programs, as well as a knowledge of the characteristic development path or experiences of particular countries. The prevailing preference in policy research for cross-sectional aggregate data analysis does not usually permit one to address questions of this kind.

Third, policy researchers should be especially wary of the constraining implications of the *model or conceptualization of the policy process* that underlies their work. Policy research has seen policy variously as basically a function of demands emanating from socio-economic environments, or of the internal processes whereby public actors make choices and respond to their consequences, or of processes of rational choice and calculation, or of relationships between public and private power, or of characteristics of particular policy arenas, or of international dependencies and transnational diffusion or penetration, or of the state as an autonomous actor responding to its own (or to capitalism's) "reproductive needs." At this early stage in systematic comparative policy research, we should, to quote Philippe Schmitter,

> eschew premature closure; emphasize the high degree of uncertainty, indeterminism and experimentation involved in policy choice; make very modest and tentative pretensions to understanding; admit a considerable plurality of types, concepts and motives; not be excessively concerned with or restricted to immediately empirical and especially quantitatively measurable indicators; and to recognize clearly its limitations in dealing with the accidental and/or brilliantly innovative act.[5]

Fourth, we must learn more about the relationships between policy content and *the characteristic institutions of capitalism, and about differences in the historical evolution and specific forms of the capitalist state.* Failure to move to this macroanalytic level, and to divest ourselves of our reluctance to name the system of capitalism will seriously limit the power of policy research to contribute meaningfully to an understanding of the issues of the day. In my view, Wilensky's very important work suffers in this regard. He specifically rejects political system, economic system, or elite ideology as useful explanatory variables, preferring more "concrete, sharper contrasts" in social, political, and economic organization. The middle-range structural variables to which he looks for explanations of differences in public policy (centralization of government, shape of stratification order and mobility rates, corporatist styles of politics, organization of the working class, cleavage structure, position of the military) are, of course, important. But they are treated by Wilensky essentially as separate autonomous analytical variables. Yet they can be meaningfully seen also as *configurations* indicating different patterns of capitalist development and different forms of the capitalist state, and hence as reflective of social class interests and dominant ideologies. Such middle-range factors then represent to some extent, as yet undetermined, the impacts of past policies and historical accretions of power. We are not only interested in centralization-decentralization, but in the origins of such arrangements, how they are kept in place in the face of change, and who gains or loses. The fact that public bureaucracies differ in power and assertiveness from one country to another or one issue area to another is interesting in itself but may also have to do with political and economic system characteristics, especially with the power and ideologies of organized private interests.

Finally, focus at this level may enable us to explore more thoroughly the complex origins of the policy paradigms, or schema, or language systems that define for any set of policy makers what will be seen as problemmatic and as the range of acceptable policy alternatives. There is reason to suppose that such policy paradigms derive not only from the historical experience of particular polities, but more importantly, from the general forms of economic and political organization and of ideological hegemony in a society. Policy paradigms, then, not only guide and rationalize the decision process; they may also reflect and seek to justify and perpetuate the power resources and relationships of the dominant groups in society.

Notes

1. Geoffrey Vickers, *Freedom in a Rocking Boat* (Harmondsworth, Middlesex: Penguin Books, 1972), Ch. 8.
2. Charles E. Lindbloom, "Integration of Economics and the Other Social Sciences through Policy Analysis," in James C. Charlesworth, *Integration of the Social Sciences Through Policy Analysis* (Philadelphia: American Academy of Political and Social Science, 1972), p. 12.
3. Harold Wilensky, *The Welfare State and Inequality* (Berkeley: University of California Press, 1975).
4. Hugh Heclo, *Modern Social Politics in Britain and Sweden* (New Haven: Yale University Press, 1974), p. 312.
5. Philippe C. Schmitter, "Notes Toward a Political Economic Conceptualization of Policy-Making in Latin America" (unpublished manuscript), p. 30.

**Part I
Planning Versus the Market**

Introduction to Part I
Robert R. Alford

The chapters in part I can be analyzed fruitfully at two different levels: first, for their substantive content, and, second, for their theoretical or (to use the currently popular term) paradigmatic implications. The expansion of state activity and specifically the increasing involvement of the state in overall economic planning and actual production of a number of vital services are taken as given by all the authors in this part, but they give diverse answers to the question of the meaning of this growth, its consequences, and its future. The answer from a pluralist perspective is that this growth is an undesirable and dysfunctional expansion of the traditional state functions of mediating social conflicts and maintaining the basic conditions of social order and economic growth. The answer from a liberal-bureaucratic or elite perspective is that this growth is a necessary elite response to the increasing complexity of the tasks of coordinating the industrial economy. The answer from a class perspective is that this growth simultaneously performs the functions of maintaining capital accumulation, but also of mystifying that function by legitimating state activity as a solution to social problems. Unfortunately, none of the chapters presents a full-fledged pluralist position, since all of their authors believe that expanded state activity of political authority is inevitable. The authors disagree, however, on how and why this expansion is related to the structure and functions of a capitalist economy, and this disagreement brings up the theoretical or paradigmatic issues—what are the appropriate assumptions and hypotheses that will clarify the issues and lead to greater understanding?

My introduction is intended to sharpen the issues by pointing to the differences in substantive assumption, theoretical interpretation, and implications in the chapters, not to blur the issues and resolve them by verbal synthesis. The questions involved are critically important and they must be posed sharply and clearly before answers can be sought systematically.

Political Scientist Andrew Martin's chapter and Economist and Urban Planner Stephen Cohen's and Regional Planner Charles Goldfinger's chapters are substantive analyses that start from accounts of the strategies of political parties and governmental elites to control social policies, and the ways in which these strategies stem from the interests of social groups and classes. Cohen and Goldfinger deal with social security in France; Martin considers full employment, incomes policy, pensions, and inflation in the United States, Britain, and Sweden. The authors of both chapters are dissatisfied

with the assumptions and questions that underlie mainstream economics and
political science in the United States, and they counterpose alternative assumptions and questions. For Martin, the question that is not ordinarily asked is:
Is democratic control of capitalism possible? For Cohen and Goldfinger: How
can we explain structural change and not merely incremental changes in the
political economy?

With Economist Robert Solo's chapter we move more directly to a challenge of the inadequacies of the orthodox economics paradigm to deal with
problems of political authority. Theodore Lowi, a political scientist, questions
whether Solo has moved far enough away from those assumptions. Sociologist
Claus Offe, starting from the standpoint of class analysis, attempts to integrate
the pluralist and elite paradigms into the framework of a theory of the basic
functions and structural characteristics of the capitalist state. Finally, my own
chapter attempts to disentangle the bases upon which various paradigms of
the state define its essential characteristics in relationship to a theory of social
structure and social change, although it does not assess the historical or substantive grounds for the various claims made, explicitly or implicitly, by the
three paradigms.

Without repeating the argument made in greater detail later in my own
chapter, I will use the analytic concepts presented there to comment upon the
issues raised by the various papers in this part. My purpose, of course, is to lend
to those concepts greater credibility by showing their analytic usefulness in
exposing the latent structure of argument and evidence in these chapters.

Andrew Martin's chapter is an excellent example of the comparative
method used by political scientists. He contrasts, coherently and logically,
the United States, Britain, and Sweden with respect to the electoral fortunes
of the Democratic, Labor, and Social Democratic parties throughout their
history, and he relates those fortunes to the general economic situation facing
them during critical elections. From these three cases he draws lessons relevant
to the general issues in the pluralist theory of the requirements for democracy:
some chance for alternation of parties in office, some significant degree of
responsiveness of political elites to social groups, particularly those less fortunately provided for by the capitalist economy. The classic argument that votes
(potential political power) can compensate for wealth (private economic power)
is assessed in the context of the relevant question: Is it necessary for a working-
class-based party to be in power *permanently* in order for the inherent structural
advantages of capital over labor to be offset, and for policies insuring reasonably
full employment and reasonably humane welfare systems to be continued?

Martin's answer, based on the period up to the 1960s, is pessimistic for the
United States and British experience but qualifiedly optimistic for the Swedish
experience. The Social Democratic party in Sweden, benefiting not only from
political skills and good timing, but also from a favorable economic situation,
managed to institute a policy favoring full employment without paying the

price of excessive inflation that would erode the benefits of welfare state policy. Martin's ultimate evaluation of this historical case, however, is negative because of the dependence of the national economy upon the world system.

Martin's pointed contrast of the varying success of United States, British, and Swedish labor-controlled political parties is directed, as already indicated, to the question: Is democratic control of capitalist economies possible? He rejects without argument or even mention the conservative position that there is no problem in maintaining democracy in capitalist economies because capitalism itself *is* democracy, because a free market in jobs, social and geographic mobility, and a responsiveness of firms to consumer preferences constitute an indispensable component of, as well as condition for, democracy. He also rejects by implication the possibility of transcending permanently the structural characteristics of Western capitalist economies by not dealing with the potential politics of socialism that might go beyond the traditional welfare state position of the Social Democratic regimes of Britain and Sweden. Yet, he ends with the pessimistic observation that the growth of multinational firms and the breakdown of the world monetary system have made national political power impotent, even if semipermanently held by a working-class party. Surely this observation must be the starting point for a contemporary analysis of the prospects for democracy, not the end.

One analytic comment might be made. The term "counter-elite" used by Martin to describe the political leaders of the Social Democratic or Labor parties may be misleading if it assumes the analytic equivalence of any and all "elites." The term suggests that the leaders or officials of large organizations, whether party, business, or labor, can be compared as if different structural locations are essentially equivalent. Such a usage may not be useful if the potential power of the organizations is not equivalent, that is, if one form of organization possesses "systemic" power (power based upon the dominant institutions of the society) greater than that of other organizations. Martin's concept of a "capitalist economy," although theoretically at the macrosocietal level, is reduced operationally to the micro level: the behavior of capitalist firms, of business interest groups in politics, or of the peak organizations negotiating with government and labor over economic policy. He makes the assumption that such organizations and groups share durable interests in profit and capital accumulation, but the conceptual decision to deal with specific actors allows him to equate their participation with that of labor or a political party. This theoretical stance seems somewhat incompatible with his substantive position that private economic control over the basic resources of the society is fundamentally incompatible with social policies designed simultaneously to reduce income inequality, guarantee full employment, and maintain inflation at a minimum level.

Martin is certainly aware of the limitations of public policy in dealing with intractable problems of managing a capitalist economy, particularly the combination of unemployment and inflation. His analytic position, however, assumes that gradual, incremental, bargaining politics focused upon maintaining or shifting electoral majorities is the appropriate strategy. At least he does not mention an alternative for the 1970s. At this point he neglects the implications of his own analysis, which showed that the Democratic, Labor, and Social Democratic parties emerged as the consequence of an economic crisis and the emergence of powerful new movements. There seems to be no reason to assume that these political possibilities no longer exist.

However, what is striking from Stephen Cohen's and Charles Goldfinger's evidence, given in the next chapter, is the continuing capacity of the French political system to withstand the demands of strong Left unions and parties. The path of crisis in French social security, growth, reform, demands, and further crisis is, at least in its general outlines, remarkably similar in the two countries, however much the details of events differ. The Cohen-Goldfinger chapter calls for, if only by implication, serious comparative investigation of these similarities and differences in the politics and economics of developments in the service sector. In a system like the United States, where Left parties and unions have not emerged with self-consciously independent political programs, there are few ideological defenses against the liberal arguments for individual compensation for unemployment, low income, and poor health.

Significant reform of health care has been impossible in France, as in the United States, because of a basic structural fact: private provision but public funding without controls, as Cohen and Goldfinger point out. In effect, risks and costs for the providers have been socialized, but the benefits and profits have been privately appropriated. Subsidy of demand by the state, but a failure to control supply, is the basic tension or contradiction leading to the explosive rise of costs. Simply to leave the analysis there, however, is to make plausible the technocratic recipe for reform: control supply also through additional bureaucratic regulation. This strategy for reform falls within the elite paradigm: faith in the potential power of knowledge to guide and control organizational elites independently of economic forces. This potential power of elites is relied upon to cut through the stalemate of pluralist bargains and compromises and to establish rational and planned social policies. Whether this is Cohen's and Goldfinger's position is not clear from the chapter.

Cohen and Goldfinger suggest that there are two political systems: one, the traditional political arena focused upon by the pluralist model of "normal" politics—participation, demands, party and elite strategies of response—that result in incremental growth of social security budgets. This model, they argue, does not recognize the second political system: the symbiosis of the giant corporations with segments of the state bureaucracy, which successfully insulates critical decisions affecting the economy from the first political system. Labeling this a second *political* system evades an important theoretical and methodological question: How can a theoretical framework be created to deal adequately with both the "traditional" political system and

its internal processes and the larger economic and social structure that has pervasive effects upon it. A model of parallel and interpenetrating structures of
power—part of the elite paradigm—seems to be implicitly what Cohen and
Goldfinger mean by the concept of two political systems.

However, the third alternative—class analysis—is also compatible with their
argument. Cohen's and Goldfinger's implicit theoretical framework seems
consistent with the assumption that the class relations and class structures of
French society have conditioned in specific ways the historical emergence and
form of the social security system in that country. The Left unions and parties
have an ideological commitment to a class definition of "solidarity" and do
not want welfare and social security to be redefined as compensation for the
social costs of capitalism. Both the loading of the costs of various social programs onto the social security budget since 1962 and the successful attempt to
insert a means test into the "salaire unique" were first steps toward a transformation of social security from a "universalistic system of mutual social protection to a selective system of compensation for injustices and inequalities."

Cohen's and Goldfinger's chapter contrasts the paradigm of "normal" or
pluralist politics with an alternative approach that is never explicitly specified
except by contrast. The alternative approach emphasizes structural rather
than incremental change, the domination of essential social forces as the key
to power rather than bargaining among relatively equal parties, and the insulation of critical decisions from influence by a coalition between business and
the state bureaucracy rather than the interplay of interests, demands, and
elite response within traditional political arenas. By implication. Cohen and
Goldfinger reject the possibility of long-range capitalist planning because of
the presence of forces beyond the control of the state.

Economist Robert Solo, representing a point of view beginning from
traditional economics but critical of its paradigm, assumes that the "political
authority" is obliged to play a central role in all advanced industrial economies. He traces three stages in the growth of the role of the political authority,
from "housekeeping" the emerging industrial order, to "offsetting" by state
activity deviations from optimum market functioning, and finally to "participatory planning"—the last stage in which the state itself has no alternative
but to plan the economy as a whole. Solo blames the traditional economics
paradigm for being unable to handle these changing historical functions of
the state and, in fact, attributes much of the "paralysis," "panic," and "stumbling" responses by political leaders to the rigidity and narrowness of the market
paradigm.

Solo's basic perspective is a "utopian elite" analysis. Properly critical of
the failures of the market, of limited government activity, and of theories
that enshrine the market and limited government, he substitutes a faith in the
redeeming power of a rational political elite, called to action by increasingly
visible and obvious "problems" (transportation, health care, energy, inflation),

and enabled to plan by an increasingly available and usable scientific and social technology. He criticizes "offset planning" because it has no "conceptual basis," no "coherent and accepted set of values." This view assumes that an underlying rational theory is a requirement for good planning and is both possible and desirable. Faith in the rationality of the market has been replaced by faith in the potential rationality of the political authority as planner. And the analytic weapon of the planner will be a revitalized structure of thought. This assumption is part of the utopian elite view that knowledge and theory are important causal forces, justifying research and underlying a search for better public policies.

Solo's chapter, while using the same language of paradigms as mine, assigns considerably more causal importance to the structure of thought than I do. He explains the failure of France to invest in the international economy as a "paradigmatic inhibition" and says that "economics" must tear itself free from neoclassical theory without, however, embracing Marxism, an equally partial and merely critical theory. Here Solo is assuming that it is possible for "economics" fundamentally to change its basic assumptions. My view, on the contrary, is that the social bases for the dominance of a given paradigm are found within the history of a specific political economy and are not free-floating and disconnected intellectual forces that can be changed easily after being rationally criticized. The view held both by Solo and by Daniel Bell emphasizes the distinctive new role of knowledge as a source of social and political power in postindustrial society. This assessment of the potential rationality of the state assumes that the rationality of the market can be transferred wholesale over to the political authority, as if it were endowed with the capacity, the knowledge, and the instruments to act in the interests of the growth of the whole political economy.

Political Scientist Theodore Lowi, commenting on Solo's chapter and offering his own concept of the "state of permanent receivership," asserts that *all* industrialized societies have a plan, although in many if not most cases it is not publicly debated or labeled as such. Lowi here deals explicitly with what Solo calls the ideological functions of the economics paradigm to conceal the new functions of the state by justifying them in terms of strengthening the market. Whereas Solo has a vision of a new, more accurate, and comprehensive paradigm that recognizes the need for expanded political authority, Lowi—with a political scientist's tolerance for the ambiguity and inconsistencies of political action—accepts the need to create rationales for public action in order to maintain leeway for political elites to maneuver. Lowi's view here is in accord with both Solo and Offe, that the state now *must* accept the responsibility for guaranteeing the continuation of capital accumulation, although he does not use that language. Lowi recognizes that the large monopoly firms are the chief beneficiaries of such state policies, but he is optimistic that the form and content of state intervention can be reconstructed to serve more than the monopoly sector of the capitalist economy.

Lowi gives several examples of the way in which the new forms of state activity function to protect existing monopolies—both corporate and labor—at the expense of the unorganized competitive sector—consumers and small businesses. Given this political and economic reality, what are the grounds for optimism that a call for rationality will be heeded? Lowi has the same faith that knowledge and criticism are potentially usable by political elites that Solo does—an informed electorate, led by a liberal labor party, can wisely balance the political economy between those sectors most rationally organizable along market principles, those sectors requiring government regulation and supervision, and those requiring direct government ownership and control. Lowi says that we have the worst of all possible worlds: bureaucracy where markets should exist, and markets where strict bureaucratic controls should be. The result is a proliferation of irrational, cumbersome, unworkable government activity.

Lowi suggests that the only alternatives are a socialist revolution—which he dismisses as both unlikely and a cure worse than the disease—and the creation of a neo-laissez-faire system. Lowi rejects Andrew Martin's basic proposal—to have a Social Democratic political elite, supported by the organized working class, administer essentially the same system, but redirect its benefits, and add more control, planning, and central coordination. Lowi rejects this as unfeasible because of the intrinsic tendencies of bureaucracies toward inertia.

Lowi asserts that if both widespread consensus on the need for fundamental change *and* a powerful political party led by thoughtful leaders existed, it would be just as possible to move the system toward neo-laissez-faire as toward socialism. This argument contains a very large assumption that a "consensus" upon political action is easily malleable and can be shifted by political elites toward the ideal solution that Lowi proposes—to have the market function properly in certain sectors under the protection of government. Lowi's position here neglects both the power of monopolies to salvage protection from the political process at every stage from legislation to implementation (as his own examples indicate), and also the sources of the popular consensus that change is needed. It seems unlikely that an opposition political movement or party could generate the popular support necessary to give government the actual—rather than potential—power to decide where the market should operate without challenging the basic institutional sources of private control over the economy. Once that kind of consensus, movement, party, and leadership existed, it seems unlikely that it would stop at a rational and moderate assessment of market versus bureaucratic mechanisms in different sectors. Lowi seems here to minimize the fundamental inequalities and injustices in capitalist societies that are sustained and reproduced by the state, as Offe argues. Liberal political elites may not be able to direct and control parties and movements seeking change once they are in motion with mass consensus behind them.

Starting from a synthetic class perspective, Sociologist Claus Offe next shows how each perspective on the state can be regarded not merely as a general analytic paradigm, but also as a *strategy* for control of policy in a capitalist state, constrained to engage in actual production of health, education, transportation, and other services necessary for the continuation of capitalist accumulation. He argues that the four separate functions that define a capitalist state are incompatible and therefore that its function and structure are inherently unstable. The three main "modes of operation" that he distinguishes can be seen usefully as separate strategies. Offe calls the pluralist paradigm the strategy of "democratic consensus-building and immediate political conflict" for controlling state production, that is, Cohen's and Goldfinger's "normal politics." The elite paradigm Offe calls the "bureaucratic" mode of operation, stressing administrative control and the enforcement of rules as the main strategy for control of state productive activities. The utopian version of the class paradigm Offe himself recognizes in the image of rational policy formation by experts and scientists—the "purposive rational" strategy for controlling state production. This strategy takes the form of cost-benefit analyses, program budgeting, and social indicators. Presumably Offe would argue that these mechanisms for rational policy planning could succeed in a socialist society but are impossible to implement in a capitalist society.

Offe's theoretical approach combines both structural and functional categories into a definition of the capitalist state, in a way that avoids the implication of stability usually found when one or the other is emphasized. An exclusive emphasis upon the "state" as a cluster of institutions—legislatures, courts, administrative agencies—tends to ignore the peculiar mode in which these structures operate in order to maintain capitalist accumulation, Offe argues. Conversely, an emphasis upon the functions served by these structures—rule making, rule adjudicating, rule implementing—abstracts these functions from the structural forms that have emerged in the history of particular capitalist societies and that shape the consequences of the functions in decisive ways.

Offe's chapter is unusual in that he employs the language of both pluralist and elite paradigms easily and comfortably, even within the framework of a class analysis. This could be regarded as an eclectic and even theoretically incoherent usage, but seems to me instead to be a way of recognizing the analytic potential—even if partial and distorted from a class perspective—of other paradigms. "Allocative" state activities, for example, are understood quite well by a pluralist mode of analysis (Cohen's and Goldfinger's "normal politics") since the state already controls the necessary resources, and the use of these resources "can be directly derived from manifest interests and power relationships which become apparent in the process of politics and political conflict." Within the framework of this type of state activity, the pluralist language of "interests," "actors," "groups," and "decision rules" is appropriate and useful. Difficulties can arise, however, and Offe is not always careful enough on this score when the character of state production is being analyzed, and quite different social and political relations become critical. For example, he argues that "decision rules about state activity . . . substitute for the lack of class consensus within the ruling class." Just how those decision rules can substitute for class consensus is not clear. Offe says that the "determinants and dynamics" of the institutionalized production rules of public policy are "the key problems in the study of policy formation," and this chapter may be a theoretical prospectus for further studies that will clarify what is meant.

Theoretical assertion of connections between these "decision rules about state activity" and class relations and domination is not enough, however. Those connections must be demonstrated historically and empirically. If they are not, then this kind of theoretical reasoning falls back into "merely" paradigmatic statements, opposed by parallel assertions from the pluralists that decision rules are the product of complex political responses to conflicting social demands, or from the elite analysts that decision rules are the product of strategies of domination by powerful elites. Such paradigmatic debates cannot be resolved by serious and systematic historical and comparative studies of the state and the economy since paradigms neither arise from nor change as a result of rational debate, but at least such research can clarify the intellectual and political issues that lie beyond and behind each paradigm of the state. These chapters are all rich and serious contributions to clarification of these issues.

1

Is Democratic Control of Capitalist Economies Possible?

Andrew Martin

Introduction

What does democratic control of a capitalist economy involve? What does it take to establish and maintain it? Is it even possible? This chapter explores some answers to these questions suggested by ideas advanced from time to time by leading figures in the Swedish Social Democratic Party. These ideas imply a general argument concerning the requirements for democratic control of a capitalist economy, to wit: A capitalist economy can be subjected to democratic control only if the state is continuously controlled by a labor movement party. The obvious political relevance in Sweden of such an argument is that it provides a rationale for the Social Democrats' unparalleled continuity in office, which has now lasted well over four decades. During the 1973 election campaign, for example, Olof Palme, the Prime Minister and leader of the Social Democratic Party, invoked an argument along such lines in urging his followers to do their utmost to get the party returned to office yet again.[1]

Although the ideas that suggest it crop up recurrently, the argument does not seem to have been systematically elaborated in the party's ideological literature, in which there is not much sustained theorizing anyway. Nonetheless, the argument clearly has far-reaching implications. Of these, perhaps the most challenging, and discouraging, is the possibility that capitalist economies cannot be subjected to democratic control except under conditions that can only be met very rarely, if at all. Accordingly, it might be worthwhile to try to see for ourselves how the argument might be set forth. Since we are concerned with its wider relevance, we shall illustrate what seem to be the main steps in the argument by drawing on evidence from the United States and Britain as well as Sweden. Essentially, our purpose is to try to make an initial case for the view that nothing less than continuous control of the state by a labor movement party can suffice to accomplish democratic control of a capitalist economy. The various counterarguments that might be made to the effect that the persistent political hegemony of such a party is unnecessary, undemocratic, or insufficient to accomplish that control is noted at pertinent points in the discussion but is not considered in detail.

The argument takes certain assumptions for granted and is directed to issues that arise beyond them. Before proceeding to the argument itself, however, we should state these assumptions at least briefly. To begin with, it is assumed that the purposes of the few who control capitalist firms are bound to come into

13

conflict with those of the many who do not. The roots of this conflict are seen
in the imperatives built into the operation of capitalist firms, so that their interaction tends to generate insecurity, inequality, and a socially irrational allocation of resources. Those suffering the consequences of these tendencies are
expected to seek protection against them in various ways, including political
action aimed at using the state to counteract the tendencies and, perhaps,
ultimately to eliminate their sources.

The scope for such action and the degree to which it can be successful is
seen to depend on the extent to which the political process is effectively democratic. To the extent that it is, the assumption is that the state can be used to
redirect the economic process in accordance with the collectively determined
purposes of the majority who do not control capitalist firms as opposed to the
purposes of the few who continue to retain control of the firms. Where the
purposes of the latter prevail, as they could by virtue of the structure of politics
in a predemocratic liberal polity, for example, it is assumed that the state would
be used to institutionalize economic roles exclusively in terms of property rights
and to restrict economic actors, by force if necessary, to market transactions
based on the bargaining power accruing to them from such property rights as
they have. This, of course, is the laissez-faire pattern of state intervention in
a capitalist economy. The controllers of capitalist firms can obviously see other
patterns of intervention as essential to their purposes, as defined by the imperatives built into the operation of the firms under different circumstances. Whatever pattern of intervention they succeed in getting the state to carry out, its consequences for the levels, distributive effects, and composition of economic activity
are assumed to be different from what they would be if the state were used in
accordance with the collectively determined purposes of the majority who do
not control capitalist firms. Democratic control is understood to occur when it
is the purposes of that majority that prevail.

The requirements for the political process to be democratic in at least the
minimal, formal sense are understood in standard, familiar terms. Control of
the state—the power to decide how public authority is to be used—must be
genuinely contingent on elections in which suffrage is universal and in which
alternative outcomes are possible. For alternative outcomes to be possible, it
is assumed that the organization of efforts to mobilize support for competing
candidates—that is, competing parties—must be protected by the necessary
structure of civil liberties, while the integrity of the ballot must be provided
with the necessary safeguards. In addition, the distribution of support among
voters has to be approximated in the distribution of successful candidates
among the positions in which the authority to control the machinery of state
actually rests. While it is accepted that a political process cannot be effectively
democratic unless requirements such as these are met, however, it is assumed that
satisfying such requirements will by no means suffice to make the process effectively
democratic in the sense that it serves to subject the capitalist economic process
to democratic control. It is essentially the further requirements of an effectively

democratic structure of politics with which the argument is concerned. We shall start with the most obvious of these requirements and go on to those that are progressively more problematic.

Participation, Political Parties, and Democratic Control

Even if there is universal suffrage in a polity, and it satisfies all the other formal requirements of democracy, the political process still falls short of being democratic to the extent that actual participation in elections is not approximately universal. This is not simply a matter of the overall level of voting. It is also a matter of the extent to which differences in the level of voting among different segments of the population correspond to differences in their proximity to control of capitalist firms. Typically, those closest to such control, who consequently tend to have the most economic power, wealth, and status, also tend to have the highest turnout in elections, not to speak of other forms of political participation. The more that this is the case, the more possible it is for winning majorities to be concentrated toward the upper end of the scale of economic power, wealth, and status, and the less necessary it is for winning majorities to include people toward the lower end of the scale. But it is the latter who would presumably have the greatest stake in the use of public authority in ways opposed by the controllers of capitalist firms or, more briefly, business elites. To the extent that turnout varies with proximity to control of the firms, then, the effectiveness of the political process as a mechanism for subjecting a capitalist economy to democratic control is likely to be minimized. The scope of actual electoral participation literally falls short of being democratic when the variation in participation makes it more likely for control of the state to be won by political elites supported by business elites, who would hence be least likely to use public authority in ways that the latter oppose.

By the same token, public authority is most likely to be used in such ways if control of the state is won by political elites who are independent of business elites and who have mobilized winning majorities by maximizing the electoral participation of people toward the lower end of the scale of economic power, wealth, and status. For this to happen, of course, political elites with a stake in maximizing such participation would have to be present in the first place. In addition, however, sufficient resources to mobilize that participation would have to be available to them from sources other than business elites. In other words, there would have to be a party or parties bringing sufficient resources to the tasks of mobilizing electoral support for these political elites, or counter-elites as we can call them, to compete successfully with the political elites sustained by parties drawing their resources principally from business elites. In the absence of a party or parties through which such counter-elites can mobilize sufficient support to gain control of the state, the problem of democratic control of capitalist economies may be insuperable.

This step in the argument can perhaps be illustrated most usefully by referring to American experience. As is well known, there is far from universal participation in American elections inspite of the existence of universal suffrage in
principle. In the 1972 presidential election, for example, more than four out of
ten people of voting age cast no ballots. As important for the argument as this
low average turnout is its wide dispersion around that average, depending on
income levels. The 1972 turnout among those in income units with $15,000
or more per year was close to twice as great as it was among those in income
units with less than $3,000 per year—79.3 percent as opposed to 45.7 percent.
When we compare turnout among the people old enough to vote in the top fifth
of income units with turnout among those in the bottom fifth, we find that
almost four-fifths of the people in the top fifth of income units voted while a
little less than half in the bottom fifth voted—79.3 percent as opposed to 49.4
percent.[2]

Both the overall level of the turnout in the United States and its distribution have long been roughly similar to what they were in 1972. Confining our
discussion to overall turnout for the time being, we find that American presidential election turnout has fluctuated around its 1972 level throughout the
twentieth century. During the first two decades of the century, it averaged 65
percent, then fell to a low of 52 percent during the 1920s, rose gradually to a
peak of 64 percent in 1960, and declined in each of the succeeding presidential
elections to 57 percent in the most recent. These turnout levels are markedly
lower than they typically have been in West European parliamentary elections,
especially in the post-World War II period in which turnout has averaged between
80 and 90 percent.[3]

This contrast is even sharper when congressional off-year rather than presidential elections are compared with European experience, for close to six out of
ten Americans of voting age have typically failed to cast ballots in twentieth
century off-year elections for Congress. Even more striking, however, is the
fact that twentieth century American turnout levels are substantially lower
than they were during the post-Reconstruction decades. The average presidential election turnout between 1876 and 1896 was nearly 79 percent—almost
exactly the same as the turnout of voters in the highest income quintile in 1972.
Thus, participation in American elections during the present century has not
only been low by recent European standards but has also declined from nineteenth century American levels quite comparable with recent European levels.
Thus, there has been something like a demobilization of the American electorate.

According to Walter Dean Burnham, the political scientist who has analyzed
the phenomenon most thoroughly, the decline in turnout is a major consequence
of what he calls the "decomposition" of American political parties. His conception of party decomposition refers to the declining ability of parties not only to
mobilize the electorate but also to structure it—that is, to aggregate election
results along consistently partisan lines. The clearest evidence of declining partisanship that Burnham cites is a prolonged secular trend toward increased

ticket-splitting, resulting in increasingly divergent outcomes in concurrent presidential and congressional elections. Along with the declining function of parties in the electoral arena reflected in these trends in turnout and partisanship, there has also been an erosion of their function in the policy-making arena, as illustrated by the replacement of party organization by seniority in determining the congressional leadership structure. Burnham stresses that all of these trends marking the decomposition of parties during the twentieth century constitute a reversal of the preceding pattern of development in which American parties assumed an increasingly important role in organizing the political process. The significance he attaches to this reversal has a direct bearing on the argument.

Burnham interprets what has happened to American parties in the light of a general view of the strains generated by industrialization and the political mechanisms that can enable it to go on inspite of those strains. "Whether managed by capitalists or commissars," he reminds us, industrialization imposes dislocations and deprivations that give rise to resentment and resistance. "Industrializing elites" of all kinds must accordingly seek "insulation" against the resulting "mass pressures" that threaten them with "displacement by a coalition of those who are damaged." Such insulation can readily be provided by an authoritarian political order, whether it be a "totalitarian monopoly of power in the hands of Communist industrializing elites" or a "less coercive . . . personalist dictatorship." It can also be provided by a predemocratic liberal political order, within which much of capitalist industrialization occurred, through the "persistence of feudal patterns of deference and especially the restriction of the right to vote to the middle and upper classes."

In a liberal political order that has been democratized prior to industrialization, however, the elites who manage the process are much more vulnerable. This was the situation in the United States and, as Burnham argues, the American industrializing elites faced a "crisis of vulnerability" in the last decade of the nineteenth century. Before that, the democratization of American politics posed no threat. The elimination of the principal restrictions on suffrage—the economic ones prior to the Civil War and the racial ones, temporarily, as a result of it—was followed by increasing mobilization of voters by parties and strengthening of party organization. But both major parties came to be dominated by the industrializing elites. Even so, that domination was rendered insecure by the possibility that one of the parties could be taken over by a coalition of the discontended. When existing discontents were intensified by the depression of 1893, that threat became serious, and when the Populists captured the Democratic party in 1896, the threat appeared to have materialized.

In fact, of course, William Jennings Bryan's candidacy failed to forge an effective coalition of those who bore the burdens of economic change. Instead, it helped to establish precisely that insulation the industrializing elites needed but had lacked. Essential to this result was the massive switch of workers in the industrialized Northeast from the Democrats to the Republicans, producing a major realignment along regional lines. The onset of the depression during a

Democratic Administration evidently initiated the switch; Bryan's campaign
reinforced it both by its "nostalgic" agrarian appeals and its nativist overtones
of hostility to the ethnically heterogeneous Northeast; and economic recovery
during the McKinley Administration consolidated it. While the realignment's
immediate consequence was to bring victory to the party still controlled by
the industrializing elites, it also had a number of effects that reduced their
political vulnerability over the long run. Republican control of national
government facilitated the transformation of the federal judiciary into a means
of safeguarding business activity from legislative restraints. At the same time
the very likelihood of such restraints was diminished by the decomposition of
parties that set in. The realignment itself contributed to that decomposition
by sharply reducing party competition. Partisan mobilization and electoral
participation was further inhibited by changes in "the rules of the game,"
ranging from Progressive reforms like primaries to outright disfranchisement
of Blacks in the Old Confederacy. In turn, reduction of the Democratic
Party in the South to an instrument for preserving the Jim Crow subsystem
severly disabled the party as a mechanism for counter-elites in the policy-making
arena long after the Republican hegemony in the national electoral arena ended.

     The long-term impact of the "system of 1896" on the Democratic Party
deserves particular emphasis. Burnham contends, along lines proposed in the
argument here, that the only known alternative to the "concentration of political power, locally or nationally, in the hands of those who already possess
concentrated economic power" is the mobilization of those without concentrated economic power within a party, or parties, that can gain control of government. The American Constitution, which divides policy-making authority among
politically separated institutions, makes such a party acutely necessary, for it
alone could "coordinate the presidency and Congress as component parts of the
national policy-making process." Whatever possibility there was for transforming the Democratic Party into such a party in the 1890s was closed off by the
1896 realignment. As Burnham sees it, even the New Deal realignment "did not
terminate or even reverse the dispersion of the potential resources of the public
sector"entailed in the decomposition of parties that ensued from the system of
1896. He recognizes that, during the period of the New Deal some reallocation
of political power did in fact take place from business elites to "a more pluralist,
welfare-oriented coalition of elites and veto groups." This did seem to reopen
the possibility that the Democratic Party could become an "instrument of collective social action," through which "the many who were individually powerless
could pursue collective political objectives under elites identified with them."
But "partisan organization and processes seem scarcely to have changed at all"
and "the process of disaggregation in policy structures inaugurated during the
1890s" continued virtually without interruption during the New Deal era, while
"the march toward electoral disagregation" was resumed in the subsequent
period. "The Democratic Party and electoral politics in general had become
very blunt instruments for governing" long before the New Deal, and the political

forces mobilized by Franklin Delano Roosevelt evidently could not be organized in such a way as to transform the party into a lasting mechanism for using public authority to redirect the economic process.

In the absence of a party that could enable counter-elites to govern in America, political elites supported by business have had no compelling need to organize a party capable of mobilizing mass support and governing either. With no party capable of governing, it is impossible to overcome the institutionalized fragmentation of public authority and establish "domestic sovereignty" in the American polity. Under these conditions, "the business elite and their political ancillaries" have no strong incentive to resist the decomposition of parties. All that is needed to keep public authority from being used in ways opposed by business is the kind of veto power that political elites supported by business can bring to bear at so many points in the American policy-making process. In other words, the "pluralistic" American political process makes it possible for the political power relevant to controlling the economy to remain concentrated in the "holders of concentrated economic power," without having to be organized through a cohesive national political party. The American situation, then, is one in which a capitalist economy cannot be subjected to democratic control inspite of a formally democratic political process, because there is no party through which the power to exercise democratic control can be deployed.

Organized Labor and Democratic Control

Under what conditions can a party, or parties, capable of serving as a mechanism for subjecting a capitalist economy to democratic control exist? The answer proposed in the argument is that organized labor is the single most important source from which such a party could draw the resources needed to mobilize support, and that only where organized labor provides it with sufficient resources can such a party compete successfully with a party that can rely on business for most of the needed resources.

To the extent that unions organize the labor force and enforce wage determination by collective bargaining, they become the only nongovernmental institution with a capacity to tap the flow of funds through the economy that even begins to approximate the capacity of capitalist firms to do so. From the incomes that their bargaining power wins, or is credited with winning, for their members, unions elicit the funds with which to sustain their activities not only in the labor market but the political arena as well.

Impelled into the political arena by purposes ranging from organizational survival, through social and economic policies directly geared to member interests, to more far-reaching social change that may be conceived in terms of Left ideologies, unions tend to channel their activity through political parties with which they establish durable links, whether formal or informal. To such parties, unions can bring not only funds for financing party activity but also other important resources. The unions themselves tend to function as political organizations in mobilizing the electoral participation of their members and using their own personnel in mobilizing support in the wider electorate. Their access to their members enables them to cultivate partisan identifications that make for increased receptivity to the associated parties' appeals and facilitate the recruitment of party cadres. Through common partisan identifications, members of particular unions can be linked within a wider mass movement, sharing a political subculture that provides a distinctive frame of reference in which the political meaning of social experience can be defined, and alternative interpretations in the appeals of other parties can be resisted. Thus, labor movement parties can provide counter-elites with the financial, organizational, and psychological resources with which to maximize the mobilization of people toward the lower end of the scale of economic power, wealth, and status. Where this has happened to a substantial extent, notably in Britain and Scandinavia, counter-elites sustained by labor movement parties have been able to control the state over extended periods.

Obviously, however, organized labor need not necessarily develop to this extent and in ways that result in the development of labor movement parties. Their failure to do so in the United States is a prime case in point, with decisive consequences for the course of party development discussed earlier. The crisis of vulnerability faced by America's industrializing elites in the 1890s would undoubtedly have been more serious if organized labor had not been as weak as it was at the time. A farmer-labor alliance was clearly envisioned in the Populists' 1892 Omaha Platform. But unions embracing a mere three percent of the labor force could not provide an effective organizational channel for the labor component of such an alliance, nor bring to the alliance a significant accretion of strength, nor even give sufficient weight to that vision of an alliance within the Populist movement to keep it from being displaced by the narrower one symbolized by the issue of free silver.[4]

Subsequently, of course, American organized labor did grow substantially, with a large but temporary surge in membership during World War I, while Republican policy made the American Federation of Labor's official nonpartisanship impossible in practice. But neither its scale nor its strategy contributed much to the return of Northern workers to the Democratic Party, which Alfred E. Smith's ethnic appeal encouraged and Herbert Hoover's response to the Great Depression massively accelerated. As Irving Bernstein points out, "Roosevelt owed the labor movement nothing for his victory." Instead, it was the New Deal that enabled union organization to break through the barriers that employers had maintained with the help of public authority and to which the AFL had accommodated by confining itself to a defensive craft unionism. With the legislative and psychological support of the New Deal, unionization was finally extended on a significant scale to the mass of semiskilled and unskilled workers without which a labor movement could not be a significant political force. In Britain the equivalent transformation of the labor movement from a narrow craft basis to a wide industrial basis had already been brought about by the "New Unionism" of the 1890s, which laid the groundwork for the creation of the Labor Party shortly thereafter.[5]

Once the breakthrough to industrial unionism occurred in the United States, the size and political activism of organized labor in this country also grew, with a major stimulus given to it by World War II as by World War I. By the early 1960s the AFL-CIO's political activity came to be highly integrated into the Democratic party organization, not only in a number of states and cities but also in the congressional legislative process. But the function performed by organized labor in the latter context, important as it was, was less a sign of labor strength than a symptom of the persistence of the structural weakness that the Jim Crow subsystem had so long inflicted on the Democratic party. Moreover, even at the peak of its influence, before the disarray into which controversy over the Vietnam War threw the Democratic party, organized labor could not serve as the principal source of the Democratic party's resources. With union membership stagnating at less than a quarter of the labor force, the portion of the electorate to which American unions had direct access fell far short of that enjoyed by the labor movements with roughly double the coverage in Britain and Scandinavia, apart from the greater cohesiveness of the labor movements in those countries. Nor could American unions compensate with money for their weakness in numbers. While business has continued to contribute more money to Republicans than to Democrats, it has provided anywhere between twice and three times as much to Democrats than the unions have.[6]

Whatever else may be said about organized labor's role in American politics, then, it has not been able to come anywhere near to providing the resources needed to enable political elites independent of business to win control of the state. If organized labor cannot do so, it apparently cannot be done at all. While other sources can and perhaps must supplement the resources organized labor can provide, there appear none that can fill the gap if organized labor cannot provide the bulk of the resources.

Problem Solving Capacities of Counter Elites

So far, then, the argument is that democratic control of capitalist economies depends on the ability of political elites independent of business to win control of the state. This depends on whether these counter-elites are sustained by parties through which they can mobilize sufficient electoral support to win, and this depends on maximizing the electoral participation of those with least economic power, wealth and status. This, in turn, depends on whether sufficient resources to mobilize that support are available to these parties, and this depends on the development of labor movements able and willing to provide most of the necessary resources.

But if all these requirements are met, it still does not necessarily mean that democratic control is established. All it means is that counter-elites sustained by labor movement parties can win control of the state. For this to result in democratic control of a capitalist economy, the counter-elites must prove able to use the public authority at their disposal in ways that are effective in redirecting the economic process in accordance with the purposes collectively defined through the political process. Obviously, they need not necessarily find ways of using that public authority that are effective. But if they do not, their control of the state clearly fails to serve the purpose of democratic control. The short-run result may well be that they lose control of the state to political elites supported by business in the next election. In the longer run, if the counter-elites again win control of the state but fail to use it effectively, the result may be an erosion of the resources available to them, possibly culminating in the decomposition of the parties on which their ability to mobilize support depends. In addition, then, democratic control depends critically on the counter-elites' capacity for solving the whole range of complex policy problems involved in redirecting the capitalist economic process.

For illustrations of policy failures by counter-elites and their consequences for democratic control, we can turn to British experience. The clearest case is provided by the response of J. Ramsey MacDonald's Labor Government to the Great Depression. By 1929, less than three decades after its founding, the British Labor Party had become a major political force. Much of the impetus for this development came from the extension of unionization to cover two-fifths of the labor force during World War I, accompanied by the Labor Party's decision to make an independent, nationwide bid for power. Inspite of the subsequent sharp decline in union membership, the Labor Party succeeded in vastly enlarging its electoral constituency, primarily by mobilizing new working class voters, including those enfranchised by the 1918 suffrage reform. In the 1923 election the Labor Party displaced the Liberal Party as the second largest, in both votes and seats, and briefly formed a minority government. In the 1929 election it won the largest number of seats, with a share of the vote just short of that won by the Conservatives. On this larger but still minority parliamentary base, it again formed a government, headed as before by MacDonald. The most pressing domestic policy problem faced by that government was unemployment.[7]

Unemployment had been a recurrent consequence of the cyclical fluctuations that capitalist—and perhaps all—market economies tend to generate. After World War I unemployment became first chronic and then acute as a consequence of the fundamental dislocation and, finally, the breakdown of the international capitalist economy. If democratic control was to be established over the capitalist economic process in Britain, or anywhere, it would surely involve the use of public authority to counteract the inability of the process to provide stable, full employment. The extent to which the British Labor Party succeeded in doing so after coming into office in 1929 would accordingly seem to provide a decisive test of its ability to function as an instrument of democratic control.

To meet the test the MacDonald Government had to come up with solutions to the technical problem of what to do to reduce unemployment and the tactical problem of how to do it inspite of its lack of a parliamentary majority. At the time, as is well known, the prevailing view among capitalist elites, particularly in the financial sector, was that nothing could be done about unemployment that would not make matters worse by interfering with the alleged curative powers of the market mechanism. The only possible exception was some income maintenance for the unemployed, but at levels low enough not to impede the downward pressure of market forces on wages and only in aggregate amounts compatible with balanced government budgets. As the number of unemployed rose and government revenues fell, this conception of the narrow limits on policy was invoked in support of increasing pressure for cuts in unemployment benefits. The unions opposed such cuts as an intolerable increase in the burdens already being borne by the unemployed, thereby defining the concrete issue in terms of which they came into conflict with the prevailing economic ideology. If for no other reason, the counter-elites sustained primarily by the unions might have been expected to resist the prescriptions based on this ideology and to search for and welcome alternative ideas about what could be done.

Such ideas were in fact available. In particular, the necessity of balanced budgets was challenged, and the use of loan-financed government expenditures to increase employment, directly and indirectly, was being advocated by John Maynard Keynes long before he spelled out the rationale for what has since become the principal technique for reducing unemployment. Lloyd George made this idea of expansionary spending the heart of the 1929 Liberal Party campaign program; Oswald Mosley urged an ambitious version of it within the Labor Cabinet and Party; and, most significant from our standpoint, Ernest Bevin and other leaders of the Trades Union Congress insisted that it removed any justification whatsoever from the demanded cuts in unemployment benefits. In other words, a solution to the technical problem consistent with the immediate, perceived interests of the Labor Party's core constituency was available.

At the same time the fact that Lloyd George and his supporters in the Liberal Party were committed to that technical solution also made available a solution to the tactical problem posed by Labor's parliamentary minority. For even though the Liberals remained bitterly divided, Lloyd George could evidently bring enough votes to a coalition with Labor to provide the majority needed to implement an expansionary budget policy.

However, MacDonald could not bring himself to challenge the wisdom of the established financial elites who formed a policy community that embraced the Treasury bureaucracy as well as the private sector, and that extended to the United States as well as to Britain. Instead, MacDonald chose to be guided by their insistence that the British currency's exchange rate had to be maintained, for which a balanced budget was deemed essential, which in turn made the cuts in unemployment benefits supposedly necessary. Since Labor resistance to the cuts could not be overcome, MacDonald agreed to head a "national" coalition government, actually dominated by the Conservatives, to enact the cuts. This failed to achieve its ostensible purpose of maintaining the exchange rate, but it did bring the second Labor Government to an end. In the election that shortly ensued, the Labor Party suffered a severe setback, rendering it incapable of mounting a serious challenge to Conservative rule for the rest of the decade.

As a result, economic policy during the Depression was shaped in accordance with the requirements of British capitalism as they were perceived at the time. This certainly did not mean leaving matters to the curative powers of the market. As Samuel H. Beer points out, Conservative economic policy was highly interventionist during the 1930s. But it was interventionist on terms defined by business rather than by any counter-elites, and policy evidently did not in practice compel British businessmen to do anything they did not want to do, inspite of all the talk of rationalization as a quid pro quo for tariffs.

Because of its leaders' policy choices, then, the British Labor Party proved unable to serve as a mechanism for democratic control when it had its first real opportunity to do so. We can only speculate about how effectively it could have done so if the alternative choices had been made. At a minimum, a coalition including the Lloyd George Liberals but dominated by Labor would have enjoyed the freedom of maneuver in economic policy that abandonment of the gold standard and devaluation gave the Conservatives. Beyond that, a Lab-Lib expansionary expenditure policy would probably have stimulated economic recovery more than the Conservatives' expansionary monetary policy could. In addition to the distributive effects of the somewhat lower unemployment levels that would probably have followed, the benefits and burdens of a more rapid recovery might have been more equally distributed by a greater development of welfare state institutions than took place under the Conservatives.

Major increments in the capability of government to shape the economic process beyond this would probably not have occurred. But enough might well have been done to convince a majority of the electorate of the Lab-Lib coalition's ability to govern effectively. Accordingly, instead of a long period of uninterrupted Conservative rule, the consequence might well have been a like period of Labor rule, with the support of the Lloyd George Liberals or, after a subsequent election, even without them. This would at least have enabled the counter-elites to retain the control of the state needed to try to work out ways of dealing with the problems of controlling a capitalist economy as those problems evolved over time. This scenario of what might have been may be recognized as describing essentially what did happen in Sweden as a result of the Swedish Social Democrats' responses to policy problems that were approximately the same, in both technical and tactical terms. Before turning to the Swedish experience, however, the British Labor Party's performance in its more recent periods in office must be discussed for the further light it sheds on the interaction of power and policy.

Can Alternation in Power Assure
Democratic Control?

World War II transformed the tasks of government and the political climate in Britain in ways that opened up a second opportunity for the Labor party to serve as an instrument of democratic control, with prospects for success undoubtedly better than in the first instance. Already at the very beginning of the war, there had been what Beer characterizes as a major shift in the distribution of power between classes in favor of "the organized working class." During the interwar years the institutionalization of union power was sufficient to withstand a good deal of the impact of mass unemployment. Therefore, once "manpower became the ultimate scarce resource" whose mobilization and allocation was critical to the war economy, union cooperation with government became indispensable. In a strong position to bargain for the terms on which that cooperation was granted, the same TUC leadership that MacDonald had refused to heed won a role among the top economic policy makers, the continued determination of wages by collective bargaining, and changes in the social services that amounted to a "revolution in social policy" even while the war was going on. But the terms included commitments to greater equity and effectiveness in social and economic policy after as well as during the war. The extent to which a postwar Conservative Government would have fulfilled the terms of this "new social contract" negotiated by the wartime Coalition is nevertheless uncertain. Doubts on that score, particularly with respect to full employment, may well have contributed to the massive support for the Labor Party that gave it its first parliamentary majority in 1945.[8]

As is well known, the postwar Labor Governments of 1945 and 1950 carried out a comprehensive program of reforms, including a major reconstruction and expansion of welfare state institutions as well as some nationalization, and could point to sustained full employment throughout Labor's time in office, although the high level of employment may have been as much the product of the unanticipated course of the international economy as of policy. In fact, the main problem of economic policy confronting Labor from 1945 to 1951 proved to be different from those of either the interwar or wartime eras. It was no longer unemployment, which was now understood to be curable by simple Keynesian demand stimulation. Nor was it an inflationary strain on resources rendered manageable by the battery of controls that wartime solidarity permitted. Instead, continued full employment was associated with persistent inflationary pressures intermittently intensified by producers' market power, supply bottlenecks, and adverse changes in the terms of foreign trade, all in a domestic political climate and international economic regime that compelled rapid dismantlement of the wartime

apparatus of controls. Under these circumstances the postwar Labor Governments were faced with the necessity of evolving a new strategy for managing a
capitalist economy consistent with its commitments to and the perceived interests of their core constituency. Exhausted by the strain of trying to cope first
with the crises of postwar economic reconstruction and then the problem of
inflation, the Labor Party lost office before it found the strategy it needed when
it was defeated in the ill-timed election of 1951.

In losing control of the state again, did the Labor Party once more fail to
serve as an instrument for subjecting British capitalism to democratic control?
It obviously did not fail under Clement Attlee as it had under MacDonald. However, a good deal more than that could be claimed for it. Thus, it could be
argued that the maintenance of full employment, expansion of social services,
and universalization of income maintenance under the Labor Governments
demonstrated that public authority could be used to control the level, composition, and distributive effects of economic activity as never before. Once this
had happened, responsibility for the course of economic activity could no
longer be escaped by any government in the future, regardless of which party
controlled it.

Arguing along lines very much like these, C.A.R. Crosland, a leading spokes-
man of the "revisionist" position in the ideological controversies that wracked
the Labor Party during the 1950s, contends that the postwar period of Labor
rule brought about an irreversible transformation of the economic function of
the state. In his view what is particularly important is that full employment
became a permanent imperative of policy because voters generally had been
convinced by the experience of continuous full employment under Labor as
well as during the war that policy can guarantee it. Because that expectation
compels any government to preserve full employment, power in the labor
market is permanently shifted in favor of "the organized workers." In addition
to compelling employers to offer acceptable terms in collective bargaining, this
makes it necessary also for governments headed by any party to bargain with
the unions and provide an acceptable quid pro quo in return for the cooperation of unions that continues to be necessary in the postwar full employment
economy as it was in the war economy. Union strength sustained by full
employment in turn provides the Labor Party with a secure underpinning.
This, together with the demonstration of its capacity to govern between 1945
and 1951, preserves the Party's credibility as an alternative government. Consequently, no Conservative Government can afford the electoral risk of not meeting the expectations, concerning welfare benefits and social services as well as
full employment, established by experience under the Labor Governments.
Crosland therefore concludes that "the basic structure of the full employment
welfare state" developed by Labor when it was in office will remain intact even
when it is not in office.[9]

To Crosland this marks a fundamental change in the British political economy. The state rather than the interaction of individual firms has become

decisive in shaping the economic process. This new economic function of the state is enforced by the logic of democratic politics. In addition, control of individual firms has passed from traditional capitalist owners to modern managers who accept the new economic function of the state, as well as the power of unions, because they recognize that both contribute in essential ways to steady and orderly growth. At the same time the policies that maintain steady growth and provide a universal floor of economic security raise the general level and reduce the difference in living standards. In combination these developments are said to have "transformed capitalism beyond recognition" and attenuated the ideologically charged controversies of the past over the performance of capitalism and the economic role of the state.

What Crosland is most concerned with is the implications all this has for the Labor Party's basic political strategy. He argues that the Party must adapt to the changed situation by recognizing that traditional socialist appeals, including the traditional socialist remedy of public ownership, have ceased to be relevant. It must instead base its claim for support on its ability to manage and improve the full employment welfare state for which it was largely responsible, making the further changes toward social justice that the Conservatives are not likely to make but that require no more fundamental changes in the structure of the political economy. It is this position, of course, that makes Crosland part of the postwar "revisionist" effort within most European labor movement parties, as well as the "end of ideology" mood that was more generally prevalent in the West.

However, the end of ideology view and its fate does not concern us directly. What does concern us are the implications that Crosland's interpretation of the Labor Party's postwar period of rule have for the question of democratic control. His view can be seen as an argument for the proposition that a capitalist economy is effectively subjected to democratic control once a labor movement party is able to control the state intermittently. In other words, when there is alternation in office between political elites sustained by parties drawing their resources primarily from business and counter-elites sustained by labor movement parties, the imperatives of electoral politics compel the former to match the latter in using public authority to redirect the operation of the economy in accordance with collectively determined purposes. However, a labor movement party that is only intermittently in office may not suffice to maintain democratic control. Thus, by losing office in 1951 and again in 1970, the British Labor Party may still have failed to serve as an instrument for subjecting British capitalism to democratic control. This possibility is suggested by developments that have become increasingly clear since the mid-1950s when Crosland was elaborating the view summarized here.

Inflation and the Erosion of Public Sector
Welfare Institutions

The "basic structure of the full employment welfare state" did not prove as durable as Crosland's analysis would lead us to expect. However, this was not because Conservative Governments between 1951 and 1964 proceeded to dismantle it. Although they did make decisions that weakened it, it has been eroded largely by processes that seem to have been inherent in the operation of the Western capitalist economies in the postwar period. All that was necessary to undermine the full employment welfare state was for the Conservative Governments simply to do nothing to counteract these processes. In large part and in various ways these processes have operated through the inflationary tendencies that have characterized the economies throughout the period, even before the recent appearance of "double-digit" inflation. The impact of inflation is clearest in connection with those British welfare state institutions so constructed as to make them most vulnerable, the income maintenance system introduced by the postwar Labor Government.[10]

That system was universal and compulsory, financed partly by funds to which all persons were obliged to make flat-rate contributions, providing to all the right to flat-rate benefits in a variety of circumstances, like retirement, unemployment, sickness, and disability, in which people are ordinarily deprived of income from work. Modelled on the proposals in the famous report by William Beveridge that was part of the "new social contract" made during the war, this national insurance system, as it was called, was supposed to guarantee a subsistence minimum to all. This was understood as a level of income that would make it unnecessary for anyone to seek means-tested benefits from a simultaneously reformed national assistance system except those who fell through the national insurance "net" because of special circumstances. Over time, it was anticipated that the net would be made finer by taking into account more and more of such special circumstances. As income maintenance by right was thereby made more nearly universal in practice as well as in principle, means-tested national assistance benefits were expected to virtually disappear.

Instead, however, the number of people receiving means-tested benefits rose steadily. This implied a still larger number of people for whom benefits by right failed to provide a subsistence income, since many who were thereby entitled to assistance were unwilling to go through the means-test required to get it. Far from being eliminated by the version of the welfare state that had been set up, then, poverty actually increased, even by the low standard incorporated into the income maintenance system itself. The main reason for this, of course, was that national insurance benefit levels were not raised sufficiently to compensate for increases in the cost of living either by building in an automatic mechanism for doing so or by successive government decisions. Even the initial benefit levels set by the Labor Government were somewhat below those Beveridge had recommended, and they fell progressively further relative to rising incomes and prices during the subsequent years of Conservative Governments.

While the public sector welfare institutions provided benefits too low to keep those dependent solely on them from falling into poverty, a multiplicity of corporate and occupational welfare schemes have grown up, providing highly differentiated benefits to those in a position to participate in them, ranging from marginal supplements to national insurance all the way to amounts vastly greater than national insurance benefits. These "miniature welfare states" came into being, primarily in the private sector, partly because firms and occupational groups found them effective in attracting and keeping employees and members, and partly because they proved to be an effective means for channeling savings into the private sector of the capital market for financial firms like insurance companies. The strong incentives to develop this private sector welfare system are paralleled by incentives for those who can to take advantage of them that grow stronger as public sector benefit levels fall further behind those available from the private sector schemes, at least for the better-off.

As the divergence in benefit levels grows, the public sector welfare institutions become less and less a system on which most members of society depend, and in which they consequently have a stake. Instead, these institutions become increasingly a system providing inferior benefits to those who are relatively disadvantaged in other respects as well, including exclusion from economic roles that bring with them more generous benefits. Concomitantly, those who have such roles have a declining stake in the public sector welfare institutions and tend to drop out of the political constituency that supports them.

In this way the political constituency of the public sector welfare state is eroded along with its universality. The most powerful force generating this process is the capacity of capitalist firms to channel the funds flowing through the economy, in a volume continuously increased by inflationary growth, in directions determined in accordance with their private policy. To be sure, the proliferation of private sector welfare institutions has not been independent of public policy. Public policy contributed to an environment favorable to their proliferation to the extent that it reinforced inflationary growth while failing to integrate public sector welfare institutions into that growth. In addition, public policy has provided direct encouragement in various ways, particularly with favorable tax treatment. Indeed, as Richard M. Titmuss pointed out, tax law amounts to one of three distinct though overlapping welfare systems—a fiscal welfare system alongside the corporate and public sector systems, each of which influences the "social distribution of welfare" by different mechanisms and according to different standards of equity.

Insofar as public policy has laid the public sector welfare system open to erosion in these ways, changes in public policy would seem to offer the obvious remedy. Beyond a certain point, however, the process may be irreversible. If it goes on unimpeded long enough, the political constituency for the public sector system might be reduced to a minority consisting of the most disadvantaged, so that sufficient support to implement the measures needed to reverse the process might be very difficult to mobilize. Undoubtedly, there is bound to be a division

between those with a stake in solidaristic, collective solutions to personal problems, arrived at through public policy, and those able to rely on particularistic,
individual or group solutions, arrived at through situational advantages and
private power. What is important politically is where the division lies: whether
it divides the participating portion of the electorate between a majority that is
in the constituency for the public sector and a minority that is not, or between
a minority that is in it and a majority that is not. The balance may be close,
and it may not take much to shift it. Under conditions of inflationary growth
in a capitalist economy, there may be ample opportunities for political strategies capable of bringing about such a shift.[11]

Whether the erosion of the public sector welfare state can be reversed
accordingly depends on whether a party with a stake in reversing it gains control of the state and implements the necessary measures before the balance is
tipped against a solidaristic, collective approach. In Britain this obviously means
that the Labor Party returns to office and reconstructs the system it introduced
in the late 1940s in time to make the difference. There was evidently still time
to do so when Labor returned to office in 1964, although private pension
schemes, for example, had already grown so much as to complicate the task
immensely. In that connection Labor had even worked out plans for reform of
the public sector pension scheme that could have gone some way toward counteracting its erosion. But Labor was voted out of office again in 1970 without having
carried out its pension reform plans or substantially offsetting the erosion of the
full employment welfare state in some other respects, and after having even reinforced the process in still other respects.[12]

What prevented the 1960s Labor Government from making the most of its
opportunity to reconstruct the welfare state, and what probably contributed
most to its loss of office in 1970, was its preoccupation with and failure to find
a viable solution to the problem of inflation. In other words, it was again
defeated in the effort to cope with inflation as it was in its previous period in
office. The nature of the problem as it has been distinctively defined for the
Labor Party and the consequent requirements for a solution that is viable for
the Party therefore calls for discussion.

The Unemployment-Inflation Trade-off Dilemma

That the maintenance of full employment, by whatever combination of
deliberate policy and other factors, has been associated with inflationary pressures, and that Keynesian techniques of demand management can curb such
pressures only by increasing unemployment, thereby confronting governments
with an unemployment-inflation trade-off dilemma, are all well known. The
postwar British Labor Government tried to get around that dilemma in the same
way as most Western governments have: It tried to get the unions to agree to

wage restraint. It got that agreement in 1948 in exchange for dividend restraint by business and some control of prices by the Government, in addition to its already established commitments on employment and welfare policies. It thereby succeeded in putting into operation one of the many ventures in what has come to be called "incomes policy." However, an anti-inflationary strategy that relies on wage restraint is not likely to be a viable one for a labor movement party.[13]

It is commonly believed that such a party is in the best position to carry out that kind of strategy because it can draw on the loyalty and interest in its survival that the unions associated with it have, and because it is most ready to give the unions the social and economic policy quid pro quo on which their acceptance of wage restraint seems to be contingent. Short of a national crisis approaching the scale of total war, however, it is virtually impossible even for a labor movement party to offer terms on which wage restraint can be acceptable to unions, for the experience of wage restraint has generally convinced unions that it entails serious organizational risks to them. Unions that comply are likely to find either that their members' earnings are increased without their help by wage drift—as employers bid up wages to attract and hold scarce labor and in other ways—or that their members' earnings fall relative to others' because their members are not in a position to benefit as much or at all from wage drift. In either case the failure of unions to perform the wage functions expected of them is likely to evoke member discontent.

In addition to the disturbance of established differentials caused by the uneven incidence of restraint on different groups of workers, restraint of non-wage income tends to be less effective than restraint of wages generally, making it likely for income inequality to be increased. For example, dividend restraint may enhance rather than limit shareholder income if plowed-back profits increase share values, aside from the possibility of larger future dividends to make up for earlier limitations. Even an incomes policy that effectively achieved the equality of sacrifice typically set as a condition for union compliance cannot be expected to elicit general acceptance, for it would simply leave unchanged inequalities over which there is no social consensus and which at least some unions may be strongly committed to reducing. Thus, unions can have important ideological as well as organizational stakes that are likely to be threatened by wage restraint.

In any case, differential incidence ordinarily leads to a progressive breakdown of compliance and compels even the most "responsible" union leaders to withdraw their consent to wage restraint. The "wage explosion" that tends to follow the collapse of an incomes policy, as unions try to catch up in whatever ways they allegedly have fallen behind, together with the possibly negative allocational effects of a period of restraint, call into question the effectiveness of such a repressed inflation strategy from a general economic standpoint.

Whatever is to be said from that standpoint, the political costs of wage restraint to a labor movement party that resorts to it are likely to be high. If it yields to the pressures building up in the unions on which it is largely based and abandons wage restraint, it gives up the strategy on which it relied to curb inflation without increasing unemployment. To the extent that it resists the pressures and tries to maintain wage restraint over the objections of unions, perhaps by even resorting to legal compulsion, it jeopardizes the support of its principal source of resources and ultimately risks the disintegration of the party. If it instead falls back on restricting demand sufficiently to curb inflation, it is likely to bring about an increase in unemployment equally unacceptable to its core constituency. If it abandons both the repressed inflation and demand restriction strategies and fails to come up with any alternative, continuing price rises and probable balance of payments difficulties cast strong doubt on its capacity to manage the economy and drain away support, particularly among those least committed to the party but who may nevertheless provide the margin of electoral victory. Failure to cope with inflation in a way that is capable of retaining the support of both its core constituency and those beyond it is there-fore likely to result in the party's loss of office—as it naturally would in the case of analagous policy failure by any party.

Just how much its failure to find a politically viable strategy for improving the unemployment-inflation trade-off contributed to the British Labor Party's defeat in 1951 is uncertain. Better timing in calling the election and a more favorable distribution of support among parliamentary constituencies might have sufficed to avert defeat and prolong Labor rule indefinitely, for then Labor rather than the Conservatives would have been in the position to reap the politi-cal benefits of the much less taxing economic conditions that prevailed for several years once the Korean crisis was over. What is certain is that Labor would eventually face again the dilemma that it could get around only with a strategy different from the one it relied on during the late 1940s.

As it happened, Labor did not return to office until after an unprecedented period of continuous Conservative rule. When it did so in 1964, however, it was still not equipped with an alternative strategy, nor were its leaders apparently aware of the need for one. That the intervening Conservative Governments had tried and been forced to abandon several variants of incomes policy could not convince the Labor leadership of the futility of the approach, for on the assumption that Labor could win the union cooperation that the Conservatives could not, the latters' failures could be dismissed as irrelevant. The course of economic policy dur-ing the thirteen years of Conservative Governments is nevertheless relevant to our understanding of what was at stake in the decisions facing the subsequent Labor Governments, so it must be briefly reviewed before discussing what the latter did.

Political Stalemate and "Stop-Go" Economic Policies

The Conservatives were not seriously confronted by the unemployment-inflation dilemma until just after they were returned to office with an enlarged majority in 1955, after having stimulated a preelection boom. Their initial response was to try negotiating an agreement among producer groups like that obtained earlier by Labor. Having failed to win the TUC's agreement, because it rejected the TUC's terms, the Government briefly joined with employer associations in an effort to impose wage restraint. But it felt compelled to retreat in the face of the resistance the unions were able to mount in the labor market. The Government was then thrown back onto lowering aggregate demand, but the resulting increase in unemployment led the Government to reverse itself to overcome the correspondingly increased prospect of defeat in the impending 1959 election. Defeat was avoided by the new boom, but it presented the returned Conservative Government with renewed inflationary pressures, to which it responded with a sequence of initiatives much like that followed between 1955 and 1959, each of which was also frustrated, including another preelection boom, which this time failed to avoid defeat. Driven back to demand management after each incomes policy attempt broke down, Conservative policy switched back and forth abruptly between restriction and expansion.

This "stop-go" pattern sheds further light on how the "basic structure of the full employment welfare state" has remained vulnerable inspite of the shift in power toward the labor movement or, more precisely, because of the limits of that shift. Just as Crosland predicted, the three postwar Conservative Governments apparently felt compelled to meet approximately the standard of full employment set when Labor was in Office after the war because the Labor Party's continued presence in the political arena threatened any Conservative Government failing to meet that standard with electoral defeat. Under these conditions the unions retained sufficient power in the labor market to frustrate any strategy for reconciling full employment with greater price stability that they regarded as unacceptable. Lacking the power to impose an unacceptable strategy and unable or unwilling to design one that was acceptable to the unions, the Conservatives fell back on stop-go demand management to steer the economy between a severe balance of payments constraint and politically enforced full employment constraint. Thus, while the British labor movement lacked the kind of power needed to prevent the erosion of the welfare state while the Conservatives were in office, it did retain the kinds of power in both the political arena and the labor market needed to prevent the Conservatives from carrying out anti-inflationary policies that threatened full employment or the union's narrower stakes.

In other words, the shift in power to the labor movement organization in the labor market, resulting from the full employment begun during the war and continued thereafter, was only sufficient to produce a stalemate over economic policy when the labor movement organization in the political arena was unable to control the state as well. Although this stalemate cannot protect the welfare state from erosion, it can protect full employment. But full employment can be protected this way only over the relatively short run. The stop-go pattern of economic policy that results from the stalemate has destabilizing effects that make it progressively more difficult for full employment to be reconciled with a level of price increases that is politically tolerable and consistent with balance of payments requirements. This renders full employment itself vulnerable to attrition in the longer run, both economically and politically. For example, a decline in employment may begin in export industries as a result of weakened international competitiveness, and pressures for lowering the level of policy aspirations with respect to employment may mount because of increasing concern over prices. Again, under conditions of inflationary growth in a capitalist economy, and especially under conditions of inflation accompanied by stagnation, opportunities may arise for political strategies that can restructure the electorate in such a way as to make a retreat from full employment possible.

Over the longer run, then, a shift in power toward the labor movement's organizations in the political arena and labor market that is sufficient only to produce a stalemate can protect neither full employment nor the welfare state. Both can evidently be protected only if the labor movement party breaks the stalemate by regaining control of the state. But this will obviously not suffice, nor persist, unless the party can come up with a politically viable economic policy strategy. This, as already noted, the British Labor Party was not able to do after it was returned to office in 1964.

The Failure of Wage Restraint Policies

As soon as it took over, Harold Wilson's Government found itself saddled with a balance of payments deficit, aggravated by its predecessor's preelection boom, that was the largest in the postwar period. Its immediate response was to reject devaluation, and it thereupon embarked on an effort to avoid devaluation that ultimately proved futile after three years. During that period the effort subjected the Party's relationship with the unions to severe strains. The pattern of policy on which that effort rested was pursued after devaluation as well until those strains reached the breaking point. At that point, the Government retreated. By then, however, even the limited protection that the postwar configuration of power had given the full employment welfare state had been seriously impaired. Only the briefest sketch of how this happened is possible here.

While engaging in various holding operations to deal with the immediate and subsequent payments crises, the Wilson Government apparently expected to overcome the economy's underlying vulnerability to such crises by a form of "indicative planning," expanding on what the Conservatives had begun. It was regarded as essential to this planning that an incomes policy be put into operation, which the Conservatives had been unable to do. The Labor Government's confidence that it could win the union cooperation that the Conservatives could not received initial confirmation in December 1964, when the TUC joined with it and organized business in a Joint Declaration of Intent to observe voluntary restraint in wages and·prices. But tension between the Government and the TUC soon began to build up as the Government pressed the TUC to secure greater compliance from its affiliates than the TUC could deliver, while the Government's commitment to planned growth which was part of the bargain seemed to waver in the face of continuing payments difficulties.

Dissatisfied with the TUC's ability to bring about restraint, the Government turned increasingly from a voluntary to a compulsory approach. Beginning with obligatory prior notification of impending increases, the Government went on to take legal power to postpone implementation of increases and then to impose an across-the-board wage-price freeze in July 1966. This was in turn followed by several phases in which compulsory restraint was enforced with varying degrees of severity. Each step the Government took in the direction of compulsory restraint was strenuously opposed by the TUC. It reluctantly acquiesced in the 1966 freeze as the only available alternative to deflation and higher unemployment, given the Government's renewed rejection of devaluation in response to the eruption of yet another payments crisis. In the event, the unions got deflation and unemployment anyway, and neither that nor the freeze proved enough to stave off devaluation. Having been forced to devalue in November, 1967, the Government sought to make the most of the breathing space devaluation afforded by continuing an incomes policy backed by legal sanctions. For its part, the TUC continued to oppose any role for legal sanctions. Meanwhile, the TUC tried to build its capacity for coordinating wage policy in accordance with its own views of what was equitable and possible.

But neither with respect to incomes policy nor collective bargaining generally was the Government satisfied that the TUC or its affiliates had sufficient authority to perform the functions it felt to be necessary. Accordingly, it moved to extend the role of legal sanctions to areas of collective bargaining well beyond wage settlements that violated incomes policy criteria. Late in 1968, it announced its intention of introducing legislation that would, among other things, penalize wildcat strikes. The Labor Government's industrial relations legislation proposals were mild enough compared with what its Conservative successor was to enact. But coming on top of the imposition of wage restraint, the proposals aroused such intense union hostility that, as one observer put it, "the traditional alliance of trade unions and politically based socialists in the Labor Party was threatened as perhaps never before."

In the face of this resistance, formally set forth by a special Congress of the TUC in June, 1969, the Government shortly thereafter dropped its legislative proposals in exchange for a face-saving formula in which the TUC pledged to take more responsibility for dealing with wildcat strikes. Parallel with this development, the Government was in the process of dismantling much of the authority and machinery for enforcing wage restraint. However, while the Government retreated from its reliance on legal sanctions to make industrial relations

conform with what it conceived to be the requirements of economic policy, its
conduct of economic policy was more unsatisfactory to the unions than ever.
A record balance of payments surplus was achieved, but throughout the first
half of 1970, unemployment hovered at levels higher than in any comparable
period since the end of the Great Depression.

As in 1951, it is uncertain how far Labor's defeat in the 1970 election can
be explained by dissatisfaction with its management of the economy within
Party as well as union ranks. Against the view that the abstention of Labor
voters caused the Party's defeat, it has been pointed out that the decline in
turnout in the 1970 election was fairly evenly spread among Conservative as
well as Labor constituencies. But lack of enthusiasm for Edward Heath among
Conservative voters need not necessarily have been matched by an equivalent
measure of apathy among Labor voters. The ability to mobilize its potential
supporters more fully than the Conservatives could their own is precisely what
it would have taken for Labor to win. That Labor failed to do so can hardly be
unrelated to the still raw wounds, in the constituency organizations as well as
the unions, inflicted in the battles over Labor's approach to the problem of
inflation. For the Labor Party to elicit the necessary electoral support, its
performance in office would presumably have had to confirm its credibility
as a preferable alternative to a Conservative Government. This it signally failed
to do with respect to aspects of policy crucial to its distinctive claim to support.

Towards a Permanent Stalemate

Whatever they may have contributed to its 1970 defeat, Labor's policies
prior to that defeat gave the Conservative Government that followed much more
room for maneuver in economic policy than the earlier postwar Conservative
Governments had. To begin with, the belated devaluation and huge payments
surplus provided an extremely favorable starting position. In addition, the
full employment constraint was considerably relaxed by the increase in unemployment under Labor, which the Heath Government evidently felt it could
let rise even higher. Moreover, Labor's abortive industrial relations law initiative made it politically possible for the Conservatives to enact a much harsher
measure. Ironically then, Labor's policies between 1964 and 1970 did break
the stalemate of the preceding years, but by diminishing the labor movement's
power in the political economy rather than by increasing it.

However, the Heath Government squandered the advantages it had inherited,
ultimately by pressing its advantage over the unions too far in its confrontation
with the miners' union, over which Heath gambled on an election and lost. Thus,
by a further irony, Conservative policies went a long way toward restoring the
stalemate or, perhaps more accurately, restoring it in a different and potentially
more persistent and paralyzing form. While the unions came through retaining

much of their capacity to resist unacceptable policy through their power in the labor market, the Labor Party had not regained its capacity to mobilize electoral support sufficiently to win a parliamentary majority while the Conservatives were deprived of theirs. In fact, Labor as well as the Conservatives won less votes in 1974 than in 1970 inspite of a larger turnout. Labor's policy capability was evidently still discredited in the eyes of many of its supporters at a time when the Conservatives had lost the confidence of many of their supporters, leaving no party with a parliamentary majority for the first time since 1929.

The considerable success of the Liberal and regional "nationalist" parties in attracting those disillusioned with the Labor and Conservative parties has been seen as indicating that a process of "decomposition" has begun in the major parties. If this is so, and if the process continues, particularly in the Labor Party, it could have far-reaching implications for the possibility of subjecting British capitalism to democratic control. If there is no longer much prospect that a labor movement party can win control of the state, even temporarily, such constraint as its presence in the electoral arena can impose on how public authority is used to influence the economy must be substantially diminished.

But what is to determine how that authority is to be used if a party drawing its resources primarily from business is also unable to win control of the state? One possibility is that business support is spread to one or more of the parties eroding the major parties' electoral constituencies, in the expectation that a governing coalition could be formed with the business supported major party. Such a coalition might well use public authority as consistently with the perceived interests of business as a government controlled by a single business-supported party, and it would be in a position to do so without being subjected to the constraints imposed by a labor movement party that was a potential alternative government. However, there is another possibility that could conceivably restore such constraints or even establish democratic control. That is the formation of an alternative coalition of one or more of the rising minority parties with the weakened labor movement party. On the other hand, if the labor movement party could not find a policy strategy capable of reconciling the perceived interests of its union core constituency with those of the rest of its constituency while it was in office on the basis of its own parliamentary majority, it is probably less likely to be able to find a policy strategy that can meet this requirement and at the same time also be acceptable to one or more other parties.

While such a coalition may therefore be unable to govern or, consequently, even act as a constraint on a governing coalition of business-supported parties, it may be just as difficult for a coalition of the latter type to govern. The rising smaller parties might be reluctant to be identified with either of the erstwhile major parties of whose decomposition they are the beneficiaries. Stable government on the basis of parliamentary majorities might then be rendered impossible. This need not necessarily preclude the use of public authority consistently with business' perceived interests insofar as its use can be determined through

bargaining between public bureaucracies and business. Yet, if party fragmentation occurs in such a way as to make it impossible for elections to yield governing
majorities, whether of one or more parties, it may become impossible for anyone
to use public authority to control the capitalist economic process, even in ways
that business may have come to regard as essential. Under such conditions, the
temptation, though not necessarily the possibility, of an authoritarian resolution
of stalemated politics might well be increased. The decomposition of a labor
movement party as a consequence of its policy failures may therefore not only
make it impossible to control a capitalist economy through the democratic
process but also threaten the very existence of the democratic process itself.

Accordingly, very much may depend on the ability of labor movement
parties to come up with politically viable solutions to the problems of economic
policy as they are distinctively defined for those parties, given their specific
sources of support and particular ways in which capitalist economies tend to
operate at various times. Can such solutions be found or are the problems as
intractable as they appear to have been for the British Labor Party?

As indicated earlier, the Swedish Social Democrats' response to the Great
Depression suggests that a policy strategy that was politically viable for labor
movement parties was available at least in that context. The Social Democratic
Party also seems to have been able to develop politically viable responses to the
policy problems characteristic of the postwar era. This seems to have played
a large part in enabling the Party to remain in office virtually without interruption for over four decades, longer than any other party subject to the
repeated test of free elections. In this way it seems to have met more effectively
than any other labor movement party the requirement for subjecting a capitalist
economy to democratic control that some of its spokesmen have declared to be
essential. But there is some doubt about whether the Party can continue to do
so, at least on the basis of the kind of policy strategies on which it has relied
successfully until now. Even if it succeeds in extending its unmatched continuity
in office, however, there are doubts about how effectively that has served as a
mechanism for the democratic control of Swedish capitalism in the past and
even greater doubts about how effectively it can do so in the future. These
doubts call into question the possibility of ever subjecting the capitalist economic
process to democratic control under any conceivable circumstances. The nature
of these doubts can best be indicated after reviewing the Swedish experience
until now.

Swedish Social Democratic Response to the
Great Depression

Like the British labor movement, the Swedish labor movement had become
a major force in the political economy by the time the Great Depression struck.

From their late nineteenth century beginnings, the development of the central federation of manual workers' unions, the LO, and the Social Democratic Party had been intimately linked. In 1930 the LO unions included almost all industrial workers and about a fifth of the total labor force. The Party had already become the largest in the Second Chamber by 1918 and had thrice formed minority governments of varying duration in the 1920s. Although a substantial gain of Second Chamber seats in the 1932 election left it still short of a majority, it formed another minority government. That government had to deal with a combination of technical and tactical problems almost exactly analogous to those faced just a little earlier by the British Labor Party.[14]

The Swedish Social Democrats' contrasting response to the technical problem of coping with unemployment had already been formulated two years earlier. Led by Ernst Wigforss, who was to become Finance Minister, the Social Democrats repeatedly urged an expansionary, loan-financed public works program, paying normal wages, in place of the orthodox policy of balanced budgets and poor-law type relief for the unemployed. The fact that the three so-called "bourgeois" parties together still had the parliamentary majority to block the program after the 1932 election posed the tactical problem facing the Social Democrats. They found a solution to it in a split within one of the three parties. In 1933 a dissident wing of the Agrarian Party agreed to support the Social Democratic program in exchange for Social Democratic acceptance of agricultural tariffs and price supports. Having won what the Agrarian Party's core constituency wanted most, the dissidents were able to take over control of it and provide the Social Democrats with the necessary margin of support. This the Agrarian Party did not only throughout the rest of the 1930s but also well into the postwar period.

At the same time that the 1933 realignment established the configuration of power on which Social Democratic rule rested for a long time thereafter, the response to the Depression which that configuration made possible set the basic pattern of policy elaborated by the Social Democrats since then. That pattern relies primarily on the instruments of public finance to maintain full employment and also to pursue a variety of allocative and distributive policies of the kind that characterize the welfare state—in short, a pattern much like that pursued by British Labor. The economic recovery Sweden experienced under the Social Democrats in the early 1930s seemed to confirm the effectiveness of that pattern, although increased exports probably had more to do with the recovery than the public works program. In any case, the political consequences were registered in the 1936 election, which gave the Social Democrats more seats than the combined total of the three bourgeois parties for the first time, though still not quite a majority because of seats won by Communists and dissident Socialists.[15]

The combination of solutions to the technical and tactical problems confronting the Social Democrats when they came into office in 1932 thus provided them with a political formula that enabled them to increase their power and build up an initial version of the Swedish full employment welfare state. However, this version was threatened during the early postwar years by the same kinds of processes that undermined the similar version built up by the 1945-51 Labor Government in Britain. Although it is more complex, the contrast between Swedish Social Democratic and British Labor responses to these processes is no less significant than the contrast between their responses to the Great Depression. This can be seen in terms of both of the broad policy areas in which the operation of the processes in the British case was discussed.

A Structural Strategy of Economic Management

Like its British counterpart and most other Western governments, the Swedish Social Democratic Government first tried to cope with the unemployment-inflation trade-off dilemma with a form of "incomes policy." Much as in Britain, a bargain was struck among the producer organizations and the government in the late 1940s, and it similarly broke down under pressures made acute by the Korean crisis. But there were no more ventures of this sort in Sweden, because the LO refused to consent to any more and no Swedish Social Democratic Government ever tried to impose any form of wage restraint over the LO's objections. Instead, when inflationary pressures became intense again toward the end of the 1950s, the Government began implementing an alternative strategy along lines that the LO had already laid out in considerable detail at its 1951 convention.

Essentially, the LO's position was that a structural change strategy, relying on the shift of labor and capital from the less efficient to the more efficient activities in the economy, could improve the unemployment-inflation trade-off in a more acceptable way than a repressed inflation strategy, relying on wage restraint. The latter was rejected because it threatened organizational and ideological interests of unions of the kind cited in our earlier discussion. On the other hand, the LO held, structural change could be facilitated by the interaction of government fiscal and manpower policies and a union wage policy that was consistent with the unions' basic function. First, profits could be squeezed between fiscal policy and union wage pressure. By greater use of indirect taxes, fiscal policy could be made flexible and restrictive enough to inhibit employers' efforts to pass on increased wage costs in the form of price increases, reinforcing the inhibition imposed by international competition. At the same time, the LO could coordinate union wage pressures so as to enforce high, standard rates—equal pay for equal work, regardless of employers' ability to pay. Second, to assure alternative employment for workers in firms forced out of business by the profits squeeze, the government would have to carry out a large-scale, flexible, and multifaceted manpower policy. This would embrace a wide range of measures including the provision of retraining, increased flows of information in the labor market, and financial benefits to cover living costs during the transition from one job to another.

The acceptability of the whole strategy hinged particularly on whether the government pursued an "active" manpower policy sufficient in scope and magnitude to shift the costs of economic stabilization and structural change from the specific workers whose jobs were threatened to the society as a whole that benefited from the results. Thus, the strategy was directed primarily at facilitating labor mobility on acceptable terms. It was assumed that capital mobility could be left to take care of itself, except that an increase in public sector savings that more than offset a decline in business savings anticipated from the profits squeeze was called for to assure an adequate supply of credit for new investment. Over the long run the strategy was expected to have the additional result of reducing economic inequality as workers shifted from low- to high-wage employment and as public savings increased relative to private.[16]

What the LO had proposed was clearly a long-term strategy for managing the economy so as to make it progressively less vulnerable to inflation and balance of payments crises. Accordingly, the British Labor Party did not have the option of adopting a similar strategy to deal with the immediate balance of payments crisis it encountered upon entering office in 1964. But it did have the option of a devaluation that might have bought the time needed to put a similar strategy into operation, at least after winning a substantial parliamentary majority in 1966 if not after its extremely narrow victory in 1964. While the LO alternative required time to build up, this was hardly less true of any "incomes policy" that there was any chance of being accepted by the TUC. And even if a structural approach proved to be no more effective in economic terms than a repressed inflation approach, its political costs to the British Labor Party were bound to be far less than the clash with the unions to which it led by its quest for wage restraint.

Inasmuch as the LO strategy not only takes time to put into operation but is one to be pursued on a continuing basis, such effectiveness as it might have evidently presupposes a government continuously controlled by political elites willing to pursue it. Given the substance of the strategy, it seems likely that the only political elites who might be willing to pursue it would be those independent of business—that is, principally those sustained by labor movement parties. To the extent that a major function of wage restraint in practice has been to prevent a squeeze on profits and maintain the rate of business savings, it would seem that any pattern of policy that ruled out both wage restraint and enough unemployment to subdue union wage pressures would necessarily involve a shift of the capital accumulation function from the private to the public sector, as envisioned in the LO strategy. But insofar as the public sector takes on the savings end of the savings-investment process, it may also have to concern itself increasingly with the investment end of the process and to develop decision-making mechanisms capable of performing allocative functions to replace those performed by the private capital market. If so, capital mobility cannot be indefinitely left to take care of itself as assured in the initial formulation of the LO strategy.

In fact, Swedish economic policy has been increasingly addressed to the composition of industrial investment since the later 1960s, and the LO position has come to be that this is essential to the effective implementation of its basic economic policy strategy. In itself, public sector intervention in the savings-investment process need not necessarily be opposed by business, particularly by those segments that can benefit directly. But if the intervention is carried out in such a way as to serve the purposes of an overall strategy like the LO's, it might very well be opposed by business, as it generally has been in Sweden. Accordingly, effective implementation of the LO strategy would seem to require that the Social Democrats be continuously in office. By the mid-1950s, however, it was becoming increasingly doubtful whether they could remain in office much longer.[17]

Having won an absolute majority of votes and seats in 1940, the Social Democrats subsequently suffered a steady decline in electoral support, making them again dependent on parliamentary support by the Agrarians. This was formalized by bringing the latter into a coalition government in 1951, as in the period between 1936 and the formation of a four-party wartime coalition in 1940. But the Social Democrats could not expect to rely on Agrarian support for much longer. The secular decline of the agricultural sector was steadily reducing its strength by depriving the party of its social base. This naturally posed the prospect of political oblivion to the Agrarian Party leadership. To avert that it set out to redefine the party's constituency and give it a new identity, clearly dissociating it from the Social Democratic Party. This was done by, among other things, changing the name of the Agrarian Party to Center Party and pulling out of the coalition government. Thus, the configuration of power on which Social Democratic rule had intermittently depended since the 1933 realignment was undermined by the changes in social structure inherent in Sweden's transformation into an advanced industrial society.

Over the longer run these changes threatened the social basis of the Social Democratic Party itself insofar as it was confined to blue collar workers, for their proportion in the labor force was also bound to decline and was already beginning to do so. For the time being, however, the Social Democrats could cope with the tactical problem as it had been redefined for them in the mid-1950s if they mobilized their traditional blue-collar constituency more fully than they had, provided that they gradually enlarged their support among white collar workers at the same time.

A solution along these lines was made possible by the political controversy that was aroused around a Social Democratic proposal for a basic reform of the national pension scheme. In addition, the reform provided a way of counteracting the erosion of the public sector welfare state where it was particularly vulnerable. Furthermore, it embodied financial arrangements that proved to be a very powerful mechanism for increasing the public sector savings called for by the LO economic strategy. For these reasons, the pension controversy was a decisive turning point in the postwar development of the Swedish political economy.

Counteracting the Erosion of Public Sector
Welfare Institutions

The first version of the Swedish welfare state provided for universal flat-rate pensions much like those in the Beveridge scheme introduced in Britain by the postwar Labor Government. The Swedish scheme became somewhat better designed to fulfill the promise of protection against poverty in old age that it shared with the British scheme when the benefits were price-indexed in 1948. Inspite of indexing and successive discretionary increases, however, benefits in Sweden also failed to keep old people out of poverty even as defined in the needs-based social assistance programs. Moreover, there was likewise a growing gap between pensions and the real incomes that sustained economic growth enabled increasing numbers of people to earn during their working years.

In Sweden as in Britain, therefore, the low level of public sector pension benefits made supplementation through private schemes increasingly attractive. The development of such schemes, particularly through collective bargaining, was urged by the Swedish employers' association, the SAF. But the LO rejected this approach in favor of legislation on the grounds that it would achieve improved pensions more quickly and equitably, since legislation could do it for everyone at the same time and on the same terms. To that end, the LO and Social Democratic Party jointly proposed a universal, compulsory scheme to supplement the existing flat-rate pensions with earnings-related benefits, which would in combination be equivalent to about two-thirds of average earnings in the fifteen best years, up to a limit of more than double the median income. The supplementary pensions were to be financed entirely by employers' "contributions"—that is, a payroll tax—to accumulate in a fund that would build up a large surplus during an extended transitional period while the number of recipients grew.

It was especially these financial arrangements that were attacked by the SAF and the liberal and conservative parties as a dangerous extension of the state's power in economic life that would, among other things, give it "absolute domination" of the capital market. After discounting the polemical exaggeration in these charges, it remains clear that a choice between the growth of public or private sector channels for capital accumulation was at stake in the conflict over alternative approaches to provision of retirement income. At the same time such charges helped to polarize political conflict along ideological lines more sharply than it had been for years, with the Social Democrats defining the issue in terms of a choice between solidaristic and particularistic solutions to social problems. In this way they were able to reassert their reformist claims and to mobilize their traditional supporters more effectively than ever before, while the specifics of their pension proposal enabled them to attract additional support beyond that constituency.

The result was that the postwar decline in the Social Democrats' electoral

fortunes was reversed in a special election in 1958, called after their proposal
was defeated in parliament. They made additional gains in the regular 1960
election after their proposal was enacted by one vote and after they restored
a sales tax that they defended as essential to finance further improvements in
the welfare state. Still short of an absolute majority, they nonetheless won
more seats than the three bourgeois parties again. And again they could govern
alone and were in a position to manage the economy in accordance with the
LO strategy. This they apparently did with considerable effectiveness, at least
in the next few years.[18]

During the 1950s as in the 1930s, then, the Social Democrats seem to have
found a combination of technical and tactical solutions to the key problems of
economic policy with which they had to deal. This combination of solutions
provided them with a political formula for continuing in office and establishing
a new version of the full employment welfare state that was less vulnerable to
erosion by the processes that threatened the initial version. At least thus far,
then, Swedish experience seems to confirm the possibility that labor movement
parties can come up with politically viable policies that enable them to serve as
effective instruments for subjecting capitalist economies to democratic control.
But does it really? Although the Social Democrats' policies may have been
politically viable in the literal sense of enabling them to remain in office, it is
not necessarily the case that the Social Democrats have thereby maintained
control over Swedish capitalism that is either democratic or effective. Serious
questions can be raised on both counts.

Can There Be Democracy Without
Alternations in Power?

Are the uses to which public authority is put determined democratically
when it is continuously controlled by the leaders of the same party? It could
be argued that the answer must be no if the democratic process only works
when there is alternation in office among two or more parties. The accountability of those who govern to the governed is presumably enforced through
elections precisely because elections make it possible for those who govern to
be replaced by others—others who challenge the way in which they govern and
propose to govern differently. Hence the necessity for a party or parties to
sustain the challenge and compete effectively with the party of those who govern,
and for the whole array of civil and political rights designed to keep those who
control public authority from using it to frustrate the challenge and perpetuate
their control. As indicated at the outset, the Social Democratic argument takes
all this for granted. The claim is that democratic control requires that the Social
Democrats be continuously returned to office, but only under these conditions.

However, what happens to the constraint imposed by the possibility of losing office if that possibility is never realized? Conceivably, the credibility of that possibility is diminished, and with that its effectiveness. To the extent that the Social Democrats succeed in staying in office by convincing enough of the electorate that they must do so to prevent those with economic power from also having political power, and also that the Social Democrats alone are capable of governing, they can perhaps free themselves of the risk of losing office. Their accountability could no longer be enforced and they could become, in effect, a governing class.

It could be countered that this need not be the case as long as they are repeatedly subjected to the test of free elections. For the opposition to remain a permanent one does not matter as long as the opposition parties can repeatedly press the challenge and renew the possibility of replacing the Social Democrats in office. In fact, the opposition parties have been highly successful in keeping the possibility real by sharply limiting the Social Democrats' margin of victory most of the time and making it so small the rest of the time that the Social Democrats have been unable to rule without parliamentary support from at least one other party. But even if the possibility is kept real, its effect on how the Social Democrats govern may be limited if it is never realized because their definitions of the issues and available policy options as well as their policy effectiveness can never be tested against those of an alternative government; there is no experience on the basis of which the electorate can weigh the Social Democrats' claims and performance against those of the opposition.

Under such circumstances, it could be argued, it becomes all the easier for economic policy to be made by a relatively closed, stable set of elites who head the organizations that manage the major economic functions: the state, unions, and business. In Sweden the organizations in each of these areas are highly centralized, putting those who head them in a position to bargain effectively with each other and giving them a common stake in finding agreements that keep things running smoothly and leave their respective positions secure. Business is not subjected to control by the state in this context any more than the unions are. The state cannot be used in any ways unacceptable to the elites that control either; both find it possible to agree with those controlling public bureaucracies on how the latter can be used in mutually supportive ways. Within the legitimating framework provided by Social Democratic control of public authority, these elites actually determine what is done with public authority without being genuinely accountable to the electorate or even their own organizational constituencies. From this standpoint, the Social Democrats are not so much a governing class as the politically necessary brokers in an essentially corporatist rather than democratic political economy.

The democratic character of the Swedish political economy has been called into question along lines like these by critics of the Social Democrats at various points on the political spectrum, especially left socialist or liberal in orientation. There is much that lends plausibility to the corporatist description in particular, which helps to explain the Center Party's success in becoming the second largest party on the basis of its call for decentralization. There is also much that deprives the corporatist description of its plausibility, which helps to explain why, while hedging its bets, business generally continues to hope that the Social Democrats can finally be ousted from office and to funnel its support in whatever directions offer the best prospects of bringing that about. A more adequate characterization of the Swedish political economy might be provided in terms of a class power configuration as in our discussion of Britain, with the shift in power toward the "organized working class" in Sweden conceived as having gone beyond stalemate to something approaching dominance by that class.[19] However, the relative adequacy of the corporatist or class descriptions cannot be evaluated apart from a systematic analysis of how economic policy has actually evolved. In any case, even if such an analysis would lend more support to the class than the corporatist description, the question of whether alternation in office is essential to make the political economy democratic would remain.

How this question is answered would have to depend a lot on one's general conception of democracy and how the issue of class power is handled within that conception. But the position that alternation in office is essential is not necessarily fatal to the Social Democratic argument, at least in principle, for continuous control of the state by any one party is not required by the argument. What is required is continuous control of the state by political elites who are independent of business. As long as they satisfy that criterion, these political elites, or counter-elites, can be sustained by two or more parties. There can accordingly be an alternation in office among them or any coalitions into which they may form. Something like such coalitions have occurred in Sweden and the other Scandinavian countries. But these coalitions have not involved anything that would qualify as alternation in office, for the same labor movement parties have typically been the dominant partners in all of them. And as we saw, the argument does go on to hold that, in practice, only where labor movement parties sustain counter-elites is there much prospect that they can compete successfully with business-supported political elites. The possibilities for alternation in office by different sets of counter-elites would therefore seem to be rather limited. There are, of course, labor movements that are divided along ideological and confessional lines, organized politically in separate parties. But such divisions seem to make it more likely that no counter-elites can control the state than that different ones can do so at different times. It may then be that control of the state by counter-elites, stipulated as necessary for the democratic control of a capitalist economy, is not likely to occur except where, as in Sweden, a single labor movement party is continuously in office. So, if alternation in office is a requirement of the democratic process, control of capitalism is not likely to occur where that requirement is met. In short, democratic control of a capitalist economy is not likely to be possible under most conceivable political circumstances.

Evaluating Social Democratic Policy Performance

If one rejects both the notion that alternation in office is essential to democracy and the description of the Swedish political economy as corporatist, one could accept the Social Democratic argument concerning the political conditions for democratic control of a capitalist economy and agree that these conditions have been met in Sweden, at least more fully than elsewhere. But this would still leave open the question of whether the power this has given the Social Democrats to determine how public authority is used has in fact been used by them to control Swedish capitalism effectively. This is an extremely complex question. What we need to know in order to answer it is itself problematical, and if that can be settled there again remains the need for an extensive analysis of economic policy to tell us what we need to know. It is possible here only to point most crudely to some of the things that raise the question.

At a minimum, as the argument implies, policy that is effective makes some difference to the operation of the economy in those respects in which its operation is identified as unsatisfactory through the political process. Which respects are thereby turned into the concerns of policy is presumably a function of the issues around which the contenders for political power mobilize support. The Swedish Social Democrats have clearly made the inability of a capitalist economy to assure employment the most salient issue most persistently, and have staked their claim to effectiveness more on remedying this defect in the operation of the economy than on anything else. On the face of it, they seem to have made good on this claim, for on a comparative basis, unemployment in Sweden during the Social Democratic era has been very low overall and has varied within narrow limits. But how much has policy contributed to this?

During the 1930s, as noted earlier, the Social Democrats' expansionary public works program probably contributed too little too late to make much difference, however innovative the program was in principle. They reaped the political benefits of Sweden's recovery, but its main source was apparently increased export demand. Then and since, the relatively late, specialized, and export-oriented industrialization of the Swedish economy (compared with others in the West) made the conventional tasks of economic policy relatively easy, notably when compared with Britain. Thus, Swedish industry was in an excellent position to take advantage of the buoyant demand that characterized the international economy throughout most of the postwar period until recently. The economic growth that has made possible rapidly rising living standards in Sweden, including the expansion of generous welfare benefits, may then have been largely the product of domestic economic development prior to, and a favorable external environment beyond the control of, Social Democratic policy.

On the other hand, there seems to be little doubt that policy contributed to the stability and composition of this growth, particularly in certain periods in the postwar decades, and that the expansion of the public sector helped

maintain the high level of demand for labor. The impact of policy emerges
clearly in view of the ways in which policy has been geared to reconciling full
employment with other goals that have been given priorities nearly as high.
One important example is provided by the course of housing construction.
Although it has been varied to stabilize employment within the construction
sector, it has been shielded from the impact of tight credit periods in order to
maintain one of the highest overall rates of housing construction in the world.
Another example is the rapid build-up of manpower policy to levels not
approached in any other country. This reflects the effort not only to achieve
such price stability as is necessary to safeguard employment over the long run
but to do so on the terms laid down by the LO. Furthermore, the relatively
tight budgetary policy called for by the LO strategy was not implemented in
such a way as to hold back the growth of the public sector. On the contrary,
by 1972 the flow of funds channeled into the public sector by all forms of
taxation had risen to nearly 44 percent of the gross domestic product (GDP),
while total public sector revenues from all sources were equivalent to 52
percent of GDP. Thus, the stabilization policy options chosen were those
that also furthered politically determined priorities concerning the composition of activity.[20]

In these and other respects, then, Social Democratic policy has evidently
made a difference. But its effectiveness in remedying those defects in the
operation of the economy to which it has been directed has been called into
question increasingly since the mid-1960s. Moreover, it has been charged with
neglecting other defects over which there has been increasing concern. A sharp
setback in the 1966 local government elections shocked the Social Democrats
into recognizing the rapidly emerging economic discontents. What appeared
to be a comprehensive policy response to them, coupled with the impact of the
Soviet invasion of Czechoslovakia, enabled the Social Democrats to more than
recover by the 1968 parliamentary election. But since then a more persistent
decline in electoral support has accompanied the Social Democrats' apparent
inability to match their previous performance, while controversy over newer
issues has intensified. After the 1973 parliamentary election ended in an
exactly even division between the three bourgeois parties, on the one hand,
and the Social Democrats and Communists, on the other, the Social Democrats have been able to just barely hang onto office with the help of one of
the other parties, initially the Communists and now the Liberals. The political formula evolved by the Social Democrats by the beginning of the 1960s
had clearly ceased to work, and their prospects for coming up with a new
policy mix that is politically viable seem increasingly doubtful.

The Social Democrats' difficulties in coping with economic policy problems since the mid-1960s stem partly from flaws in their execution of the
pattern of policy they were pursuing, pretty much as had been urged by the
LO. Most serious was the mistiming of fiscal policy in the middle of the decade

and again at the end. The use of fiscal policy for stabilization purposes is, of course, the least distinctive feature of that pattern of policy as well as one with which governments generally have had trouble. In the Swedish case mistimed fiscal policy made it more difficult to fulfill the promise of the more innovative features of the pattern. However, even if it had been carried out precisely as prescribed, it may still not have been adequate to its assigned tasks, not to speak of the broadening range of tasks economic policy was being called upon to perform.

Structural change in industry accelerated but the massive expansion of manpower policy proved insufficient to shift the burdens of mobility from the affected workers to society as fully as anticipated. For some, especially older workers, the employment and income effects were not offset. For others, even new jobs and higher pay did not always compensate for giving up satisfying social and physical environments for strange and often more congested surroundings. The population shifts involved also gave rise to new discontents among both those who were left in declining districts and those already in the rapidly growing urban conurbations. Yet, the improved unemployment-inflation trade-off that the structural change was supposed to bring was not forthcoming. On the contrary, established expectations concerning full employment were being less consistently met than before while prices were nevertheless rising fast—which is not to say that the worsening of the trade-off would not have been greater in the absence of the policies pursued.

Obviously, Sweden was not escaping the kind of economic difficulties being experienced elsewhere. Quite apart from recent broad trends, structural change is undoubtedly bound to be socially disruptive. But Social Democratic policy had generated expectations about the distribution of the burdens and benefits of economic change that it was not satisfying. Instead of shaping the process of economic change in accordance with politically determined priorities, policy now seemed merely to be accommodating the requirements of change as defined by the autonomous decisions of capitalist firms. If so, the capitalist economic process was evidently not being subjected to democratic control.

At the same time such consensus over priorities as there had been seemed to be diminishing. Distributive issues were becoming salient to an unprecedented degree. Growing awareness of the fact that there had been virtually no reduction in economic inequality led to increasing LO pressures to improve the relative position of low-income groups and demands for more redistributive tax and transfer policies. This in turn evoked intensified resistance by upper-income groups. Greater LO aggressiveness in this connection was partly a reaction to declining acquiescence in the structure of authority in industry. Wildcat strikes challenged the binding character of collective agreements, thereby threatening both the labor movement's highly centralized organization and managerial prerogatives at the plant level. The latter, it should be pointed out, have since been circumscribed by Social Democratic legislation. Controversy over the distribution of power in industry has thus joined controversy over the distribution of income. While this could be seen as the reemergence of long latent issues, the eruption of environmental concerns evidently posed issues for economic policy that were largely new. Already complicated by employment considerations, environmental issues have been made more intractable by the recent emergence of energy supply as an urgent problem. The accumlation of all these issues has been making economic policy formation ever more complex.

Their 1966 electoral setback already convinced the Social Democrats that they were not equipped to cope with the economic policy problems facing them at the time. The result was a shift in the direction of development of policy. The pattern of policy elaborated since the 1930s has been essentially macroeconomic. As noted earlier it has relied primarily on the instruments of public finance to influence the overall level of activity. It has, of course, done so in such a way as to enlarge vastly the public sector share of the national product. Moreover, the "general" techniques of fiscal policy have been supplemented by "selective" techniques, particularly in the credit and labor markets for the purposes of manpower and housing policies. Beyond that, however, the composition of activity has been left to the private sector, especially as far as the industrial core of the economy is concerned. The cumulative consequence of this pattern of policy is that Sweden's "mixed economy" is marked by an exceptionally sharp contrast between the growth in the financial dimension of the public sector and the relative stagnation in its entrepreneurial dimension. As indicted above, over half of the GDP is channeled through the public sector in all forms of revenue, more than in any other Western country. However, public enterprise has only accounted for between five and six percent of GDP and roughly the same portion of total employment for a long time, which is lower than in several West European countries.

In one respect, however, the growth in the financial dimension of the public sector was bound to make the composition of industrial activity an issue of public policy sooner or later. The extremely rapid accumulation of funds in the supplementary pension scheme enacted in 1959 was making it the single largest source of loans in the credit market by the late 1960s. This created an enormous potential for influencing the pattern of investment, but the government had made no use of that potential except to assure sufficient finance for housing. The policy crisis that emerged in 1966 brought the issue of industrial investment to the surface. The Social Democrats responded by turning to a much greater degree of microeconomic intervention than they had ever attempted in the past.

Early in 1967 they announced a "new industrial policy." Its declared aims were to establish control over the process of technological change and its social consequences, so as to assure both long-term economic development and a just distribution of its burdens and benefits. While the policy's aims were ambitious, its implementation was limited by the need to build up the instruments for doing so almost from scratch. A beginning was made right away with the establishment of a state investment bank, followed by a ministry of industry, a holding company for managing and expanding public enterprise, some new research and development organizations, the expansion of the regional planning apparatus, and creation of a new agency for sectoral planning. The process of equipping the government for microeconomic intervention has been slow and uneven, so that its concrete results have so far been small. Its initial impact was primarily political. The new industrial policy sharpened ideological controversy much as did the pension conflict a decade earlier, and contributed to an even more marked improvement in electoral support for the Social Democrats in 1968, except that the improvement was also more short-lived, precisely because industrial policy could not bring quick economic results.

But even over the long run there is serious doubt as to whether the development of economic policy along the lines begun in the later 1960s could provide the Social Democrats with the capacity for shaping economic change that seems to have largely eluded them so far. This doubt does not rest primarily on the complexity of economic policy arising from the proliferation of issues cited earlier. These issues will be recognized as by no means unique to Sweden. Nor is there anything exceptional about the attempt to come to grips with these issues by greater intervention in the process of structural change. Indeed, most governments in Western Europe, of diverse political identities, have been pursuing "industrial policies" in one form or another, some much more ambitious than Sweden's. By itself the multiplication of issues involved makes it difficult for any of these governments to find a policy-mix that would be viable politically even it it could be effective economically. But it now seems increasingly doubtful that any of these governments can find an economically effective pattern of policy.

This doubt rests on the changing character of the international economic environment of national economic policy. For a large part of the postwar period, that environment seemed to provide at least some scope for governments in the industrialized capitalist societies to influence the economic process within their own jurisdictions, while the level of domestic activity benefited from the sustained growth of international trade. From the perspective of the argument here, such influence may not have subjected capitalism to democratic control in most cases because the domestic political conditions for that were not met. Control of the state nevertheless put at the disposal of those who had it the instruments through which some influence over the economic process was possible, even if it could only be for purposes that were acceptable to domestic business elites. In recent years, however, such scope as there was for national economic policy seems to have been sharply diminished.

Transformations in the International Economy

The main features of the transformation of the international economy, or at least the advanced capitalist portion of it that is most pertinent here, are familiar. One of the crucial features, of course, is the growth of multinational firms, spreading what Richard N. Cooper refers to as the "decision-making domain of business enterprise" across the jurisdictions of many governments, impairing the domestic sovereignty of all of them.[21] Another related feature is the breakdown of the monetary arrangements on the basis of which international transactions were carried out since the end of World War II. As a result of such trends the capitalist economic process may have become transnational to such an extent that no national governments can control its operation effectively within their own jurisdictions, short of closing their borders and attempting autarky. If this is so it no longer matters whether the configuration of power within a national political arena meets the requirements for subjecting capitalism to democratic control as stipulated by the argument. Even if national governments are controlled by counter-elites, democratic control of the capitalist economic process has become impossible if national governments can no longer serve as instruments through which such control can be exercised, and there is no transnational political authority coterminous with the decision-making domain of capitalist firms, not to speak of one whose uses can be determined through a democratic political process.

On the other hand, whether the capitalist economic process effectively escapes beyond the control of national governments may depend on which governments are controlled by counter-elites. Even in the absence of governmental authority coextensive with the scope of transnational business activity, that activity presupposes some kinds of governmental authority even if it is exercised by national governments, jointly or individually. And in this connection some national governments are more important than others. Indeed, as has been widely observed, Britain played a decisive role in organizing the pre-World War I international economy, and the United States has played a similar role since World War II. If the postwar international economic order was largely a function of American hegemony, whether it is now ending or not, the character of that order was shaped not simply by the sheer magnitude of the American economy but by the way in which American policy structured its impact. Thus, the environment favorable to the expansion of multinational firms—predominantly though not exclusively American—as well as the postwar monetary system are primarily the results of American policy.[22] While that policy certainly cannot be understood apart from the dynamics of power in the world as a whole, the particular course of American policy and its consequences for the structure of the capitalist portion of the international political economy has undoubtedly been conditioned by those very aspects of the structure of politics within the United States that we discussed earlier. We suggested then, it will be recalled, that the configuration of power in the American political economy clearly falls short of the requirements for subjecting American capitalism to democratic control, or for even establishing domestic sovereignty within the country. Accordingly, it may be that the democratic control of capitalism has become impossible elsewhere because it remains impossible in the United States.

Notes

1. Speech at Visby, July 26, 1973, supplied by Prime Minister's Office. An earlier example is an essay by Ernst Wigforss, former Social Democratic Finance Minister and a major contributor to the development of party ideology as well as policy, "Demokrati, parlamentarism och klasspolitik," written in 1944 and reprinted in his *Frihet och gemenskap* (Stockholm: Tidens förlag, 1962).
2. U.S. Bureau of the Census, *Current Population Reports,* Series P-20, no. 253, "Voting and Registration in the Election of November 1972" (Washington, D.C.: U.S. Government Printing Office, 1973), pp. 7, 96, and computations based on p. 93. Average turnout based on actual votes, dispersion according to income based on survey data. See also Sidney Verba and Norman Nie, *Participation in America: Political Democracy and Social Equality* (New York: Harper, 1972).
3. Walter Dean Burnham, "The Changing Shape of the American Political Universe," *American Political Science Review* 65 (December 1965), pp. 10-11. The discussion in the rest of this section is based on this article, esp. pp. 24-26, and other works by Burnham, principally his *Critical Elections and the Mainsprings of American Politics* (New York: W. W. Norton, 1970), esp. pp. 100-11, 131-33, and 183-87. A fuller discussion and detailed citations are provided in my, "The Politics of Economic Policy in the United States: A Tentative View from a Comparative Perspective," *Sage Professional Papers in Comparative Politics* 4, 01-040 (1973), pp. 25-32.
4. The Omaha Platform is reprinted in John D. Hicks, *The Populist Revolt* (Lincoln, Nebr.: Bison Books, University of Nebraska Press, 1961), pp. 439-44. The relation of labor to populism and socialism is discussed in Gerald N. Grob, *Workers and Utopia* (Evanston: Ill.: Northwestern University Press, 1961) and John Laslett, *Labor and the Left* (New York: Basic Books, 1970). Proportion of union members in labor force based on data in U.S. Bureau of the Census, *Historical Statistics of the United States* (Washington, D.C.: U.S. Government Printing Office, 1960), pp. 70 and 97; and U.S. Department of Labor, *Handbook of Labor Statistics 1971* (Washington, D.C.: U.S. Government Printing Office, 1971), p. 307.

5. Irving Bernstein, *The Lean Years* (Baltimore: Penguin Books, 1966).
    The quotation is from p. 512. See also his *Turbulent Years* (Boston:
    Houghton Mifflin, 1970). A summary of the developments discussed
    is provided in J. David Greenstone, *Labor in American Politics* (New
    York: Vintage Books, 1970), chaps. 1 and 2. The British developments
    are summarized in Henry Pelling, *Origins of the Labour Party*, 2nd ed.
    (London: Oxford University Press, 1965), chaps. 5 and 10.
6. Greenstone, *Labor in American Politics* surveys labor's role in the
    Democratic Party with particular emphasis on the first half of the
    1960s. Comparative data on labor movement coverage are provided in
    my "The Politics of Economic Policy in the United States," p. 36. Data on
    labor's share of party finance in the United States are summarized in Harry
    M. Scoble, "The Magnitude and Method of Labor's Financial Involvement
    in Politics," in Charles M. Rehmus and Doris B. McLaughlin, eds., *Labor and
    American Politics* (Ann Arbor: The University of Michigan Press, 1967),
    pp. 363-74; and David Nichols, *Financing Elections* (New York: Franklin
    Watts, 1974), pp. 117-18.
7. The Labor Party's history is sketched in Henry Pelling, *A Short History of
    the Labour Party*, 4th ed. (London: Macmillan, 1972), and its mobilization
    of working class support is analyzed in David Butler and Donald Stokes,
    Political Change in Britain, col. ed., (New York: St. Martin's, 1971), chap. 7.
    The following discussion of the MacDonald Government draws on Alan
    Bullock, *The Life and Times of Ernest Bevin* 1 (London: Heinemann, 1960),
    chaps. 16-18; and Robert Skidelsky, *Politicians and the Slump* (London:
    Macmillan, 1967). See also the analysis in Dennis A. Kavanaugh, "Crisis
    Management and Incremental Adaptation in British Politics: The 1931
    Crisis of the British Party System," in Gabriel A. Almond et al., eds., *Crisis,
    Choice, and Change* (Boston: Little, Brown and Co., 1973). Samuel H.
    Beer's discussion of policy in the 1930s is in *British Politics in the Collectiv-
    ist Age* (New York: Alfred A. Knopf, 1965), chap. 10.
8. Samuel Beer, *British Politics,* esp. pp. 212-16. See also, Richard Crossman,
    "The Lessons of 1945," in Perry Anderson and Robin Blackburn, eds.,
    Towards Socialism (London: Fontana Library, 1965).
9. C.A.R. Crosland, *The Future of Socialism* (London: Jonathan Cape, 1956),
    esp. pp. 56-62; and *The Conservative Enemy* (New York: Schocken Books,
    1962).
10. The following discussion draws heavily on the work of Richard M. Titmuss
    and his associates, including Brian Abel-Smith, Tony Lynes, and Peter
    Townsend, the basic direction of which is best indicated in Titmuss' essay,
    "The Social Division of Welfare," in his *Essays on "The Welfare State"*
    (London: Allen and Unwin, 1958). That the Titmuss approach can evidently
    stimulate a somewhat different interpretation is indicated in Hugh Heclo,

Modern Social Politics in Britain and Sweden (New Haven: Yale University Press, 1974).

11. The shifts in the relative strength of solidaristic and particularistic conceptions of interests in Britain are suggestively discussed in T.H. Marshall, "The Welfare State and the Affluent Society," in *Class, Citizenship, and Social Development* (New York: Anchor Books, 1965); and W.G. Runciman, *Relative Deprivation and Social Justice* (Berkeley: University of California Press, 1966), esp. pp. 50-119.

12. J.C. Kincaid, *Poverty and Equality in Britain* (Harmondsworth: Penguin, 1973).

13. The discussion in this and the following sections is based primarily on my "Labor Movement Parties and Inflation: Contrasting Responses in Britain and Sweden," *Polity* 7 no. 4 (Summer 1975), and the sources cited there.

14. The discussion of the Swedish case is drawn from my forthcoming book, *The Politics of Economic Policy in Social Democratic Sweden.* The Social Democratic Party's growth and mobilization of working class support is described in Raymond Fusilier, *Le Parti Socialiste suédois* (Paris: Les Editions ouvrières, 1954); and Leif Lewin, Bo Jansson, and Dag Sörbom, *The Swedish Electorate 1887-1968* (Stockholm: Almqvist & Wiksell, 1972).

15. A brief description of the politics of the 1933 realignment is provided in Dankwart A. Rustow, *The Politics of Compromise* (Princeton: Princeton University Press, 1955), pp. 90-110. Recent controversies concerning the origins of the economic policy innovation are summarized in Bo Gustafsson, "A Perennial of Doctrinal History: Keynes and "the Stockholm school," *Economy and History* 17 (1973), pp. 114-28; and Carl G. Uhr, "The Emergence of the 'New Economics' in Sweden: A Review of a Study by Otto Steiger," *History of Political Economy* 5 (1973), pp. 243-60. Somewhat different estimations of the actual effects of Social Democratic economic policy in the Depression are provided in H.W. Arndt, *The Economic Lessons of the Nineteen-Thirties* (London: Oxford University Press, 1944), pp. 207-20; and Erik Lundberg, *Business Cycles and Economic Policy* (Cambridge: Harvard University Press, 1957), pp. 54-55.

16. On the LO inflation strategy, see my "Labor Movement Parties and Inflation."

17. The political developments are sketched in M. Donald Hancock, *Sweden: The Politics of Postindustrial Change* (Hinsdale: Dryden Press, 1972), chap. 5.

18. The substance of pension system developments is described in Carl G. Uhr, *Sweden's Social Security System* (Washington, D.C.: U.S. Government Printing Office, 1966); and Thomas Wilson, ed., *Pensions, Inflation and Growth* (London: Heinemann, 1974), chap. 4; the politics in Björn Molin,

"Swedish Party Politics: A Case Study," *Scandinavian Political Studies* 1 (1966), pp. 45-58; and Bo Särlvik, "Party Politics and Electoral Opinion Formation: A Study of Issues in Swedish Politics 1956-1960," *Scandinavian Political Studies* 2 (1967), pp. 167-222; while both the substance and politics are considered in Heclo, *Modern Social Politics,* pp. 228-53.

19. Critiques of the Social Democratic regime as corporatist are noted by Olof Ruin, "Participation, Corporativization and Politicization Trends in Present-day Sweden," paper presented at the 1972 Annual Meeting of the Society for the Advancement of Scandinavian Studies. Philippe C. Schmitter, "Still the Century of Corporatism?" *The Review of Politics* 36, no. 1 (January 1974), pp. 85-131, is a rich and challenging discussion of corporatism as a highly varied but widespread structural tendency in societies with capitalist economies, including Sweden, resulting from the "decay of pluralism" where it had long histories or the "abrupt demise of incipient pluralism." pp. 107-8. While the issue cannot be pursued here, it may be that the notion of corporatism obscures as much about different configurations of power as the notion of pluralism has. For some attempts to understand the Swedish political economy in class terms, confined primarily to the structure of the industrial relations system, see James Fulcher, "Class Conflict in Sweden," *Sociology* 7, no. 1 (January 1973); and Walter Korpi, "Conflict, Power and Relative Deprivation," *American Political Science Review* 68, no. 4 (December 1974), pp. 1569-78.

20. *The Swedish Economy* 1 (1973), p. 162. See this and other issues for data on Swedish economic trends. See also *The Swedish Budget,* annual issues; and Assar Lindbeck, *Swedish Economic Policy* (Berkeley: University of California Press, 1973).

21. Richard N. Cooper, *The Economics of Interdependence* (New York: McGraw-Hill, 1968), p. 6 and chap. 4. See also Raymond Vernon, *Sovereignty at Bay: The Multinational Spread of U.S. Enterprises* (New York: Basic Books, 1971).

22. The relation of the postwar American hegemony, and its apparent decline, to the international economic order is discussed in David P. Calleo and Benjamin M. Rowland, *America and the World Political Economy* (Bloomington: Indiana University Press, 1973); and Robert Gilpin, *The Multinational Corporation and International Politics: The Political Economy of Foreign Investment* (New York: Basic Books, 1975).

2

From Permacrisis to Real Crisis in French Social Security: The Limits to Normal Politics

Stephen S. Cohen and *Charles Goldfinger*

Growth creates stress; stress, reform; and reform averts crisis and sustains permacrisis. While the fate of the critical intellectual has often been likened to Prometheus, the role of the rationalizer-planner in this "normal politics" view seems better to resemble the labors of Hercules in the Augean Stables.

French social security is big and growing bigger. It transfers over twenty percent of disposable income, mostly through three programs: health insurance, family allowances, and old age pensions. It is growing faster than gross national product (GNP), faster than wages, faster than the government budget. Only the rate of efforts to reform it grows faster.

Though the subject of this chapter is the French social security system, the theme is methodological: How can we make sense out of a perfectly ordinary political process such as efforts to reform social security? The method is to contrast, concretely, the understanding that comes out of a normal politics approach with that derived from an alternative approach. As this is not a demonstration of the Rashomon effect—an exercise in the multiplicity of views and the ambiguity of perceived truth—normal politics is found to provide an incomplete, and hence distorted, analysis when compared with the alternative approach.

The term normal politics is used to designate the mode of political analysis that has become dominant in American social science. More like the system of the modern American economy than the poor little match girl, it really doesn't have a name; sometimes pluralism is used, occasionally, liberal pluralism. It is well represented by such authors as Arthur Bentley, David Truman, Robert Dahl, David Braybrooke, Nelson Polsby, and Aaron Wildavsky. Normal politics sees political change in terms of marginal adjustments. "The decision," its unit of analysis, is determined by the vector sum of competing forces. The budgetary process, its view of how the public purse is opened, is an endless saga of compromise among competing groups. It is endless because, as compromise engenders stopgap and as fundamental choices are continually postponed, new cracks appear in the structure and new compromises are necessary. It is marginal

Research for this essay was aided by grants from the Institute for International Studies at the University of California, Berkeley, and from the American Philosophical Association. The generous cooperation of several French "technocrats," as they refer to themselves these days, especially M. Henri DeLapparent and M. P. Potier at the Plan and M. René LeNoir, Secrétaire d'Etat, à l'Action Sociale, was indispensable. M. Max Stern (the Jean Monnet of French Urbanism) provided important explanations of fact and context as well as invaluable aid in helping us penetrate the French administration. Though without the help of these good people we would have gotten nowhere, they bear no responsibility for what has been done to and with the information and explanations they provided.

change because the rules are known; the players, though not completely
equal, all hang in. No one dominates the game; no one wins. Groups, not
classes, are the relevant units. Bargaining among them—not domination of
the essentials—is the important dynamic. The game goes on. The structures
get bigger and bigger, and sometimes rather funny looking, like Victorian
houses. But the structures do not change. If anything should lend itself well
to explanation through this approach, it is French social security, especially
efforts to reform it.

The awesome size of French social security is nicely complemented by
its labyrinthine complexity. J.J. Dupeyroux, the leading academic expert on
the subject, finds that the system is built of some 25,000 rules and regulations.[1] No one has questioned his count. As complexity itself is a favorite
theme of normal politics, we can take it as an appropriate starting point.

Origins and Compromise

The system is a wonderfully Weberian bureaucracy, laboring to express
through rigid rules and regulations a moving balance of political forces and
social strains. That is one major reason for the system's complexity. It is a
trajectory of political compromise.

The social security system was created in the very special political climate
of 1944-45 when social and economic crisis—present, past, and anticipated—
plus political truce forged compromise decisions on major questions of how
to rebuild France. A double compromise was at the origin of social security.[2]
The first was an organizational compromise between the universal, egalitarian,
and unified system proposed in the Laroque report, and the existing structures
of restricted, unequal, and categorical funds—one for civil servants, one for
railway workers, etc. A Régime Général was created, embodying those basic
principles of the Laroque report. But the critical integration of the existing
categorical funds was postponed, and the creation of still more categorical (or
complementary) funds was pretty much assured by the adoption of a ceiling
on assessed wages.

On a deeper level the system represented a political compromise between
the two major parties of the 1944 government: the Communists (with the
labor units behind them) and the Gaullists (with business huddled in their
camp); the Socialists and Radicals, representing among others important elements of the civil servant class, kept compromise from being too neat.

For the Communists the creation of an extensive system of social security
represented an extension of concessions won from the employers during the
period of the Popular Front. Social protection had become a right; social
security a mechanism for organizing it under workers' control (until 1967
unions had seventy-five percent of the seats on the governing boards of the
social security funds). Many Gaullists—conservative but enlightened and

fervently nationalistic—were concerned with the demographic decline of France,
for them a major cause of the French military humiliation. They saw the new
system as a means of rebuilding the Nation and increasing its productive and
military potential. They also perceived social security as a means of maintaining social peace and stability, first as a cushion against the full impact of fluctuations in economic activity, and second as an example of the association
between capital and labor—the ideal form of social organization in Gaullist ideology. Furthermore, those Gaullists who did not see it in positive terms at least
recognized social security as a political necessity: Going back on that key piece
of the Resistance promise would be politically impossible. At the same time
they did not want a fully socialized system, and they also had to think about its
impact on labor costs. Hence, for example, no steps were taken toward nationalizing the health industry. The Socialists and the Radicals had important class
distinctions to preserve for their white collar supporters, so categorical funds
were maintained and the ceiling on assessed wages was instituted.

Solidarity

The existence of an ideology for social security to which the major parties
could subscribe—the ideology of solidarity—further facilitated the convergence.
Ideology may or may not be the driving force behind the actions of "madmen in
power," but it certainly provides constraints on them and defines the boundaries
of permissible conduct and utterance. The persistence of Social Darwinism plays
an important role in the success of the welfare-baiting and "blaming the victim"
rhetoric of United States politicians; the broad, public acceptance of the ideology
of solidarity helps make similar statements very rare in France.
Solidarity is not an ethic of redistribution, of providing income or assistance
to the poor. The latter is grounded in a liberal vision of the state and in the so-
called voluntary exchange theory of public finance, which postulates the separation of the allocative and distributive branches of the economy, and only minimal
state intervention. Solidarity is grounded in an organic vision of the state, in
theories of general interest (which is not the sum of individual interests), and in
an ideology of nationalism. Solidarity is an egalitarian, unifying concept, blur-
ring—sometimes desperately—social divisions and distinctions and emphasizing
instead the unity of the nation. It stresses the sharing rather than the transferring
aspects of social protection.[3]
In the framework of solidarity social protection is a constitutional right:
The Constitution of 1946 states in its preamble (reasserted in the Constitution
of 1958):

> The Nation assures the necessary conditions for the development of
> an individual and a family. It guarantees to everybody, especially to

a child, a mother and an older worker, health protection, material
security, rest and leisure. Every human being who, because of his
age, mental and physical condition, or economic situation is unable
to work, has a right to obtain from the community, appropriate
means of existence.

Solidarity thus charges the public authorities with responsibility for the
social protection of the disadvantaged. However, the main thrust of social
protection lies elsewhere. Its goal is not to compensate ex-post inequalities
generated by the allocative process, but to contribute to, regenerate, upgrade,
and develop the nation's human capital. The labor force is the focus of the
social security system. Healthier workers and more children guarantee a bigger and better working population, a bigger and better army, and a greater
France; health insurance and retirement pensions, plus a sharing of social risks
such as disability and unemployment, assure a greater sense of social cohesion
and interdependence. To the extent that human capital is an essential guarantor of national independence and grandeur, and a well-developed system of
social security a necessary ingredient of social peace, the ultimate beneficiaries
of social security are the nation and the state. Stressing national unity and
strength, and also the values of work and large families, solidarity rings the
familiar tune of enlightened, conservative *sozial politik* in the tradition of Bis-
mark and LePlay.

But solidarity also emphasizes equality of social protection, shared protection against social risks, the *right* of citizens to adequate health care, and to
proper means of existence, and those themes are attractive to labor unions
and left-wing parties. Thus, solidarity was a broad enough concept (perhaps
one should say vague enough) to provide common ground for differing views
of what social security should be. It has been, and still is, the official ideology
of the system, even if, in the changing context of societal development, diverging interpretations of what solidarity really means have emerged. Solidarity is
being qualified now. It becomes *class* solidarity for labor unions opposing
proposals to have social security pick up the deficit of health insurance for the
self-employed; it becomes *horizontal* solidarity for the family allowance lobby
fighting attempts to link family allowances to levels of income.[a] It may also
become categorical solidarity (within a social category) in the government's
proposals for a social security fund for self-employed workers in which the

---

[a]Horizontal solidarity means the redistribution of resources from those who do not
have children to those who have them. It is rooted in a clear vision of some families taking
on the socially necessary burden of producing and raising children. It is therefore only right
that the financial burden of this effort in the general interest be shared by the nation. Horizontal solidarity is the legitimating ideology of the nationalist family allowance system,
and the battle cry of the family lobby, in whose hands it assumes away questions of income
differentials and concentrates exclusively upon burden sharing by family size.

young and well-to-do self-employed would have to support their aging and poorer colleagues. And this proposal could be vehemently and at times violently resisted by large factions of self-employed in the name of national solidarity. Thus, the French are increasingly asking, is solidarity national, professional, proper to an industrial sector, a group, a class? without being able (or willing) to fully answer the question.[4] However, in spite of this semantic evolution, which reflects the conflicting positions of different social groups, and which also takes us a bit ahead of ourselves, the basic tenets of solidarity as an ideology—equality of service and social security as a right—remain firmly entrenched, and no one dares to attack them frontally.

Growth and Stress

The motor, or perhaps merely the most immediately nerve-wracking manifestation, of the permacrisis of social security is the system's rapid growth compounding away upon its fearful size. Extrapolations read as though they were taken from a pop-ecology article: Towards the end of the 1980s, if recent trends continue, social security will absorb all of GNP![b] Such extrapolations are at least good for one thing. They point to the distinct possibility that normal politics—as both a phenomenon and as a method of political analysis—cannot tell the whole story.[c]

First, some dimensions of the problem. During the ten years, 1959-69, social security expenditures increased by 345 percent, faster than prices, faster than GNP. Social security benefits rose far faster than primary income (wages and salary) so that the percentage of total household resources coming from social security transfers rose from 15.1 percent in 1959 to 19.5 percent in 1969.[5] And the trend is continuing. From 1969 to 1970, social security expenditures rose by 12 percent; from 1970 to 1971 by 13 percent; from 1971 to 1972 by 11.6 percent[6] while GNP rose by about half that rate and the state's general budget rose by 9 percent. In 1972 the social security budget became the biggest thing in France: It was larger than the state's general budget.[7]

---

[b]No less an extrapolator than President Pompidou declared in his press conference of 22 September 1969: "In 19 years, it will absorb our entire national product!"

[c]Aaron Wildavsky's *The Politics of the Budgetary Process,* (Waltham, Mass: Little Brown & Co., 1964) is an excellent example—indeed, it has become an exemplar—of the normal politics approach to analyzing budgeting. It demonstrates the profoundly political—as opposed to any nonpolitical or technical nature of how public money is allocated. As do all true exemplars, the book also illustrates the defects of its virtues. It demonstrates that the central political process is all about marginal movements rather than structural changes. The moral of the story is that in spite of the good-willed efforts of structural reformers, in the budgetary process the most likely outcome is much like what has prevailed in the past plus a few percent. But in this particular case such an outcome is impossible. So the most likely is impossible; therefore, something less likely is more likely, or else normal politics has its limits. It can deal with only part of the process of political change, and the easy part at that.

Composition of Growth

The growth of social security expenditures has been uneven among the
different funds. Galloping increases in health and pensions, the two largest
items, have dominated at the relative expense of family allowances, which
have barely kept even with price index; as a result the composition of social
security benefits has slowly changed.

Between 1959 and 1969:

Health insurance expenditures grew by 470 percent (in current francs);
Pensions rose by 376 percent.
But family allowances, the third largest component of social security
transfers, rose by only 234 percent (about half the rate of health).

So that by 1969:

Health benefits accounted for 29 percent of all social security transfers;
in 1959, health represented 21 percent.
Pensions equaled 43 percent of social security transfers in 1969; in 1959,
39 percent.
And family allowances fell to 19 percent of social security transfers in
1969, from 28 percent in 1958.
None of the other social security categories (including unemployment)
accounted for more than 5 percent of the total in either year.[d]

The growth of the social security system can also be seen by looking at
data on the number of persons covered. Coverage varies somewhat among
funds. For health insurance our information shows that in 1960, 75.8 percent
of the total population was covered; by 1972 it had risen to 98 percent, and
coverage has been extended since.[8]
These are numbers. But behind them there are structural phenomena that
give the growth process its momentum, its potential for creating conflict, and
its meaning.

---

[d]All data from Perrot, "Salaries" table 27. See *Liaisons Sociales,* 16 June 1969, for
slightly different data based on different sampling techniques. An additional social transfer
program called Assistance (or Aide Sociale) is not part of the social security budget; it provides
aid for the down and out, and has been studied at times by Americans as somehow analogous
to our welfare system. In 1965 assistance was about 5 percent of social security budget
and about the same in 1969. See Cindy Stevens, *A Study of Public Assistance and Allied
Benefits in France,* New York University, under HUD 05-69-94, for a very monographic
description in English of the program, or "Ministère de la Santé et de la Sécurité Sociale,"
Statistiques Sociales, Supplément D 2, December 1969, p. 47, for Assistance data.

Sources of Growth

The growth of social security does not take place all by itself in a static, ceteris paribus world. It is not pure, self-contained growth, whatever that may be. It cannot be isolated and then analyzed; it must be situated—in its political-economic context—in order to be understood. It is a corollary, a by-product of the overall reorganization of the French economy which, since the end of World War II, has been growing at the average real rate of about five percent per year. This growth entailed a profound and traumatic transformation of the French economic and social fabric: sectoral shifts away from agriculture (from thirty-six percent in agriculture in 1946 to under thirteen percent in 1968)[9] and away from small, family-owned and operated shops and business to giant corporations and supermarket chains; shifts in ways of life: the Paris region in 1946 had a population of about 6 million, and now it counts over 10 million,[10] of which over 7-1/2 million are in the suburbs!

Losers

Joseph Schumpeter has characterized economic development as a process of creative destruction. And, indeed, development in France has been destructive, GNP has grown mightily, but blood has been spilled all over the place: Agricultural workers too old to migrate barely make a living, peasants watch their world being destroyed, small shopkeepers and artisans get wiped out by the sweep of industrial and commercial concentration.[11]

Rapid growth exacerbates inequalities, for its logic is to encourage and reward the already strong and resourceful. But at the same time it generates rising expectations and thus increases pressures for greater equality. Disparities and privations passively accepted in a static context are now perceived as unbearable. Peasants demand institutional guarantees of parity of income with industrial workers. The self-employed want social protection that offers the same coverage as salaried workers. These demands cannot be ignored, especially when a rapid growth policy is promoted by a politically conservative government, as in France. Here, the losers of the creative destruction game—the peasants, small shopkeepers, and artisans—still constitute one of the main blocks of the Gaullist electorate. Something has to be done for them and done quickly, before they stop the whole growth machine.[e]

Providing social services and transfer payments is one obvious thing that can

---

[e]The dangers that these groups present to the all-out growth strategy are clear. However, whether the Gaullists whom they support are necessarily more responsive to their demands than any other likely governing group is highly problematical. One could just as well—on the same basis, political wisdom—argue the opposite. And political statistics will not help either. They show that the Gaullists wipe them out, and the Socialist Democrats too. Perhaps the important point is the way they get wiped out.

be done. Thus, the law of 25 January 1961 extended the benefits of health insurance to the agricultural population. Another law of 12 July 1966 extended social security benefits to the self-employed.[f]

Nonlosers

It is easy to see why the economically bypassed—the losers—made desperate demands on social security. But theirs were not the only new claims on the system generated by the economic transformation. The winners, or more accurately, those employed in the mainstream of economic growth (because the real winners do not have to worry about social security benefits) also made new claims on the system. Industrial workers detached from the social protection provided by a now wiped-out peasant and shopkeeper society turn towards its new rationalized, bureaucratized successor for pensions and social protection because for them, in the new economic system, there is no accumulated savings in the form of economic capital nor in the soft capital of family or social structures to guarantee survival in old age and care in the face of misfortune.

The nonlosers demand that social security not merely replace the social protection lost in the passing of the old society, but that it provide *compensation* for the failings, the frustrations, and the disillusionments of the new society. White collar workers—very new to the white collar status[12]—find bitter disappointment in the realization that they are, in spite of their new social mobility, still "proletarians"; sometimes that disillusionment is expressed dramatically,[g] but it always generates increasing claims on retirement benefits, on health benefits, and on the preservation of differentials with whatever the working class has won. The working class increasingly focuses on "getting out quick." Lowering the age of retirement has become a top-priority trade union demand, one that is vigorously pushed by the rank and file.[13] And the new form of French society seems to generate a very high income elasticity of demand for health services and pharmaceutical products—though, fortunately, not necessarily such a high rate of sickness. Thus, between 1959 and 1969 health expenditures grew at a rate almost double that of household expenditures. As a result the percentage of health expenditures in household expenditures increased from 8.3 percent in 1959, to 11.8 percent in 1969, to 12.8 percent in 1971.[14]

The final force on the demand side is demographic. The arithmetic is simple.

---

[f]The implementation of this law, which began in 1969, was an immediate cause of widespread disturbance by shopkeepers, artisans, etc., which forced the government to reconsider the onerous contribution rates the special fund created for the self-employed who managed to stay in business. These disturbances clearly put in evidence the vehement sensitivity of the self-employed to the issues of social protection and security. See Le Monde, 13 January 1967, 24 June 1969, 5 August 1969, 23 August 1969, 4 September 1969, 1 November 1969, and 4 December 1969.

[g]As in the recent bank strike that centered on these themes.

Recently France has been stuck with a small and stable working-age population supporting rapidly growing numbers of old people and young people. In 1946 people 64 years or older represented 11 percent of the population; in 1972 they represented 13 percent. On the other end total population rose from 40.1 million in 1946 to 50 million in 1968, while at the same time the "active population" barely increased: from 19.4 to 20 million.[15] The heavy burden of this demographic situation—an additional 10 million dependents, all of whom receive medical insurance plus either family allowances or old age pensions—is most keenly felt in the social security system, which is financed out of payroll taxes on the same 20 million working population.

Along with these different and powerful forces pushing for the growth of social security expenditures there is the compounding problem of an apparent inability to realize any economies of scale on the supply side. Unit costs in health just don't seem to decrease,[16] while pensions and family allowances are straightforward cash transfers.

All these forces together translate into one basic political-economic fact: An increasing absorption of national resources into the social security sector—a movement that, as we shall see, runs counter to the basic direction chosen for French economic development. It provokes, therefore, vigorous and determined (if not very effective) responses from those responsible for the overall direction of the French economy.

Logic of Economic Development in France

Each form of development has its own logic. And the logic of the rapid French development—what they have taken to calling the "industrial imperative"—provides the backbone for opposition to growth in social security expenditures just as it generates claims for more and bigger expenditures. It is a simple logic, but powerful. And it is consistently put forward by big business, the Gaullist political class, and the technocrats of the state and of big business. In their present form, the argument goes, social security expenditures are labor costs. Higher labor costs mean reduced competitiveness in international markets. The French economy is locked into a serious competitive struggle that it has entered on a weak footing compared with its principal competitors, the awesome Germans. It cannot afford to increase its burdens relative to the competition.

The policy implications are quite as clear: (1) Hold down increases in expenditures, and (2) what cannot be held down should be reformed to serve, as well as possible, the end of increasing productivity. The problem, of course, is that these simple economic imperatives must pass through the complex mediation of the political system, which does not always obey the "obvious logic of development." Indeed, the lack of a smooth fit between

the imperatives of the economic system and the necessities of the political
system is the key to understanding the contradictions of social security—and
much more—in modern France. It might be useful, therefore, to step back for
a moment, and examine the recent evolution of this tension.

Economic Imperative and Political Power

In place of the general Malthusianism of the prewar economy, the postwar
economy, before, during and after DeGaulle, has been increasingly dominated
by a central core of large, modern, rapidly growing firms and a still powerful,
still interventionist but now growth-oriented state bureaucracy. The Plan has
come to symbolize this new economy—the modernizing partnership of the
technocrats of big business and of the state.

This partnership has reshaped France since the war. But it is important
to see how this was done. It reshaped the economy primarily through long-
term actions on the supply side, for example, through the restructuring of an
industry from many small, high-cost, low-growth noncompetitive firms into a
modernizing oligopoly. In reshaping the structures of industry, it has, over
twenty-five years, also reshaped the economic, social, and even political landscape of France. But it has been on the supply side through "industrial policy"
that the power of this group (or subsystem) has been directly exercised: The
potent impacts on every other aspect of French life have been second round or
indirect effects of the industrial policy. The agricultural programs of the first
Plans constitute a perfect example. The "agricultural problem" of marginal
producers, Byzantine subsidies, medieval land tenure (all kept alive in a hot-
house of infinitely complicated protectionism) was an economic rationalizer's
dream-playground. But a direct assault on the structures of the agricultural
sector—on land tenure, and on the subsidy system—was beyond the political
capabilities of the political subsystem that controlled investment. Recognizing
this blatant fact, the Plan chose not to attack agriculture directly. Instead,
the early Plans, after devoting pages and pages to the complexities of the
agricultural problem, limited their agricultural programs entirely to the construction of more tractor factories and more fertilizer plants. They let the
tractors fight the peasants. There are other possible explanations to the Plan's
approach to rationalizing agriculture. None, however, seems so simple and so
satisfactory. It clearly highlights the basic political fact—that power to build
a tractor factory is different from that needed to change subsidy systems, and
that the political-economic subsystem that controlled investment (our partnership between the technocrats of big business and of the state) could not hope
to control farm subsidies. That belonged to a much broader political system:
the traditional political arena.[17]

It is important to an understanding of the political process to see where,

and how, and why it has been able to change things *directly,* and, where its
influence has been felt, has resulted in profound change but only through
indirect impacts; finally it is necessary to understand what permitted the relative independence of that political subsystem, and what is limiting that
independence. For participation in the "industrial policy" approach, which
has shaped so much of French life, has been as narrow as its direct objectives. When you restructure an industry, you need only the managers of that
industry, the state (to organize, to provide the goodies, and sometimes to
prod), and the passive acquiescence of the trade unions. Nothing else, and
crucially, no one else, is needed. Indeed, broader participation could only
endanger things. The nature of their direct objectives (industrial modernization) permitted the state-big business partnership to concentrate on the supply
side (and there only in certain areas), and the nature of their political power
(strong in just those areas, weak in direct confrontations with broad-based
political movements) kept them far away from the active concerns of the
major political groups and even farther from the machinery of day-to-day,
broad participation politics. The big business-technocrats partnership that
is the Plan in its day-to-day operations is essentially a device to keep the state
actively involved in the management of the industrial core of the economy
while keeping broad participation politics out. Thus, in spite of their enormous power in one vital area, the big business-technocrat partnership has
never been able to control such vital, direct concerns of traditional politics
as short-term, demand-side policy, agricultural subsidies, and social security
benefits.

The general problem of incoherent economic policy—of short-term
demand policy differing from longer term supply side policy—illustrates
this situation rather well. Many reasons have been offered to explain the
disparities between the targets of the successive Plans and actual results:
econometric errors and the youth of that rapidly developing science; the
impossibility of planning several years ahead in a market based economy;
a series of unique, exogenous forces that intervened, etc. There is something to each of these explanations, but the partial insights each offers comes
at a high price: They lead nowhere. The simplest answer takes one furthest
into an understanding of the political process that is the Plan. One big reason that the Plan's targets were not in fact realized is that short-term demand
policy was never exercised with the realization of them as a principal objective. The two were never coordinated. Successive governments simply did
not follow the Plan. They inflated and deflated, increased or held back on
pensions, subsidies, and defense expenditures, and toyed with interest rates
with a general disregard for the targets of the Plan. The reason they
repeatedly did this is also simple. They were neither too stupid to appreciate
the complex tool that was the Plan, nor were they particularly at odds with
its objectives. It is just that the Plan was the product of a rather small

political subsystem—largely the one we have been describing—whereas the exercise of demand side policy is the focus of broad participation, of conflicting interest politics. The incongruence of these two political systems is the principal reason for the complete failure to coordinate short-term demand side policy with the longer term supply side programs of the Plan.[18]

The absence of a strong government (prior to 1958) further increased the tendency for industrial policy to have a certain independence. It left almost all long-term policy (especially that on the supply side) to the stewardship of the technocrats.[h] The semiclosed nature of the pre-Common Market French economy helped even more; it left open the alternative of relative inflation, which was an important factor in insulating industrial policy from more general economic and social policy.[19]

The opening of the French economy into the Common Market has been the principal external pressure for big business "doing something" about what they see as the heavy and growing burden of social transfers. The Common Market is many things, but it is well to remember that it is a liberal (small "L") Common Market: goods and money move fastest across borders; laws and harmonization of social policy more slowly. The implications for business are simple and direct. When the union asks Lucy (president of Lucy's Lemonade Lounges) for a raise, she replies, "Gee, people, I'd love to, but if I gave you the extra 7½¢ an hour, the competition would drive me out." And she is not lying. French business now has to compete with its Common Market partners (especially Germany). And this fact dominates all. They can now say, "I'd love to, but if we do, the Germans will clobber us. So why don't you get German business to increase what it pays for family allowances (and the Dutch and Italians too, while you're at it), and then we'd be delighted to go along with it."[i]

They can say that, and they do, pretty much in those words. The Sixth Plan provides some excellent examples. It includes an impressive report on social

---

[h]Later, under Gaullist governments, for different reasons, the technocrats were to have their greatest moment, which now seems to be threatened by the new Giscard d'Estaing-Poniatowski Government.

[i]Each time a major move for reform of social transfers gets under way (e.g., 1967, 1969, 1971, etc.) it is blurred by a flurry of speeches and reports proving that the burden of transfers on French business is greater (or lesser, depending upon which side is talking) than elsewhere. In general, French public spending is not appreciably higher than among its principal trading partners (United States and Sweden are highest, but United States is heavily military). Straight social transfers do not seem to be higher in France than in Germany (nor does the "burden on business" seem higher, whatever that means). France does have the highest rate of social budget paid directly by business firms and employees (Germany has a higher proportion of its social budget paid out of the general tax till (see EEC, *Social Accounts,* 1962-65). But "social expenses" were 21.9 percent of GNP in Germany, and only 19.3 percent in France, and 17.1 percent in Italy. All in all the problem with this game is that it is the wrong game. The argument over absolute amounts is not crucial. In competitive economics it is the change—the direction and amount of the disturbance to the going equilibrium—that matters. (For vintage examples of great debate on how much the French pay compared with the Germans, see *Le Monde,* 23-24 July 1967, 7 August 1969, 10 September 1969, and 27 May 1969.)

transfers, some 200 pages (plus reams of annexed materials) that present all the good ideas—absolutely all of them: aid to newborn babies, the lame, the blind, the halt, the bored; the day care centers; the at home services for the old; the electronic aids to add comfort to troubled lives; new professions to absorb the new professionals the last Plan's educational reform is now producing. The trouble is that it is a very long document. If hurried one can turn instead to the Plan's Finance Committee's report. They boil the whole social program down to a manageable seven pages, and still find time in their busy lives, and space in their crowded pages, to acknowledge that the Social Action report was a splendid document, and represented a fine piece of work, and that its authors (and there were many) ought to be congratulated. Then, after the congratulatory paragraphs and the inspirational opening, the Finance Committee breaks the news—under the heading *Les Limites de la Solidarité*:

> The drive for international competitiveness brings things into question . . . for policies derived from the idea of *solidarité* there is a new imperative. . . . The opening of the economy necessitates that the burdens on the French economy not be heavier than those of its principal trading partners, especially those in the Common Market. . . . Doubtless the burden of salaries and social charges is not heavier in France than in other Common Market countries. But the total of obligatory payments is reaching one of the highest rates. It is true that, following a similar line of reasoning, each of the member states of the EEC could only be apprehensive at the prospect of granting new social benefits. Hence the idea of the Plan's Commission on the General Economy and Finance, that NO REAL PROGRESS CAN BE MADE IN THIS DIRECTION BY INDIVIDUAL STATES, and that it is only by concerted action, going beyond the idea of harmonisation, which in practice is very limited, that the European countries can begin to give a new dynamism to their social policy. (page 41, emphasis added.)

The Plan then goes on to proclaim the new social policy: What is really and truly in the interest of each and all is to increase productivity, and the principal and overwhelmingly most important means of social redistribution is to better "develop the earning ability of each person . . . enhance the capacity of each individual to increase his personal gain." (p. 42.)

By the mid-sixties the limited industrial policy of the technocrats of the Plan and big business, had overflowed the boundaries of their own political subsystem and had become the dominant economic policy of the whole government: the industrial imperative of adopting the whole French economy—and society—to the requirements of all-out international competition.

Many reasons lay behind this movement so loudly trumpeted by the Fifth

and Sixth Plans. The most important was the internal dynamic of the successful industrial policy. The industrial core of the economy had become quite
modernized: GNP had grown at 4.8 percent per year between 1959 and 1964
and labor productivity had grown even quicker—at an annual rate of 5.1 percent.[20] The critical economic problem no longer concerned the reorganization
of the industrial core. It now centered about extending the breadth of the
rationalization process to new sectors (such as distribution) and in maintaining
overall economic balance and price competitiveness. Both politicians and
planners alike feared the newly acquired economic vitality to be fragile. For
one thing, inflation—the perennial foe of the French economy—was still alive
and well. From September 1958 to June 1963 French prices rose by 24 percent
while German prices rose at about half that rate.[21] The economic logic was
clear: A more general economic policy—to increase productivity—would have
to replace the narrow but deep investment and restructuring policy of the old
Plans. The political system would have to accommodate that new orientation.
Much had changed in the political system. Years of stable Gaullist rule had
strengthened the hand of the political class. Ministers could expect to be in
office long enough to act. More important, perhaps, the new economic strength
of big business was rapidly translating into a realization that they no longer
needed so much tutelage and interference from the state. The precrisis Giscard
d'Estaing presented himself as the mighty sword of France's very minor flirtation with neoliberalism—with small disengagements of the state from its ubiquitous involvement in the economy in favor of greater selectivity in its economic
intervention. In particular, the state should cease its draining of savings and
diverse liquidities from the private sector and from banking circuits and let
those structures play a more normal role in channeling investment funds—as
befits a healthy capitalist economy. Important efforts were made in this direction.[22] Similarly, the tax burden, of "fiscal pressure," was to be reduced.[23]
An all-out attack on nonproductive uses of national resources would follow,
and social security along with education and farm subsidies would be the
prime targets. Efforts to hold down social security expenditures and to rationalize the system so as to serve the end of productivity better became more numerous and more serious but not, apparently, more successful.

Reforms of Social Security

At first glance it would seem as though normal politics—both as a phenomenon and as a method of political analysis—beautifully captures these efforts to
reform social security.
    The offensive began in earnest in later 1966. But the infrastructure for the
operations began to be constructed in the early sixties with prestressed reports
by official commissions on different aspects of the social security system. Some

of the more important were the:

Commission Prigent on Family Allowances, 1960
Commission Laroque on Problems of Old Age, 1961
Commission Canivet on Health Insurance, 1964
Commission Friedel, on the whole system, 1964
Commission Bordaz on Social Transfers, 1965

These blue-ribbon commission reports were purely advisory; their recommendations were not binding. But they provided important political ammunition: expertise, objectivity, technological capability. Apart from any specific recommendations, they legitimated the basic idea of reforming the social security system.[j]

Normal politics tells us that the increased intensity of government action was triggered by the financial situation of the General Regime. From a surplus through 1962 to quasi-equilibrium in 1963, the budget of the General Regime went into the red by 584 million francs in 1965, and ran a 1.5 billion franc deficit in 1966. The projected deficit for 1968 was 4 billion francs and prospects for still further growth were frightening.

Thus in late 1966 and early 1967, armed with a budget crisis and a ream of advisory reports, the Minister of Social Affairs, Jeanneney, and the Prime Minister, Pompidou, proclaimed the need for urgent and truly fundamental reform. On 27 September 1966 Pompidou declared, "The reform of social security is a fundamental problem. It demands a very large debate, for which the Deputies will be perfectly informed." Three days later M. Jeanneney told the National Assembly to prepare for the "opening of a great debate" on social security reform. And M. Bourges, representing the Government before the Senate, proclaimed on 14 December 1966, "The reform will be of such magnitude, that it cannot be carried outside the Parliament."[24]

While the government was preparing its campaign, the opposition also got to work. And it had a big advantage—an election. When the legislative elections were over in March 1967, the government and its allies were still in power but with a much reduced majority. Several groups, including the Communists, the trade unions, the white collar unions, the doctors, the family lobby, and the shopkeepers were opposing the reform of social security. Anticipated reforms had something to alarm everyone. The government became increasingly reluctant to open so explosive a dossier. Thus began the semantic retreat.

---

[j]The Canivet, Friedel, and Bordaz reports were especially helpful. As to specific recommendations, those which could be used by the government to support its own projects were used or "enacted." The others were buried; for example, the Bordaz recommendations for increasing workers' contributions (taxes) to health insurance and for having the patient pay a higher share of medical costs were accepted; recommendations for having the state budget, instead of the social security budget, pay housing allowances (Friedel), and recommendations for major increases in prenatal and maternity benefits (Prigent) were rejected.

The "very large debate" (in Parliament!) that Pompidou had announced in the fall, had become by spring "a question which will be treated comprehensively."[25] The government then asked Parliament for the power to legislate by executive decree to bypass Parliament because the question was too political. Arguing that further liberalization of the Common Market was scheduled to take effect in 1968, the Executive asked for power to legislate by decree until 31 October in order to solve the urgent economic problems facing the nation, among which the social security budget figured prominently. After a heated debate the majority held and the special legislative power was voted on 12 June 1967.

The Communist Party claimed that "the dismantling of the social security system is on the agenda."[26] The left-wing unions organized a day of protest for July 27 against the anticipated government projects and cautioned the faithful "despite the vacation period, to keep vigilant and prepare to act."[27] Opposition to the anticipated reforms did not only come from the Left. The white collar union (CGC) expressed its categorical opposition to any attempt, no matter how small, to raise the ceiling on contributions. The professional association of doctors expressed their alarm that some of the anticipated reforms would threaten the basic principal of liberal medicine.[28]

The executive decrees on social security reform were adopted by the Cabinet on 31 July 1967, the traditional day for political nasties. The first day of vacation, it is a tough day for street demonstrations, and by the time everyone has returned from his month of camping, the storm is over and forgotten and there is a new crisis. There is no need to enter into detailed analysis of the reforms. No one could possibly detect in them anything like a fundamental reform of the system. They constituted a set of expedients geared towards reestablishing the short-run financial equilibrium of the system. Thus, "medical care was made a little less free," as the out-of-pocket participation by the patient (le ticket-moderateur) was increased from 20 percent to 40 percent.[k] Contribution rates for workers were raised from 6 percent to 6.5 percent and the ceiling for health contributions was raised.[l] The Government promised to participate in the financing of certain special funds, especially the miners' fund, until then entirely supported by the Régime Général. And following the recommendations of the Friedel and Canivet commissions, as well as the persistent and vehement demands

---

[k]Following the "Events of May 1968" it was lowered to 25 percent.

[l]From 1968 to 1969 the ceiling on wages assessed for social security contributions was raised from 11,400 francs to 16,320 francs, a hike of 13.3 percent. This may look like a sizeable raise. But it should be pointed out that by law (decree of 29 August 1962) the ceiling is indexed to the progress of hourly wage rate. In 1968 (a very special year) those rose by 15.8 percent. Thus, the ceiling fell behind the progression of hourly wages, and behind the legislated index. The lag was obtained by pressure from big business (the CNPF). As Le Monde put it: "The public authority fixed this number (13.3%) halfway between the demands of the CNPF and the 15.8 percent required by law" (1 October 1969; see also, 17 December 1969).

of the family lobby, a separate management of risks was instituted with three basic funds: health, family allowances, and old age benefits. The practice of "perequations" (shifting resources from surplus to deficit funds) was to be definitely and definitively abandoned.[29]

The decrees did not succeed in even beginning any process of fundamental reform, let alone in implementing any such thing. The compromise actions did not even succeed in achieving a ceasefire on the social security front; in their own modest way the social security reforms contributed to May 1968. Even the most explicit goal, the financial equilibrium, was achieved only for a very short time—exactly one year until the next "crisis" budget. For 1968 the General Regime had a surplus of 600 million francs, but in 1969 the new Minister of Health and Social Security announced that the deficit would be 1.5 billion francs in 1970.[30] The policy of separate management of risks so earnestly affirmed in 1967 was quietly abandoned two years later.[31] *Le Monde,* reviewing the great reform wave of 1967 from the vantage point of the beginning of the 1970 round of reforms, summed up the 1967 effort as finally resulting, not in any fundamental reforms, but rather in "a vague papering-over."[32]

The 1967 reforms—which seem to provide a classic illustration of normal politics in action—were followed by the 1969, the 1970, and the 1971, etc. reforms, which seem to confirm further the soundness of that approach, so rooted in political experience and empirical observation. Nothing is more normal than a social security budget crisis leading to solemn calls for drastic budget cuts and programs of fundamental reforms. Thus, in 1970 the Government announces, "It is no longer a question of retouching a facade: important choices must be taken."[33] The Sixth Plan (for 1971-75) issued its call to battle cited above, and M. Boulin, head of Social Security, rhetorically asks the National Assembly, "Expenditures on social security represent 19.5% of National Product [sic] — the highest level in the Common Market. Can the Nation afford almost 20% of its product for social spending?"[34] And nothing is more normal than the unrelenting growth of spending (up 12% for 1970) and the absorption of those fundamental reforms into a patchwork of expediential stopgaps, shaped by the interaction of the different political vectors that converge on the social security budget process. As choices are continually postponed, new cracks appear in the structures and new compromises are necessary. The pluralist vision of normal politics—an endless soap-opera of mock-crisis and compromise, repeating itself round and round with an awesome stability and predictability—seems to fit this most ordinary of political processes. The budgetary process is a game of marginal movements. The rules are known. The players, though not completely equal, all hang in. No one dominates the game; no one wins. Bargaining—not domination of the essentials—is the important dynamic. The budget grows. The structures do not change.

We can stop here with a summary conclusion that because of the balance of political forces, reform efforts are ineffective: one more case study showing the staying power of liberal pluralist, normal politics.

One problem (among many others) with such an approach is that it is very uninteresting. Like econometric models, it has its uses, especially as long as the ceteris paribus conditions do not move. But like those models, normal politics has absolutely nothing to say about what our econometrician friends call "inflection points." Such an approach precludes inquiry into how—and why—structures change. And sometimes structures do change. Normal politics deals with only one part of the political cycle, and the easy part at that. Yet, the simple arithmetic of social security expenditures points to the distinct likelihood of some kind of inflection point, some kind of structural change, because the spending curve simply cannot continue along the same trajectory.

Perhaps we can take the summary conclusion of blocked reform and use it as a point of departure. After all, given the strength and stability of the Fifth Republic, given the publicity and frequency of the government's stated intentions to restructure the system, and given the economic logic behind those intentions, the political equilibrium sustaining the present arrangements could change. And actions could be aimed at changing it.

Let us then look a bit closer at these responses to the growth of the system. There are three major kinds of responses: first, simple stopgap expedients of the kind we have been discussing; second, "rationalization"—reforms to contain cost increases and bring the service closer into line with the perceived demands of the economy; and, third, reorganization—fundamental changes in structure and function.

All three responses come through the mediation of the political system. But each generally has its own sublogic, its own mode of operation, and its own group of primary "change agents." Each influences the other. And it is impossible to make sense of the whole process of reform without seeing all of these pieces and how they interact.

In order to see the full dimensions of the three-front war, let us examine three different pieces of the social security system: first, the problem of "undue charges," a pure case of expediential window dressing; second, the dynamic of health expenditures, a classic case of blocked reorganization; and, third, the story of the reform of the salaire-unique (the single wage earner allowance), an example of successful rationalization.

Undue Charges

The government loads the social security budget with items that many feel should be charged to the state budget. As a result, estimates of these "undue charges" vary greatly, depending upon what one considers undue. In 1970, for example, the Plan put the estimate at 1.3 billion francs, while the left-wing union estimated them at 6 billion francs. In 1972 the CGT put the bill at 12 billion francs.[35] Some items commonly cited include medical education, medical research, and hospital buildings. Other lists include as well expenditures for the elderly who never contributed to retirement funds and special funds for declining professions.

Undue charges present more than purely accounting interest. They are the eminent domain of normal politics, and make sense only in its terms. They also help to make sense of normal politics. By itself undue charges as a category makes no sense at all. They are not economic questions, merely accounting questions. But they highlight the symbolic dimension of the apparently pragmatic response of normal politics, and symbolic responses can be serious. Symbolic political acts are tools for ideological reform, and ideological reform—not hard-headed budget cutting—is the key to the long-term reorganization of social security.

The dispute over undue charges is rooted in two particular symbolic factors: first, the peculiar constitution of French social security and its symbolic value to different parties; and, second, the important ideological and therefore practical dimension of neoliberal symbolic acts to recent governments.

One pecularity of the French system of social security is its hybrid constitutional status: semimutualistic, semipublic. Officially, the general regime is not a public institution, not part of the state, but rather a mutualistic association of salaried workers and employers.[36] This means that spending on social security does not count as official public spending; it is not part of the budget. Social security expenditures are not voted by the Parliament; from a public expenditure viewpoint, the social security budget (so long as it is in balance) is invisible.[m]

We have already noted (pp. 69-70) that the all-out industrial policy to which the government turned in the sixties included a determined effort to channel resources through the banking and financial circuits into private investment at the expense of a relative withdrawal of the state from its heavy domination of savings and financing sources. This approach obviously implied serious efforts to limit public spending—especially in areas that would not serve as "infrastructure investment." Limiting public expenditures and reprivatizing control of a greater portion of savings funds are concrete means to transfer real resources towards the private sector. But symbolic acts are also necessary in pursuit of such a policy, necessary to create a climate in which such real transfers become possible, and also necessary sometimes to compensate with expectations for failures to achieve substantial real results. The imagery and

---

[m]The general regime is included in a document called "The Social Budget," but the latter is only a purely informational accounting document, having no binding value.

rhetoric of holding down spending and of preserving or attaining balanced budgets
are an integral part of such an overall economic policy.

Thus, the old neoliberal theme of dismantling the state's grip on the economy
and especially of "lowering the fiscal pressure" on both individuals and business
has been making a strong comeback. Valéry Giscard d'Estaing, beginning with
his Stabilization Plan in 1963 and continuing on through his stronghold over the
economy as Minister of Finance and now as President, has been the acknowledged
champion of this neoliberal approach. One of his greatest claims has been that
(contrary to trends in other competing countries) he has arrested the steady
increase of fiscal pressure, and even turned the tide from 24 percent of GNP in
1962 to 23.8 percent in 1970.[37]

Whatever its political worth, this stability of public spending and fiscal pressure is more apparent than real. Thanks to "debudgetization," important items
do not appear in the budget. Social security is one of them. Social security
spending, as we know, has been growing faster than GNP; in 1962 social security
payments represented 13.9 percent of GNP; in 1970, 16.5 percent.[38] If this
spending and its "fiscal pressure" were to be included in official presentations
and discussions of public spending, the picture of the latter would conform much
less to the image the Ministry of Finance is seeking to project.

This pattern of loading social programs onto the social security budget seems
to have become a systematic policy since 1962.[39] It permits the government
to respond to social demands it cannot repress, and take political credit for the
response, while preserving the illusion of fiscal soundness politics, and keeping
the state budget for what it considers more productive uses. Every now and
then, when the accumulation of "undue charges" on top of other expenditures
brings about a major social security budget crisis, the government admits that
some charges are indeed undue, and agrees to include them in the general budget. This happened in 1967. However, the pattern reasserts itself quickly:
Thus in 1971 the deficit for the special fund for railway workers was transferred
to the general regime (412 million francs). As recently as fall 1972 the government announced with a maximum of publicity a series of social measures concerning the aged and lagging regions. The cost of those measures was put at 2.5
billion francs. When asked about their financing, Prime Minister Messmer
responded that this is a "complex problem." However, in a few days it became
apparent that the measure was to be financed almost entirely by the surplus
accumulated in the family allowance fund.[40]

The real question about all this is, so what? Who cares if they finance it
out of social security taxes or out of general taxes—unless the incidence is
radically different?

The left-wing unions care. And they care for two different reasons: The
first is the easier to see, but the less important: defense of their constituency,
the working classes. The general regime is financed out of payroll taxes; it is
paid for out of the wages of working people.[41] Were it not for undue charges,

workers would be getting better social protection for their money—better medical care, higher pensions, and especially higher family allowances. The second basis for their opposition is ideological. It is somewhat more difficult to understand, but it is more important and takes us an important step closer to understanding the real dynamic of social security reform.

For the trade unions social protection is a right. It represents a hard-won victory of the working class against capitalism and it must be constantly defended. Social security is a mechanism for organizing it under working class control. It is emphatically not a device to smooth over the contradictions of capitalist economic relations. It is not "an automatic stabilizer"! It is not to be co-opted to conform to the rationality of the capitalist system. Social security is rooted in the ideology of solidarity as the Left understands it and emphatically not in any voluntary exchange notion of public finance. Its unique function is social protection. It is not supposed to compensate for the malfunctioning of the allocation system. If the allocation system malfunctions, one should get a better allocation system, and failing that (i.e., while waiting for more revolutionary change), the burdens of compensating for the inhumanity and irrationality of the allocation system should be placed on the back of the existing allocation system—especially on those who most benefit from it. It is the responsibility of the government, and not of the mutualistic social protection scheme to make that compensation. Thus, if the twisted logic of capitalist development creates masses of human debris in the form of wiped-out shopkeepers and farmers, the government has to find a way to take care of these victims of creative destruction. The trade unions must resist attempts to push those costs onto the social protection scheme. Similarly, because the allocation system is so unjust and irrational, it creates poor people. The answer is not compensatory social benefits out of the workers' wages; it is higher wages in the first place for those people! The ultimate integration of the social security system into the logic of the neocapitalist state would be to means-test all social payments—thus using social security benefits as the balance wheel for the injustices and irrationalities of capitalism, and doing so in such a manner as to get the most social payoff per buck while dividing the working classes. Undue charges is merely one small step down the fatal path.

Health Care

Health care lies at the heart of the permacrisis of social security. Containing rising costs (health expenditures have been increasing almost twice as fast as GNP)[42] is the main problem. But the need to maintain standards of quality while preserving inequality of service complicate the problem dramatically.[43]

Unlike pensions and family allowances, the other main components of the social security budget, health insurance is not a simple transfer payment; it is not merely the provision of a check. It is basically the provision of a complex service. Reform of health insurance confronts, therefore, not only the relatively simple, though impossible, problem of what size checks to send out to how many people, and where to get the money for those checks, but also the complex and substantive matter of organizing, or rather reorganizing, a major sector of economic activity. And it is a big sector, several times bigger than, say, the steel industry. It is a sector that has, over the past ten years, created more new jobs by itself than *all* of industry combined. It is the sector that more than any other major sector—except possibly education—has contributed to inflation, to rising taxes, and to a rising rate of reforms.[44]

There is no room in this chapter for an analysis of the causes of that growth or of the responses it has triggered.[45] Suffice it to say that in France, as in the United States, there is no fully satisfying, single explanation for the rapid growth. The usual factors making for cost increases are eminently present:

1.   A high income elasticity of demand for health services.[46]
2.   Increasing factor inputs—*both capital and labor.* Unlike most sectors of the economy a large percentage of cost increases in health seem to be, especially in the hospital segment, due to increases of factor inputs per day of hospital care.[47]
3.   Increased costs of those factor inputs.

These headings include such diverse phenomena as new, very high cost medical technologies (kidney dialysis machines, open-heart surgery units, heart-lung machines, etc.), that reflect advanced, albeit expensive, methods of prolonging life, and thus the necessary price to pay for improved care, as well as inefficient use of expensive facilities, monumentally wasteful fee-for-service billing to third-party payers, and rapacious proprietary hospitals, labs, and pharmaceuticals. In brief, they are descriptive economic categories: They are causal only in the econometric sense but not in any serious way.[48]

Limited space precludes discussion of these categories, which means avoiding serious discussion of why costs rise so much and simply pointing to the existence of all these "usual" expenditure generators and confining our brief remarks on factors peculiar to the French health system and, of those, to the factors that are most germane to the theme of this chapter.

Were we to ask a class of young systems designers to model an inflation maximizing health care system, the better projects would integrate the essential architecture of the French system—public payment and private provision. The outstanding projects would add the critical details: fee-for-service payment and supplementary insurance benefits for certain large groups.

It is the mismatch of these two conflicting modes of economic organization— on the one hand socialized demand and on the other what *Le Monde's* J. Dumont calls "the flourishing industry" of health care:[49] liberal medicine, private hospitals, laboratories, and pharmaceuticals, which are all connected through third party, fee-for-service payment— that generates increasing expenditures and reduces all reforms and efforts at "rationalization" to relative impotence.

To be sure, there is omnipresent state control and regulation aimed at preventing abuse. But this certainly does not prevent costs from soaring, nor does it prevent funny things from happening. For example, an agreement is periodically contracted between the health insurance fund and the doctors' union setting maximum-level fees per medical act that doctors can charge and still be paid by social security; but this cannot control the number of medical acts a doctor deems necessary for the treatment of an illness. Similarly, there are price controls on pharmaceutical products, but the pharmaceutical industry seems to be particularly inventive in France and comes out with new products that differ only slightly, if at all, from the old product almost as fast as the government comes out with new controlled prices.[n] The day rate in private hospitals is indexed on the cost of a day in the public hospitals, but the private hospitals cream the surgery market, leaving the costly and messy jobs to the public system. This has the immediate effect of keeping their real costs down while pushing up the costs in the public hospitals, and hence the per day rate of reimbursement from social security.[50]

The result is that, according to the Bordaz Commission of the Sixth Plan, it is in France and in Belgium where the mixed system of health care delivery (public payment, private provision) operates that the average cost of health care per protected person is by far the highest in the Common Market. According to the Commission this cost was 440 francs in France against 320 francs in Italy and 281 francs in Germany, which also provides better coverage and better care.[51]

The normal politics approach to containing health care costs becomes ever more difficult. On the demand side, for the reasons given above, more and more of the population has had to be included in the insurance system inspite of the actuarial unsoundness of bringing them in. Now coverage is pretty much universal, and it is simply out of the question to try to kick any major group out. The government tried to make the consumer pay a greater share of each bill hoping thereby to reduce the number of medical acts as well as its own outlay per act. This reform was passed in 1967, and in May 1968 as a major part of the Grenelle agreements, the trade unions reversed it and made it perfectly clear that they would not tolerate any major moves in that direction. All that remains, therefore, is a steady increase in "contributions" (social security taxes) whether through higher rates or higher ceilings. But higher social security taxes are ever more fiercely resisted by both the labor unions and the middle class unions, and also counter the government's

---

[n]In constant prices, medical spending doubled between 1950 and 1960; spending on pharmaceuticals quadrupled: J. Doublet, *Sécurité Sociale*, p. 547.

basic policy not to see still more national resources pulled out of productive use
and eaten up in the health system.

As a result there are recurrent spasms of rationalization and reform on the
supply side: more computers, more paramedical personnel, new health administrators, and new administrative technologies (program budgeting, better cost
controls, facilities location models, etc.). But the thrust of these reforms and
rationalizations is quickly lost in the structural flaw at the heart of the system
and costs continue to climb.

Real reform, such as an end to fee-for-service, is viewed by all players as a
system change. It is not a marginal question to be resolved through a liberal-
pluralist compromise. It is a victory for one side (or at least a wipe-out for one
side): It goes beyond normal politics.[52]

Thus, the margin for political maneuver is narrow. Alternatives look all too
clear, and therefore unpalatable. The system—politics as usual—struggles on.
Contribution rates go up; so do ceilings. In 1968 a 2.5 percent tax is slapped
on pharmacy profits; in 1970 it is "renegotiated." Computers are mobilized to
establish a "medical profile," which is supposed to curtail abuse by doctors of
their power to determine which and how many medical acts are needed.

Behind this patch-work of pragmatic, incremental intervention—the outputs
of normal politics—there appears to loom a definite, although weak, strategy
aimed at imposing self-discipline on the runaway sector. The government declares
its desire to preserve the present system, but threatens that if present trends continue it will not be able to. M. Jeanneney, Minister of Health, was very explicit:

> I desire ardently that we succeed in saving our liberal medicine, but
> its fate is entirely in the hands of doctors themselves. If they know
> how to impose over their whole profession a discipline such that
> their expenditures represent the necessary, without the superfluous,
> then the nation will be able to carry the burden. . . . If not, one day
> or another, liberal medicine will disappear.[53]

This unusually blunt statement drew indignant outcries from the medical associations, but similar statements continue to be made. M. Boulin, Jeanneney's successor, also stated that "the *survival* of liberal medicine implies that doctors
closely control health consumption expenditures"[54] (emphasis added).

The Bordaz Commission of the Sixth Plan stated: "It is impossible to reconcile a liberal organization of health delivery, whatever its merits may be, with
collective, compulsory insurance, without significant increases in costs." The
Commission's decision to consider "offering clear choices . . . between the maintenance of the present system with the cost it implies . . . and a study of a new
mechanism" can also be considered a part of this strategy.[55]

Thus, all players persevere, trying desperately to preserve the permacrisis of
health care and to push off the necessity of making it into a real crisis.

Salaire Unique

The family allowance program is the weakest of the three major social
security programs,[o] and the salaire unique is the weakest piece of the family
allowance package. As the name "single-wage earner allowance" indicates, the
program distributes money to families with only one wage earner, presumably
the husband.[p]

According to official sources the program originated in the natalist framework of family allowances. Its initial purpose was to compensate mothers who
were performing an important, though unpaid, task for the nation: staying
home and having children. According to others—especially Keynesian economists and feminist sociologists—it was designed essentially as an incentive program to keep women out of the labor force and in the kitchen. According to
all, its effects are very weak, if not negligible. The amount (about $20-$25 a
month on the average) is too small to offset a second income, so the program
fails as both an incentive and a compensation. Its net effect is simply to pass
along a small sum of money to families where the wife would not be working
in any case.

Furthermore, though a relatively small program (by social security standards),
the sums of money spent are not at all negligible: about $1 billion per year.[q] It
is clear then why, for the past fifteen years, the salaire unique has been the favorite target of reformers. But though it fills no economic or social function, the
form through which it fails to fulfill those functions has important political
characteristics: it is a check sent out each month to almost four million families.
As a result proposals for reforming the salaire unique have become familiar ruins
on the political landscape. The scenario rarely changes. A blue-ribbon commission demonstrates the uselessness of the program. A Minister announces a
thoroughgoing reform, usually consisting either of the total suppression of the
program, or else a plan to means-test it either directly or indirectly by including
the payment in taxable income. The Prime Minister backs him resolutely.
Then the family lobby swings into action. The Prime Minister abandons the
Minister, who in turn abandons the reform. The 1969 round provides a perfect illustration, but the 1960, 1964, 1966, and 1967 rounds were almost as
good.[56]

In January 1969 a new crop of commission reports appeared demonstrating the necessity for basic reforms.[57] In August 1969, just after Pompidou's

---

[o]As its steadily declining share of total social security expenditures indicates:
See above, p. 62.

[p]The equivalent program for nonsalary incomes was called the mère-au-foyer
allowance!

[q]Unofficial estimate for 1970 provided by the Commissariat du Plan; about 4 percent of social security expenditures.

decisive victory in the presidential elections, the Minister of Labor, Fontanet, declared that the salaire unique was to be fundamentally reformed.[58] In September the Prime Minister officially proposed the reform as part of a major declaration of policy, constituting a "Plan de Redressement." He said that the "salaire unique will be significantly increased for low-income families, but correspondingly reduced for better-off families and even suppressed for those who do not need it."[59] At the conclusion of the parliamentary debate, the government demanded a vote of confidence. The new program was scheduled to go into effect in 1970. At that point the family lobby (which is also the backbone of the Gaullist parliamentary party) mobilized against this serious threat to the core principle of "solidarité." By 26 September 1969 (ten days after the Prime Minister's resolute words and vote-of-confidence grandstanding) the CGC (the white collar union) had obtained a public retreat from the Prime Minister who declared to the union's officials that the reform of the salaire unique would not be enacted "precipitously," but instead would be submitted to "a profound examination."[60]

The rationalizers went back to their drawing boards and came back with a true masterpiece, in time for the *successful* 1972 effort at reform. The reform was voted on 3 January 1972 and decrees of application were published June 29. The reform exhibits all the finesse of fifteen years of accumulated technocratic expertise at preparing reforms for the salaire unique plus an absolutely devastating dosage of political compromise. The old salaire unique allowance is not suppressed; it is maintained at its old level. On top of it, a new, increased allowance is added for families with lower incomes. But ceiling of resources (an eligibility requirement) is established for the old allowance. Its effect will be to exclude 700,000 out of an estimated 4½ million families who would have received the allowance under the old system. But an additional 1,800,000 families will receive the new supplementary allowance (all numbers for 1973). The net additional cost of the reform for the first year was estimated at 1¼ billion francs—to be, of course, paid out of surpluses in the family allowance fund.[r] But the real ingenuity of the reform lies in expectation of future developments. The ceiling on income for elibigility will stay fixed. Thus, inflation will effectively kill off the old allowance program as money incomes rise, and successive cohorts earning more, but lighter francs, will rise through the trapdoor in the ceiling.

The difficulties of reforming the salaire unique, the weakest piece of the weakest social security program, would seem to indicate that the road to reform of the major programs will be extremely long and extremely rough. It also seems to bear out the wisdom of normal politics: Influence vectors converge on compromise, which begets further compromise and only marginal change.

---

[r] All data in this paragraph from unofficial estimates by Commissariat du Plan.

In our opinion that is not the only moral of the story. Once again, the symbolic, or ideological, dimension provides the key. The real problem of the salaire unique was not one of the efficiency of budgetary allocation. The government paid too high a price—1¼ billion francs per year plus a guarantee of massive increases in administrative costs—to purchase the possibility, and it is only a possibility to increase the efficiency of budgetary allocation (or to save some money) several years down the road.[s]

The real reform was not about improving the efficiency of budget allocations—in the limited sense of getting better use of the salaire unique money. The real reform was not in the sphere of short-term allocation policy, but rather in the ideological sphere. It consisted of transforming the ideology underlying the attribution of the allowance.

The crucial success of the reform is this: The old allowance was not related to income; the new one, in its convoluted way, is. The old allowance was an expression of the ideology of solidarity; the new allowance is rooted in an ideology of compensation and assistance. This is the critical shift—the one the government was willing to pay so high a price to get. If assistance and compensation—and means-testing is their ultimate expression—become the prevailing principles of social security, that is, if the social actors accept them as such, it would pave the way for a major rationalization of the social security system. An attempt to achieve such an ideological shift is the crucial element behind the government's persistent efforts to reform social security. It is what gives the disparate elements their coherence. It explains the peculiar compromises they are willing to accept and translates an apparent drift-course through the vagaries of normal politics into a strategy aimed at transcending that arena and producing a structural change in the role of social security in French society.

The transformation of social security from a universalistic system of mutual social protection to a selective system of compensation for injustices and inequalities created by the allocation system is not an easy task. It requires considerable political skill, continuous pressure, and time, especially so when the prevailing view is backed by an impressive array of entrenched social forces. It also requires a strong faith in the worthwhileness, the ultimate superiority, perhaps even the inevitability, of the new approach. One must believe that the new ideology is more "rational." Fighting for fundamental changes in ideology is no game for cynics—even in France.

---

[s]Savings of about $5 billion francs per year assumes a steady inflation (a safe assumption), but also the power to hold the ceiling on the old allowance; if they would be able to hold the ceiling on the old allowance in the face of inflation, they might almost as well be able to hold its rate—and save 1¼ billion francs per year right from the outset.

Distribution

A campaign to shift discussion of social security towards the realm of assistance and compensation would have little difficulty showing that the giant transfer system is not playing a very major role in redistributing income from richer
to poorer. But as a major effort by the government to show how social security
taxes and expenditures are distributed risks creating greater problems than those
it already has to contend with, there are few official studies of the full redistributive effects. Indeed, there seems to be none. In official documents there is rarely
a serious discussion of the redistributive impact of social security transfers in
spite of the fact that the system transfers about 22 percent of disposable income.[61]
A few semiofficial and unofficial studies exist, but none is complete. None ana-
lyzes the redistributive effects of the total system on meaningful categories.[62] One
of the few partial analyses prepared for the INSEE on the basis of new household
survey data[63] deals only with the benefit side. It does not include tax incidence.
And it does not include retirement pensions, nor does it fully take into account
family size.

Using this data, if we look at benefit distribution by social-occupational
category in terms of percentages of primary household revenue, we find no sur-
prises. Income from transfers represents a greater proportion of total income for
the lower social categories and a lesser proportion for the upper groups.

> For agricultural workers (the lowest group), social security transfers equal
> 42.5 percent of primary income (i.e., add 42.5% to what the average agri-
> cultural worker's family earns and you get their total income).
> For industrial workers (no breakdown between skilled and unskilled), the
> percentage declines to 38.6 percent.
> For *cadres moyens* (middle white collar) the percentage of primary income
> accounted for by transfers declines still further to 22.7 percent.
> And, finally, for *cadres supérieurs* (upper white collar and executive, the
> highest occupation group), transfers represent only 10.6 percent of pri-
> mary income.[64]

Thus far we get the comfortable feeling that this is how it ought to look. But
then, when you get upset at using percentage numbers and begin to search around
for some absolute amounts, a very different story begins to come out of the same
numbers. Just as the percentage of primary income represented by transfers gets
bigger as you go down the socioeconomic ladder and a warm glow of distributive
justice sets in, so, the absolute numbers, convey the opposite conclusion about
the scale of benefits. It goes up with social group, and the warm glow gets
replaced by that (really) more reassuring feeling of indignation. These same social
security transfer payments per family when measured in absolute amounts for
1969 come to:

for *cadres supérieurs*
>   (upper white collar and executive)   6,145 francs
for *cadres movens*
>   (middle white collar)   6,106 francs
for *ouvriers*
>   (industrial workers)   5,720 francs
for *employés*
>   (low clerical and white collar)   4,880 francs
for *personnels de service*
>   (domestics, menial services, etc.)   3,973 francs
>   (or 65% of transfers given
>   to a *cadre supérieur*)

In brief, when you examine the distribution of benefits in real cash, you find
that they are distributed inversely with "need" (or at least what appears to be
need to your sociological intuition).[t]

Now, while these results are disturbing, they are not complete for they do
not consider social security contributions (taxes).[u] The basic social security contribution (tax) paid out of wages (part by worker, part by employer) and subject
to a ceiling is outright regressive. As one's income rises way above the ceiling
on assessed income, one pays a dramatically lower proportion of total income
to social security than does a worker whose entire salary is below the ceiling.[v]

The foremost French academic authority on social security, J.J. Dupeyroux,
provides an example of how the ceiling works. Suppose we have two families
with identical composition: father, mother, and four children. In the first
family one father is employed as a *cadre supérieur* at 5,000 francs a month. He
would pay 655 francs in contribution to social security. In the second family
four persons work: the father earning 1,300 francs, the mother 800, and two
children, 800 and 700 francs, respectively. Their total social security contributions would be 1,667 francs per month, two and a half times (1,012 francs)
more than the first family even if their total income is 1,000 francs less.[65]
Dupeyroux also noticed that this counter-redistributive effect of the ceiling
becomes more pronounced as the ceiling rises slower than the salaries. Thus,

---

[t] Roze, "Prestations Sociales," Table 5. Your "sociological intuition" can be
verified by multiplying the two tables to get absolute income levels in order to show
correlations of these socioeconomic categories with income. The estimates of total
income are totally unreliable for the highest brackets—very understated. Data for self-
employed are omitted, because income data for self-employed in France are simply not
to be taken seriously.

[u] Nor, it is important to remember, do they include old-age pensions.

[v] Both parts—employer contribution and worker's contribution—can be treated,
for economic analysis, as coming out of wages. This is even done by such true-blue economists as the Brookings Institution: See *Brookings Bulletin* 9, no. 4, 1972, p. 2.

between 1963 and 1969 the average salary rose by 60.2 percent, but the ceiling by only 56.3 percent. A study by the Confédération française démocratique da Travail shows that as income rises, the percent of social security contributions declines. A bachelor earning 6,000 francs per year will pay 6.9 percent in contribution to the social security (this is his direct contribution; when the employer part is also considered, he will pay 44.3 percent of his total wage to social security), but if he earns 50,000 francs per year he will pay only 2.6 percent of it to social security (14.8 percent if the employer's part is included).[66]

It is difficult to compare these results with those of Roze, for the breakdown is difficult in the two studies (Roze used socioprofessional categories and the CFDT uses incomes). An attempt to assess the distribution effect globally has been made by B. Mourre who analyzed the distribution of transfers in function both of household income and family size.[67] But among transfers he included family allowances, health insurance (but not pensions), and he also added education and all taxes, direct and indirect (not just social security taxes). On the basis of the data Mourre provides we established a table (Table 2-1) indicating combined redistributive effect of family allowances, health insurance, and contributions to social security.

It is not easy to interpret these results. The main reason for the difficulty is their inconclusiveness. If we hold family size constant, we can claim that there is a redistribution of income from the richest to the poorest, albeit very little. Thus, for each family size, a household with an annual income of 50,000 francs receives a smaller absolute amount of transfers than a household with an income of 6,000 francs. On the other hand, if we take, for example, the category households with one child, all income levels pay in more than they get out. But the highest income level is paying in a smaller percentage of its income than any other level. In that sense it is regressive. The same is true for all levels of single person households, and childless couples. It is also true for all but the very lowest income level of the category two child households.

But the true nature of the system only becomes apparent when one begins to compare across family sizes. We see, for example, that a couple with two children and an annual income of 50,000 francs receives bigger absolute amounts of transfer payments than a couple with one child and an income of 6,000 francs per year. This can mean only one thing: that the horizontal redistribution, that is redistribution which transfers resources from smaller families to larger families, is much stronger in the system than the vertical redistribution of income, that is from the richer to the poorer.[w]

---

[w]The horizontal redistribution effect of family allowances is compounded by the regressive vertical distribution of health insurance. Here, the pattern is extremely clear: The higher the income, the higher the absolute amount of health insurance transfers (even if the relative amount is declining). This finding is corroborated by a wealth of studies and even by official data. The following list shows health expenditures by socio-professional category in 1967.

The Left and the Reform of Social Security

If we shift discussion of the social security system into the terms of compensation and assistance, even a cursory analysis of its distributional effects provides powerful justification for major reforms to make the system favor the needs of the disadvantaged. And once that shift is made—a shift that assumes away the big question—the normal politics explanation of the positions of the various competing groups has a solid ring of realism to it.

From this perspective the government's reform efforts appear to be laudable in terms of "equity" as well as understandable in terms of "efficiency." One can also easily understand that the CGC—the white collar union—staunchly defends the status quo against efforts to use social security for vertical income redistribution. After all, they hardly ever miss an opportunity to take a stand against equalization of revenues, whether through wages or through transfers. Similarly, one is not surprised to find the UNAF—the Union Nationale des Allocations Familiales, the organized arm of the family lobby—coming out vigorously against the introduction of means testing. Means testing would threaten the whole rationale of family allowances, the benefits of its constituents and the existence of the Union Nationale. It is a bit more difficult, however, to explain the opposition of the left-wing unions such as the CFDT and the CGT to the "most disadvantaged first" thrust of the proposed reforms—but only a bit. Within a normal politics framework one explains their behavior as traditional interest group activity in spite of their class politics rhetoric. Thus, one accuses them of either the higher cynicism or the lesser cynicism. The higher cynicism indictment would hold that they are really rather like American labor unions—interested overwhelmingly in the interests of their membership, "organized labor," and not in the welfare of any underclass. Were this the case, their opposition to the social security reforms would need no further explanation, just documentation to show a consistent pattern of behavior. The second alternative, the lesser cynicism, finds that the labor unions do try to represent, as they claim, a working class movement and not just "organized labor." But the exigencies of day-to-day politics, especially the need to make and hold political alliances, forces them to this "antiprogressive" position. This force—the logic of their role in a

cadres supérieurs	1633 francs (724 francs for pharmaceuticals)
cadres moyens	1319 francs (502 francs for pharmaceuticals)
agriculteurs	940 francs (444 francs)—the average
employés	935 francs (463 francs)
ouvriers	866 francs (396 francs)
inactifs	811 francs (456 francs)
professions indépendantes	768 francs (374 francs)

Source: *Tableaux: Santé et Sécurité Sociale, 1970-71*, p. 380. For similar findings more extensively discussed, see C. Michel, *La Consommation Médicale des Français*, 1969.

Table 2-1

Combined Redistributive Effect of Family Allowances, Health Insurance, and Social Security Contributions

Household Income		Single	Childless Couple	Couple 1 Child	Couple 2 Children	Couple 3 Children	Couple 4 Children	Couple 5 Children
6,000/year francs	1	—	—	372	2,959	5,607	7,343	9,110
	2	781	1,484	1,570	1,968	2,070	2,343	2,624
	3	-417	-417	-417	-417	-417	-417	-417
	4	364	1,067	1,525	4,510	7,260	9,269	11,317
		(-1,535)	(-762)	(-324)	(2,681)	(5,431)	(7,440)	(9,488)
12,000/year	1	—	—	235	1,518	5,013	6,801	8,681
	2	802	1,524	1,612	2,021	2,125	2,406	2,624
	3	-834	-834	-834	-834	-834	-834	-834
	4	-32	690	1,007	2,995	6,304	8,373	10,471
		(-3,626)	(-2,968)	(-2,651)	(-673)	(2,646)	(4,715)	(6,813)
20,000/year	1	—	—	130	2,080	4,037	6,050	7,848
	2	864	1,642	1,737	2,177	2,290	2,592	2,903
	3	-1,002	-1,193	-1,188	-1,108	-1,078	-1,053	-1,028
	4	-138	640	679	3,149	5,519	7,589	9,723
		(-4,374)	(-4,509)	(-4,448)	(-1,595)	(-1,081)	(-3,115)	(-5,362)
30,000/year	1	—	—	113	1,894	4,051	5,757	7,507
	2	1,004	1,908	2,018	2,530	2,661	3,012	3,373
	3	-1,103	-1,450	-1,392	-1,303	-1,213	-1,167	-1,192
	4	93	805	739	3,121	5,509	7,602	9,688
		(-4,531)	(-5,297)	(-5,083)	(-2,273)	(545)	(-2,857)	(-4,817)
50,000/year	1	—	—	129	1,913	4,001	5,656	7,373
	2	1,194	2,269	2,400	3,009	3,164	2,582	4,012
	3	-1,305	-1,535	-1,548	-1,439	-1,493	-1,425	-1,305
	4	-106	964	981	3,483	5,672	6,823	9,934
		(-4,948)	(-4,982)	(-5,028)	(-1,999)	(-70)	(1,406)	(-4,381)

Source: All data from B. Mourre, "Repartition de Certains Transferts Sociaux, Suivant la Taille et le Revenu Des Menages Salaries," Statistiques et Etudes Financieres, no. 5, 1972, tables A-G, pp. 51, 54.

1 = Total of family allowances (average)
2 = Health insurance
3 = Contributions to the social security (employee part)
4 = The balance (in parenthesis: balance includes employer contributions to social security)

political system and not their ideological claims, however sincere—becomes the primary determinant of their behavior. There is much to recommend this interpretation; it explains a good deal, convincingly.

Certainly the labor unions' opposition is motivated by the demands of day-to-day politics. The left-wing unions are associated, more or less formally, with the left-wing political opposition to the present regime: the CGT, the largest union, very strongly and closely with the Communist Party; the CFDT, more loosely and informally, with the non-Communist but radical Left. The unions are rivals. They compete for membership and for influence. But they are also allies; they must act together if any successful labor action is to succeed. And they are close allies at the political level in an ever-tenuous united Left coalition that aims at assembling an electoral majority: over 50 percent. In the last election the left coalition got 49.3 percent of the vote! The electoral route to power means that divisiveness must be avoided. The Left is painfully aware of the growing importance of white collar workers in the work force and of their even greater importance in the electorate: The four million foreigners, unofficially estimated to be working in France at blue collar or menial service jobs do not vote. Traditionally very solidly based in blue collar workers and voters, the Left must enlarge its constituency if it is to conserve its power and conquer new leverage. But white collar workers are better paid, and they also frequently benefit from complementary social insurance schemes assessed on that portion of wages above the social security ceiling. To press for greater progressivity in the social security system risks antagonizing this much-sought-after constituency. Thus, normal politics has its own dictates that the unions must follow.

The CGT tries especially hard to attract white collar workers, in line with the Communist Party's strategy of unifying all working people against the domination of monopoly capital. Sometimes their willingness to please white collar workers carries them amazingly far. Thus, the UGIC, the small white collar union affiliated with the CGT, asserts that the reduction of wage differentials will not improve the fate of disadvantaged categories. Instead, "any real salary improvement can only be made at the expense of capitalist profits, and for the public and nationalized sector, by reducing massive and unproductive state expenditures such as the nuclear striking force."[68]

Given their need for unifying rather than a divisive strategy, it is much wiser to emphasize the need to extend the system than to dwell upon the modalities of reducing benefits. They demand larger benefits: pensions at sixty, better health protection, bigger family allowances, greater influence for working people in the decision-making process of social security. And these larger benefits are for everyone—including the disadvantaged. They find no need to reduce workers' benefits or to increase their "contributions" in order to finance these extended benefits, let alone to maintain present benefit levels. For them there is no financial crisis in social security. Better benefits should be paid not out of workers' wages, but rather out of monopoly profits, out of the massive public spending that is undertaken purely to support those profits, and out of undue charges that create the illusion of deficit and provide the government with a pretext for trying to steal back what the working people won through struggle and for trying to divide the Left.

There is nothing false in this normal politics interpretation of the Left's position, and certainly the factors it illuminates cannot be ignored in any solid analysis of the problem. Only it is incomplete, and an incomplete analysis is a distorted analysis. Its partial, though solid, truths do not lead to an understanding of what the whole battle over social security is all about. It fails to elucidate the more fundamental basis for the labor unions opposition or for the economic rationalizers' persistent initiatives. It even fails to explain such concrete anomalies as the government's willingness to pay so high a price to reform the salaire unique.

The unions consider the present regime as their adversary, as basically inimical to their interests, the interests of the working class. They disagree with its neoliberal philosophy, of which the social security reforms are just one faithful expression. And they a priori distrust its actions. But beyond their instinctive distrust of the present regime and the tactical necessities of alliance with the white collar workers, there looms a more profound disagreement.

The unions do not perceive the problems in government terms. They do not see social security as an either/or dilemma: either the disadvantaged or the middle class. There is no industrial imperative for them. Nor is there a prejudice against expanding the public sector or increasing "fiscal pressures." Nationalizations and socializations are not only perfectly acceptable to them, they are desirable. There is, for them, no reason why social security should not be able to provide higher benefits for its contributors and their families. The justice in the system should be reestablished not by cutting benefits for those better off, but by increasing benefits for all—and by financing those new benefits out of profits or out of the vast sums the state spends trying to shore up an irrational economic system, and not out of the wages of the worker. As for the health sector and the health industry, they should be socialized. There are some differences as to the extent of the socialization. Both unions favor nationalization of the high profit, high price pharmaceutical industry, but they diverge on their strategy towards doctors. The CFDT advocates far-reaching reforms, in particular the suppression of the principle that doctors should be paid per medical act, which for supporters of liberal medicine represents the keystone of the present system. Following its "united front" line, the CGT is more conservative here.

The unions view social security and income redistribution as two different problems. It is not the role of social security to compensate for inequalities of income generated by the present irrational allocation system; it should not have to pick up the human debris of the system's creative destruction. These problems derive from the allocation system and should be handled at that level. The best place to start is with the fiscal system. It is through higher taxes, especially on capital gains and unearned incomes, that major inequalities should be corrected.

The problem of distribution is that of redistributing from capital to labor, not from workers' wages to the poor. The problem of public spending is its inhumane irrationality: to stop spending the ever-growing amounts of money needed to keep the neocapitalist system afloat and to spend that money on the needs of the system's victims. Monopoly capital must be made to pay the full social costs of its activity. This is the form of redistribution that they are willing to accept through social security reform, yes! But what to reform first is a big—perhaps *the* big—political question, one that theorists of normal politics do not seem to address.

The unions reject not only the government's concrete proposals, but also the vision of social security they feel sustains those proposals. For them the issue does not concern giving a little more to the poor and a little less to the middle. The reforms are not about marginal adjustments: They are about structural changes. They are about changing the organizing principles of social security from solidarité to assistance, and this they reject. Assistance means means-testing of some kind, and that implies a loss of dignity; it means abandoning a right for a dole. It can also mean long-term reductions in benefits to workers by opening the gates to skillful manipulation of indices and ceilings by creating more and more categories and granting increases to some categories and not to others until a coalition supporting benefits is shattered. Most important, means-testing is invidious: It means pitting the disadvantaged against the workers, the workers against the white collars, the better off workers against the worse off, and so on through splintering differences. Indeed, this is the critical problem for the unions—and the big attraction of the system, as the unions see it, for the government. It could splinter the united movement of working people against capital, and divert it into factional squabbles among working people for the crumbs being dished out by the dole. The specter of the American welfare backlash reinforces their misgivings about assistance and means-testing. To the unions, means-testing represents a big step towards the end of the Left.

Conclusion

The complex history of efforts to reform social security is not a drift course within the confines of normal politics, but rather a slow development towards fundamental reform. Within the tangle of budgetary compromise and the feverish but stalemated motion of normal politics, we can see one marginal change that is unlikely to remain marginal: It is the thin end of the wedge of structural change. The important methodological problem is to be able to see why some changes stay marginal and others grow to be structural. Normal politics is unable to aid that critical determination. Though it focuses on movement, it cannot deal with change.

We have already examined the forces shaping that structural change and discussed its substantive character. The permacrisis of social security is the result of the impasse between the imperatives of the economic system and the necessities of the political system that mediates economically imperative reform. It is a transient state. The social security spending curve cannot continue along the same trajectory. Some kind of structural change—either in social security or in the general orientation of the economy—is necessary.

The long-run functional objective of reform is to make social security better serve the ends of the newly modernized economy, to "rationalize" it. In ideological terms the goal is to shift from solidarity to assistance and compensation. The chief instrument is means-testing.

From the economic rationalizer's view, the ultimate integration of social security into the logic of the neocapitalist economy is to means-test all social payments. The force of social security spending would then be directed at compensating for failures of the allocation system. In that way it serves the rationality objective of helping the neocapitalist economy to run ever faster. It also serves the equity objective of helping those who most need help. And it meets the efficiency criterion of achieving those ends with the greatest payoff per buck (or per franc), while at the same time providing the extra bonus of serving to divide the working class.

The path towards this end will be long and difficult. Small victories must be won and accumulated, and there is the ever present risk of big defeats—such as the sustained crisis that began in the depression and ended in 1947, which first established social security, or the smaller crisis of May 1968, which reversed many of the 1967 reforms. Nothing is sure. But precedents can be accumulated. First is the ideological level: Cultural hegemony must be won. Means-testing must gain legitimacy and familiarity. Hence the importance of the salaire unique victory. Then, one at a time, others can be added to the list; aids to the handicapped are now on the agenda along with housing allowances. Conquests must be made a step at a time, but that does not mean that they are made mindlessly: The gains accumulate. No conspiracy is needed to generate the consistent long-range strategy: That is the function of the logic of a form of development; how well the strategy is pursued is the measure of the ability of those leading the economy along its development path.

Normal politics will continue to dominate the day-to-day scene. The stalemate will continue; a focus on the dynamic of structural change does not imply visions of imminent catastrophy or impossible pressures. Some pressures on the system might even relent. As almost everyone is now in the system, there will be no new influx to accommodate; one major source of growth in the past is thereby eliminated for the future. Demographic pressures might also relent. The birth rate is falling suddenly, and the postwar baby boom is now entering the labor force. The proportion of the population in the labor force will likely rise before it again shrinks. On the other hand, some pressures might intensify. Unemployment benefits that until now have been trivial[69] might rise, hitting the financial equilibrium from both ends by dramatically increasing the outgo while simultaneously cutting the income. Similarly, the large number of foreign workers (somewhere between 2½ and 4 million) might shrink, and that might increase the financial pressure on the system.[x] Social security will not suddenly explode and be rebuilt from scratch. The permacrisis will continue. And so will the conquest of structural reform. At some future date an analyst will look back on the system and explain how the whole thing had become quite different—quite naturally, quite imperceptably, through the smooth sum of marginal movements and, perhaps, a few decisive environmental changes (population, etc.).

Along with means-testing (the ideal tool) comes the proliferation of complementary funds (both public and private). The growth of complementary funds, which take as their floor the social security ceiling, generates inequalities. By slicing the population into more categories and smaller groups (by income and by industry) it weakens the overall solidarity created by the general fund. The wedge cuts two ways: into the economic problem, but also into the political problem. It divides the political forces that have thus far blocked social security reform. It goes even further: In its own modest way it helps to splinter the left coalition in general.

If ultimately successful this strategy will bring about a dual system. One part will increasingly serve the poor, the crippled, the bypassed—all those left out of the benefit stream of the new economy; both the force of economic development and the stronger force of manipulating the ceiling on means-testing will isolate them as a distinct minority. The other part will be a set of funds,

---

[x]The role of foreign workers in social security and in the social transfers system in general is very complex, quite unexplored, and in many essentials, unprovable. All pay full social security taxes. All enjoy full coverage. That much is simple. Then the complexity begins. Their dependency ratio (dependents per worker) is much lower than that of the rest of the work force. Second, they are not permanent residents; it is expected that most will return home. Third, a web of special treaties between France and the supplier states defines their position vis-à-vis social security benefits—and those treaties are still being made and amended. Finally, since very few, if any, have reached the age to qualify for old-age pensions—and so many things can change before they do—it is extremely imprudent to speculate on their long-term impact on the system. Even short-term impacts need very careful study. Several basic points would include: (1) the use of health insurance by relatively young foreign workers without families who fear losing their right to stay in the country if they stop working for very long, and (2) the arrangements actually in force for sending family allowances back home that vary from country to country and change from time to time. In the short run it would seem that they pay in more than they take out.

both public and private, serving—at carefully differentiated rates—those in the
mainstream of the economy.

French has no word for "policy analysis." What you see depends upon how
you look at things, on your approach, or method, or as one too often hears,
"your methodology." Normal politics traces the drift course of budgeting
within the permacrisis. It spotlights the marginal adjustments that come about
through the complex interactions of competing interests resulting in stop gap
compromise, which leads to further and more complex compromise. It is all
reminiscent of classical economics with its fixation on marginal price competition generating marginal adjustments that oscillate around an equilibrium path.
The resemblance is not purely coincidental.

The alternative view presented here provides a different understanding.
Movement through the permacrisis is not a drift course. It leads to change,
and not by the simple accumulation of marginal gains. It shapes the permacrisis into a real crisis, into structural, not marginal change. The marginal budgetary movements keep score for the game of competing interests; they are
real, important, and quotidian. But if we may continue our analogy to economics, they give as distorted a picture of political reality—especially the
crucial element political change—as do marginal movements among competing
corner grocery stores when a supermarket moves in. To use Joseph Schumpeter's
phrase, "the powerful level is made of other stuff."

Notes

1. Cited in *Le Monde*, 20 September 1972, p. 33.
2. The following paragraphs draw upon H.C. Galant, *Histoire Politique de la
   Sécurité Sociale Française* (Paris: Cahiers Sciences Politiques, No. 76,
   1955). Written by an American, it is the basic work on the politics of setting up the social security system, especially the key period through 1947.
   See also: the decree of 4 October 1944, the cornerstone legislation, and
   law of 17 January 1948, the keystone legislation; Pierre Laroque, the
   "Father of French social security," "La Sécurité Sociale de 1944 à 1951"
   Révue Française des Affaires Sociales, April-June, 1971, pp. 11-15; Jacques
   Doublet, *Sécurité Sociale*, 4th ed., (Paris: Presses Universitaires de France,
   1967), pp. 31-39.
3. For a somewhat different and very brief discussion of this concept, see
   Alvin Schorr, *Social Security and Social Services in France*, U.S. Social
   Security Administration, 1965, pp. 2ff. For a labored history of the
   concept, there is J.E.S. Hayward, "Solidarity: The Social History of an
   Idea" *International of Social History* 4, 1959, p. 2, pp. 261-84. See also
   Pierre Drouin's articles in *Le Monde*, 10 April 1967 and 18 September 1969.
4. *French Report on the Efficacy of Social Security* to European Institute
   of Social Security, Hague, November 1969, p. 28.

5. Marguerite Perrot, "Salaires, Prestations Sociales et Pouvoir d'Achat. . ." *Les Collections de l'INSEE*, Series M (Menages), No. 9, table 26. Total household resources are primary revenues (salaries, wages, etc., plus transfers). Social security transfers as a percentage of primary incomes (income before transfers) are 24.2 percent.
6. *Annuaire Statistique*, 1973, p. 550.
7. See 1972 budget, p. 66 and p. 69.
8. P. Pezant's 1960 estimate, "La population couverte par les assurances sociales," *Consommation* 1, 1963; 1972 estimate from J. Brunet-Jailly, *Essai sur l'économie Générale de la Santé* (Paris, Cujas, 1971); INSEE estimates for 1971 48 million covered out of a population of 51 million. See *Annuaire Statistique*, 1973, pp. 14 and 551.
9. *Annuaire Statistique*, 1966, p. 107; 1973, p. 60.
10. *Schéma Directeur* de la Région Parisienne, p. 14.
11. See E. Malinvaud et. al., *La Croissance Française* (Paris: Seuil, 1972) pp. 218, 229-31, and 232-35, for a statistical picture.
12. See S. Cohen and J. Dyckman, *Evolution des Services et Aménagement du Territoire*, 1975, Service Régional de l'Equipment de la Région Parisienne.
13. See *Année Politique*, 1971, p. 180.
14. *Tableaux de l'Economie Française*, INSEE, 1970, p. 289 and *Annuaire Statistique*, 1973, p. 569. See also Comm. du Plan, *Dépense du Secteur Santé*, 1960-67, (Sixth Plan).
15. See Malinvaud et. al. *La Croissance Française*, pp. 58-80 and *Annuaire Statistique*, 1966 and 1973; also Pezant, "La Population couverte."
16. See below, pp. 77-80.
17. On this theme, see Stephen Cohen, *Modern Capitalist Planning*, 2nd ed., Berkeley, (University of California Press, 1976), especially pp. 112ff.
18. C.f. ibid., 152-75 and 96-103.
19. See *Projet de Rapport sur les Principales Options du Ve Plan*, J.O. Lois et Décrêts, 24 December 1964; and J. Benard, "Le Marché Commun et l'Avenir de la Planification Française," *Revue Economique* 5, 1964.
20. A. Vasconcellos and B. Kiker, "The Performance of the French Economy Under Planning, 1959-64," *Economics of Planning* 3, 1968.
21. L. Stoleru, *L'équilibre et la Croissance Economique* (Paris: Dunod, 1967), 199ff.
22. See Maurice Parodi, *L'Economie et la Société Française, 1945-70* (Paris: Colin, 1971), pp. 53-60, for an introductory discussion of this process.
23. See below pp. 76 ff.
24. Quotations from *Le Monde*, 28 March 1967, p. 21 and 14-15 May 1967, p. 9. For the build-up on the Great Debate, see *Le Monde* of 19 April 1967, 20 May 1967, 14-15 May 1967, 27 April 1967, and 3 June 1967.
25. Pompidou's speech to the National Assembly, 19 April 1967.
26. See, *l'Humanité*, 29 March 1967, 23, 24, and 27 July 1967.
27. *Le Monde*, 23-24 July 1967.

28. On the opposition build up, see *Le Monde*, 28 March, 14–15 May, 12, 13, 14, 21, 23, 28 and 29 June 1967.
29. On these decrees see *Le Monde*, 28 May, 14 May, 29 July 1967, and 3, 4, and 5 March 1970.
30. *Le Monde*, 7 November 1969.
31. See below p. 76.
32. "replatrage," *Le Monde*, 3–5 March 1970.
33. Ibid.
34. *Le Monde*, 23–24 November 1969.
35. For Bordaz Commission estimates see *Le Monde*, 28 March 1967, p. 21; *Le Monde* 5 July 1967 provides a summary of the Cour des Comptes' findings on the subject. The CGT prepared a brochure, "Les Charges Indues et les Transferts, 1974," which states their position and their estimates. See also CGT, *Courrier Confédéral* 310, 30 Dec 1971, pp. 18–19, and 333, 9 May 1972, pp. 29–30. The CFDT presented their views and estimates at a press conference of 24 May 1972, p. 3. See also *Le Monde*, 5 March 1970.
36. See, Jacques Doublet's standard juridical manual on social security, *Sécurité Sociale*. "les Caisses de sécurité sociale . . . doivent être considerées comme des *organismes privés gérant un service public*. . . . La formule qui tend à se répandre desormais est différente en ce sens que la création de l'organsime auqual est confiée la gestion du service public est généralement l'oeuvre du législateur, bien que l'organisme reste de nature privée et que les rapports entre la personne privée et l'administration soient d'ordre réglementaire. ("The social security fund should be seen as a *private* organization providing a public service. . . . The formula which has tended to develop until now is different in that the creation of the organization to which the leadership of public service has been conferred is generally the work of the legislature, even though the organization remains private by nature and the relationships between the private person and the administration are of a regulatory nature.") (pp. 261-62.)
37. See "Projet de Rapport sur les Principales Options du Ve Plan" where reducing fiscal pressure and increasing the share of private financing is presented as an absolutely top priority. The government's success in this domain—compared with that of other nations—is trumpeted in such documents as Ambassade de France, Service de Presse et d'Information, *France 1959-66, Main Developments in the Administrative, Social and Economic Fields*, p. 3. One sees the effects in various places, such as Peter Coffey, *The Social Economy of France* (London: Macmillan 1973), table 40, which shows the national budget as a declining percentage of GNP.
38. From P. Martel et al., "Le Modèle de Projections des opérations de la Sécurité Sociale," *Statistiques et Etudes Financières*, 1972/6, p. 8.
39. See *French Report*; and CGT, *Les Charges Indues*.

40. *Le Monde*, 6, 7, 9 September 1972.

41. Even mainstream United States economics generally treats payroll taxes such as social security as a wage cost. See, for example, *The Brookings Bulletin*, 9, no. 4, 1972.

42. Martel, *Le Modèle*, p. 8.

43. See Robert Alford, *Health Care Politics: Ideological and Interest Group Barriers to Reform* (Chicago: University of Chicago Press, 1975), on this important theme.

44. Cohen and Dyckman, *Evolution*.

45. This question is treated in Stephen S. Cohen, *The Permacrisis of the Service Sector*, to be published at Berkeley: University of California Press in 1976.

46. Karen Davis, "Rising Hospital Costs: Possible Causes and Cures," *Brookings Reprint 262*, provides a clear and simple review of the major usual factors making for cost increases, as do Canivet Commission report and Bordaz Commission report, but in a less concise form.

47. See S. Waldman, *The Effect of Changing Technology on Hospital Costs*, 1972, U.S. Social Security Administration, and Canivet Commission.

48. M.S. Feldstein, "Hospital Cost Inflation" *American Economic Review*, 1971, for demand side oriented econometric analysis; also Waldman, *Effect of Changing Technology*.

49. In *Le Monde*, 3–5 March 1970.

50. See the article of Dr. Bernard, "La Surconsommation Medicale" in *Le Monde*, 3 January 1970 for similar practices, or else see any of the numerous analyses of common "abuses" of medicare in the United States, for medicare incorporates the same basic structural defects of the French system—with similar results.

51. Quoted in *Le Monde*, 3 March 1970, p. 24.

52. For how doctors view the end of fee-for-service, see *Le Monde*, 24 June 67 and 30 June 67.

53. *Le Monde*, 20 June 67. Speech to "Congrès National des Classes Moyennes."

54. *Le Monde*, 29 Jan. 70.

55. See Sixth Plan, Commission des Prestations Sociales (Bordaz) Subcommittee report on health insurance systems in Europe, or *Le Monde's* detailed summary, 5 March 70.

56. See *Le Monde*, 2 February 64 for a careful analysis of the imminent, basic reform of the salaire unique; *Le Monde*, 24 March 64 reports on a similar reform package, as does 29 July 67.

57. *Le Monde*, 4 January 69, and 19–20 January 69.

58. *Le Monde*, 27 August 69.

59. *Le Monde*, 17 Sept. 69.

60. *Le Monde*, 29 September 69.

61. INSEE, *Annuaire Statistique*, 1973, estimates 1970 disposable income at 553 billion and social security payments at 121 billion (page 632).

62. A brief article signed "A.R.N.": "Réflexions sur les transferts économiques," *Problèmes Economiques*, 8 April 1971, remarks "le sujet est pratiquement vièrge en ce qui concerne l'approche globale," ("the subject is almost untouched as concerns the global approach") p. 6. See also *French Report*, pp. 26-27.

63. Hélène Roze, "Prestations Sociales, impôt direct et échelle des revenus," *Economie et Statistique*, INSEE, February 1971.

64. Roze, "Prestations Sociales," table 4.

65. J.J. Dupeyroux, *Sécurité Sociale*, (Paris: Dalloz, 1971), p. 676.

66. *Etudes Economiques de la CFDT* 58, April 1970.

67. B. Mourre, "Répartition de Certains Transferts Sociaux, Suivant la Taille et le Revenu Des Ménages Salariés," *Statistiques et Etudes Financières* 5, Paris, 1970.

68. *Le Monde*, 7 December 1966. For a simple presentation of the CGT's position, see CGT, *Courrier Confédéral*, no. 310, December 1971 and no. 333, May 1972.

69. See page 62 above.

3

The Economist and the Economic Roles of the Political Authority in Advanced Industrial Societies

Robert A. Solo

This chapter deals with the situation of the economist, specifically of those trained in the conventional paradigm of the Anglo-American academic establishment, faced with the realities and confronted by the central role the political authority is now obliged to play in all advanced industrial economics.

What follows is a discussion of the relationship of the economist to the prevailing ideology and to the economic roles of the political authority as those developed from the period before the Great Depression, through the so-called Keynsian Revolution, to the economic deterioration and crisis in the 1970s. The dilemma of the economist appears in the incapacity of his analytic heritage to grasp the character of economic organization or to encompass the changed and changing configurations of economic power in our time. It is shown that the very cognitive structure of his discipline excludes from consideration and awareness the omnipresent realities of the political economy, that is, that universe of economic phenomena that expresses collective choice and political directive, control, or influence. It is argued that this institutionalized blindness is the consequence of an epistemological commitment to a pretended universality, the embrace of an "essence" cloaking itself as a "science."

Ideological Liberalism and the Housekeeping Function

During the nineteenth and early twentieth centuries a set of beliefs were dominant in Europe and were universally accepted in the United States: belief in the omniscience of the market, and in its self-regenerative, self-equilibrating power, belief in self-seeking individualism as the unique and necessary motive force for efficient and creative economic activity, belief in the individual as beginning and end, and in individualized choice as the sole viable criterion of well-being, and belief in privately held, individually controlled property as the necessary form of economic power. Moreover, and this is what must be insisted upon, economics then was specifically the expression of that ideology. Neoclassical theory, which today remains at the heart of the discipline, constitutes the most evolved and logically coherent expression of that ideology, though in recent decades the assumptions at its base have become so laden with complex deductions

and esoteric symbolism as to be quite hidden from view. The question remains
as to whether a system of thought that came into being as an argument against
government "meddling," against political "interference," a system of thought
that is essentially an apologia for laissez-faire and a glorification of the market,
can ever transcend itself and comprehend within its framework that process of
political choice and the table of collective values that are increasingly central
to organization of the economy in our time.

In the years of the Republic up until the Great Depression of the 1930s,
American thought was absolutely dominated by ideological liberalism; and under
the imperative of that ideology, the political authority was held to the outer
confines of the market system at the rim of the economic universe. The market
system was taken to be the sacrosanct criterion of worth and of value and the
proper arbiter of equity. During the long epoch of ideological liberalism the
political authority functioned as a kind of housekeeper in a house of many
rooms. In common expectation and therefore in fact, she was a slothful and
stupid wench and something of a whore. She cleaned the corridors, locked
the doors, put out the dog at night, did errands for and variously serviced the
boarders, giving the key to her bedroom to a favored few. On the festive occasions when the pig who grazed and grubbed on the common ground was
slaughtered, she divided up the pork—and the ones who got the biggest chunks
were those with the longest arms and the quickest reach.

Thus, in the first phase of our economic history, the political authority
performed the *housekeeping function*: (1) protecting liberty—which is to
say, securing a safe and settled haven for individualized choice and the unin-
hibited exercise of the property power, (2) providing a rag bag of residual
services that the market did not make available, and (3) divvying up whatever surpluses might appear in the public domain. The only positive economic role of the political authority, the only one demanding complex
analysis and independent initiative, was that of keeping the market competitive, a task laid down in the Sherman and Clayton Acts and only seriously
undertaken in the United States. Under the rubric of industrial organization
and public control, economics in the United States has certainly concerned
itself with antitrust policy, and economists have participated with lawyers
in the formulation of antitrust strategy.

During this period the most complex and significant economic function
of the public authority was not outside of the market system, but was rather
a part of the market, intrinsic to and necessary for its operation: namely,
in making rules for the exchange relationship, and in arbitrating disputes
between and, hence, setting boundaries to, the power of the parties to
exchange. This was a task for the lawyer, and in a government of lawyers,
the only branch of government that then developed any significant and
particular competence was the judiciary. The processes of collective choice
expressed in the Congress and implemented by the President were virtually

irrelevant to the activities of the judiciary and to the complex framework for private and corporate power and market exchange that its decisions created.

The Keynsian "Liberation," and the Offset Function

Ideological liberalism was shattered by the Great Depression of the 1930s. Perforce as it lost its hold the old constraints on political action were dissipated and a new idea of the role and function of the political authority took form.

It is as part of this ideological liberation that Keynsian economics should be understood. Keynes made no new discoveries, nor did he propose new policies. His was an apologia for policies into which governments had been driven step by step, through the force of catastrophe. Nor did Keynes invent techniques of choice or control. Then and now governments used costly and clumsy tools that are the chance baggage of another age, designed for other purposes entirely. The only new tool that has been devised to implement "Keynsian" macroeconomic policy is that of French indicative planning.

Keynes' accomplishment was of another order. What he and his followers did was to offer economic orthodoxy a schemata in which the realities of mass unemployment could at long last be recognized without rejecting the neoclassical faith. In the Keynsian conception of things the market system was taken without reserve as the proper, indeed as the only viable, allocator of resources, distributor of income, organizer of production and consumption—all was left as before except that it was now conceded that the aggregate of expenditures spontaneously generated in the private economy might be too little, producing unemployment, or too great, producing inflation. The private economy was seen as a world afloat in an ether of aggregate spending, pressure too high and the sphere rose to the skies of inflation, pressure too low and it sank to the mire of depression. Hence, it becomes the task and responsibility of government to maintain the proper pressure by compensating for or *offsetting* deviations from the normative level of aggregate expenditures generated in the market economy, possibly by spending more than it taxed or by taxing more than it spent. Thus, a new economic role for the political authority; to the housekeeping function, an offset function is added.

There was a hooker in all this, a fundamental contradiction. Central to the Keynsian rationale is the assumption of a set of prices that are not responsive to changes in supply and demand, but are determined in some other way. Only if such policy-determined prices are prevailing and pervasive, can Keynsian theory work, so that changes in aggregate expenditure will produce greater or less employment rather than upward or downward swings in price. But neoclassical theory holds as its major tenet that prices universally move in automatic and autonomous response to conditions of

supply and demand, with free moving price patterns directing the allocation of
resources and determining the distribution of income throughout. The essential
Keynesian assumption and the fundamental neoclassical condition are opposite
and contradictory. Keynes did not resolve the contradiction, but hid it away
in the labyrinthine convolutions of his argument. Contradiction or not, the
Keynesian breach in the old ideological walls opened for the economist a path
to the citadel of political power.

Keynesian economics was only a segmental expression of a much larger
ideological change, and compensatory spending was only one of whole range
of offsets. In this regard consider the response of the American political authority faced in the 1930s with a collapsed economy and a society in crisis, once
the inhibiting force of the old ideology had weakened and the old constitutional
constraints had vanished. The WPA, PWA, CCC, RFC were all massive spending
programs to relieve the victims of the depression, workmen for years without
work, the young without opportunity, the old without hope, business in bankruptcy. Now that it could no longer be believed that the poor were to blame
for their poverty or that the lash of unemployment was needed to drive the
laborer to his task or that every man could and must be left to make it on his
own, there were spending offsets to protect the weak and the aged against the
harshness and exigencies of the system. There were offsets against the disabili-
ties of functional groups whose position and power in the market system had
been thrown out of kilter by the growing importance and ultimate dominance
of giant corporate organizations in industry. These were victims of an organizational revolution as well as of the depression: thus, parity payments for
agriculture for whom the terms of trade had steadily worsened and turned
catastrophic in the years of depression, and the NLRB and minimum wages
for industrial labor no longer able to bargain individually against the massive
corporation.

What had been difficult for the political authority was to cross a psychological threshold, to overcome the ideological inhibitions and folklore of
laissez-faire. This Congress did. It spent massively for compassionate causes.
Wonder of wonders, there was no retribution. The prophecies of doom did
not come to pass. But note, the political authority remained outside the
nexus of economic activity. It did not organize complex processes. It under-
took no social engineering. What it did was offset some of the effects of
individual and corporate choice in the market economy by occasionally changing the legal parameters of individual decision and corporate policy, or by
transfers of income, or by measures intended to affect the level of aggregate
spending. What now distinguished reform from reaction, left from right,
warm from cold, was the willingness to appropriate monies for compassionate
causes. The worth of an administration was now measured by the monies it
it succeeded in appropriating for good causes. Such was the outlook and
character of the New Deal, Fair Deal, Square Deal, New Frontier, and even
of Nixon's New Revolution.

The Economist and Offset Planning

Does the offset function of the political authority require a form of public planning? Surely so, and economics in its Keynsian incarnation and economists in their numbers have entered into the process of offset planning. Offset finance has become their professional domain.

Offset planning in all its forms has this special character. It must respond to what happens to happen in the market economy. It is a system of counterpunching. Effectiveness depends on a capacity to anticipate what is coming in a highly variable universe of private choice itself permeated with uncertainties, and as well on the capacity to foresee the responses of the private economy to whatever the political authority attempts. Hence, offsets require forecasts. The contribution of economics and economists to the technology of offset planning has largely been in the development of forecasting techniques and the systematic accumulation of information useful in such forecasts. Thus, since the 1930s, the proliferation and development of national income and related statistics, including input-output studies, and the econometric models maintained and operated as the in-house property of the University of Pennsylvania, Yale, MIT, and elsewhere are alike efforts to improve the performance of offset planning. Within government it has been the primary task of the Council of Economic Advisors to evaluate forecasts and itself to forecast as a basis for a fiscal and monetary policy intended to offset inflation and unemployment. *French indicative planning* is an offset technique that bases itself on the ex ante investment intentions expressed by private firms and public agencies.

Participatory Planning and the Planning Programming Function

But offset planning does not suffice. It is only the start of a greater transformation in the economic role of the political authority. By the force of events and under the pressure of necessity the political authority has been and will increasingly be obliged to participate in the organization of economic activity in the market system (call that *participatory planning*) and itself to undertake the organization of production and/or consumption on public account (call that *planning-programming* in the political economy).

The requisites of modern weaponry and the exploration of outer space (also a strange product of the cold war) have, in the American case at least, made the political economy into the source and center, progenerator and disseminator of the most "advanced" technologies in the world. There in recent decades some two thirds of all the science-trained and research-engineering manpower of the nation have been employed. This is to say that the technologically creative capacities of the American economy have been organized and deployed by the political authority—a fact of great consequences to which academia, the public, and officialdom itself has been strangely blind.

And participatory planning: Faced with the degradation of the railroads,
the collapse of the passenger lines, the overloaded airways, an air transport
technology that is a function of government R&D, the breakdown of urban
transit and the strangulation of the cities by the automobile, the political
authority—helter skelter, acting with foresight or pulled by the seat of its
pants—is drawn into the rationalization, the organization, planning, and development of a national transportation system. An instance of this is the crippling
of the economy by an energy crisis, unforeseen and unnecessary. The flounder-
ing political authority, already the R&D source of the nuclear technologies and
evidently the only agency capable and motivated to develop other energy
resources, is driven by public expectation and economic necessity to begin to
rationalize or create a viable national energy system.

The political authority tried to deal with health care in offset terms—
another law and another money bill. It could not work. It produced only a
crop of millionaire physicians and degraded medical care. Given the ideological
recognition of health care as a social responsibility, the political authority has
no alternative other than to enter into the planning of every element of a
national health system: research and the dissemination of information, the
recruitment, training, and deployment of doctors and medical aids, the development and deployment of hospitals and care facilities, and the upgrading of
management and the increase in the productivity of each of these, the standardization and universal control of health records, and all the rest. Nor, faced with
the blight of the cities, can the political authority for long avoid the fundamental rationalization, the planning, and the massive restructuring of locational
patterns, community organization, and whatever else turns out to be required
to create a secure, livable environment. And it is precisely in these terms that
the internal structure of political organization, faced with emerging responsibilities for health and education, transportation and energy, communication and
urban organization, is taking new forms.

President Nixon's price control floundered out of Phase III, and inflation
became rampant. And we are heading evidently back to something like Phase I
again. So it will be, out of control and back into control again, frying pan and
fire, politicians trying to avoid what cannot in the end be avoided. In the circumstances of the modern market economy, given that for a dominant sector
of that economy, prices and wages are a function of corporation and trade
union policy, public control, or rather public participation in the control of
prices and wages is ultimately necessary.

Keynsian offset planning fails to satisfy the public demand for full employment and price stability. And now the economist tells us that "price-wage
controls won't work" either. And certainly it is true that the controls imposed
hitherto are not workable. Without a conceptual basis, or any coherent and
accepted set of values by reference to which essential judgments can be made,
they are no more than the paralysis of society in panic: a "freeze." There is
not yet the consciousness on the part of the politician, the bureaucrat, the

public, or the economist that the issue is not one of sitting tight, but rather is one of how to allocate resources, to distribute income, and to preserve incentive through a yet-to-be invented but necessary system of co-participatory planning.

It is not necessary to argue that the interpenetration of public and corporate planning in the market economy or that public planning and programming in the political economy are desirable. It suffices that they exist and their massive extension is not to be avoided. The question is not whether, but how, and for whom. There are certainly grave problems to be resolved and terribly difficult questions to be answered. These questions will not be of the order of "shall we have a free market or shall we have planning?" We have and we will continue to have a market economy co-existent with a political economy, and there will be planning within and in respect to each. Market-based enterprise and politically directed agencies alike will face the question of when to centralize and how and how far to decentralize power and decision. Both confront the perennial dangers of rigidification and the suppression of innovation. Each must keep alive the capacity for initiatives in the organization of change and the opportunities for individual participation in the complexities of organizational or social choice.

The Blight of Ignorance, the Burden of Knowledge

Up until the mid-1930s lawyers dominated public life in the United States. The role of the economist was marginal and other social scientists were even further removed from the loci of authority and decision. This is surely understandable. The inculcated outlook and advocacy skills of the lawyer prepared him for the role of pleader and adjudicator in divvying up the public pork. It prepared him to articulate and continuously to reformulate the boundaries of private (that is to say, property) power and the legal parameters of private choice. It prepared him to pursue, prosecute, judge, and punish those who deviate from established norms (including the norms of market competition). But the lawyer and the government of lawyers were entirely unequipped to comprehend complex social processes, economic organizational and technological changes, and were impotent in the face of structural deterioration and breakdown.

The economist was better prepared than others for the analysis of complex and dynamic social processes. He was trained to analyze and explain the flux of price, the flows of income, the movements of trade. But, he sought to see and he saw perfection in the market's inner workings, and his ideological commitment was to protect the market's autonomy from the subversive force of government meddling. He was sealed off by his theory from an awareness of institutional variability or from any serious consideration of institutional reform or significant structural change. It was Keynes,

as we saw, seeming to turn the trick of scrambling the egg without cracking the
conceptual shell, who offered an egress, an escape hatch that permitted the
economist to take the deviant phenomenon of mass unemployment into positive account, and thence to engage in every phase of offset planning.

Since then the economist has shared with the lawyer the rostrum of political power and decision. And, if his analytic capabilities account for this
favored place, that selfsame structure of thought explains in good part the
failure of a political authority stumbling blindly from crisis to greater crisis.

Neither the economist nor anyone else has developed the conceptual
frame required to comprehend and to deal rationally with group behavior
and collective choice in a multisectored economy where planning and programming in the political economy and participatory planning in the market
economy have, by force of circumstances, become a commonplace necessity.
But, if all alike share the blight of ignorance, the economist additionally bears
the burden of his knowledge. His cognitive framework positively excludes and
rules out of account a priori those functions and values that are now at the
heart of economic organization and control in all advanced industrial societies.

Institutionalized Blindness: Three Examples

Built into the system, nay more, into the very manner of "economic
thinking" is the incapacity to conceive of collective choice and political direction as a rational instrument for the organization of economic activity, indeed
an incapacity to admit the very existence of the political economy and its
potentials as a center for the massive organization of production and consumption. Consider a few current instances of this institutionalized blindness.

International trade policy and international finance policy are mysteries
beyond the grasp of practicing politicians and outside of the direct experiences
of their constituencies. For that reason these matters have been particularly
the domain of academic economists. In this light consider (1) the Marshall
Plan, and (2) recent American trade deficits and international trade imbalance.

After World War II our former allies and our former enemies were allegedly
in difficult straits. Clearly their economic problems were more superficial
than we were then led to believe. Undeniably there was bombed out industrial
plant and ruined transport facilities, worn out equipment, a shortage of housing, and a general state of disorganization—but, after all, the Germans and the
Japanese were able to maintain enormous war machines and rising levels of
output until months before the cataclysm of defeat.

In any case, subjected to a propaganda that played at once upon our
heart strings and upon our fears, the Americans moved by compassion and
motivated by anticommunism, poured billions upon billions of dollars into
refurbishing and modernizing European and Japanese industry—of old friend
and of old foe alike.

This was a magnitude of government to government giving entirely without precedent. What is even more unprecedented, no repayment was asked. Such was the famous Marshall Plan.

Now, of course, there was a kind of repayment. American diplomats and visiting politicians could strut in Europe or Japan like kings for a day, and foreign governments were sensitive to their whims and whimsy. But, for the American worker, producer, consumer, taxpayer, citizen it was all grant, gift, pure give-away. Why so? Is the American really that unselfish? Do we pave our streets with bricks of gold?

The economist's rationale behind the Marshall Plan would have been stated thusly. Europe and Japan cannot repay so massive a sum without grave damage to the American economy. This was established by the experience with American war debts after World War I. To raise the funds for repayment to the United States, the debtor nations would be obliged to generate a great—and transitory—surplus of exports to the United States over and above their imports from the United States. This could be done only by reducing foreign markets for American goods and/or by flooding American markets with Japanese and European goods sold at desperation prices, which would produce grave dislocations in the American economy, probably generating irresistible demands for protective tariffs and quotas and hence causing world trade to spiral downward. That decline of trade would not only itself be detrimental, but it would also keep an ultimate debt settlement forever out of sight.

The classical though perhaps apocryphal story to illustrate this point of view is of Lloyd George who, as British Premier during the World War I, advocated a hard peace and demanded heavy reparations from the Germans in cash or in kind. When he came to realize that the Germans would try to pay through the export of coal, and when he considered that cheap or free coal would ruin his already impoverished Welsh constituencies, he changed his tune and became a champion of a soft peace and advocated a lifting of reparations.

Moreover, besides those dislocations in production and employment that would be created by the necessity for these transitory trade surpluses, the influx of cash through debt repayment into the American banking system could be nothing but disruptive of government's efforts to stabilize the level of aggregate spending.

For all these reasons the Marshall Plan was conceived and installed as a gigantic give-away. As it turned out the United States has run enormous trade deficits with its European and Japanese trading partners, so that there would have been in fact no problem at all in arranging for repayment, and then we in the United States would have been spared the inflation-producing pains of successive dollar devaluations.

Still, to be fair, rather than ask whether the Marshall Plan was justified in the light of subsequent American trade deficits, a different question should be asked: Was the analysis just described, that led to the Marshall Plan being proposed as a gift rather than a loan, reasonable, rational, sensible in its time?

It was *if* it is assumed that trade adjustments can be made only through the market economy. But there is another side of the story. Something was left strangely out of account. In every Western society there is also the political economy organizing under government direction the production and/or consumption of goods and services on a scale that approaches that of the market economy. More than one observer has noted that in this age of relative affluence, it is the public sector where the greatest need to expand consumption exists. There is indeed no limit in sight to those enormous and unsatisfied values, for example, in upgrading health, education, and the environment, where choice is collective and consumption is organized through the political economy. So also there is no inherent limit to the capacity of the political authority to organize the use of increased consumption of imported goods and services in the public sector.

Suppose that the Marshall Plan had been a loan instead of a gift with repayment systematically provided for, either as an offset of such trade surpluses as might occur in the international market economy or alternatively through imports made on public account with consumption organized through directive in the political economy. The latter alternative could have provided the finest medical equipment for tens of thousands of clinics and hospitals in the United States, or research equipment for American universities over and above the normal level of procurement. Such increased consumption of imported goods and services on public account could have been planned with no disruption of the private sector, but with real benefit for American society. Why not?

This is not an argument made with the benefit of hindsight. I argued the point with Jacob Viner, one of the grand mandarins of international trade policy in 1946. He and his associates could not admit the existence of the political economy as an instrument for organizing consumption. It was outside the economist's realm of consideration and choice.

Consider again Lloyd George. It would have indeed been disastrous to have allowed German coal to be dumped in the British domestic market. That would have dealt a terrible blow to a coal industry already desperate and declining. But if Lloyd George had arranged to take as reparations German equipment designed to modernize operations in a nationalized British coal industry and to make the mines safe for those who work in them, he might have saved that industry from the disastrous years that in fact lay before it.

The Fullbright-Hays Bill is an example of the publicly organized consumption of goods and services received in the settlement of a government debt. In this instance a partial repayment of American lend-lease deliveries were used to support American research and teaching abroad; an arrangement that made no small contribution to the postwar preeminence of American science, art, and scholarship. It might have served to establish the general value of this technique not only for intergovernmental debt settlement, but also for offsetting trade imbalances generally. It did not. The political economy remained for the economist invisible as a sphere where the consumption of foreign imports could be deliberately planned and organized on public account.

It will be recalled that 1972-73 was a time when repeated trade surpluses with the United States were leaving great dollar piles and heaps of gold in the vaults of the central banks of France, Japan, and Germany. This outflow of cash and gold was moving the world to another drastic dollar devaluation that could not be justified by relative price levels, that was not wanted by the Americans and was dreaded by their trading partners, and that could only introduce new shocks into the tottering edifice of the international economy.

Those heaps of dollars and gold, immured in the vaults of the treasuries and central banks, were quite useless to those who possessed them, a mass of unutilized claims that bespoke the incapacity of the international market system to gear together the trade of the world's diverse private-sector economies. But why could those claims not have been utilized for imports on public account?

I was in France that year. For them to have so increased private consumption across the board sufficiently to bring trade into balance would have been impossibly inflationary, and the cutting down of their foreign markets as a consequence of dollar devaluation was equally a threat to economic stability. Why not, then, bring trade into balance through the systematic consumption of foreign outputs organized through the French, German, and Japanese political economies? Why should France not put to use a portion of that heap of dollars and gold immured in its treasury vaults to refurbish its antiquated and collapsing nationalized telephone industry, or to fortify its nationalized electrical power industry with a range of imported nuclear reactors, or to build pipe lines to feed cheap natural gas from the Soviet Union into the nationalized French energy system, or to send twenty or thirty thousand students and faculty to American universities to bolster their training in particular areas of French academic and scientific weakness? Why not? Such measures could cause no market dislocation nor pose any inflationary threat in France. So far as I could see there could be nothing but benefits for the French. So I raised these questions and knocked on doors, and spoke with the mandarins. I proposed no panacea, but only that the consumption of imports planned through the political economy be considered as another string in the bow for international monetary policy. No one challenged my reasoning. No one gave me a reason why not. And no one noticed what I was saying. Le Monde accepted an article that dared to raise the question, had me thrice revise and develop it, got cold feet about publishing it (and, characteristically, never paid for it).

Why this refusal not simply to act, but to take any conscious account of the possibility for action? It is only to be explained as an institutionalized blindness, a paradigmatic inhibition that plots out the very possibility of a policy and a strategy of import-export control through consumption organized under political direction on public account, in spite of the massive existence of the political economy as an organizer of production and consumption in modern society.

A final example, that of the "Russian Wheat Deal": Here was an instance of an enormous intergovernmental economic exchange. Yet, from the American side, the transaction was thrust into the hands of private brokers in a strange, ritualistic obeisance to the workings of the "free market," with the result that all capability for foresight and control, and any possible rational reckoning of the consequences of the exchange for the American consumer and the American economy, was lost. We blindfolded outselves in an ideological reflux, a psychic inhibition built into the neoclassical paradigm that blocks out the recognition of the political economy as a field of action and of public planning as an option for choice.

The Obstructed Vision

It could be said that wherever the anthropologist looks he sees a tribe, that wherever the sociologist looks he sees a family, and wherever the economist looks he sees a business run by a hardnosed profit-seeking entrepreneur in a price-competitive market. So, too, when economists have looked at the political economy, the image of the price competitive market has been the reference base and they have analyzed the operation of the political economy by an extension or elaboration of the neoclassical theory of price-competitive markets. Oscar Lange, Abba Lerner, and those who followed them in the late 1930s and 40s conceived a socialism that would install under governmental directive a regime of pure and perfect competition with managers ordered to follow the rules of entrepreneurship as laid down in the neoclassical text, thereby realizing those beatitudes, dreamed of but never witnessed in any capitalist economy. William Baumol and a host of others have proposed that marginal-costing, marginal-pricing rules be applied according to the neoclassical text in public utility rate making under public regulation. Following in the footsteps of John R. Commons, Warren Samuels and Allan Schmid analyze the interpenetration of property power and judicial interpretation in determining the rules of the market game. Kenneth Arrow, J. Hirshliefer, Paul Samuelson, William Vickery, Otto Eckstien, Jacob Stockfish, and others have concerned themselves with extending the entrepreneurial rules of investment, according to the neoclassical text, to the evaluation of public expenditures.

In the 1930s economics, in imitation of physics, declared anathema on all value judgments (a declaration that was itself a supreme value judgment). But no policy science, no discipline that would gear into individual or social choice, can do without a value base. What the anathema on value judgment did was to narrow quite arbitrarily the value base and push it into the obscurity of mathematical symbolism, eliminating evidently considerations of justice and equity in the distribution of income. Nevertheless, even in its most stripped-down form, economics is geared to the formulation of the conditions of efficiency, on the assumption that the full and efficient use of resources in an intrinsic good. Efficiency is conceived from the standpoint of the balance of costs and benefits as these are expressed and evaluated by the individual on private account. Economics accepts that certain costs and benefits consequent upon individual choice and action may fall outside (and hence be "external" to) the system of private accounting. It is in this penumbra of "externalities" that economics admits the possible value of public intervention. In this light E.J. Mishan, W. Baumol, I.M.D. Little, K.J. Arrow, Paul Samuelson, Gordon Tullock, Mancur Olson, James Buchanan, and others have wrestled over the alleged ethical neutrality of Pareto Optimality as a welfare rule and the possible limits on its spontaneous achievement through market exchange, hence defining the boundaries "this far and no further" of the permissible in the exercise of the political authority. Kenneth Boulding's effort to promote the study of the "grants economy" has produced a considerable number of studies intended to assimilate public transfers into the theory of market exchange. Thus, invariably, the economist's analysis of the public sector follows the strictures of neoclassical thought in deducing models, analogies, and criteria as guides for the formulation of public policy, with the initiatives, outlook, and opportunities for public action understood and explained as no more than residuals in an occasionally imperfect universe of private choice and market exchange. None of this has in any way clarified the complexities or explained the phenomena of the political economy as these exist, nor contributed to the development of policy or to the improvement in techniques of participatory planning or of planning and programming in the political economy.

In fact, we are still deep in the ruts of neoclassical thought. We have not yet escaped from habits of mind and patterns of analysis that are inherently and profoundly antipolitical, that cannot conceive of the political authority except as an instrument of the last resort and that have no place for the analysis of collective values or of collective organization or of the economy as a form of human community.

What can be done?

The Grip of Essence

We cannot escape the neoclassical heritage, or the Marxian heritage. We would be wrong to try to do so. Yet, each of these great bodies of thought must be seen in a different perspective. What is required, rather, is that we abandon the idea of and the commitment to any unique, universal, unilinear system conceived as pervading and prevailing in the whole universe of economic relationships. In its epistemological rationalizations, economics would be an analogue of physics, aspiring to the model of classical mechanics. But the system of relationships postulated by neoclassical theory or that which is postulated by Marxist theory are never visible in or refutable by reference to the specific observation or event. They are alleged to underlay the flux of specifics. Neoclassical economics posits a universal, unique equilibrium underlying the surface flux of economic phenomena, unachievable, invisible, yet the sum and end point of all tendencies. This is specifically the idea of essence. So also, the Marxian historical dialectic, moving inexorably beneath and in spite of the flux and cross currents of observable events, is an idea of essence.

It is hard to escape the grip of essence, for two reasons: First, because economics and other social sciences rationalize themselves in quite different terms. We conceive of our disciplines as dim and imperfect approximations of the physical sciences, when in fact they are based on a fundamentally different principle of statement. And second because this principle of statement, that has the character of an essence, is necessary. We have no choice but to propose certain hypotheses as "tendencies" that cannot claim to be true in every (hence any specific) case and, therefore, that fall outside the scope of experimental refutation and hence verification, and that likewise fall outside any stable universe of probabilities and hence that must be accepted or rejected as a matter of judgment. That said, we can still reject (as a matter of judgment) the idea that the universe of economic phenomena can be explained by any single system. In the face of the facts of our experience, we can choose rather to see that the economic functions are everywhere performed by numerous and coexisting systems—by political agencies and by households and by tribes and by individual proprietors in competitive markets and by great corporations suspended in a different context of relationships and by universities and by churches—each of these with distinctive structural elements, each with a modus operandi and an evolutionary path proper to itself. Unless the economist takes this step, he can never comprehend the operations of, nor enter into the development of the new functions of the political authority.

This has been an essay about Western academic economics but I would suggest that Marxist like neoclassical thought reflects the same nineteenth century episteme, which cloaked the judgment of essence under the absolute and universal claims of a deified science, and that the current impotence of the Marxist economist is to be accounted for on the self-same grounds as that of his neoclassical protagonist. It is more than half a century since the Russian revolution. Half the world is already "socialist." These diverse socialist societies have in their formation been variously distorted by terror, failure and conflict. Yet, within or outside of those societies, Marxist economics remains no more than a critique of capitalism quite unable to comprehend or contribute to the development of socialism in all its complexities, variabilities, and travail, leaving that task to bureaucrats and engineers. How can this grotesque fact be explained except as the incapacity of the Marxist to step outside the universalist, absolute, and scientific pretentions of his theory in order to enter into the diverse forms and multiple dimensions of organization and behavior?

When Daniel Bell proclaimed the end of ideology but insisted upon the need for utopias, he was making the same point.

> The end of ideology is not—should not be—the end of utopia as well. If anything, one can begin anew the discussion of utopia only by being aware of the trap of ideology. The point is that ideologists are "terrible simplifiers". Ideology makes it unnecessary for people to confront individual issues on their individual merits.
>
> There is now, more than ever, some need for utopia, in the sense that men need—as they have always needed—some vision of the potential, some manner of fusing passion with intelligence. Yet, the ladder to the City of Heaven can no longer be a "faith ladder", but an empirical one: a utopia has to specify *where* one wants to go, *how* to get there. . . .[1]

What Bell calls a utopia is, in our terms, an ideology: Called one thing or the other it cannot be dispensed with. The sense of his argument is, I believe, that no social theory should be enthroned as unique, universal, "scientific," above the fallibilities of judgment, and sufficient unto the diverse and changing configurations of the social universe.

To comprehend and to enter into the functions of the political authority, economics must tear itself free—not to abandon but to achieve a state of detachment from the assumption of neoclassical theory that choice, behavior, and learning are uniquely functions of the individual. There are also processes of group, corporate, collective choice, learning, and becoming that cannot be understood by analogy to the individual but that are fundamentally of another order. Moreover, an economics that would enter into and provide the framework for the development of the new economic functions of the political authority must open itself to a table of values that does not now fall within our analytic focus.

Note

1. Daniel Bell, *The End of Ideology,* rev. ed. (London: The Free Press, 1965) p. 405.

4

Toward a Politics of Economics:
The State of Permanent Receivership
Theodore J. Lowi

Introduction

Chapter 3 by Robert Solo provides some brilliant discussion of important
economic ideas. It is especially a pleasure for a political scientist to read about
the shortcomings of economics written by an economist.

Solo tries in a number of useful ways to point toward the needs of modern
government in the last quarter of the twentieth century. He sees the central
problem with economics as its inability or unwillingness to take into account
what he calls political authority. He seems to believe rather strongly that
economics also has to get away from a focus on individuals and individual
motivation and go toward some kind of concept of collective decision making,
groups, and group motivations—if such there be.

However, the chapter is lacking in specifics about political authority, its
character, and its modes of behavior. It refers to political authority as an
abstraction, as a simplistic force, virtually as a variable. It offers us little on
the actual pattern of governments, politics, and other public institutions as they
intervene in the economic life of a country. These public institutions are treated
almost as the residuum of the difference between what economists predict and
what actually happens. The facts in the chapter tend to be facts about shortcomings or facts about real economic patterns rather than facts about public
institutions and their behavior in the market. For example, Solo provides one
of the best brief histories available on the phases of public outlook toward the
market, but he ends with what he calls the "offset" function, which was a stage
of public policy that the United States was already reaching in the 1930s. And
I think Solo would agree that the failure of this "offset" function is exactly what
has led him to make his very worthy appeal to economists to focus on the role
of political authority.

Solo seems to conclude that the most recent stage of political-economic
development possesses two characteristics. One of those characteristics is a
considerable increase in direct government provision of goods and services
to the society, either by government corporations or by government contracting.
The second characteristic is "permanent crisis." It is difficult to learn from Solo
or from real-world situations whether this more direct government involvement
is a cause of the crisis or a response to the crisis, although my guess would be
that Solo would see these two characteristics as interdependent, perhaps mutually
causative in a kind of spiraling effect.

He recognizes that the crisis involves the science of economics as well as
real economies. Systems of thinking are not so useful if the variables in the
systems are inexhaustive. Still more unfortunately, the distinction between
private and public goods does not promise much improvement because,
although it is a very worth while distinction in and of itself, it is not parallel
to the distinction between public and private spheres, between planning and
the market, between any two institutions that are having some important effect
on the society.

Thus, it would be very difficult to disagree with Solo's eloquent argument
that we abandon the quest for economic universality. But it seems to me we
are under equal obligation to go further and to begin immediately the effort
to adopt particularistic models that are loyal to the political-economic patterns
of one or more real countries at a time. This is to say that we need a political
theory of economics rather than an economic theory of politics, and I am not
absolutely certain that Solo would be ready to go this far with the implications
of his arguments. Not only does it imply a jump from the universalistic to the
particularistic, it also implies an abandonment of assumptions about the nature
of economic man and his motives. In the past generation political scientists
have proved, if nothing else, that assumptions about the nature of man and
his motives in public are unnecessary and probably harmful and misleading.
But what we need and do not find in the chapter are timely propositions about
political facts. It has not been able to break away fully from the economist's
commitment to universality, even though Solo is chafing at the bit to get on
with it.

This chapter is a response, not a critique. It is inspired by weaknesses as
well as strengths in Solo's arguments. It attempts to pursue on a preliminary
basis some of the very directions expressed and implied by him.

The State of Permanent Receivership

An important starting proposition for a politics of economics is that all
advanced industrial countries have a plan. They do not publish their plan
because it would never gain consent. Yet, it is not what one ought to call a
conspiracy, even though there is a great deal of conspiracy in every ruling
class. The plan is not entirely conscious or systematic, and it cannot be as
long as it is not written, published, debated, revised, and so on. But it is not
what you could call a secret. Every government, or prevailing majority in
every government, can draw on innumerable lawyers and economists to rationalize whatever part of the plan is to be made explicit as a matter of policy. There
has not been and there is not likely to be a program of any sort that does not
have its economists to support it. In fact, we ought to employ a term like *for-
ensic* economics to designate this whole subsection of the science of economics.

In an important sense it is the job of political science, of a politics of economics, to discover what the plan is, and in discovering it, stopping it or improving it as the case may be. Discovery is indeed within the power of intellectuals. Stopping it may not be, although making it explicit may go farther towards stopping a bad plan than is generally appreciated.

For purposes of conceptualization and for easy reference, the plan will be called the "State of Permanent Receivership." A bolder approach would apply the same conceptualization to all advanced industrial countries. But for reasons of space as well as incapacity, the focus will be almost entirely on the United States.

The State of Permanent Receivership is a logical, if not necessarily natural, outgrowth of the politics of offsetting, providing, and contracting by government in the economy. And if not logical in terms of historical development, it is certainly logical to the extent that it was constructed and rationalized by Keynesian economists even as they were talking of aggregate demand, national growth, full employment, etc.

Receivership is a means of maintaining social order during a crisis involving the bankruptcy of a business. When a business is on the verge of dissolution, the public takes an interest in it for the obvious reason that the various creditors might fight over the remaining assets. A court is given power to appoint a receiver, to administer the properties of the bankrupt. A receiver may be appointed to administer any properties that are subject to suit. Receivership is apparently an indispensable means of providing for an orderly process of disposing of assets.

Permanent Receivership involves maintaining the assets and never disposing of the organization at all, regardless of the inequities or costs of its maintenance.

If we expand a bit further on the notion of bankruptcy to include all large organizations—not only profit-making ones—and if we expand the concept to include potential as well as actual bankruptcy, we can then begin to appreciate modern government and its primary policy outputs as a State of Permanent Receivership. It is a state whose government maintains a steadfast position that any institution large enough to be a significant factor in the community shall have its stability underwritten.

The stress here is on organizational stability, not upon individual or elite stability, although these things are not always easy to separate in practice. It is an answer to "permanent crisis." Conceptually and in practice, the State of Permanent Receivership is comfortable to large groupings of any sort. It is also comfortable to large state bureaucracies, because in concept and in practice it is deeply conservative. It respects all skills and all existing social contrivances, and above all, it respects established subject-matter lines of doing government business, that is, the lines of jurisdiction that are the almost total preoccupation of bureaucracies. And, as we shall see, the State of Permanent Receivership is also extremely comfortable with all of the economic technology that we have developed in the past 200 years.

Underwriting may be the key to what national planning and positive government are coming to mean today in the State of Permanent Receivership. In such
a state there is very little socialization of production or distribution. There is
not even an overwhelming need for the socialization of delivery of essential
services. The State of Permanent Receivership works through the *socialization
of risk.*

The conduct of government in such a state may leave most of private property in individual hands and most of corporate activity in private hands. France
could always be a nation of shopkeepers. What is planned in the State of Permanent Receivership is not private activity as such but the environment of that
activity. Older approaches emphasize subsidies to keep things going, bounties
to encourage activities that did not exist, regulations to head off bad conduct,
and outright direct provision where none of the other techniques was available
or effective. These categories continue to contain significant examples of government policy. But in the State of Permanent Receivership they are used in very
special ways, and they are becoming less important with the rise of underwriting
and the socialization of risk.

The Lockheed case will serve as a significant albeit small entrée into the
analysis. Lockheed, on the brink of real bankruptcy, was neither allowed to
dissolve nor saved by a direct subsidy, two policies characteristic of the old days.
The government took positive steps, but it spent no money at all. It simply
guaranteed a $250 million loan Lockheed was seeking. With that guaranteed—
which was no more than a signature of a higher bureaucrat on a slip of paper—
Lockheed could then get private bank money at decent interest rates and remain
in operation for at least a while longer.

There are of course many antecedents, in the sense that traditional policies
could be and still can be used in a framework of Permanent Receivership. The
National Recovery Administration was a system of Permanent Receivership
whereby the leading voices in each sector of the economy would name their
own conditions for survival. In a more constitutional manner, the Federal
Trade Commission (FTC) works almost completely in the spirit of Permanent
Receivership. Organizational conservatism was the original approach of the FTC,
and amendments of the late 1930s were even more explicitly in the direction of
establishment, competitive policy. Elaborate studies of the history of the FTC
by Professor Alan Stone of Rutgers University confirm beyond any doubt this
"pattern or practice." According to Stone actions brought by the FTC have
overwhelmingly been against smaller firms seeking a larger share of their markets
by use of vigorous competitive methods. These have been called "unfair competition" only by those who are already in established market positions and do
not care to advance in those positions. The posture of the FTC is matched
and more by the Antitrust Division and by the FCC. As one former member of
the FCC put it, "Without government protection, the market would very
quickly provide a good deal of competition with AT&T. . . ." He goes on to

suggest that there could still be a great deal of competition in the communications industry if the FCC would loosen up "the monopolistic protection given to AT&T."

These and many other traditional policies of positive government anticipate the State of Permanent Receivership. In some ways we could say that these policies help produce the "offsetting" function. However, it provides this function in a very biased and special way, and it is that manner of use rather than the function itself that needs the careful analysis.

During the period of Keynesian dominance of policy making in Washington, an almost entirely new category of public policies was added to the federal government's kitbag for tinkering with the economy. These are of course the fiscal and monetary policies. (Here they are referred to by the single term fiscal policies.) Now, fiscal policy is not in and of itself a policy of Permanent Receivership. As with the more traditional types of government policies, it all depends on how fiscal policies are used and whether they are used systematically for organizational conservatism.

Fiscal policy in Solo's "offsetting" was concerned largely with the creation of structures around the economy—floors, ceilings, frameworks, forward pricing, etc.—within which economic activity would operate. During the formative period these structures were thought to work more or less automatically to "counterpunch" or would work through some fairly stable rules of administration, such as discount rates, tax rates, or budget balances. Rates or structures in an orthodox offsetting plan could even be set by Congress, either as permanent and unchanging rates or as rules to govern the activities of central bankers and other agents, public and private. Whether this is called "full employment planning" or "the stabilizing budget policy" or "offset planning," it could be supported in some form or another by such diverse personalities as Paul Samuelson and Milton Friedman.

But that changed during the 1950s and 1960s largely with the emergence of *discretionary* fiscal power. With increasing frequency following the election of John F. Kennedy, Congress began delegating to the President and to other top members of the Executive Branch the power to use fiscal policy in a specific case and not necessarily in relation to a framework or to a longer range trend at the aggregate or macro level. It is now legally and technically possible for the President to manipulate the entire economy in order to produce a single loan guarantee—for a new town, for a real estate developer, for a city doing redevelopment, or for a conglomerate in trouble. Along with the power to guarantee loans there is also the power to arrange mortgage insurance, mortgage refinancing, and otherwise to underwrite the risk of a long-range private venture. And the interesting thing is, these government policies do not cost the government anything except the maintenance of the administrative agency that handles the paperwork. Yet, their effect is obviously vast upon the aggregate economy, and beyond that, the policies are capable of infinite subdivision and dispensation

according to whatever standard of privilege or justice the President may wish
to develop. And it would be impossible to overemphasize the vastness of the
effect. The value of all the economic decisions made on the basis of this kind
of underwriting must be far in excess of all of the direct federal expenditures
on domestic, social, and socioeconomic policies.

Planning in the State of Permanent Receivership has also available to it
the discretionary use of welfare money. Once this was very much a part of the
structural and highly defined system of government transfer payments to the
dependent. As a welfare technique it was designed to meet specifically defined
situations, and as a fiscal technique its aim was the support of aggregate demand.
But during the 1960s the "categoric welfare" system was provided with an
extremely important overlay of government activities that are called welfare
but are very much more a part of the system of Permanent Receivership. Specific cases in point are the War on Poverty and general Revenue Sharing. These
throw out the definitions and leave entirely at the discretion of executive agents
and local governments the allocation of federal revenues. This way there can
truly be a system for "regulating the poor." In a study done by the American
League of Cities completed in the spring of 1973, the reports on allocations
under the Revenue Sharing Act were so somber that the League never published
its tabulation because they were "convinced that by releasing the figures they
might be misunderstood." What their figures show is that there was definitely
a drainage of federal monies away from dependent persons and toward the
support of local institutions. The biggest gainer in all of this was the law enforcement agencies. Another big gainer was the interest rates on local bonds. This
means that capital improvements got a new lease on life. However, these were
not capital improvements in the social welfare area of public housing and community facilities. During this same period the federal government became far
and away the largest holder of urban property, most of which was abandoned
and for the moment nonfunctional.

Wage control is another very interesting aspect of Permanent Receivership,
although the technique involved here is more like the regulatory approach of
the old NRA. Study of wage-price control shows a definite connection between
permanent receivership and mercantilism, although the State of Permanent
Receivership has the advantage of many techniques that were not available to
the old monarchs. Under wage and price control the plan was to declare all
wage and price increases illegal and then grant individual exceptions as a matter
of individual privilege. (This is called "on the merits.") This is exactly the way
mercantilism worked, by declaring a whole area of endeavor illegal and then
granting licenses to certain favored persons to engage in the activity. The
result of wage control under the 1970 Wage-Price Control apparatus has to be
seen at two levels. (We are dealing here only with Phase II, the regulatory phase.)
The first level is the macro level, and generally it has been concluded that the
aggregate effect of wage control was noninflationary. But then there is also

the micro level. From the very beginning of Phase II the Pay Board was permitted to consider individual wage decisions "on the merits" as well as in terms of the general guidelines. As a consequence, during the first full year of Phase II, ending at the time of the "labor walk-out," the Board disposed of 975 cases involving firms employing 1,000 or more workers. Many of these requests were almost automatic in that they came very near the five to seven percent range. And since many other actions and requests fell below the five percent mark, the aggregate inflationary effect was probably kept within the seven percent ceiling. However, note the exceptions. They were all granted in response to requests made by established labor unions. The Gulf and East Coast Longshoremen got increases ranging from 9.8 to 12 percent. The West Coast Longshoremen asked for 20 percent and got 14 percent. The Board turned down the Aerospace Workers' request for 12 percent, but awarded them 8 percent. United Transportation Union got a 10 percent increase, while the Organized Coalworkers got 11 percent. Exact figures were not available on the disposition of requests made by the Building Trades Union, but the average increases handed out by the Wage Board's Committee on Construction Industry Stabilization were so large that even one of the top United States labor leaders, I.W. Abel of the Steelworkers, was publicly critical.

In the fields of defense and space industry, Solo may be correct that the United States government is the progenitor. But most of the production nevertheless works on a system of contracts, disposition of which are highly, though not completely, discretionary. And a review of the data on the defense and space industries to be found in various studies, such as those of Adam Yarmolinsky, and Richard Barnet, as well as such semiofficial sources as *Congressional Quarterly*, will show well enough the extent to which this area of policy can be handled on a receivership basis. And so much as to provide injury to insult, there is in the international field an Overseas Private Investment Corporation (OPIC) that has for years been insuring large, multinational corporations against risks abroad. (OPIC was established in 1969 but took over many of the same functions from AID.) The purpose was to provide incentives to investment in developing nations. But the administration of it ended up by providing 80 percent of the $3.4 billion in insurance guarantees to large multinational corporations.

Alternatives: Revolution or Neo-Laissez-Faire

Are there alternatives to such a system of government, such a method of planning?

Most readers will find the arrangement rather clever, not very newsworthy, and in need of no particular answer. If there were time and space, I think it could be shown that this is the worst possible position to take, because discretionary government power, especially on the scale of discretionary fiscal policy, has produced many of the features of politics in advanced industrial societies that we are beginning to call "permanent crisis." In a companion work I shall be arguing that the vast increase in discretionary fiscal power in the Presidency has contributed directly to that crisis of executive power popularly known as Watergate.

In any case, others will respond to the problem presented here in a typical American fashion by suggesting that we kill this form of planning by taking the plan out of it. That is, we can kill privilege by universalizing access to it. Unfortunately, however, that is about what we have now. Each area of privilege is rather well known among those who have a special interest in each particular area of governmental activity. The result is a very unequal distribution, and it always will be.

Another answer that would be typical of "occidental rationality" would be to leave the system intact but to take it over with a social democratic elite group, which will then break the pattern without breaking the system by turning over the services used to other clientele groups. But we already know that will not work because of the bureaucracy problem. It also will not work because all of the social democratic parties of the West have been deradicalized by their existing access to the privilege system. The trade union basis of most social democratic parties has already been overwhelmingly corrupted by their access to the present governmental elite, even when these unions are not themselves a part of the elite, as in France today.

Thus, there seem to be only two violent breaks away from the State of Permanent Receivership. One is along orthodox Marxist lines, but only if the revolution deeply transforms the bureaucracy. And it is probable that this will not happen in highly developed countries. Nevertheless, it is one possibility.

The other possibility of a violent break away from Permanent Receivership is *neo-laissez-faire*. There is a limit to how much a government can do to influence the economy, even when there is no constitutional limit to the amount of power, policy, and appropriations the government can summon up to each task. On the other hand, there is probably no limit to the amount of abnegation of power a government can engage in. And just as we could easily radicalize the communications market by removing the regulations of the Federal Communications Commission, so we could perhaps radicalize a number of other markets. And this suggests that the abolition of a variety of government programs may be more radical even than a Marxist approach, if one looks, with Dahl, "after the revolution."

A direct deflationary approach to government would amount to nothing but laissez-faire and could be supported only by return to all of the assumptions made by nineteenth-century liberals and thoroughly rejected by twentieth-century liberals and others. But neo-laissez-faire may be another matter. Coupling a gigantic deflation of government in general with an expansion of certain aspects of government in particular, we may provide the basis for a break with the present State of Permanent Receivership, including the gigantic and conservative bureaucratic apparatus.

We could do this in three moves, preferably taken simultaneously. The first, of course, is to abolish as many large discretionary economic programs as possible. This would include the so-called porkbarrel and subsidy programs, but would also include virtually all of the discretionary fiscal apparatus identified herein.

The second feature would be to tighten up the original "offsetting" policies, that is, the framework within which modern economic activity takes place. Most of this activity was from the very beginning nondiscretionary, and required an administrative apparatus far smaller than what we have today in the politico-economic field. Much is truly self-executing. There was once upon a time something quite truthful in the notion of the "built-in stabilizers."

The third move is an enormous expansion of federal police power. That is, a very elaborate addition of regulatory laws concerned with bad conduct in the economy. This is truly the *neo* part of neo-laissez-faire. There is no reason on earth why planners and social democratic parties cannot identify those features of corporate activity that should be declared illegal and against public policy. And a definition of bad conduct is not to be considered simply a statement like "unfair competition," the merits of which are to be left in each case to the administrator. If there is in fact bad conduct in the economy, planners, independent social scientists, and government bureaucrats ought to be able to identify rather precisely what it is, or the conduct should not be proscribed.

To this last proposal many would answer that modern economies are too complicated for any precision in the definitions of laws. But if that is the case, then planning itself is impossible, and everything that is said against precision in regulatory laws applies equally if not doubly to the more complex and interdependent statements that make up a planning document. What these people are really saying is that legislators and other politicians are incapable of stamping out bad conduct and should rather delegate all of the power to affect conduct to a series of bureaucratically organized experts. That is not a plan. That is government by persons who call themselves planners. And it will always be just as conservative as it would be were it monarchs or generalissimos asking for broad delegation of power on the basis of their superior ability to decide what is bad and good conduct.

If, for example, we have come to the conclusion that there is no way to escape some kind of price system in production planning, then why not recognize the existence of a price system, leave it to do its work, and then attempt in every way possible to stamp out through regulatory devices those activities that either hamper the working of the price system or bias it in favor of those who are already too well established in the market and can influence the price system to their own benefit. We already do this exceptionally well with laws concerning counterfeiting, credit, contracts, etc. There is no reason why we cannot change these or expand on them to serve new and more democratic definitions of the workings of the price system. Those who are skeptical and dubious ought to spend a few minutes studying nineteenth-century legislation in the American states. Between 1820 and 1850, there was very little understanding of banking, insurance, corporations, etc. There was no modern economic theory. "Capitalism" was not even coined as a concept until the end of this period. Consequently, nineteenth-century industrial society must have appeared to the nineteenth-century eyes as far more complicated and in flux than our society appears to us. Yet the states, with their amateur and corrupt legislators, passed law upon law that created the economic system as we know it today. There is no reason why we cannot do for our own system the same thing, and do it in terms of more democratically inclined values.

On the basis of the earlier critique, especially if the description of how we plan is an accurate one, the compelling question should be: Why not take the next logical step, to socialism? Indeed, one could properly argue that the United States is already socialized, only badly, with socialism for the rich and capitalism for the poor.

The answer is that if there were in the United States the consensus and the political party capable of that transformation, there would also be sufficient power to deal with capitalism in the neo-laissez-faire manner proposed above. And the advantage would be that civil liberties would not have to be sacrificed during, or after, the transformation to a system of effective "command planning." Anyone who imagines that an industrial economy as gigantic and as interdependent as that of the United States could be transformed without the sacrifice of civil liberties is displaying far greater naivete than any displayed in a neo-laissez-faire approach.

The neo-laissez-faire route is a statist, but a "liberal" statist, solution, and as such it is caught on a profound contradiction: Stress on civil liberties is likely to work to the benefit of those who already have wealth and power. We are all too familiar with the equal access to the chicken yard provided by liberal laws to the elephants and the chickens, or the equal justice meted out by the liberal state to the rich man and the poor man who takes shelter under the bridge at night. This is a true contradiction, not merely in the mind of the analyst.

The socialist or "command planning" solution provides a way out of the liberal contradiction—but only by encountering another. Central planning must sacrifice civil liberties—by imposing real interest on false consciousness— or it must attempt to maintain a semblance of civil liberties through "participation." But participation, if it is to be effective, must subvert central planning.

Choice in the political system may never be a matter of selection among alternative solutions but only a choice among contradictions: Which contradiction are we best able to abide?

5

The Theory of the Capitalist State and the Problem of Policy Formation
Claus Offe

State interventionism is the key concept that has been as the center of contributions to the theory of the state, and it has been used as such by both liberal and Marxist authors. The fact, in other words, that the state is an *interventionist* one in advanced capitalist societies, has been and is undisputed. The only controversy that one could think of in this respect is not as to whether the state is *interventionist* or not, but as to whether it has always been so in the history of capitalist society, that is, whether state interventionism is a relatively new fact (say, fully emerging only after World War II) or something that, as a regular case, can be traced back to the earliest stages of capitalist society. The latter is usually admitted. It is argued, however, that the quantity and scope of state interventionist strategies has increased to an extent that makes it justifiable to speak of a new phase of capitalist development in recent decades.

In order to put this "quantitative increase leads to new quality" argument on more stable grounds, we want to develop a model that can be applied in the historical study of the functions of the capitalist state, and of capitalist societies in general, and that tries to avoid the related though opposite mistakes of describing change of state functions as either nonexistent or irrelevant (the orthodox Marxist version) or as total and pervasive (the postindustrial, social democratic version). By concentrating on the latter, that is, the theoretical purpose of the model (no attempt at a historical test of the model is undertaken here), we explore a way in which both continuity and change of the functions of the capitalist state, as well as the contradictions of its mode of operation, can be understood.

The Concept of the Capitalist State

Before we speak of a *capitalist* state, or the state in capitalist societies, we should specify which characteristics we postulate for such a state. This is not done in institutional terms (that is, for example, by reference to parliament, bureaucracy, guaranteed property rights, etc.) although those elements may be present in all or most capitalist states that we find in history. The criterion of definition will rather be taken from the relationship between the state and the accumulation process. Central to our definition are therefore not structural attributes to a sector of society (the state), but the way it is functionally related to and dependent upon the accumulation process. The elements of the definition are four:

125

1. The state has no authority *to order production* or *to control* it. Production/accumulation takes place in *enterprises* that are said to be *free* in the sense of *"exempt from state control."* The basic prerogative of *free enterprises* is a negative one: the right not to produce unless production is at the same time accumulative, that is, not only production of useful things but simultaneously production of surplus value, or profit. The first and most important element in the definition of the capitalist state is thus: The state cannot *initiate* production within private enterprises that is thought to be *not* accumulative by the private accumulating unit, and it cannot, conversely, *stop* production that *is* considered accumulative (profitable) by the accumulating unit. The state is no capitalist itself, and accumulation takes place only in private accumulating units. State and accumulation *are* divorced, so that production and accumulation can*not* be divorced.

2. However, the state does not only have the authority, but the *mandate* to create and sustain *conditions* of accumulation. There are different levels of specificity in which the function of creating and maintaining conditions of accumulation can be performed, for example, individual accumulating units, categories of accumulating units (industries, regions), and capital as a whole. There are also different categories of *threats* that cause *problems* of accumulation, that is, threats coming from other accumulating units (interfirm, interindustry, and international competiton) and threats coming from noncapitalists, that is, the working class, but also from actors engaging in *deviant, criminal,* or other kinds of behavior that are considered incompatible with the orderly pursuit of surplus-value production. Having mentioned these various sources and levels of potential threat, we can also say that the function to "create and maintain" conditions of accumulation is equivalent to establishing control over these destructive possibilities and events.

3. The third element of the definition of a capitalist state is this: Its power relationships, its very decision-making power *depends* (like every other social relationship in capitalist society) upon the presence and continuity of the accumulation process. In the absence of accumulation, everything, and especially the power of the state, tends to desintegrate. If we think of the budgetary obligations of the state in advanced capitalist societies, its extensive reliance on resources created in the accumulation process and derived through taxation from wages and profits, this becomes immediately clear. Thus, every interest the state (or the personnel of the state apparatus, its various branches and agencies) may have in their own stability and development can only be pursued if it is in accordance with the imperative of maintaining accumulation; this fundamental dependency upon accumulation functions as a selective principle upon state policies. The criterion of the stability of accumulation is thus incorporated in the pursuit of interests and policies that, considered by themselves, may have little or nothing to do with accumulation. Accumulation, in other words, acts as the most powerful constraint criterion, but not necessarily as the determinant of content, of the policy-making process.

We can call these three elements of the concept of the capitalist state the principles of *"exclusion, maintenance* and *dependency,"* respectively. *Exclusion* means, as we have pointed out, that the state is not a capitalist itself, that is, something that has its existence outside the accumulation process. *Maintenance* implies that this process cannot perpetuate itself in the absence of this external being, that there are threats and possible disturbances to the process of accumulation that require some state-organized protection of the process. And *dependency* means that this protective device itself would be threatened if it engaged in policies inconsistent with its protective functions. The question now becomes: How is such a highly precarious combination of conditions at all possible? How is it possible that, at the same time, the state *gains* power, *applies* this power in a way conducive to and maintaining the conditions of accumulation, *without* thereby *subverting* its own existence as a capitalist state by adopting policies that would transcend the reciprocity relationship between state and accumumation? The above definition spells out under what conditions we speak of the state as a capitalist state; now we talk about what is responsible for the coincidence and harmonious coexistence of these conditions (or, conversely, the absence of what would destabilize this harmonious coexistence).

The answer to this question, which cannot be explored in detail here, is *legitimation.* Legitimation, or the need for legitimacy, adds an important *fourth* element to the concept of the capitalist state. The idea is that only if (and only as long as) the capitalist state manages, through a variety of institutional mechanisms, to convey the image of an organization of power that pursues common and general interests of society as a whole, allows equal access to power and is responsive to justified demands, the state can function in its specific relationship to accumulation. This is equivalent to saying that the state can only *function as* a capitalist state by appealing to symbols and sources of support that *conceal* its nature as a capitalist state; the *existence* of a capitalist state presupposes the systematic *denial* of its nature as a *capitalist* state. (This, incidentally, comes fairly close to a reformulation of the Marxian concept of ideology.)

Allocation Versus Production

We now want to leave the purely conceptual level of discussion and try to deal with some long-term trends of developments that can be generalized from the history of capitalist societies. In specific, we are interested in the causes and consequences of the change in the functions of the state that have been observed by many authors, Marxists and liberals. *State interventionism* is the label usually applied to describe the state in advanced capitalist societies, whereas, by contrast, nineteenth-century capitalism is described as *liberal capitalism* in which the role of the state was of minor and almost

negligible importance. Social historians, however, emphasize that the image
of a purely market-regulated capitalist economy is highly "ideal-typical" and
has never and in no place been an accurate description of historical fact. An
adequate account of real changes and developments (rather than of deviations
from an idealized model that never existed in reality) would therefore have
to address itself to the question of qualitative rather than quantitative changes.
The argument of historical changes of the capitalist state would have to be
based on the *extent* to which the state created and maintained the conditions
of accumulation, but on a concrete description of what these *conditions* themselves were, the maintenance of which required state intervention, and in which
ways their creation and maintenance was undertaken by the state. Two modes
of state intervention are therefore discussed in the following analysis (allocation and production); they are linked to a changing pattern of *threats,* or structural problems, that emerge out of the accumulation process and to which these
modes of state activity can be seen as responses.

Allocation is a mode of activity of the capitalist state that creates and maintains the conditions of accumulation in a purely authoritative way. Resources
and powers that intrinsically *belong* to the state and are at the disposal of the
state are allocated. Certain industries received protective tariffs. Money and
money lending are determined by certain rules issued by the state. The repressive apparatus (military, police, courts) is employed according to certain legal
rules and decisions. Roads and bridges are built, land is given to railway lines,
and attendance in schools is made compulsory for certain age groups. What
do these examples of state activity have in common? All of them can be said
to be *interventionist,* in so far as they impose a certain order created by the state
on an area of social and economic activity. But this does not distinguish them
from activities like manpower training, antiinflationary or R&D policies. What
distinguishes the former from the latter is the *method* by which state activity
is designed. The method in the former case is authority—whether the authority
is based on constitution, on a system of legal norms, or on consideration of
political majorities and political affiliations. From the point of view of the
particular actor in such a state activity, there is no criterion for the goodness
of such activity other than his own interests, the interests of his respective
constituency and the legal norms that support or prohibit the pursuit of such
norms and interests. A "good" decision, from the point of view of the decision maker, is a decision that coincides with his legal or political power. There
is no alternative or additional criterion for decision making. What characterizes
allocative policies, then, is that politics and policies are not differentiated:
Policies are congruent with politics. This is due to the fact that, in all of the
above mentioned decisions, the state creates and maintains the conditions of
accumulation by measures that require simply the allocation of resources (land,
taxes, repressive force) which are already under the control of the state. In a
way they can be described as "state property," and the question of political

decision making that goes on internal to the state apparatus is to whom or to what purpose these already available resources should be allocated. This question can be resolved by the method of power struggle over the resources of the state, that is, through politics.

The distinctive features of allocative mode of state action is thus: (1) economic conditions under which a suitable environment for accumulation can be created and maintained merely by authoritative allocation of resources and "things" that are already "state property"; (2) the elements of this environment do *not* have to be produced themselves, but merely have to be *allocated*; and (3) political power, or power in and over the state apparatus and its parts is the sole criterion and determinant of allocation, that is, there is no method of policy making other than politics needed. The importance of these features of allocative decision making will become better understood after we have contrasted allocative mode of state action to the other type, *productive* state action. It should be noted at this point, however, that the notion of a allocative method of state action is by no means restricted to the earliest stages of development of the capitalist state. For instance, Keynesian economic policies belong to this category, too. The creation of autonomous demand as measure to stimulate economic growth essentially makes use of a state-owned resource, namely, the power of government to vary the level of taxation and expenditures; at what phase of the business cycle, to what extent, and in what combination these powers of government are utilized is a decision that emerges from political conflict and consensus, and one that does not require additional criteria.

The second major type of state activity is *productive* as opposed to allocative. The *productive* mode of activity of the capitalist state becomes preeminent under—and corresponds to—certain situations of the accumulation process. This situation is made up of the following elements:

1. In order to keep the accumulation process alive (either on a firm, industry, regional, or national level), there is more and something *different* required than the allocation of resources and things that the state has already under its control. In order to create and maintain the conditions of accumulation, the allocative means of state action (allocating state owned resources, taxation, state demand, tariffs, repression, subsidies etc.) is insufficient. In addition to the state-organized *framework* of production/accumulation, some physical input into production is required in order to maintain accumulation.

2. Of course, physical input is always needed—either in the form of human labor power or raw materials or fixed investment for production/accumulation. Under normal circumstances, those inputs are provided by markets on which they appear as commodities: Labor, or variable capital, is to be found on the labor market, and raw materials and machinery, or constant capital, is to be found on the market of investment goods, produced for this market by capitalists who specialize in investment goods industries. In the particular situation that we are describing, and to which the *productive* mode of state

activity is to be seen in correspondence, the quantitatively and qualitatively sufficient supply of variable and constant capital fails to appear on the market. Why? Because for both the supply of variable and constant capital that is required, an investment would have to be made that is not considered profitable from the point of view of any accumulating units. Why is it not considered profitable to make such investment? Because the accumulating units that could produce such supply have reason to believe that for the potential buyers of their supply the supply would be too costly to buy at a price that is profitable for the supplier. The resulting situation would be the *failure* of some capitalists to *produce input commodities* on which the accumulation of other capitalists depend.

3. This failure can be due to either of three facts: Either the input commodities are so *costly* that the accumulating units who need them for the purpose of their own accumulation cannot afford to buy them; or there are *risks and uncertainities* involved in the buying of such input commodities, and because the individual accumulating unit cannot be reasonably sure that the use of such input commodities will prove to be profitable for itself, it refrains from buying them; or the technical nature of the input commodities involves *externalities,* that is, it prohibits the buyer of the input commodity from making exclusive use of the usefulness (use-value) of the input good. All of these possibilities, or any combination thereof, would be sufficient to explain why there is an actual lack of demand for, and hence absence of incentive for accumulating units to supply, such input commodities.

4. So far, however, we have not given any indication as to why this theoretically imaginable situation of insufficient supply of input commodities should be a likely case in the real world. Why should it not be possible either to avoid this unfortunate situation altogether or to correct it through the automatic forces of the marketplace once it occurs. In order words, why should the accumulating units permanently depend upon input commodities that permanently tend to be too costly for them, too costly either in relation to their *absolute financial capacities,* to their ability to *absorb risks and uncertainties,* or *relative to the internalized portion* of total benefits derived from the input commodities? In order to fill this apparent gap in the course of our argument, we remind ourselves of the competitive nature of capitalist accumulation. That is to say, accumulation can only take place if and to the extent that individual accumulating units find ways to protect themselves against the *constant competitive pressure* coming from other accumulating units. Only those who are sufficiently immune against the competitive pressure of the market (more specifically: the competitive pressure exercised on them by other accumulating units on goods markets, labor markets, and capital markets) have a chance to continue their production/accumulation. If accumulation in an individual enterprise is going to continue at any given point in time, there must be certain *defensive mechanisms* available to the enterprise that allow it to protect itself.

Examples of such protective mechanisms, which are employed in order to minimize the threat of others to accumulation, are productivity increases through introduction of labor-saving technology, price competition, advertising, limitation of market access, advertisement, product differentiation, market research, cartelization. A history of capitalist industrialization could be written as a process in which those—and many other—defensive mechanisms are developed by individual capital units. The never-ending and self-propelling process in which new defensive mechanisms are evolving is due to the fact that a defensive mechanism, say advertising, becomes a dull and ineffective weapon as soon as it is diffused and universalized. The relative competitive advantage and the relative security of the "creative entrepreneur" (as Joseph Schumpeter described the process in 1910) tends to destroy itself in the process of universalization of a defensive measure, and the process starts anew.

In this sequence: competitive pressure—defensive mechanism—universalization—competitive pressure, two levels must be distinguished. On one of these logical levels, the dimension of countercompetitive, or defensive, mechanisms remains the *same* throughout the spiral. Take process innovation, product innovation, or the opening up of new markets as examples of such dimensions: The events change, but the *strategic dimensions* by which the accumulating units keep themselves in the market remain identical over time. Innovation takes place *within* dimensions, (the dimension being, for example, the opening up of new markets, and the successive innovations being that one country after the other is made accessible to the market of a firm). The other level is, logically speaking, a "meta-level." Here, the innovation does *not* take place as an innovation *within* a dimension of competition and countercompetitive strategies, but as an innovation *of* the strategies by which accumulating units gain a relatively superior position vis-à-vis other accumulating units. For example, assume that in a given industry competitive relations and strategies between individual firms take place in the framework of price competition, process innovation and product differentiation. Each advance of one of the competitors in one of these three dimensions means both a relative protection of accumulation of the one and a new competitive pressure on all others. So far, only the first level of competitive relations is concerned. But now, one of the firms in the industry does not invent a new manufacturing process, but a new *dimension* of competition; for instance, it opens a branch plant in a low-wage country, gets the government of its region to build a transportation system that is suited to its needs, engages in industry espionage, bribes a union leader or finds some other way to getting ahead of the others. In other words, it changes the rules of the game by incorporating new means, or new dimensions, of competition. Using the distinction between the two levels—innovation *within* established dimensions and innovation *of* these dimensions—we can hypothesize that whenever the potential of one dimension is exhausted, accumulation will be continued by opening up new dimensions of competition and defensive mechanisms.

If we think of the dynamics of competitive accumulation that is to say, of the pattern of development of capitalist industrialization in terms of these defensive strategies in the course of which each accumulating unit protects itself from threats coming from others (thereby in turn posing threats to others), we can foresee a point in this development at which the ability of accumulating units to create new protective mechanisms by and for themselves becomes exhausted. At what point in time, to what extent, and in what particular industries this happens is an empirical question. Analytically, at this point accumulation can only go on if productivity gains and other advantages by which an individual accumulating unit protects itself from the competitive pressure of others can be derived from sources other than the accumulation process itself. In other words, at this point some or all accumulating units become, for the sake of their continued accumulation, dependent upon "help" in their strategy of competition; they become dependent upon means that the accumulation process itself cannot supply. At this point, *productive* state activities, in addition to the allocative ones, emerge, since the state is the only organization in capitalist society that could provide such *inputs* that are required in order to sustain accumulation and production.

In state productive activity the state fulfills its function as a capitalist state (to create and maintain the conditions of accumulation) not only on a broader scope, but in a *new way*. By such activity the state responds to situations in which labor and/or capital fail to operate in the accumulation process by producing material conditions that allow the continuation of accumulation. By its material production the state creates conditions that are essential for the accumulating units but that cannot be achieved by their own activity. Such productive state activity is initiated by the actual or anticipated, sectoral or general absence of accumulation (or disturbances in the accumulation process). The rationale is to restore accumulation or to avoid or eliminate perceived threats to accumulation.

We now want to concentrate on the following question: What are the decision rules by which the state operates in such a situation? As we have seen before, the decision rules for allocative state activities can be said to be directly derived from politics. Here the problem is relatively simple, because the conditions of accumulation can be created and maintained by state-owned resources (like police power, law making capacity, tax money, etc.). Seen from the point of view of the state (or one of its agencies or branches) as an actor, the decision problem is a minor one because directives as to what use is to be made of these state-owned resources can be directly derived from manifest interests and power relationships that become apparent in the process of politics and political conflict. This is different in a situation where the state does not respond to demands, but, as it were, to *negative events,* namely, the absence or disturbance of an accumulation process. It is always easier to respond to positive demands: They can either be rejected or accepted. In a situation where one wants to *avoid* something, that is, where one *reacts to a manifest or anticipated danger,* there is no clear-cut course of action that could either be followed or rejected. Even though it is unlikely that the state as an actor is the only one who wants to avoid a certain condition, the state cannot afford to rely on the directions of action recommended or demanded by the most powerful (or politically dominant) groups in society; for to satisfy the interests of one group is one thing, and to restore the accumulation process as a whole is another thing, and it is by no means certain that the two will coincide. Consequently, the state has to devise decision rules of its own in a situation where the primary concern is to avoid disturbances of the overall accumulation process. The rules and laws that govern *politics* are not sufficient to solve this problem. An additional set of decision rules is required that determines *policies.*

Schema

A general definition of the activities of the capitalist state is the creation and maintenance of the conditions of production/accumulation.

Types of activity

1. Allocative

    a)   Allocation of state-owned resources
    b)   In response to demands and laws ("politics")
    c)   Demands are positive and specific in regard to time, space, group, type, and amount of state resources
    d)   Decision reached by politics

2. Productive

    a)   Production of inputs of accumulation (organized production process required) in response to perceived threats to accumulation
    b)   There are no demands, or conflicting or incompletely articulated demands, that cannot be expected to eliminate threats to overall accumulation
    c)   Decision reached by policies based on state-generated decision rules.

State activity takes on the form of policy making when the process of competitive accumulation becomes too fragile to regenerate itself within the framework of allocative state activities and when the state is required to produce (rather than merely decide upon) the conditions of continued accumulation. The basis for productive state activities in the form of policies (i.e., separated from the process of politics) is a twofold weakness of competitive accumulation itself: first, the economic weakness of being unable to produce the necessary inputs of accumulation through accumulation itself; and, second, the weakness that the ruling class, being made up of essentially *competitive* accumulating units, is unable to develop a class consciousness containing consented and workable directives as to how the state should operate. This twofold deficiency (both sides of which are based on competition) is attempted to overcome by (a) the development of productive state activity, supplementing the material input that is needed for accumulation, and (b) state activity in the form of policies (or decision rules about state activity), substituting for the lack of class consensus within the ruling class.

The state produces education, skills, technological change, control over raw materials, health, transportation, housing, a structure of cities, physical environment, energy, and communication services. The emphasis on the productive character of these state activities is because all of them differ sharply from the allocative ones since what is needed in a given situation is not already at the disposal of the state but must be *produced* by the state in the first place. The state-owned resources (like money and legal and repressive powers) are, so to speak, merely the raw materials out of which certain outputs have to be manufactured according to decision rules (or "production rules") that the state cannot take from its environment but has to generate for itself. The institutionalized production rules of public policy, their determinants and dynamics, are the key problems in the study of policy formation.

Production Rules of Public Policy—Form Versus Content

In order to explore the problem of policy formation in the capitalist state more fully, a distinction of form and content might be useful. Most studies of public policy in the area of "productive" state policies have been dealing with the content aspects of such policies. These *content* aspects can be divided into three complexes of questions that lead to (1) the analysis of processes in the environment of the political system that lead to the recognition of certain "problems" as a matter of public policy and hence to the expansion of the agenda of the political system, (2) the analysis of the interests that determine the process of policy formation, and (3) the material outcomes and the distribution of tangible benefits that result from policies and their implementation.

In contrast to this set of questions, we postulate here that public policy cannot be understood fully by these content-related questions, but that, in addition, the formal procedures, or the institutionalized method processing problematic states of affairs of the environment, are equally important determinants of state activity. The usual conceptualization of state activity visualizes the state as a "problem solver": Problems are recognized, and more or less adequate solutions are produced. This image is not wrong, but one-sided and incomplete. For what the state does if it works on a problem is a *dual* process: It organizes certain activities and measures directed toward the *environment* and it adopts for *itself* a certain organizational procedure from which the production and implementation of policies emerges. Every time a state deals with a problem in its environment, it deals with a problem of itself, that is, its internal mode of operation. It seems obvious that both processes of problem solving are interconnected in a circular way: Social and economic problems, as items on the state agenda, may trigger off changes in the formal strategies according to which the state operates, and conversely these formal strategies may substantially determine both the ability of the state to perceive problems and the nature of the ensuing policies.

It is important to note that the relationship between the two types of strategic rules is strictly a *symmetrical* one. That is to say, the formal rules that give structure and continuity to the operation of the state apparatus are not merely instrumental procedures designed to carry out or implement political goals or to solve social problems. They rather do determine themselves, in a hidden and unexplicit way, what potential goals are and what problems have the chance to come up on the agenda of the political system. Thus, it is not only true that the emergence of a social problem puts into motion the procedural dynamics of policy formation, program design, and implementation, but also, conversely, the institutionalized formal mode of operation of political institutions determines what potential issues are, how they are defined, what solutions are proposed, and so on.

After having discussed now (1) the general characteristics (or functional requirements) of a capitalist state, (2) the distinction between "allocative" and "productive" activities of the state, and (3) the distinction between form and content rules of operation of state institutions, we now turn to the question: How can the formal rules of policy production be described that determine the activities of the capitalist state in the area of "productive" activities? Our aim in asking and discussing this question is to explore potential discrepancies between the functions attributed to the state as a *capitalist* state and its internal structure, that is, its institutionalized mode of operation. To put it in the most formal way, our problem is the balance or imbalance in the relationship between internal production rules and functions referring to the accumulating process. Is there a "fit" between these internal and external aspects of the state's activity? If so, what kind

of mechanisms reproduce this functional congruence? If not, what are the
systemic causes of this failure of reciprocity?

The basic types of formal decision rules according to which public administrations can operate seem to be limited to three: These three "logics" of policy
production are bureaucracy, purposive action, and consensus. In the case of
bureaucracy sequences of action are informed and determined by those structural elements that are, in an idealized form, described in the Weberian type of
bureaucracy. In the case of *purposive action* technical rationality inspires the
mode of operation. Finally, in the case of *consensus* the main determinant of
administrative action is the conflict over interests or the agreement on common
interests that exists either among the members of an administrative body or
in their environment (internal versus external consensus).

For both empirical and theoretical reasons it seems reasonable to assume
a close correlation between a bureaucratic mode of operation of the state
apparatus and what we have called "allocative" activities of the capitalist state.
As long as the required functions of the capitalist state were predominantly
allocative, its internal structure, or institutionalized mode of operation, was
predominantly bureaucratic. The reason for this assumption is that in *allocative* activities, in which state-owned resources are distributed, the bureaucratic
mode is both best suited and sufficient to administer the allocation process in
accordance with the functional requirements of the capitalist state.

The bureaucratic mode of operation, however, fails to operate sufficiently
and adequately (according to the requirements of the capitalist state) as soon
as *productive* state activities appear on the agenda of the state. The problem is
that application of predetermined rules through a hierarchical structure of
"neutral" officials is simply insufficient to absorb the decision load that is
implied by productive state activities. In other words, the administration of
productive state activities requires more than the routinized allocation of
state resources like money and justice. Additional questions have to be
answered in order for productive state activity to begin, for example: What is
the final product, or purpose, of state production? How much of it is needed
in a particular situation? What is the most efficient way of producing it? Who
should receive it? At what point in time and for what length of time? How
should it be financed, and what priorities should be followed in case of cost
increases and/or revenue decreases? All of these questions are beyond the
scope and the responsibility of a bureaucracy in the strict sense. A bureaucracy is controlled by *inputs*—be it the will of a ruler or the law. This input
is to be applied strictly, faithfully, and without exception, and the result is
supposed to be "order." In contrast, what productive state activity presupposes is control by *output*: An activity is "adequate" not if it conforms to
certain established rules and procedures, but mainly if it leads to certain
results.

In various policy areas one could easily investigate the change from merely allocative to additional productive types of the state activity. In the case of health, for example, allocative health measures would consist in laws that make a certain *behavior mandatory* (for landlords to provide water and sanitary installations in their buildings; for doctors to register the incidence of contagious diseases with a department of health; for employers to install protective devices for industrial accidents, and so on) or in regulations that make certain *claims legal* (e.g., a claim of certain categories of people to receive public health insurance, or of certain private hospitals to receive state subsidies). On the opposite polar point there are purely productive state activities, or health policies in the proper sense, such as the management of public hospitals, a medical training system, or state-directed medical research. Although in most cases the actual health policy will consist of a combination of both, the preponderance of one of the types, and a historical development from the first type toward the second one will be recognized. In the first case, the state regulates behavior through the administration of negative or positive sanctions on a routinized basis, and it is exactly this that bureaucracies are so perfectly suited to do. In the second case the state pursues a concrete production, which in the case of our example includes the organization of physical investment and equipment, the qualification of manpower, and the production of the required knowledge. It seems obvious that, in the second case, the scope of data and events that take place outside the administrative structure and must be taken into consideration is relatively much broader. This is the reason why the procedures of an organization of the second type cannot be standardized, routinized, and channelled through rigid hierarchies in the same way as this is possible in bureaucracies in the strict sense that deal with the peculiarities of their environment on a much narrower and much more abstracted basis.

Bureaucratic structure seems inadequate as the basis for the productive type of state activity. This, incidentally, is the major result of numerous theoretical works pointing out that what is held to be the hypothesis in Weber, namely, the superior efficiency of bureaucratic structure, is wrong: Bureaucracy is inefficient and ineffective, and effective structures of government are nonbureaucratic. This point of view also has inspired numerous critiques of bureaucracy as well as proposals for its reform that aim at a stricter control of state activity by output and objectives, rather than inputs and rules. The critique of the "spending-service-cliche" inherent in bureaucratic structures is a case in point.

If we now look at the alternatives, the two possible structures seem to be the purposive-rational one and the one based in democratic conflict and consensus. In the history of sociopolitical doctrines, both of these solutions have been advocated under the phrase "from the rule over men to the administration of things," a formula that Saint-Simon first coined in order to demand the replacement of officials by experts and scientists, and that

later was used by Engels as a description of what the mode of operation in a
classless and democratic society would be. Let us first consider the purposive-
rational or technocratic mode of operation of productive state activity. To
what extent is it applicable as a viable solution to the problem that is posed
to the capitalist state by the fact of discrepancy between the predominantly
bureaucratic structure of the state apparatus and its function as required by
the accumulation process?

To substitute bureaucratic rules of policy production by purposive-rational
ones would make the state apparatus—in its internal procedures—similar to what
goes on in production of commodities in industry. However, while the choice
of ends in *industrial commodity* production, namely, a certain quantity and
kind of commodities, is (pre)determined by market forces, there is no such
mechanism in the case of the state that sets and corrects the goals of *state*
production equally automatically. This difference is most important. Only
if the goals of purposive rationality can be taken for granted in a given situation, can purposive rationality become the organizing principle of the structure
of an organization. An individual accumulating unit derives its goals from its
environment, or at least it derives very stringent criteria from its environment
as to what its range of decision making about goals is. So its main problem
remains to implement these goals efficiently and effectively, that is through
instrumental rationality. This is something the state cannot do: It does not
have unequivocal, uncontroversial, and operational cues as to what the goals
of its productive state activities should be; at least it is unable to derive such
definitions of goals and goal related criteria from its environment. For the
state there is no calculus that allows it to interpret data from the environment
and transform them into strategy. The state is, in other words, not itself a
capitalist accumulating unit, and therefore the problem of its internal decision-making structure is much more complicated to solve than in the case of
a capitalist firm. The variety of needs, interests, demands, crises, etc. that
appear in the environment of state activity are of a contradictory nature,
especially under conditions of advanced forms of competition discussed before,
to allow the derivation of operational goals. Conversely, the state in its specific
capitalist form is unable to impose on its environment its *own* definition of a set
of goals that it then could pursue according to instrumental rationality.

The lack of operational political goals that could be implemented in a
purposive manner is not the only obstacle to the adoption of a purposive
mode of operation. In addition to clear-cut goals there must be two additional
conditions in order for this mode to be applicable: First, there must be a relative stability of conditions at least for the length of the production cycle. If
a dramatic change of cost and price, or means and end, is to be expected during
the course of production of a commodity, its production can hardly be organized in a rational instrumental way. While for the individual firm the relevant segment of the environment is relatively small and the fact, direction, and rate of

change in relevant variables can relatively easily be anticipated, the state's relevant environment is broad and hence less predictable. This greater turbulence of the environment is aggravated in its effects by the fact that production cycles of productive state activity are often very long, so that the implementation of goals (even if they are sufficiently operational) is likely to be a process that is affected by changes in the relevant environment that escape rational instrumental calculation. The familiar phenomenon that long-term programs are blocked by short-term fluctuations of the business cycle is a case in point. Second, the purposive-rational type of action is applicable only where side-effects of the production process itself can be safely ignored (or compensated for) by the organization. To treat the elements of a situation as means and ends is simply to ignore all aspects of the "means" except those specific ones that can be utilized as instruments for the "end." The question of what happens to the *means* except and after being utilized can be *externalized*. This is, at any rate, easier for a private capitalist organization to do than for a capitalist state, especially as far as the need to legitimize its power and conceal its real functions is concerned. Finally, there is the well-known problem of finding a common denominator for means and ends, a task that can only be solved in a more or less arbitrary way as soon as reforms of state production cannot be calculated in monetary terms since they are not sold on a market. For this reason it is always easier to achieve *technical* rationality, or effectiveness, than economic rationality or efficiency in productive state activities. But it is exactly this possibility of achieving benefits regardless of cost considerations that is made most unreal (with the relative exception of defense) by fiscal constraints that in turn are aggravated by the number and costs of productive state activities. We conclude from this brief summary of the obstacles to instrumental rationality as the organizing principle of productive state activity that the adoption of this principle cannot be considered as an adequate and viable solution to the structural problems of the capitalist state and its internal organization except under very limited and unlikely conditions such as: clear-cut, uncontroversial and operational goals; stability of the environment and/or short production cycle; ignorable externalities; no fiscal constraints; and others.

The third principal method for organizing the decision-making process in the area of productive state activity is to allow for a highly decentralized process of political conflict and consensus to determine the production process. By this method production would not be made dependent upon a set of rules generated at the top of a hierarchical structure, or by a preconceived goal that is to be achieved by rules of technical effectiveness and economic efficiency, but by a *simultaneous determination of inputs and outputs* by the clients of state administration or the recipients of its benefits. Such a model of decision making, at least in its pure form, would mean that not only the logical and institutional distinction between politics and administration, but also the basic distinction between state and society, becomes negated: The authority to organize and decide upon productive state activity would reside in its clientele. The difficulties that such a loss of differentiation would entail for the ability of the state to function as a *capitalist* state are rather obvious. First, the permanent interference of conflict of interest and the dynamics of consensus formation into administrative action would probably make it incapable of planning and long-term action. Second, even if the time horizons of demands and planning would coincide, it remains highly questionable whether a policy process that is directly dependent upon democratic pressures could any longer converge in a policy that is consistent with the functions of the state that are required in a capitalist society. In other words, too much responsiveness towards its clientele would almost necessarily push administrations beyond the limits of what they can do and are required to do within the framework of a capitalist organization of the economy. At least, such responsiveness would not only *reflect* conflicts most directly, but also *create* conflicts in case its pretended reliance upon democratic decision making is not paralleled by its ability to act according to the emerging decisions of its clientele. In other words, conflict is created by the fact that the adoption of social conflict and consensus as the basis for policy production does *invite* more demands and interests to articulate themselves than can be *satisfied* under the fiscal and institutional constraints that the capitalist state is unable to escape.

Policy Analysis and Public Administration

We have argued that the study of policy formation is fundamentally incomplete as long as its main emphasis is on matters of policy content. The formal structure, or method, of policy making is of equal significance, especially since it predetermines what can and does become the content of a policy. We have further argued that there are three principal methods by which the administration of productive state activities can be undertaken. Checking each of them, we have found, as it seems, that each might be viable as a structure of decision making, but that none of them is adequate for solving the specific problem of the capitalist state, which is, as we have argued, to establish a balance between its *required functions,* which result from a certain state of the accumulation process, and its dynamics on the one side and its *internal structure* on the other side. It thus seems that the problem of the capitalist state is *not* how to solve certain problems that are brought by the accumulation process, like how to control inflation or unemployment or how to produce technological change and education. The problem of the capitalist state is rather one that has to be solved before any of those changing problems can be dealt with, namely, how to establish and institutionalize a method of policy production that constitutes a *balance* (or reciprocity) between required state activities and the internal structure of the state.

Liberal policy research and policy analysis tends to ignore this problem altogether, because it assumes that the right course of action relating to a specific social problem is what is most urgently needed, and not what mode of operation is adequate for a capitalist state. These branches of social science deal with ways to cure what are seen as the ills and deficiencies—rather than the nature—of advanced capitalist society. In most cases these perceived problems fall into one of the three categories that constitute the framework for the *liberal* critique of capitalism: (1) failure of the market-controlled accumulation process to take into account externalities and social costs; (2) failure of the accumulation process to produce staple levels of income and employment over time, and (3) failure of the accumulation process to produce a distribution of income that is in conformity with standards of social justice and the requirement of social peace. Implicitly, in such perspective of policy research the state is seen as a *neutral* actor who lacks knowledge as to what to do at what time. Conversely, another branch of liberal political science, namely public administration, is concerned exclusively with the most "rational" or "responsive", or "efficient") mode of organizing and managing public organizations. In this view the *environment* of state activity, namely a capitalist society in which the accumulation process poses certain problems and requires certain state activities, is neutralized. In both fields of study, policy research and public administration, the problem of reciprocity versus discrepancy between external function and internal structure is ignored due to its respective specialized and one-sided point of view. This is why both disciplines tend to become normative, abstract, and voluntaristic in their recommendations: the problem-solving approach of policy analysis to the extent that it fails to take into consideration the problem of the internal mode of operation of the state, and the public administration approach because it ignores the functional aspects of the state as a capitalist state.

We have argued before that none of the three principal modes of organization and decision making can be said to provide the adequate structural basis for the performance of those functions that characterize the capitalist state. In the rest of this chapter I discuss the questions: (1) how the problem of this structural discrepancy between structure and function can be observed empirically, and (2) the observable responses to this problem by which an attempt is made to reconcile or minimize the structure/function discrepancy.

If we look at the major doctrines of administrative reform and reorganization, it is interesting to note that they do correspond closely to the three main modes of operation. The bureaucratic mode of operation is the model after which all these recommendations are designed that call for a stronger centralization of administrative structures. Centralization aims at a stricter enforcement of rules for a broader range of units and administrative subsystems so that rules, directives, and informations are accepted more reliably by more actors. Second, the purposive-rational mode or operation is the model that inspires all those suggestions that call for stricter control by objectives, outputs, and outcomes by such techniques as program budgeting, cost benefit analysis, and social indicators. Finally, there is a school of reformers of administration who seek to improve responsiveness, equity, and the consideration of democratic values of meaningful participation. The guideline in these proposals is obviously the conflict/consensus model that is either meant to imply greater participation on the part of the lower ranks *within* the organization and/or on the part of the *clientele.*

If we are right to assume that all of these modes of operation are in specific ways inadequate to solve the structure/function problem of the capitalist state under conditions where the state's function can only be performed through productive state activities, then the pursuit of such nonsolutions on the level of internal modes of operation should lead to empirical phenomena of friction or to failures in the performance of state functions. In other words, if it is true that each of the three models of internal structure are inadequate as the organizational form for the functions required by a capitalist state, such inadequacy must be demonstrable on the level of empirical phenomena.

This seems to be most easy to do in the case of the purely bureaucratic mode of operation and its marginal extension through stricter centralization, etc. Bureaucracy means hierarchy, fixed division of labor, input orientation, abstraction of concrete events occurring in the environment into "cases", and the routinization of procedures. While one could argue that this arrangement is perfectly suited for the purpose of allocating state-owned resources to certain categories of receivers, it has often been observed that it does not work in the area of productive state activities, that is, in all those cases where resources have not only been handed out to legally specified recipients, but where those resources have to be combined into a production process of, for instance, health, defense, education, or industrial innovation. For such state activities, the pure type of bureaucratic organization is either altogether ineffective or, at least, highly inefficient. The strategic alternatives that remain in this situation are *either* to reduce drastically the quantity and scope of state organized productive activities (a solution that is typically advocated by conservatives who believe in "incrementalism" as one of the organizational forms that emphasizes input orientation), *or* to innovate and transform bureaucratic structures in a way that makes them more rational for their productive task. Since the incrementalist solution is inconsistent with our basic assumptions, namely, that extensive productive inputs organized by the state are an indispensable prerequisite for the accumulation process in advanced capitalist societies to take place, the adequacy of this solution can be dismissed as irrelevant within our present framework of assumptions. The second solution contains itself a critique of the bureaucratic mode of operation, which can be summarized as follows: to the extent that bureaucracies are employed as organizational structures dealing with the performance of productive state activities, they are neither effective nor efficient and hence produce outcomes that are insufficient in quality and quantity, relative to the functional requirements of the accumulation process in advanced capitalism.

Second, the rational-purposive mode of operation (commonly associated with the concept of planning) seems to cause disturbances of the capitalist accumulation process for opposite reasons: It is not, as in the case of bureaucracy, insufficient to perform productive state activities; rather, it seems, if applied rigorously and comprehensively, to be most adequate for the design and implementation of productive state activities. However, such an instrumental-rational mode of operation presupposes, as we have seen before, a degree of control over relevant variables that is atypical for the capitalist state. The typical case, rather, is that the amount of state power required for comprehensive planning of the production process is denied to the state by the accumulating units themselves. Planning thus seems to be inherently impossible to the capitalist state as an internal mode of operation—impossible not in itself, but because of the acts of retaliation that planning provokes on the part of capital as a whole or individual accumulating units. Such acts of retaliation (the major forms of which are *absolute* disinvestment, or investment strikes, and *relative* disinvestment, or displacement of investment in time and space) tend to make the cure worse than the disease under capitalism, and are thus self-paralyzing in regard to state activity.

Third, the contradiction inherent in any attempt to base state productive activities on democratic consensus-building and immediate political conflict (either within state agencies or between them and their clientele) tends to exacerbate the problem rather than to create solutions. Participation and unfiltered conflict tends to interfere with the institutional constraints, under which state agencies have to operate, and, as could be demonstrated in the cases of participation-based welfare policies, urban policies, and education policies, lead to a highly unstable situation. Participatory models of the organization of state productive activities that aim at increasing administrative responsiveness are as inadequate as the two others because they tend to crystallize conflict and protest and can thus easily become *subversive* of the balance between the state and the accumulation process.

Each of the three sets of institutionalized decision rules that we have discussed contain a specific contradiction: the bureaucratic mode of operation is wasteful at best and ineffective at worst and thus *insufficient* as a structural model for productive state activity. The purposive rational model may be both efficient and effective in itself, but its application requires interference with the prerogatives of the private accumulation process, the resistance to which on the part of the accumulating units makes its application impossible (except where it is almost congruent with private investment decisions in the first place). The main reason for this impossibility is the resistance of the accumulating units and their power to retaliate. Resistance, protest, and political conflict on the part of the working class (and other groups that are deprived of control over investment decisions) are the major reason for the subversive effects of participatory structures.

This line of argument seems to suggest that, among the three major strategies of establishing a balance between the structure of decision rules and the functions of the state for the accumulation process, there is none that has the potential for success. Whichever is pursued, it tends to violate rather than to establish the balance of the state and the accumulation process. Moreover, since all three of these strategies, which aim at the adaption of structure to function, seem to be followed by current proposals for administrative reform simultaneously in different branches of the state apparatus, the occurrence of second-order contradictions, namely between those strategies among each other, can be hypothesized. No agency can simultaneously open itself to directives that come from the top of the bureaucratic hierarchy, from the experts, and from its clientele.

Conclusion

A better understanding of these structural problems of the capitalist state, its inability to reconcile, without paralyzing side effects, its functions as a capitalist state, and its internal mode of operation, may oblige us to redefine the concept of the capitalist state itself. In the beginning of this chapter we said that a capitalist state is defined (a) by its exclusion from accumulation, (b) by its necessary function for accumulation, (c) by its dependence upon accumulation, and (d) by its function to conceal and deny (a), (b), and (c). If the analytical propositions we have developed are at least partially valid, it is hard to imagine that any state in capitalist society could succeed to perform the functions that are part of this definition simultaneously and successfully for any length of time. If this is true, what entitles us to talk about the capitalist state as if it were part of social reality? What is real about it is the constant attempt to reconcile and make compatible these various functions with its internal structure, or mode of operation. But what is equally real is the fact that there is neither visible nor to be anticipated a strategy that actually *does* reconcile these functions and thus achieve a balanced integration of the state and the accumulation process, that is, a reliable and workable strategy of "systems maintenance" (as many radicals believe).

The reality of the capitalist state can thus best be described as the reality (and dominance) of an unrealistic attempt. There is no method of policy formation available that could make this attempt more realistic, at least if it is true that element (b) in the above definition spells—under conditions of *advanced* capitalism—the need for productive state activities.

6

Paradigms of Relations Between State and Society
Robert R. Alford

Three paradigms of the relations between the state and the society in industrialized capitalist democracies can be labeled *pluralist, elite,* and *class.* This chapter sets forth the basic assumptions of each paradigm and considers the possibility of transcending their limitations as partial analytic models.

Several alternative key terms besides "paradigm" might be used, implying different degrees of rigor, comprehensiveness, and self-consciousness: model, theory, or perspective. The word "paradigm" avoids the inferences of logical coherence and deductive consistency that the terms "theory" and "model" suggest. The term "perspective" is too weak, indicating simply some assumptions or hypotheses that are untested and perhaps untestable. Although the argument requires thorough justification not possible here, the term "paradigm" is appropriate because of the implicit but powerful influence of the assumptions upon all aspects of the intellectual processes involved: selection of the problem, the unit of analysis, or the key terms (such as "power"); definition of the relevant data; interpretation of those data; and generalization beyond the data.[a]

Each paradigm selects certain aspects of state-society relations for emphasis and focus, but at the boundaries must deal with data and explanatory factors central to other paradigms. In any comprehensive substantive study ideas and evidence appear that are inconsistent with the paradigm that organizes the material for the particular author. The test of the paradigmatic location of a work is in the underlying decision rules that are inferred to have guided the

---

I am indebted to a great many students and colleagues for their comments over several years on various drafts of this chapter, which is still a tentative statement that has not resolved some of the issues my critics have regarded as important. This chapter was originally delivered at the 1973 meetings of the American Sociological Association in New York City and, in somewhat revised form, to the University Seminar on the State at Columbia University in December 1973, with the title "Toward a Critical Sociology of Political Power."

[a]For the original presentation of the paradigm concept and subsequent critical comment, see Thomas S. Kuhn, *The Structure of Scientific Revolutions* (Chicago: University of Chicago Press, 1962), and Imre Lakatos and Alan Musgrave, eds., *Criticism and the Growth of Knowledge* (Cambridge: Cambridge University Press, 1970). Kuhn's response to the criticisms appears in the Lakatos and Musgrave volume and also in a 1969 postscript to a 1970 reprinting of the original volume. My application of the term indicates my disagreement with Kuhn's position that the social sciences do not have paradigms. I believe that paradigms are characteristic not of fields as a whole, but of clusters or subareas within fields, and can be identified by analysis of the dominant journals, works of leading figures, control over sectors of a professional association, and recruitment to leading departments and universities.

overall selection and organization of materials and their interpretation, not whether all of the facts or generalizations included are consistent with the paradigm.[1]

Three major points are made: First, the three paradigms focus upon distinct social and political forces that shape the state and legitimate its actions: individuals and groups for the pluralist paradigm, bureaucratic organizations for the elite paradigm, and social classes for the class paradigm.[2] Second, each paradigm gains its explanatory power by focusing upon a particular context of action—a situational context within which individuals and groups choose to mobilize to influence political decisions, for the pluralist paradigm; an organizational context within which bureaucracies deploy their resources, for the elite paradigm; and a societal context within which social classes shape institutions that reinforce their rule, for the class paradigm.[b] Third, the domination of pluralist and elite paradigms in political sociology has led to neglect of a key hypothesis that flows from a preliminary attempt at synthesis: The potential democratizing consequences of the emergence of a mass electroate, parties, and parliaments have been nullified by the proliferation of fragmented networks of administrative agencies and interest organizations.

Three Paradigms of the State

The *pluralist* paradigm assumes that diverse groups and interests intermittently present demands to political parties and other elite coalitions that in turn aggregate and represent those demands to leaders and officials. The state comprises a mosaic of agencies and organizations, each of which is an institutionalized response to the historic sequence of demands and responses by elites to those demands. Through a complicated process of political, social, and economic competition, these demands are filtered or screened in order to define the essential commitments and goals of the various components of the state. The highest level of authorities—political leaders and statesmen—mediate and compromise between those demands that attain the visibility and level of support to warrant reaching the level of authority that can make binding decisions. The issues entering the political arena for decision are relatively limited in number, scope, and intensity because they occur within the narrow boundaries of a fundamental consensus among all social groups on basic values and the institutions embodying those values. Power is held by those who win in a particular struggle within the legitimate political arena.

---

[b]For reasons of length, no specific citations to works exemplifying the three paradigms are given, although in a longer work in progress, of which this chapter is an outline, a number of studies are subjected to detailed analysis to show how the paradigmatic assumptions of the author have led to choice of particular units of analysis and selection and interpretation of relevant data. See Robert R. Alford, *Political Sociology* (Englewood Cliffs, New Jersey: Prentice-Hall, forthcoming).

In the pluralist view the state is not a single "bureaucracy" but a multiplicity of overlapping jurisdictions, each competing for more resources—manpower, functions, and money. Each is linked to a public and private constituency and seeks to broaden its constituency to the maximum degree while simultaneously retaining maximum autonomy.

In the pluralist paradigm bureaucratic organizations are assumed to be ultimately responsive to a clientele, controlling agency, or democratic political process. If such organizations act in ways that seriously violate popular or elite expectations of justice, equality, and freedom, they will be forced to change in the long run. Social classes in the pluralist paradigm are assumed to be one of many clusters of interests in the society, with more political resources than some groups, but counterbalanced by the adult franchise and the capacity of minorities to mobilize public opinion and influence political elites, even in the absence of decisive majority support.

The *elite* paradigm assumes that large-scale complex organizations tend to form in almost every sphere of social life in these societies: factories, universities, government agencies, labor unions, and political parties. All interest groups, in order to have an impact in such a bureaucratized society, must themselves reach some threshold of size, homogeneity, and organizational capability, or else they will be helpless. Unorganized groups must thus be represented by organized ones. The combination of expertise, hierarchical control, and the capacity to allocate human, technological, and material resources gives the elites of bureaucratic organizations power not easily restrained by the mechanisms of pluralistic competition and debate. The competition between organizational elites is held to be, if not the hallmark, then at least an essential requirement for democratic politics in societies dominated by industrial and political bureaucracies. Power is held by those who hold dominant positions within the organizations that control key resources.

In the elite paradigm the pluralistic diversity of social groups and demands is assumed to result in a political arena in which few decisions of real consequence for the structure of power are made. Social classes in the elite paradigm are assumed to be a crucial base of power for certain elites, but have lost their independent control over both the economy and the state because of the emergence of a social stratum possessing expertise and managerial skill that are functionally required for such a society. The state is thus seen as a cluster of large-scale organizations, each based upon a separate institutional sector, the elites of which have come to manipulate and control their political base, not the other way around.

The *class* paradigm views neither the debates and decisions occurring in pluralistic political arenas nor the battles of organizational elites to maintain their control over material and human resources as exhausting the crucial facts about the relations between the state and the society. Both group interests and organizational elites are operating within a framework of economic appropriation and cultural hegemony that seldom challenges the principles defining the basic structure of the society. These principles guarantee the continued disproportionate allocation of the social product as well as its control to a relatively small portion of the population of the society that constitutes the "ruling class." Power is held by those classes benefiting from the structure of society in a given historical period.

In the class paradigm a pluralistic diversity of social groups representing a wide variety of interests and values is real but relatively unimportant since the issues and demands that arise seldom challenge the basic institutional framework. The "consensus" applauded by the pluralists as preventing "demand overload" is, in this view, a manifestation of the cultural domination of intellectual and political life by ideas and attitudes congruent with the maintenance of that institutional framework. Bureaucratization in the class paradigm is a technological requirement for the necessary coordination and administration of a class society, but seldom, if ever, do the elites manning bureaucracies challenge the premises of the institutional allocation of the social product.

To summarize, within the *pluralist* paradigm the core function of the state is to achieve *consensus* and thus social order through continuous exchanges of demands and responses by social groups and government and a continuous sequence of bargaining processes. Within the *elite* paradigm the core function of the state is the maintenance of *domination* by existing elites. Within the *class* paradigm the core function of the state is the *reproduction* and management of existing class relationships, via both formal processes (the operations of courts, police, army, administrative and legislative agencies) and informal processes (socialization within schools and family to accept the limits of political participation and political action as inevitable, pragmatic, and even desirable).

Utopian and Pathological Images

Each paradigm has both a utopian and a pathological image of state-society relationships, and each has both empirical (predictive) and normative (ideological) aspects.

The utopian image of the pluralist paradigm might be called *pluralist democracy*. Groups can freely form within the larger society and have open access to authoritative bodies to express their interests and values and seek support for them. The political process as a whole consists of a moving equilibrium of demands and responses, resulting in a gradual evolution toward a more just, more humane, more equalitarian society. No group has a dominant role in the society as a whole.

The pathological variant might be called *mass society*. Groups have lost their capacity to act as intermediaries between their members and other groups, to soften the demands of their members, or to negotiate reasonable bargains with other groups. As a result, some groups present unrestrained demands upon other groups and upon the leaders of the largest group of all, the society. The societal leaders become unable to mediate or negotiate effectively between the groups, and the "rules of the game" governing the bargaining process break down. The pluralist paradigm, being a model essentially of the "normal" processes of group formation and representation, cannot deal with these pathological developments except to criticize them from a normative perspective.

The elite paradigm also has its utopian and pathological images. Its utopian image might be called the *planned society*. In such a society elites are not so bound by the short-term demands of the groups that keep them in office or in power that they cannot develop long-range rational planning of the direction of investment of the social resources that they command. The elites of the many giant organizations that dominate the society are responsible and farsighted enough to realize that they must coordinate their activities with others and work out arrangements for the orderly exchange of needed personnel, services, and other resources because they realize that they are dependent upon each other in the long run, regardless of how competitive they may be in the short run. Thus, the elites of various organizations cooperate in supporting the overall development of societal resources that benefits them all: education, science, technology, transportation, health care. These resources are sometimes to be developed by the state and sometimes by private action, depending upon the most rational use of social resources. Through the coordinated activity of these elites, economic growth continues, and basic group demands are met.

The pathological image is *totalitarianism*. The top elites lose any effective sanctions over their behavior, and they begin to act in such a way as to maximize the benefits accruing either to them personally or to their organization, rather than to work together with other elites. Also, they begin to manipulate the opinions and preferences of mass publics in order to maintain their own control. In the extreme case this manipulation takes the form of outright repression and terror and use of police or military force against any attempts to replace them. Within the elitist paradigm it is very difficult for elites who have attained this degree of control to be overthrown (this is almost Max Weber's image of "normal" bureaucracy), and it is only counter-elites who have even this potential. The best safeguard against elitist totalitariansim is thus the maintenance of a system of competitive elites. Mass democracy is merely utopian in an era when the society is basically controlled by giant corporations, and decisions are inevitably made by relatively few people because of the lack of interest and information among the mass electorate about the complex and technical grounds of decision making.

The class paradigm also has utopian and pathological images. The utopian image is *anarchism*. The enormous productive capacity of a capitalist society is assumed to be convertible to rational human uses instead of being consumed by military production, advertising, packaging, useless commodities, and the various social expenditures such as those on police and television that may be necessary to mystify and control a population potentially aware of alternative possibilities. It assumes that a complex division of labor based on advanced technology can be based on rational knowledge and thus consent, not authority and domination. It assumes that the common interests of the entire society can be translated into resource investments without requiring either a structure of authority relationships—with the problems of selecting and training elites associated with such structures—or a diversity of specialized interest groups whose needs and demands would necessitate some structure of participation, representation, and access to ultimate decision makers. This is the classic image of a communist society and is essentially an anarchist image of a simultaneously decentralized and cooperative society.

The pathological image of the class paradigm is *fascism*. In such a society the ruling class, no longer capable of maintaining its rules through the peaceful political processes of parliamentary debate and electoral competition, resorts either to repression of dissent and organized opposition by various techniques— wiretapping, bribery, legal harassment, agents provocateurs, co-optation or intimidation of opponents—or to open abolition of representative institutions. More subtly, the political culture is manipulated by symbolic distortions of events through the mass media to turn, in Orwellian language, repression into law and order and defeats into victories—resulting first in popular revulsion, then depoliticization, and finally apathy, all dubbed concensus and mass support.[3]

The Strategic Focus of Each Paradigm

Aside from its political and ideological content, each paradigm can be regarded as an analytic strategy allowing a focus upon what are assumed to be key relationships, ignoring other factors. The class, elite, and pluralist paradigms identify societal, organizational, and situational contexts of action, respectively. The pluralist paradigm focuses upon the conditions of mobilization of particular groups and individuals for political action and upon the strategies of influence and the outcomes of action in particular situations. As already noted, power is defined as the winner in a pluralist combat between potentially equal opponents. The elite paradigm focuses upon the stable coalitions of resources in organizations manned by elites and emphasizes the limited range of possible decisions within the organizational parameters. Power is defined as the long-range capacity to deploy organizational resources. The class paradigm focuses upon the basic institutions of property and the objective class relations arising from those institutions. Power is held by those who continuously benefit from the functioning of those institutions, regardless of what their particular structural forms are or who makes decisions within them.

The explanatory power generated by focusing upon a particular context of action is gained at the cost of neglecting certain questions. Because these definitions of state-society relations are paradigms and not merely models or theories, each tends to explain away the independence of the phenomena of central concern to the other paradigms or to subsume them under its core concepts and variables.

The pluralist paradigm neglects some important questions: First, the origins of those "preferences" (interests and values) of individuals that lead them to form groups: These are essentially taken as given, and their historical or institutional origins are not problematic. Second, the sources of inequalities in the basic resources or capabilities of groups to act in defense of their core interests or values: No inherent institutional or resource barriers to the formation of any groups are assumed to exist if potential members have some felt interests or values in common. Third, the extent to which groups are actually created and then sustained by the actions of other groups, or by institutions at the level of the society as a whole, mainly the state: The voluntaristic image of group creation neglects the extent to which positive legal or political action at higher levels actually generates social groups.

The elite paradigm also ignores some questions that are crucial to the other paradigms. First, because it assumes that the structures of power commanded by elites have become severed from their possible origins in group demands and needs, it tends to ignore the concrete social and economic interests actually served by bureaucratic organizations. The maintenance of power and domination by elites is seen as having become an end in itself, and the consequences of elite decisions and policies for social groups and classes tend to be slighted. Second, the differences in power of different bureaucratic organizations are neglected. Because the focus tends to be upon separate organizations with relations between them defined as exchanges of resources, rather than upon the consequences of the operation of the bureaucratic organizations for specific social groups, the social origins of the differences in the amount of resources and what they are used for tends not to be analyzed. Third, the origin of bureaucracies in past critical decisions and outcomes of social conflicts is not seen as an analytic problem. Once in existence, giant organizations become social actors, but their origins in past conflicts as attempts by social groups or social classes to solve their problems or to establish a claim upon a part of the social product tend to be neglected.

Thus, both the pluralist and class paradigms would criticize the elite paradigm for artificially isolating giant organizations—whether corporations, trade unions, universities, or government agencies—from their social milieu or context. The pluralist paradigm sees organizations as arising from and representing the legitimate needs of social groups; the class paradigm sees organizations as attempts by segments of social classes to defend their interests within the range of possibilities and limits imposed by a given set of class relations and type of productive system.

The class paradigm also fails to deal with some important questions. First, the extent of social and cultural diversity within classes is played down, although this class heterogeneity may have decisive implications for the potential for class

consciousness, solidarity, and conflict. Second, the persistence of authority relationships and the requirements of hierarchical and disciplined organization of
labor under conditions of high technology and industrial production are minimized, if not ignored. If these requirements are not in fact simply an epiphenom-
enon of capitalism, but are endemic to industrial organization, both the image
of the future society and the means to get there would have to change sharply.
Third, the problem of stable representation of diverse group interests is neglected
or simply assumed to be easily solvable, once the fundamental distortions resulting from class rule are done away with. However, even given a productive system
capable of meeting everyone's basic needs, there would still have to be mechanisms
for articulating, representing, mediating, and ultimately deciding between alternative forms and modes of satisfying human needs. These potential modes of participation and response are neglected in the class paradigm.

Each paradigm has a tendency to claim more explanatory power than it
possesses and to extend the domain of its concepts to answer those questions
it is actually unable to deal with. For example, the pluralist paradigm sometimes
collapses the societal and organizational contexts of action into the situational
context, regarding no causal factor as being important if it is not reflected in
overt, current behavior. This occurs when class hegemony over the definition
of public versus private spheres of activity, for example, is regarded as a cultural
consensus, manifest in an acceptance of the limits of action by all participants in
the political arena. This also occurs when organizational dominance over key
resources such as money, personnel, and legality is regarded as only an attribute
of individuals who choose whether or not to use their resources. In such instances
the historically developed societal and organizational constraints upon action are
denied as such or are reinterpreted as cultural values internalized by actors. In
the pluralist paradigm the potent analytic emphasis upon the contingencies of
action in the *present,* the varying motives of actors, and the widely varying probabilities of different outcomes can thus become a way of concealing organizational
and societal constraints.

Similarly, the class paradigm can lead to a merging of the three levels or contexts of action if it is assumed that class interests are always perfectly reflected
in class organizations, which in turn always act in ways that serve underlying and
long-range class interests. The reputational school in the study of community
power, for example, comes close to assuming that discovery of a banker sitting
on a city council is not only evidence of his personal interests and motives (as
the pluralists would conclude), but also evidence for the power of the banks
as organizations and even for the power of the capitalist class in the society.

Methodological Implications

Two sets of methodological implications can be drawn from the previous argument, suggesting either an additive or an interaction model of relations between different levels of social organization. In the additive model, individual, organizational,

and societal levels are not perfectly correlated with each other. An important element of contingency or "slippage" exists between these levels, each of which is causally important and cannot be reduced to the others. This independence provides each paradigm with its explanatory potential within its own level or context.

The variance in the predictability of the behavior of historically specific, concrete actors, even within similar class and organizational contexts, gives the pluralist paradigm its independent analytic potential. The elite paradigm derives its independent analytic potential from the narrow range of possible alternatives for action once a set of organizations and their elites exists, and because the class relations in a society do not absolutely determine the possible forms or mode of organization of political parties, trade unions, legal structure, etc. Because neither pluralist combat nor elite domination frequently challenges the underlying class relations of production in a given capitalist society, and because the actions of the state can plausibly be interpreted as reinforcing those relationships, the class paradigm also has independent analytic potential.

Using an additive model, each level of "structure" sets limits upon the other levels, but does not completely determine structures within them. That is, the class structure of a society sets broad limits upon the types of organizations that can easily arise and those that are deterred, fought, or opposed by economic, legal, and political power. However, one cannot predict from the fundamental character of the class structure the particular array of organizations that will exist in a given historical period: political parties, a particular form of state agency. Nor can one predict the life history and internal dynamics of those organizations; they behave according to "laws" of organizations, not of societies. Nor can one predict the ways organizations will act in particular situations or the ways individuals within groups will act. The organizational structure of a society in a given period sets broad limits upon the kinds of situations that are likely to arise, but does not predetermine the outcome of those situations.

Thus, within an additive model of the three paradigms, a pluralist paradigm is a powerful tool for analyzing the situational context of action and the conditions of mobilization of individuals and groups to influence particular political decisions within a framework of a cultural consensus. The elite paradigm provides a means for understanding the structures of power of complex organizations constituting the state and their bargains, exchanges of resources, personnel, and impact on general policies that set the parameters for particular decisions. The class paradigm enables us to understand the limits of policy formation and of the state structure within the class relations of a given society. The translation of class interests (or a cultural consensus) into organizational form and then into action is problematic and contingent, as are the consequences of specific actions and events that may challenge and change only particular decisions in some circumstances, the structure of organizations under other conditions, and the general structure of social relations under other conditions.

This formulation contains, however, an unresolved ambiguity in the possible relations between these "levels." If each level of structure sets limits on the other levels but does not completely constrain their internal relations, then the relationships between levels are additive. That is, social class variables affect some organizational variables, and both organizational and class variables affect some situational variables. Social class variables do not affect the relations among the organizational variables, nor do class and organizational variables affect the relations among situational variables. If these conditions in fact hold empirically, then legitimate grounds exist for analyzing the three levels in isolation. Although an isolated analysis results in only a partial view of the system, the results can at least be generalized to similar parts of other systems.

However, an interaction model can be specified starting from any of the paradigms. Within the class paradigm the internal relations within organizations change as the class structure changes, and political situations become fundamentally different if both the elite/organizational structures and the class structure change.[c]

Within the pluralist paradigm a change of political circumstances and situations alters the outcomes of action not merely temporarily, or within the confines of an overdetermined set of structural relationships, but permanently, and the probabilities of such contingent outcomes cannot be predicted from a knowledge of organizational and class structures. From this viewpoint the diversity, complexity, and variation between empirical situations of action produce a prediction of intense interaction effects from the other "direction" than that which the class paradigm predicts. The complex combination of situational factors changing almost from moment to moment produces gross consequences not predictable from knowledge of structure.

The degree of independence of the three different levels is not a question that can or should be resolved by sheer assertion or theoretical assumption but is ultimately an empirical question to be addressed by systematic comparative studies that include variations in each level as part of the research design. The additive model hypothesizes that the internal relations between variables is the same at different levels although the probability for the occurrence of conditions under which those variables will be found together may differ, depending on the context. The interaction model hypothesizes that not only will the probability of the variables occurring together differ, but also the correlations between them will be sharply different, even reversed.

To settle the claim of each paradigm to be a truly general description and explanation of state-society relations in these types of societies may require an interaction model of the relations between levels of analysis. If pluralism is a valid general theory and not just a set of decision rules for analysis of specific political situations and decisions, then organizations and classes, regarded by the other paradigms (under certain historical conditions) as homogeneous social and political actors, are really temporary coalitions of diverse groups and

---

[c]I am indebted to Paul Allison for this point.

individuals held together by a fragile consensus and a set of beliefs that successfully cause them to act as a coalition. That is, the apparent unity of resources
and interests that we label an "organization" or a "class" is actually created by
the successful strategies of elites and leadership and has no "structural" reality.
Conversely, if class theory is valid generally, then the apparent diversity of
individual and group interests conceals an underlying logic of an institutional
structure that imposes similar principles of action upon all components of the
society, and in fact the surface diversity and complexity may be highly functional in legitimating and reproducing a given set of class relations. Both theoretical and methodological aspects of these issues are obviously complex and
beyond the scope of this chapter.

Synthetic Problems or Paradigm?

A synthetic analytic paradigm, given these issues, may not be possible.
Pending some fundamental theoretical advances, however, there should be,
in serious comparative studies of the state and processes of policy formation,
recognition of the empirical reality of the differentiation of interest groups,
the expansion of all forms of state and bureaucratic activity, and also the
appropriation and control of the social product by a small segment of the
population. The dichotomies of "state" and "society," "public" and "private" sectors, "elites" and "masses," and "political" and "nonpolitical" must
be transcended. Such terms are all useful, but must be incorporated into a
method that does not beg the most important questions in the act of defining
concepts.

To state some of the apparent paradoxes of a more inclusive perspective
(not yet a paradigm) more specifically, in many respects the contemporary
state itself creates the society, the public defines what is private, and the
political determines the nonpolitical. Conversely, the society is insulated
from the state by the very fact of state action, and the private is preserved
from the public by public action. Social groups are literally created by
government action—welfare recipients, students, research workers (by federal
grants), suburbanites (by housing subsidies). Once created, they become
privatized and see government as an alien force, taxing, regulating, but then
presenting itself for democratic validation in election after election. The
very institutional separation of the public from the private spheres, together
with the continuous creation of new groups by state action, has produced
an explosion of political demands by both the new and the old social groups.
The response by the state has been a continuous expansion of political production: programs and agencies that gesture toward the demands but mainly
produce symbols.[4] Both the demands and the responses are the political
analog of economic demands and production: Relatively simple human needs

for housing, food, transportation, leisure time, and satisfying work become transformed by mediating symbols into demands for packaged status. The response, in the polity as in the economy, is a surface diversity of product concealing an underlying uniformity.

The intellectual domination in political sociology and political science of the elite and pluralist paradigms has led to neglect of an important hypothesis about elite and class reactions to mass democratization. The conceptual path followed by researchers has paralleled the objective institutional separation of the state from the society, the public from the private, and the elites from the masses. The consequence of paradigm separation, with most social and political research being guided by either pluralist or elitist assumptions, has been that studies of the processes of mass mobilization and elite formation and behavior have been severed from each other. Because the formation of nations and the crucial problems of production, distribution, political integration, and social control have been assumed to be solved in the industrialized nations of the world, it has been possible intellectually to divide studies of elites from those of pluralist political participation. It has been assumed that if the electorate participated, the elites would respond appropriately in a way that would both preserve their capacity to rule and still satisfy the minimum demands of the electorate in a way compatible with political stability. Conversely, if there was a reasonable circulation of elites, a capacity to respond to mass demands would remain because elites were susceptible to losing power. That is, it has been assumed that the actions of elites were sufficiently visible to the mass electorate that gross failures or incapacities would bring down the worse offenders.

Given those assumptions, "elite" research could then focus upon the concrete decision-making processes in bureaucratic agencies, in legislatures, and in courts, and neglect the actual impact of these processes upon the mass electorate, and also neglect whether or not these processes were a substantial and tangible response to the demands of various publics. "Pluralist" research could focus upon the factors affecting participation of various segments of the electorate in parties and voting, without worrying about whether or not this participation had any consequences for elite behavior. Dividing the political system into two parts—the elites and the mass electorate—allowed neglect of some crucial questions about the relationships between those parts.

A major hypothesis has thus been neglected and can be stated briefly as follows: Elite response to mass enfranchisement has been to establish decision-making processes that fragment policy-making authority into decentralized bureaucracies incapable of formulating, let alone carrying out, possible solutions to the problems they are charged with.[5] This process has blurred the understanding of political processes for the mass electroate; it is now almost literally impossible to understand how decisions are made and how they could be made in more rational ways. The net result has been for many voters cynicism about politicians and withdrawal and for many leaders cynicism about ignorant voters and careerism.

This hypothesis requires some all-too-brief elaboration. In Stein Rokkan's words, paraphrasing an unpublished article written in 1960 by Peter Rossi,

> the three basic strategies used by economic elites in countering the effects of this growth of electoral power will be these: 1) the promotion of non-partisan electoral systems and of technically neutral administrative agencies; 2) the intensified proliferation of privately controlled community institutions and voluntary civic associations serving as instruments of influence and pressure in conflicts over local policies; and 3) the development of state-wide or nation-wide interest organizations to influence policies beyond the control of the local political elite.

Rokkan goes on to broaden the applicability of these generalizations:

> . . . the extension of the suffrage increased the chances for a status polarization of national politics, but this very polarization brought about a proliferation of sectional and functional organizations which in turn tended to soften the overall strains in the system and reduce the level of polarization. What we tend to find is a cumulation of forces making for a narrowing of the alternatives for national politics, a fragmentation of the networks of policy-influencing organizations, and a consequent decline in the importance of the decisions of the electorate-at-large. This may tend to lower the level of general political participation and to alienate from politics sizable sections of the once enfranchised citizenry, leaving the basic decisions to a bargaining process between interest organizations, parties and agencies and departments of the national bureaucracy.[6]

This is a crucially important statement because this perspective on the "strategies used by economic elites in countering the effects of this growth of electoral power" has been forsaken in the 1960s by much research on national as well as local community power and decision making. If the diversion of power from the mass electorate to a fragmented network of interest organizations and bureaucratic agencies is an inevitable part of the modernization process, if it is part of the "end of ideology" in Western polities, if it is a healthy component of a functioning pluralist polity, then it is not necessary to look to the "functions" of such a political system for the continuing domination of the allocation of values of dominant elites and ruling classes. One must simply accept the structure of the society as given and attempt to keep open the channels of influence and access available to less privileged groups. This latter emphasis has in fact been the concern of much of the work on political participation and local community decision making in the last decade or so. However, events of the last few years in the West have challenged an easy acceptance of this perspective. Without going into detail to state an alternative view, it seems more likely now that this kind of political system is not inevitable, not a success, and not a component of a healthy society, polity, and economy. In spite of the increasing centralization of power at the national level, the "narrowing of the alternatives for national policies" has meant, in the United States as well as in other Western societies, the avoidance of the public definition, let alone the solution, of crucial problems of the priorities for allocation of the national product, or of the development of nonexploitative relations between nations, to mention only two.

From a short-term point of view, the softening of the strains in the system by the reduction of polarization might be regarded as positive, as a way of avoiding conflicts that might result in "system overload." Such has indeed been the underlying implicit assumption of much research on bureaucratic decision making and on the nature of partisanship. It has been assumed that cross-pressures on individuals minimized extremism and that the system consequences would be moderation. In fact, the system consequences of institutional and organizational fragmentation may have been mainly to free political elites to act with fewer constraints, and as a result to place them *more* under the influence of the most strongly organized interest groups and social classes. Thus, a principal consequence of the democratization of the electoral process may have been the development of mechanisms by political and economic elites to neutralize or cancel out the consequences of that democratization.[7]

Depriving the mass electorate of channels for the expression of preferences about clearly defined national policy alternatives is not an accident of history or the inevitable result of the technological imperatives of large-scale industrial and political organization or the ineluctable consequence of the differentiation of the mass electorate. Turning the potentially democratic instruments of party and parliament into a means of consensus formation rather than policy making has been the result of a series of strategic choices by dominant elites and a mechanism for maintaining basic class relations intact.[8] If this is the case—and the question is by no means settled—then social and political movements capable of both understanding and action may still arise to define and create alternative modes of social, economic, and political organization. Critical analysis of paradigms of state-society relations may contribute something to that understanding.

Notes

1. With this qualification, I can give examples of some of the theoretical or empirical works that represent one or another paradigm: *Pluralist*—S.M. Lipset, *Agrarian Socialism: The Cooperative Commonwealth Federation*

in Saskatchewan; A Study in Political Sociology (Berkeley: University of California Press, 1950); Robert A. Dahl, *Who Governs? Democracy and Power in an American City* (New Haven: Yale University Press, 1961); Arnold M. Rose, *The Power Structure: Political Process in American Society* (New York: Oxford University Press, 1967); *Elite*—C. Wright Mills, *The Power Elite* (New York: Oxford University Press, 1956); John Kenneth Galbraith, *The New Industrial State* (Boston: Houghton Mifflin, 1967); *Class*—Paul A. Baran, *The Political Economy of Growth* (New York: Modern Reader Paperbacks, 1957); Floyd Hunter, *Community Power Structure: A Study of Decision Makers* (Chapel Hill: University of North Carolina Press, 1953). Attempts at synthesis that basically start from one or another paradigm include the following: *Pluralist*—Samuel P. Huntington, *Political Order in Changing Societies* (New Haven: Yale University Press, 1968); *Elite*—Ralf Dahrendorf, *Class and Class Conflict in Industrial Society* (Stanford, California: Stanford University Press, 1959); *Class*—James O'Connor, *The Fiscal Crisis of the State* (New York: St. Martin's Press, 1973); Claus Offe, "Political Authority and Class Structures: An Analysis of Late Capitalist Societies," *International Journal of Sociology* 2 (Spring 1972), pp. 73-108. Ralph Miliband's *The State in Capitalist Society* (New York: Basic Books, 1969), and G. William Domhoff's *The Higher Circles: The Governing Class in America* (New York: Random House, 1970) are interesting fusions of elite and class assumptions explicitly critical of pluralism from both other viewpoints. For reasons of space no detailed references are given in this Chapter, nor should it be assumed that every work mentioned above includes every aspect of the paradigm to which it is closest.

2. For an article making similar distinctions, see Milton Mankoff, "Power in Advanced Capitalist Society: A Review Essay on Recent Elitist and Marxist Criticism of Pluralist Theory," *Social Problems* 17 (Winter 1970), pp. 418-30.

3. See George Orwell, "Politics and the English Language," *A Collection of Essays* (Garden City, New York: Doubleday Anchor Books, 1954), pp. 162-77.

4. See Murray Edelman, *The Symbolic Uses of Politics* (Urbana: University of Illinois Press, 1964), and also his *Politics as Symbolic Action: Mass Arousal and Quiescence* (Chicago: Markham Publishing Company, 1971).

5. For a case study that applies this perspective to health care policy in the United States, see Robert R. Alford, *Health Care Politics: Ideological and Interest Group Barriers to Reform* (Chicago: University of Chicago Press, 1975).

6. Stein Rokkan, *Citizens, Elections, Parties* (New York: David McKay Company, 1970), pp. 41, 43.

7. For an expansion of this argument, see Robert R. Alford and Roger Friedland, "Nations, Parties, and Participation: A Critique of Political Sociology,"

Theory and Society 1 (Fall 1974), pp. 307-28, and by the same authors, "Political Participation," *Annual Review of Sociology*, vol. 1, 1975, forthcoming.

8. See Claus Offe, "Political Authority," for an elaboration of this point.

**Part II
Inequality Versus Opportunity**

Introduction to Part II
Colin Crouch

"Votes are more equally distributed than pound notes." This assertion, made by one of the participants in the Monterosso conference[a] during a discussion of the role of the state in the reduction of inequality, could well serve as the one abiding *credo* of social democracy. It expresses its abiding faith in the possibilities of parliamentary democracy under universal suffrage. It expresses the antagonism between polity and economy that was born with the political mobilization of the working class, replacing the earlier form of that antagonism between aristocracy and bourgeoisie. And at the same time it gives a hint of the historical debt owed by social democracy to liberal utilitarianism. Furthermore, the questions begged by the assertion are those begged by social democracy. With what confidence can it be assumed that the state will be responsive to "votes" rather than to the other, frequently conflicting, pressures imposed upon it, including those to maintain (rather than counter) the patterns of inequality established in the economic sphere? How likely is it in fact that votes, however equally distributed, will actually be used to demand the pursuit of equality?

In their different ways the three chapters included in this section present some of the substantial arguments behind these expressions of skepticism, though none of them challenges the fundamental claim that the political mechanism is likely to be more egalitarian than economic forces. To gain some perspective on the respective contributions of the chapters it is useful to establish a theoretical framework within which the interrelationship of the various forces involved may be analyzed.

The sources of inequality are many and various, but in industrial societies it is possible to trace many of them back to the fundamental inequalities that stem from the organization of work. The foundation of this lies in the scarcity of the material resources that men desire, their need in all societies to organize themselves in order to work to increase these resources and prepare them for consumption, and the tendency for these organizations to generate positions of domination and subordination that in turn imply conflicts of interest over both the organization of work and the distribution of its proceeds. In other words, the class relationship stands at the center of inequality; the distribution of material resources and positions in the crucial institution of occupational

---

[a]Michael Stewart, Reader in Political Economy, University College, London.

163

organization have wide implications, generating inequalities across the whole range of life chances and life styles.

The ideas of domination and subordination imply the dichotomous model that several theories of class adopt. However, the empirical form taken by this relationship leads to a far more complex array of concrete social positions. For example, the function of "domination" may be institutionally segregated into positions of ownership and control: Workers who are in some aspects of their work employees, or subordinates, may also fulfill delegated authority functions; and nearly all workers enjoy skills and degrees of experience that increase their scarcity value over and above that of the simple concept of subordinate labor power. This last is particularly important in that it not only erodes certain aspects of the unequal exchange, making the employer dependent on the skills of the worker, but it also produces multiple distinctions among subordinates. It was of course to the erosion of differences of this kind that Marx looked when envisaging a sharply defined class society. M. Weber, in attempting to produce a model of class that would deal with actually existing societies, added the possibility of classes being formed on the basis of these divisions among subordinates.[1] A. Giddens has suggested that this raises more problems than it solves, in that it does not define discretely distinguished classes in terms of a relationship.[2] His own approach is to demonstrate how the myriad social positions identified by Weber can be assimilated to a few broad bands by examining clusters of different positions thrown up by empirical correlates.[3] This leads him to seize on the crucial manual/nonmanual division. If such an approach is to be adopted it is very important to state accurately its relationship to the underlying relationship of domination and subordination. The classes Gliddens identifies are certainly "class related," in that they are defined in terms of the dominant/subordinate employment relationship; but the specific classes in his dichotomous model do not constitute classes in the sense that they identify social groups occupying the discrete polar positions of domination and subordination. The manual/nonmanual barrier is not the domination/subordination barrier, though many of the factors that support its importance are the product of different relations to the domination/subordination dimension.

This fallacy of the attempt to find a simple empirical manifestation of the analytically distinguishable dichotomous model is seen most clearly in the approach of F. Parkin, whose argument is in fact closely followed by Giddens.[4] Parkin fits the entire population of a society into a domination/subordination model corresponding to the nonmanual/manual division, to the extent that he is able to make without qualification such remarks as: ". . . the state effectively buttresses existing inequalities of reward in favour of the non-manual or dominant class."[5] However relevant the continuing disparities in conditions and hours of work between manual and nonmanual workers may be, it is difficult to accept an analysis that would apparently treat all clerical workers as members of a relatively undifferentiated politically dominant class. What these attempts

demonstrate is the imperfect fit of the class model to empirical societies, resulting from the characteristics mentioned above. If Weber's amendment to Marx's
model presents us with a myriad of social positions, then this may be because of
the social reality. The concept of class retains its relevance because it is possible
to relate many of these differences to the domination/subordination relationship,
not because it is possible to reduce all social positions to either of the two poles
of that relationship. And we must also be prepared to accept the existence of
positions whose rank in the hierarchy of inequality cannot be related to the class
relationship at all. Modified in this way, the concept of class remains a crucial
component in any analysis of inequality.

So far class inequalities have been considered in terms of their central sphere
of origin: economic relations. It is now necessary to relate this to politics and
the state. Economic domination is, analytically, a different power from that
possessed by the state, which is ultimately the power defined by the effective
monopoly of the legitimate use of the means of violence.[6] But evidently the
power of economic domination will be greatly strengthened if it is supported by
the state and the law. *Pari passu,* a dominant class would experience considerable
difficulty if the state were outrightly hostile to the particular mode of production
that secures its dominant position. (Such is, for example, the problem for capital-
sim under both communist and feudal states.) As a result therefore we should
expect to find in stable ongoing societies a high degree of consonance between
economic and political power, the latter consolidating and supporting the inequalities generated by the former. However, at the same time there are grounds for
expecting tension between the two, especially in societies with universal suffrage
and some degree of freedom within the political system.[7] The possibility is then
opened that forces other than those of economic power will be brought to bear
on the state. It is to this point that Weber was probably referring when he identified "party," or political organization as a potential form of stratification rivalling
that of class.[8] And it is of course the point to which our original contrast between
the power base of "votes" and that of "pound notes" refers. Whether in any particular action the state can be seen as buttressing economic domination, or in
contrast as acting as a countervailing power to it, must be a matter for research.
It is in fact an area to which all three of the chapters in part II are relevant.

The third dimension of inequality, that of ideology, contributes to the
maintenance of domination, not through the imposition of material constraints
on subordinate groups as in the two former spheres, but through its effect on the
subjective orientation of subordinates themselves. If subordinates accept the
essential rightness of their position, or have very low expectations so that they
do not question it, or do not perceive their situation as being one of subsubor-
dination, the problem of the need for external constraints will not arise. This
has been a theme of several theories of domination. In Marxist terms ideology
concerns the generation of ideas supportive in a very general and total way of
the whole order of social relations that incorporates the position of a dominant

class.[9] More specifically, the Weberian concept of legitimation may be considered
to refer to a similar process: to the patterns of ideas that justify an authority to
those who are subject to it.[10] Ideology may also define certain social positions as
carrying intrinsic entitlements to recognition of superiority, or to the enjoyment
of certain standards of life; and by the same token other positions will be defined
in terms of negative entitlements. In this way the concepts of ideology and authority legitimation become closely related to the idea of social status. The crucial
intervening concept that relates them is deference, for it is deference that distin-
quishes authority relations from other social relations, and that marks the boundaries between subjectively defined and hierarchically ordered statuses.[13]

But again, as with the relationship between political and economic resources,
although class and status are clearly closely related, they may well not coincide,
and it was of course in order to draw attention to this possibility that Weber
developed the concept of status and distinguished it from class in the first place.[12]
The complex interrelation between them is therefore a further question for empirical investigation. Finally, on this point an important historical change needs to
be noted. Weber developed the status concept with special reference to the continuing prestige of the old landed aristocracy, and there is a contrast between the
nature of status and legitimation in traditional societies in which dominant elites
laid claim to a generally exalted position, which was at times legally prescribed,
and modern industrial societies where elites seek only a specifically and institutionally defined deference. In some ways modern status groups are but a pale
shadow of the stronger medieval concept of estates. Several factors are related
to this, including the declining importance of religion as a source of legitimation,
and its replacement by the prosiac and challengeable claims of rationality. At
times, indeed, modern elites seem to seek a justification for their work, not by
proudly proclaiming their superiority as did traditional elites, but by denying
their own existence.[13] The nature of legitimation therefore changes, and status
in the true sense may not always be encountered; but the question of the subjective perceptions of intrinsic entitlements to enjoy inequalities, and their relation to concrete economic patterns will always be an issue.

Patterns of Inequality

The study of inequality and changes in its patterns may be defined in terms
of the above framework: What patterns of inequality are generated within each
of the three spheres—economic, political, ideological—and how do they relate to
one another? Within capitalist societies an important starting point historically
has been the firm institutional segregation between the three spheres: A strict
distinction was drawn between polity and economy, and questions of value were
considered irrelevant to the determination of material inequalities, which were
seen as the rational and impersonal product of the laws of the market. This does

not mean that the three spheres were unrelated: The state underpinned and guaranteed the operation of the market and the acquisition of private property through a framework of law; and the idea of the rationality of the market was itself an ideology.[14] The process can be seen as one of differentiation and reintegration, but the fact of institutional reparation did imply a relative looseness that left scope for the generation of antagonisms between the different spheres; for example, the attempt to use the state to regulate economic power and the development of an ideological critique of capitalism. In some ways the process of institutional segregation has continued, so that by the early 1960s it was possible to see it as one of the main factors reducing the level of tension in class relations.[15] However, at the same time it is possible to identify the very opposite processes: a reintegration of political, ideological, and economic spheres of society, occurring at different points from the process of separation. At the present time, in the wake of the renewal of a series of economic and political crises in most advanced Western societies, it is this process that seems most significant. Each of the chapters included here can be seen as dealing with some aspect of this reintegration, and in particular with the question of its likely implications for the structure of inequality.

Manuel Castells tackles an area widely thought to be the very center of a previous triumph of egalitarian politics over market inequalities: collective, usually publicly provided, consumption. But he contends that in fact market inequalities reproduce themselves in the allocation of collective resources, and that elsewhere new criteria of inequality are generated by the administrative process of regulating access to them. Perhaps the most telling of his arguments is where he shows how the role assigned to collective provision, far from challenging the market economy, actually strengthens it in two paradoxical respects. First, it takes on tasks that the market is unable to perform but that capitalism needs for its own operation, such as the provision of a reasonably healthy, educated work force able to live in and travel from the great urban concentrations generated by the large scale of modern economic organization. But second, the very fact that collective, public provision takes care of the difficult, less attractive, unprofitable tasks means that is becomes associated with inefficiency, mean services, and sometimes stigma. By contrast the private sector is able to present itself as efficient, comfortable, and luxurious. Thus, capital feeds on collective provision and then benefits from the adverse character which that provision thereby acquires. Castells illustrates this in detail with examples from housing and transport, but other examples could also be chosen, such as nationalized industries, the contrast between state and private education, and state private health and insurance services.

But his chapter also opens some issues to be resolved by future debate. Castells relates all the phenomena he describes to the nature of modern capitalism. This gives him some difficulties when he confronts the problem that urban patterns similar to those he describes can be observed in Eastern Europe, a phenomenon that leads him to warn against generalizations of a no more sweeping kind than those that he himself applies to capitalist societies. The problem is in fact less severe for those who, unlike Castells, do not treat Eastern European societies as "societies in transition," but as patterns of economic domiation that incorporate a different interrelationship between political and economic forces than capitalism, but that nevertheless constitute patterns of domination and inequality, hence in which urban inequalities of a similar kind may be found.

At the same time one may wish to question the universal application of a class analysis. Certainly, the inequalities of class relations may be seen at work affecting collective consumption as Castells describes, but does the evidence really justify the attribution to class of the simple determining role that is ascribed to it? Following the less deterministic approach to class outlined in this introduction one seeks a more thorough demonstration that all the processes affecting urban change are in fact those of class. Similarly, bearing in mind the scope for countervailing power and the complex nature of the interrelationship between polity and economy that has been outlined here, one would like to see at least some consideration given to these possibilities in the analysis. Castells acknowledges the role of popular pressure as one of the factors affecting the operation of the modern state, and at the end he points to the recent emergence of urban conflict in several countries. But more attention could be given to the extent to which the current pattern of collective provision is an outcome of a compromise of forces. After all, as is implied in the quotation at the start of this introduction, the attempt to use politically established forms of collective consumption as a counter to economic inequalities has been the central battleground between established Left and Right in most Western countries for many years. Castells' chapter is valuable in reminding us of the naivety of seeing the issue solely in these terms, but it would be better still to see the complex and shifting interplay between the rival forces.

The two other chapters consider the growing realignment of all three spheres of social relations identified above: economic, political, and ideological. Martin Rein and Peter Marris describe how decisions about income, still often seen by many interpreters in terms of economic theory alone, have not only become politicized, but also, as a further consequence of that development, have become directly implicated in debates over justice and equity. The factors leading to this development are not all recent. In practice it has never been possible to persuade people to treat their incomes as the impersonal results of an objective economic process; in particular, considerations of status have been important in the role of "comparability." And the process described by Rein and Marris whereby pay decisions have become increasingly *administered* rather than market-determined dates back to the growth of large-scale managerial enterprise. But the more recent massive growth in political intervention associated with economic crises has considerably intensified these developments.

As with Castells' chapter, one does not need assumptions of socialist or egalitarian intent to account for this increasing politicization of and introduction of "ethical" criteria into pay determination. Primarily the state intervenes to assert an order that, in conditions of full employment, the economic system can no longer provide for itself. But in doing this the state needs consent at a series of levels; it cannot operate through coercion alone. It therefore makes heavy use of moral exhortation, and it is at this point that the questions of fairness, including those of equality, which Rein and Marris consider, necessarily become involved. Status criteria are able to assert their demands on the administrative and political process when they conflict with the results of simple market processes, and the occassional introduction of egalitarian pressures completes a complex triangular conflict.

Somewhat underemphasised in the chapter is an important point that perhaps strikes more directly at the structure of inequality within the occupational structure itself than any of the arguments in this or the other chapters. Quoting John Goldthorpe, Rein and Marris refer to the possibility under certain kinds of incomes policy of "restructuring the entire occupational dimension of labour." In other words, given the steep involvement of the state in both pay determination and the acquisition of vocational qualifications, and making certain assumptions about the strength of egalitarian pressures on the state, it is possible to envisage policies aimed at eroding the very differences in skill levels and relations of domination, which constitute the mainstay of inequalities among the occupied population, as noted in the theoretical discussion earlier in this introduction. To what extent are the particular skill demarcations of particular occupations strictly necessary to the performance of the task, and to what extent do they simply establish the labor-market position of a group? How necessary are existing hierarchies of authority, involving as they do the exclusion of most workers from decision making in their work? To what extent could the apparent scarcities of skills produced by educational and training systems be eroded by changes in educational policy (as occurred historically, for example, as the spread of universal literacy undermined the priveleged positions of clerical workers)? So far questions of this kind have been directed against one form of occupational privelege alone: that of the skilled manual crafts. This can have only minor implications for overall inequality. But if similar questions were directed at professional and managerial occupations throughout the hierarchy the implications could be radical indeed.

Several of the points raised by Rein and Marris are also discussed in my chapter, but my main focus is elsewhere. Whereas Rein and Marris concentrate on the state and its problems, I examine the possibility of an egalitarian mass movement emerging to take advantage of the opportunities presented by the

increasing politicization of economic affairs. Again the point of departure
is the conflation of economic, political, and ideological dimensions. It may
be objected that the chapter lays down unnecessarily severe conditions for
the generation of such a movement, assuming that it would be dependent
on a large-scale development of egalitarian perspectives among ordinary people. In this the chapter follows the current preoccupation of British sociology with questions of workers' subjective perceptions, but perhaps these
are not so important. Perhaps one should look more at the likely objective
consequences of the fact of widespread industrial militancy as a form of
political pressure on governments and industry, irrespective of the views
that happen to be held by the rank-and-file participants in that militancy.
One of the interesting features of the current resurgence of industrial conflict in various European countries is that it is not necessarily distinctively
new or more ambitious demands by workers that create the crisis; familiar
demands for a stable, slightly growing standard of life acquire radical political implications because of the changed economic circumstances within
which they arise. Just as when studying the role of the state it is essential
to look behind the expressed statements of intent and motivation, so one
should examine the objective implications rather than the subjective intent
of workers' actions. Some attention is given to these possibilities in the
chapter, but they are perhaps underemphasized.

A further question raised by my account is whether the phenomena
I described are general or subject to cultural variation. My evidence is
drawn exclusively from Britian. Is the particularism that I describe peculiar to the British, or at the most only some, working classes, or is it more
general? In particular it would be interesting to compare the British evidence with that from France and Italy where, on the face of it, workers
have a more strongly developed sense of overall class identity and are more
readily mobilized for specifically political causes.[16] Indeed, the very act
of union membership in those and some other countries involves an apparent
ideological choice. Is it the case that some societies—perhaps those with
Catholic and communist backgrounds—generate more universalistic mass
cultures, whether of the allegiant or the oppositional kind, than do certain
others? On the other hand it may be that the distinction between "official"
and "concrete" value systems also operates in these societies, intervening
between the frequently expressed statements of political identity and the
perspectives that govern everyday life. This is an area in which there are
several existing studies, if with conflicting conclusions, but it would be interesting to know more about changes that may have occurred with the recent
resurgence of conflict and attempts at increasing the political integration
of the working class. In particular, can one identify in any of the countries
concerned the emergence of new popular egalitarian ideologies, and how do
these relate to the previously existing situation?

Future Research

The chapters collected here cover just a few, albeit central, issues in the debate over inequality. By setting them in the wider context of the changes taking place in the role of the state and the breakdown of the institutional segregation of the political, the economic, and the ideological, one becomes aware of some of the areas in which further detailed research would be valuable. These have been mentioned at certain points in the previous discussion. In conclusion these will be summarized.

1. Emerging from all three chapters, but most explicitly from that of Castells, it is important to test certain thesis concerning the changing role of the state, to replace the postwar thesis of the welfare state as democratic socialism's challenge to the laissez-faire economy. From Castells's own work emerges the argument that the state's function is to take on those tasks that capitalism needs to have performed, but that it is unwilling to tackle itself. In other words, the reengagement of state and economy leads to a new division of labor in which the state takes on capitalism's "dirty work"—carrying on unprofitable, inefficient, unglamorous tasks, controlling the labor force, providing the infrastructure. Against this can be set the rival thesis (elements of which can be seen in Rein's and Marris' chapter and to a certain (extent in mine) that the same reengagement renders certain economic processes (such as pay determination) vulnerable to political action for the first time; and that this, returning to the "votes and pound notes" hypothesis, has egalitarian possibilities. One can envisage a range of studies of the welfare state, of incomes policy, of state economic planning, of the policies of nationalized industries, in which these rival arguments could be applied to empirical data.

2. In all the chapters one can read the message that the egalitarian possibilities of political action are limited given the nature of the labor market. However, as noted in the discussion of Rein's and Marris' chapter, the state is now involved in several areas relevant to the nature of the labor market: incomes policy, vocational eduation, training and retraining programs, the professions. What in practice are the possibilities of systematic action to affect the supply side of the labor market, reexamining the nature of skills and the means of making more universal their acquisition? Relevant here would be studies of the nature of qualifications and occupational skills and educational studies. These are fields in which literature exists, but it rarely covers this perspective, being limited to existing managerial needs for work study and job evaluation.

3. At the end of Castells' chapter he hints at distinctive protest movements that emerge to counter the urban inequalities he describes. My chapter is also concerned with the scope of mass movements countering the changing patterns of politico-economic power. Are there yet common

themes in these disparate points of opposition? Is it possible to discern distinctive ideologies that contest the new forms of domination? Within the new configurations of political, economic, and ideological involvement, are popular pressures yet striking at new points?

The democratization of industrial societies that has occurred so far has been curiously lop-sided. At a few points there have been major breakthroughs: political citizenship (primarily universal suffrage); the decline of traditional ideologies of deference that legitimated the positions of old elites; and most impressive of all the enormous increase in mass prosperity, accompanied by an acceptance of the countervailing power of organized labor within industry. But each of these developments can be characterized as *passive* democracy. The most successful aspect of political citizenship has been the periodic exercise of the right of suffrage within carefully managed and controlled election campaigns that are carried on rather like advertisement campaigns. The more active levels of political participation—pressure-group activity, the direct wielding of political influence, personal participation, even the acquisition of detailed knowledge about politics—continue to be marked by considerable, class-based inequalities. The erosion of deference to established elites has not been succeeded by the widespread development of radical popular ideologies, but by an atomised instrumentalism of the kind described in my chapter. Passivity also characterises the form taken by mass prosperity. It has primarily been an extension in the power to consume, and to consume within markets that are increasingly managed and oligopolistic. Mass wealth has not led to a "property-owning democracy" in the sense of large numbers of people wielding some form of power of ownership. To the extent that the masses participate in industrial investment they do so through insurance schemes, unit trusts, banks and similar institutions that appropriate for themselves the decision-making power that once accompanied the ownership of the wealth itself. Finally, while labor's organizations have been associated with the growth of prosperity they have tended simply to pursue further increases in purchasing power rather than a share in power and decision making.

Further research would be needed to substantiate this contention of the passive nature of existing forms of democracy; but what would be more interesting at the present time would be studies of the extent to which, if at all, this is changing. Are contemporary forms of protest and countervailing power continuing in the same patterns or are they trying to move towards more active forms of power?

Notes

1. M. Weber, "Class, Status and Party," in H.H. Gerth and C.W. Mills, *From Max Weber: Essays in Sociology* (Oxford: Oxford University Press, 1946).

2. A. Giddens, *The Class Structure of the Advanced Societies* (London: Hutchinson, 1973) pp. 78-80.
3. Ibid., ch. 10.
4. Frank Parkin, *Class, Inequality and Political Order* (New York: Praeger, 1971) ch. 1.
5. Ibid., p. 28.
6. M. Weber, "Politics as a Vocation," in Gerth and Mills, *From Max Weber.*
7. The clearest expression of this position is in T.H. Marshall, *Class, Citizenship and Social Class* (Westport, Conn.: Greenwood 1973).
8. M. Weber, "Class, Status and Party," reprint of 1964 ed.
9. K. Marx, "The German Ideology" in C.J. Arthur, ed., *German Ideology, Pt. 1 & Selections from Pts. 2 & 3* (New York: International Pubs. Co., 1970).
10. M. Weber, "Politics as a Vocation."
11. E. Shils, "Deference," in John A. Jackson (ed.), *Social Stratification* (Cambridge: Cambridge University Press, 1968).
12. M. Weber, "Class, Status and Party."
13. C.W. Mills discussed this possibility in *The Power Elite* (Oxford: Oxford University Press, 1959).
14. N. Poulantzas, *Political Power and Social Classes* (London, New Left Books and Sheed and Ward, 1970).
15. These ideas were developed in, for example, R. Dahrendorf, *Class and Class Conflict in Industrial Society* (London: Routledge and Kegan Paul, 1973).
16. For a useful survey of British, North American, and European sources, see M. Mann, *Consciousness and Action among the Western Working Class* (London: MacMillan, 1973).

7 Advanced Capitalism, Collective Consumption, and Urban Contradictions: New Sources of Inequality and New Models for Change
Manuel Castells

Social inequality is the most obvious expression of any class society insofar as the place occupied in the system of production determines the distribution of the product among social groups. For, from the moment that we deny the entire identification between the system of social stratification (related to the economic and symbolic distribution of the product) and the system of social classes (based on the system of production and, hence, on the power relationships between the classes), and make the former depend on the latter, it becomes necessary to spell out the specific form of this social inequality according to the phases of a mode of production and the historical formation of a social system. Thus, the history of eternal disparity between the rich and the poor, based on a fatalism with perfect results for the dominant classes, gives way to the precise analysis of the social production of differentiation at the level of consumption and to the study of the basic logic of a certain type of social relations that are experienced in the form of oppressive daily life.

From this point of view, in advanced capitalist societies one begins to perceive the importance of new forms of social differentiation and new contradictions upon which they are based, particularly on the economic level, in the still poorly defined domain of "collective consumption", often expressed in terms of the "urban problem." Indeed, insofar as the indirect salary (i.e., the salary coming not directly from the employer but in the form of general social allowances) increases in importance, both relatively and absolutely, and at the same time as the conditions of life for the individual become objectively interdependent by socialization and technological concentration (both economic and organizational) of production and consumption, it seems that the traditional inequality in terms of incomes, which is inherent in capitalism, is expressed in new social cleavages related to the accessibility and use of certain collective services, from housing conditions, through the type and level of health, educational, or cultural facilities, to working hours. This appears all the more paradoxical in that in many countries collective services are reputed to be administered by the state, with priority given to the social interest they represent rather than to their profitability from invested capital. But our hypothesis is precisely that, apart from the superiority granted by the highest levels of income (including housing and collective services), there is a new source of inequality inherent in the very use of these collective goods that have become a fundamental part of the daily consumption pattern.

These problems are treated as urban problems to the extent that residential

175

agglomerations constitute the units of collective consumption and that their management is directly allied to the organization and management of the various collective holdings. Urban organization is not then a simple arrangement of spatial forms, but rather these forms are the expression of the process of collective treatment of the daily consumption patterns of households.[1] This is why the "crisis of the cities" is profoundly felt, for rather than deterioration of the environment the deterioration of the quality of life itself is involved, not so much of the physical surroundings but of the way of living, of the very meaning of life.[2]

This said, to go beyond a description of events and attempt to reach the structural tendencies susceptible to more precise investigation we must take the question in reverse, not starting from expressions of inequality but from the evolution of advanced capitalism and the new position occupied by the goods of collective consumption in this evolution. It is only after this that we will be in a position to explain some of the instances of structural disparity between the users of such services.[a]

The Strategic Role of Collective Consumption in Advanced Capitalist Economies

The transformation of consumption in advanced capitalism is directly determined by the long-term structural tendencies upon which it is based: to wit, the concentration and centralization of capital and its constant battle against the tendency toward a lower rate of profit, the socialization of the forces of production, the development of the class struggle and the growing power of the workers' movement that extends its bargaining power to all areas of societal life, finally and above all, to the massive and decisive intervention of the state into the totality of economic activity.[3]

Indeed, the search for new markets for capital is not achieved simply by the penetration of capital into countries under imperialist domination, but by its penetration in precapitalist or archeo-capitalist sectors of the economy of "metropolitan" countries, by dissolving the social and economic relationships

---

[a]The analyses presented here will not be supported by statistical data but only by some bibliographical references showing a certain amount of generally known social facts; we accept from the start a certain *schematism* in this text: Such is the price we must pay to sort out the grand tendencies of social evolution, to reach beyond the nuances connected with particular historical situations.

Besides, the problems evoked here are too vast and too unknown for one to be as affirmative from a scientific point of view as we have been for the sake of clarity in our text. The attempt here is above all to present a certain number of ideas and hypotheses that can only be truly clarified by a series of concrete systematic analyses. It is hoped that these will have been made possible by the presentation of the general perspectives to which we address ourselves here.

that exist there. Such is the case specifically in the sector of the production of means of consumption for the popular classes, a sector until recently differing from country to country, and largely dominated by nonmonopolistic capital.[4]

On the other hand, the class struggle and the growing bargaining power of the worker and popular movement imposes a certain level of consumption and changes the historical definition of need, both qualitatively and quantitatively.[5] So much the more so in that it is relatively easier for the dominant classes to cede to popular demands in the domain of consumption than it is at the level of production or in matters concerning political power.

Finally, technical progress produces several important effects in matters of consumption: It raises the capacity for response to the demands for consumption, thus permitting its expansion; at the same time it necessitates, on the one hand, the convergence of this consumption with the reproduction of a labor force that has been rendered specific and noninterchangeable for specialized positions; on the other hand, for the large mass of the nonspecialized labor force, the socialization and interdependence of production determined by technological progress requires the smooth functioning of the conditions of collective reproduction of the labor force (thus, for example, a specialized worker can be replaced easily, but it is important that transportation assure manpower mobility such that several million workers can be simultaneously on time at their jobs). In fact, the more important constant capital becomes in its size and in relation to the labor force, the more essential its smooth functioning becomes in rendering cybernetic the most unpredictable element of the productive process, that is, the work force.[6]

Thus, we arrive at the phenomenon called *mass consumption,* that is, the fundamental importance of household consumption, both for making use of accumulated capital and for the smooth functioning of the productive process, even when the production and distribution of these consumer goods is concentrated and achieved on a grand scale and when the ensemble of the sector is subject to the special interests of monopolistic capital. This latter aspect is the basis for the principal contradiction between the increasingly collective and interdependent character of the process of consumption and its domination by the interests of private capital.[7]

Such a contradiction not only conditions consumption, reinforcing the use of certain products (through advertising, styles, etc.) and determining the lifestyles of people as a function of the greatest profit from capital investment in such-and-such a type of product; but above all, it provokes lacunae in vast areas of consumption that are essential to individuals and to economic activity. Such is the case, for example, in housing, sociocultural facilities, collective transportation, etc.; that is, the whole sector that the economists call "collective goods" and that are characterized (in terms of liberal economics) by the fact that they do not meet the price of the market, that they are not governed directly by supply and demand. Manifestly, this characteristic does not depend on the type of product (the production of housing is not more or less collective, in itself, than the production of automobiles), but on the type of capital invested that is determined in the last instance by the relation between the rate of profit of the productive arm and the average rate of profit in each branch. Thus, we will see, for example, certain goods (housing itself) fluctuating from one category of consumption to another as a function of the capital cycle and the supply created by demand.[8]

It is at this point that the intervention of the state becomes necessary to take charge of the sectors and services that are noncompetitive (from the point of view of capital) but necessary for the functioning of economic activity and/or the appeasement of social conflicts.[9] Such is the history, repeated in all countries, of public housing,[10] but such is also the case for other types of consumption that are less explicitly public (for example, certain sports, "art cinema," etc.).[11]

This intervention of the state is functional and necessary to the monopolies, even though it is often done in opposition to some capitalist interests. In effect, it assures the necessary reproduction of the working force at a minimum level, it lessens the cost of direct salaries (for example, the effect of rent ceilings to combat high salaries), at the same time easing demands. Besides, public investment, as we know, is an essential form of "devaluation of social capital,"[12] the principal recourse for counteracting the tendency toward a lowering of the profit margin. By investing "at a loss," the general rate of profit of the private sector holds steady or increases in spite of the lowering of profit relative to social capital as a whole. In this sense social expenditures of the state not only thus favor big capital, but they are also indispensable to the survival of the system.

This said, the intervention of the state in the production and administration of a collective good is not permanent or "normalized" in the functioning of the economy. It is always done in articulation with private capital, be it in making a sector competitive and in transferring it afterward to the private sector, or be it in assuring a continuous interlacing where the intervention of the state covers the functional or economic "holes" making it possible for private capital to take over (thus the public highway infrastructure that makes use of the automobile possible, or urban renewal operations that permit the actions of private promoters, etc.).

The massive intervention of the state in the organization of collective consumption has specific and decisive effects on this, for if the state intervenes in the economy on the part of the interests of the monopolies, one cannot forget, on the one hand, that it acts in the interests of the ensemble of the capitalist system and not only as a servant for a given group, and, on the other hand, that it has, above all, a logical *political* apparatus and that each intervention, even economic, will be marked by that.[13] This double relative autonomy of the state, both in the interests represented and in the accomplished function, has two

principal effects on the process of collective consumption and on the urban
organization that flows from it: (1) It maximizes the *regulation* function of
the state, which will be expressed specifically through the process of *planning,*
under the double aspect of a technical rationality and calculations in terms of
social interests; and (2) it *politicizes* the urban question in that the state is the
principle responsible agent, which is to say, on the one hand, that collective
consumption will be put directly into politico-ideological competition rather
than treated in economic terms, and on the other hand, that the demands called
urban will be strongly articulated towards the question of power.[14] Besides, the
systematic intervention of the state in the domain of collective consumption
takes on decisive importance in the current phase of capitalism characterized by
the internationalization of capital[15] and, at the level of the daily functioning of
the economy, by structural inflation that results from the specific intervention
of the multinational firms. In fact, for floating capital the assumption by the
national state of responsibility for the hidden expenses of production becomes
even more advantageous. Able to play on interstate competition, dependent
on the good will of private investment, the multinational firms shift the responsibility for infrastructures onto different local or national authorities. This
mechanism is well known when it concerns recourse to national credit, which
has permitted American enterprises to become implanted in Europe by borrow-
ing from private and *public* European banks. But although this aspect is little
studied, it functions still more clearly with collective goods, all the more so
since multinational firms (because "apatriated") can be less mindful of the
social consequences of neglecting the needs of the population.

Another phenomenon, namely, "growth within inflation,"[16] entails still
more important consequences for collective goods. Inflation, as we know:
(a) hits the least favored categories of the population, and (b) encourages the
purchase of goods already on the market. Or, put in different words, inflation
makes people more consumption-oriented at the same time as it differentiates
them according to their capacity for consumption. In these conditions, two
problems, among others, must be resolved:[17] (1) avoiding important bottlenecks in the reproduction of the labor force, in particular for goods outside
the market or for which the sale is founded on long-term credit and that are
therefore made more valuable by monetary devaluation (housing among others),
and (2) preserving guaranteed savings capacity in order to have available at the
proper moment new complementary resources. Thus, it is necessary to assume
differential costs of reimbursement of stagnant money. In both cases public
intervention in collective consumption is essential: It attenuates the effects
of inflation for the economy as well as for social relations, while at the same
time it preserves the mechanism of monopolistic accumulation that is known
as inflation. In fact, it is clear that the financing of this intervention is achieved
by an increased burden of taxation that has a much greater relative effect on
the work force than on capital. Thus, the gains in salary obtained by social

struggles are not only obliterated by the rise in prices but counteracted by tax laws. Certainly buying power is increased by the combined effect of technical progress and economic growth, but the negative effects of consumption appear essentially at the level of collective goods that are profitable for private capital and that will be provided by the state and thus by the taxpayers. Then, one has only to blame problems on the negative aspects of urban growth, "ineluctable gangrene of industrial civilization," and the game is won, one can continue the epic of capitalist accumulation and develop individual buying power, all the while intensifying the contradiction between these grandiose perspectives and the historically dated reality of the standard of living and style of life of the populace. To close the circle, necessarily individualized, personalized in daily life, in case of "failure," there will always be a psychiatrist. Or a cop.

Let us then try to see the more concrete consequences of such an economic and social evolution of the relationship of social groups to collective consumption, limiting ourselves to a review of some examples as case studies of a general structural logic.

Class Structure, Urban Structure, and Collective Consumption: The Social Determinants of the New Inequality

The processes of collective consumption simultaneously express the growing contradiction between their objective socialization and their management as a function of the interests of capital, the contradictory exigencies of capital, the confrontation of the different factions of capital, and the confrontation between popular demands and the rationality of the dominant class to which the state necessarily subscribes.[18]

This group of contradictions forms the basis for new expressions of social inequality that derive from the importance of collective consumption in advanced capitalist societies.

Thus, in matters of *housing,* the primary inequality concerns the income level that conditions access to the type of housing market, but it does not stop there. It is extended by economic and social considerations at each step in the conferment of a property. And this from the point of view of housing as a product as much as of housing as a means of social expression, or, if you will, as much from the quantitative as from the qualitative point of view, aspects that are, anyway, closely related.[19]

Thus, the most common case in the United States, and a similar tendency is discernible in Western Europe, is for access to the bulk of the private housing market to depend essentially on the capacity to have access to credit. This itself is also a function of income level (excluding the highest strata) the stability and the predictability of income in the long term, or in the last analysis, on the possibility of a *career,* that is, a predictable succession of employment positions.[20]

In effect, lifetime indebtedness is the mechanism that permits the majority of
American families (and also Germans) to have access to ownership of their
suburban homes.[21] But the ability to predict employment is not only a function of occupational qualifications; it also depends on the situation of the business and position occupied within the enterprise. Thus it is that employment
within large organizations and the functionality of the position for the enterprise (and not for the productive process) establishes new cleavages. Still more,
it is clear that this stability is a direct function of politico-ideological integration
in the productive system and in the social hierarchy: One thus finds oneself
faced with this characteristic of the "new society"—the allocation of a certain
type of housing according to the level of social integration.[22] If it is true that
there has always been repression against "agitators," what is new is the size
of the phenomenon, made massive by the generalization of recourse to credit
as well as the refining of the repressive procedure that not only takes place via
the blacklist, but also via the systematic application of a banker's morality in
the routes of access to housing.[23]

But the specificity of these new inequalities in housing is even more clear
in housing called "social," that is, public or semipublic, that arises theoretically
from a logic of service and not from criteria of profitability. For, to consider
the public and the private as two autonomous economic spheres is to forget the
dominant structural logic. In fact, the intervention of the state is accomplished
within the limits of mobilizable resources, and besides, is distinguished by a
subordination to the interests of the monopolies in two ways: First, social
investments come only after direct aid to industrial enterprises has been effec-
tuated; second, the constant tendency is to make the sectors of public subsidi-
zation profitable in order to bring them into line with the criteria of private
capital so as to be able to transfer them gradually over to it.[24]

Thus access to public housing is limited by a whole series of criteria of
selection (ability to pay rent regularly, aptitude for maintenance, size of family,
etc.) that are also calculated on the private market even if they are put quantitatively at a lower level. Sources of inequality based on income, employment,
and education are thus reinforced once more in public housing.

But added to these economic cleavages are new criteria of selection dependent on the social and institutional organization of access to public housing.
Thus, the insertion into the system of social security, though it seems consistent, leaves aside a whole series of situations (youth, the unregistered unemployed, the unrecognized sick and handicapped, etc.) that we lump together
too quickly in a "marginal" category, whereas they are in each case the result
of a precise mechanism of social production.[25] Particularly revealing in this
sense is the practice of limiting access of immigrant workers to public housing
(in France they cannot be more than 6.75 percent whereas they are 30 percent
of the construction force): Equality in housing is thus skewed and the allocation of public housing is the occasion for new disparities.[26]

In the same way the ability to maneuver inside the bureaucratic network

of public assistance in order to win one's case is a socially determined cultural acquisition and the ability to "make it" is nothing other than the capacity for adaptation to a certain model of behavior prescribed by dominant
values.[27]

As a whole, these informal criteria for selection come from the very same
model that governs competition for public housing: It consists basically of a
concept of charity that could well be forgotten and that is addressed to "little
people."[28] At the extreme of this logic one finds formulas such as those represented in France by the "cités de transit," slums run by and, above all, controlled by, the outcasts of the poorly housed, where are assembled all those
who do not qualify under any criteria of selection (even if most of them are
regularly employed workers) and who are left "in transit" during several years,
sometimes as many as ten or fifteen.[29]

Besides, insofar as housing is not simply a means to "satisfy a need," but
is a social relationship, public housing as a formula for privileged intervention
of the state makes the style of life of these classes and income levels directly
dependent in an area where they ought to have an escape from the economic
and ideological direction of the dominant classes. Thus, for example, in France
the delay incurred in the years after the war, the popular demands and the
opportunity for a strong public voice instigated the policy of construction of
large housing projects from 1954 on. As emergency policy it was distinguished
by the basic choice to construct the maximum amount of housing as quickly
as possible for the lowest possible cost. The result, on the urban level, was the
construction of inexpensive property in the far suburbs, badly equipped and
poorly serviced, and the building of a series of large housing projects of poor
quality that were filled even before the installation of minimum household
equipment.[30] At the same time the image of collective public housing deteri-
orated because such undertakings were also generally associated with leftist
municipalities. In 1973 the policy of making housing competitive, of extension of the market toward the middle class, as well as renewed efforts toward
social integration through urban organization focused on the myth of the
suburban petit-bourgeois, led the government to legislate against the big housing projects as "negators of the individual." Can one do today what was not
possible in 1954? Let us say rather that the financial concentration of housing
has become sufficiently consolidated to undertake the rationalization and the
extension of a new housing market over the long run.[31] Public housing is used
in the same way in the United States, simultaneously as a response to urgent
need and as a starting gate to feed publicity for parcelling out suburban subdivision.[32]

Because of differential ability to gain access to the market, inequality in
housing is thus reinforced by the inequality that results from the differential
treatment of each class and social level by economic, institutional, and cultural
mechanisms of production and administration in public housing. Besides, each

of these classes and levels is thus submitted to specific forms of manipulation that accord with the competitive interests of the dominant class.[b]

A similar analysis can be developed concerning the system of communications and the organization of transportation in large metropolitan areas. In fact, at the root of the complexity and the importance of these intraurban transport systems, one finds the spatial separation of residence and place of work, urban concentration, and the daily rhythms of activity depending on a certain organization of work. We know that such phenomena are produced directly by specific forms of social and technical division of work in a period of monopolistic capital. It is not a matter here of any sort of technological determinism, but a real expression of a social relationship. In fact, technical progress is very often considered to be basic to the metropolis. Inspite of all the arguments that we will bring to bear on this point, the role played by technology in the transformation of urban models is indisputable. Influence is exerted at the same time by the introduction of new activities of consumption and production, and by the near elimination of the obstacle of space, due to an enormous development in the means of communication. At the time of the second industrial revolution the generalization of electrical energy and the utilization of the tramway permitted an increased concentration of manpower around more and more vast unities of production. Collective transport insured the integration of different zones and activities of the metropolis, dividing the internal fluctuations according to a tolerable time/space relationship. The automobile has contributed to urban dispersion, with enormous zones of individual residences extended over the whole region, connected by routes of rapid transit to various functional areas. The daily transport of products of current consumption benefit equally from such mobility; without the daily distribution by truck of agricultural products harvested or stored in the region, no large metropolis would be able to subsist. The concentration of business headquarters in certain regions, and the hierarchical decentralization of centers of production and distribution are possible because of the transmission of information by telegraph, radio, and Telex. Finally, the development of air navigation has been fundamental in reinforcing the interdependence of the various metropolitan regions.

Thus, technical progress permits, on the one hand, the evolution of urban configurations toward a regional system of interdependencies, due to intervening changes in the means of communication, and on the other hand, it reinforces this evolution directly by the transformations created by fundamental social activities, particularly as concerns production. Industry is more

---

[b]An extreme case is perhaps the construction of the large housing project of Grande-Borne in Grigny, near Paris, by the "official" architect of the French government, Emile Aillaud. He was commissioned to construct there, in the name of decor, petrified forms of his personal fantasies. Under the pretext of artistic creation, he has imposed on the life of several thousands of families who violéntly object to his personal psychic universe.

and more liberated from factors of rigid spatial localization, such as primary material or specific markets, whereas it is, on the contrary, more and more dependent on qualified manpower and a technical and industrial milieu that stretches across the chains of functional relationships already established. Thus, industry is looking above all for insertion in the urban system, rather than for localization in relation to the functional elements (primary materials, resources, outlets) that determined its placement in the first period.

At the same time the growing importance of administration and information, and the liaison of these two activities in the urban milieu, reverse the relations between industry and city, making the former depend more and more on the complex of relationships created by the latter. Thus, technological evolution (in particular the development of nuclear energy and the key role of electronics and chemistry) favors the spatial regrouping of activities, reinforcing internal ties to the "technical milieu" and diminishing dependence on the physical environment. It follows that development starts from extant urban-industrial cores and that activity becomes concentrated in the network of interdependencies thus organized.

Finally, changes in the construction industry have also permitted the concentration of functions, in particular functions of administration and exchange, in a reduced space accessible to all parts of the metropolis, thanks to high-rise construction. The prefab has been the basis for the mass construction of individual houses and, through that, for the phenomenon of residential diffusion.

Yet, the metropolitan region is not a necessary result of simple technical progress. For technical knowhow, far from constituting a simple factor, is only one element of the ensemble of productive forces, which themselves are primarily a social relationship, and thus also constitute a cultural mode of utilization of the work resources. This liaison between space and technology is thus the most immediate material manifestation of a profound articulation between the ensemble of a given social structure and the new urban configuration. Urban dispersion and the formation of metropolitan regions are closely allied to the social model of advanced capitalism, designated ideologically by the term "mass society."

In fact, the monopolistic concentration of capital and the technico-social evolution toward organization of very large unities of production are at the root of the spatial decentralization of functionally related establishments. The existence of big commercial firms, with standardization of products and prices, permits the diffusion of residences around shopping centers, easily connected by a system of rapid communications.

On the other hand, the standardization of a growing mass of the population (salaried workers) as concerns their position in the production hierarchy is accompanied by a diversification of levels and by hierarchisation within this category—which, in terms of space, gives rise to a real segregation in terms of status by separating and "labelling" the different residential sectors. Hence, they become a vast field of symbolic display.

The ideological integration of the working class in the dominant ideology goes along with the separation of the activities of work, residence and leisure, a separation that is at the root of functional metropolitan zoning. The value put on the nuclear family, the importance of the mass media, and the dominance of individualist ideology react in the direction of an atomization of relationships and a segmenting of interests in terms of individual aspirations, which, in terms of space, is translated into the dispersion of individual residences, be it in the isolation of the suburban home or the solitude of the big housing projects.

Finally, the growing concentration of political power, as well as the formation of a technocracy that assures that the long-run interests of the system gradually eliminate local characteristics and tends, through urban planning, to deal with the problems of the functioning of the ensemble from the beginning by cutting it up into significant spatial unities based on networks of interdependencies in the productive system. But this contributes to the regulation of the rhythm of the urban machine by the real functional unity that is the metropolitan region.

The metropolitan region as a central form of organization of the space of advanced capitalism diminishes the importance of physical environment in determination of the system of functional and social relationships, annuls the distinction between rural and urban, and places in the forefront the dynamic space/society, the historic meeting place of social relations that form its basis. We could address ourselves, eventually, to a major objection concerning this analysis of the production of the metropolitan region as a certain type of space derived from the logic of capitalism as a particular method of production and capitalism in a specific stage, that is, monopolistic capitalism. Are there not socialist countries in which analagous urban forms develop? Then how can one deny that these are the product of a certain level of technological-economic development, independent of the principles of social organization? Well, first of all, one must avoid approaching these problems from a capitalist/socialist dichotomy that is not a theoretical category but a historic pseudo-globalization that confuses and combines very diverse social processes. We do not use the term capitalism to describe a historical reality that would be immutable and directly determined by profit in all social occurrences. We make reference rather to a particular social matrix, economic, political, and ideological, which is determined in the last analysis by an organization of social relationships founded on the separation of the worker from the means of production and on the appropriation of the surplus value by the only holders of the means of production. In posing thus as a point of departure for the analysis the determination of social organization by capital, we have not said all there is to say. But we have said something essential because we can start from a specific hypothesis concerning the logic and the contradictions inherent in a certain type of urban organization. It is this that we have outlined in our analysis of the metropolitan region, it is this that tends to prove the ensemble of urban research we have cited throughout the text. If in the noncapitalist countries there are similar urban forms, that does not weaken the analyses we have made. Our analyses can only be discussed in relation to themselves, by referring to the methods that have been used to demonstrate that metropolitan configurations are derived from specific laws regarding the conversion of capitalist social relationships. In addition, such an observation allows us to pose a problem that could not be resolved except by means of specific research. The problem is that of knowing how there is reproduction of analagous social forms on the basis of different social relationships. The answer would require:

1. Determining if the content of these urban structures, their practice, and not only their spatial appearance is effectively the same
2. Seeing which is the concrete articulation of the different modes of production in each socialist society, for indisputably the capitalist mode of production is present there in varying degrees, in particular at the level of the division of labor logical to society in transition, if one does not assimilate a mode of production to a simple political regime[33]
3. Establishing the theoretical basis for analysis of a society in transition, for we do not yet have the equivalent of *Das Capital* by Marx for the societies in transition
4. Elaborating a theory of the determination of urban space by different types of articulation of the methods of production in a postcapitalist society of transition, and being thus in a position to explain, for example, why there is a strong urbanization in the USSR and disurbanization in China, or again, why the underurbanization in Hungary plays a very different role than that in Cuba.[34]

We see thus that we are facing a very different problem than that of opposing capitalism and socialism in general terms so as to unify them in the common semblance of some historically determined urban models. We proceed otherwise: We start from hypotheses concerning the structural arrangement of the laws of the capitalist mode of production in several phases and stages of development of this mode, and proceed to several levels (economic, political, ideological) in specific historical periods of which it is necessary to take account. It is not a matter thus of finding a moral responsibility for all social inequities, but of studying the validity and the transformation of the social laws that have been established up to this point by research, by specifying them and modifying them if new observations require. Thus, for example, the American model of the dominant class and middle class fleeing the city and leading to residential dispersion is in the process of being replaced in large European cities (but also

in the United States) by a model of a quasi-village community reserved to the
leading elite right in the heart of the big metropolis: Living in new modern
super-deluxe and self-sufficient buildings, built in the central city (very often
across from urban renewal projects), working in the headquarters of established
big businesses, and monopolizing the leisure activities and cultural opportunities
concentrated in the central city, everything happens as if the delocalization and
internationalization of capital is accompanied by a quasi-communitarian and
strongly localized closing off of the executive milieu for whom spatial mobility
then comes to mean primarily air travel.[35]

On the other hand, for the mass of employed workers, the tendency is
toward the growing spatial diffusion of activities, to the separation, more and
more strongly evident, between residence, work, recreation, shopping, etc.,
and thus to an increased daily dependence on the means of transportation. Such
a dependence sets up new cleavages and gives rise to new contradictions.[36]

The social predominance of the market, reinforced by the inevitable necessity for a collective response to the problem is found in transportation even more
clearly than in housing insofar as this differentiation is expressed very precisely
by the different methods of transport: the individual, taken in charge by the
market (even though partially, for automobiles need roads, generally public),
and the collective taken on, in general, by the public sector.[37] But what is specific to this differential treatment of transport is the fact that for a large part
of the population, there is a combined use of the two types; this produces
diverging effects, for on the one hand it generalizes the problems flowing from
the use of transport and on the other hand, it creates new cleavages according
to the combination that can be made of the use of the two methods by such
and such sector of the population.[38]

Each of these types of transport produces specific problems that come to
bear on equally specific social categories.

Thus, for *public transit,* the main problem is its extreme dependence on the
social function that has made it necessary, to wit, the daily travel from home to
work at hours and locations that are extremely *concentrated* for the large mass
of salaried workers, who have no possibility of arranging their time or space.
Consequently, in the same way as public housing develops at the minimum level
that is historically, socially, and economically possible to maintain, public
transit operates at a minimum level, that is, predominantly at the times we
call "rush hour." Thus, spatial mobility is worked out according to the time-
tables of the big organizations, even when the urban structure of the large metropolises makes autonomy of activity in the crowded zones or districts almost
impossible.[39]

This dependence on the timetable of collective transportation is reinforced
by dependence stemming from the routes of the transportation network, itself
also conceived according to the capacity to resolve certain problems of spatial distribution of place of work rather than the attempt to increase intraurban mobility.[40]

One manifest example is the route of the new Réseau Express Régional (RER) in Paris, designed to connect the new business center of La Défense (in the northwest periphery) to zones of heavy residential density of employees in the near southeast suburb, even when the growing difficulties of traffic in the suburbs require other priority measures (for example, the lengthening of various lines of the Paris metro towards the townships of the nearby suburbs).[41] The concrete result for the nearly ten million inhabitants of the Paris Region is to see the budget for public transport disappear in operations that increase mobility for only a special segment of the market of tertiary employment and only as concerns mobility for work.

Thus, collective transport becomes a synonym for discomfort, for congestion, for oppression, for compulsory timing, if not, as in the New York subway, for personal insecurity. Then one thinks only of escaping it, of autonomy, of the capacity for individual unrestrained mobility: The need is thus created and the market is there, ready to satisfy the demand of the consumer: It is the reign of the "car for individual freedom." And once the cycle is begun, it is impossible to stop it. Cities explode under the weight of a traffic pattern individualized to the point of being absurd; congestion is a constant menace;[42] this becomes the principle cause of air pollution;[43] massive investments in road-building equipment grow continually without even catching up with the problems created; traffic accidents become accepted as a necessary massacre, resulting in a growing number of physically handicapped people. Technically, socially, the reign of the individual automobile as a privileged means of transport in the big metropolitan areas is one of the greatest absurdities of our society. However, economically it is a necessity for the present structure of capitalism, ideologically an essential trump card for the development of the individualism and aggressiveness at the base of the dominant culture: Here we have a concrete expression of what is called the contradiction between the forces of production and the relationships of production.

Nevertheless, the big automotive firms and the oil trusts have nothing to fear: The demand for cars, both in quantity and in quality, has continued to increase over the years and in spite of the oil crisis does not seem to be seriously threatened in the long run. It seems clear that in the present state of urban organization, in the situation predominating in public transit, in the framework of capitalist social relationships, it cannot be otherwise. The automobile, outstanding social absurdity, is at the same time one of the strongest social demands as a mythical means for individual autonomy.

And this need for the automobile as a means for mobility made necessary by urban organization and by the way common transport is managed is in turn a new source of inequality: on the one hand, because the level of income thus comes to order the capacity for mobility and individual security, depending on the quality of the vehicle used and the physical and psychological mastery of its operation (also socially conditioned); and on the other hand, because this extreme dependence on the automobile creates new sources of discrimination: All nondrivers are seen as virtually handicapped, even more impaired in that intraurban transportation is based on individual means. Such is the case for the aged, for adolescents, for housewives when the husband has gone to work in the car, for the sick, but also for the great segment of the population not equipped with a car: One forgets (beclouded by an American image) that almost one French family in two does not possess an automobile. So many groups stuck in the underequipped residences, so many immobile people destined to consume little else but television, so many "living dead," and so many future buyers (or thieves) of individual automobiles. Such are the everyday forms of oppression and social disparity in advanced capitalism.[44]

A New Historical Model of Urbanization

Such analyses, even though rough and schematic, could be extended to other domaines, for example that of educational facilities[45] or sociocultural ones.[46] But even more significant is the generation of new social constraints by the very type of urban structure that unifies and organizes the whole process of collective consumption.[47]

In fact, the big metropolitan areas characteristic of advanced capitalism represent a type of city qualitatively different from the city of capitalist industrialization:

First, the different elements of the basic urban system are strictly connected and interdependent. Thus, for example, transportation and the localization of its activities, equipment and housing, the center and the symbolic signals, as well as each of the elements cited in relation to the others, form an indissoluble ensemble in constant interaction. It is not a matter of dealing with such and such an element of the collective consumption process, but with the process as a whole; there is no longer the possibility of organizing housing without intervening in transport or vice versa; there are no more "urban problems" but crises and contradictions of the urban system.

Second, the structure and the processes of this urban system are directly ordered by the logic of capital expressed in a specific way, that is, according to the dominant function transmitted to each urban system by capital in the collective consumption process (thus, a city controlled by heavy industry or a center of tourism will have its own forms of conformity to the logic of the capital that determines them). For what is important is that monopolistic capital in the present phase is itself caught in a pattern of interdependencies, simultaneously by economic sector and at the worldwide level, and that it responds to a logic of long-term profit. This in turn implies the objective necessity for the smooth functioning of the various units of production and consumption according to a logic not accessible to these units but answerable only to the process as a whole.

Third, the intervention of the state in the domain of collective consumption, and the economic and political importance of the centralized regulation of these processes, determine the taking in charge of the organization of the units of collective consumption. This is done by regulatory entreaties, more or less formalized, that correspond in general to the apparatus of urban planning. The metropolises of advanced capitalism thus are not only submitted to a rigid capitalist discipline, but then organized according to the very requirements of the state intervening in this domaine.

Such is the completely new urban model that we propose to call "Monopolville" (Monopol-City).[48]

The consequences for the consuming agents across such collective units are numerous and complex, but they can be summarized in three points:

1. Collective consumption and the routines of daily life that depend on it become extremely rigid, standardized, constrained. This is what we call the installation of veritable cadences in the area of consumption, similar to the cadences of production line work in a factory. The personal sensation of distraction and rush in life in the big cities is a concrete expression of this.

2. The ensemble of these problems appears as a coherent whole dominated by an implaccable logic. Monopolville is, in this sense, a completely totalitarian universe.

3. The supplier, the organizer, the interlocutor, the agent of central initiatives, appears to be the apparatus of the state. It globalizes and politicizes all the problems in making their collective treatment more necessary and visible, but, at the same time, in making their confrontation by the individual more difficult. The impression of powerlessness on the part of the isolated citizen is thus increased. As a totalitarian universe, imposing the daily cadence, ruled by the centralized power of a far-away machine, "Monopolville" exacerbates to the maximum its internal contradictions, destroys all protective mechanisms, causes continuous strain in daily life, to such a point that it becomes a fetish, a structure that oppresses by an ineluctable process. Such a process of alienation, in the classical sense of the term, reminds one of the making a fetish of money and the natural predominance of capital in the relationship of men to the production process. Still, the contradictions and the inequalities created by this process are of another order and it is there that the new sources of social inequality produce specific effects on the class structure of advanced capitalism.

Social Inequality and Class Power: New
Contradictions and New Models of Change

We have traced the general lines of the structural evolution of advanced capitalism by showing the new strategic role that has devolved from the process of collective consumption. We have shown, through several examples, the new contradictions that are born in the process and in the urban systems that constitute the real unit of operation. But, where is the social inequality to which we made reference at the start of our report? How do we make reference to an inequal distribution of the problems raised among the positions defined in the social structure? For the theme of inequality carries in fact an implicit reference to the relative positions of the agents in relation to each other. In this sense have we really demonstrated that the workers, the employees or the bourgeois have their own relationship to collective consumption different from other classes or levels? Such is the question we must pose in order to relate the analysis of the emergence of new social contradictions to the appearance of new forms of social inequality.

At the first level the income, educational, and professional occupational level, dependent directly on the position occupied in the relationships of production, strongly prescribe the level and style of collective consumption and their relationship to the urban system. We have seen, in fact, not only that the capacity for access to this consumption by the market offered a greater autonomy, but also and above all that the internal cleavages of the public sector were calculated on criteria of more or less great proximity to the market. From this point of view one can say that collective consumption prolongs and specifies the social stratification determined by the class system.

But aside from these effects of reinforcing the class structure, one finds new disparities also, emerging from the historical mode of dealing with collective consumption, that do not correspond to the position occupied in class relationships but to the position in the consumption process itself, as well as in specific elements of this process and in the unities of the urban system where it operates. Such is, for example, the case in the organization of urban transport, discrimination against old people, or the access to housing for immigrant workers (or for black Americans), or, again, the maladaptation of cultural facilities to the routines of young people following their differential insertion simultaneously into the scholarly machine and the urban structure. Such inequalities among social groups are not entirely autonomous of the class system since its logic determines the organization of consumption, but the positions defined in the specific structure of inequality do not correspond one-to-one to the structure of class relationships. It is in this sense that there is specific production of new effects of social inequality.

Furthermore, at a certain level it can be said that the ensemble of social groups are caught in the problems (bottlenecks or contradictions) created by collective consumption and, in this light, if there is not equalization in the result experienced there is, in fact, a rapport that is not antagonistic between the agents but rather partakes (differentially, surely) of the same difficulties. Let us think for example of the problems of urban traffic: Here it is a matter of questions that become obsessive for nearly the whole population. Also, if for housing the number of privileged people is larger, the crisis of housing

largely transcends the frontiers of the popular classes. That is to say that in
urban problems, social inequality articulates a question of more general scope:
Structural contradiction between the model of collective consumption and the
model of relationships of production that is at the root of the class system,
for the collective character, objectively socialized by this process of consumption, makes the crises and difficulties more solidified, less dissociable among
the agents. Certainly, one can escape more from pollution and the rhythm of
urban traffic above a certain income level, but one is no less aware of the difficulties. That is, it is at the level of urban problems that one can see most
easily how the combination of the logic of capital oppresses not only the working class but the ensemble of possibilities for human development.

This objective community of interests, this partial interclassism of contradictions at the level of collective consumption, provides the objective basis for
the ideology of environmentalism, which tries to naturalize the urban contradictions welding the ensemble of classes and social agents into a single army of
Boy Scouts unified by the high purpose of the preservation of the species. This
also conduces to efforts toward social integration in the form of experiments in
citizen participation in the administration of daily affairs, thus reconfirming
the old Anglo-Saxon tradition of the community as an instrument of social
cohesion that has stood the test of time in the service of the dominant structural
logic.

But at the same time the accentuation of contradictions, their globalization,
and their direct connection to political power, form the basis for a practical
articulation of the more general demands for transformation of the societal
model. Thus it is that the growing emergence of what are called urban social
movements in advanced capitalist societies is a major element of the social
dynamic insofar as they permit the progressive formation of an anticapitalist
alliance upon a much broader objective basis than that of the specific interests
of the proletariat or than that of the alliances depending on the convergence of
political interests in each conjuncture.[49]

For if the stated contradictions at the level of collective consumption do
not correspond exactly with those springing directly from the relationships of
production, it is essential to understand the gestation of these contradictions
beginning with the dominant logic of monopolistic capital. Analysis in terms
of class is thus depersonalized and one can speak of the domination of capital
without referring necessarily to the consuming habits of the bourgeoisie. It is
at just that historical moment that capital progressively loses any concrete
incarnation, that its logic becomes diffused on the world scale, and that its
power is identified more and more with that of the worldwide political powers,
that the conditions are ripe for a collective coming to awareness of the obstacle
represented by the social relationships structurally dominated by production
for the qualitative transformation of the societal model made nevertheless
necessary by the transformation of productive forces and the leaps forward of
political and ideological practice.

Some people will speak then of stopping growth and returning to nature. Caught between their awareness of the crisis and their class membership, they will choose the flight into utopia.

Others, by contrast, will find in the appearance of these new contradictions a field of choice in which to incorporate the great majority of the people in the political battle against capitalism, the only real historical practice leading to a qualitative transformation of social relationships of production that are the basis for the expressions, old and new, of social inequality.

Notes

1. For a theoretical and empirical argument along these lines, see Manuel Castells, *La Question Urbaine* (Paris: Maspéro, 1972), esp. chap. 3.

2. On the relation between urban organization and style of life, see Murray Brooklin, *The Limits of the City* (New York: Harper and Row, 1973).

3. For these analyses I refer to Paul Boccara, *Etudes sur le capitalisme monopoliste d'Etat, sa crise et son issue* (Paris: Editions Sociales, 1971); Jean-Pierre Delilez, *Les Monopoles* (Paris: Editions Sociales, 1972); Philippe Herzog, *Politique économique et planification en régime capitaliste* (Paris: Editions Sociales, 1972); Paul A. Baran and Paul M. Sweezy, *Monopoly Capital* (New York: Monthly Review Press, 1966).

4. For an analysis of this problem, see André Granou, *Capitalisme et mode de vie* (Paris: Le Cerf, 1973); and for statistical sources that enable an appreciation of this transformation, the studies of CREDOC (Paris) on the consumption patterns of the French.

5. See Jacques Brière, "La dialectique des besoins." *La Nouvelle Critique* (Paris April 1974); and Agnes Heller, *La teoria dei bisogni in Marx* (Milan: Feltrinelli, 1974).

6. On the transformations of the utilization of the labor force in relation to the new economic requirements, I refer to the general trends developed by Massimo Paci, applied by him in his study on Italy: Massimo Paci, *Mercato del lavoro e classi sociali in Italia* (Bologna: Il Mulino, 1973); also F. Indovina, (ed.), *Lo Spreco edilizio* (Marsilio, 1972).

7. See the problematique elaborated on this point by Michel Freyssenet and Françoise Imbert, *Mouvement du capital et processus de paupérisation* (Paris: C.S.U., 1973) (mimeo).

8. See J.P. Page, "L'utilisation des produits de la croissance" in Darras, *Le partage des bénéfices* (Paris: Minuit, 1966).

9. See the excellent work of James O'Connor, *The Fiscal Crisis of the State* (New York: St. Martin's Press, 1973), both for its analyses and the statistical and economic sources that are cited as a basis for his thesis.

10. See Renzo Stefanelli, "L'intervento Publico. Confronti internazionali" in *Le leve del sistema* (Bari: De Donato, 1971), pp. 263-84.

11. See the different sectors where public intervention becomes necessary in the collection of essays assembled by Alan K. Campbell, *The States and the Urban Crisis* (New York: the American Assembly 1970).

12. We have allowed ourselves to use here, without repeating the basic concepts, works that have become classics in Marxist economic theory. For more information we refer the reader to *Capital* by Marx, especially book 3, sec. 3, or, closer to us, the works of Charles Bettelheim or the *Traité Marxiste d'Economie politique* (Paris: Editions Sociales, 1971).

13. See Nicos Poulantzas, *Classes sociales et pouvoir politique de l'Etat capitaliste* (Maris: Maspéro, 1968).

14. See M. Castells, *Luttes Urbaines et Pouvoir Politique* (Paris: Maspéro, 1973).

15. See Christian Palloix, *Les firmes multinationales et le procès d'internationalisation* (Paris: Maspéro, 1973).

16. We are familiar with the direct connection between the importance of the multinational firms and the structural inflation of advanced capitalism. See Charles Levinson, *Capital, Inflation and the Multinationals* (London: George Allen and Unwin, 1971).

17. See J.L. Dallemagne, *L'inflation capitaliste* (Paris: Maspéro, 1972).

18. On the relationship of determination between classes and the state, I rely on the very precise, very subtle, and very new analyses contained in the book by Nicos Poulantzas, *Les Classes sociales dans le capitalisme aujourd'hui* (Paris: Seuil, 1974).

19. I refer for some basic facts to the following works: Michael Young (ed.), *Poverty Report 1974* (London: Temple Smith, 1974), especially Chapter 7, written by Peter Willmott, for England; F. Ascher and D. Levy, "Logement et construction," *Economie et Politique,* May 1973, and to the "Rapport de la C.N.L. sur la situation du logement en France," Colloque de Grenoble, N° spécial de *La Nouvelle Critique* sur l'Urbanisme, 1974, for France; the statistics and sources assembled by Francesco Indovina in *Lo Spreco Edilizio* (Padova: Marsilio, 1972), for Italy.

20. See for France, the analysis of Christian Topalov, "Politique monopoliste et propriété du logement," *Economie et politique,* March 1974.

21. For the basic facts, see C.I.E.C., *Le Financement du logement en France et a l'étranger* (Paris: P.U.F., 1966).

22. On this point see the extremely important book of David Harvey, *Social Justice and the City* (London: Edward Arnold, 1973), especially pp. 55-84; for empirical evidence on the Paris region, see M. Freyssenet, T. Regazzola, and J. Reter, *Ségrégation spatiale et déplacements sociaux* (Paris: C.S.U., 1973) (mimeo.)

23. See Danielle Combes and Etienne Latapie, *L'intervention des groupes financiers dans l'immobilier* (Paris: C.S.U., 1973) (mimeo).

24. This point is fundamental and perhaps already proven in the present state of

research, at least for France. We refer for this to the basic texts that we
cannot review here in detail: Suzanna Magri, *Politique du logement et
besoins en main d'oeuvre: analyse de la politique de l'Etat en relation avec
l'évolution du marché de l'emploi avant la deuxième guerre mondiale*
(Paris: C.S.U., 1973), (mimeo); Claude Pottier, *La logique du financement
public de l'urbanisation* (Paris: Mouton, forthcoming); Edmond Preteceille,
La production des grands ensembles (Paris: Mouton, 1973); Christian
Topalov, *Les promoteurs immobiliers* (Paris: Mouton, 1973); D. Cornuel,
Politique de logement dans le C.I.L. de Roubaix-Tourcoing, Ministère de
l'Equipement, Paris, 1973 (mimeo).

25. See Paul Hermand, *L'avenir de la sécurité sociale* (Paris: Seuil, 1967).

26. G. Pierre Calame, *Les travailleurs étrangers en France* (Paris: Les Editions
Ouvrières, 1972).

27. See, in this sense, the very pertinent observations contained in the study
of Franco Ferrarotti on Rome: *Vite di baracatti* (Naples: Liguori Editore,
1974).

28. See Frances Piven, *Regulating the Poor* (New York: Harper and Row, 1971);
for France, the report of Suzanna Magri on "Le logement des travailleurs"
at the Colloque de C.E.R.M. in 1973 in *Urbanisme monopoliste, urbanisme
démocratique* (Paris: Cahiers du Centre d'Etudes et de Recherches Marxists,
1974), pp. 143-91.

29. See Collette Petonnet, *Ces gens-là,* (Paris: Maspéro, 1970); Gerard Heliot,
"Le logement des travailleurs immigrés," *Espaces et Sociétés,* n° 2, 1971.

30. See Edmond Preteceille, *La production des grands ensembles* (Paris: Mouton,
1973); for the ensemble of sources and references on this theme, very signi-
cant in the social logic of housing in France, we refer to the commented
bibliographic synthesis by Bernard Lamy, *Les nouveaux ensembles d'habita-
tion et leur environnement* (Paris: CSU, 1971) (mimeo).

31 I refer for an analysis of the social bases of the transformation of housing
policy in France to a text that caught this transformation at its beginnings:
J. Bobroff and F. Novatin, "La politique Chalandon: nécessité tactique et
stratégie de classe," *Espaces et Sociétés,* n° 2, 1971.

32. See the classic work of R.M. Fisher, *Twenty Years of Public Housing* (New
York: Harper Brothers, 1959), as well as the very interesting inquiry of
Louis Kriesberg, "Neighborhood Setting and the Isolation of Public Housing
Tenants," in P. Meadows and E. Mizruchi (eds.), *Urbanism, Urbanization
and Change* (Reading, Mass.: Addison-Wesley, 1969), pp. 276-91.

33. Charles Bettelheim has made the greatest efforts in this direction, especially
in his book *Calcul économique et formes de propriété* (Paris: Maspéro, 1969).

34. The best analysis we know of this sort of problem is that of Ivan Szelenyi
and Giorgy Konrad, *The Social Conflicts of Underurbanization* (Budapest:
Institute of Sociology, unpublished), relative to Hungary; for China, we refer
to the article of Micheline Luccioni, "Processus révolutionnaire et organisation

de l'espace en Chine," *Espaces et Sociétés,* n° 5, 1971, and await the book being written by the same author and the publication of the text that Ana-Maria Echevarria (Ecole Pratique des Hautes Etudes) has written on the same subject.

35. See in this regard the fairly new viewpoint of the development of the suburbs that appears in the collection of Charles M. Haar (ed.), *The End of Innocence: A Suburban Reader* (Glenview, Ill: Scott, Foresman and Co., 1972), taking up again in a forward-looking manner the themes that were introduced ten years before by Raymond Vernon in *The Myth and Reality of Our Urban Problems* (Cambridge, Mass: MIT Press, 1962).

36. See Franco Ferrarotti, *Roma, de capitale a periferia* (Bari: Laterza, 1971); Jean Remy, "Utilisation de l'espace—Innovation technologique et structure sociale," *Espaces et Sociétés,* n° 4; David Harvey, *Social Justice,* pp. 96-120.

37. See Jean-Noël Chapulut, Jean Frébault, Jacques Pellegrin, *Le marché des transports* (Paris: Seuil, 1970).

38. See for the basic statistics (American), the classic by J.R. Meyer, J.F. Kain, M. Wohl, *The Urban Transportation Problem* (Cambridge, Mass: Harvard University Press, 1965); and for a theoretical analysis of the question, Nicole Julien and Jean-Claude Veyssilier, "Transports urbains et contradictions sociales," *Architecture d'aujourd'hui* (Paris) 1, 1974.

39. See the documents assembled on this problem by the Italian trade unions: *Una Nuova politica per: transporti. Atti della Conferenza nazionale GIL-CISL-UIL. Ariccia, April 1972* (Rome: Edizioni Sensi, 1972).

40. See the very concrete analysis concerning the social determination of the Parisian metro routes in Alain Cottereau, "Les origines de la Planification urbaine dans la région parisienne," *Sociologie du Travail,* n° 4, 1969.

41. See the detailed analysis of the underlying social logic at the RER in Jean Lojkine, *La politique urbaine dans la Région parisienne* (Paris: Mouton, 1973).

42. See a good resumé of some important research in this field in John F. Kain, "Urban Travel Behavior," in Leo F. Schnore, *Social Science and the City* (New York: Frederick Praeger, 1968), pp. 162-96.

43. See the statistics presented by Roger Revelle, "Pollution and Cities," in James Q. Wilson (ed.), *The Metropolitan Enigma* (Cambridge, Mass: Harvard University Press, 1968), pp. 96-144 (paperback edition).

44. See specific analyses and observations of this kind assembled by Michel Bosquet in his *Critique du Capitalisme quotidien* (Paris: Editions Galilée, 1973).

45. See Monique Segré, "Politique scolaire et aménagement du terriroire en France," *Espaces et Sociétés,* n° 5, 1972, pp. 105-28.

46. See, for example, Jacques Ion, *Les équipements socio-culturels et la ville* Paris: Ministère de l'Equipement, 1972.

47. See specific analyses and observations of this sort in the Rapport du CERM,

Urbanisme monopoliste. Urbanisme démocratique, Paris, 1974, cited above. This problem is approached from a different perspective by Jean Rémy and Liliane Joyé in *La ville et l'urbanisation* (Brussels: Editions Duculot, 1974), particularly in the first part.

48. For an analysis that is both concrete and theoretical of this type of process of urbanization, we refer to our book, written in collaboration with F. Godard, *Monopolville* (Paris: Editions Mouton, 1974).

49. See the analyses of social movements assembled in numbers 6, 7, and 9 of the review *Espaces et Sociétés* (1972 and 1973), as well as several studies already in this domain: Christopher Pickvance, "On the Study of Urban Social Movements," University of Manchester (mimeo); Enzo Mingione and others, *Citta e conflitto sociale,* (Milano: Feltrinelli, 1971); Andreina Daolia, "Le lotte per la casa," in F. Indovina, ed., *Lo Spreco Edilizio* (Padova: Marsilio, 1972); Maurizio Marcelloni, "Le lotte sociale in Italia," Rome, 1973 (unpublished); Giuliano della Pergola, "Le lotte urbane," *Archivio di Studi Urbani et Regionali* 3, 1973; M. Castells, El Cherki, and D. Mehl, *Sociologie des mouvements sociaux urbains. Enquete sur la région parisienne.* I. (Paris: EPHE, 1974); J. Borja, *Estructura urbana y movimientos urbanos* (Barcelona: Universidad Autonoma de Barcelone, 1974).

8 Equality, Inflation, and Wage Control
Martin Rein and Peter Marris

Anxiety about the rapid growth of inflation has riveted attention in a number of advanced industrial countries on the effectiveness of statutory wage and price controls as an anti-inflationary policy.[a] Yet, wage controls, as an instrument to prevent unions and employees from entering into labor contracts that promote inflationary expectations, require both a fair measure of consensus about goals and a willingness to comply with established regulatory controls.

The British miners' strike of 1974 and the general election it provoked, dramatized a profoundly challenging issue: By what right are wages determined? The question is both political and moral: What legitimizes a wage settlement? And what wages are just? The two aspects are inseparable, for any government that intervenes in the process of settlement begins to assume responsibility for the structure of wages themselves, and so in the end must confront the justice of that structure. And, conversely, once the issue of justice has been raised, it draws into question the legitimacy of all those assumed, established rights of bargaining and organization by which the structure perpetuates itself. Hence, a government impelled by public resentment against inflation to curb wage demand risks becoming entangled in fundamental issues of justice that it cannot handle within the established institutional framework of a democratic, capitalistic society. In this chapter we explore some of the principles, theories, and pragmatic compromises by which British and American governments have tried to resolve this dilemma.

Inflation always presents a government with moral choices: It can let it alone, hurting those dependent on fixed incomes; create more unemployment; subsidize prices; or increase interest rates. The fairness of any policy depends, of course, on whom inflation harms; but the consequences are not necessarily obvious. An American analysis, by R.G. Hollister and J.L. Palmer,[1] using information from the 1961 survey of consumer expenditures, concluded that

---

We wish to thank Clint Bourden for his many insightful suggestions. In addition, Mike Piore and John Goldthorpe offered useful comments on an earlier version of this chapter.

[a]At the same time it has provoked a vigorous controversy among economists. Keynesians argue that wage control is crucial; Monetarists (led by Milton Friedman) argue that wages are less important to inflation than the question of the money supply; hence, wage controls are irrelevant and an increase in unemployment is inevitable as the money supply is held down. This chapter does not address the merits of these conflicting interpretations of the causes of inflation. We limit our discussion to the dilemmas that arise when governments act on the assumption that wage rates are important in the fight against inflation.

price changes were about the same for all products; hence, rich and poor suffered alike from inflation, although their patterns of expenditure were different. The analysis implied that a deflationary policy would harm the poor disproportionately, since they would lose more income by higher levels of unemployment and a slack labor market than they lost in purchasing power by inflation. A "tax on employment" was worse than the "tax on inflation"; the cure worse than the disease. But a more recent staff report of the Joint Economic Committee, using the same differentiated indices of consumption, concluded that between August 1971 and December 1973 "low income persons suffered about one-fourth more from inflation than did middle and upper income consumers"[2] largely because of disproportionate rises in food, housing, and fuel costs. If this is so the social justice of letting inflation take its course is much weaker.

Such arguments concern the use of conventional economic regulators, and fall within the accustomed controversies of political debate and budgetary manipulation. These familiar regulators, seeking to stimulate investment or reduce demand, do not preempt the processes of bargaining and accommodation by which wages are negotiated. Even a temporary wage and price freeze can be seen, more doubtfully, as an emergency regulator, imposed only so long as need be for other measures to restore the economy to a balance.

But we are faced now with inflationary trends that seem to defy regulation by traditional means. Unemployment and inflation have risen together, and regulators that assume an inverse relationship between levels of unemployment above four percent and rates of inflation seem less and less reliable. Disillusioned with monetary methods of economic management, governments are drawn to intervene directly in the control of wages and prices, with no assurance that they can ever extricate themselves from this control without a resumption of the inflationary spiral. In principal, of course, only the curbing of prices is crucial when wage increases are justified as a means to prevent an erosion in current living standards. But since food, fuel, and raw materials respond to an international market beyond the control of any government, the hope of restraining inflation comes to rely largely on that component of prices accountable by the cost of labor. This raises more far reaching and disturbing questions of justice than balancing the social impact of budgetary incentives.

Wage Differentials and Inflation

How, first, are wages believed to contribute to inflation? If goods are really becoming scarcer, the demand for wage increases to meet their rising price becomes an inflationary scramble to escape the consequences. A policy of wage restraint is then a straightforward recognition that the standard of living must fall. But controls have characteristically been imposed in the belief that the prosperity of society is still growing; and inflation is a self-reinforcing aberation,

independent of any general scarcity. In the first place, once people perceive
an inflationary trend, they demand wages that will protect them against the
price increase they expect before their next settlement, and so help to fulfill
that expectation. But this general movement, which might be held back by
an automatic adjustment to a price index, is compounded by a continual,
complex adjustment of wage differentials to each other. Wages in one sector
set standards for another, and as these increments disturb the frame of reference for rates of pay elsewhere, the whole structure of wages is defined in
higher and higher amounts of money. Since rates of pay scarcely ever fall,
the adjustment is always upwards, and every attempt to restore a difference
risks setting off a further chain of increments. If this is so the structure of
wage differentials itself becomes the crucial concern of any policy of wage
restraint. The structure must somehow be brought into balance, so that
changes reflect only increases in productivity, or a redistribution of rewards.
And once government takes on this task, it has to answer, sooner or later,
for the justice of the balance it is seeking.

Even a short-term wage freeze raises questions that must be decided by
fair and impartial principles. On the day it is imposed some workers will have
just received a raise, others are about to secure one; must the latter accept
their bad luck? Should workers in low-paid occupations, whose ability to
meet their essential needs is most threatened by inflation, be subject to the
same restraint? Should workers who are about to realize large increases through
their cooperation in raising productivity be denied their reward? Should the
wages of workers committed to long-term bargaining agreements, or in jobs
where demand has temporarily declined, be allowed to deteriorate, compared
with those who made substantial gains just before controls were imposed?
Arnold Weber, who was responsible for managing phases one and two of
America's wage control policy under the Nixon administration, observed that
"any system of wage controls must have sufficient flexibility to accommodate
the needs created by . . . different situations" that arise when control is initiated. The policy towards discretionary exceptions, he suggests, depends on
the standard chosen for permissible increases:

> Where there is a tight standard—defined by a large gap between a
> permissible increase and that which might be expected under current
> economic conditions—there must also be a flexible approach to
> exceptions. On the other hand, the promulgation of a generous
> standard means that most individual cases can be accommodated
> within this regulatory framework and that the goals of the control
> program will have to be served by an austere approach to excep-
> tions.[3]

When public policy seeks to control the average rate of wage increase, it

confronts a conflict between equity considerations from a political point of
view (i.e., everyone with very few exceptions should get the guideline rate of
increase) and the economic need to reward productivity or attract workers in
some sectors and not in others. As time goes by either discretionary awards
will undermine the credibility of impartial control, or the rigidity of the standard becomes intolerably oppressive. Anomalies are bound to multiply, the
grievances demanding exception become more widespread, and the need for
explicit, acceptable principles more pressing. Hence, if a short-term wage
freeze cannot quickly head off the critical pressures—and this seems a poor
hope—it leads relentlessly towards the search for a fair wage structure, rather
than merely for impartial wage constraint. But what are the principles of a
fair structure, and where does government look for them?

The Principles of Wage Policy

In the debate about the British miners' pay, three kinds of argument were
put forward by the National Coal Board, the Pay Board, and the miners' union.
Firstly, all parties agreed that there was a crisis in recruitment, which threatened
the production of coal even at the levels foreseen before the spectacular rise in
oil prices. Coal, now, might rescue the nation from a crippling dependence on
foreign fuel, if enough men could be attracted to the pits and held there. For
that, wages would have to be high enough to draw recruits from other occupations; and, at the same time, low enough to hold coal to a competitive price.
But this straightforward argument about supply and demand led into the issue
of differentials. What point of reference determined whether wages would seem
attractive? Mineworkers' pay had been falling relative to pay in other manufacturing industries: A substantial increase would be needed only to restore their
position, and it might have to be increased still further to attract more men. But
here the Pay Board became nervous: Would such a rise create a precedent for
other wages, setting off a chain of inflationary adjustments and eroding the
attraction of minework? This in turn leads to another level of argument: Mineworkers deserve to be especially well paid, to compensate for the dangers and
hardships of their occupation. This principle raises a further problem of equity.
The threats to health and the unpleasantness of the job apply only to miners
who work underground in the pits. Only two-thirds of manual workers in the
industry work underground. To limit the wage increases to these workers would
alter the internal relativities of wages between the underground and surface
workers. Since relative earnings of the underground workers had declined compared with surface workers, a case could be made for returning to the customary
differentials. But such an arrangement posed new difficulties. A widening of
differentials threatened recruitment by decreasing the attractiveness of mine-
working as a lifetime career, because men who move from underground to the

surface experience a sharp decline in their earnings. To meet this difficulty a supplementary principle is brought forward: The dangers are all underground, but a man too old or physically unable to do underground work should not suffer a drop in pay, retaining still a proportion of his underground allowance. (The amount recommended was one half.) Since thirty-two percent of surface manual workers have worked underground, this arrangement increases the cost of production (2.5 million pounds annually), while creating new inequities among surface manual workers, who perform similar work but receive different pay. To take account of the past is to create inequities in the present.[4]

The "equity" question is thus complex and multifaceted. What was at issue was a conflict between the demands for equity of the internal wage structure and the implications of these requirements for the external wage structure. While the basic issue was the earnings of the men who work at the pit-head, an increase just for them (in relation to the need to attract workers from outside who were looking at the external wage relations) conflicted with the need to retain "equitable" relations for the internal wage structure. In order to keep the internal wage structure consistent, the miners had to sell their case to the nation on the basis of average external differentials (miners versus average wage in manufacturing, etc.).

Thus, three kinds of argument were used in debate: an argument about the efficient price of labor; argument about the equitable position of miners in relation to other wages in manufacture, and between different jobs in the industry; and an argument about compensation for hardship. All were recognized and exploited by the three parties, though with differing emphasis. The union seemed especially concerned with equity, reluctant to make too much of the claims of hardship, for fear of discriminating against its surface workers. The Pay Board, on the other hand, made the most of hardship since it wanted to establish miners as a special case, whose settlement could not be used as a precedent elsewhere. The Coal Board, naturally enough, was preoccupied with incentives. But no one followed any one line of argument exclusively, although they are not necessarily mutually reinforcing, or consistent. The first is a pragmatic argument; the others are both, in different ways, concerned with justice. And all of them, perhaps, were largely rationalizations of the bargain that all parties saw might be struck. But they suggest the interplay of argument from which a comprehensive wage policy might derive its theories and principles. Explicit arguments about differentials do not exhaust the grounds on which pay claims are advanced. Workers, for example, lay claim to higher wages on the basis of changes in the cost of living, where the reference system is workers' past circumstances, or the inability to survive because the wage levels are below welfare standards, taken as a crude measure of subsistence. The crucial point is that whatever rationale is put forward to justify pay increases, they can disrupt established patterns of differentials and hence create difficulties for the conservative view.

Wages as the Market Price

First, any policy must be reasonably efficient in distributing labor productively. The wage structure, from this point of view should represent a sensitive mechanism of incentives, continually adjusting supply to demand. Inflationary pressure from scarcity of labor can then be corrected by reducing demand. But this apparently simple principle becomes increasingly difficult to interpret, the more closely we examine the meaning of its terms. The demand for labor is demand at a given price; and this price is not established, in any direct way, by the supply. "Wage theory has tended historically to disintegrate on the supply side. . . ," writes John Dunlop. "The supply function tends to be pushed outside the analytic system. The amount of labour supplied and the wage rate come to be determined by social custom or institutional considerations."[5] Trade unions, professional associations, conventional expectations, minimum wage laws insure that the price is at least maintained. Hence, the adjustment is made in the rate of employment, rather than the rate of pay. When demand is slack, people are laid off, fewer shifts are worked, graduates search longer for a tolerable job, married women cease to look for work, fewer immigrants arrive. When demand is high, the trends are reversed, and at the same time there is an irreversible investment in capital to eliminate unnecessary, scarce labor, which establishes permanently higher rates in those jobs which remain. Thus, the structure of wages is governed by conventional expectations, reinforced by protective institutions, which prevent both an absolute fall in money wages, and any ready transfer of labor from one sector to another.

The origins of this structure can be traced back to the social, political, and economic circumstances that have shaped it. As new occupations evolve they attach themselves to points of reference within the existing structure, establishing their relative status. The distribution of employment shifts as the economy develops, and children learn to perceive different occupational chance from their parents. But the structure itself endures. It does not seem to represent the resolution of supply and demand. Rather, it is the given framework within which the market adjusts.

If this is so a wage policy that sought to restore an antiinflationary equilibrium through mechanisms of the market would have two choices: It could restrict demand so drastically that unemployment rose until people were ready to abandon their expectations. Or it could attack the protective institutions directly—rescinding rights to collective bargaining or minimum wages. Neither seems politically feasible or tolerable, on a scale to be effective. For these institutions have arisen just because the purely economic determination of wages seems unbearably insecure and inequitable.

Wages as Equitable Treatment

In practice when people claim higher pay, they characteristically present a grievance. That is, they are not—or at least pretend they are not—testing the market price of their labor, but protesting an injustice. The injustice is defined as an inequitable relationship between their wages and the wages of others. The comparison is selective. The claimants usually refer to a particular set of rates, in occupations analogous to their own, where wages are better. But they may also argue that their relative advantage over some properly inferior occupation has decreased. It is almost as much of an affront to discover that some lower status occupation has caught up with your pay, as to see an occupation of equal status drawing ahead. Such arguments imply that there is a recognized customary structure of wage differentials, which represents a right to a position in the hierarchy of wages, and it is unjust to deprive an occupation of its position.

This principle of equity suggests a partial theory of wages. Jobs are typically categorized in clusters, where differences in pay reflect gradations of status, skill, and authority within a firm or industry. These job clusters—at least in the short term—can be treated as given "by the technology, the managerial and administrative organization of the wage determining unit, and by the social customs of the work community".[6] Within each cluster one job category sets the key rate, around which the other categories are arranged as a scale, representing their conventional status. In negotiating the internal wage structure both management and unions use these rates as an explicit reference point. But these key rates are also related to corresponding rates in other firms, setting the standards to which the overall structure of wages is expected to conform. This broader cluster of a stable group of firms—linked together by similarity of product markets, by resort to similar sources for a labor force, or by common labor market organizations (custom)—form a wage contour with common wage-making characteristics. Job clusters and job contours are concepts used to relate the internal wage structure of a firm with the wider external wage structure of a stable group of firms. Like the job cluster, the wage contour is a group of wage rates organized around a key rate. "At the exterior of the contour, furthest from the key rates, the firms may only remotely follow the leadership." The overall wage structure is shaped by a "limited number of strategic rates depicted by the job clusters and wage contours."[7]

Wage inflation, then, arises at least in part from distortions in the structure represented by these clusters and contours. That is, when these conventional expectations of relative status are eroded, people demand that they be restored, and since wages can only, in fairness, be raised upwards, the search for a new equilibrium may set off a chain of inflationary adjustments. If, for instance, key rates rise faster than the productivity of the economy as a whole can sustain, the recovery of balance will be inflationary, even though the keyrates themselves may not be. Or if there is a dispute between two trades over their relative status, the competition between them to assert or deny the appropriateness of a differential can lead to a spiral of claims and counter claims that sets inflationary standards for other occupations. Or if, obliged to accept the constraints of long-term contractual obligations, the principle unionized occupations

forego wage claims while nonunionized occupations gain ground, the structure
is again distorted. For instance, in the late 1960s in the United States, non-
union workers' wages were rising faster than those of unionized workers, but the
trend had reversed by 1971: "The interpretation suggested by this pattern is
that wage increases in the non-union sector were responding to increased slack in
the labour market, while wages of unionized workers increased more rapidly as
agreements expired and previously eroded relative wage positions were restored".[8]

From this point of view, therefore, an antiinflationary policy of wage control should seek to restore the equilibrium. Rather than set any overall limit to
increases, it needs to hold back leading key wage rates, while it permits lagging
wages to catch up. Such a policy may have to tolerate a considerable short-term
inflation while the structure recovers its balance. But once the balance is restored,
people will be receiving what they expect: Their pay will reflect the occupational
status they recognize. This policy assumes an inherent conservatism, which
leads people to identify with these familiar expectations. Not that they are
necessarily content with their life chances; nor that they think the inequality of
rewards is, in some larger sense, just. But within the setting of their everyday
lives, they accept the fairness of their treatment compared with others of their
kind. To be paid less than a workmate of equal status is a personal affront, a
legitimate grievance in the system's own terms; to be paid less than people in
comparable work elsewhere is an arguable, collective grievance; but to be paid
less than someone of a conventionally recognized higher status is, rightly or
wrongly, how things are. We do not expect to be able to challenge the system
itself through the negotiations of wage claims.

American wage control policy in the last few years has tried to exploit these
conservative assumptions, taking the restoration of accustomed differentials as
its guiding principle. A paper by Quinn Mills, deputy director of the Cost of
Living Council, when John Dunlop was its director, discusses the theoretical
framework for administering such a wage stabilization program. The most urgent
task is to relate average wage increases to individual changes, since it is by controlling the latter that policy hopes to influence the former. The rate of increase
in the aggregate wage index is dependent upon three factors: "The rate of change
in the consumer price index, the long run rate of change in output per manhour
and the degree of distortion in the structure of wages. . . . During a period of
inflation, increases in wages made as a result of adjustments of wage structure
become more important than the cost of living or productivity factors. This is
so because it is the essence of a period of inflation that wage relationships
become distorted and require readjustment." For instance, carpenters in the
building industry received a fifteen percent increase in the late 1960s. This
upset the traditional differentials between carpenters and bricklayers, who set
about catching up the lost ground. "The task of stabilization authorities," says
Mills, "is to begin to return the structure of wages as quickly as possible (without undue effects on industrial relations or productions) to one appropriate for

the long run." The worst kind of wage control policy is one that allows each
rate to rise by some unvarying percentage, thereby freezing "a badly distorted
wage structure."[9]

But "distortion" is clearly a matter of judgment—a conservative metaphysic,
denying either that tradition might have entrenched injustice; or that the relative value of skills might be changing. However subtle, pragmatic, and unobtru-
sive the restoration of the traditional structure, its assumptions are not readily
translatable from the context of particular wage negotiations to a national policy.
Since wages are always being revised somewhere, there is no obvious point of
equilibrium that policy might take as a reference. Does it choose the year when
fewest claims were presented, average the differentials over a period of years,
or assemble an ideal configuration from the trend of wage settlements in various
sectors? As soon as we ask such questions we begin to need criteria of choice
that cannot be derived from the conservative assumptions themselves. The
American approach is not only inherently conservative but short run. We can
rationalize wage policy based on customary wage differentials for only so long;
then, new and obvious distortions arise and the longer run actions of the market
pose difficult supply and demand questions as well as new equity issues. Under
the Mills-Dunlop view, where one is trying to control wage differentials and
accommodate changes by reference to a given customary structure, a tension
between short- and long-run aims is inevitable. While we can accept the structure as given in the short run, where custom legitimates it, in the long run it is
obvious that the structure is continuously changing and hence the system of
wage control must recognize, accede to, and even lead these changes. These
longer run or market dominated changes are, of course, understood by those
who embrace a conservative approach to wage controls. They are, however,
very difficult to handle on a systematic basis. Coherent policies to cover these
long-term equity questions defeat the principle of restoring customary wage
differentials.

These questions lead to the still more fundamental question of the legitimacy of any conservative principle. Criteria of fairness acceptable within the
terms of a structure cannot be applied to the maintenance of the structure itself. By analog the precedents established under a law can only guide the hear-
ing of a case: They cannot justify the law. Hence, the American policy would
be hard to justify, once it is challenged. Its success seems to depend on a series
of discrete interventions, whose underlying principles are never examined
critically.

The British Prices and Incomes Board also recognized the importance of
differentials. It, too, believed that wages responded to claims of equity, rather
than supply and demand, and that equilibrium depended on a generally accepted
structure of differences. "If the labourer (earning £10 a week) works alongside
a skilled man earning no more than £11," it argued in one of its reports, "it might
be economically unwise and socially unjust to give the labourer an increase of £1

and leave the skilled man's pay untouched." But unlike its American counterpart, the Board did not equate justice with tradition. It sought to rationalize differentials by the criteria of skill and responsibility. In principle these criteria implied some radical changes in the existing structure: The Board was impatient, for instance, with the accustomed difference in status between manual and nonmanual work, where these did not reflect real differences of quality. In practice, it compromised: "The Board's main concern in pursuing rationality was to seek structures which would be *accepted* as internally coherent rather than a precise substantive rationality according to its own criteria of skill and responsibility. . . . its overriding concern in this matter was to produce structures which those directly concerned would accept as rational and hence (and in the Board's view *ipso facto*) as equitable."[10]

Thus, both British and American policy recognized that the equity of the structure of differentials was crucial to the stability of the wage structure. But while the Americans tended to define equity in terms of the differentials to which people were accustomed, the British reversed the relationship, and defined the ideal structure of differentials in terms of equitable principles, as people perceived them. But once these principles are established independently of custom, the argument is open to other considerations of equity, which do not take the rationalization of differentials as their starting point. Once it is conceded that differentials should represent, not merely custom, but rational justice, then the inquiry into the justice of wages cannot logically be restricted to questions of skill and responsibility.

Wages as a Socially Just Return

In the Pay Board's report on the miners' wage claim, much emphasis was placed on dangers and "unsocial hours." Shift work, dirt, danger, are all fair reasons for compensation. But once we are launched on this line of argument, the competing principles of justice begin to multiply. The Pay Board itself, in urging special recognition of the hazards of underground work, argued, as we have seen, that men too old for the pit face should not be forced to take a drastic cut in earnings. In the United States, too, the Cost of Living Council approved a twelve percent wage increase for coal miners on grounds of need and protection of income later in life—though the circumstances were quite different. Because of a persistent, sharp decline in the work force, 130,000 active workers were supporting a pension fund paying benefits to half a million recipients. The Council could not have refused the wage increase without "denying retirement and health benefits to incapacitated miners, widows, and orphans."[11] Seniority, need, effort are all valid, respected claims. Once we look at the overall structure of wage differences in the light of these broader claims, we cannot help noticing how arbitrary and inconsistent the differences are.

The approaches to wage stabilization we have discussed try to evade these issues, seeking to contain the principles of wage control within the framework of a given tradition. If only "inexact moral judgement" (in Quinn Mills' phrase) can be kept out of the debate, "formal symbolic representation of the inter-relationship among wage rates allows rigorous definition of wage structure adjustments." But the hope seems illusory, for the traditional structure does not represent any coherent principle, but the outcome of continual, discrete, pragmatic adjustments of a very partial equity, whose overall fairness is not at issue. Once this structure is taken to represent a consensual justice, public policy is trapped in the defense of an essentially irresponsible system. As Barbara Wootton says: "The picture which emerges is . . . of a community determined, on the one hand, to fix standards of remuneration that are fair and just as well as economically defensible; and no less determined, on the other hand, to abdicate from all responsibility . . . engaged in the impossible task of attempting to do justice in an ethical vacuum."[12]

It seems that wages policy, in its search for principles, must sooner or later reach this point. The control of inflationary trends in wages cannot ultimately be divorced from fundamental questions of justice. But as yet, amongst the industrialized capitalist democracies, only Sweden has insistently asserted a morally ethical policy towards existing differentials. The Swedish experience suggests that although wage solidarity policies provoke political controversy and labor unrest, such strife can be overcome, and the principle of reducing earning differentials accepted in negotiation.

Can Wage Policy Evade the Question of Justice?

We have tried to show how the attempt to restrain wage inflation leads to a search for principles that would insure a stable wage structure. The conceivable principles seem to be of three kinds—economic, conservative, and ethical. The policies of governments can be seen in these terms; American policy has tried to steer wages into a stable, historically determined structure of differentials; Swedish policy has tried to assert egalitarian principles in its approach to wage solidarity. British policy, under the last Conservative government, started out with a desire to limit the power of trade unions and give the most play to free competition—and when driven to wage controls, treated them as stop-gap measures until the economy recovered its balance. The new labor government is committed to the voluntary control of wages, through a social contract with the unions.

The "social contract" represents an agreement to moderate wage demands in return for a broad range of social and economic reforms. Moderate wage demands mean wage increases that do not exceed the cost of living. Thus, if government can control price it can slow down inflation, confident that wage bargaining will not generate an inflationary spiral. The social contract corresponds, in effect, to a conservative, equity approach since bargaining will tend to maintain the existing structure of differentials.

In its commitment to leave wages untouched, the social contract returns to the principles of the welfare state: that social purposes should be developed through fiscal policy and social service policy. But, as Titmuss noted many years ago in his seminal inaugural lecture, the sector of occupational policy serves many of the same purposes as do taxes and social services. The contract could, in principle, serve as an important vehicle to promote equality in the nonwage aspects of income, for example, equality of educational and occupational opportunity. And, as John Goldthorpe suggests, the contract might contribute to the "restructuring of the entire occupational dimension of labour. National job evaluation schemes could, for example, open the door for such a major reassessment."[13] The effectiveness of such a social contract is an open question. If Edward Heath, the former conservative party leader, was right in saying that wage increases already negotiated before the October 1974 election would lead to inflation of thirty percent for the coming year,[14] the contract would not curb the present inflationary trend, and past attempts to create greater equality in the nonwage dimensions of economic well-being have not been very impressive.[15]

Neither British nor American policy has been obviously successful in its anti-inflationary purpose (though to be sure, one would have to compare actual rates of inflation with a guess at what would have happened without any policy: By this standard, American policy in phases one and two did seem to contain inflation while they lasted). But the issue, especially in Britain, is wider than inflation: The economy is continually disrupted by strikes, and at least part of this disruption seems to spring from a widespread sense of injustice at the class divisions and inequities of society. America may be under less pressure, for in spite of comparable rates of price inflation, wages have risen more slowly there than in Europe—7.9 percent compared with Britain's 17.9 percent and Sweden's 12.2 percent. Wage control and union reluctance to strike probably contributed to this moderation.[16] But if average wage increases begin to follow the European trend, in America, too, the need for a new, more radical approach may emerge.

We have argued thus far that the interplay of supply and demand cannot provide a stable basis for adjusting wages because of the institutional and customary constraints on the movement of wages and labor. But custom itself, though it is the characteristic point of departure in wage negotiations, cannot be used as a justification of the wage system as a whole. Hence, in the end, wage policy is led to issues of social justice.

Governments are likely to resist this conclusion. They tend to regard wage controls as an unfortunate, temporary necessity—and so (since they disclaim any long-term responsibility for the wage structure) try to evade the underlying issue. But if wage controls cannot be temporary, if their relaxation only sets off an alarming inflationary spurt, governments may find the incoherence of their

principles increasingly challenged. Hence, the wage structure itself is likely
to become a much more central issue of reform. Since World War II, the
search for greater equality has tended to concentrate on the nonwage aspects
of income under government control—taxation, social benefits, social services,
educational opportunity, and public housing. Most European countries redistribute over a fifth of national income through social insurance and public
assistance; but though this makes the poorest tenth of the population better
off than it would otherwise be, these policies have scarcely affected the
inequality of incomes in the past decade.[b] Now a more radical challenge to the
wage structure itself begins to seem politically conceivable. Unwittingly, perhaps, and reluctantly, even conservative governments are being drawn by a
muddled expediency to confront crucial injustices in the social structure.

Equality as the Basis of Justice

Once the question of justice has been raised, is there any ethically rational
principle on which to found a wages policy that does not assume a basic egalitarianism? All the arguments that seek to justify inequalities of treatment
must, surely, presuppose some yardstick, against which the claims to extra
rewards are measured. They accept that it is inequality, not equality, that
needs excuse. Other things being equal, the arguments imply, everyone should
be paid the same; and their principles then seek to define how other things may
not be equal. But these factors can only be given a quantity and developed into
formulae against a universal norm. Each claim represents a basic wage, plus an
increment for overtime, productivity, danger, unsocial hours, dirt, discomfort,
need, reimbursement for earnings lost and costs incurred in training, seniority,
skill, responsibility or whatever. The inequalities are all supplementary adjustments, which seek to correct a perceived unfairness in too rigid and absolute an
egalitarianism. But the arguments only make sense if the underlying egalitarian
premise is first assumed. And it seems certain that any structure of wage differentials built on such a foundation would be radically different from the present,
where inequality is taken for granted.

These principles of justice could, ideally, reconcile the three kinds of argument we have reviewed. Economic incentives to attract workers and encourage
their productivity can be taken to represent fair compensation for extra effort
and the trouble of moving one's workplace; some structure of differentials seems
to reflect a common understanding that some people by skill, responsibility,
length of service, contribute more than others to the success of everyone's
endeavours; and some compensation for accepting unusual hardships seems

---

[b]This inference is derived from projecting the I.L.P.'s 1967 account of the cost of
social security into the 1970s.

obviously fair. At the same time the claims of each have to be defined against some basic, general standard of reward, and justified because they are either self-evidently fair, or in everyone's interest.

If we assume that tradition is not inevitable, and that economic forces function within a wage structure determined independently of supply and demand, then it should be possible to manipulate the wage structure in the interests of justice. In the long run such a structure would be more stable. The restraining of inflationary wage demands may only be possible within the framework of an explicit ethical rationality.

Would an egalitarian incomes policy be accepted as a move in the direction of greater social justice, or would it exacerbate the problem of income inequality? Goldthorpe notes "that through increasing information about, and interest in, differences between occupational rewards and conditions, the actual operation of an incomes policy will serve to broaden comparative reference groups among the mass of the population, and at the same time bring issues of equity and fairness into greater subjective salience. Thus . . . one would expect, in the case of the working class at least, a growing sense of resentment and grievance over the *status quo* and, in turn, an even greater unwillingness to accept restraint or to hold back in any way from the direct pursuit of their own maximum advantage."[17] Managerial and professional groups may also revolt against policies to promote greater equality in wages and salaries. Each group pursuing its own interest may thus threaten the stability of wage solidarity policies. But the Swedish venture into solidarity policies suggests that such opposition can be overcome, at least in the short run.

No wages policy could succeed—except in a revolutionary context—if it attempted to abolish wage differentials abruptly. Hence, policy probably has to respect the accustomed expectations about the status of jobs. But within that framework it should be possible to assert the principle that wages should move towards equality as an ideal. That is, higher pay raises would be endorsed for low-paid workers, and at the highest level a net reduction of the real value of salaries would be sought. One way towards this is to express all pay increases in amounts of money rather than percentages, and to give higher paid workers little or no more than their lower paid colleagues by way of increase. Another might be to reduce the number of categories of jobs; and to reclassify certain occupations altogether—so that they disappear from the hierarchy, and their occupants are reinstated with a differently defined status. A workable strategy would have to combine incremental changes, that would not be too hard to adjust to, with an explicit emphasis on the aim of social justice. At the same time some pragmatic adjustments to attract labor where the demand is greatest are probably inevitable. But our essential point is that however pragmatic, flexible, and complex a working policy is likely to be, it cannot succeed unless it is seen to be just. And we cannot imagine any argument of justice, broad enough to define the structure of wages as a whole, that was not drawn from a basic principle of equality.

Notes

1. R.G. Hollister and J.L. Palmer, "The Impact of Inflation on the Poor," in K.E. Boulding and M. Pfaff eds., *Redistribution to the Rich and the Poor* (Belmont, Calif: Wadsworth Publishers, 1973).
2. "Inflation and the Consumer in 1972," staff report prepared for the Joint Economic Committee, 92nd Congress, 1st Session, January 14, 1974.
3. Arnold R. Weber, "Making Wage Controls Work," *Public Interest* 30, Winter 1973, p. 30.
4. For a full account of the arguments see *Pay Board Special Report: Relative Pay of Mineworkers*, HMSO, Command 5567, 1973.
5. John T. Dunlop, "The Task of Contemporary Wage Theory," in Dunlop ed., *The Theory of Wage Determination* (London: Macmillan, 1957), p. 15. He explains that while it may be true that wages tend to measure the marginal productivity of wages "this is not a theory of wages rate determination. It does not explain particular wages nor the general wage levels" (p. 10).
6. Dunlop, ibid., p. 16.
7. Dunlop, ibid., pp. 18-20.
8. Marvin Kosters, Kenneth Fedor, and Albert Eckstein, "Industrial Relations and Inflation: Collective Bargaining Settlements and the Wage Structure," *Labour Law Journal*, August 1973, p. 519.
9. D.Q. Mills, *Government, Labor, and Inflation*, (Chicago: University of Chicago Press, 1975). Copyright © 1975 by the University of Chicago.
10. Colin Crouch, "The Ideology of a Managerial Elite: The National Board for Prices and Incomes 1965-70," in Ivor Crewe, ed., *British Political Sociology Yearbook, vol. 1; Elites in Western Democracy* (London: Croom Helm Ltd., 1974).
11. Arnold Weber, "Making Wage Controls Work," p. 37.
12. Barbara Wootton, *The Social Foundation of Wage Policy* (London: Allen and Unwin, 1962), p. 120.
13. Correspondence with John Goldthorpe, July 29, 1974.
14. Terry Robards, "London Testing a Pact with Unions", *New York Times*, October 6, 1974.
15. For a detailed review of this experience in Europe and the United States, see S.M. Miller and Martin Rein, "The Possibilities of Income Transformation," *Social Policy* (forthcoming).
16. See "The Great American Wage Puzzle," *New York Times*, May 26, 1974, p.F2.
17. John H. Goldthorpe, "Social Inequality and Social Integration in Modern Britain," in D. Wedderburn ed., *Inequality and Class Structure* (Cambridge, Cambridge University Press, 1974), p. 228.

9 The Drive for Equality: Experience of Incomes Policy in Britain
Colin Crouch

The recent experience in several European societies of inflation, renewed militancy by organized labor, and an increasing state involvement in the determination of pay, prices, and profits has reopened one of the classical issues of sociological debate: Is society becoming more equal? The question is a large one, and this chapter considers only one aspect of it: What have been the implications for the forces seeking a reduction in material inequalities of the development of incomes policy in Britain?

This inevitably neglects several issues. No matter how strong a demand for more equality might be, such major constraints as the role of rewards to capital, the scarcity of trained skills in the division of labor, and other sources of antiegalitarian power will inhibit the translation of that demand into action. Second, it is not only direct political pressures that can affect the structure of inequality; economic developments, changes in technology, and the unanticipated by-products of political and other action may all have far more important practical consequences. Third, the emphasis in this chapter is on the reduction of inequalities, rather than on the pursuit of a state of equality. This avoids philosophical questions on the nature of equality as a condition, and difficult problems of the point at which, say, an inequality of material reward merely compensates for a complementary output of effort, skill, or risk. I am assuming (1) that we live in societies in which the inequalities of wealth, income, and life chances are sufficiently large for us to be able to speak of inequalities and the political feasibility of their reduction without rapidly reaching the point where a state of equality may actually be attained; and (2) that important though the "compensation" argument is, it can itself serve as a legitimation of inequalities and is hence part of the problem to be studied rather than a scientifically established constraint on the formulation of that problem. A final limitation is that the chapter is heavily concentrated on recent British experience in one major area of policy, that of incomes policy and workers' pressures for increased pay. This has its handicaps, because many aspects of British politics and industrial relations are not readily comparable with those of other countries. But little of substance can be said on a major comparative basis in a chapter of this length, while an entirely abstract discussion of logical possibilities would be worth very little.

I am grateful to John Goldthorpe (Nuffield College, Oxford), Professor Ernest Gellner (London School of Economics and Political Science), and Professor Ronald Dore (Institute of Development Studies, University of Sussex) for comments on earlier drafts of this chapter, although I am of course solely responsible for its contents.

It is therefore hoped that, distinctive though British experience might be, certain lessons of a more general nature may emerge from it, if only perhaps by contrast.

The State and Industrial Conflict

In concrete terms the immediate question becomes: to what extent can one identify in Britain forces pursuing a reduction in major material inequalities? Is egalitarianism a vital political force?

Ostensibly the relevance of industrial conflict to major questions of overall material inequality is not in doubt. But in practice it has only rarely touched such questions. At several different levels of social structure industrial conflict has been channelled and institutionalized so that it relates to a narrow set of issues. Historically the most fundamental source of this narrowing has been that segregation of economic, political, and ideological dimensions of social structure that is so characteristic of a capitalist economy. "Industrial" issues are separated from "political" ones; the polity avoids a direct economic role, and it is difficult for an immediate economic conflict to acquire universal and political implications. Similarly, in the ideology of laissez-faire such economic matters as income distribution are conceived as being "rationally" determined by the market and therefore free of ethical implications.[1]

The larger structural phenomenon to which these processes relate is the essential invisibility of class structure in capitalist society, especially a liberal capitalist society in which institutions of universal citizenship have been established and the incorporation of working-class organizations has been achieved.[2] This factor is probably closely related to the interesting phenomenon that it is societies which have retained elements of a feudal and rural structure during the rise of capitalism that have developed revolutionary working-class movements. In countries where the emergence of capitalism has been more thorough-going class conflict takes on a far less aggressive political form.[3] Capitalist society may here be contrasted with previous societies in which elites buttressed their rule through their visibility, their overt combination of economic, political, and ideological dominance, and their rejection of demands for universal citizenship. Such ruling classes made major claims to intrinsic superiority; no pretense at equality could even be presumed (at least, not this side of the grave). To a certain extent it is true that early capitalism sought explicit religious legitimations, but with time these were transformed into mundanely rationalistic claims. Inequalities of material reward became divorced from any consideration of moral deserts; the distribution of income was an objectively determined consequence of the labor market.

In subsequent development the economic dimension has been subject to further internal fragmentation. The functional separation of ownership and management means that the social relationship around which conflict is in practice articulated—manager and managed—is separated from that where the most obvious conflict over distribution occurs—owners and employees. Workers' demands for higher wages have been further diverted from major conflicts over distribution by the availability of such alternative means of their satisfaction as increases in overall productivity, minor short-term redistributions between different groups of workers, and (temporarily and superficially) inflation.[4]

Finally, as has been discussed by R. Dahrendorf and others,[5] industrial conflict has become institutionalized as employers and organized labor recognized the legitimacy of each other's role, organized their conflict through stable institutions, and developed a set of recognized procedures for resolving disputes.

But for several years now the British state has moved from its position of noninvolvement in questions of income determination and has challenged several traditional practices of the institutionalization of conflict. If the tensions potentially generated by the inequalities of a capitalist society could be defused by the structural articulation of that society and by the network of institutions that developed around industrial conflict, what are the implications of such a major shift in that balance of structures and institutions? In what circumstances should we expect an intensification and spread of conflict over issues of inequality?

To account fully for this new activity by the state, which is by no means limited to Britain, is beyond our present scope, but it is possible to indicate certain important proximate causes.[6] First, there is the generally increasing role of government in the modern economy, related to such factors as the scale and complexity of modern industrial development and the importance of planning at the national level. Second are the implications of the state's commitment to the particular interventionist policy of full employment. Full employment removes from the economy one of the main fingers of the "invisible hand" with which capitalism restrains subordinates, and this provokes a search for alternative mechanisms. The state becomes involved in policies of income restraint, which increasingly come to mean income determination in the wider sense.

It is easy to see how this development disrupts the pattern of structured conflict described above. At the superficial level of institutionalization, expectations about the behavior of conflict-regulating institutions become disappointed; the state moves away from its traditional conciliatory role. More profoundly, the division between polity and economy—which has already been undermined by several twentieth-century developments—is threatened; what will be the implications if the state is seen as directly supporting a particular structure of occupational inequalities; or as extending unequal treatment to different factors of production or different kinds of occupational groups? At the same time the other crucial component of the invisibility of capitalism—its ethical agnosticism—is also at risk. A state incomes policy cannot long remain merely a policy of restraint. In a pluralistic society the state cannot depend on coercion; it relies heavily on attempts to create a voluntary consensus; this involves the use of moral suasion and the allocation of moral praise and blame. Definitions of selfish and unselfish behavior are developed, and particular practices become defined as "unfair." The most dramatic example of a government being drawn, against its initial will, towards policies of this kind was the Conservative government 1970-74. In Opposition the Conservatives had warned against introducing the language of fairness and social justice into income determination;[a] by February 1974 when for various reasons they had been moved to readopt an incomes policy they were ready to launch an entire general election campaign on the theme of fairness in incomes policy.[b] A second reason incomes policies rapidly involve ethical questions is that a policy of restraint has to consider criteria for increases. Since income determination by collective bargaining in Britain has much to do with "fair comparisons," it is difficult for a policy to become engaged in this area without involving itself in these same questions;[7] and the implications of seeking to apply such criteria at the level of a national state policy are of course much wider than their existing use at the level of various autonomous bargains.

There are at least two major alternative ways in which the reemergence of the state, and its associated disruption of the insulation of industrial conflict, might be considered to reawaken the pursuit of equality as a political issue. Most of the remainder of this chapter explores the potentialities of these alternatives. First, it is often argued that this state intervention is itself egalitarian. In this view a state incomes policy certainly disrupts the balance achieved in the earlier compromise between capitalism and trade unionism in collective bargaining, but it does so in the direction of increasing equality. This is a common assumption about the role of the state in Britain, which one may trace to several sources. First, the concern for equity that invariably accompanies incomes policy is seen as having something to do with equality. Second, an important part of the political rhetoric surrounding incomes policy has been concerned with the role of that policy in protecting the weak. And, third, there is the general association between state intervention, socialism, and social welfare policy.

A very different argument sees the pressure for equality coming not so much from incomes policy itself as from reactions to it. It is argued that the

[a]For example, Mr. Edward Heath said in 1966, when Leader of the Opposition, ". . . wages are in future to be governed as a major element, by social justice. . ... This will not give confidence to anybody abroad or anybody in this country who is trying to produce an efficient and effective economy. They will immediately see that economic decisions are always to be pushed to one side in favour of a vague criterion of social justice. Surely the House must agree that, if social problems have to be dealt with, they should be dealt with by social policy and not by interference in economic policy as such." *Hansard*, December 1, 1966, vol. 737, col.660.

[b]The Conservative manifesto for the election, entitled, *Firm Action for a Fair Britain*, called for "a fair and orderly policy for pay and prices . . . . " and for "a morality of fairness without regimentation."

process of throwing income distribution open to political debate will increase the salience of the overall structure of that distribution; people in subordinate positions will become more aware of inequality, and will seek to reduce it.[8] This argument is sometimes linked to a further one: that a modern economy requires a closer degree of integration and social solidarity than earlier industrial society, because of the importance of co-operation and mutual effort; that this solidarity is only likely to be achieved if there is a greater degree of moral consensus over such matters as income distribution; and that this consensus will only be forthcoming in the circumstances of a modern society if there is a considerable degree of overall equality.[9]

These two rival approaches are examined in turn.

Have Incomes Policies Sought to be Egalitarian in Their Effects?

A full discussion of whether incomes policy in Britain has in practice been egalitarian would be a complex technical task; it also involves ultimately speculative conjecture about what would have occurred over the period concerned had the policy not existed. One is thus studying two very different questions: on the one hand the results of the policy when it was effectively applied, and on the other the extent to which it was, or could be, so applied. Since our primary concern is with the direction of policy it may be more relevant as well as simpler to consider the intentions of policies rather than their measurable practical consequences. For this purpose we shall consider in turn the implications of certain aspects of various recent incomes policies, as follows:

A crude and limited egalitarianism to be achieved by concentrating on the "extremes" of the income hierarchy, principally the lower extreme. This includes measures to restrain or tax higher incomes and concentrations of private wealth, with fiscal and other measures to help the lowest paid. In 1964-70 this formed an important part of the rhetoric of incomes policy.[10] In practice the main organ for administering the policy, the National Board for Prices and Income (NBPI), did not give priority to this aspect of its task.[11] However, towards the end of the period low pay became a political issue and some more purposeful government action was taken: Low pay was allowed as a criterion for exceptional increases; encouragement was given to pay settlements that concentrated raises on the lowest paid; and measures were taken to enable the lowest paid to be protected from the essentially inegalitarian effects of a policy based on percentage increases (this last point is discussed more fully below). Assistance to the poor was also claimed to be an objective of policy in 1972-74, largely through the benefits that would accrue to them if the pressures of organized labor for higher incomes were restrained and inflationary pressures thereby reduced.

These policies really had to do with relative poverty, which is often confused with inequality in British debate; a kind of egalitarianism was involved, but it was limited to a redistribution between the very poor and those not far above them in the income hierarchy. The view implied by such a policy is therefore that the overall structure of inequality is acceptable, but that those at the very bottom should be assisted to move a little closer to those immediately above them, on the grounds of concern for their overall standard of life.

Attempts at either persuasive delegitimation of, or measures for the legal limitation of, particular means of protecting or advancing pay levels. The means most often singled out for attention has been industrial action by organized labor, though "windfall" profits and gains from land speculation have also come under heavy rhetorical attack.[12] Economic strength secured through such means as professional organization, hierarchical position in organizations, the possession of scarce skills and most forms of capital investment have not been subject to this kind of criticism. This policy therefore seeks to reduce or eliminate one of the means used by people in the lower and middle (but not high or the lowest) ranges of the income structure to advance their position. As such its implications for equality are ambiguous, but they are certainly not overwhelmingly egalitarian; and by implication the remaining modes of advancing one's economic position are legitimated.

These themes have been present throughout the development of incomes policy, but attacks on industrial action become most prominent from 1968 to 1974, during which period both Labor and Conservative governments sought to impose legal restraints on the activities of organized labor. From 1970 to 1972 measures of this kind were the Conservative administration's main strategy on incomes, more explicit incomes policies having been temporarily rejected.

Attempts at the construction of a rationalistic hierarchy of occupational rewards, based primarily on criteria of skill and responsibility, and making use of such techniques as job evaluation, work study, and measured day work. The National Board for Prices and Incomes attempted this task piecemeal with the references that were submitted to it, treating its cases, that is, as though such a hierarchy could be constructed. This hierarchy was seen explicitly as corresponding to both rational and ethical criteria.[13] The policy of "relativities" that appeared at the very end of the 1970-74 Conservative government's incomes policy constituted a different approach to a similar question.[14] Provision was to be made for examination of the cases of those who had slipped from an earlier relative position in a particular earnings "league table," or who felt that circumstances had altered sufficiently to warrant their moving up such a table. The policy was primarily concerned with manual workers, and certainly did not embrace all income earners; to extend the league table analogy it more accurately should be regarded as a policy for dealing with the lower divisions of a league, rather than an entire league. This policy did not involve such detailed application of the rational criteria to particular cases as did the NBPI, but it proceeded on the assumption that rationality and fairness were characteristics that could be attributed to the income structure. The notion of fairness maintained here was that of equity in the strict and essentially conservative sense of that term: One may lay claim to the rights and rewards associated with one's established station, but there is little scope for challenging the hierarchy of stations itself or the criteria that support it.

These policies were the most detailed that have been developed so far in Britain, and they constituted both an ambitious attempt at imposing a framework for settling levels of income and a compromise with existing practices. They reflected a managerialist approach to income determination, which bears a complex relationship to the classical capitalist method of market allocation; in so far as skill and responsibility (the main criteria of the hierarchy) are deemed to be related to scarcity, application of these principles may be seen as the *ersatz* recreation of a market situation in a society where the actual process of market determination is considered chaotic, inflationary, or too unstable for managerial requirements.[15] But at the same time the application of skill and responsibility criteria, together with the structure of comparisons erected by the relativities policy, went some way towards meeting traditional trade union demands for fair comparisons and the maintenance of certain patterns of differentials. But if there was an attempt at compromising with trade-union criteria, there was no willingness to compromise with trade-union power, or with union verdicts on what would compromise proper differentials. It is in this way that these policies become implicated in those given above. They were attempts at constructing rationally legitimated hierarchies of income inequality that would stand some chance of winning the agreement of a trade unionists, but they sought to appropriate for official administrative determination questions that had hitherto been the province of bargaining.

Another relevant aspect of these attempts at constructing administered hierarchies of inequality is the limited nature of the universe of application of the rationalistic criteria. Objective measures of the relative worth of jobs can be applied more readily the more the job is subject to detailed control and able to be costed; involves routine as opposed to discretionary operations; and makes use of physical as opposed to intellectual effort. They are therefore most applicable to subordinate jobs, and to manual rather than to nonmanual ones. This becomes clear from an examination of the difficulties experienced by the NBPI when it tried to apply its approach to professional earnings. And of course neither the NBPI nor the Pay Board could treat profits as in any way comparable to earned incomes, that is as incomes accruing to individuals in exchange for the application of skill, responsibility, and effort.

The establishment of a percentage norm of permissible income increases. This has always been a predominant feature, because the objectives of incomes policies have often been conceived in terms of the relation between annual percentage increases in incomes, prices, and productivity. Various percentages were established as the norm, varying between nil and 3.5 percent between

1962 and 1969. A major readjustment in line with the important increase in
the level of inflation that became noticeable at the end of the 1960s came with
the Conservative strategy 1970-72 (that is, before the formal readoption of
statutory incomes policy). This was the policy that became known as the
"n - 1", the objective of which was to insure by a variety of pressures that
each major wage settlement would be about one percent less than the previous
one. Interestingly this was seen as unfair, because the percentage to which
one was entitled depended on the arbitrary chance of position in the queue.
The readoption of a formal policy in 1973 saw a return to percentage norms.
As these policies have flourished over the past decade,[16] increasingly sophisticated safety valves have been developed to cope with (and contain) exceptions, including provision for exceptional increases for the lowest paid, productivity bargains, and special provisions for working "unsocial hours." In 1973
provision was made for threshold agreements under which specified flat-rate
increases would be awarded automatically if the retail price index reached a
specified point by a certain date.

The strategy of the percentage increase has an apparent universalism. It
combines equality of *process* (subjection to an equal percentage norm) with
inequality of *substance* (a percentage increase being notoriously antiegalitarian).
The major exceptions to the principle of the equal percentage have occurred in
deference to strategy action on the extremes of the income distribution. Under
the 1965-70 policy the government looked favorably on agreements with
"tapered" percentage increases, under which a full increase would be given to
those at the bottom of the scale, with the percentage being reduced at each
step above the floor. In this way a differential could be maintained, though
eroded, while the increase was concentrated on the lowest paid. A more rigidly
defined version of this followed in 1973 with the principle of £1 a week plus
four percent (the flat-rate element obviously entailing a positive if minor diminu-
tion of differentials in percentage terms), together with an absolute ceiling of
£250 increase in any one year.[17] The ceiling (and also the flat-rate thresholds
discussed above) did constitute a positive egalitarian move and indicate the
viability of the proposition that a move to lessen inequalities is likely to be
involved in incomes policy. This may have been particularly important for
the government of the time that had entered office with a declared policy of
increasing certain inequalities. When they came to develop an incomes policy
they were vulnerable to the criticism that they had not created the kind of
environment in which this would be possible. However, it is important to
note the limitations of these egalitarian moves. They were limited in application to earned income and were in any case intended only to be temporary
policy instruments. For them to have a material effect on pay structure they
would need to be in operation for several years. Further, it is inaccurate to
regard fairly universal percentage increases at regular annual intervals as having
been the common practice under voluntary collective bargaining. Figures show

wide variations in percentages, a tendency at some periods and in some industries to agree to flat rate instead of percentage increases, and rather irregular time spans. In fact it is probably the rise of government incomes policy that has led to a greater standardisation of percentage awards and of timing.[18]

Voluntary understandings between government and organized labor, under which union restraint in the pursuit of wage claims would be exchanged for government pursuit of certain social policies. These policies have included specific measures to aid collective bargaining, action to restrict rises in the cost of living, improvements in social welfare and, significantly, fiscal measures to redistribute wealth and income.

A strategy of this kind had been part of the rhetoric of incomes policy between 1964 and 1970, but even at this level it was only vaguely conceived. It took further shape while the Labor party was in opposition (1970-74) as the "social contract" between government and unions. The minority Labor government of March 1974 adopted this theme as its sole incomes policy, and in the October 1974 general elections it became the party's central platform.[c] The policy is best interpreted as an extension of collective bargaining into politics. The unions make certain political demands in exchange for which they offer a measure of wage restraint. As such it is a reciprocal action for the steady intrusion of politics into collective bargaining. In principle it has more powerful egalitarian implications than any of the other forms of policy discussed, not so much in the nature of the income restraint which it provides as in the political demands that accompany it (such as demands for a wealth tax or for subsidies of basic foods financed by progressive taxation). These policies do not concern just the narrowing of income differentials, but affect a whole range of social and economic issues.[19]

However, against all this has to be set the extreme vagueness of the policy in practice. Nowhere are the terms of the contract properly set out, and the identity of the parties to it is not even clear. One side is clearly the government, but there is ambiguity whether the other party is the trade union movement or as implied in some Ministerial speeches, the country as a whole. The fact that the terms are so nebulous suggests a lack of confidence by both government and the unions in their capacity to fulfil undertakings of any specificity.

Setting aside the potentialities of this last strategy, it would be difficult to conclude from the foregoing discussion that incomes policy has had as other than an ancillary purpose the overall reduction of inequality; the reverse proposition has indeed at least an equal claim to consideration. The

---

[c]"At the heart of this manifesto and our programme to save the nation lies the Social Contract between the Labour Government and the trade unions. . . ."

"The Social Contract . . . covers the whole range of national policies." (Labour Party Manifesto, October 1974).

central preoccupation of all these policies had been restraint, particularly on
the activities of organized labor. To the extent that they went beyond that
their concern was with insuring a stable structure of inequality, oscillating
somewhat between a concern for the maintenance of existing relationships
and a more ambitious attempt at securing rational inequalities—with the main
emphasis on manual and routine white-collar workers. There was some concern with the position of the lowest paid, largely in relation to those not far
above them in the scale. But the policies could be claimed to correspond to
certain conceptions of equity, and also to certain limited kinds of universalism:
the universalism of equal subjection to a percentage norm; universalism in the
application of work measurement to various grades of worker; and the universalism of those who accept the application of the policy to themselves, in
contrast with those who use industrial action to evade it.

Have Incomes Policies Politicized Industrial Relations?

Incomes policy itself may be inegalitarian, but it may evoke an egalitarian
response. It involves a politicization of industrial relations issues that may
contribute to an intensification of union militancy; and it may make the contours of the incomes hierarchy more evident and vulnerable to political action.
Such a response could come about in several ways. One might assume a general
desire for more equality among the population as a whole, and several commentators have interpreted the general increase in industrial militancy to mean just
this. For example, Aubrey Jones, the former chairman of the NBPI, has
written:

> The franchise is now universal, . . . it would be surprising, then, if
> "everyman" did not attempt to extend into the economic field
> the political equality to which he has become accustomed. . . . . why
> should somebody with a nominal political right equal to everybody
> else's be content just with an equal minimum [as in the Welfare
> State]? Why should he not try more insistently to try and climb
> the mountain? The struggle for economic equality is to the 20th
> century what the struggle for political rights was in the 19th
> century.[20]

Alternatively it may be argued that a reduction in inequality may be an
objective consequence of militancy whether or not it is explicitly sought. The
various ways in which these two arguments operate can best be explored if one
considers the different forms of practical action that have lent credence to them.
    1. There is clear evidence that the Trade Union Congress and certain
national unions have come to take a deeper interest in the overall distribution

of income and wealth. Of course, this could be written off as the rhetoric of a trade union movement that on formal public occasions likes to lay claim to a mythical socialist past. But there is distinct evidence that since the late 1960's, trade unions have engaged seriously in the formulation of alternative economic policies, in which demands for egalitarian policies have been important.

One can see this shift in the TUC and union policy as a direct consequence of the increase in state intervention in income determination. So long as the state was content to leave voluntary collective bargaining alone, the unions were happy to play a relatively nonpolitical role. Their political commitment to the Labor party has never involved them in a serious and continuing concern for political issues.[21] But once the state began to interfere in collective bargaining and to express a view about criteria for increases and appropriate levels of pay for different occupations, the unions were perforce thrown into a wider arena. And their response was, in part, to point at sections of society outside organized labor, and richer than its members, who were not being subjected to what they saw as equivalent restraints. A major item in this direction was the institution of the Annual Economic Review by the TUC in 1968, which was used not only as a basis for lobbying government but as guidelines for the TUC's own incomes policy.

The social contract can be considered as a development of this constituting the nearest approach yet of the unions actually making political demands (in exchange for wage restraint). To a certain extent this strategy depends heavily on there being a general demand for equality, for it is assumed in the contract that workers will be willing to exercise wage restraint if certain reforms are carried out. However, some aspects of the contract do not depend on this. For example, action to stabilize the cost of living through subsidies or through profit controls, assuming the measures take certain forms, have redistributive implications. Here it is not necessary that workers recognize the egalitarianism and hence wage restraint in exchange; it is simply that, if they recognize a stabilization of their cost of living, they may not agitate so strongly for wage claims.

2. Certain developments in collective bargaining have made it more possible for workers and unions to challenge managerial control. Nationally, unions have sought changes in company law that would make more knowledge of company affairs available to union negotiators.[22] Organized labor has started to emerge from the narrow range of issues with which it was for so long preoccupied. Wider demands on conditions and security of employment, challenges to the exercise of managerial prerogatives, and attempts at regulating management's disciplinary powers, have all been involved in this process. In some cases these developments have been related to the highly ambiguous process of productivity bargaining, currently out of favor in Britain but an important aspect of collective bargaining during the 1965-70 incomes policy.[23] There is little doubt that the main intention of government and employers in advancing productivity bargaining was to regain managerial control by offering workers

shorter hours, greater security and, sometimes, higher incomes in exchange for their relinquishing certain areas of unilateral regulation, craft rules, and traditional working arrangements.[24] However, once the concept of involving work practices in negotiations over pay and conditions had been promulgated, it was possible for alert unions to build on it to their own advantage. In particular the Transport and General Workers' Union turned productivity bargaining into a means of securing union and workers' control over a wider range of aspects of employment conditions, bringing into bargaining issues that management had normally sought to retain as its prerogative.[25]

Although these various developments in collective bargaining do not relate directly to overall inequality, they are potentially relevant to it. They raise workers' activity above a concern for short-range issues, small pay increases and relative differentials. They may involve important challenges to the scope of managerial authority (which is after all a major factor in the structure of overall inequality throughout an individual enterprise), and may bring under scrutiny such issues as a firm's allocation of resources, and distribution of profits.

An important aspect of the resurgence of activity has been the increase in shop-floor militancy in many industries.[26] Workers have been increasingly willing to take action, with or without union support, to defend their standard of living and work patterns, and aggressively to seek means of securing further improvements. Of course, this upsurge of activity is not a consequence of incomes policy, but it may be considered to have potential implications for inequality, in that it means that formerly passive sections of the working population are more determined to seek improvements in their living standards.

3.   During the major intensification of inflation of the past two years, those two previously described processes have come together in an apparent pincer movement. Unions and unofficial groupings have pressed major wage claims, while government controls on prices and profits, introduced partly as a response to union pressure, have limited the ability of firms to pass on the increases in price rises, at the same time that rising commodity prices have placed further strain on them. Profit margins have been squeezed, and although this has been associated with a reduction in investment rather than in distributed profits,[27] it has been implicated in the decline of company valuations, which has reduced the paper assets of many wealth holders. All these processes would seem to reduce inequalities of wealth. Finally, on a slightly different point, these developments have all served to make industry heavily dependent on government, raising the possibility of major state appropriations of privately owned industry at low rates of compensation. Though wage militancy is far from being the only factor in the economic crisis that has generated these developments, it is certainly one of them, and it has been in an attempt to control that militancy that governments have imposed some of the pressures on companies. It was the early development of this process in the late 1960s

that led some Marxists to proclaim wage militancy as a potential contributor to the "final crisis of capitalism."[28]

However, certain other tendencies in the existing situation work against the various interpretations that might proceed from the three phenomena discussed. These are as follows:

There must be come scepticism over the extent to which unions would be able and willing to deploy their strength for wider socio-political objectives than the narrow concerns of collective bargaining. Historically the main reason British unions have entered the political arena has been to ward off attacks from government on their traditional freedoms in bargaining; once the battle has been won or lost they have again subsided into political quiescence.[29] This was true of the occasion of the union's original formation of their own political party, and has remained so throughout this century with the exception of wartime.

Of course, if it is really true that we are at present on the brink of a major historical change, then these lessons of past history may no longer be relevant. But examination of unions' most recent use of a wider political strength suggests that the traditional interpretation still holds. Almost without exception the evidence given by unions to the Royal Commission on Trade Unions and Employers Associations in 1965-68, was preoccupied with the defense of free collective bargaining. Disagreements with the 1964-70 Labor government over incomes policy concerned not so much the fact of restraint or the application of certain kinds of criteria as the statutory nature of the policy; and the major confrontation with that government, involving an unprecedented use of political strength by the unions, concerned an Industrial Relations Bill that sought certain limitations on the legal freedom of industrial action. Although during the subsequent Conservative government the unions opposed a renewed statutory incomes policy, they rarely sought to defy or destroy the application of that policy; but the Industrial Relations Act introduced by that government, which imposed legal controls on bargaining, met with almost complete noncooperation. Finally, it is noteworthy that the major confrontation between government and unions that precipitated the general election of February 1974, that with the National Union of Mineworkers, was essentially a confrontation over the *means* of settlement of the wage claim; the government tried to insist on the use of its new administrative machinery for fixing pay, while the union wanted to return to the traditional method of collective bargaining backed by the sanction of industrial action. Even this major increase in the involvement of unions in political conflict was therefore consistent with the traditional stance of British unions. Each episode in their apparent move towards political militancy can be more accurately seen as a defensive response to a new militancy from the state that was threatening traditional bargaining. It remains an open question whether unions have either the will or the power to press aggressive as opposed to defensive political demands.

Commentators on the resurgence of industrial conflict in Britain speak
frequently of an increase in workers' "expectations," and of a "wage explosion"
dating from late 1969. In fact, little is known of the nature of these expectations, and this remains one of the most important gaps in knowledge on these
questions that should be filled by sociological research. There has certainly
been a change of some kind, but rash statements that it constitutes evidence
that formerly narrow reference frameworks of manual workers have been
transcended are premature.[30] The somewhat indirect evidence[31] that is available suggests that workers have been seeking to maintain a certain standard
of life and have therefore sought to anticipate inflation—in other words, they
have transcended "money illusion." They have probably also come to expect
a slight rise in their living standards each year, and are not simply protecting
a static level. Finally, there is evidence that wage claims have sought to counter
the effects of increased taxation on "take-home pay"; this is a fairly novel
phenomenon, since it is only in recent years that the great bulk of wage earners
has been earning enough to become liable to income taxation. Now, these
developments may well indicate a new assertiveness by workers in their demands
for a certain standard of life, and in many cases a greater willingness to use
industrial action to achieve that standard, but none of them necessarily implies
a concern for or even an awareness of the wider inequalities of the society as a
whole; indeed, all these actions could take place within an already highly egalitarian society.

Closely related to this point is the fact that it is precisely at the level of
shop-floor wage determination, that level at which the new militancy is most
evident, that frames of reference are most narrow. The evidence of several
studies of shop-floor bargaining[32] demonstrates that it is predominantly concerned with fractional increases, the protection of existing securities, and minor
exercises in comparability based on the relative movements of closely related
occupations. This evidence is also interesting in displaying the complex nature
of workers' pressures at this level. In part it is a highly opportunistic pressure;
workers will simply take what chance they can to secure minor improvements
in their position. But it is not merely a matter of alertness for opportunities.
There are also strongly held notions of fairness, which affect workers' strength
of feeling on an issue, their judgements of whether management is acting properly, and whether they are being treated justly in relation to other workers.
The fact that ethical judgements are so important at this immediate level
emphasizes the absence in practical industrial relations of their application over
a wide social perspective. To assume that militant shop-floor wage pressure has
anything to do with the overall pattern of income and wealth is to make a large
assumption for which there is little established support.

Obviously, the weaknesses of the former two developments automatically
affect the possibility of the "pincer movement," and certain further points
need to be made on this issue. Although many commentators draw sweeping

conclusions on the implications for wealth distribution of the current inflation, the available evidence on which groups suffer most from inflationary pressures is much more ambiguous.[33]   Many managerial and white-collar occupations, even if not unionized themselves, have their pay scales linked to the movements of manual wages, because managements seek to insure the "integrity" of their payment systems. It would also be premature to draw long-term conclusions based on very recent experience. Research has shown that, in the past, periods when organized labor or specific occupations have made major advances up the pay scale have been followed by periods of readjustment to previously existing relationships.[34]

Finally, the arguments concerning the fate of companies under pressure need reexamination. It is clear that a modern government will take action of some kind in the face of a declining viability of major firms. The question is, will its action consist simply of assistance to and subsidy of existing institutions, with an easing of the price controls that have been part of the pincer movement? Or will it move to a policy of acquisition and intervention as described above? The easier course is the former one, and special pressures would need to be present to shift state action in a crisis towards the second, more controversial strategy. Such a pressure is apparently present in Britain today in the unions' political demands within the social contract. But that pressure is heavily dependent on the unions' ability to deliver their side of the bargain—wage restraint. If that collapses the pressure for policies to please the unions declines. Except in the unlikely circumstances that unions would then be able and willing to use industrial action directly to demand such measures, government would be under considerably stronger compulsion to concede the demands of companies facing bankruptcy rather than those of unions that can offer nothing in return. Much therefore depends, if not on the existing social contract device, on the viability of some kind of political bargaining. It is at this point that the paradox discussed above becomes crucial again: the points of strength of the current militancy are poorly deployed for a strategy that relates to overall social inequalities. The basis of its power is at shop-floor level, but it is here that its objectives are narrowest; its ability to comprehend the wider issues is at the level of national leadership, but in many of the most important unions this is no longer the main source of power. Overall, the points at which the intensiveness of militancy are concentrated do not correspond to those at which it is most extensive.

It is reasonable to conclude that if there is any drive for a reduction of inequality in the current situation it is as an objective by-product of attempts by government, unions, and workers to stabilize the cost of living. These possibilities are real, but limited. Evidence of a drive for equality in the sense of the subjectively intended action of a movement is much more doubtful. This is not simply the familiar discussion of whether people "want to be equal"; that debate itself is dependent on certain more fundamental assumptions concerning the nature of popular political orientations and aspirations. Before we can consider whether people "want" equality or inequality we have to ask whether questions of that kind have any meaning to ordinary people in the light of the narrowness of perspectives revealed in industrial relations activity as discussed above.

Worker Perceptions and Perspectives

There are two complementary sets of explanations of the narrowness of perspectives: concerning (1) the structure of industrial relations activity and (2) workers' attitudes and perspectives. The structural explanations concern points made earlier in this chapter on the institutional segregation of industrial conflict; not only are industrial conflicts insulated from expansion into wider spheres, but also the fact that small-scale but positive gains are realistically attainable within this limited framework channels activity into well-known paths.

Workers and unions are unlikely to launch a major contentious challenge to criteria for the overall structure of incomes if claims based on short-run comparisons or the cost of living can provide the basis of a dialogue with management, making an actual increase in wages much more likely. Although much is said about the power of industrial workers, within an economy governed ultimately by market constraints and based on private ownership and managerial hierarchy, that power is only operative within limits. Were a union to step outside the framework of claims that can be met without disturbing the overall structure, it would encounter major obstacles to its power and waste its substance in fights that it would lose. For example, although solidarity and militancy are important to an explanation of the considerable industrial power currently enjoyed by coal miners, one cannot neglect the relevance of the shift in their market position afforded by the rise in oil prices. At a certain point, presumably, miners' demands would exceed the scope that this affords them and they would encounter more powerful government resistance, or would run the risk of a shift in policy away from coal.

The structural aspects are intensified by the question of workers' subjective perceptions. Here, it is valuable to relate the conclusions drawn above on the nature of industrial militancy to the evidence of sociological research on workers' attitudes and perceptions of their world. W.G. Runciman's study[35] of the social standards of comparison against which perceptions of inequality are judged showed that notions of fairness and equity do have meaning for people; but that for manual workers the universe of comparison rarely extends beyond a very local and limited range; and that the only major examples of frames of reference crossing "class" boundaries occurred when various middle-class respondents listed manual workers as those in the society who were doing better than they were.

The series of studies of "affluent" workers in Luton by J.H. Goldthorpe,

D. Lockwood et al[36] was not so directly concerned with perceptions of overall social structure, but described a set of attitudes called "instrumentalism,"
which was contrasted with the solidaristic collectivism of more traditional
workers. Instrumentalism carries the implications of opportunism and assertiveness discussed in the previous section; but it also conveys the same sense of
limitation and *narrowness* of perspectives. The fact that the Luton workers
had cut themselves free from various traditional constraints on their perspectives did not mean that they now had radical horizons for their ambitions or
radical criteria for judging their relative social position.

The Luton workers were predominantly Labor party voters; but it is interesting to note how studies of working-class Conservative voters reveal a similar
shift in the basis of attitudes from traditionalism to a narrow opportunism.[37]
In the case of the Conservatives the tradition away from which research detects
a movement is that of deference, not the solidaristic working-class tradition of
Lockwood and Goldthorpe's traditional workers. But the "secularism" or
"pragmatism" that is described as the attitude of modern working-class Conservative voters is strikingly similar to that of instrumentalism. And what is
noteworthy here is that "pragmatism," "secularism," and "instrumentalism"
are all essentially *particularistic* dispositions. This is not stressed in the studies
themselves, because they are concerned with contrasts with other forms of
particularism but it is an important point.

Particularism merits analysis as a form of orientation towards action. It
comprises a set of limitations imposed on an actor's perception of available
goals and means by the local nature of his major sources of information about
the social world. Two important questions are raised by this: the relation
between particularistic action and rationality, and the range of forms that particularism may take.

Rational action may appear to be starkly contrasted with particularism in
that the former is often seen as action that is taken after *all* available ends and
the means thereto have been weighed carefully in the balance against each other.
But this abstract model is rarely followed in everyday life. The sheer complexity
and infiniteness of calculations needed to make a fully rational decision render
perfect rationality out of the question for most human situations, constrained
as they are by limitations of time, knowledge, and facility. In everyday life,
and indeed in more exalted action contexts, we cope with this problem by
limiting the arena of choice and calculation (i.e., of rationality) in our actions
to a few crucial points, using various more or less unexamined (and hence
strictly speaking nonrational) shorthand formulae in order to treat the rest
of our situation as "given," or as taken for granted. This process is likely to
be unconscious. Most practical social action therefore has a rational component,
shaped by the operation of attempts to make conscious relations between selected
means and selected ends, and an unexamined component, shaped by "givens"
in the social context of the action. There are many potential different kinds of
such a context including those defined above as "particularism."

In turn, particularistic constraints on rationality may take several forms. The most familiar is the constraint of tradition. In traditional action deeply entrenched values or stereotyped patterns of behavior, instilled through early socialization and reinforced by subsequent experience, heavily limit the operation of conscious choice. When the values are backed by powerful institutions and sanctions, and when alternative experience is very limited, the scope left for discretion may be extremely small, and traditional action may indeed be treated as distinctly nonrational. So important is tradition as a form of particularism that it is often seen as its only form, and any emergence from its constraints is proclaimed as an advance in rationality.[38] This assumption has been made in the classical literature and in modern discussions alike, but it is highly misleading. It is not simply old-established community patterns that impose a narrowness on working-class perspectives. The conditions of modern working-class life are just as conducive to constraints of localness as those in the communities with which it is more usually associated. Particularism persists; it merely takes novel forms.

None of this is to imply that dominant groups in society have, in contrast, a consistently rational, universal vision. It would be an interesting, though separate, exercise to study typical constraints on perspectives in that section of society too; one recalls the Bourbons who "learned nothing and forgot nothing."[39] But there are some reasons for suspecting that limitations of localness are not such a severe handicap at that level. First, through socialization and education most members of social elites are encouraged to act on a wide, national or even global, scale. Second, their occupational positions, greater scope for personal mobility, and so forth, remove them from the constraints of a single limited context. And third, since their interests are secured by the existing system there is not the same need to perceive alternatives.

It is important for sociology, essentially the sociology of culture, to interpret and conceptualize these varying forms of consciousness and its constraints. For the purposes of the present discussion our needs are more specific. Before we can establish the likely implications of industrial militancy and the interpretation that workers will place on incomes policy, we need to consider carefully the particular limitations of social perspective with which they are likely to be operating. These limitations have been explored by Michael Mann[40] in an article that, besides throwing further light on the substantive issue, criticizes certain kinds of sociological research for their neglect of this important question. He demonstrates that studies of political culture have tended to exaggerate both the degree of consensus on core values that exists in advanced capitalist societies, and the extent to which social cohesion depends on such a consensus. By means of a reanalysis of the results of research on popular attitudes, he argues that whereas working-class respondents are likely to give assent to formal abstract statements embodying what are seen as the dominant class consensus on certain key questions about social and political inequality, when asked to react to concrete everyday situations they may well express deviant or radically critical values. Mann goes on to argue that since in their everyday lives these people rarely encounter these major questions, little more is required of them; the societies in question maintain cohesion, not because of any great consensus on core values, but because of an absence of any powerfully articulated countervalues.

A point that stands out from this analysis is the evident difficulty that is experienced in generalizing from the concrete experience of working-class life to universal and political statements; what critical consciousness there is remains at the level of the concrete experience. Similar points are evident from a recent study of working-class politics in Liverpool by Barry Hindess.[41] The main lesson the author sought to draw from his study was the way in which the local politics of the Labor party had become remote from the experience of working-class people because it had adopted an essentially middle-class mode of discussing political issues. This same process was interpreted as one of a "betrayal" of class loyalties by the Labor party, and Hindess' study became generally known as a study of elitism and the neglect of working-class interests. However, if one examines his detailed evidence on the differences between working-class and middle-class politics it is by no means simply a question of the latter being less "radical"; the "working class politics" is usually heavily rooted in a concrete and particuliaristic mode, and it is the distinction between abstract and universal on the one hand, and concrete and particuliaristic on the other, that seems more relevant than an attempt at distinguishing between "conservative" and "radical." For example, discussions of housing policy among middle-class party activitists would be in terms of abstract questions of government action, finance, and the roles of various bureaucratic officials, while in working-class areas housing problems would be seen in much more immediate, specific, and personal terms of particular cases that people were experiencing.[42]

Hindess warns against a tendency to see working-class views as "nonpolitical" merely because they do not use the formal language of orthodox politics; but it is also true that such a phenomenon as a popular movement for a reduction in overall social inequality cannot easily emerge from a localized and limited perspective that does not even perceive matters outside the immediate context.

Even more directly relevant to questions of incomes policy is a recent study of shipbuilding workers by J. Cousins,[43] which noted a combination of conservative attitudes and militant behavior among shop stewards. The author concluded:

> It is as if workers had two separate systems of understanding: one reflected in general attitudes and responses to the industrial and normative systems of order and drawn from public attitudes; the other with potentially more radical implications, reserved for concrete, interpersonal interpretations, and drawn from specific experience of injustice and conflicting life styles.

These studies indicate the strength of the limitations that concreteness and specificity of time and place impose on working-class consciousness, not only within the bounds of rural deference or the conservatism of an entrenched proletarian community. The determinants of these limitations rest deeply in the structuring of perceptions of reality and their articulation, which render the work of Basil Bernstein[44] on the social bases of linguistic forms relevant to further exploration of this question.

The immediate context of Bernstein's work has been that of educability and different forms of speech communication between parents, teachers, and children. But as he would probably agree, his findings can be extended to other and wider social relationships. He has described two modes of speech communication, a restricted code based on limited grammatical and syntactical forms, to which nearly all members of a society have recourse, but to which manual workers and their families may be limited; and an elaborated code, with extensive grammar and syntax, use of which is limited to middle-class groups. At one point Bernstein distinguishes his two codes thus:

> A restricted code is generated by a form of social relationship based upon a range to closely shared identifications self-consciously held by the members. An elaborated code is generated by a form of social relationship which does not necessarily presuppose such shared, self-consciously held identifications with the consequence that much less is taken for granted.[45]

And elsewhere he says:

> An elaborated code is universalistic with reference to its meaning inasmuch as it summarizes *general* means and ends. A restricted code is particularistic with reference to its meaning inasmuch as it summarizes *local* means and ends. . . . Access to an elaborated code will depend not on psychological factors but on access to specialised social positions within the social structure, by virtue of which a particular type of speech model is made available. Normally, but not inevitably, these positions will coincide with a stratum seeking, or already possessing, access to the major decision-making area of the social structure."[46]

Of course, form and type of speech do not necessarily reflect (or indeed shape) total perceived experience; and as Mann's article showed, it is possible for the language of immediate and concrete social relationships to express such concepts as inequality with considerable clarity and vigor. But again, if we are considering the likelihood of the overall structure of inequality of rewards becoming politically salient in the same sense that immediate and local disparities already are, then the implications of Bernstein's analysis cannot be avoided. And, as he explicitly recognizes, the linguistic shaping of perception will be a major factor in shaping the rationality of action. The differences between restricted and elaborated frameworks of perception will affect the extent to which different social groups are capable of asking in the universalistic sphere of national politics.

This embarrassing aspect of social differences is usually ignored in political discussion. The well-established fact of universal suffrage, and the existence of such entrenched working-class institutions as trade unions, enable politicians, political commentators, and academic observers alike to assume that the society comprises a political community of equality in cognition and perception, but this is fundamentally misleading. As Mann[47] shows, such a study as that of G. Almond and S. Verba,[48] which seeks to demonstrate the maturity of the "civic culture" in Britain, ignores the wide social-class differences that were revealed by their own results. A more recent and critical examination of the civic culture concept, on the other hand, brings out fully the essential remoteness from politics of ordinary people in that country.[49]

These arguments have strayed from the initial point of reference—workplace militancy—but an important recent contribution by Alan Fox makes it possible to relate them.[50] Fox describes what he calls the "low-discretion" nature of most of industrial work, and the low level of trust that exists between employers and workers in consequence, and relates these to the extreme division of labor and the concentration of powers of control and organization in management that have been central to economic development. An aspect of this division of labor is a distinction between those whose lives and responsibilities concern only their immediate personal (or familial) context and those who relate to a wider universe of issues. Fox's analysis has further implications for the present discussion that will be considered shortly, but at this stage it is necessary only to note its contribution to the general conclusion of this section: that the ordinary people of as well-established a liberal democracy as Britain remain extremely limited in their perception of and ability to manipulate the political world. The mode of participation made available to them by socialization, work roles, and other experience hardly equips them for the kind of role that is assumed for them in discussions of the political implications of shop-floor militancy, the response to incomes policy, and a politicized collective bargaining.

The Search for Moral Reintegration

Evidence has been accumulated from several sources: from consideration of the structural location of collective bargaining in the British economy; from the facts of industrial militancy; from knowledge of workers' subjective perceptions; from Bernstein's sociology of early socialization; and from Fox's elaborations of the findings of industrial sociology. Its conclusions concern essentially

the uneven and limited nature of the entry of the working class into political
citizenship. The apparent universalism of the modern political community as
embodied in its formal institutions conceals vast disparities of both structural
position and subjective orientation. As such this argument will be unsurprising
to, say, Marxist observers who would see these limitations as highly functional
to the perpetuation of an existing class society. But it is at this point that
an important paradox must be considered. In this chapter the context for a
discussion of particularism has been the handicaps on a popular movement for
greater universal equality. But particularism has recently been creating equally
severe problems for defenders of the existing economic order. Here the problem is that of enjoining concern for a "national interest" on a working population that is now wielding its power to protect its standard of life in a time of
economic crisis.[d] Though this appeal is not exactly "universalist," it is one
that transcends localism, and it has encountered the same obstacles as the very
different project of trying to mobilize the forces for equality. Indeed, the social
contract incurs both difficulties, being dependent on both a commitment to
an ostensible national interest and a concern for egalitarian reform.

In the past various mechanisms have limited the dependence of the political
system on the active participation and positive consensus of the masses: high
unemployment, a relatively easy rate of improvement in the standard of living,
Disraelian combinations of reform and the manipulation of deference, simple
legal restraints, all have served their turn at various times in enabling an advanced
level of popular liberty to co-exist with a low level of overall social integration.
But now none of them seems able to operate. Increasingly, direct appeals have
to be made to "the people" voluntarily to impose self-restraint, but there is
little response. During the long postwar period the forces of conservatism and
order constituted the party of optimism and prosperity. But it is as though,
behind the relatively easy cohesion afforded by prosperity, the final remains
of traditional deference were withering away. And now conservatism is adopting a different mood, once familiar enough throughout Europe, but absent for
many years. Old fears of the power of the masses are returning. Hobbesian
and Malthusian echoes can be detected in recent political utterances: How
may the masses by restrained? What will limit their appetites?[51]

At a different level, sociologists and industrial relations specialists[52] have
begun to find renewed relevance in Emile Durkheim's *Division of Labour in
Society*. The concept of moral integration has become a practical question.
No doubt Durkheim would have pointed out that the pursuit of economic
growth and prosperity did itself rest on moral or ideological foundations.

---

[d]The most significant (and unsuccessful) example in Britain to date of such an
attempt at mass mobilization in the interests of order was the Conservative election
campaign of February 1974.

But when that growth seems fundamentally threatened the society appears strangely impoverished in ideological resources.

Some voices appeal for a new morality of order. Others, to return to our original theme, insist that the only relevant morality of order in modern society must be an egalitarian one.[53] But, given the existing state of affairs described in this chapter, all these arguments resemble complaints that the destination would be easier to reach were the starting point elsewhere than it is. At a time when the opposing political forces of egalitarianism and defense of the existing order have both felt the need for recourse to the active support of the mass of the people, they have both encountered a political vacuum. The intensity of political conflict is greater than for many years, and the issues at stake are central ones. But the popular response is confused and anomic.

It is against this whole background that speculation on the outcome of the apparent present resurgence of a concern for equality has to be made. It is not simply a matter of predicting the success of a reactivated Left, but of setting that against a reactivated Right and an anomic center. Everything depends on the eventual configuration of that triangular relationship, which will in turn be dependent on the emerging economic situation. In conclusion one may illustrate this point by the bald indication of certain alternative possibilities.

First, it has been noted at several points in the above discussion that certain tendencies in the present situation seem to have mildly egalitarian consequences, regardless of the problems of subjective motivation. To the extent that the leaders of working-class movements have egalitarian objectives, and to the extent that they can wield the militancy of their members as a weapon at least partly under their control, they may well use that militancy to achieve certain political ends. Indeed, there is evidence of that process at work in Britain at the present time. It is therefore possible that, provided economic conditions do not impose too severe a strain on the mechanism, policies of the social contract type may mark a limited shift towards egalitarianism in various spheres of policy. In this sense therefore one may speak of the resurgence of a drive for equality.

However, if the economic situation continues to decline, a second possibility arises. Government will make more pressing demands for restraint, and workers will become increasingly dissatisfied with their standard of life. The dependence of political institutions on positive mass co-operation will then intensify. Governments may offer increasingly radical policies in exchange for wage restraint; and measures may be taken to give reality to the notion of a shared community interest. It is then that the weaknesses of reliance on subjective orientations discussed in this chapter would become very relevant. If such weaknesses were transcended, the possibilities of a radical egalitarian movement would be very strong.

If they did not, and on the basis of this chapter this must be considered a more likely eventuality, then a third course of development becomes probable. The situation would be one in which egalitarian forces had raised powerful

demands but had completely failed to mobilize either popular support for them
or popular acceptance of the restraint that had been offered in exchange for the
reforms. The forces, namely the unions, would then be in a highly exposed
position, having evinced both an extreme radicalism and an ultimate powerlessness. The likely consequence of this would be a political move to the right,
with state action against organized labor. Whether this took the form of direct
legal controls, state incomes policy, or high unemployment, it is not possible
to predict; but it would be pursued more powerfully than the restrained experiments of the past. This would presumably see the end of the drive for equality.

Two final and contrasting changes of economic situation complete the
available alternatives. A sudden improvement, with a major revival of economic
growth, would probably mark a return to the patterns of the postwar decades,
with largely neutral consequences for inequality. Alternatively, a major slump
would lead quickly to high unemployment, an erosion of the power of organized
labor, and the removal of the question from the political agenda.

Notes

1. For an excellent discussion of this last phenomenon see Reinhard Bendix,
   Work and Authority in Industry (Berkeley: University of California Press,
   1974) chaps. 4 and 5.
2. C.W. Mills makes this point with particular reference to contemporary
   United States elites in *The Power Elite* (Oxford: Oxford University Press,
   1956). See also Nigel Harris, *Beliefs in Society* (New York: International
   Pubs. Co., 1968).
3. M. Mann, *Consciousness and Action among the Western Working Class*
   (London, Macmillan, 1973).
4. E. Phelps Brown and M. Browne, *A Century of Pay* (London: MacMillan,
   1968); G. Routh, *Occupation and Pay in Great Britain, 1906-1960*
   (Cambridge: Cambridge University Press, 1965).
5. R. Dahrendorf, *Class and Class Conflict in an Industrial Society* (Stanford:
   Stanford University Press, 1959); C. Kerr, *Labor and Management in Indus-
   trial Society* (New York: Doubleday, 1964), esp. the essay, "Industrial
   Conflict and its Mediation"; A.M. Ross and P.T. Hartman, *Changing Patterns
   of Industrial Conflict* (New York: Wiley, 1960).
6. Fuller accounts of different aspects of this question will be found in:
   J. Barbash, *Trade Unions and National Economic Policy* (Baltimore: Johns
   Hopkins Press, 1972); J.K. Galbraith, *The New Industrial State* (Boston:
   Houghton Mifflin, 2nd rev. ed. 1971); and A. Shonfield, *Modern Capitalism*
   (Oxford: Oxford University Press, 1969)
7. G.T. Saunders, "Problems of Incomes Policy," (Konferenz des Institute für
   Weltwirtschaft, Universität Kiel, May 1965.)

8. J.H. Goldthorpe, "Social Inequality and Social Integration in Modern Britain," in D. Wedderburn, ed., *Poverty, Inequality and Class Structure* (Cambridge: Cambridge University Press, 1974).

9. Ibid.; See also A. Fox, *Beyond Contract: Work, Power and Trust Relations* (London: Saber, 1974), ch. 8.

10. See, for example, Ministerial contributions to debates on prices and incomes policy at Labour Party Conferences 1966, 1967, 1968; and speeches made by several Ministers (R.H.S. Crossman, Mrs. B. Castle, R. Gunter, R. Marsh) in September 1966.

11. C.J. Crouch, "The Ideology of a Managerial Elite: The National Board for Prices and Incomes 1965-1970," in I. Crewe ed., *Elites in Western Democracy: British Political Sociology Studies Yearbook* (NY: Halsted Press, 1974), vol. 1. Also A. Fels, *The British Prices and Incomes Board* (Cambridge: Cambridge University Press, 1972).

12. Examples can be given from official and party documents and political speeches over several years, but a particularly concentrated discussion will be found in the record of the February 1974 general election campaign.

13. C. Crouch, "Ideology."

14. Pay Board, *Relativities* (London, H.M.S.O. 1974).

15. C. Crouch, "Ideology." See also the concept of "bureconic" pay structures developed by R. Marris, *Economic Theory of Managerial Capitalism* (NY: Free Press, 1964); and the arguments developed by J.L. Meij, "Wage Structure and Organisation Structure," in J.L. Meij, ed., *Internal Wage Structure* (Atlantic Highlands, N.J.: Humanities Press, 1963).

16. See various White Papers on incomes policy: *Machinery of Prices and Incomes Policy*, Cmnd 2577: 1965; *Prices and Incomes Standstill: Period of Severe Restraint*, Cmnd 3234: 1967; *Productivity, Prices and Incomes Policy in 1968 and 1969*, Cmnd 3590: 1968; *Programme for Controlling Inflation: The Second Stage*, Cmnd 5205: 1973; *The Counter-Inflation Programme*, Cmnd 5267: 1973.

17. *The Price and Pay Code*, SI 1973 no. 658, paras. 109, 121.

18. D. Layton, "Low Pay and Collective Bargaining," in F. Field (ed.), *Low Pay* (London: Acton Society Trust, 1973).

19. See, for example, the policies set out in *Economic Policy and the Cost of Living* (TUC–Labour Party Liaison Committee, 1973), which was one of the documents subsequently designated as being part of the social contract.

20. A. Jones, *The New Inflation* (Harmondsworth, Middlesex: Penguin, 1973).

21. Irving Richter, *Political Purpose in Trade Unions* (Totowa, NJ: Rowman & Littlefield, Inc., 1974).

22. See the evidence presented by the TUC and several unions to the Royal Commission on Trade Unions and Employers Associations, 1965-68.

23. R.B. McKersie and L.C. Hunter, *Pay, Productivity and Collective Bargaining* (NY: St. Martin's Press, 1973).

24. A. Flanders, *The Fawley Productivity Agreements,* (Levittown, NY: Trans-atlantic Arts, 1967), was a highly influential work in encouraging manage-ments and eventually, the government, to adopt productivity bargaining. E.J. Robertson, *Productivity Bargaining and the Engineering Industry* (London: Engineering Employees Federation, 1969), is an example of employers' (in this case the Engineering Employers Federation) concep-tion of productivity bargaining. Discussion of the use made of the pro-cess by the NBPI will be found in Crouch, "Ideology." For a Marxist perspective, see T. Cliff, *The Employers' Offensive: Productivity Deals and How to Fight Them* (London: Pluto Press, 1970).

25. Transport and General Workers Union, *Plant and Productivity Bargaining* (London, no date).

26. Much of this discussion was summarized in the *Report* of the Royal Com-mission, 1968.

27. A. Glyn and R. Sutcliffe, *British Workers, Capitalism and the Profits Squeeze* (Harmondsworth, Middlesex: Penguin, 1972).

28. Ibid.

29. I. Richter, *Political Purpose.*

30. See, for example, T. Cliff, "The Class Struggle in Britain," in H. Harris and J. Palmer, ed., *World Crisis* (London: Hutchinson, 1971), and R. Hyman, *Marxism and the Sociology of Trade Unionism* (London: Pluto Press, 1971).

31. N. Bosanquet, *Pay, Prices and Labour in Power* (London: Fabian Society, 1969); D. Jackson, et al, *Do Trade Unions Cause Inflation?* (Cambridge: Cambridge University Press, 1972).

32. S. Lerner et al., *Workshop Wage Determination* (Oxford: Pergamon, 1969); W. Brown, *Piecework Bargaining* (London: Heinemann, 1973); H.A. Turner et al., *Labour Relations in the Motor Industry* (Clifton, NJ: Augusta M. Kelley Pubs., 1967).

33. C.S. Maier, "The Political Contexts of Inflation: Some Tentative Considera-tions," unpublished manuscript presented at conference on Twentieth Century Capitalism, Council for European Studies, Cambridge, Massachusetts, 1974.

34. Routh, *Occupation & Pay.*

35. W.G. Runciman, *Relative Deprivation and Social Justice* (Berkeley: Univer-sity of California Press, 1966).

36. J.H. Goldthorpe et al., *The Affluent Worker* (three monographs) (Cambridge: Cambridge University Press, 1968). Also relevant to this discussion is Lock-wood's theoretical account of different forms of working-class consciousness: "Sources of Variation in Working Class Images of Society," *Sociological Review* 14 (November 1966).

37. R.T. McKenzie and A. Silver, *Angels in Marble* (Chicago: Univ. of Chicago Press, 1968); E. Nordlinger, *The Working Class Tories* (London: MacGibbon & Kee, 1967).

38. Two examples of this may usefully be cited, coming from very different ideological standpoints and relating to rather different specific issues: J. Westergaard, "The Withering Away of Class: A Modern Myth," in P. Anderson and R. Blackburn, eds., *Towards Socialism* (Ithaca: Cornell University Press, 1966); and A. Flanders, "Trade Unions and the Force of Tradition," Sixteenth Fawley Foundation Lecture, University of Southampton.

39. For a more modern instance, see J. Winkler, "The Ghost at the Bargaining Table: Directors and Industrial Relations," *British Journal of Industrial Relations,* (July 1974).

40. M. Mann, "The Social Cohesion of Liberal Democracy," *American Sociological Review,* 35, 3 (June 1970), pp. 423-439.

41. B. Hindess, *The Decline of Working-Class Politics* (London: MacGibbon and Kee, 1971).

42. Ibid., pp. 72-76.

43. J. Cousins, "The Non-Militant Shop Steward," *New Society,* February 3, 1972.

44. B. Bernstein, *Class, Codes and Control* (Boston: Routledge & Kegan Pane, Ltd. 1973).

45. Ibid., "Linguistic Codes."

46. Ibid., "Linguistic Codes and Grammatical Elements."

47. M. Mann, "Social Cohesion."

48. G. Almond and S. Verba, *The Civic Culture* (Princeton: Princeton Univ. Press, 1963).

49. B. Jessop, *Traditionalism, Conservativism and British Political Culture* (Atlantic Highlands, NJ: Humanities Press, Inc., 1974).

50. A. Fox, *Beyond Contract.*

51. See, for example, the speeches made in November 1974 by Sir Keith Joseph MP, relating to each other the economic crisis, industrial militancy, "moral decline," and the birth rate of the lowest socioeconomic groups.

52. J.H. Goldthorpe, "Social Inequality"; A. Flanders and A. Fox, "The Reform of Collective Bargaining: From Donovan to Durkheim," *British Journal of Industrial Relations,* 7, 2, 1968.

53. Goldthorpe, ibid.; Fox, *Beyond Contract.*

**Part III
Legitimacy Versus Efficiency**

Introduction to Part III
Claus Offe

The attempt to describe structural problems of advanced capitalist societies through conceptual dichotomies such as they are used in this book is, at best, a starting point for discussion and analysis. Professor W. Baldamus, the British sociologist, has pointed out in an unpublished work that such dichotomies play a vastly different role in liberal social theory on the one side and Marxist theoretical tradition on the other. Whereas in the former tradition, they are employed either for descriptive classification of social phenomena (e.g., low versus high educational status) or as theoretical constructs that conceptualize polar opposites of a historical continuum (e.g., mechanic versus organic solidarity), such dichotomies are used in Marxist thought in order to point to an *asymmetrical* or hierarchical social relationship: for example, capital versus labor, exchange value versus use value, ruling class versus proletariat. What the analyst is interested in within the latter tradition is not merely descriptive or conceptual *distinctions,* but historical *contradictions* that exist within relationships of domination in general and particularly in the capital/labor relationship.

The Concept of "Contradiction"

It is not obvious at first glance in which of these two strategic perspectives of social theory the dichotomy of "legitimacy versus efficiency" actually belongs. One can argue, on a descriptive level, that to maintain both legitimacy and efficiency is a major task of modern democratic regimes, and that various branches and institutions of the political system do specialize in providing either one of these functional prerequisites. One can argue that providing legitimation and providing efficiency are separate though simultaneously performed functions of the political process; this is what Edelman has analyzed as the "symbolic" and the "instrumental" aspects of state agencies. One can argue, on a more theoretical level, that the need to perform those two functions simultaneously tends to cause certain strains and tensions in such political systems that hence must be resolved through strategies which are able to reconcile the two requirements. For instance, the German political scientist Fritz Scharpf has argued that the real and most important obstacles to efficient performance of governments is in the institutionalized and fragmented pressure of specific demands to which governments have to comply in order to maintain their basis of legitimation and popular support.[1] Other authors argue that a solution to this dilemma becomes increasingly difficult to find, because exactly those values (like instrumental rationality and intellectual discipline) that are necessary for the efficient conduct of government are subverted and paralyzed by "irrational" cultural trends.[2]

Whether or not this contributes to the sharpening of a dilemma or actually constitutes a "contradiction," as Bell maintains, is probably largely a matter of what we mean by the term "contradiction." If we mean the incidence of opposing demands and conflicting pressures that have to be absorbed by a particular institutional setting (be it a political system, a family, or a business enterprise), then the term approximates the term "dilemma." Dilemmas, however, are fairly common and virtually universal in social relationships, and it adds little to our understanding of social reality if we call them "contradictions."

An alternative use of the concept "contradiction" might be sketched out in the following way. Any human society operates through an institutionalized set of rules. A part of these rules determines the process by which the society reproduces itself materially, by which the society trancends the lifetime of its individual members. More specifically, these institutionalized rules of material reproduction regulate three things, namely, the effective control over human labor power, over the material means and resources of production, and over the product itself. Numerous mechanisms of control, or modes of production, which regulate these three elements of material reproduction, can be distinguished historically. Each has its own specific economic, political, and cultural requirements on which it depends in order to secure its continuity as a societal mode of production. Now, a contradiction is not simply a situation in which these indispensable requirements of a certain mode of production are absent or inadequately fulfilled. If that were the case catastrophies (like floods or epidemics and also "social catastrophies" like wars) would indicate contradictions. This would hardly be an adequate use of the term. What we mean by contradictions is rather narrower and more precise. A *contradiction* is the tendency inherent to a specific mode of production to destroy those very preconditions on which its survival depends. Contradictions become manifest in situations where, in other words, a collision occurs between the constituent preconditions and the results of a specific mode of production, or where the necessary becomes impossible and the impossible becomes necessary.

Without a single exception, all Marxist theorems that try to elucidate the nature of capitalism are based upon this concept of contradiction. To name just a few such theorems that have been explored by Marx and Marxist authors (without implying that all of them are valid or remain valid under the conditions of advanced capitalism): The "law" of the falling rate of profit maintains that what is necessary for the accumulation process of capital (namely, the introduction of labor-saving technical change) turns out to make further accumulation impossible (due to the decreased share of variable capital out of which surplus value and hence profit can solely be extracted). Similarly, the theorem of underconsumption maintains that what is necessary to maximize profits (namely, the reduction of wages of labor) renders impossible further capitalist accumulation because of the resulting decline in "effective demand" and the consequent "realization" problem. In the same way the organizational strength and political struggle of the working class is analyzed in various Marxian theories as a direct consequence of the very mode of capitalist production that systematically creates the conditions under which the working class can engage in anticapitalist struggles.

Numerous other theorems could be mentioned that are based on the same concept of contradiction. For the purpose of illustration, however, it may be sufficient to point out that in all of them the term contradiction is not used as an attribute of a particular actor in a particular situation, or as a condition that prevails in a specific institutional sector of society. The term contradiction is rather used as an analytical concept related to the dominant mode of production by which a society reproduces itself. Contradictions are not contingent, but rooted in the mode of production, which is *itself* seen to be contradictory, that is, self-paralyzing and self-destructive.

Here the obvious question comes up: How can something exist at all in historical reality that is inherently contradictory by nature? How can it become and remain operative as a mode of production? Does its very existence (and duration over time) invalidate the concept of contradiction as applied to a mode of production? Such paradoxical conclusions can only be avoided if we assume that (a) the structural contradictions of the capitalist mode of production are not *uniform* throughout the history of a capitalist development, but become larger and more prevasive as accumulation proceeds; and if we keep in mind that (b) the concept of "contradiction" does not imply any automatic "breakdown" or "crisis" of the capitalist mode of production. In other words, the self-destructive tendencies of the capitalist mode of production evolve in a historical process, and their destructive and revolutionary potential can well be controlled and kept latent through various adaptive mechanisms of the system, at least temporarily. The expectation that the ability to reconcile emerging contradictions through such adaptive measures is limited, and that contradictions will finally result in a *crisis* of the capitalist mode of production, is not based on any utopian hopes, but on the consideration that there is no actor or agency within the capitalist mode of production that is sufficiently unaffected by those contradictions that are to be reconciled to be able to act in such a way as to counteract them.

Whatever the particular contributions of Marxist theory of society are, it should have become clear by now that this theory proceeds according to a fundamental theoretical model in which the concepts "mode of production," "contradiction," and "crisis" are closely and inseparably interconnected.

But what does all of this have to do with the problem that is alluded to by the dichotomy of legitimacy versus efficiency? We argued a moment ago that the theoretical link between contradiction and crisis is to be found in the fact that such corrective or adaptive mechanisms in society as could perform the function of repressing or reconciling contradictions are themselves involved in the contradictions inherent in the capitalist mode of production. Both liberal and Marxist theorists see the state as the major institutional system in advanced capitalist society that could assume the function of overcoming contradictions. The central analytical controversy, however, concerns the question of whether the state is actually able to perform this function effectively or whether there are systematic contradictions *on the level of state activity itself* that prevent the state from dealing successfully with the contradictions of the capitalist mode of production. It is this controversy that provides a theoretically relevant background for the discussion of "legitimacy versus efficiency." The exploration of these two concepts, or aspects of state activity, may contribute to the resolution of the controversy between liberals and Marxists about the nature of the state.

Legitimacy and Efficiency

Before we discuss this question in the light of the contributions by Isaac Balbus, Murray Edelman, Michael Mann, and Renate Mayntz, let us first consider some alternative meanings of the two terms legitimacy and efficiency. Since the famous typology of Max Weber, legitimacy is conceived as the essential and indispensable basis of political authority. According to Weber there are different historical modes of legitimating political authority, and one of these modes, the legal-rational one, tends to become the dominant one in the modern world. The great advantage of this mode of legitimation[3] relative to the historically older ones consists in the fact that authority becomes legitimate independently of who is the incumbent in political office or what the intentions of the incumbents are. The only thing that decides about the legitimacy of political authority is whether or not it has been achieved in accordance with general formal principles, for example, election rules. These legal principles endow political power, whatever use is made of it, with legitimacy. Compared with those older forms of legitimation, the legitimating mechanism is shifted from the *substance* of authority of the *person* of the ruler to the *mode* by which office holders are recruited.

Those selection principles[4] that regulate the access to political authority and that carry the burden of legitimating it operate in two directions. They constitute binding directions both for the rulers and the ruled. In modern democratic regimes these formal principles oblige the (prospective) office holders to pass the test of general elections, to obey the rules of the constitution while in office, and to resign from power as soon as a competing party elite achieves an electoral victory. Conversely, such constitutional rules of democratic government do also bind the behavior of the citizens who are subject to state authority. This is most obvious in the obligation to comply with the laws made by government, and it is also clear in the fact that the citizenry is prohibited from promoting individual and collective interest through political means other than those provided by the constitution. In other words, the legitimating power of formal constitutional rules reaches as far and only as far as the governing elites comply with these rules *and* as the ruled are willing to refrain from modes of political behavior that are not covered by the set of options provided to them by the constitution.

If this is true, the question now comes up: What are the conditions under which these legitimating rules find universal *acceptance,* and under what conditions do they fail to find such acceptance (either on the part of the rulers or of the ruled)? Exactly because these rules are formal, they cannot win acceptance because of the advantages they imply. Their acceptance must depend not upon what *they* are, but what the *consequences* or likely *results* of their application are. We do not drive on the right-hand side of the road because there is any inherent preferability for doing so, but because we assume that general compliance to this formal rule will result in greater safety of transportation, etc. In the same way the preferability of democratic government is not based on the rules itself but on the expectation that this form of government will contribute to common and individual welfare and other desirable ends. The ability of governments actually to produce such ends—or at least to create the appearance that it is able to achieve such ends—may consequently be considered as one major determinant of what we have called acceptance of the legitimating rules that, as formal rules, have themselves to be legitimated. The problem of legitimacy thus turns out to be caught in the dialectic of form and content.

The concept of efficiency is equally in need of some clarification. In the academic disciplines of business administration and organization theory a distinction is made between *efficiency* and *effectiveness.* Marginal gains in efficiency occur if the same amount of output can be produced at lower costs. Effectiveness, on the other side, measures the ability of an organization to achieve its stated goals. The typical dilemma of the management of a private firm is to find a combination of the two—often inversely related—performance criteria that maximize profits. Both efficiency and effectiveness are subgoals relative to the overarching goal of *profitability* of private firms who buy and sell their inputs and outputs on *markets.* Where—as in the case of governmental organizations or the state in general—both the criteria of profitability and market relationships are absent, it becomes difficult to attribute a clear-cut meaning to such terms as efficiency and effectiveness. If, for instance, the postal services and mail distribution are closed on Saturdays in order to save costs and to reduce the chronic deficit of most government-run post offices this measure looks like an economizing, hence efficiency-increasing, act. Upon closer inspection, however, we see that this is not necessarily the case: It implies greater inconvenience for the users of postal services as well as a reduction of the number (or wages) of postal employees, and only a government that was in a position to consider these side-effects as irrelevant (both politically and economically) could congratulate itself on having achieved a gain in efficiency. In the absence of this highly unlikely condition of irrelevance of side-effects, the state agency would have to take into account the trade-off that exists between the saving of expenditures and the increase in user inconvenience. But since only one of these variables, namely expenditures, can be calculated in monetary terms, whereas the other one (user inconvenience) does not reflect a market process, the comparison between the two is not amenable to calculation. Hence, it is hardly demonstrable that in fact an efficiency gain has been achieved through any particular government measure.

A similar difficulty occurs in the case of *effectiveness* of government activity. Within the jurisdiction of a particular agency and within the framework of given goals, the effectiveness (or ability to achieve stated goals) of a given agency can easily be determined. However, since the governmental system of organizations does not receive its goals from the market (like a business firm), it has to organize a process by which goals are defined, their priority in time and funds is determined, and the responsibility for the achievement of this goal is assigned to a particular agency. Again, in the absence of market relationships and the profit criterion, the term effectiveness becomes ambiguous. For instance, a particular agency may be highly effective in implementing goals that are determined through a highly ineffective political process of decision making. School administrators may be very effective in implementing a program of school reform that turns out not to serve the purposes it was designed to serve in the first place, and a similar judgement may be reached in respect to NASA and the decision to send a man to the moon.

We conclude that the rationality operating in the capitalist state (or normatively postulated for its operation) cannot be the type of rationality that prevails in private organizations. The goal that inspires the capitalist state and its detailed operation is not a substantive one and cannot be justified as a substantive one. That is to say, the capitalist state is not oriented towards doing anything efficiently or effectively (because there is no way to determine whether efficiency or effectiveness has actually been advanced through any measure or program) but it is oriented towards putting private actors in a position to increase their efficiency and effectiveness according to the criteria of private exchange and accumulation. Due to the constitutional arrangements that we find in liberal democracies, the state is not even allowed to pursue any substantive ends other than those that constitute the preconditions for universal commodity relationships.

This important point can easily be demonstrated. Schooling and training do not have the purpose of providing knowledge and abilities to young persons; they do have the purpose of putting individuals in the position to use their labor power as commodities on the labor market, and for this purpose knowledge and abilities are thought to be instrumental variables. How efficiently and effectively educational policies do operate can only be determined by looking at the increases in efficiency and effectiveness that appear in the private sector, that is, in the market interaction of the owners of labor power and the owners of money capital who are willing to pay wages for the use of this labor power. There is no "internal" criterion of a "good" policy, independent of commodity interaction. Not only will a policy that manifestly fails to put private units in the commodity form (or to help them to survive in that form) be considered a failure by policy makers, but also the budgetary basis of such policies will decline. Important trends in the discipline of policy analysis and its practical recommendations point in the direction of modernizing policy design in a specific way, namely, to reduce those benevolent welfare-state measures that consist of handing out goods and services to certain categories of people in "need," and to replace them by measures that are expected to put them in a position to take care of their needs themselves through the sale of their labor power.

The capitalist state is efficient and effective not by its own criteria, but to the extent that it succeeds in the universalization of the commodity form. The ideal state of affairs is a situation in which every citizen can take care of all of his or her needs through participation in market processes, and the inherent test of rationality of policy making in the capitalist state is the extent to which it approximates this situation. There is no need to equate the capitalist state, either empirically or theoretically, with a political alliance of the personnel of the state apparatus on the one side and the class of the owners of capital (or certain segments of this class) on the other side. For the abstract principle of making a subject of permanent market exchange relationships out of every citizen does more to keep state policies in tune with the class interests of the agents of accumulation than any supposed "conspiracy" between "overlapping directorates" of state and industry could possibly achieve. As the most general strategic rule, which is the key to most observable policies and changes in the method of policy making, the imperative to universalize the commodity form means nothing but to do two things: first, to put every owner of labor power in a position that makes him or her able to find employment on the labor market, the demand side of which is directly or indirectly determined by profitability criteria of owners of capital; as soon as labor is made employable under these criteria, the surplus-value extracted from the labor power under conditions of equivalent exchange is guaranteed; second, to put individual units of capital or capital as a whole in a position in which it actually appears to be profitable to buy labor power. In this sense full employment of all units of value under the exploitative conditions of the capitalist mode of production is in fact the supreme purpose of the capitalist state and the substance of its observable activity.

From this discussion of the concepts of legitimacy, efficiency, and effectiveness we wish to suggest one conclusion. There is only one point of general equilibrium in the relationship between legitimacy and efficiency, and that harmonic balance is achieved if (a) the acceptance of the legitimating rules of democratic and constitutional regimes is reinforced by the material outcomes of governmental measures and policies, and (b) if these measures and policies are "efficient" in the only way a capitalist state can be efficient, namely in succeeding to provide, to restore, and to maintain commodity relationships for all citizens and for the totality of their needs. This definition of the state of general balance serves us, however, only as a starting point for the attempt to explore causes of possible deviations from this "harmony" that then could explain the supposed contradictory relationship between the requirements of legitimacy and efficiency.

Hypotheses About Contradictions Between Efficiency and Legitimacy

There are three broad categories of empirical phenomena that could disturb such idealized balance of legitimacy and efficiency of the capitalist state. They can be very briefly distinguished and illustrated as follows.

First, the problem of securing the commodity form of both labor and capital becomes both more urgent and more difficult to solve in the course of capitalist development. The monopolistic structure of industry that we find in the dominant sectors of most advanced capitalist economies best illustrates this situation. Monopolies tend to make larger profits relative to industries in competitive situations, and hence they need larger investment opportunities in order to maintain their operation on a given level of employment of both capital and labor.[5] In the absence of easy-to-occupy new markets, it becomes more costly for the state to open new investment opportunities for monopoly profits (e.g., by socializing parts of their private costs or by relieving them from the burden of paying for their social costs), and hence to maintain their rate of growth. But even if state economic policies succeed in keeping the monopolistic sector in operation, they do so at the risk of declining employment of labor due to the constant introduction of labor-saving technological change taking place in the monopolistic sector. Moreover, the further the process of monopolization has already proceeded at a given point in time, the more difficult it becomes for corporations to find investment opportunities on markets that are already "closed" by monopolistic practices. These structural problems lead to a situation that is characterized by the existence of a large and permanent "surplus population", consisting of both owners of labor power unable to find employment and owners of capital unable to find profitable investment opportunities.

The political alternatives that are likely to come up in this situation are either a violation of the legitimating rules (for which support can no longer be provided through state policies) by the occupants of the state apparatus, or a violation of those rules by the ruled. In both cases the dual constraining power in which, as we have seen, the constitutional arrangements of liberal democracy consist, is weakened. If the constitution is broken by the rulers, the commodity form is restored by such measures as increased regressiveness of taxation, the repeal of the right to strike, to engage in union activity, or to form militant organizations; and, finally, forced labor for those parts of the labor force that do not find employment on the ordinary labor market. If the constitution is broken by the ruled, the commodity form is tentatively abolished in mass struggles using means of political power that are declared illegal by the constitution and constitutional authorities, and in which the workers insist that their work, their income, and their life should no longer be controlled by capitalist "market forces," but by rights based upon popular power. One contradiction within the operation of the capitalist state is that by supporting capitalist commodity production it cannot but support those forces of accumulation that result in the opposite of full employment, namely, the irreversible "dropping out" of growing parts of both labor and capital.[6]

A second contradictory relationship between legitimacy and efficiency is this: In order to prevent the erosion of the commodity form (as well as ruptures in the accumulation process that is based on the equivalent exchange between labor and capital, that is, on the commodity form) numerous and still increasing measures have been initiated by capitalist states and their governments to increase the ability of value units to engage in exchange relationships and to perform as commodities. The already mentioned policies of schooling and training are designed to increase the saleability of labor power. Recent innovations in industrial relations regulations[7] and labor market policies[8] in Western countries pursue the goal of (a) instituting flexible and at the same time responsible frameworks of wage determination and arbitration that are expected to safeguard both sides in their existence as commodities, and (b) facilitating the integration and, if necessary, repeated reintegration of labor power into an economy that is characterized by unforseeable and abrupt economic and technical changes. A similar rationale seems to be pursued in the area of R&D policies (which are expected to provide the chance to participate in competitive accumulation processes to individual capital units and whole industries) as well as in the area of regional development, where policies are also designed to keep capital and labor competitive, that is, connected with exchange opportunities.

Such state-organized provisions for exchangeability do imply two alternative contradictions. Such "far-sighted" programs may fail to win the support of those parts of the capitalist class (and occasionally the working class, too) who are the beneficiaries of the status quo of actual or imminent disappearance of certain values from the market. For it is by no means self-evident that there is a universal and consistent interest in the general "commodification" of value. For instance, if one firm has the prospect of achieving a monopoly position

and outcompeting its former competitors, it will hardly be in favor of state measures that help the prospective victim survive. Similarly, if one industry derives
its profits mainly from the employment of cheap and unskilled youth labor, it
will be opposed to state training programs that would increase the range of
alternative market options open to its workers and hence threaten its profits.
The political creation of market options for certain categories of labor or capital
or both (as in the case of regional development) will always be at the expense of
some others, and where competitive relationships among categories of labor
prevail (professionals versus semiprofessionals, male versus female workers),
there is no exception to this rule. The fact that such programs of political and
administrative commodification tend to be costly in their share of the budget
and have to be financed out of tax money often makes it easy for the specific
opponents of such programs to win allies among the mass of taxpayers and to
launch vigorous political resistance and obstruction to such programs. The
underlying contradiction of such familiar political issues and conflicts is that
the attempt of the state apparatus to maintain and universalize the commodity
form is not only in the common and long-term interest of capital as a whole,
but also clearly against the particular and short-term interest of many owners
of both labor and capital who are negatively affected by such programs. To
the extent the capitalist state fails to impose its policies upon resisting factions
of capital and labor, we are at the same point as before, namely, in a situation
where there is a manifest surplus population of both labor power and capitalists
unable to participate in exchange relationships.

But even if state policies succeed in restoring and maintaining commodity
relationships (at the expense and against the resistance of those in whose particularistic interest the absence of options of exchange of others lies), the problem
is by no means settled. The contradiction that becomes apparent under these
conditions is the following one: The restoration of commodity relationships
through the state and its administrative agencies takes place under social arrangements that are themselves external to commodity relationships.[9] The problem
with which experts in public economies and infrastructure investment have
dealt in various ways can be summarized in the question: How can state authorities serve the market by means that in fact suspend market relationships? How
can commodities be created in a "decommodified" way?

Obviously, the relationship between a worker and an employer or between
a department store and its customer, on the one side, and the relationship between
a teacher and a student, or a highway authority and the users of highways, on the
other side differ in one crucial aspect: In the first case the transaction is determined through effective demand, supply, and individual profitability criteria,
whereas in the second case the transaction is structured by such parameters as
politically perceived and determined needs, budgetary decision making, and
administrative expertise. Occasionally desperate attempts that we find, especially
among the conservative political forces, in all advanced capitalist countries are

directed towards turning back the wheel of supposedly unproductive state expenditures for public goods and public services, to "reprivatize" them, or at least to create a public goods market so that the rules of production and allocation of public goods may eventually become analogous to those rules governing the exchange of commodities.

The powerful political thrust to get rid of this administrative mode of control over labor and material resources is often, but not exclusively, motivated by the need to relieve the economy of the burden of taxation, and to overcome the fiscal crisis of the state.[10] A second argument is of similar importance: It is the fear that the administrative form of control over material resources could become politicized to such an extent that it is no longer subservient to, but subversive of the commodity form. This fear is well grounded in many facts. We see that wherever the state expands services and infrastructure, they become the focus of conflicts that, on the most general and abstract level, can be described as conflicts between the function of commodification such services are designed to serve and the decommodified form in which they try to do this.

Such conflicts cannot occur under pure commodity relationships, because the great virtue of the commodity form of social organization is that it settles conflict automatically: If two individuals need the same good, no conflict can arise because it is given to the one who is able to pay a higher price; and if two suppliers compete for the money of one purchaser, no conflict can arise between them, because the purchaser decides according to individual quality or price considerations. It is exactly this peace-making function of the market mechanism that is removed from the administrative form of providing goods and services. There is no accepted formula by which it could be decided what is to be learned at school, how many miles of highways should be built in what region, and so on. Sometimes the resulting political conflicts are merely about what specific category of capital or labor should be served by such investments and services to maintain their commodity existence, but often the very commodity form is at issue in such conflicts: This is the case when the question is brought up—and sometimes fought out in militant struggles—whether schools, universities, hospitals, welfare systems, prisons, housing authorities, conservation projects, etc. should aim at providing or restoring marketable labor power and material resources, or whether they should serve some alternative needs and social purposes.

The contradiction within state-organized production of goods and services is one of form and content. By their origin and functional content, such organizations are designed to create options of exchange for both labor and capital. By their formal administrative mode of operation they are exempt from commodity relationships: use values are produced and distributed without being controlled and dominated by exchange values. This tends to open up such state agencies to demands that sometimes (as was the case in the student revolt) are directed against the commodity form itself as well as against a state apparatus that is seen to be subservient to this form. By expanding social services and infrastructure investment, the state does not only exacerbate the symptoms of the fiscal crisis, but makes itself the focus of conflict over the mode in which societal resources should be utilized.[11] The state does not so much, as liberal reformers believe, become a force of social change and social progress, but rather it becomes increasingly the arena of struggle; it provides the rudimentary model of organization of social life that is liberated from the commodity form without being able to live up to the promise implicit in that model. State agencies project an image of themselves that suggests that use values like education, knowledge, health, welfare, and other ingredients of a "decent" life actually are the final purpose of its measures and policies. The experience that this image is misleading, and that the state produces all these services not in order to satisfy the corresponding needs, but only to the extent that is required to keep in motion the universe of commodities with its implicit exploitative relationships of production—this experience must cause specific conficts and attitudes of frustration over "false promises."

The more and more visible conflict between promise and experience, form and content of state policies can lead, and this is the major hypothesis related to the legitimacy/efficiency dichotomy, to growing difficulty for state policies to win acceptance for the legitimating rules on which political power is based. The most active state policies that try to maintain and to restore exchange opportunities for every citizen through a huge variety of economic and social strategies of intervention are—by their form and according to the image they project of themselves—a model of social relations that is liberated from the commodity form. In actual fact, however, these policies are forced to operate as supportive mechanisms of the commodity form, and within the fiscal and institutional limits of the universe of commodity relationships. What results from this structure is a dual and inconsistent standard of "goodness" of policy making. Policies will be measured both by the exchangeability they produce for labor and capital and by their promise to satisfy needs of people through alternative, nonmarket means of social production. The very concepts of health (ability to work versus physical well-being) education (marketability of labor power versus personality development) and all other social services are characterized by this dual reference to the commodity form *and* to need. This duality makes it increasingly difficult for the political system to gain support and acceptance for those legitimating rules of democratic government on which political power is based.

A third contradiction must be briefly mentioned. It has been argued[12] that the terms of acceptance of legitimating rules of political power do undergo a structural change that itself is propelled by the consequences of some state services. For instance, expanded education is said to exert effects upon the moral consciousness of people, and these effects tend to make them unwilling to accept the apparent universalism inherent in the rules of liberal democracy and representative government. Consequently, the terms of acceptance become more demanding and the preparedness of people to engage in "nonconstitutional" forms of struggle is increased. This makes the difficulties of the political regime even greater.

Exploring the Hypotheses

The general hypothesis that the specific kind of efficiency that characterizes the capitalist state, namely, the maintenance of the commodity form for all citizens, cannot be achieved to the extent that is needed in order to win acceptance for the legitimating rules of liberal democracy—the hypothesis of a structural and increasing "imbalance" of legitimacy and efficiency—is interestingly refuted in three of the four contributions in this Part, namely those by Mayntz, Mann, and Edelman. Let us briefly summarize and discuss their main arguments.

First, Mayntz argues that there is no such dialectical relationship between what we have called legitimating rules and policies of the state. Rather, she maintains, stable acceptance of the legitimating rules does *not* require reinforcement through policy outcomes in all cases: "Belief in the legitimacy of a political system makes . . . for a willingness to accept its decisions, *irrespective* of the positive or negative evaluation of specific measures in terms of one's own interests" [her emphasis]. She agrees, however, that this "belief in the legitimacy of a political system" can not be taken for granted either by political analysts or by actors in the political system, and that a possible weakening of that belief must—and can!—be compensated by "other factors producing mass loyalty," such as material benefits. Mayntz reminds us that "social systems can operate quite well on a minimum of normative consensus"—if only they have some alternative way to induce people to comply. But it is exactly this "if" that is at issue. Mayntz suggests that a "shift to other sources of generalized support" is generally unproblematic and easy to achieve for the modern state. We have argued that this optimistic assumption is highly questionable, because the only measure of effectiveness for the capitalist state is the extent to which it puts citizens in the position to engage in exchange relationships and that this kind of effectiveness (as an alternative source of support) is either unavailable due to the resistance of individual capital units or counterproductive due to the decommodified form in which such efforts necessarily take place. The question remains unresolved and is in need, as Mayntz emphasizes, of much further research.

Mayntz also points out that the vanishing of legitimating beliefs can be counteracted by governments through the "management of symbols" and the strengthening of both specific and general support resulting from such management. Here the question comes up, as in the contribution of Edelman, to what extent political symbols that provoke some kind of trust and confidence are in fact available to governments, and to what extent the management of symbols is immune to "reality testing." In order for a symbol to become useful as an instrument of support building, there must be some positive meaning associated with it. It is not evident that there are many symbols available to the governments of capitalist states that actually do have this supposed mobilizing power. But even if they do mobilize strong positive sentiments, their use may involve the risk that governments create expectations that they turn out to be unable to live up to, and consequently produce conflict rather than support. As a description of what governments attempt to do in terms of "management of symbols," Edelman's chapter contains a highly illustrative catalog of the tactics of support building; but that does not mean that governments already succeed in doing what they attempt to do, namely, to create confidence. The reference to psychic needs and anxieties that induce people "to want to believe the message" hardly settles the question empirically, and neither does it take into consideration research findings that point to symptoms of widespread political scepticism and cynicism, that is, immunity against effective "management of symbols."

Whereas the dominant line of argument in Mayntz' contribution is that the supposed imbalance of legitimacy and efficiency of the capitalist state is unproblematic because alternative modes of winning support are open to the state; and while Edelman argues that this imbalance is unproblematic because "strong mass beliefs" can be essentially produced and manipulated by the dramaturgical tactics of the state apparatus itself according to its needs, Mann follows a third line of argument: Supportive attitudes in respect to political power are not needed for most people most of the time, and hence the observed or hypothesized absence of such attitudes does not constitute any structural problem or contradiction. In his view the problem of legitimacy can be of concern only for intellectuals, whereas ordinary people do not base their acceptance of the institutional arrangement of the state on any coherent set of explicit ideological views and attitudes. Instead, they live in a state of mind that Mann aptly calls "institutional fit," "stable implication," and "pragmatic acceptance."

This, again is quite convincing as a description of the mode of political integration of most people most of the time. The question, however, is, whether the vast generalizations of this finding that Mann suggests are valid. There is no functional need for explicit legitimation as long as "everything goes well" and role acceptance is forced upon citizens either by their own utilitarian/instrumental motives and/or, at least, by the absence of feasible alternative roles and social mechanisms. To put it in slightly different terms, as long as every citizen takes part in market relationships that allow him to do so continuously, there is no apparent reason to challenge the legitimating rules of political power or even to think about them in cognitive terms. As everyday experience teaches, and as we have argued in the preceeding section of this introduction, this happy condition of normality can hardly be assumed to be the normal case. Either the "commodity existence of every citizen" is visibly and clearly threatened, or the organizational arrangements by which state policies try to maintain and to restore exchange relationships do themselves open up political alternatives by which those half-conscious attitudes of "institutional fit" become subverted. While it is true, as Mann cogently demonstrates, that "capitalism is distrusted by intellectuals," he fails to give any indication as to why, after all, intellectuals are not the only ones to distrust capitalism and the legitimating rules of the capitalist state.

Notes

1. F. Scharpf, *Planung als politischer Prozeß* (Frankfurt: Suhrkamp, 1973).
2. cf. D. Bell, "The Cultural Contradictions of Capitalism," *The Public Interest* 21, Fall 1970.
3. For recent discussions of the concept of legitimacy cf. P. Graf Kielmannsegg, "Legitimität als analytische Kategorie" *Politische Vierteljahresschrift,* 12 (1971), no. 3; P. Green and S. Levinson, eds., *Power and Community* (New York: Vintage Books, 1970), pp. 276-327, and J. Habermas, *Legitimationsprobleme im Spätkapitalismus* (Frankfurt: Suhrkamp, 1973).
4. The concept of selection principles is used and elaborated in C. Offe, "Structural Problems of the Capitalist State," *German Political Studies* (London: Sage Publications, 1974), pp. 31-57.
5. This is the key argument in P. Baran and P.M. Sweezy, *Monopoly Capital* (New York: Monthly Review, 1964).
6. For a very detailed and original analysis of the emerging "surplus population" see various works of J. O'Connor, most of all his *Fiscal Crisis of the State* (New York: St. Martins Press, 1974).
7. cf. J. Goldthorpe, "Industrial Relations in Great Britain, A Critique of Reformism," paper prepared for a conference on "Sources of Discontent and Institutional Innovation in Advanced Industrial Societies," Columbia University, March 1974.
8. C. Offe, *Berufsbildungsreform—eine Fallstudie über Reformpolitik* (Frankfurt: Suhrkamp, 1975).
9. For an elaboration of this point, see C. Offe, "The Abolition of Market Control and the Problem of Legitimacy," *Working Papers on the Kapitalistate,* 1973, no. 1, and idem., *Strukturprobleme des Kapitalistischen Staates* (Frankfurt: Suhrkamp, 1973).
10. cf. O'Connor, *Fiscal Crisis.*
11. cf. O'Connor, *Fiscal Crisis,* ch. 9.
12. See Habermas, *Legitimationsprobleme.*

10

Legitimacy and the Directive Capacity of the Political System

Renate Mayntz

Introduction

For a certain time the concept of legitimacy played a relatively minor role in modern social theory, except where reference was made to Max Weber. For several decades the preferred concept has rather been consensus, or, in political theory, support. The interest in the concept of legitimacy has recently been revived by Left or neo-Marxist analyses of the role of the state in maintaining the given social order in advanced capitalist societies. The major thesis is that in this context, legitimacy is becoming critical, that is, a crucial yet scarce resource, so that a "crisis of legitimacy" can be diagnosed or at least predicted.[1]

However, the meaning of this thesis remains somewhat vague, since in the highly abstract discussion the empirical referents of the concept of legitimacy are not sufficiently specified. In fact it is not even always clear whether the legitimacy of the capitalist system as a whole or the legitimacy of the political order or of state action is at issue. This distinction may be largely analytical, but in the context of a discussion of state functions it is meaningful to choose explicitly the second reference point.

Social scientists of different political convictions are largely in agreement that in highly developed capitalist societies the active direction of social and economic processes by the political subsystem has become a functional necessity. *Active direction* implies the ability to develop and implement policy that is not only reactive in nature, as in short-term crisis management, but also of an active kind, that is, comprehensive and long-range in scope, autonomously determined by the political system, and oriented toward structural change.[2] Such an active political direction meets with a set of external restrictions. Most frequently discussed among these are the restrictions inhering in the economic system, including the need for economic growth that the system generates. An active policy furthermore meets with limitations that inhere in the constitution and restrict the right of governments to intervene in certain spheres of life or to change constitutionally guaranteed institutions. Most pertinent to the present discussion is yet another type of restriction that follows from the nature of the political system. In a parliamentary democracy where the government depends on majority support, consensus becomes a resource of crucial importance. Moreover, the need for popular support is a restriction of active direction not only because support, being contingent, is scarce, but anticipation of such scarcity already militates against the development of an active policy

261

wherever this threatens hallowed traditions, affects vested interests, or necessitates a deferral of immediate gratifications for the sake of future welfare.

The dilemma between the need for active direction and the dependence
of the political system's directive capacity on support appears to be a reformulation of the "crisis of legitimacy" thesis in system theoretical language. The
question is whether "support" and "legitimacy" are interchangeable terms, so
that speaking of legitimacy instead of support is only a semantic trick that
imputes to the rather value-neutral process of losing support the negative moral
significance of a loss of legitimacy; while the first may be sad, the second is
clearly bad and can even serve to justify revolutionary ambitions. We hold that
to reintroduce the concept of legitimacy into the discussion makes sense only
if legitimacy means something different from consensus or support.

Using this as a starting point, the following remarks aim first of all at
conceptual clarification. In this process, however, the issue itself will appear in
a different light. Beginning with the question of *in what sense* the thesis of a
crisis of legitimacy might be true, (i.e., the question for the empirical referents,
the exact content of the concept of legitimacy,) we are therefore led to a
second question, namely, whether the thesis *is* indeed true. This question is
discussed under three headings:

1. Does the directive capacity of the political system really depend on legiti-
    macy? And if so, why and to what extent?
2. Is legitimacy in fact becoming a scarce resource, and if so, why?
3. Can a crisis of legitimacy not be avoided by the use of strategies that
    increase (or produce) legitimacy?

Legitimacy, Support, and Directive Power

The directive capacity of the political system depends on its ability to
implement policy effectively. Effective implementation in turn depends on
the compliance of those who are affected by a policy, even though compliance
may be only a necessary, but not a sufficient, condition of success. This is
due to the fact that a policy that is based on false assumptions about causal
relationships may produce an outcome that deviates from its goals even if the
governmental directives are compiled with fully.

Compliance can be secured by coercion or can be voluntary. A government that depends on elections can make only very limited use of coercion
to implement its policies. Effective implementation depends therefore largely
on consensus, or on the support that the government can muster. This is true
even if we take into account that coercion is not to be understood simply in
terms of "naked force." A well functioning system for the detection and
punishment of tax evasions is as much part of the government's coercive or

law enforcement apparatus as a strong police force. This makes it clear that more control based on the availability of sanctions need not necessarily mean less support and vice versa. In fact different societies might be distinguished by the characteristic balance between coercion and support in policy implementation.[a]

By implication we have already defined *support* as willingness to comply. More exactly, support is here taken to mean the willingness of the citizens, irrespective of what motivates them, to:

1. Tolerate the interventions of the government (including its administrative branch)
2. Accept its decisions where these are meant to commit individual citizens or groups to a certain behavior
3. Cooperate where the government sets goals or defines critical limits, as in indicative planning

Support can be general or specific. *General support* means a generalized willingness to comply with previously unspecified measures of the government. The concept thus refers to the probability of compliance and is related to Chester Barnard's "zone of acceptance" as well as to Niklas Luhmann's concept of membership role.[3] For certain purposes it may be important to distinguish further between the general support enjoyed by a political system, as expressed in the willingness to uphold the present institutional arrangement and to abide by its rules, and the support accorded a specific government. Though considerable transfer may take place between the two types of support, system support cannot make up for lacking governmental support, which implies the willingness to return a specific group of incumbents to office.

In contrast to general support, *specific support* refers to substantive agreement with specific governmental measures and is not granted in advance, but ad hoc. Such specific agreement can obviously follow from general support, which otherwise would not become manifest, but specific support does not presuppose general support; often it is given because a policy or governmental action is positively evaluated by the affected citizens in terms of their own perceived interests.

The general support that a government commands importantly extends its sphere of action by enabling it to develop and implement policy that does not find the full acclaim of the affected citizens. This makes general support the crucial resource it is. It also accounts for the importance of legitimacy. By definition legitimacy refers to the belief that a source of control has the right

---

[a]Four basic types could be derived by combining the "high" and "low" values of the two variables in the manner of a fourfold table. See for this Amitai Etzioni, *The Active Society*, (NY: Free Press, 1968), p. 480-82; instead of coercion and support Etzioni uses the terms controi and consensus and speaks of the control-consensus "mix".

to issue authoritative directives, which puts their recipients under the obligation
to comply. Belief in the legitimacy of a political system makes therefore for a
willingness to accept its decisions, irrespective of the positive or negative evaluation of specific measures in terms of one's own interests.

In the present discussion about the crisis of legitimacy no systematic distinction is made between the political system's need for consensus (support, mass
loyalty) and its need for legitimacy. In fact, these terms are often used synony-
mously. To insist on the distinction between support and legitimacy is more
than semantic quibbling. Max Weber already observed that the belief in the
legitimacy of an authority is but one of several reasons for compliance. If
legitimacy is but one factor of support, and if not legitimacy in particular but
support in general, no matter what its motive, is the decisive limit for policy
making, other factors producing mass loyalty could make up for a weakening
of the legitimating belief. This possibility is of too much theoretical and practical importance to be obscured by failing to make the appropriate analytical
distinction.

The main argument for a distinction between general support and legitimacy
is that general support can derive from other factors and does not depend only
on the political system's legitimacy. Legitimacy may be equated with a normatively motivated willingness to comply. In addition, such willingness may be
motivated instrumentally; it may be bought with favors or exchanged for other
goods. This could be interpreted to include the conversion of specific support
into general support. Figure 10-1 shows the relationships so far described.

The diagram indicates that for the directive capacity of the political system, there is the possibility of a substitution of specific agreement for general
support (which would correlatively lower the dependence on legitimacy as factor
of general support). Obviously such a substitution is limited, especially in view

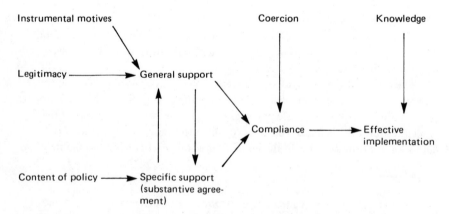

Figure 10-1. The Directive Capacity of the Political System

of the importance of general support for the autonomy of political decision making, which becomes of great importance particularly in the case of active rather than reactive policies.

At least in the present context, however, the main problem is not the posibility of functional equivalence between different factors of compliance, but the possibility of functional equivalence between different factors of general support. To question such equivalence means of course to question the concept of general support. If general support is a real phenomenon, its quality should be independent of the particular factor that produced it in a given instance. More likely, however, general support is but a conceptual construct of a kind similar to the concept of (summary) social status, whose empirical existence as an entity is open to doubt.

Considering the concept of general support to refer to a summary category for differently motivated kinds of willingness to comply, the question can be rephrased in the following way: Does it make a difference whether the general willingness to comply is motivated normatively, that is, through a legitimating belief, or in some other way, for example, instrumentally? To put the question in this way suggests that at least a certain amount of substitution should be possible; especially in the theory of organizations, but also in criticisms of Talcott Parsons' view of system integration where it has been pointed out that social systems can operate quite well on a minimum of normative consensus.[4] In this connection the hypothesis might be advanced that what we are at present experiencing is less a crisis of legitimacy than a shift in the basis of mass loyalty from legitimacy to other sources of generalized support. It may well be that in the area of politics something analogous to the general secularization process is taking place (though one would have to be careful not to take a change in the content of the legitimating beliefs for a disappearance of such beliefs).

This does not mean to say, of course, that other factors of general support could be completely substituted for the legitimacy of the political system. It may be true, as Jürgen Habermas argues, that the political system needs legitimacy in particular where it deliberately changes and shapes areas of life that until now were governed by unquestioned cultural traditions.[5] It is also plausible that in crisis situations the legitimacy of the political leaders secures compliance more easily than other kinds of generalized support. Finally there is the general advantage of legitimacy over other motives for compliance, that is, its stabilizing effect; this was observed already by Max Weber and later emphasized indirectly by Talcott Parsons in the argument about the system stabilizing effect of normative consensus. For these reasons it may well be that legitimacy can be substituted for primarily in the short run, but to a lesser extent in the long run. For practical political purposes such long-run requirements may of course be less interesting than short-run possibilities. At any rate, given even a limited measure of functional equivalence, a decrease in legitimacy need not be tantamount to a correspondingly large decrease in general support and hence in the directive power of the political system. To go beyond such a summary formulation we would have to know more about the nature of the currently held legitimating beliefs, as well as about other mechanisms generating mass loyalty.

Such knowledge, however, will hardly be gained if attention remains fixed at the systems level of analysis and at the question of functional prerequisites (whether for active political direction, or for maintaining the capitalistic system). It should also be asked how much the individual needs to believe in the political system's legitimacy in order to render it general support in the sense of the definition given above. It may well be that legitimating beliefs are more important for the behavior of some social groups, such as intellectuals or highly educated professionals, than of others, as Michael Mann suggests in his contribution to this book. The absence or minor importance of legitimating beliefs for complaint behavior should not be confused with a second aspect of the problem, that is, the undoubtedly existing differences between social groups in the coherence and complexity of the beliefs they hold and in their ability to verbalize them. Finally, it is likely that different sectors of the population concede the government legitimacy on different grounds, so that one should not only have to inquire into changes in the dominant legitimation of a political system, but also into the "mix" of legitimating beliefs that coexist at a given point in time. Since active political direction does not make the same demands on all sectors of the population (neither quantitatively nor qualitatively), empirical knowledge of existing legitimating beliefs, specified by content and holder, would doubtless be of considerable importance for political decision makers.

The argument in this section started with the statement that the political system's directive capacity depends cn its ability to implement policy effectively. It must now be said that this is only part of the truth. It would be a much too objectivistic view to assume that every policy that has the perceived chance of effective implementation is in fact being developed. Political decision makers who depend for their continuation in office on the results of the next election and on the permanence of the parliamentary majority are compelled to consider the reactions of the electorate to their policy decisions. The development of an active policy thus depends importantly on the anticipated effect of such a policy on voting behavior. As briefly suggested in the introductory section, this has a restrictive effect on active policy making that sets in long before implementation could become a practical problem.

It would be an interesting research question to explore the assumptions that political decision makers make concerning the determination of voting behavior. Even so it is clear that policy impact, that is, the consequences of effective program implementation, is only one, quite likely a relatively unimportant, and at any rate not a very visible, determinant of voting behavior in a given

election. Being afraid first of all of losing votes, the chance of effective implementation tends to become a secondary criterion in the policy choice of
politicians.

Figure 10-2 represents the relationships as they are probably also perceived
by politicians.

By judging the effects of a specific policy on voting behavior there is therefore a tendency to neglect long-term program impact in favor of the anticipated
immediate reaction to program content. One important reason for this is that
the effect of a new policy may become felt only in a later legislative period,
while the parliamentary system generates pressure to act in such a way as to
maximize short-term, visible success. Long-range reform strategies are often
not politically attractive, though they may have a perfectly good chance of
effective implementation; but not being popular, to pursue them would mean
that the government endangers its chances of being reelected and invests in an
enterprise from which the opposition will earn the profit. The constraints generated by a political system that is characterized by competition between parties
and democratic elections thus act as restrictions for an active policy and hence
as limitations of the political system's directive capacity. In this connection
specific governmental or majority party support is of more importance than
legitimacy, because where the political system as such and all its component
parts are considered legitimate, election success depends on the "marginal
differentiation" between competing parties in other respects than legitimacy.

The Erosion of Legitimacy

Having discussed to what extent the directive capacity of the political system depends on legitimacy, we now turn to the question whether legitimacy, as
generally postulated in the current discussion, is in fact eroding, and why.

One argument is that the political system produces more demands, or

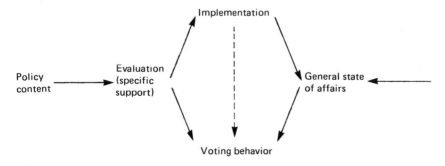

Figure 10-2. Determinants of Voting Behavior

expectations, than it can satisfy, and that the resulting disappointment affects the system's legitimacy negatively. The first part of this argument is convincing: With the expansion of governmental intervention the state assumes increasingly more responsibilities, from providing for the old and the sick to preventing an economic crisis. The level of expectations may also rise in response to election campaigns where the parties vie with each other in making promises to the electorate. On the other hand the resources that the government can dispose of are obviously limited. The successive satisfaction of the demands of different groups necessarily produces a feeling of relative deprivation among those whose demands are not immediately fulfilled. The disappointment due to unfulfilled expectations may be even more acute because the wide publicity of political action makes failures more visible, as presently for instance in the control over inflationary developments. Habermas questions whether the level of expectation must inevitably be higher than the chances of satisfaction, so that disappointments must result; but should this be the case, he concludes that a crisis of legitimacy must ensue.[6]

This is not necessarily so. It is quite possible that the disappointments which are produced diminish the general support for the political system, but do not affect its legitimacy. In the long run disappointments may also lead to a revision of the level of aspiration, thus reducing the negative effect of a given situation on mass loyalty. The way in which passengers have accommodated to the effects of the German air control personnel's slow-down that the government was long unable to stop may provide an instructive example. Only under one condition would the disappointment of specific expectations have a deleterious effect on legitimacy, and that is when legitimacy is claimed—and conceded—on the basis of a superior ability to satisfy (material) demands. This applies at present at least as much to the situation in socialist countries as it does to our type of society. Again we lack empirical knowledge about the prevalent legitimating beliefs to come to a more precise conclusion.

A slightly different version of the previous argument has been advanced by a group of authors from the Max-Planck Institute in Starnberg.[7] In the stage of advanced capitalism, they argue, policy making is governed by a specific selectivity with respect to the topics (or problems) approached and the interests (or social groups) favored, and this selectivity generates conflicts with delegitimizing effects. The first part of the argument is again convincing. There are undoubtedly policy-induced conflicts that grow out of the nonsatisfaction of specific demands and the nonsolution of problems. A policy that selectively favors specific interests can also contribute to the development of new organized groups that then fight for a change of current policy. The authors fail to make clear, however, why such conflicts must have a delegitimizing effect—over and beyond the mechanism already discussed in the previous paragraph. To have a delegitimizing effect policy-induced conflicts must be destructive of legitimating beliefs. Conflicts between the political system

and client groups pressing for the satisfaction of specific demands have a delegitimizing effect only if the government has staked its claim to legitimate power
on the satisfaction of these interests. So far this argument reduces to the one
previously discussed. It remains to be shown that there are other important
ways in which the very selectivity of policy produces conflicts that undermine
existing legitimating beliefs. That there are social processes that have this
effect is the main point of the following two arguments, but it is usually difficult,
if not impossible, to explain these processes as the direct result of conflicts deriving from the selectivity of policy.

The strongest argument for a crisis of legitimacy growing out of processes
that undermine the normative basis of legitimation is made by Habermas.[8] In his
view legitimation is produced by the sociocultural system, which used to generate
motivational patterns that were functional for the persistence and operation of
the political (and the economic!) system. Habermas describes these functionally
important, but disappearing, motivational patterns as "privatistic" both in the
sphere of political behavior and in family and occupational life. Elements of
these motivational patterns are for instance the belief in elites, the belief that
rewards must be earned by performance, the ingrained achievement motivation,
or the voluntary renunciation of claims for participation. Habermas devotes
himself mainly to showing how these motivational patterns are indeed eroding,
and he demonstrates that the political system itself has unintentionally contributed to this development, for instance, by its policies of social welfare, social
security etc., which have served to weaken the perceived relationship between
individual performance and well-being.

This is not the place to repeat the argument in more detail. But while it is
quite plausible that the motivational patterns Habermas describes gave attitudinal
support to the socioeconomic and political status quo, it is often less evident why
the change of these patterns must have specifically delegitimizing effects for the
political system. Habermas is in fact more concerned with the cultural context
that may support a specific legitimating belief than with this belief itself. His
concept of legitimation is so wide that it shades over into the concept of culture, and his crisis of legitimacy is really a crisis of traditional culture.

To pinpoint those changes in the normative system that directly involve
elements of the legitimating belief which supports the existing type of political
system one would first have to know what this legitimating belief is (or has
been) like. But political scientists have been content to work with theoretical
assumptions rather than with empirical data about the contemporary legitimating belief(s). Often Max Weber's concept of legal-rational legitimation has
simply been accepted as a description of the prevalent legitimating belief. But
Max Weber's ideal type of legal-rational legitimation has quite likely never
been a good empirical description, nor indeed is this what an ideal type is meant
to be.

An instructive parallel to Weber's concept of bureaucracy might be drawn at this point. This concept was also formulated as an ideal type (i.e., in a certain sense a theoretical model), but it was largely misunderstood to claim descriptive validity and was therefore sharply criticized on this account.[9] The empirical research thus stimulated contributed much to our knowledge of the structure and functioning of concrete bureaucracies. Unhappily the ideal type of legal-rational legitimation has not provoked similar attempts of empirical refutation (misplaced as these might have been as a criticism of the ideal type), and we are therefore largely restricted to theoretical assumptions if we are to describe the currently held legitimating beliefs.

This notwithstanding it is possible to identify at least two focal components of our type of political system whose legitimacy is being challenged ever more widely, namely, the principle of representative rule and the principle of bureaucratic authority. Not only is there a large body of critical literature dealing with these two principles, but the criticism manifests itself also directly in social reality. Both are familiar topics. The critique of the parliamentary system[10] concludes with the claim for more and new changes of direct participation, which indicates that direct participation is assuming legitimating functions that formerly adhered to the principle of representation. The critique of bureaucracy focuses around the element of formal, hierarchical authority that inheres in the rights of the position rather than in the demonstrated competence of its incumbent. The hierarchical principle comes under attack both for contradicting democratic values and for being inefficient. The critique of bureaucracy concludes with claims for co-determination and intraorganizational democracy on the one hand, and with the substitution of functional authority for the formal authority of the office as a legitimating principle.[11] To the extent that the political system does not adapt to these changes, its legitimacy will diminish.

It may be concluded that there are indeed changes in the legitimating belief that so far supported the political system of parliamentary democracies with a highly developed state bureaucracy, as well as in the cultural underpinnings of this legitimating belief. It is clear that these are not only autonomous developments following from the internal dynamics of the sociocultural system, but that the actions of the political system have contributed unwittingly to this erosion of its own legitimacy. It is not immediately evident, however, that the effects of policy induced conflicts have played the major role in this. Nor is it certain that the "revolution of rising expectations" has a specifically delegitimizing effect.

Legitimizing Strategies

The final question concerns the feasibility of strategies for increasing the legitimacy of the political system. Of interest in this context are only the strategies that the political system can choose, not developments endogenous to the sociocultural system.

One strategy that has been much discussed recently is the adaptation, especially of public administration, to the demand for direct participation of relevant sectors of the population in administrative decision making and particularly in planning. This strategy can not only build up specific support for administrative measures and programs, but can also have a legitimizing effect generally where participation has become a widespread demand and a value in itself. The net effect of this strategy on the political system's directive capacity is, however, ambivalent. Frieder Naschold sees in the mobilization of support through participation primarily a means to extend the political system's sphere of action, but this presupposes that only "progressive" interests are being mobilized. A general strategy of participation can, however, mobilize as well the resistance of those who defend the status quo against reform policies.[b]

Another set of strategies for building up political support might be grouped together under the heading "management of symbols." This includes all forms of persuasion as well as political impression management. Habermas maintains that the political system cannot procure its own legitimation, the main reason being that the deliberate and purposeful creation of symbols (or "meaning") is impossible because it destroys the very basis upon which their effect depends.[12] But historically it is not evident that this must be so, nor is it psychologically convincing. Why should it not be possible for politicians to reaffirm through persuasive argumentation the waning belief in the capacity of the representative system to express what lies in the common interest? Why should not skilfull political impression management enhance specific legitimating beliefs, as for example the belief in the historical mission of a political leader, or in the superiority, the exemplary nature of the particular country's political institutions?

It is true, though, that the management of symbols can only contribute to, but not create the system's legitimation from scratch. Moreover, the political importance of these strategies lies not primarily in reaffirming legitimating beliefs. The management of symbols influences directly both the specific and the general support for the political system without involving legitimacy in this. Specific support for an initially unattractive policy can for instance be gained by deliberately stimulating the subjective feeling of a state of crisis in the population, which makes disliked interventions acceptable because it is believed that they prevent worse from happening. The

---

[b]This has not only been shown in several studies of citizen participation in urban planning, which have for instance been reported in the *Journal of the American Institute of Planners* since the middle of the sixties, but also in a study of participation in planning processes at the central state level; see Renate Mayntz, "Funktionen der Beteiligung bei öffentlicher Planung," in: *Demokratie und Verwaltung* (Berlin: Duncker and Humblot, 1972, pp. 341-53). For the more global positive evaluation see Frieder Naschold, "Gesellschaftsreform und politische Planung," in: F. Naschold and W. Väth, eds., *Politische Planungssysteme,* (Opladen: Westdeutscher Verlag, 1973).

development of pollution control policies might provide examples here. A government can similarly bolster its general support if it creates the impression of effective crisis management, for instance by developing elaborate plans as long as the topic is hot, even if it later desists from putting them into effect when the public interpretation of the situation as a crisis has subsided. Even if such strategies do not contribute to legitimation, they do increase the system's directive capacity, since this depends largely on the specific and the general support the system can muster. Persuasion and political impression management finally, have, a direct influence also on voting behavior. To the extent that politicians and leading administrators realize these potential influences of a skilful management of symbols, their use of such strategies may diminish the dependence of policy choice on the evaluation of program content in terms of the immediate interests of those affected, and this can significantly extend the political system's directive capacity.

Aside from legitimizing—or at least support building—strategies that are deliberately used to these purposes, the very way in which the political-administrative system operates can also contribute to its legitimacy. This at least is the thesis advanced by Niklas Luhmann, who assigns the function of legitimation to the specifically "political" and the function of utilizing legitimacy for program development and implementation to the "administrative" component of the political system.[13] Luhmann, too, considers consensus a scarce resource for the political system, and he differentiates explicitly between consensus (agreement to specific decisions), and legitimacy as a generalized willingness to accept political decisions that lie within a certain range. His main argument is that this general willingness to accept decisions issuing from the political system, whether this is the government, the parliament, the courts, or the administrative organizations, is significantly enhanced by specific effects of the formal procedures employed in elections, jurisdiction, and administrative decision making.[14] The only objection that could be raised against this theory in the present context is that it applies to general support rather than to legitimacy. In fact, Luhmann's concept of legitimacy focuses on its consequence (i.e., general support) rather than its basis (i.e., certain beliefs).[c]

These few remarks cannot be more than opening notes for a discussion that must be pursued elsewhere, but that would obviously have to differentiate between the various components of the political system and inquire into their specific chances and limitations in building support. We can only conclude at

---

[c]This could mean that Habermas' rejection of Luhmann's thesis is essentially correct, except for the fact that Habermas' own concept of legitimation also shades over into that of general support. Habermas argues that formal procedures can have the effects that Luhmann attributes to them only if the institutions that use such procedures are already accepted as legitimate; see ibid., p. 138. But applied to general support, this objection is psychologically mistaken and empirically incorrect.

this point that the political system might in fact have more chances to enhance the general support it enjoys than specifically to build up legitimating beliefs. This, however, is less problematical than is often assumed, since the political system's directive capacity depends in fact much more on support in general than on legitimacy in particular. At this point the argument returns to the questions raised in the section, "Legitimacy, Support, and Directive Power," of this chapter, which will probably find no definite answer without much additional research effort.

Notes

1. See mainly Jürgen Habermas, *Legitimationsprobleme im Spätkapitalismus* (Frankfurt: Suhrkamp Verlag, 1973), who also summarizes other relevant literature. See also Claus Offe, "The Abolition of Market Control and the Problem of Legitimacy," in: *Working papers on the Kapitalistate,* 1973, no. 1, pp. 109-16, and no. 2, pp. 73-75.

2. For a more extended discussion of this concept see Renate Mayntz and Fritz Scharpf, "Kriterien, Voraussetzungen and Einschränkungen aktiver Politik," in the book edited by the same authors: *Planungsorganisation– Die Diskussion um die Reform von Regierung und Verwaltung* (München: Piper, 1973).

3. Chester Barnard, *The Functions of the Executive* (Cambridge: Harvard University Press, 1938); Niklas Luhmann, *Funktionen und Folgen formaler Organisation* (Berlin: Duncker & Humblot, 1964).

4. See for instance Niklas Luhmann, *Funktionen und Folgen formaler Organisation,* p. 68 ff.

5. Ibid., p. 103.

6. Ibid., p. 105.

7. R. Funke, M. Glagow, C. Offe, V. Ronge, F. Schmieg, *Erzeugung und Verarbeitung von Krisen durch politisch-administrative Handlungssysteme* (Starnberg: Max-Planck-Institut zur Erforschung der Lebensbedingungen der wissenschaftlichtechnischen Welt, June 1972).

8. Ibid., see esp. pp. 106-27, and pt. 3 of the book.

9. See for this Renate Mayntz, "Max Webers Idealtypus der Bürokratie und die Organisationssoziologie," *Kölner Zeitschrift für Soziologie und Sozial- psychologie,* vol. 17 (1965), pp. 493-502.

10. As one illustrative example see Winfried Steffani, ed., *Parlamentarismus ohne Transparenz,* (Opladen: Westdeutscher Verlag, 1971).

11. For a more detailed discussion of the content and the implications of the contemporary critique of bureacracy see Renate Mayntz, "Bürokratische Organisation und Verwaltung," in: *Die Moderne Gesellschaft,* Freiburg, 1972, esp. pp. 482-86.

12. Jürgen Habermas, *Legitimationsprobleme im Spätkapitalismus,* p. 99.
13. Niklas Luhmann, *Theorie der Verwaltungswissenschaft* (Köln and Berlin: Grote, 1966).
14. Niklas Luhmann, *Legitimation durch Verfahren* (Neuwied: Luchter- hands, 1969).

11

The Ideology of Intellectuals and Other People in the Development of Capitalism

Michael Mann

Ideology and the Ordinary Citizen

There is a widespread assumption that an erosion of the legitimacy of Western governments is now occurring. I wish to dispute this assumption, however, and to argue that no such fundamental change in the realm of values is occurring. Therefore this chapter offers no support to theories of structural change in the West. Furthermore, the assumption is based on a misleading view of the nature of belief systems themselves. I shall argue that ideology, in the sense of an abstract system of values concerned with the legitimacy of the overall social structure, is normally found only among the intelligentsia. What are labelled the "ideologies" or belief systems of the mass of the citizenry are generally abstractions by the intellectual from the concrete actions and experiences of the citizen. It is necessary to distinguish sharply between these two types of belief systems in any analysis of the legitimacy problems of Western societies.

The 1960s have seen the reawakening of the repressive side of Western society. A savage war in Asia — in which most Western governments were implicated to some degree — racial turmoil in the United States, and an increase in working-class action in most European countries, have demonstrated that advanced capitalism must still encounter force and reply with force to survive. When workers, students, and ethnic groups are involved in street fighting against the forces of law and order, a loss of governmental legitimacy is obviously involved. Yet, this is not a new problem for Western societies. The violence of industrial relations in the prewar period in the United States — measured, shall say, in the number of deaths or troops involved — was greater than in recent racial or university unrest.[1] Racial disturbances have themselves been part of the American way of life, intermittently exploding until repressed, and in this way they are paralleled by Britain's troubles with the Irish and Belgium's community strife. The current situation in Northern Ireland is, of course, worse than ever before, but numerous deaths have occurred before, in 1916 and 1920-22. The use of troops in Britain in 1918 and 1926 has not recently been paralleled in industrial relations. And, of course, Britain and the United States have been relatively stable capitalist democracies in the twentieth century, compared with Germany or Italy or even France. Rather than breaking up in the late 1960s, Western society was perhaps slowly returning to its normal mode of existence, and its normal mode of suppressing enemies.

The abnormally peaceful period was, paradoxically, the result of war. The experience of total war for those countries that thought they were fighting reasonably well (Britain and its white Commonwealth, the United States, USSR, and Germany) was an extraordinarily cohesive force. In the free countries national governments, the forcing of employers to negotiate with trade unions, the levelling effect of rationing, the opening up of elite officer castes to outsiders, social welfare legislation, all gave substance to the propaganda of national solidarity. This resulted after the war in the only substantial bout of income redistribution ever experienced by most Western countries. The social quiet of the 1950s was the after-glow of the fires of war.

If it takes total war to produce social harmony within capitalist nations, the role left for ideology is rather different from that envisaged by the organizers of the conference upon which this book is based. For neither social harmony nor a shared sense of régime legitimacy may be necessary conditions for the persistence of capitalism outside of wartime. Research done even amid the relative harmony of the 1950s and early 1960s shows that value consensus did not exist to any significant degree in Britain and the United States, beyond perhaps a general adherence to the values of nationalism.[2] Indeed, most citizens of the West do not normally possess any very coherent set of norms, values, or beliefs. Such beliefs as they have are contradictory in their tendency, can change rapidly and almost randomly, and appear to be of a very low salience to them.[3] One could regard this as a distinctive feature of contemporary capitalist society — comparable survey data obviously do not exist for any other type of society — but a more plausible view of the ideological confusion, pragmatism, or lack of interest of the citizen would be that it is common to all complex societies.

This implies a very different view of ideology than is normally found within either "bourgeois" or Marxist sociology. In a sense we have been looking for ideology and its sources in the wrong place, in the stable consciousness of the citizen and in the formal agencies of socialization. But ideology normally operates in a much less direct way. What the observer calls an "ideological disposition" on the part of the citizen is more likely to be the observer's own abstraction from the citizen's concrete attitudes and activities than the latter's own philosophizing. It is very misleading to assert, as Antonio Gramsci does,[4] that all men are philosophers, for there is generally little abstraction beyond the use of language itself. Naturally, there are worker intellectuals — the category of "intellectual" blurs at the edges so that individuals from most social classes may be labelled as such. In this chapter I do not attempt to use the term in a precise and restrictive sense. In fact I argue that the blurred limits of the intelligentsia in capitalist society prevent the creative writer from being able to see his audience, and lead to his worrying about the nature of "anonymous" market relations. However, the gap between those who are clearly intellectuals, in the sense that they ponder the abstract nature of truth and morality in society, and the ordinary citizen is very large. The latter is "unconscious" — the patterning of his life comes because his concrete experience is actually linked to the central institutions of society.[5] It is the "institutional fit" and not "values" that give both coherence to the citizen's life and stability to society. This fit is never perfect and must contain contradictions. The point at which the contradictions become glaring, and concrete experience is felt to no longer fit into the central institutions, is critical for a ruling class, for this "revolutionary" situation may call forth more explicitly ideological and radical responses from the citizens. Economic dislocation and defeat in war are the obvious twentieth century instances of this in the advanced societies, and the process of industrialization itself is the nineteenth century instance.

Perhaps an example will make clearer the distinction between "ideology" and "institutional fit." The educational system of capitalist society has been viewed traditionally by radicals and conservatives alike as a propaganda medium, teaching children the virtues of culture and citizenship. It has also been seen as functionally necessary for the occupational system and this led to a great emphasis on its positive role in social mobility. When, however, the liberal dream of equal educational opportunity for all was exploded by research findings, it was seen that the most important socializing role of the school lies not in its explicit values but in its negative mobility effect. The lower class child is taught less of the virtues of capitalism (or, if he is taught more, he does not listen) than that he is a lower class child, destined for a particular social level and occupational niche. The ideological effect of school is not so much normative acceptance of society as pragmatic acceptance of a role within it. The efficiency of capitalist schools is not to be found in explicit ideology at all, but in the extent to which it is functionally related to the occupational world. A lack of fit between Western universities and middle-class occupations has recently caused problems of social order that are discussed later.

A stable society is, therefore, one whose central institutions interlock and involve the activities of its citizens. In the West there are two supreme institutions, capitalism and the nation-state, and the "ideological spirits" that inhabit them are possessive individualism and nationalism. The key to institutional and ideological stability is to be found in the way these jointly permeate the concrete lines of those whom Nicos Poulantzas has so aptly termed the "individus-citoyens" of the West — whose individuality in conferred by the economic structure of capitalism, and whose collective identity is conferred by citizenship in the nation-state.[6] Other senses of collective identity, whether deriving from religion, class, or race are normally subversive of this structural configuration. In the twentieth century these twin features have moved closer together as foreign policy has become increasingly viewed in terms of capitalist competitiveness and as the ubiquitous economic league tables have become major weapons in domestic policy. Thus, the twin props of Western society can be united in the concept of economic property, and the allegiance of the citizen viewed in terms of his implication in the property system of advanced capitalism. Again, let me stress that I am not interested primarily in whether the citizen believes in private property, but in whether he is factually and stably implicated in it. Ideology for most people is not a system of values, norms, and beliefs, but an abstraction from the ground of their social being.

Viewed in this way there seem to be three major sources of instability in Western society that would bring forth dissident ideologies:

1. The traditional conflict between the institutions of private property and the collective action and interests of (primarily) subordinate social classes and (secondarily) subordinate racial and religious groups

2. The slowly growing conflict between the interests of the individual citizen and the emerging monopolistic, oligopolistic, and étatist tendencies of capitalism

3. The very recent development of conflict in Europe between capitalism and the traditional framework of the nation-state — a reversal of the tendency, noted earlier, towards the enmeshing of capitalism and the nation-state.

The first of these is still the most important source of social conflict in the West. In all countries except the United States the proletariat is still the major opponent of the status quo, though the incorporation of social democratic parties and trade unions has attenuated the class struggle. Whether the proletariat can actually overthrow capitalism in any country is a more doubtful question, though an optimistic revolutionary might see the second tendency as producing potential allies and the third tendency as weakening the ruling class itself. For if corporate capitalism backed up by the coercive power of the state no longer has much in common with individualism, then large sections of the middle class — equally controlled by bureaucracy, incomes policy, etc. — might feel as oppressed as the proletariat. And if the ruling class suddenly abandons nationalism in the effort to increase industrial profits, as Britain has done in entering the EEC, then it is jettisoning a large part of its traditional legitimation.[a] We must not fantasize, of course. The barriers are very great between the working-class movements, on the one hand, and the new middle-class movements for consumer and ecological protection plus white-collar trade unionism on the other. And if the conservatives in Britain are losing the label of the national party, this is not true of the Gaullists, for example. It will be many years, if it happens at all, before capitalist international pressure groups rival the nation-states in influence within the EEC. And for the viable nation-states of

---

[a]For a brilliant analysis of Britain's entry see T. Nairn, "The Left Against Europe," *New Left Review* 75, 1972.

However, it seems that the lineup for or against entry was even more complex than Nairn suggests. Splits within both the political parties and most economic sectors meant that the concept of the "national interest" was almost inoperative in the debate other than at a romantic level.

Japan and the United States, international economic trends can only strengthen the ideology of national economic property.

Moreover, there are other countervailing trends, which may be strengthening the ideology of capitalism. Principal among these is the spread of property ownership itself. Patterns of consumption and saving differ greatly between nations, but we can trace common increases in certain spheres. Shareholding itself may as yet be widespread only in the United States (twenty-five percent of families owned common stocks in 1969), but is is increasing in most countries (e.g., from five percent in 1961 to eight to nine percent in 1965 in Western Germany). The involvement in private pension and insurance schemes is also increasing. Owner occupation of housing involves two-thirds of American families, one half of British and two-fifths of German. Consumer debt since the war has increased at a much sharper rate than government or business debt, and consumer demand has been perhaps the major determinant of good or bad economic years.[7]

This may have had negligible effects on inequality. The argument is not that greater prosperity, either absolute or relative, brings more commitment to capitalism, for the latter clearly cannot guarantee this in the future. But privatized consumers and small-scale investors will not be the shock-troops of socialism in an economic crisis. They are more likely to turn to conservative guarantors of capitalism, to more étatism, perhaps to Fascism. The more the lives of the citizens are factually implicated in capitalism the less they can conceive of an alternative to it. And to the extent that citizenship is dominated by consumption patterns, the less the possibility of grasping the totality of capitalist production.

In the sector of consumption, therefore, the implication of the ordinary citizen in the institutions of private property is growing. The attempt is now being made at a political level to convert this into commitment. The recent growth of "law and order" campaigns are a definite attempt by conservative groups to persuade the citizen that criminals and political radicals represent a joint threat to his property stake. More subtly they attempt to link together the house and the car of the citizen to the private fortune of the large-scale capitalist. As yet the campaigns do not seem very effective, except in the United States where they are anyway more plausible: whereas the United States President's Commission on Law Enforcement found that citizens picked crime as one of the two major social problems (the other was race), repeated National Opinion Polls have shown that "law and order" barely figures among the concerns of British citizens.[8] Perhaps we should not expect such dramatic political dividends just yet. A more typical product of the spread of private property might be the fate of the 1966-70 British Labor government's pension bill, considerably watered down in the face of the attachment of many trade unions to the private occupational pension schemes of their members.[b] Here is a case

---

[b]The bill was not enacted, its passage through Parliament being almost complete when Labor lost the 1970 election.

of trade union sectionalism extended to protect the capital investments of its members!

Predicting the future of the West on the basis of these conflicting tendencies is not possible. Rather, I have hoped to illustrate how "ideology" is maintained, and how it might be disrupted. Western citizens are not committed in any significant degree to a set of values that might legitimate the status quo. Instead, their commitment is to be found in the extent to which their daily lives are functionally related to the central institutions of society. In this view there is no general "crisis of legitimacy" in the West. Indeed in countries where there is a good fit between the citizen, private property, and economic nationalism, there is exceptional stability. Hence, the United States, in spite of pockets of violence and chaos, is structurally highly stable, for private property is widespread and is not greatly threatened by state or monopoly control, while the nation is a cohesive and successful economic unit. Less successful nations, like Britain, might expect more dislocation, and then ideology in the abstract sense would become more problematic for many citizens. As the condition for economic success in the United States may well be the failure of other Western nations, it is fruitless to talk, even in this sense, of ideology as a general problem for the West as a whole.

Ideology in the abstract sense exists for most people only in revolutionary situations, where institutional dislocation forces upon them the problem of their relationship to the social totality. In the twentieth century the two most common types of "total" consciousness have been socialism and Fascism, where the individual feels that his social identity stems from membership in class and nation respectively. These still seem to be the most likely outcomes of revolutionary situations in the future for the West.

In Chapter 10, Renate Mayntz invokes the support of Max Weber and Talcott Parsons in arguing for the integrating effect of normative consensus. In a sense I am arguing the reverse. To the extent that consensus exists it is the *product*, not the cause, of institutional stability. When classes, nations, religions, etc. become dominant over others, their domination is at first based on coercion. If their domination is secure and stable over a long period it attains a tremendous facticity. "What is" becomes what is *natural* (perhaps the domination of men over women is the extreme example). The borderline between what is and what is *right* is, of course, blurred. Hence, moral commitment by subordinates is normally the product of long factual subordination. For example, what is called social deference occurs in situations where the deferred-to group can guarantee the continuance of its protective power.

Yet, in a dynamic, competitive economy this power is always uncertain. Eugene Genovese has pointed out that the "slave mentality" and the slave-owners' normative power is restrained by the uncertainties of the world market. A contradiction develops between the patrimonialism of the slave master and the dynamics of the wider economic system, and slave revolts can follow apparent moral acceptance of subordination.[9] The experience of the modern industrial worker is equally contradictory — sudden redundancy and instances of arbitrary managerial powers are as much part of the average worker's history as periods of security, stability, and amicable industrial relations. Contradictory consciousness is the reflection of contradictory reality, and for most of the population ideology *is* epiphenomenal.

Intellectuals and the Division of Labor

If there is not a general crisis of legitimacy, why is it that this is talked about? Here we come to the malaise of the intelligentsia. There are a large number of people whose job is ideology. Whether intellectuals choose to attack or defend society, or perhaps apparently to ignore it, they probe its moral values, its relationship to ultimate levels of religious, scientific, and aesthetic meaning, the quality of its everyday life. They have been doing so since the institution of the division between mental and manual labor. The continuity of the Western intellectual tradition can be traced back to the earliest surviving written records. These records have insured that modern intellectuals can consciously place themselves in that tradition. For example, neither the sociologist nor the novelist (the two categories on which I will be concentrating) interact directly with modern society; rather their views and experiences are filtered through existing sociological or literary traditions. Thus, the intellectual is somewhat removed from the material practices of his society, living in a "house of ideology" with its own house rules and traditions. For him, the conception of ideology as a more-or-less disembodied set of norms, values, and beliefs may be appropriate. This is arguing for more than the "relative autonomy" within a mode of production that Marxists grant to ideological activity, for the autonomy of intellectuals exists outside of particular modes of production in the division of labor itself, and in the "symbolic power" that their supposed command of knowledge and ethics grants to them in society.

Naturally the degree of independence they enjoy varies greatly between societies. In theocratic societies they are also in control of crucial economic, military, and political power and this may make their "symbolic" role less credible. In societies with powerful symbolic elites that do not wield overall political control, considerable conflict may result — as in the relations between king and church (and emperor and pope) in medieval Europe. The case of capitalist society is particularly interesting, for in this secular, materialistic society we may expect symbolic power to be at its weakest. Yet, even so we see below that in certain crucial respects capitalism has failed to control its intellectuals.

This is not to argue, however, for Karl Mannheim's "unattached" intellectual, who is closer to attaining objective knowledge than anyone else in society.[10] We see that the intellectuals' knowledge of modern society is often inaccurate. Nor is their knowledge independent of social practice. It is rooted in their historic role in the division of labor, as well as in their position in their own society. But neither type of role may be typical of society at large. Their views of contemporary society may be more appropriate to their own situation within it than to society as a whole. I argue later that the "moral crisis" of capitalism, so beloved of contemporary intellectuals, is to be explained less in terms of the overall nature of capitalism than in terms of a contradiction between (a) their conception of their universal symbolic role and (b) their relationship to the particular economic structure of capitalist society.

Intellectuals and Capitalism

As it would be an enormous undertaking to trace the attitude of intellectuals toward capitalism from the late eighteenth century to the present day, I will examine three rather disparate forms of intellectual activity and seek to establish sufficient similarities between them to support my argument about intellectuals in general. The three are sociological theory, the novel form, and the practices of universities. I will attempt to bring these together in discussing the recent spurt of intellectual discontent in Western societies. The argument is that — quite contrary to the traditional Marxist argument about the role of intellectuals in reproducing the social relations of production[c] — intellectual activity has been, on balance, subversive of the capitalist structure of the West.

Perhaps the first point to be made about the nature of intellectual activity in this period is its progressive specialization. This has two aspects: the separation of types of knowledge from each other, and the separation of knowledge in general from more practical social concerns. The writers of the Enlightenment claimed that all knowledge hung together, and they dabbled in a wide variety of fields. For as Hume said, "We cannot reasonably expect that a piece of woollen cloth will be brought to perfection in a nation which is ignorant of astronomy, or where ethics is neglected. . . . Thus, *industry, knowledge,* and *humanity,* are linked together by an indissoluble chain."[11] This seems an astonishing statement to us today. Hume's choice of example shows one type of activity favored by the *philosophes:* concerned to attack the traditional forces of privilege and religion, they believed in extending freedom and enlightenment to the classes associated with the emergence of capitalist production. Activity, restlessness, and *inquiétude* were regarded by

---

[c]Though Lucien Goldman, to whom I refer below, has emphasized the critical role of the literary intellectuals.

Hume, Locke, and Condillac as the essence of human life, and this is also how the spokesmen for the new capitalists saw their own superiority to traditional ruling classes. Yet, specialization was embodied in both Enlightenment thought itself and in the economic system it supported. Hume's separation between fact and value, however we interpret it, laid open the possibility of a dissociation between moral and scientific enquiries, with literary activity becoming the major arena appropriate to the former. Empiricism, with its tendency toward relying on "facts" (or in Hume's case, on relationships between individual facts) standing in isolation from overall "systems," attempts to build up knowledge from careful, detailed studies in different areas. If the Enlightenment stood fundamentally for the *"esprit systématique"* rather than the *"esprit de système,"* this spirit contained the seeds for the growth of specialized intellectual activities. And if the social system of capitalism was also developing an elaborated division of labor, then the practical role of the intellectual depends on contacts with a specialized elite in the outside world. Would "industry" in fact listen to "knowledge" and "humanity"? Capitalism would listen to neither the novelist nor the sociologist after about the middle of the nineteenth century, and hence their relationship to, and support for, capitalism became increasingly problematic after that date.

We have two ways of interpreting this disassocation. In the first place we can note that rising classes need ideologists in order to legitimize their capture of state power, but that once they successfully institutionalize their rule, their need for ideological justification declines. But, second, we might agree with many of the social theorists of the late nineteenth century that capitalism is a relatively "amoral" form of social system that is unusually uninterested in ethical justification. An example of this is Max Weber's claim that the Western society of his time, dominated by scientific rationalism, capitalism, and bureaucracy, was "disenchanted," Though based on the moral precepts of individualism, it did not actively embody and teach them: Under laissez-faire individualism, the social good is the by-product, and not the conscious goal of individual "selfish" action. In Marxian terminology social structure embodies exchange value, but not use value. It is helpful to contrast it in this respect with the state socialism of the Soviet Union, where socialist morality is directly inculcated in its citizens (moral incentives, pioneer corps, etc.). Later on I qualify this view of capitalism as "disenchanted," but whichever interpretation we wish to stress we would hypothesize that, when dominant, capitalism does not actively seek the moral legitimation that intellectuals might provide. We can glimpse this change in the development of the novel form.

The Bourgeois Novel

The novel is often considered to be, in its eighteenth- and nineteenth-century form, the bourgeois art form par excellence. As a general statement this may conceal as much as it reveals, for it obscures the variety of novels in this period as well as systematic change within the period, However, the following individual characteristics of the novel may be considered as having some affinity with capitalism.

1.   As developed in England it was aimed specifically at the growing literacy within the urban middle-class household — the readership was bourgeois.

2.   This mass literacy produced the first mass market, the first extension of bourgeois entrepreneurial activity into the sphere of high culture in modern times — the novelist as bourgeois entrepreneur.

3.   From the eighteenth-century English novel onwards, novelists showed a great interest in individual psychology and character. However, this could take a diversity of forms, of which the extremes were subjectivism and a failure to provide an authoritative account of character and motives (e.g., Samuel Richardson), and the device of an omniscient narrator able to account rationally for all character and motives (more common, in the nineteenth-century novel). The individual as the unit of inquiry was also basic to eighteenth-century empiricist and sensationalist philosophy, and was central to capitalism's own view of itself, political economy — the unit of inquiry is bourgeois.

4.   In the early nineteenth-century novel, the narrative becomes more orderly, and the flow of time predictably chronological. The use of clocks was closely related to the degree of merchant activity in the preindustrial period, and this objective presentation of time may be considered as bourgeois.

5.   Moving away from the earlier picaresque novel, and the late eighteenth-century concern with the social life of fringe groups like criminals and whores, the setting of the novel becomes both socially precise and in the mainstream of the life of the English upper stratum. It is as likely to be set among the country gentry as the urban bourgeoisie, but the two are becoming closely entwined.[12] The setting is realistic, and contemporary conflicts between sexes, classes, town, and country, etc. are carefully explored — the subject matter is bourgeois.

Singly, some of these qualities may be found in literature in other periods, but as a combination they dominate the English tradition increasingly from Defoe, Fielding, and Richardson to George Eliot, Dickens, and Trollope.[d] The moral purpose of the tradition is evident: to explore the meaning of the life of of the bourgeoisie, and to relate the quality of everyday social life to universal

---

[d]On the eighteenth-century novel, see Ian Watt, *The Rise of the Novel* (London: Chatto & Windus, 1957). On later novels in England and elsewhere, see the works cited elsewhere in this section. As this "bourgeois novel" is an ideal type, individual novelists can be found who possess very few of these qualities — for example, Emily Bronte. And the "realistic" elements of the English novel endured long after its social setting changed (Hardy, Conrad, Lawrence).

standards of morality. The moral content is also vouchsafed by the importance of women characters in the novels. Often the novelist is critical of society, but the moral and political criticism is from within. Merchants, capitalists, professional men and their families might be thought reprehensible, but standards for judgement are felt to exist within their own world. This is the authorship of the involved intellectual whose involvement is evidenced most directly by the relative absence of mediating "alienated" artistic characters in the novels themselves.

The high-water mark of this "bourgeois" novel is the first half of the nineteenth century in England, slightly later in France (it never appeared in Germany). During this period, however, the novel remained clearly separated from poetry, where the social involvement was somewhat different. The romantic poets usually were connected more closely to other fields of intellectual inquiry in other countries, especially philosophy and political theory, then were most of the novelists (George Eliot being the main exception). Hence, they drew on a larger number of Enlightenment ideas, especially on the "nature versus society" contrast and on political liberalism. In the wake of the post-Napoleonic political repression in Europe, these traditions were forced apart: Romantic poetry became increasingly concerned with "nature" divorced from "society," while liberalism was expressed by commitment to Greek freedom rather than the freedom of the domestic working class. The Romantic poet felt increasingly removed from his society, and from this eventually flowed Bohemianism, and the cult of the artist as first "disinterested" in society and then "alienated" from it.[13]

Perhaps the novelist was relatively well-integrated into society because of the secure nature of his audience. All educated people were assumed to be in the potential audience, though the actual readership was largely female. While the businessman was pursuing his "disenchanted" role, his wife was expected to carry the moral burdens of the family unit. "Improvements" (or very often "depravity") was expected from the novel. Novelists like Dickens or Scott were well aware of the characteristics of their audience and exploited their knowledge in a conscious business-like way. Though this was increasingly a middle-class audience, and not perhaps the "elite" that earlier forms of patronage implied, it embedded these novelists in the world of the dominant class of industrial society. Yet, mass literacy threatened this integration, for under the pressure of journalism, the market disintegrated into different levels indicating relatively "low" and "high" culture.[e] The novelist regarding himself as being in the direct line of descent

---

[e]Q.D. Leavis, *Fiction and the Reading Public* (London: Chatto & Windus, 1932), chap. 4.

These "levels" were not clearly demarcated from each other, however. Publishers oscillated greatly in the extent to which they identified an elite audience or a mass audience for (popular) classics R.D. Altick, *The English Common Reader* (Chicago: University of Chicago Press, 1963 ed.), esp. chaps. 12-13.

from the earlier major novelists now became subjectively uncertain of his readership and objectivity confined to a relatively small, ill-defined intelligentsia stratum
of the middle class. I am not aware of detailed researches into the reading public
in other countries, but it seems likely that this stratification spread throughout
Europe, affecting those countries whose literacy requirements were aimed at staf-
fing large bureaucracies (like the Austro-Hungarian Empire) as well as those rapidly industrializing. This is important, because it produced similar problems for
novelists living in very different social conditions, which I explore later.

The novelist's uncertainties about his own audience and his contacts with
more Romantic literary forms began to influence the novel form. The theme
of the sensitive, artistic type at odds with a more materialistic world had already figured in the novel (e.g., Ladislaw in *Middlemarch* or Julien Sorel in
Le Rouge et Le Noir). Both G. Lukacs and L. Goldmann have placed this
theme at the heart of the bourgeois novel tradition — the search for authentic
"use values" amid the "degraded" materialism of a capitalism concerned only
with "exchange values".[14] This is an overstatement as far as the English tradition is concerned, but becomes more appropriate in the late nineteenth
century in all countries. The protagonists are now increasingly and specifically "the artist" and "materialism," "the business world," or "money." The
problem was treated in a variety of ways by novelists. Proust and Henry
James, for example, could still discuss the possibilities of reconciling art with
money from well within the perspective of contemporary, conventional
society. In two other instances, André Gide and the early Thomas Mann, relative pessimism was the result. These are rather interesting cases (particularly
as Thomas Mann developed a somewhat different position in his later works)
and I will examine them as illustrations of the argument that capitalism has
gradually lost the support of the novelist. It should be borne in mind that
these two men were by no means left-wing politically (though Gide's position
is complicated by a late and "religious" flirtation with communism). That
they were troubled is suggestive of very wide malaise.

The main protagonists of many of Gide's novels are outside of society
in the obvious sense that they are bastards or outcasts. Their bohemian world
is contrasted to the world of the *haute bourgeoisie* and in certain respects is
found superior. However, Gide is aware of their problems in developing a
moral sense without social ties, and his dislike for the materialism and status
consciousness of the bourgeoisie, and the occasionally expressed contempt
for the reading public, is tempered by this. Yet, he is apparently blind to the
way that his bastards and outcasts are well-cushioned by both the private
means and the status of the class they despise. The counterposing of the
artist and society is false, because the artist actually incorporates definite
social positions that do not allow the possibility of real failure. Interestingly
enough, Gide recognized this hypocrisy in himself during his later communist
period, when he was to compare unfavorably his own private income with the

earnings of the "honest workman."[15] But in his novels the sense of distance and distaste for the vulgar world is threatening the social sense of the novel form. At the same time Gide is able to convey very powerfully the moral restlessness of the artist who at least *feels* that he is outside society, and whose only transactions with society are mediated by a disliked and anonymous market. The explicitly political stances to which this attitude could lead were various. Among the "Bohemians" it was perhaps more likely to lead to a contempt for ordinary people than to political opposition to capitalism. For Gide, on the other hand, a sense of the amorality of the modern business world led him through both religion and communism, searching for a counteracting church. The sense of contradiction between use values and exchange values could lead to virtually any political position except ideological support of laissez-faire capitalism.

Similar themes are dealt with more explicitly and with greater variation by Thomas Mann. More ambivalent than Gide, he sees greater defects in the artistic side of the dialectic between artistic and material qualities. Artistic and aesthetic leanings are consistently associated with physical weakness, disease and death in *Buddenbrooks, Death in Venice, The Magic Mountain, Dr. Faustus,* and *Tristan* and with immorality in *Dr. Faustus* and *Tristan.* In fact, the relationship between art and society is a true dialectic, with health, either for an individual or for Germany, coming only through an interplay of the two worlds. Yet, in spite of the ambivalence and the variation between early and late works, Mann remains consistent in his portrayal of one aspect of the business world: He consistently denies a true social morality to it. Here, for example, is Thomas Buddenbrooks reflecting on his financial crisis of 1866:

> For the first time in his career he had fully and personally experienced the ruthless brutality of business life and seen how all better, gentler and kindlier sentiments creep away and hide themselves before the raw, naked, dominating instinct of self-preservation. He had seen that when one suffers a misfortune in business, one is met by one's friends — and one's best friends — not with sympathy, not with compassion, but with suspicion — cold, cruel, hostile suspicion.

But why, he asked himself, should such thoughts bother him? ". . . unless, indeed, he were a feeble visionary and not a practical business man at all!"

Note the author's tone of finality in Buddenbrooks' perceptions: Buddenbrooks had seen "the truth" about the business world, not merely experienced certain thoughts in misfortune. Note also the contrasting of the business man with the visionary, one expression of the persistent contrasting of the business man with the creative artist. The decline of the Buddenbrooks is the ostensible story of the novel, and for this three reasons are advanced — the decline in their physical strength (Christian Buddenbrooks), the decline in their mental activity (e.g., the failure to vet Tony's husbands properly), and their moral superiority to the business world and, in particular, to the rising Hagenstroms. In a sense an author can portray a world as he likes, but this outsider's view of the business world — the denial of morality and companionship in it — leads to an unconvincing account of the decline itself. To view capitalism as amoral (as did the contemporary social theorists to be discussed later) is acceptable to a degree. But in a traditional social novel that empathizes and sees into charac- ter, to portray business men blaming their ruin on the lower moral standards of their rivals is to use a stereotype based on ignorance, or, in this case, on an idealized image of the conflict between the traditional cultured burgher class and the *nouveau riche*. That this is not just an isolated example is revealed in *The Magic Mountain,* a later and greater work. Here the intellectual values of the mountain sanatorium are contrasted with the materialism of the "flat- lands" below, and though the novel ends with the death of the main intellec- tuals, Settembrini and Naphta, and the return of Hans Castorp to the flatlands, he is taking with him the knowledge and the morality learned in the sanator- ium, for, as he says

> One must be rich down there . . . if you aren't rich, or if you
> leave off being, then woe be unto you . . . . It is a cruel atmo-
> sphere down there, cruel and ruthless. When you lie here and
> look at it, from a distance, it makes you shudder.

It is pertinent to note here, as did Lukács, that Settembrini, the essence of Enlightenment liberalism, is continually reproached by Naphta with being merely an apologist for capitalism. Yet, he never ever replies to the charge. As Lukács remarked, Thomas Mann apparently "never connected a genuinely free, fully consistent bougeois democracy with the defence of the capitalist upper stratum."[16] With such an unsympathetic view of capitalism, Mann could not continue within the tradition of the bougeois novel, and it is partly a cause of his greater success than Gide that he had moved from realism to allegory, and from portrayal of society to portrayal of the intellectual by the time he wrote *The Magic Mountain.*

The shifts in Thomas Mann's attitude toward the problem of the artist in society are highly significant. Though he started from the traditional anti- thesis, he was later to describe it as "the romantic sickness of the nineteenth century."[17] As he continued to write his own ability convinced him of the sympathetic qualities of the burgher, and as he lived he recognized his political commitment to Germany and the Weimar Republic. In the later works the artist (especially the composer Leverkühn in *Dr. Faustus)* actually embodies society in both his personality and his works. In *The Magic Mountain* hope lies with the burgher Castorp who has yet imbibed the humanist lesson: *"Man must, for the sake of goodness and love, cede to death no dominance over his thoughts"* the only wholly italicized sentence in the writings of Thomas Mann). Yet, the optimism is tinged with a certain archaism. The only wholly involved character in the novels is the Biblical Joseph. And in Germany Mann looks back frequently at the Weimar of Goethe for his ideal. This is not unconnected with his attitude toward the ideal burgher, who seems to be the cultured merchant of the past rather than the capitalist of the twentieth century. Mann rarely deals with this animal, and when he does the reference (as we have seen) is derogatory. Hence, for all his commitment to liberal society, one element is missing — a defense of the modern capitalist enterprise. The parallel with Max Weber is obvious and is made later.

These two novelists illuminate a turning-point in the role of literature within capitalism. Facing up to the opposition between art and society and denying social morality to the latter, they can no longer pretend to reflect social issues directly. The artist is interposed between the reader and society, and the view of society is explicitly his view. There is now a greater chance that independent sociological evidence will not confirm this view: Business men do *not* view themselves as do the Buddenbrooks; there *is* a connection between capitalist society and moral values (which I explore later); artists are *not* outside of society as Gide claims. The strain may be felt on the opposite side of the symbolism too. Adrian Leverkühn's music seems more acceptable as a symbol of the political state of Germany than it is as music (which understandably irritated Schoenberg, the supposed model for Leverkühn).

We might regard this transition as being the natural exhaustion of a particular literary form, if it were not parallelled in other art forms. The growing distrust of capitalism is found among most writers, whatever their chosen medium. Here, I am not thinking only of avowedly left-wing writers, but also of the reactionary ones, who (like Pareto and Mosca in social theory) viewed democracy, significantly, as the rule of the dollar, and who saw Fascism, or at least "leadership," as the only remedy for an aimless laissez-faire system.[18] Again, capitalism is distrusted by intellectuals from both Right and Left for supposedly lacking a moral purpose. The retreat from realism has been even more widespread, not only in painting but also in music, where Stravinsky has reacted against nineteenth-century program music by declaring that music is powerless to depict anything at all, and where today only conservative composers like Britten use the opera form extensively. It is a banality to observe that modernism is opposed to the direct depiction of the social world.

However, the social relevance of artistic production is not thought to have disappeared, and even the most abstract modernism is interpreted as containing a social message. Samuel Beckett presents perhaps the most extreme example of this in literature today, for his heroes are stripped of all

social identity. Their sense of time and place is rudimentary. Their problems
are universal, relating to human existence itself rather than to any particular
social reality. Birth and death, sex and excretion oppress them. They compare
themselves with universal figures like Odysseus and Christ, and are mocked for
it. Even Molloy's contact with the "social" authority of the policeman and the
court (for violating "I don't know what, public order, public decency" by lean-
ing on the handlebars of his bicycle) is so undermined by a failure to understand what is going on, that it is nightmare rather than social reality both for
Molloy and for us. And, yet, critics note, the hero is a "mid-twentieth century
Everyman," "alienated from society," "a social exile."[19] Does this mean then
that Beckett considers alienation to be the normal feature of the mid-twentieth century? No one knows whether he has any specifically social intent – his
somewhat cryptic pronouncements lean towards the universal meaningless of
life. Yet, we may ask why this view should arise in the mid-twentieth century.
After all, Beckett does not stand alone. The quest for authentic values by the
individualized hero has become generally more pessimistic in the twentieth-
century novel. And in the writings of Kafka and Musil the potential tragedy
of this situation had already been undermined by the quest's meaninglessness,
which strips the protagonist of tragic dignity. Beckett also draws specifically
on the "underground" tradition of Russian literature that substitutes the tramp
from the lower depths for the bohemian artist, and emphasizes his passive
stance vis-à-vis society. The influence of existentialism is also evident in such
a philosophically-inclined writer. The dislocation of time and memory has
been a central concern of the French novel from Proust to the *nouveau roman*,
while the combination of naturalism of detail with a highly abstract overall
environment has often characterized the same tradition. There are, of course,
major twentieth-century Western novels that are less "modernistic" – Faulkner,
the German successors of Thomas Mann (Böll and Grass). But the exceptions
are found more often among the novelists who have not been accorded major
status by the intelligentsia, the Graham Greens and Kingsley Amises of every
country whose works are largely ignored abroad.[f] The quest for authenticity
has been largely unsuccessful, and the major novelists have retreated from the
social form. Why?

The most tempting answer is the one that Beckett seems to invite – that
the hero is an "Everyman" reflecting the social reality of the twentieth
century. This has been argued most forcefully by Lucien Goldmann in relating the modern novel, and especially the French *nouveau roman* to the change
from liberal to monopoly capitalism. Robbe-Grillet, for example, is said to be
in the realist tradition in that he reflects accurately the plight of the modern

---

[f] And American novelists have generally stuck close to the traditional social novel, and
its mass market, more than have the Europeans.

man confronted by the reifications of planned monopoly capitalism.[20] I disagree with this for two reasons.

First, as a statement about the consciousness of "everyman" today, it is highly suspect. Does the average citizen feel alienated, oppressed by the meaninglessness of life and the rigidity of structures? Perhaps no very precise answer can be given to such a general question; yet, it is worth casting an eye upon relevant sociological evidence. Most empirical studies indicate that one area of modern life may fit this picture — the work situation of the manual, and (increasingly) the white-collar, worker. Yet, the nonwork lives of the working class probably serve to compensate for work alienation, providing for most people their sense of life's meaning.[21] It seems highly improbable that Robbe-Grillet and his novelist colleagues should actually know about work alienation levels! How many important novels have been written about work in the twentieth century? Two more distant spheres of activity than novel writing and factory life can hardly be imagined in modern society. Perhaps, however, the argument might be expressed rather differently — that the citizen feels the economic system as a whole to be out of his control and oppressive. Yet, this is contradicted by evidence referred to earlier, that in normal times the citizen lives at a very concrete level, with little conceptualization of overall structures. In times of economic dislocation he may change, but is this any different in kind to the experience of war, famine, and plague in other societies (and economic dislocation has probably declined since the nineteenth century)?[g] It would seem that, if modern novelists are commenting upon general social experience today, they are largely wrong.[h]

The second difficulty with the "reflectionist" argument is that the modern pessimistic novelists themselves came from astonishingly diverse social locations. What common social problems would possibly stimulate the Russian underground tradition, Kafka and Musil from the Austrian Empire, the novelists of France from 1910 to 1970 (including an expatriate Irishman)? Kafka is a central figure in this tradition. Why should we regard his heroes' struggles with authority as having anything to do with capitalism, still a minor part of his own social environment?[i]

A more plausible version of the reflectionist view concerns not the work of art itself but its reception by others. Kafka's work might be the product of

---

[g]Anyway, Goldmann makes the opposite argument — that the experience of reification increases with the advent of the successfully planned, self-regulating economy.

[h]A.J.P. Taylor makes this same point about British interwar writers, who, he says, convey the feeling that "the barbarians were breaking in." Yet, "By any more prosaic standard, this was the best time mankind, or at any rate Englishmen, had known." *English History 1914-1945* (Oxford University Press, 1965), p. 180.

[i]Malcolm Bradbury criticizes the obsession of Marxists with capitalism, but his substitution of "modernisation" is too vacuous to allow real connections to be made between it and "alienation": *The Social Context of Modern English Literature*. p. 6.

an extraordinary individual or situation, but its translation into the literary
pantheon would reflect the experience of its readers. This would necessitate
proving that Kafka, Musil, Gogol, etc. were more popular in advanced capitalist societies than locally, and we would still be left with the problem of explaining the extraordinary sympathy between the writer in one situation and
readers in a completely different one. Even if we modify the reflectionist view
to that of the "maximum possible consciousness" argument expressed elsewhere by Goldmann,[22] it is distinctly odd that expressions of the maximum
possible consciousness of the bourgeoisie should occur in societies that had not
even entered the bourgeois era.

Yet, there is a common social element uniting the experience of all these
novelists. Though living in societies characterized by very different modes of
production, *their own* was remarkably similar. None experienced significant
patronage. All wrote for the market, and all for the peculiarly undefined "high
culture" market.[j] Though the dependence of the intellectual novelists on an
anonymous market was originally the product of British capitalist development, it spread to all Western nations regardless of their stage of development.
The contradiction between use values and exhange values was experienced
more by the writers than by their societies at large, but their isolation from
social classes and particularly from ruling elites, help transform this into a
universal view of the human condition. Though it appeals to us as readers
because it clearly does correspond to elements of our experience, we should
be wary about generalizing to the experience of humanity at large, or about
taking it too seriously as precise social theory of the twentieth century.

Yet, as social theory it may have social force. The argument about the
novel form can now be concluded. Anyone now immersing himself in the literary traditions of the capitalist era would imbibe from them a growing view that
capitalism, or the business world, or, even more vaguely, the material world,
was separated from, and morally inferior to, the literary world. While this is
not exactly a critical social theory, still less is it supportive of capitalist society.
Under the circumstances outlined below, it could give rise to a more coherent
criticism of society. First, however, I wish to chronicle a similar story within
the development of social theory itself.

Sociological Theory and Capitalist Society

It rather detracts from the claim of sociology to be the "science of society"
that its history closely resembles that of the art of the novel. For sociology has
also moved from being the handmaiden of capitalist development through

---

[j]Kafka is the exception to this, of course, as most of his work was published post-
humously.

worried concern about the dehumanizing effects of capitalism, to a strange ignoring of the presence of capitalism. But in this movement individual theorists have fared worse than novelists for they can be *wrong,* and the price of being regarded as mistaken by subsequent generations is oblivion. The history of European sociology is now conventionally portrayed as being a romatic reaction against capitalist industrialization and the French Revolution by the conventional device of forgetting all about those theorists (all Enlightenment thinkers except Rousseau, and nineteenth-century thinkers like St. Simon, Comte, and Spencer) who do not fit this pattern.[23] Indeed, this interpretation has involved the killing off of British social theory, the refusal to acknowledge the contribution of a tradition that from Hume and Ferguson through Adam Smith and Bentham to J.S. Mill, Spencer, and T.H. Green was committed to exploring the possibilities for a social ethic of capitalist society.[24] One of the peculiarities of modern thought is the extent to which it has been dominated by German figures — and, to a lesser extent, those from France and Russia. The most advanced capitalist societies, Britain and the United States, have apparently contributed little to intellectual advancement. I wonder whether one of the reasons for this is the intellectuals' distrust of capitalism. Certainly, the neglect by subsequent theorists of a tradition sympathetic to capitalism needs explaining.

However, one part of the explanation lies in the behavior of the British governing elite. Though extremely responsive to this social theory, its interest begins to change around the mid-nineteenth century, when it begins to channel theory into two unconnected areas, empirical inquiries into public sanitation, drunkenness, poverty, and the like, and anthropological investigation of the colonies. And both begin to reflect the social and political prejudices of the ruling class itself.[25] Again we see that after becoming hegemonic, capitalism requires technicians not intellectuals — through it has never really succeeded in eliminating the latter. The theory of liberal democracy was now largely complete, and though it has continued to develop in the academic study of political theory (e.g., Michael Oakeshott) it has been largely ignored in other fields of inquiry, even indeed in other branches of politics.

It is this theory that provides the social ethic of capitalism. The integrity of the individual is the starting point, and his freedom the aim of society. Freedom is both negative and positive — freedom from the state and other individuals, and freedom to use one's creative abilities (or, to use C.B. MacPherson's terminology, freedom to maximize both utilities and powers).[26] The social institution that best insures these freedoms is the competitive market. The best safeguard against slavery is to guard against totalitarianism, to separate human power and provide separate markets for political, economic, and cultural endeavour. The interpenetration of economy and polity are obvious: Political freedom is only possible within a broadly laissez-faire economy (though Mill and Green noted that positive freedom needed some state intervention as well).

What might appear remarkable is the complete neglect or dismissal of this theory among the French and German theorists now generally recognized as the founding fathers of sociology — Marx, Durkheim, and Weber. Marx's dismissal was well-considered, of course, and the socialist tradition has always taken great pains to deny the connection between human freedom and a capitalist market economy. But Durkheim and Weber are far more "bourgeois" theorists in many respects, and their neglect is puzzling. Emile Durkheim was a republican, an ardent Dreyfusard, and a political appointee to his chair. One of his purposes as a sociologist was "to contribute to the moral consolidation of the Third Republic." [27] An avowed positivist, he was in the center of the tradition of bourgeois philosophy. Yet, his writings on the economy do not fit into this pattern, and they are the reason he has often been labelled a romantic conservative (e.g., by Nisbet). The increasing division of labor in the modern world is viewed ambivalently: at the end of *The Division of Labour in Society* he has come closer to associating it with anomie than with organic solidarity, which was his original purpose. In *Suicide* he relates economic activity and growth to both egoistic and anomic suicide. In various places he recognizes the inadequacies of the capitalist-worker relationship and looks to its modification by a guild system (in a way which prefigured both Fascist and socialist thought in the twentieth century). This ambivalence about capitalism, or the modern economy (like the novelists, he was none too sure), is distinctly odd for such a progressive liberal thinker as Durkheim. Indeed he was never able to integrate it into his general theory, and these unpleasant aspects of capitalism were labelled by him as "abnormal." Why did he not connect the economic system to the liberal ethic of freedom? The answer is an ironic one: that Durkheim missed one of the major aspects of the division of labor in his time — the separation of the intellectual from the economic sphere. Though politically and philosophically committed to contemporary bourgeois republican forces, he had no real connection with the clash between worker and employer, and could stand as a disinterested critic of that particular sector of society. In this he was parallelled by most French intellectuals of his time, who, from extreme right to left deplored the advent of capitalist individualism. [28]

The ambivalence of Max Weber toward capitalism is more easily explicable, partly because Weber spent far more time analyzing the nature of capitalism, and partly because he was aware of his own dilemma. As I have noted, Weber believed that capitalist society was "disenchanted," by which he meant that it was not consciously oriented toward substantive ethical postulates. This "substantive rationality" takes second place to "formal rationality," the selection between alternatives on technical grounds of efficiency. This analysis of the capitalist economic enterprise is largely in terms of its technical methods — double-entry bookkeeping being the most stressed part of the habitual and methodical calculation of profit and loss. Yet, he was aware of the limitations

of this technicism — that it embodies definite political purposes, that utility
satisfaction is not the same as want satisfaction, that, therefore, it can become
"an iron cage" fettering the human soul. On the political side of the equation,
he was even less of a capitalist apologist. Though identifying himself as a
bourgeois liberal, suspicious alike of conservatism and socialism, he never made
a connection between laissez-faire and freedom. This would have been rather
utopian in Imperial Germany, where, as Weber tells us, the bourgeoisie timidly
submitted to the force wielded by the traditional alliance of Junkers and Prussian bureaucracy. For Weber politics was power politics, and only positive
leadership could save Germany. Hence, the social purpose necessary for
the recovery of Germany was far removed from its economic system. In many
ways, therefore, Weber expressed sociologically the same burgher unease that
Thomas Mann expressed aesthetically.

Weber's analysis has much to recommend it; yet, we might observe that as
a general theory of capitalism, it is rather incomplete. By implicitly comparing
the religious capitalism of seventeenth-century England with the controlled
capitalism of late nineteenth-century Prussia, Weber arrives at his "iron cage"
worries. Had he taken seriously the secular ethic of nineteenth-century England, he might have modified his view. It is not clear that this form of capitalism was so disenchanted, for it embodied the ideals of individual freedom and
increasingly connected the economic market with parliamentary democracy.
Marxists tend to play down this connection, noting that capitalism has been
associated with a great variety of political systems, many of which are extremely undemocratic.[29] However, the English model has become the dominant one in the West. In almost all Western countries today, capitalism *is*
associated with parliamentary democracy, habeas corpus, freedom of the press,
and a formal separation of powers. Elsewhere I have suggested that extremes
of class conflict and the use of severe state repression are a product of uneven
development, and that where capitalism is relatively hegemonic, then institutionalized and liberal-democratic methods of compromise can be used.[30] This
is the element of capitalist society neglected by Weber. For a bourgeois writer
he is surprisingly unsympathetic to capitalism.

Not all sociological theory is Weberian (or Marxist), however, and it may
seem that much modern theory is more favorably disposed toward capitalism.
Though the disquiet of Weber and Durkheim was added to by Pareto and
Mosca (also considered significantly as "founding fathers"), has not the sub-
sequent dominance of functionalism and empiricism restored the balance?
The so-called radical sociologists would have us believe more than that:
Sociology, they claim, *is* bourgeois ideology.

I would not dispute for one moment that modern American sociology has
been profoundly conservative in its implications. But its relationship to capitalism is more problematic. Functionalism, for example, is so generally expressed that it can serve as a technicist ideology in *any* existing society, and

indeed is now in vogue in the Soviet Union. The theoretical tradition that is
often viewed as a "radical" alternative to functionalism, symbolic interactionism is equally abstract, positing individual relations as devoid of any particular
social content as the systems building of functionalism. When we leave "grand
theory" and descend to the level of empirical studies, the main difficulty is
how rarely postwar sociology (other than Marxism) describes, or even names,
the economic system of the West. The society is merely "industrial," differentiated only from "preindustrial" or "modernizing" societies. A link between
economy and polity is seen, but liberal democracy is said to result from the
level of economic development, urbanism, or literacy, and not from any features specific to capitalism.[31] The comparison with the state socialism of the
USSR is instructive, for it is generally contrasted with political pluralism (and
found wanting) — political liberalism is defended, and the link with market
capitalism is rarely made. Talcott Parsons has been virtually the only relatively
conservative sociologist who has added this vital element of true bourgeois
ideology, and even he has made the link only through analogies between economic and political systems.[k]

Academic empiricism is paradoxically preventing sociology from being
explicit bourgeois ideology. Empiricism as a scientific method (though not as
a philosophical system) tends to affirm that "the facts speak for themselves"
and can be abstracted from their social and historical totalities. Theories can
be arrived at by adding up these discrete facts, which are most efficiently arrived at by scientific specialization. The economy is the business of the economist, personality of the psychologist, the polity of the political scientist. What
this leaves to the sociologist is not to his liking, so he attempts imperialism over
the other subjects. But as economics, the most technical of the social sciences,
is well-protected against the amateur aggressor, the economy rarely figures in
sociology (or, indeed, in political science). This neglect is indeed conservative
in its implications, for sociology must take for granted an overall economic

---

[k]For example, Z. Brzezinski and S. Huntington, *Political Power: USA/USSR* (London:
Chatto and Windus, 1964). The main exceptions besides Parsons are the Marxian, C.B. Mac-
Pherson, and Rolf Dahrendorf. a true nineteenth century liberal but often viewed as a
radical by American sociologists. See his "Market and Plan" in *Essays in the Theory of
Society* (London: Routledge & Kegan Paul, 1968). A. Gouldner has claimed that even
Parsons has been sufficiently concerned by the moral emptiness of capitalism to draft
stronger normative elements into his theory: *The Coming Crisis of Western Sociology*
(London: Heinemann, 1971). Though this would support my own argument, I regard it as
implausible. Robert Dahl rejects the "classical" link between political democracy and a
decentralised capitalist economy, because countries like Sweden possess the first but not the
second characteristic. This common argument that a country is not "capitalist" if as much
as 53 percent of its GNP is public expenditure (as in Sweden) neglects the "prime mover"
role of the private sector of the economy and the effects of the international capitalist
economy. R. Dahl, *Polyarchy* (New Haven: Yale University Press, 1971), pp. 57-61.

structure of society that it cannot comprehend. But it cannot lead to an *explicit* ideology for capitalism if it cannot even *see* capitalism.[l]

This makes sociological theory today a very odd affair. Marxism offers it a firm anticapitalist possibility, though this has been largely rejected by American sociology in most of the postwar period. The explicit liberal concern with (and often defense of) capitalism, which could be found especially in the British theoretical tradition, is neglected. The other European traditions that are respected transmit unease about the capitalist element of modern society. To set against this there is abstract functionalism (with a bias towards stability), the Durkheimian concern with tradition, and an empiricism that cannot recognize either social or historical totalities. This combination of a concern with stability, tradition, and pragmatism is essentially conservative for it ignores the radical claim that society is a totality, but one that changes and therefore can be changed.[32] But is is precisely not a *theory* of modern society, for that would require conceptions of both totality and change. When combined with the traditions filtering through from Marx (usually in a very watered-down form), Weber, Pareto, and symbolic interactionism, in something labelled and taught as "sociological theory," it is largely incapable of forming a theory about modern society, and retreats into either scholarship concerning the classic theorists or empiricism. If groups then emerge within sociology or within the student body who hurl abuse at capitalism, sociological theory can do little to resist, for it contains no legitimating theory of capitalism and even its conservatism has excluded the capitalist economy (and functionalism becomes useless once there actually *is* social conflict). "Bourgeois" theoretical sociology collapsed like a house of cards in the late 1960s. If ideology, it was remarkably feeble ideology.[m]

Intellectuals and the Economy

We are now in a position to make some general observations on the role of the intellectuals in capitalist society. If we could credit societies with purposes,

---

[l]This theoretical neglect is rather baffling, given the *political* commitment of some Western sociologists to capitalism. The "end of ideology" group were particulary active in the 1950s, through the Congress for Cultural Freedom, in "the defence of freedom against Communism."

[m]The disintegration of theory into successive fads has proceeded to the point where it is difficult to distinguish spoof from serious intent. What are we to make, for example, of T.R. Young (of the "Red Feather Institute for Advanced Studies in Sociology") who argues that three recent theorists – of whom two are enigmatic and the third polemic – offer us a breakthrough, not only in sociological theory, but also in the running of our own lives? "The Politics of Sociology: Gouldner, Goffman and Garfinkel," *The American Sociologist,* 1971.

we might say that capitalism has made a serious mistake in dealing with its intellectuals. In keeping with its emphasis on specialization, it has encouraged the division between mental and manual labor, so that the pursuit of ethical, aesthetic, and social theory has become more than ever the province of distinct groups of intellectuals, each with its specialized institutions, and most of which are connected to the rest of society only by the market for their products (the exception is the University — increasingly the home of intellectuals — which will be discussed later). In these ways intellectual endeavor is no different in kind from electrical engineering, the legal system or other sectors of capitalist society. Yet, intellectuals have always considered their mission to be all-embracing — to pursue questions relating to the nature of the "whole man" and the "whole society." This is contradictory and intellectuals will attempt to meddle in other sectors in the same way as priests do in more religious societies. Unless they become entirely technical, they will seek to contravene specialization. And as it is no one else's task to actively pursue moral issues, they will complain — just as priests do — about society's utilitarianism and materialism.

Capitalism's problems in dealing with the intellectuals are heightened by the peculiar distance that exists between them and the capitalist *economy*. Even in the eighteenth century, though Enlightenment writers might welcome the advent of commercial enterprise, they had little real contact with it, because industrial capitalism was a social force that rose up beneath a cultured, intellectual world that was already in existence.[n] And, when established, capitalist enterprises were not required by any important pressure group to embody moral or social purposes themselves. These correctives to private selfish interests were to be applied by the state. Therefore the concerned intellectual might engage in political activity but not in activity within the economic sector itself. The capitalist *economy* is "disenchanted," and so is likely to be antipathetical to the intellectual. At the very least it is "alien territory" for him and he will give it little direct ideological support.

Most commentators on the role of literature or sociology in society make too direct a connection between them. The writer is said to reflect either his society, or, more modestly, only the writer's position or class in society.[o] But we must be cautious on both sides of the equation, taking into account not only the writer's position and biases but also that the "object" of his study

---

[n]Hence the patronizing ring of Kant when supporting the gradual extension of "enlightenment" to the "dumb, domestic cattle," the people, "What is Enlightenment?" International Kant Congress, 3d, University of Rochester, *Proceedings*, ed. L.W. Beck (Indianapolis: Bobbs-Merrill, 1963), and Rousseau when supporting democracy: "It pleases me to see my mason, my carpenter, my blacksmith . . . and my friend the manufacturer, all rise above their craft," quoted by P. Gay, *The Party of Humanity* (London: Weidenfeld & Nicholson, 1964), p. 95.

[o]This is true of almost all sociologists of literature; for example, Lukacs, Goldmann, and Bradbury.

may not be "society" but a specific element of social structure. Those writers and critics who have posited a dichotomy between the artist and society have been wrong not only because the artist is a social being, but also because society turns out to be primarily economy. It is only because within capitalism the economy is the major determining element of society (one does not have to be Marxist to see this) that such a plausible transition can be made. *Within* capitalist society there is a contradiction between two elements of social structure, felt by the intellectual not only abstractly and intellectually, but concretely every time he chafes at being dependent upon an impersonal market. We might also add every time his university is pressured by the needs of the economy, for intellectuals and especially social theorists have been increasingly domiciled there. To round off the argument by seeing the response of intellectuals to these pressures I now turn to the role of the universities.

Universities and Capitalist Society

Universities existed before capitalism, and therefore the latter had to come to terms with them. The traditions of the eighteenth-century universities were in many senses opposed to the intellectual currents of the industrial revolution.[33] As repositories of scholarship and religion but also concerned in a rather amateurish way with the education of the traditional governing classes, they were opposed by the thinkers of the Enlightenment, whose schemes for replacing them by professional training schools and government academies for science and arts were put into effect by the French revolutionary government in 1799. Yet, in most countries the power of the universities was sufficient to resist the encroachment of nineteenth-century governments, even when shorn of their traditional alliance with the land-owning classes. Education systems differed greatly between countries, of course. Yet, in all of them it is possible to see the same academic resistance to outside utilitarian pressures. This was most successful in England, where the nineteenth-century provincial foundations, originally intended to provide the utilitarian training despised by Oxbridge, were later forced largely into the latter's mould. Cambridge's thinking is well-revealed in the struggle in the 1870s to place modern languages upon the university's curriculum, for the innovators went to great lengths to explain that the syllabus would *not* assist those going into foreign trade! The logic of economic utility was shunned.[34] In Germany, although the revival of the university was the work of the Prussian State itself, and tight formal control was erected over the academics, the content of the teaching was in their hands, and they emphasized intellectualism rather than practical training, theory rather than knowledge. They were able, moreover, to banish utilitarian engineering to the lower status Technische Hochschule. In France the traditional university was eliminated by the revolutionary and Napoleonic reforms that lasted until 1896, and even after that date the Grandes Ecoles, with their close connections with the practical world of administration and business, have survived to provide a highly-integrated educational elite. But alongside these have remained the Paris academies dominated by conservative intellectual traditions. And even in the United States a plurality of academic systems has left many elite colleges with a distinctly nonpractical bias.

The pressures exerted by a capitalist economy, when dominant, have been very great, and not even Oxbridge emerged unscathed.[35] Yet, the adaptation was generally rather indirect. For the "training" role of the modern University has been less in supplying the captains and kings of the economic system itself than in providing its *professionals* — lawyers, teachers, civil servants, doctors, engineers. A study of nineteenth-century Cambridge has revealed that the university assisted in a considerable net outflow of personnel from the business sector — that is, the number of graduates entering business was less than half the number of university entrants whose fathers were in business. This was probably as much due to the status aspirations of the fathers and sons as to the university's prejudices, but it shows the social power of the university's traditions. Even in the 1930s the imbalance, though decreasing, still existed.[36] Later data for the university are not available, and indeed it is difficult to obtain occupational data of sufficient precision to establish this as a general trend within all capitalist nations. But United States data seem to support it. A 1960 study found that twenty-nine percent of male students' fathers were either nonfarm proprietors or business officials, yet only twenty-one percent of male graduates went into business occupations.[p] If we examine students' desired occupations instead of their actual destinations, we find business even less popular. In another United States national study of 1961-62, twenty-four percent of second-year students were sons of businessmen; yet, only six percent chose business as their preferred career.[q] And, of course, the net outflow for women is far greater (though this may reflect industry's own discriminatory practices rather than the women's own desires).

---

[p]Bureau of Social Sciences Research Inc. for the National Science Foundation, *Two Years after the College Degree* (Washington: U.S. Government Printing Office, 1963), table A-32M, p. 226. As thirty percent of students were from working-class backgrounds — and very few graduates went into working-class occupations — this is remarkable demonstration that college students do not view business occupations as an important avenue of upward mobility.

[q]C.E. Werts, "Social class and initial career choice of college freshmen," *Sociology of Education*, vol. 39, 1966. One datum that might be thought to run counter to my argument is that the number choosing business actually increases through college years. In one study only seven percent planned business careers in their first years, but this rose to seventeen percent after graduation. Yet, as the shifters were those with very low grades it is probable that this is a forced change, that they could not continue with their plans to enter professions, do research, etc.: R.R. Hind and T.E. Wirth, "The effect of university experience on occupational choice among undergraduates," *Sociology of Education*, vol. 42, 1969.

This is not unexpected, for whereas many professions require university degrees or diplomas as entry qualifications, the business world still offers chances of upward mobility to men off the shop floor. The provision of graduates for industry is only a subsidiary part of the vocational aspect of universities. Yet, if we remember that the graduates who do go into industry are generally those with below-average degrees, that those in business studies are of below-average ability, and that industry has complained persistently of inadequate recruitment from elite universities, then we can perceive a certain uneasiness in the relationship between them. The universities are happier supplying professionals, supposedly committed to the ethical principle of service, than the materialistic world of business.

That academic values are somewhat distant from those of the outside world can be seen in American studies of changing student values. While at college the importance students give to aesthetic values increases markedly while that given to economic values declines slightly; they rate "the academic goal of general education and appreciation of ideas" higher, at the expense of vocational training; and they increase noticeably in political leftism.[37]

This is not yet evidence for outright opposition between universities and business, and in many university disciplines there may be virtually no antipathy. This is so where academics can find elites either in business or in other areas of the outside world who are responsive to their results — in business administration itself, in engineering and the applied sciences, in economics, law and medicine. At the other extreme are those academics and students at the receiving end of the traditions I outlined earlier, in the humanities and in the nonapplied social sciences, especially sociology. The studies of student values would indicate that the latter are far more hostile to capitalism.[38] In these subjects and in the elite universities dominated by them and by pure science the students and staff find themselves closer together in their politics than either is to politics outside the university.[39] Hence, one of the strands of the recent "student revolt" can be traced back to the Western intellectual tradition in the humanities and social sciences that found in the universities one of its main homes. Usually this took the form of a vague distrust of the business world, but it also nourished pockets of socialism and reactionary conservatism, both hostile to capitalism and refusing to recognize a link between freedom and the market system. In recent years the encroachments of monopoly capitalism and the war economy upon the universities has converted this into a heady atmosphere of radicalism for many students and dons.

Student radicalism in the 1960s has been disproportionate among the most intellectually committed students, among arts and social science students, among children of university graduates, among children of liberal professionals.[40] In attacking their universities the students have been concerned with pointing out the discrepancy between the traditional ideals of the humanities and the social sciences, and their contemporary state of abstracted scholarly empiricism. This has considerably embarrassed their teachers, many of whom have supported them. Of course, in any explanation of student revolt we must also consider causes specific to the growing pains of adolescence and the internal administration of the universities, but I wish to note that the most radical students are those most in touch with the intellectual tradition I have described. And having been politically defeated, the student radicals have become more intellectualized than ever — as a glance at the publishing industry's steady revival of forgotten Marxists texts reveals! Of course, we must not overlook the nonuniversity intelligentsia's own political participation — in May 1968 in France, in the United States antiwar movement, and in many other recent radical phenomena. The liberal professions are heavily overrepresented in contemporary radical movements in the West.[41] The connections I have made between the various groups associated with the Western intellectual tradition have now been revealed in political movements.

I have stressed the continuity of the intellectuals' suspicion of capitalism. Even "the students' revolt" is a fairly traditional pheomenon, at least in the United States.[42] Yet, the political radicalism of the intellectuals is growing. Three causes can be adduced for this: First, as capitalism has become hegemonic within Western societies the business economy has swallowed up traditional elites in the political sphere. Thus, reactionary revulsion to it becomes increasingly impracticable. Appeals by intellectuals to the Church, to cultural nationalism, to particularistic paternalism, are less and less possible as these are swallowed up by capitalism, or become identified with Fascism. Second, the intellectuals are increasingly connected to the economic structure of monopoly capitalism. Though the arts play their traditional role of providing for "higher" aspirations than mere materialism, they are now also essential for the economic system itself (through design, advertising, the mass media, etc.). Insititutions like art schools, caught in the crossfire of art and commerce, have become politicized very recently. Third, there has been a consequent large increase in the sheer numbers of intelligentsia required by the new economy (though this need was exaggerated by educational planners in many countries). Hence, a political movement of some size could develop in the 1960s when Western capitalism was involved in a war that offended all humanitarians.

Prospects for the Future

The disaffected section of the intelligentsia does not yet constitute a very formidable political movement. Still small in absolute numbers, more interested in ideas than actions, incapable of agreeing about ideas, drawing much support from the temporary freedom of adolescence, disapproving of capitalism but not too threatened by it, dependent for its momentum upon capitalism involving itself in obvious atrocities (as in Algeria and Vietnam), the intellectuals' movement is neither capable nor willing to attack the ruling class. Yet, their overall effect is subversive rather than conservative, utopian rather than ideological. Intellectuals can, and often do, provide part of the moral fiber of a social order. This is at present absent from capitalism. We must not forget that in the modern era revolutions have been preceded by disaffection among the intellectuals.[43] If groups such as the Narodniks were remembered for their own sake it would be for their naivety, incoherence, and failure.[44] Yet, they preceded the Bolsheviks and are honored for their descendants. The sense of alienation and incoherence among the Russian intelligentsia is powerfully conveyed in Dostoevsky's novel *The Possessed*. There a provincial governor, playing with the intellectual fashions of the time, is reading anarchist literature when an anarchist plot erupts underneath him. His realization of his repressive duties is late and inadequate. Such might be the subversive role of the intelligentsia in modern capitalism.

It is unlikely that the intellectuals will become suddenly reconciled to a capitalism that is continuing to mount pressures upon their freedoms. Furthermore, as the large corporation begins to dominate the economy and the state intervenes and represses with greater regularity, the traditional equation of capitalism with liberal freedom now begins to look implausible.[r] Though I have argued that intellectuals have failed to do this justice in the past, their skepticism might be healthy in the long run. One possibility for gradual improvement in their position is provided by the new middle-class politics of the environment and consumer protection. A particularly interesting development is the political emergence of a technical intelligentsia, convinced from its own technical study of ecology, sources of energy, population, economics, etc. that present trends must be reversed by authoritative political action. This is already showing itself to be more practical and more acceptable to reformists in the political establishment than are the politics of the more "humanistic" New Left. Little "ideology" is involved – for if they are infringing "freedom" by advocating more central planning, so too are their opponents, who are increasingly identified as large corporations and national governments. Furthermore, they may be able to recruit from the traditionally disaffected intelligentsia, for control over fuel policy and urban development have the kind of absolute "rationality" that appeals to humane intellectuals (as did the appeal to "stop bombing babies") in a more immediate way than the rather complicated appeals of socialism (or Fascism, for that matter). This would appear to be the most promising area for intellectuals to effect a reformist corrective to the perceived evils of capitalism, in the absence of major upheavals stemming from other sections of capitalist society.

However, the hope of most left-wing intellectuals lies in the working class,

---

[r] As C.B. MacPherson has repeatedly stressed.

and if the latter did increase in revolutionary fervor then it might be possible
to see intellectuals playing the kind of vanguard role ascribed to them by the
Leninist tradition. This possible dénouement clearly depends on some kind of
deepening economic crisis within capitalism. As such a crisis would probably
affect each nation-state differently, the condition of success for some may be
the failure of others. The weakest link in the capitalist chain might be forced
to the wall. Great Britain is the obvious candidate for this dubious distinction.

In normal circumstances there is little in common between disaffected intelligentsia and radical sections of the working class. However, in times of
crisis they may at least share the experience of government repression. In
Imperial Russia censorship and control over education brought together many
intellectuals in the same political movements, and the same jails, as working-
class leaders. A milder parallel is to be found in 1968 in France. In modern
Britain minor economic crises have already had similar, though separate, effects
upon the universities and the trade-union movement. Attempts to make universities more efficient and useful and to upgrade Polytechnics are after all
part of the same government offensive as attempts to reduce the power of
trade unions over wage determination. They may be both mild and unsuccessful as yet, but if the crisis deepened then the government, whether Conservative or Labor (as at present constituted), would be forced by its beliefs to increase the pressure. And if we are hypothesizing an economic catastrophe,
then we must visualize social turbulence, where a government is possibly
sacking troublemakers within the universities, jailing worker militants, and
allowing mobs to attack theaters where "subversive" plays are being
performed. In such circumstances it is not just a question of some intellectuals
forming a vanguard party group to lead the workers, but also of real experience
of repression wonderfully concentrating the minds of the intellectuals themselves, forcing them to stop waffling about alienation and capitalism and to
face the concrete political enemy. Whether they would do this in sufficient
numbers, whether they would not move to the Right, whether the working
class would be sufficiently aggressive, whether the ruling class would possess
the moral fiber to stand firm, is beyond the somewhat modest powers of prediction of social science.

The reason I introduce such an apocalyptic vision is to point out the contrast between the normal and the revolutionary situation. In any elaborated
division of labor, to experience the totality of society, is a rare phenomenon,
confined perhaps to wartime and to revolutionary situations. Even the best
social theorists I have discussed, Durkheim and Weber, were aware of lacunae
in their thought. Others seem more evident to us, their descendents. The
lacunae are naturally greater among the novelists discussed, whose social
theory was more marginal to their purposes. The gap between their consciousness and that of the ordinary citizens of Western capitalism has been very large,
reflecting the distance between intellectual and industrial institutions in the

society. Given a division of labor, the only mediation possible between the two types of ideological experience – the abstract thought of the intellectuals and the patterning of the citizen's life – is provided by the political apparatus of the state, which, even in the laissez-faire society, "holds the ring." This is why the common experience of state repression is the only likely precipitator of one united radical ideological perspective – just as its obverse, the experience of a threat to the state from outside is the main precipitator of a common conservative ideology. Outside of these situations the two types of ideology are very separate.

The intellectuals do not serve as ideologists for capitalism. Because of the contradiction between their own particular role within capitalist society and their beliefs about the general moral role, and because of their dislike of the commercial market for their products, they are uneasy at what they identify as the capitalist element of modern society. Yet, this is not necessarily a serious threat to capitalism, for it is not in consciously articulated ideology that capitalism finds its support and its stability.

Notes

1. There are several useful quantitative studies contained in H.D. Graham and T.R. Gurr, *The History of Violence in America* (New York: Bantam Books, 1969).

2. M. Mann, "The Social Cohesion of Liberal Democracy," *American Sociological Review,* 35, 3 (June, 1970), pp. 423-439.

3. P. Converse, "The Nature of Belief-Systems in Mass Publics," in D.E. Apter, ed., *Ideology and Discontent* (Glencoe, Ill: The Free Press, 1964). R.M. Blackburn and M. Mann, "Ideologies in the Non-Skilled Working Class," in M. Bulmer, ed., *Working Class Imagery* (London: Routledge & Kegan Paul, 1974).

4. *Selections from the Prison Notebooks* (London: Laurence & Wishart, 1971), p. 323.

5. As Nigel Harris puts it, "Tranquility is the first duty of the citizen," *Beliefs in Society* (Harmondsworth: Penguin, 1971), p. 97.

6. Nicos Poulantzas, *Pouvoir politique et classes sociales* (Paris: Maspero, 1968), p. 134.

7. G. Katona, "The Human Factor in Economic Affairs," in A. Campbell and P.E. Converse, eds., *The Human Meaning of Social Change* (New York: Russell Sage Foundation, 1972).

8. The President's Commission on Law Enforcement and the Administration of Justice, *The Challenge of Crime in a Free Society* (Washington: U.S. Government Printing Office, 1967), p. 49; National Opinion Polls, London, *NOP Political Bulletin,* January 1971.

9. Eugene Genovese, *The World the Slaveholder Made* (London: Allen Lane, 1970), p. 98.

10. Karl Mannheim, *Ideology and Utopia* (London: Routledge & Kegan Paul, 1936).

11. David Hume, "Of refinement in the Arts," *Works*, III, pp. 301-2, quoted and discussed in Peter Gay, *The Enlightenment: an Interpretation* (London: Weidenfeld and Nicholson, 1970), vol. II, chap. 1.

12. Raymond Williams notes the enmeshing of land and trade in the fortunes of the families portrayed by Jane Austen, *The English Novel from Dickens to Lawrence* (London: Chatto & Windus, 1970), pp. 18-24.

13. M. Bradbury, *The Social Context of Modern English Literature* (Oxford: Blackwell, 1971), p. 119.

14. G. Lukács, *The Theory of the Novel* (London: Merlin Press edition, 1971); L. Goldmann, *Pour une sociologie du roman* (Paris: Gallimard, 1964), esp. chap. 1.

15. André Gide, *Journals 1889-1949* (Harmondsworth: Penguin edition, 1967), p. 580.

16. G. Lukács, *Essays on Thomas Mann* (London edition: Merlin Press, 1964), p. 43.

17. Quoted by Roy Pascal, *The German Novel* (Manchester: Manchester University Press, 1956), p. 259, from whose chapters on Thomas Mann I have drawn freely.

18. J. Harrison in *The Reactionaries* (London: Gollancz, 1967) traces these views in Yeats, Wyndham Lewis, Pound, Eliot, and Lawrence.

19. For example, J. Fletcher, *The Novels of Samuel Beckett* (London: Chatto & Windus, 1964).

20. L. Goldmann, *Pour une sociologie du roman*, chap. 4.

21. For a review of the literature, see Michael Mann, *Consciousness and Action Among the Western Working Class* (London: MacMillan, 1973), pp. 24-33.

22. For example, in L. Goldmann, *The Hidden God* (London: Routledge & Kegan Paul, 1964).

23. As. R.A. Nisbet does in his influential *The Sociological Tradition* (London: Heinemann edition, 1967). It may be doubted also whether Durkheim really fits into such an interpretation (see below).

24. Such neglect sadly characterizes Philip Abram's *The Origins of British Sociology 1834-1914* (Chicago: Chicago University Press, 1968), which starts too late and includes only Spencer of these men.

25. Ibid, "Introduction."

26. C.B. MacPherson, *Democratic Theory: Essays in Retrieval* (Oxford: Oxford University Press, 1973).

27. Quoted by J. Stuart Hughes, *Consciousness and Society* (London: MacGibbon and Kee, 1967), p. 280.

28. S. Lukes, *Emile Durkheim: His Life and Work* (London: Allen Lane,

1973), pp. 195-99.

29. Poulantzas, *Pouvoir politique et classes sociales.*

30. Mann, *Consciousness and Action Among the Western Working Class,* pp. 39-44.

31. For example, S.M. Lipset, *Political Man* (Garden City, New York: Doubleday, 1960).

32. See Nigel Harris's brilliant account of conservative thought in Britain and the Soviet Union in his *Beliefs in Society,* esp. chaps. 4, 5, and 7.

33. This paragraph is heavily dependent upon J. Ben-David and A. Zloczower "Universities and Academic Systems in Modern Societies," *Archives Europénees de Sociologie,* vol. 3, 1962.

34. S. Rothblatt, *The Revolution of the Dons: Cambridge and Society in Victorian England* (London: Faber and Faber, 1968).

35. For an account of the process in England see M. Sanderson, *The Universities and British Industry 1850-1970* (London: Routledge & Kegan Paul, 1972).

36. Rothblatt, *Revolution of the Dons,* pp. 271-72.

37. K.A. Feldman and T.M. Newcomb, *The Impact of College on Students* (San Francisco: Jossey - Bass, 1969), vol. 1, chap. 2. More detailed explanation of the data are found in vol. 2.

38. Ibid, chap. 6.

39. S.M. Lipset, "The Politics of Academia" in D.C. Nichols, ed., *Perspectives on Campus Tensions* (Washington: American Council on Education, 1970), and his *Rebellion in the Universities* (Boston: Little, Brown & Co., 1972), pp. 31-32 and chap. 6.

40. Lipset, *Rebellion in the Universities;* M.W. Miles, *The Radical Probe: The Logic of Student Rebellion* (New York: Atheneum Press, 1971).

41. F. Parkin, *Middle-class Radicals* (Manchester: Manchester University Press, 1968).

42. Lipset, *Rebellion in the Universities,* chaps. 4 and 5.

43. C. Brinton, *The Anatomy of Revolution* (New York: Vintage Books, 1965 ed), pp. 39-50.

44. F. Venturi, *Roots of Revolution* (London: Weidenfeld & Nicholson, 1960).

12 Symbolism in Politics
Murray Edelman

The Shaping of Beliefs Through Politics

Americans are taught early in life that the policies of their government reflect what the people want, but few adults can be unaware today that governments create public opinion as well as respond to it, or that they sometimes respond to it only after they shape it.

Governments influence both the quality of people's lives and their states of mind, although until recently political science paid relatively little attention to the latter process. Public policies help the poor, kill people in wars, and make some rich through depletion allowances; they also evoke common beliefs and perceptions among large segments of the population: a belief, for example, that a foreign country is planning aggression, that antitrust laws protect consumers against unfair prices, that crime is increasing or declining, that welfare recipients need to be controlled or forced to work. Such common beliefs in turn justify far-reaching public policies.

The beliefs are frequently accurate, but often they are inaccurate or problematic even though everyone likes to think of himself of herself as a political realist. Usually the beliefs are a mixture of fact and myth, and there is no way most citizens can learn which components are which. The social and psychological processes through which public beliefs come into being regardless of verifiable evidence are systematic in character, however, and we are learning what these processes are through the study of political symbolism.[1]

These symbolic processes more easily maintain confidence in the status quo than they promote disaffection and change, for the most powerful and most subtle cues come from established authorities. Though public officials and policies often become targets of criticism, the existing social structure and existing patterns of authority and status relationships typically benefit from political symbolism in advanced industrial societies. Increasing social complexity, more sophisticated electronic communications media, and greater knowledge of psychology are likely to provide authorities with ever more potent resources for reassuring the public and for socializing people into roles useful to elites.

When change serves elite interests, myths and rituals readily justify that too, typically employing traditional symbols to do so. Old nationalisms serve the interests of the new multinational corporations. Summit visits in Moscow and Peking create a widespread belief that detente has been achieved, although there is no lessening in the arms race or in the occurrence of confrontations.

The political creation of strong mass beliefs about controversial public issues takes many forms, but there are common elements whenever it occurs. There is always widespread anxiety about a potential threat (foreign attack, domestic subversion, economic insecurity, moral blight), and there is always substantial ambiguity about the facts and the causes of the problem. In consequence a large public very much wants to believe that the authorities know how to cope with the issues that they themselves find both threatening and bewildering.

For most people most of the time politics is, paradoxically, both a distraction from their chief interests and a source of deep-seated anxiety. Political leaders who appear to be competent, strong, and resolute therefore find a large audience eager to be reassured by their dramaturgical performances even if the social, economic, and foreign problems they attack remain unsolved or grow worse. Because of the pervasive ambiguity about the nature of the problems and the ready possibility of creating misleading benchmarks either of progress or of growing threat, dramaturgy rather than demonstrable results can easily shape public opinion and win a political following.

Through this psychological incentive to treat top government officials and official actions as symbols of effective and benevolent leadership, governments continuously evoke widespread beliefs about the entire range of our social and political concerns. They evoke perceptions of escalating threats and reassure us that threats are being dealt with; they create beliefs about what problems face us and what their causes are; and they instill beliefs about which people are meritorious and should be rewarded and which are incompetent or untrustworthy and need to be controlled. In short, they shape our political worlds far more completely than we recognize. Symbolically evoked beliefs are not necessarily false, but it is social cues rather than their factual accuracy or demonstability that brings them into being; and they often *are* invalid. The mode of creation of each of these forms of politically cued beliefs is worth examination.

In the wake of Watergate and the Pentagon Papers it is obvious that governments sometimes evoke false beliefs deliberately. While outright public lying can profoundly affect people's lives, it is neither as long lasting in shaping states of mind nor as scientifically challenging as those political symbols that engage the political actors themselves at least as deeply as their audiences. The discussion that follows focuses upon the evocation of public beliefs that are not consciously deceptive: those that are typically seen both by officials and by the public as having different consequences from their demonstrable ones.

The Symbolic Evocation of Threats

Some political enemies hurt their adversaries; some help their adversaries by winning wider political support for them; and some do both. For the German Jews under Hitler, the Nazis were enemies who tortured and killed; for the Nazis, the Jews were enemies who helped solidify domestic opinion behind Hitler and so were politically useful, even though the typical Nazi doubtless perceived Jews as the enemy in just as real a sense as the Jews saw Nazis as their enemies. Because political opponents *can* marshal support for a leader or a cause, it is tempting for those who share a political ideology to perceive some group as the enemy and to evoke the same perception in the population generally. In view of the ready possibility of real conflicts and the constant temptation to create symbolic enemies, it is easy to understand why so much political history is a chronicling of mass violence in the form of wars, genocidal operations, riots, rebellions, and police actions.

The forms of action and of rhetoric that create enemies in this way are readily identified. A physical attack on the alleged enemy by a government recognized by its poeple as legitimately holding power is the most potent way to create a symbolic enemy. When the Johnson Administration fired upon North Vietnamese ships in the Tonkin Gulf and began bombing North Vietnam, most Americans accepted that action as evidence for the claim that North Vietnamese ships had fired upon American ships on routine maneuvers and that North Vietnam was aggressive, dangerous, and had to be contained. When the Chicago police beat up demonstrators at the 1968 Democratic National Convention, survey research showed that most Americans at once perceived the demonstrators as subversive types needing forceful containment. To try representatives of a group for alleged subversion in publicized court proceedings similarly convinces at least a part of the public that the group is indeed subversive.

In general, any social movement most effectively enlarges its political support by identifying as the enemy a group widely regarded as different and alien and therefore not sharing the human qualities of the people we know well. Differences in color, in religion, in nationality, in ideology, and in life-style have all served as a reason for picturing some target as subhuman or, occasionally, as uncannily superhuman. Because these grounds are so readily available for the creation of support to battle symbolic enemies, it is a constant temptation for political regimes and for others who need political support to convince themselves that whatever goals they have in the way of power, status, or money for themselves are in fact means to cope with powerful threats to the population generally: that their own interest is identical with the public interest.

Once particular people are identified in the public mind as actual or potential enemies, the intensification of conflict with them can stem from other symbolic cues rather than from demonstrable aggression. "Hawks" convinced a showdown is inevitable gain wider public support for escalation and larger military budgets by observing, publicizing, and exaggerating the militant behavior of the actual or potential adversary. In this sense the hawks in the Pentagon and in the Kremlin, for example, unwittingly serve each other's domestic political interests. Doves in rival counties do too, though in their case it is typically a conscious strategy.

Escalation and detente therefore bring with them new patterns of political support and new winners of material rewards. Heightened racial tension in the cities attracts wider support for the more militant groups and tactics, both among police and among blacks. It also means larger budgets for police weapons and more support for police discretion, power, and wage increases. On the other side escalation means larger public contributions and higher status for groups like the Black Panthers and less for moderate groups like the Urban League, while detente means the opposite. Because it is easy for governments to create beliefs in threats and enemies, and because the resulting escalation brings material and political benefits, the confusion between real and symbolic enemies can be useful to authorities. Ritualistic engagement with enemies based upon plots that are often mythical brings real rewards for some, though the rewards are conventionally perceived as public costs or deprivations.

If some enemies muster political support, there is reason to change enemies from time to time, to evoke new ones who will muster even wider support in the light of new popular anxieties. And that is exactly what happens with symbolic enemies. At various periods in the nineteenth century the Pope and Roman Catholicism were widely feared enemies for Americans worried about internal subversion from alien sources. In the early decades of the twentieth century anarchists assumed this role. After the Russian Revolution it became the communists. Sometimes an ally becomes an enemy overnight. Soviet Russia, which fought on our side during World War II, became the chief foreign threat to America almost instantly after V.E. Day; and our erstwhile enemies, the Germans, became allies almost as quickly. The inevitable ambiguity about how much of the threat from such enemies is real is a prerequisite to their symbolic potency, as noticed earlier.

By a curious paradox it is the opponents who are most widely and universally feared who most easily undergo such fast conversions. When there is political debate over a public issue or the definition of an enemy, beliefs and perceptions change slowly. Public controversy forces people on both sides to defend their opinions and find reasons to espouse and maintain them. But when there is a consensus the government is the chief, sometimes the only, source of cues, and social pressures are so strong that people adopt the common view with great facility, without having to defend it or even think about it with care. This is often the case in the foreign policy area. When the government begins to redefine the situation a new consensus is as easily formed as the old one was. There is little or no ground for resistance; social pressures to conform are still overwhelming; and so the change is just as noncontroversial as was the previous consensus.

The Creation of Reassurance

Just as people are induced to see enemies who help politically but may not hurt physically, so are they induced to accept real deprivations without political resistance. Here again the possibility of symbolic response arises because the actual impacts of governmental actions are ambiguous and because people are eager to believe that the problems they fear are being effectively countered by governments they can trust.

Economists typically have little confidence, for example, that public utility laws, antitrust laws, and other statutes regulating business prices and practices in the interest of consumers make much difference for long. The regulatory agencies begin before long to reflect the interests and the point of view of the business corporations they are supposed to regulate, their information and their contacts are chiefly with these businesses, and the commissioners typically come from the same social and economic circles as the business management. Consumers, by contrast, are not organized to pursue their interests, to exert political sanctions if they are ignored, or even to see themselves as a distinct pressure group.

Laws regulating business in the interest of consumers do serve an important function, but it is chiefly political and psychological in character rather than economic. To people worried about the power of business monopolies or conglomerates to exploit them, the establishment and the publicized operations of a regulatory agency are reassurance that the government is protecting them. Politicians have often built constituencies upon these fears and their symbolic appeasement through "regulation," even if economists conclude that the regulation is largely ceremony, freeing the regulated industries to set prices and quality of service without political resistance. Because there is no other benchmark of fairness, consumers readily accept the pronouncements of the authoritative regulatory agency as constituting objective, scientific analysis, not responsiveness to the perspective and the interests of sellers.

In the same way a great deal of "law enforcement" masks bargaining, or arbitrariness, or concessions to elites behind a facade of legal certainty and objective fact-finding that render the outcomes psychologically acceptable. Law enforcement is often best understood as a game in which the basic rule is that most "violations" will not be detected or punished, but the authorities are free to decide which will be, in accordance with social norms, formal and informal bargains, and political strength. At the same time legal language and procedures legitimize the process and the outcome because they serve so potently as symbols of objectivity, blindness to privilege, and certainty. In filling out income tax forms, in observing or ignoring speed limits, in coping with antitrust laws, and in hundreds of other encounters with each other, citizens and public administrators regularly engage in a form of risk taking and bargaining while justifying the process and the result with the symbol of the rule of law. For this reason publicized emphasis upon the justice or the democratic character of a governmental proceeding is often a signal that the procedures are significant chiefly for their psychological effect: that they are justifying concessions in line with bargaining power.

A dramaturgy of zealous coping by leaders in behalf of the mass of the citizens is another powerful source of reassurance. Like formal procedures and formal declarations that the consumer is being protected, it is typically effective psychologically whether the leader's coping is real or make-believe and even when the outcome is an obvious failure. President Kennedy's popularity actually rose after the Bay of Pigs fiasco, as did President Nixon's after the 1971 wage-price freeze. When a leader's action looks resolute and decisive, it wins approval, for it reassures people that the chief executive knows how to deal with a problem or threat that worries them but also baffles most of them. A shake-up in the form of a governmental reorganization or the dismissal of subordinates; the publicized assumption by the chief of state of personal "responsibility" for a problem even though only subordinates are actually penalized for mistakes; the vigorous pursuit of a course of action that brings no results or counterproductive results—all of these have often increased a leader's popularity. President Nixon's rapid decline in popularity after the Watergate scandal is evidence that tough rhetoric and action cannot help a leader when the public perceives them as *refusal* to assume responsibility or as self-serving or self-contradictory. This stance leaves the impression of inability to cope and so creates anxiety. But a leader has wide leeway to shape a dramaturgy of competence. The test lies in how he acts, for by creating confidence in himself he also creates confidence in his own interpretation of the results of his acts, which are always ambiguous.

Symbolic gestures not only reassure the general public, but can continue to do so indefinitely, even in the face of authoritative evidence that the reassurance is not warranted. The federal antitrust laws are more than eighty years old. Public utilities regulation and other controls over business in the interest of consumers date from the early years of the twentieth century. Almost from their inception economists have questioned the effectiveness of such controls; but they continue to win votes for politicians, and any effort to repeal them would certainly bring widespread and intense protests. Tokenism has similarly been the order of the day over many decades in other areas of public policy, including many civil rights protections and guarantees of the health and safety of workers. Publicized administration and token enforcement continuously re-emphasize the message people want to believe. The hard-nosed skepticism of serious students of these policies becomes known to some and even ambivalently accepted; but in a setting of uncertainty and concern, public actions in behalf of the consumer are easier to grasp, and they exercise a psychological magic that retains its potency.

Governmental Language As Reassurance

George Orwell once observed that political rhetoric usually lulls people into an uncritical and accepting state of mind, as church liturgy does.

By what psychological devices can the language of government play its part in stilling qualms and focusing the mind upon those facets of public policy that justify it? All language is metaphorical in the sense that it highlights some aspects of a situation while ignoring or masking others. In speaking of a farm policy as "parity" we concentrate upon its alleged function of raising farm income to an equitable level but divert attention from the demonstrable fact that it chiefly helps corporate farmers rather than family farmers and that consumers pay for it. In discussing a "war on poverty" we focus upon the intention of helping the poor, but in consequence fail to notice that the war is a border skirmish at best: that its benefits to the poor are meager and highly selective, while it provides much larger benefits to such affluent groups as slum landlords, highway builders in Appalachia, and physicians whose patients are covered by medicaid or medicare.

The *form* of political language has an even more subtle, and probably more powerful, impact upon our beliefs about government than its content does. As politicians and public officials appeal to us to support candidates and policies, their exhortations implicitly convey the message that our opinions count; and that reassuring message builds support for government and public policies whether or not we like particular regimes and particular actions. The legal language of constitutions, statutes, and treaties is rigorous in its form, commanding officials to carry out the precisely expressed will of the people and their elected representatives. This linguistic style is also strongly reassuring, for it tells us that it is the people, not officials, who make policy. But legal language is highly ambiguous in application. There are always conflicting precedents conferring wide and sometimes total discretion upon governmental regimes. Nonetheless the *form* of constitutions and laws continuously reassures us that we have a government of laws and not of men.

Banality and jargon in official language are also reassuring, even when they are exasperating and objects of irony. The bureaucrat who speaks in "officialese" is certainly avoiding fresh ideas and is telling us through his language style that just as his words are banal, so will his ideas be the conventional ones in the organization he serves. He can be counted on not to question the accepted values of his organization or rock the boat; and those who absorb such jargon smoothly, without qualms or protest, convey the same message about their own values. Hannah Arendt's observation that Adolf Eichmann expressed himself chiefly in cliches therefore helps us understand Eichmann's willingness to accept the shocking goals of the organization he served; in this sense Eichmann was the archetypical bureaucrat. By the same token people who refuse to use the conventional language forms of an organization or a social group are declaring their independence of the values of their associates.

The Symbolic Evocation of Merit and Deviance

One of the most powerful, yet least obvious, symbolic functions of

government is the creation of widespread impressions about the level of merit
or competence of particular groups of people. Who are incompetent, unde-
serving, criminal, mentally sick, or otherwise deviant; and who are normal,
intelligent, admirable, or authoritative? In some degree, of course, we base
such judgments upon objective evidence, but to a considerable extent we also
base them upon governmental cues that are subtle, yet arbitrary. When government defines the consumption of alcohol as legal and the consumption of mari-
juana as criminal, it shapes public opinion regarding the respectability of consumers of the first and the deviance of consumers of the second. Similarly,
the Eighteenth (prohibition) Amendment to the United States Constitution
legitimized the way of life of rural, fundamentalist Protestants while debasing
the culture of urban Catholics, just as repeal of that amendment twelve years
later conveyed the reverse message about the relative status and respectability
of these different groups of Americans. Government constantly influences
status by exalting or condoning some norms while condemning others; and
these influential judgments often differ over time and place, as the current
state of obscenity and abortion laws illustrate.

    In many other ways as well, agencies of the state determine people's status
through procedures that purport to be scientific but are in some measure
arbitrary or problematic. Elementary school teachers and counselors define
children as intelligent or dull, high or low achievers, normal or psychologically
disturbed, using tests and observations whose validity and reliability have
repeatedly been shown to be low or doubtful. For one thing they often measure how well the children conform to middle-class norms of behavior, demeanor,
and speech. Yet, there is impressive psychological evidence that the classifica-
tions tend to become self-fulfilling prophecies, for they shape the attitudes of
others toward the child and the child's self-esteem and self-conception.

    Studies of the classification of people as mentally ill and of the decision to
charge them with crime similarly show very low reliability and the strong tendency to believe the worst of the poor and those whose social norms differ from
those of psychiatrists, social workers, policemen, and judges. An overwhelming
proportion of psychiatric patients involuntarily committed to hospitals and of
persons charged with crime are poor or black, while a far higher proportion of
middle-class crime and unconventional behavior is either overlooked or labeled
as something else, such as individuality, resourcefulness, or eccentricity. In the
first case we are cued to see a major defect of character or of mind; in the
second, either something laudatory or a yielding to transient temptation, much
less serious in its causes and in the rehabilitation measures that are appropriate.
The state not only punishes people who are categorized as deviant, but in doing
so reinforces beliefs about what is normal and what is deviant in the population
generally. Governmental and professional actions create popular fears of the ex-
mental patient or the ex-con whose original labeling was often problematic. In
doing so they strengthen biases against the subcultures of the poor and the

unconventional and so force the victims to continue to play the stigmatized role authorities have defined for them. It is understandable that recidivism rates for prisoners and mental patients are high, no matter what the mode of their "treatment" or the actual threat they pose. A five-year study in New York of the arrest rate of 5,000 former mental patients found it was one-twelfth that of the general population; and most of the arrests were for loitering, vagrancy, and public intoxication, the charges that confer the widest discretion upon police.

This role of the government in classifying people's level of merit and then making the labels a self-fulling prophecy works for the exalted as well as for the demeaned. As already noted, behavior is often officially or professionally judged according to who engages in it. The managment and stockholders of most forms of business receive large governmental subsidies in the form of tax benefits, free public services, or direct grants. The subsidies are justified on the ground that their recipients are serving the public interest, and they symbolize a high level of merit, while the resulting wealth of the recipients further guarantees their high status.

The Evocation of Beliefs About the Character of Public Problems and Their Causes

Governmental acts and rhetoric also shape beliefs about the nature of public problems and about their causes. Such beliefs underlie many of the differences just noticed in the symbolic and material consequences of governmental programs. What we see as a public problem is not an empirical observation, but rather a function of subtle cues. While a comparatively small group of liberal intellectuals saw the segregation of school children by color as a serious problem before 1954, it was the widely publicized Supreme Court decision in the Brown case in that year that defined it as a major public issue for a much wider segment of the population. The proclamation of a "War on Poverty" in 1964 made poverty in America a conspicuous and serious problem for a large number of people for whom the poor had been invisible earlier, even though there had long been as many or more poor people suffering just as intensely.

Government strongly influences perceptions of the causes of problems as well as perceptions of their existence. The 1962 amendments to the Social Act requiring some classes of welfare recipients to accept counseling from social caseworkers created or strongly reinforced a widespread belief that there is far more wrong with the poor than low wages, unemployment, or inability to work: a belief that they suffer from cognitive deficiencies and need control and guidance in how to raise their children, run their homes, and spend their money. The work requirement in the 1972 amendments created or reinforced a belief that a major cause of poverty is laziness, even though it had long been known that a very small fraction of the recipients were physically able to work, did not have to care for small children, and could find jobs when the unemployment rate was close to five percent. In this instance the symbolic function of the statute came close to being its only function.

During World War II gasoline rationing was quite deliberately used not only to conserve fuel but also to create and maintain a strong sense of urgency in the population: to remind people in a compelling way that we were at war and that a spirit of austerity and self-denial was appropriate. The shortage was in fact never serious and the rationing program flexible enough that virtually everyone who was sufficiently persistent and demanding could secure extra rations. As a wisecrack among employees of the Office of Price Administration put it, "The meek shall inherit the dearth."

It has long been clear to sociologists that reality is socially created: that people differ radically in their perceptions of the same situations because of different cues from others. But we rarely recognize or remember that fact as we go about our everyday affairs. We naturally think our perceptions are objective, identical with those of other rational people. We see the world as fact, not as a creation of "significant others" who provide cues that resolve thousands of confusing sense perceptions into simplified patterns that tell us what kinds of situations confront us and even who we are. The belief that our perceptions are objective gives us confidence in them, whether or not the confidence is warranted.

Cues from others are especially powerful in shaping beliefs and perceptions when they deal with matters that create anxiety, when they are not countered by conflicting cues from other sources, and, above all, when the cues are covert. On all kinds of issues that concern us deeply government is our chief or only source of information. When governmental leaders debate publicly among themselves or with nongovernmental opinion leaders, their views are influential because the idea that government is legitimate is inculcated in us early in life. But the very fact of open debate signals the possibility that government can be wrong and in some degree makes us skeptical and alert for confirming or falsifying evidence.

The case is otherwise when the cues from government reach us without our becoming aware that we are being influenced, as is true of most of the symbolic cues discussed in this chapter: rituals of imminent threat to national or personal security and of protection against threats; metaphors and syntactic forms embodied in the language that "describes" issues and governmental institutions; authoritative labels that demean or exalt groups of people and define the causes of their behavior and their problems; myths we learn as children that give us our political identities and roles.

Issues in Need of Further Exploration

Though it is apparent that many tenaciously held political beliefs are not empirically based, we need to know a great deal more about the social-psychological processes and the conditions that generate such beliefs. In what respects are the language and the acts of public officials distinctive in their consequences for public opinion and in what respects do they exemplify a link between language and cognition that also appears in other social interactions?

Comparison of political symbolism and its consequences in different countries and cultures should prove especially fruitful in this regard. Manifestly, the content of symbols differs among nations in the light of their respective histories, social and economic conditions, internal social conflicts, and national myths. But such differences may be fairly superficial, changing readily as new interpretations of history, new economic circumstances, and new ideologies appear. They may also be superficial, in the sense that symbols with different content are functionally equivalent, generating similar cognitive structures, as the work of Noam Chomsky and of Claude Levi-Strauss suggests.

These issues also arise with respect to comparisons of symbols over time. Words and acts that once had powerful effects upon belief lose their potency, and new ones appear. We need to learn considerably more about the conditions of such change and the extent to which new symbols are functional equivalents of their predecessors.

One of the questions that needs investigation in this connection deals with the symbolic correlates of social and economic complexity, urbanization, and functional differentiation in contemporary life. Social scientists have long suggested that these secular trends have entailed a loss in individual autonomy and increasing alienation and anomie. As people's lives are increasingly affected by remote decisions (or nondecisions), does susceptibility to political mystification grow as well? And is there a corresponding increase in the range of behaviors defined as deviant by authorities and therefore by a mass public?

In the study of individual psychology systematic exploration of the nonrational and the irrational has become an essential complement to the study of human intelligence and reason. A similar emphasis in the study of political behavior is past due.

People typically pride themselves on their realism where politics is at issue, but our political worlds are symbolically created to a greater extent than are most aspects of our lives: a joint consequence of psychological needs and of the communications implicit in governmental actions and language. Political mystification is most powerful and most dangerous when, as is usually true, it is not deliberate; and so it is vital that we apply our knowledge of politics and of social psychology to throw light on the mechanisms that create and maintain widely held political cognitions whether or not they are valid.

Notes

1.   I have discussed the issues raised in this article in more extended fashion in

these publications: *The Symbolic Uses of Politics* (Urbana: University of
Illinois Press, 1964); *Politics as Symbolic Action* (New York: Academic
Press, 1971); "The Political Language of the Helping Professions," *Politics
and Society*, vol. 4, no. 3; "Language and Social Problems," Institute for
Research on Poverty Discussion Paper 207-74, May 1974.

13

Politics as Sports: An Interpretation of the Political Ascendency of the Sports Metaphor in America
Ike Balbus

Introduction

The Nixon years in the United States have been marked by a strikingly frequent application of the sports metaphor to the realities of organized political life. State activity is increasingly being cloaked in the rhetoric of the sports world; at times it even appears as if the language of politics is being completely absorbed by the language of sports. Thus, the President becomes the "quarterback" who, along with his Cabinet and White House staff "team," pursues "game plan" policies designed to reach the "goal line" and to "win" the political "ballgame." This corruption of the discourse of politics by the discourse of sports alerts us to a possibly profound transformation in the way in which governmental activity in America is defined and understood: to envelop politics with the symbolism of sports is to transfer the meanings that we attribute to the latter to the former. Thus, the political ascendency of the sports metaphor may well signal the increasing importance of sports as a legitimating mechanism of the American State. The purpose of this chapter is to develop a tentative and unabashedly speculative interpretation of this phenomenon.

The Senate Watergate hearings have revealed the extent to which sports language has permeated the day-to-day operations of the Nixon administration. Thus, one conspirator absolves himself from any moral responsibility by claiming that he was "just a member of the team"; another informs us that his threats to expose the cover-up led to efforts on the part of his superiors to dissuade him on the grounds that he was "destroying the game plan"; and yet another confesses that his moral scruples were overcome by orders from the officers of the Committee to Re-Elect the President to "play ball" and by his consequent fears of not being considered a "team player." Those who would interpret this as nothing more than the toadying of administration sycophants before the linguistic "line" established by their boss, and thus attribute the ascendency of the sports metaphor to the idiosyncracies of an individual President who just happens to be an avid sports fan, would be hard-pressed to account for the growing use of sports language on the part of political commentators in the "independent" and often anti-Nixon press. Consider the language of a recent article in the financial pages of the *New York Times* entitled "What will Nixon Team do in Second Half?"

Let me express my gratitude to Bob Alford, Andrew Arato, Mike Brown, Claus Offe, Bertell Ollman, and Alan Wolfe for having read and criticized an earlier draft of this chapter.

The new Nixon team is in the locker room right now, getting ready for
the second half. What, Wall Street is wondering, will be the new game
plan? In a powerful scoring drive late in the first half, the veteran coach
of the G.O.P. Elephants got the economic ball rolling well. Now with the
second half about to begin, the Elephants have a tricky problem to deal
with: The economy has developed so much momentum that there's a
danger that it could run right past the goal line of full employment, clear
out of the end zone and smack into a new round of inflation. The
penalty for this kind of infraction . . . would clearly be to call the play
all the way back to tight money. . . . [But] it's a tricky business trying
to read Mr. Nixon's play book in advance.[1]

This example is extreme, but hardly unique. Indeed, the widespread adoption of
the sports metaphor for the purposes of political description and analysis recently
led a leading *New York Times* sportswriter to complain that if political analysts
insist on using sports terms, they should at least use them correctly, with a proper
understanding of and respect for their original meaning.

The ubiquity of the sports metaphor suggests that it is performing important
functions within American society, and thus obliges us to develop a structural
explanation of its significance. A clue as to how such an explanation must proceed is provided by the fact that the increasingly frequent political application
of sports language coincides with the increasingly important economic role of
organized sports in America. The rise of monopoly capital in America has transformed sports from an elite preoccupation into a giant, mass spectator industry
that more and more dominates the everyday, nonworking life of the average
American male. Paul Hoch has demonstrated how the dictates of monopoly
capital have shaped the form and content of organized sports, to the point where
all the exploitative relationships within the business world find their reflection in
the relationships among the various participants in the sports world.[a] Thus, the
paradox before us is that language drawn from sports is being used to describe
and interpret political life precisely at that point in time when sports is being
transformed into a Big Business; as sports have become in reality more and more
like work, politics is increasingly being cloaked in the rhetoric, and thus taking
on the appearance, of sports. This suggests that any attempt to understand the

[a]Paul Hoch, *Rip-Off the Big Game: The Exploitation of Sports by the Power Elite*
(Garden City, N.Y.: Doubleday & Co., 1972). Hoch's analysis of the way in which organized
sports contributes to the inculcation of the values and character structures consistent with
the interests of the American ruling class succeeds in demonstrating the centrality of sports
as a contemporary capitalist reproductive mechanism. His analysis does not extend, however,
to the specific phenomenon with which this paper is concerned: the role that sports plays,
through the political application of the sports metaphor, in legitimating the *state* activity that
establishes the necessary political framework within which ruling class interests are secured.
For a review and critique of Hoch's important book, see Isaac Balbus, "The American Game
of Life," *The Nation*, May 7, 1973.

political transformation entailed in the ascendency of the sports metaphor must ground itself in an analysis of the economic dynamics that underlie the transformation of sports themselves. An adequate explication of the legitimating role of the sports metaphor, in other words, must be rooted in the problematic of the advanced American capitalist state.

Advanced Capitalism and the Technocratic State

The efficient functioning of the American capitalist order has come to depend (as it has in other advanced capitalist systems) on a sustained, permanent economic intervention on the part of the state. The "privatized" social relations of capitalist production can no longer contain the increasingly "socialized" forces of production in the absence of a progressive extension of the state form to all spheres of economic activity, and thus a politicization of virtually all economic transactions. To begin with, "the increase in the social character of production (specialization, division of labor, interdependency, the growth of new social forms of capital such as education, etc.) either prohibits or renders unprofitable the private accumulation of constant and variable capital,"[2] and thus demands that the costs of capital accumulation be socialized through the state. Consequently the responsibility for the technological development essential to capitalist productivity increasingly falls to the state, which attempts to gear scientific research to the production of technically exploitable and thus immediately profitable knowledge. Thus, science has become a "leading productive force"[3] through the state-supported transformation of the "private" American university, foundation, and other centers of research into quasi-public institutions for the accumulation of social capital.

The same technological dynamic that requires the progressive socialization of the costs of capital accumulation demands that the state insure that this production is met by an appropriate level of consumption. Technological development has reached the point where "the expansion of goods production capacity proceeds as a function of the sustained decline of required, and possible, labor time employed in goods production,"[4] and thus threatens to undermine capitalist social relations of production: Left to its own logic capitalism progressively deprives individuals of their source of employment, yet simultaneously requires that these same individuals consume the goods that the system produces. Under these conditions the state is obliged to sustain the necessary level of consumption; it does this either through military spending, which creates jobs that would otherwise not exist, direct transfers of income in the form of welfare payments to those for whom no jobs can be created, or military support for private efforts to export capital abroad. In short, the efficient operation of American capitalism increasingly depends on the progressive expansion of the warfare-welfare state.[5]

Thus, the economic requirements of advanced American capitalism dictate that the state become a directly productive force. Whereas nineteenth-century competitive capitalism "institutionalized [the economic system] as a domain beyond the authority of the state"[6] and pre-World War II monopoly capital limited the state to regulatory functions designed to stabilize intracapitalist class relations and to encapsulate worker-capitalist class conflict, the contemporary American state is directly engaged in the day-to-day economic tasks of directing and maintaining capitalist production and consumption. Under these conditions "social processes will almost without exception no longer take place beyond politics; on the contrary, they are regulated and sustained by permanent political intervention . . . the economic system is no longer a *prepolitical* substrata but is, in fact, one of the most important areas of state action."[7] This means that economic transactions that were formerly self-legitimating—in the sense that they were governed by seemingly "automatic" market mechanisms— now require a specifically political legitimation; the expansion of the state form to embrace virtually the entire scope of economic activity leads to "an interpenetration of norms that govern activity at the base and norms that inform activity in the superstructure."[8]

This necessarily total politicization of economic activity can not be accomplished within the framework of the traditional structures of the American state. Neither the Liberal Democractic structures of representative government appropriate to the period of competitive capitalism nor the pluralist, corporatist structures of interest-group representation appropriate to pre-World War II monopoly capital can accommodate the centralized state planning that the everyday steerage of the economy requires; to gear the state to the accumulation and consumption needs of capital as a class requires a flexibility that is hindered neither by the rule of law or formal rationality characteristic of Liberal Democratic structures nor the administrative delegation and interest-group representation and bargaining characteristic of pluralist structures. This incompatibility of existing state structures with the economic requirements that advanced capitalism imposes on the state, moreover, is exacerbated by the formal (and very real) decentralization of authority characteristic of American federalism.[9]

More generally, we can say that any state structure that encourages the application of qualitative, political criteria to state authority necessarily subverts the quantitative, "technical" imperatives of capitalist system-maintenance.[10] Indeed, the smooth and uninterrupted functioning of the "feedback" relationship between the state and private capital so essential to capitalist production and consumption pre-supposes the effective elimination of serious political discussion and debate from the state arena. As long as private economic activity was largely exempt from state authority, such discussion and debate presented no real obstacle to the implementation of capitalist class interests; now that the state form must expand to embrace the totality of capitalist economic activity, however, the political conflict and controversy characteristic of Liberal Democracy and even Pluralist Democracy becomes increasingly "dysfunctional" to the successful reproduction of the capitalist order. Thus, "the new politics of state interventionism requires a depoliticization of the mass of the population";[11] that is, the creation of a centralized state structure freed from popular and interest group control.

The creation of this structure has proceeded apace since World War II. Thus, state authority has increasingly been centralized in the executive, especially in the President and his White House staff. The recent creation of a Domestic Council to direct program planning for the President symbolizes the ascendency of executive policy making and the circumvention of Cabinet-level authority that is subject to congressional and interest-group control. The gradual shift from line-item budgets to program budgets and the recent transformation of the Bureau of the Budget into the Office of Management and Budget reflect efforts to centralize the allocation of budgetary resources and thus free the budgetary process from the tenacious grip of congressional committees.[12] The Ash Council's plan to "reorganize the federal executive along functional rather than program lines" by "dismantl[ing] seven cabinet-level departments and reassembl[ing] them into four superdepartments" is designed to centralize further administrative authority and overcome the clientele politics typical of American bureaucracies.[13] Unlike previous waves of American administrative reform, moreover, these reforms have generally been initiated and elaborated by Presidential Task Forces, themselves reflecting the increasing assumption of planning functions on the part of the executive.[14] Public and even congressional ignorance of a host of recent and crucial executive decisions—including all the Watergate-related "horrors"—testifies to the extent to which state authority has been freed from the constraints of representative and pluralistic structures and thus become a force above both the law and the interplay of interest-group bargaining.

The congressional and public outcry following the discovery of these executive decisions, however, testifies to the continuing legitimating power of the traditional political structures and thus the risks of deligitimation that their abrogation entails. If these traditional structures and their corresponding ideologies have become obstacles to the state-guided reproduction of the American capitalist order, they nevertheless embody deeply rooted, evocative norms by means of which political authority is evaluated; the rule of law, "interest-group liberalism," and "grass-roots democracy" remain powerful forms of what Marx called the "illusory general interest in America."[15] The dilemma for those with an interest in the reproduction of the capitalist system, therefore, is that the creation of the state structure essential for this reproduction necessarily undermines the legitimacy of state authority and thus the legitimacy of the entire system: The efficiency functions that advanced American capitalism imposes on the American state stand in inverse relationship to the availability of appropriate legitimating mechanisms. The response to this dilemma has been the consolidation of the new state structure and the functions that it performs through the articulation of a new legitimating ideology that denies the applicability of the potentially subversive, traditional political norms to this structure and these functions.

Thus, the past decade has witnessed the academic elaboration and subsequent popularization of the technocratic model of politics, which stresses the allegedly neutral character of the economic functions imposed on the state by an allegedly autonomous technological development.[16] According to the theory of technocracy state decisions increasingly take on the nature of purely technical decisions subject only to the imperatives of scientific rationality; traditional ideological conflicts lose their relevance as political authority becomes the mere agent through which immanent technological necessities are put into practice. Both those who welcome this development and those who bemoan it agree that, insofar as state decisions have become technical-scientific decisions, these decisions are not and cannot be subject to a public discussion and debate informed by traditional normative criteria but rather become subject to the "value-free" criteria of the scientific community.

> Political norms and laws are replaced by objective exigencies of scientific-technical civilization, which are not posited as political decisions and cannot be understood as norms of conviction or weltanschaung. Hence, the idea of democracy loses its classical substance. . . . In place of the political will of the people emerges an objective exigency, which man himself produces as science and labor.[17]

Thus, as Habermas has argued, technology and science are rapidly becoming the new legitimating ideology; the functions that the American state undertakes on behalf of private capital and the structures that it adopts to perform these functions are rationalized as the inevitable by-products of immanent scientific necessities. State structures need not be democratic or even pluralistic because the functions that they perform are not political but rather "scientific"; the legitimation of the pervasive economic functions that the state performs on behalf of capitalist class interests is secured through the appeal to the allegedly common interest of all elements of the population in scientific progress. Thus, science itself increasingly vies with the rule of law and "interest-group liberalism" as the dominant "illusory general interest" in America. This transformation entails a radical depoliticization of the definition of the common interest; "the new ideology is distinguished from its predecessor[s] in that it severs the criteria for justifying the organization of social life from any normative regulation of interaction, thus depoliticizing them."[18] If successfully internalized it therefore promises to legitimate the elimination of political discussion and debate from the state arena, thus insuring the existence of a state structure well-suited to the task of reproducing the American capitalist order.

If, according to the technocracy thesis, politics has become technique, it follows that political power is (and/or ought to be) increasingly a function of technical or scientific expertise. Indeed, the technocracy thesis is typically accompanied by the argument that rulership in our "postindustrial" societies has been transformed into a predicate of a "new class" defined in terms of its monopoly of scientific knowledge and of the means of its communication; as the accumulation of capital progressively gives way to the accumulation of knowledge as the overriding systemic imperative, so do former power groups cede their position of dominance to an elite of knowledge that increasingly subordinates all branches of the society to its hegemony.[19] Thus, a new authority principle—the rule of experts—comes to replace the rule of law and the rule of interest groups as the dominant legitimator of state power. Unlike the earlier principles, however—which encouraged the average citizen to determine for himself/herself whether the state was acting in accordance with these principles—the "rule of experts" by definition deligitimates any claim on the part of the average citizen to come to a reflective judgement concerning the exercise of state power. If, in other words, the exercise of political authority increasingly approximates the model of the authority of the airline pilot, any claim to question that authority on the basis of norms that uphold the political competence of the average citizen can and must be discounted on the grounds that it constitutes a grave threat to the security and well-being of the entire society. Active citizenship, in short, becomes not only unnecessary, but also positively harmful; depoliticization is held to be essential to the very survival of the system as a whole.

Accompanying the technocracy thesis' definition of politics as technique, and its characterization of political rulership as expertise, is a specification of the function that this expertise is designed to fulfill: planning. Nothing is dearer to the hearts of the ideological apologists for the technocrats than the illusion that the ascendency of the "knowledge elite" signals the triumph of rational planning and the decline of the irrational conflicts that dominated an earlier age. As the accumulation of capital gives way to the accumulation of knowledge, the hegemony of the competitive market gives way to the superior rationality of "the plan," with the technocrats of the state working hand in hand with the technocrats of the corporations: Galbraith's "technostructure"—who, mercifully liberated from the stranglehold of profit maximization, can therefore be counted upon to join the cooperative effort to program the future needs and direction of the society? Thus, the contradiction between the private ownership of productive activity and its social consequences—formerly reflected in classical economics' distinction between the market and "externalities"—withers away as everything can be indexed by a "social indicator," all our problems can be quantified, so we may happily conclude that qualitative contradictions no longer exist and that our remaining problems are well on their way toward a rational, coordinated solution. If the definition of politics as technique and the

definition of political rulership as rule by experts legitimate each new state
structure required by advanced capitalism by persuading us that these structures
are performing purely neutral functions and that each function is being performed by those most competent to deal with them, the emphasis on global
planning legitimates the overall relationship between the totality of structures
by convincing us that they are all working together, like intermeshing gears, on
a single problem: the rational coordination of all the diverse technical functions, and the many technical experts, who might otherwise be working at
cross-purposes.

Depoliticization and the Rise of the Sports
Metaphor

We are finally in a position to appreciate the systemic significance of the
political ascendency of the sports metaphor. Sports language is becoming political language precisely at that point in time when the efficient operation of
American capitalism has come to depend on the mass internalization of a legitimating ideology that asserts the neutral, "scientific" character of state economic
decisions, the scientific competence of those who make them, and their overall
integration in the form of a plan. Indeed, my thesis is that "the increasingly
frequent application of sports language to the sphere of state activity both signals
and helps promote the internalization of this ideology" and thus the depoliticization essential for the reproduction of the American capitalist order. One way in
which the neutral, scientific character of state economic activity is being established, in short, is through the mediation of the symbolism of sports.

The form of contemporary American sports is particularly well-suited to
this mediating function. There is, in fact, a remarkable structural homology or
isomorphism between a contemporary sports contest and the model of politics
advanced in the technocracy thesis: Sports have increasingly become *technical*
activities that require participation by *experts* whose activities are subordinated
to the dictates of a pre-established *plan*.

Thus, to begin with, a contemporary sports contest is they very model of
purposive-rational or instrumental action governed by technical rules and strategies.[20] The goal of sports activity is always unambiguous and noncontroversial;
participants do not come together to discuss or debate the ends for which the
activity has been established, but rather take this end for granted and apply
themselves in a single-minded fashion to the task of developing the most efficient
means to achieve the predetermined, unchanging, and noncontroversial end:
winning. The strategic, means-oriented character of contemporary American
sports receives its penultimate expression in the advanced, maximally efficient
division of labor characteristic of American football. Football, however, is only
an extreme example of the general tendency of all organized American sports to

obey the imperatives of instrumental, alienated labor rather than those of symbolic interaction or communication.

As alienated labor, performance in organized sports is increasingly evaluated by means of abstract, efficiency criteria rather than by a concrete, qualitative criteria; nothing more dramatically signals the transformation of what was formerly known as play into alienated labor than the universal obsession with the *record*—the constant comparison of performance on the basis of a common, quantitative scale—and the concomitant neglect of stylistic and esthetic dimensions. As Pierre Laguillaumie has argued,

> The law of competition is an integral part of sporting contests . . .
> It begets, at all levels, *the search for maximum efficiency* which can
> only find its expression in the *precise* quantification of the work ac-
> complished. This quantification requires a strict, precise *measure*
> which is internationally controlled in order that a standard be estab-
> lished—a world referent, unifying the practice of all levels: the
> *record.*[21]

Sports, in other words, increasingly consists of the search for the most efficient technique by which to achieve maximum output; the taylorization of sports production has paralleled the taylorization of factory production to the point where Laguillaumie can justly claim that "The champion is fabricated in the image of the worker, the stadium in that of the factory, (and) sporting activity has become a production which takes on all the characteristics of industrial production."[22] For the athlete as much as for the worker—and for all those whose interaction is governed by purely technical, instrumental norms—"the body is lived in the mode of an efficient tool"[23] subordinated to the goal of maximum efficiency, rather than as a source of immediate pleasure and gratification.

A necessary corollary to the progressive subsumption of organized sports under the hegemony of purely instrumental imperatives is the rigid distinction that they enforce between the expert, active participant and the mass of passive spectators who lack sufficient expertise to participate in any but a vicarious manner. As the role of athlete—with its increasingly long, increasingly specialized apprenticeship—more and more determines the possibility of engaging in sports activity, participation on the part of the great majority of nonexperts becomes passive and vicarious rather than active and direct; as Marc Naison has remarked, the vast mushrooming of spectator sports since World War II—as measured by their frequency of media exposure, the length of "seasons," the number of teams, etc.—has not been accompanied by a corresponding increase in the number of persons who actively engage in, and the frequency with which they engage in, the particular sports that they follow and support.[24] Whereas there is now an average of six hours of televised sports each Saturday and Sunday during most of the year and it has been estimated that one out of three American males who read newspapers read nothing but the sports pages, a study completed in 1967 found that "on the average day, only about one percent of the American population engages in some form of genuine athletic activity. . . ."[25] Thus, the inevitable consequence of the transformation of play into organized sports is that sports increasingly assume the character of *spectacles* produced by a relative handful of experts that are ostensibly designed for the consumption of the majority of nonexperts, that is, the rest of the population.

As in the case of any technical operation, maximum sports efficiency requires a plan that serves to coordinate the activity of the various expert participants; there is in fact no clearer example of totally planned interaction than a modern organized sports contest such as American football. The nucleus of the plan is *the play*, which dictates the precise function that each player will perform over a given time span. Any deviation from the play—any failure of an athlete to perform the precise function specified—will necessarily result in a decline in team efficiency, and, if such deviations persist, the "benching" or even dismissal of the responsible player. The more efficiency, the less spontaneity; even the seemingly most spontaneous, even breathtaking movements of a football back, for example, depend on the capacity of ten other players to execute ten planned and precisely delimited functions without which no "spontaneous" individual achievement would be possible. In football, moreover, the selection of plays is not entirely the prerogative of the players themselves; rather individual play selection is normally governed by a "game plan," elaborated by the coach (that most expert of experts, the only one who "knows the game as a whole"), which establishes a hierarchy among the different plays. Thus, the drive for maximum efficiency, conducted by experts, strives to eliminate as much as possible the contingencies of individual choice and error and to subordinate all individual athletic movement to the dictates of a rational, preestablished orchestration. The activity of each part of the team is determined in terms of the function that it plays in relationship to the team effort as a whole, the functional relationships being established and coordinated by means of a thoroughly tested study that precedes the actual activity itself.

Thus, organized sports in America have increasingly taken on a technical, "quasi-scientific" form. This only suggests, however, rather than demonstrates, the plausibility of the thesis that the application of the sports metaphor to political decisions serves to internalize the allegedly neutral, "scientific" nature of these decisions. A genuine demonstration of this thesis would require evidence that sports have not only assumed a technical form, but also, and crucially, that they have been imbued with a technical *meaning* in the consciousness of those who follow them; only if sports "mean" technical activities to those who are exposed to them can we be confident that the sports metaphor is capable of transferring a technocratic meaning to politics.[b] It is entirely possible, in other

_____

[b]For this caveat I am indebted to Mike Brown.

words, that in spite of their increasingly technical form sports continue to have multiple meanings: To some they may signify "fair play," to others "competition," and so on.[c] Thus, our argument presupposes that at least one of the meanings that people attribute to sports is a technical one, and, moreover, that this technocratic meaning is evoked when political activity is described in the language of sports.

There is no conclusive evidence on this point, but at least two things can be said in favor of our interpretation. First, the dominant American spectator sport—the sport that has replaced baseball as the one that is ranked by opinion polls as the most popular American spectator sport—is football, which is, as I have already suggested, the most technical, "scientifically" organized of contemporary American sports. Since that which most distinguishes football from all other American sports is precisely its overwhelmingly technical character, and since football has become the most popular American spectator sport, it may be plausibly (but certainly not conclusively) asserted that the American public increasingly tends to attribute a technical meaning to sports. Moreover, it is precisely language drawn from football—the overtly technical language of "game plans" rather than the language of "fair play" or "competition" common to all sports—that supplies the content for the sports metaphor, suggesting that it is likely that it is above all the technical meaning of sports that is evoked by the application of sports language to political life.

If sports have taken on not only a technical form but also a technical meaning, the following considerations suggest themselves. First, insofar as the application of sports language to political reality encourages us to think of political activity as a sport, it necessarily encourages us to conceptualize political activity in purely instrumental terms. If politics is a sport, then the ends for which political activity is pursued become as unproblematic, as uncontroversial as the end of winning, and politics itself becomes nothing more than the search for the most efficient means to achieve these ends. Political choice is transformed from a normative debate over ends into a technical search for the most appropriate strategies. Thus, the conceptualization of the President as a "quarterback" or "coach" who pursues "game plans" designed to win the political "ballgame" serves to depoliticize state economic decisions by internalizing the ideology of the purely instrumental, technical, and apolitical nature of these decisions.

The depoliticizing consequences of the sports metaphor are vividly

---

[c]That sports may have multiple meanings suggests that the legitimating role of the sports metaphor may be even more complex than I have described it in this chapter. Insofar as sports signify not only technical activity, but also "fair play" and "competition," it may be that the sports metaphor is also capable of reviving the "older" legitimating ideologies of the rule of law and interest-group competition, in which case the ultimate power of the sports metaphor may derive from its capacity to simultaneously evoke, and reconcile, the major competing legitimating ideologies of the American State.

illustrated in the following exchange between then-Representative Gerald Ford and Senator Harrison Williams on the occasion of the former's Vice-Presidential confirmation hearings. Questioned about his future willingness as Vice-President to disagree with Presidential politics, Ford responds: "I learned long ago that after a play has been called, you don't go out and tackle your quarterback." Doubting the applicability of the football metaphor to the governmental process—the only public occasion of which I am aware when any such doubt has been expressed—Senator Williams objects to Ford's unqualified acquiesence to Presidential authority, but nevertheless does so while remaining within the prison of sports language. He asks Ford what he would do if his quarterback got turned around and started running with the ball to the wrong goal line. "Wouldn't you tackle him?" This led Ford to recall a college football game of some fifty years ago when a player had scored a "touchdown" but had run the wrong way, and prompted him to answer Williams' question with the argument: "But that's the exception more than the rule."[26]

Notice that the inevitable consequence of Williams' (reluctant) acceptance of the sports metaphor as the basis for his criticism of Ford's position is the implication that the pursuit of undesirable political goals is as rare as the unintentional pursuit of one's own—rather than the opponent's—goal line. The characterization of political policies as "plays," in other words, necessarily commits one to the position that such policies, like football plays, are neutral, purely instrumental strategies designed to secure the absolutely unambiguous, unproblematic goal of winning: One need only object to these means—just as one should only tackle one's own quarterback—when they clearly bear no conceivable relationship whatsoever to the end of the "game."

If the use of the sports metaphor fosters the internalization of a technocratic legitimating ideology, the widespread acceptance of this metaphor testifies to the degree to which this internalization has already taken place. Here the Watergate hearings are instructive. As I have mentioned, witness after witness invoked the language of sports to describe, explain and justify participation in activity that they were aware was illegal. Although many committee members professed a sincere desire to probe and uncover the reasons for what they considered a shocking eclipse in political morality, to my knowledge not a single senator objected to the profusion of sports language with which they were confronted: From all appearances, neither they nor the political commentators of the media were able to see any connection between the conspirators' conceptualization of their activity as a sports contest and their willingness to participate in it, between the corruption of the discourse of politics by the discourse of sports and the political corruption in which they were engaged. This connection, as I have suggested, is established by the capacity of the sports metaphor to transform the political problem of moral choice into the technical problem of strategic choice. The inability of committee members and political commentators to grasp this ideological transformation accomplished by the sports metaphor would tend to suggest that the distinction between moral choice and strategic choice has already become blurred in the American consciousness and is being replaced by a technocratic conception of politics.

By transforming politics into a neutral, quasi-scientific activity, the sports metaphor also serves to justify the exclusion from participation in this activity of all those who have not acquired the requisite technical competence. If politics is a sport, especially an extremely complex sport like football, then only those who have mastered the technical rules and acquired the appropriate skills—only the experts—are encouraged to participate. Thus, the conceptualization of the state arena as a sports arena encourages us to redefine the relationship between citizen and political leader as a relationship between spectator and expert participant. If sports is the relevant model, then the mass of the population stands in the same relationship to the state elite as the passive spectators to the football team and its expert quarterback or coach: Politics becomes a spectacle to which the masses passively react, which they may second-guess ("Monday morning quarterbacking"), but in which they can never participate actively. In short, through the application of the sports metaphor politics becomes the preserve of the expert, and citizenship is transformed into acclamation.

Finally, the characterization of political leaders as following "plays" that are set forth in a "playbook" and whose interrelationship is established by means of a "game plan" carries with it the unmistakable implication that political decision making is increasingly a *planned* activity. It leads us to conclude, in other words, that the president as expert quarterback or coach has succeeded in establishing a rational coordination among his subordinates and their activities by means of a centrally established and thoroughly tested plan that militates against "spontaneous" deviations from the most efficient possible pursuit of the unquestioned goal of "winning." If one "play" does not work, moreover, we need not fear, since we can be confident that the President and his team, like any other, have an arsenal of plays at their disposal that can be used to adapt to any possible contingency. Thus, the sports metaphor is capable of contributing to the internalization of the third and final component of the technocratic ideology—namely that state decisions are increasingly planned and coordinated— and thereby of helping to mask the continued dominance of the specifically capitalist imperatives to which this "planning" is in actuality largely nothing more than a response.

Conclusion

If the political effectiveness of the sports metaphor rests on the technical form and meaning of organized sports, then any challenge to this form and meaning will necessarily threaten to undermine the legitimating power of the sports metaphor. There are signs, moreover, that such a challenge is in progress.

The past few years have been marked by a growing resistance to the commercial-
ization and instrumentalization of athletic activity. The so-called "jock liberation movement"—the highly publicized refusal of professional and "amateur"
athletes to consent to their continued brutalization and exploitation—is but the
tip of an iceberg whose base includes the efforts of growing numbers of young
people to redefine the form and meaning of sports:

> If we look around us, we will see that there are new patterns of athletic
> participation and physical exercise *already emerging* that are radically
> antagonistic to the commercial sports scene in America. Men and
> women playing soccer, volleyball, basketball and touch football in
> newly non-competitive ways; women taking a growing interest in phy-
> sical conditioning and the martial arts (karate, judo, etc.); parents
> bringing up male and female children with the same orientation toward
> exercise, sports and physical fitness . . . these are the germs of a wholly
> new approach to sports which emphasizes collective physical health, a
> cooperative ethic, [and] the aesthetic dimensions of athletics.[27]

Thus, a curious dialectic is at work that threatens to rupture the one-
dimensional equation of politics and technique fostered by the political ascendency of the sports metaphor. Advanced American capitalism is generating
struggles that aim at a deinstrumentalization of sports—that seek to restore the
spontaneous, egalitarian character of playful activity—precisely at that point
in time when the legitimacy of state authority and thus of the capitalist order
as a whole is being buttressed by the instrumentalizing functions of the sports
metaphor. Thus, these struggles entail potentially explosive possibilities.
Successful deinstrumentalization of the form and meaning of sports, coupled
with the continued application of the language of sports to the realm of politics,
might well lead to a radical reversal in the political function of the sports metaphor: Imbued with a new meaning, the sports metaphor would be transformed
from a mechanism fostering the internalization of a technocratic legitimating
ideology into a subversive, critical standard by means of which the existing
technocratic state structure would be evaluated and condemned.

Notes

1. *New York Times*, December 13, 1972. ©1972 by the New York Times
   Company. Reprinted by permission.
2. James O'Connor, *The Fiscal Crisis of the State* (New York: St. Martin's
   Press, 1973), p. 8.
3. Jürgen Habermas, *Toward a Rational Society* (Boston: Beacon Press, 1971),
   p. 100.

4. Martin Sklar, "On the Proletarian Revolution and the End of Political-Economic Society," *Radical America*, vol. 3 (May–June 1969), quoted in Karl Klare and Dick Howard, *The Unknown Dimension: European Marxism Since Lenin* (New York: Basic Books, 1972), p. 24.

5. O'Connor, *The Fiscal Crisis of the State*, ch. 6.

6. Claus Offe, "Political Authority and Class Structures—An Analysis of Late Capitalist Societies," *International Journal of Sociology*, vol. 2, no. 1 (Spring 1972), p. 81.

7. Ibid., pp. 80, 98.

8. "An Introduction to Working Papers on the Kapitalistate," *Kapitalistate*, vol. 1 (1973), p. 4.

9. On the relationship between Liberal Democratic structures and the economic requirements of both competitive and monopoly capitalism, see Franz Neumann, "The Changing Functions of Law in Modern Society," in Franz Neumann, *The Democratic and the Authoritarian State*, ed., (New York: Free Press 1964). For an analysis of the incompatibility of pluralist structures with state planning see Theodore Lowi, *The End of Liberalism* (New York: W.W. Norton & Co., 1969), esp. ch. 5. The best analysis of the impact of Federalism and decentralization on policy making in the United States is Grant McConnel's *Private Power and American Democracy* (New York: Alfred A. Knopf, 1966).

10. Offe, "Political Authority and Class Structures."

11. Habermas, *Toward a Rational Society*, pp. 103-4.

12. O'Connor, *The Fiscal Crisis of the State*, pp. 80, 75.

13. Ibid., p. 81 and p. 38, p. 94.

14. Stephan Leibfried, "US Central Government Reform of the Administrative Structure During the Ash Period (1968-1971), *Kapitalistate*, vol. 2 (1973), pp. 17-29.

15. Karl Marx, "The German Ideology," in Robert C. Tucker, ed. *The Marx-Engels Reader*, (New York: W.W. Norton & Co., 1972), p. 125.

16. See for example Jacques Ellul, *The Technological Society* (London: Jonathan Cape, 1964) and John Kenneth Galbraith, *The New Industrial State* (Boston: Houghton Mifflin, 1967).

17. Helmut Schelsky, *Der Mensch in der Wissenschaftlichen Zivilisation* (Opladen: Westdeutscher Verlag, 1961), quoted in Habermas, *Toward a Rational Society*, p. 59.

18. Habermas, *Toward a Rational Society*, p. 112.

19. For a review of this literature and a qualified defense of its thesis, see Daniel Bell, *The Coming of Post-Industrial Society: A Venture in Social Forecasting* (New York: Basic Books, 1973).

20. On the distinction between purposive-rational action guided by a cognitive interest in technical control and symbolic interaction guided by an interest in understanding, see Jürgen Habermas, *Knowledge and Human Interest* (Boston: Beacon Press, 1971), passim.

21. Pierre Laguillaumie, "Eléments pour une Critique Fondamentale du Sport,"
    Partisans, no. 43 (July–September 1968), p. 32 (my translation).
22. Ibid., p. 33. (my translation).
23. Ginette Bertrand, "Education Sportive et Sport Educatif," *Partisans*, no. 43
    (July–September 1968), p. 79 (my translation).
24. Marc Naison, "Sports and the American Empire," *Radical America*, vol. 6,
    no. 4 (July–August 1972), p. 110.
25. J.P. Robinson, "Time Expenditures on Sports Across Ten Countries,"
    International Review of Sport Sociology, no. 2, 1967, quoted in an unpub-
    lished paper by Simon Rosenblum, "Sport: More than a Spectacle." I am
    also indebted to Mr. Rosenblum for the estimates of sports exposure on
    television and in the newspapers.
26. *New York Times,* February 15, 1974.
27. Marc Naison, "No Joy in Mudville," *Liberation* (June 1973), pp. 38–41.

Part IV

Dominance Versus Vulnerability

Introduction to Part IV
Leon N. Lindberg

So far in this book we have focused on internal stresses and contradictions in advanced industrial or capitalist societies, and upon their domestic political and policy consequences. We have largely refrained from direct analysis of the international dimensions of these societies. We have not asked how contemporary political and economic characteristics of societies and future development options are directly or indirectly influenced or determined by changes in the international environment and by dynamic interaction patterns between national and international processes and structures. We have, therefore, as the late Stephen Hymer observed at the Monterosso Conference,

> been conducting a "rear view mirror" analysis, because we ignore the "invisible environment" within which these societies are "advancing" ... the "world implosion," "the tightening web of interdependence" or the "world market crisis," as McLuhan, modern social science, and Marx respectively described it.

The chapters in this section turn explicitly to this wider framework and to the ways in which shifting the level of analysis adds to or modifies our view of the strains and contradictions of modern capitalism.

Internationalization

It has become almost commonplace to record that we live in an increasingly internationalized and interdependent world society and political economy. There is an ever-accelerating interrelatedness among countries, made up of military vulnerability, environmental and ecological factors, economic integration, psychic and cultural interpenetration and diffusion, ideological contagion and emulation. Marxists and non-Marxists alike recognize that this internationalized and interdependent system was brought into being chiefly as a consequence of the political hegemony of the United States and the economic hegemony of free-market capitalism in the post-World War II period.[1] Research has tended to focus on the processes involved—the evolution of postwar American international economic policy, the rise of multilateral organizations like the OEEC, the movement toward economic and political integration in Western Europe, the growth of overseas investment and the multinational corporation, the rise of the Eurodollar market and capital mobility generally, or on the consequences of these phenomena either for developing countries—the literature on dependencia and uneven development—or for the international economic order itself. In this latter context concern has been expressed for such topics as the international transmission of economic disturbances; the organization of world monetary, investment, and trade systems; the relationships among trade and investment, income distribution, and economic policy; trends and policies in commodity supply; international aspects of environmental problems.[2]

More recently it has been observed that economic integration seems to have outrun political integration. Or rather, that the political integration provided by United States military, political, and economic hegemony has been eroded, and that no other leadership or political ordering process or mechanism seems to have emerged to take its place. A fundamental restructuring of the international political economy is in train. A new system seems to be emerging out of the complex interactions of internationalizing forces, national responses thereto, the collapse of American hegemony/leadership, the lag of political integration behind economic integration, supply scarcities, etc. From the perspective of elites or nations that were the beneficiaries of the previous "order" or equilibrium, these changes will be viewed as short-run instability and the goal of policy will be to restore the system to equilibrium. But from the point of view of those with lower comparative advantage in the previous "order," the incentives will be to take advantage of disturbances, to resist restabilization, to embrace change even if the direction and ultimate objectives of policy are themselves inchoate or obscured. None can tell what the outcome of this restructuring will be, nor how successful will be the various competitive efforts to guide it. And scholars rightfully ask whether the interdependent world economy can survive in the changing political environment of the 1970s and 1980s.[3] Research has therefore been directed primarily toward the substantive issues that arise in this interdependent world political economy and the institutional arrangements and policy planning that can contribute to their resolution.[4]

But much less attention has been bestowed on the problems that most concern us here, namely, how do internationalizing forces, structural features of the international system, and potential transformations of that system, affect the internal political development of capitalism as a system and of advanced capitalist states themselves? It will be helpful in addressing this problem, and in integrating the concerns of the chapters that follow, to propose a simple conceptual scheme for specifying the ways in which changes in the external environment of a political system can impinge on its domestic development and stability. From the perspective of a simple cybernetic model, these effects can be conceptualized either as changes in the decision or demand load upon the state, or as changes in the response capabilities of the state.[5] Severe problems of political allocation, a system crisis, or dissynchronization can follow from a substantial change in the rate, composition, intensity of demands, magnitude and distribution of political resources available to contending elites, or from a loss of capabilities on the part of incumbent or dominant coalitions to produce appropriate allocations, or from a dialectical process of increased demands—to less effective allocations—to further loss of capabilities and more insistent demands for action—to public anxiety, disaffection, alienation, and increases in the resources of contending elites. Resources will include votes in electoral and other arenas as well as the ability to mobilize individuals or command large organizations, but also elite cohesiveness and self-confidence, legitimizing ideologies, efficacy of standard instruments of public policy or of policy paradigms, and societal consensus on criteria for the evaluation of policy.

The chapters in this section call our attention to three aspects of internationalization and interdependence that can produce the kinds of load and capability consequences suggested above.

1. *Within the nation*, internationalization and interdependence not only create new problems of public policy, but also induce policy error and allocation failures by rendering many preferred policy instruments less efficacious. They have also served to reshape the political goals and strategies of groups and organizations, and to intensify already chronic legitimacy strains or crises.

2. At the level of *relations among capitalist nations, and between them and developing countries and Communist countries*, internationalization has produced a complex pattern of interstate and intersocietal linkages that similarly have consequences for domestic politics and for the coherence of state and society as mediated by penetration, intersocietal sensitivity, contagion and emulation.

3. Enormous uncertainties about future economic development options, as about patterns of military security, or of monetary and trading systems, flow from the ongoing restructuring of the international political economy. Prospective and long-term changes in loads and capabilities must then also be sought at the *level of the global system itself.*

All of these point to a more problematic, volatile, intrusive, and potentially destabilizing international environment for advanced capitalist nations. This implies, on the one hand, increased levels and shifting parameters of interstate rivalry and conflict, and on the other hand, a heightened need for international cooperation, for the development of regimes or quasi-regimes for the management of interdependence, for guaranteed access to scarce resources, and for the orderly exploitation of international "commons." Both will markedly increase the foreign policy decision load of national decision makers, and it is not at all obvious how or if they will be able to manage the transition to a new set of international relationships and institutions without severe crises. The same international developments also seem likely to add to or intensify the internal strains or contradictions in the political systems of capitalist states that have been identified in the first three parts of this book.

Economic Internationalization

Most of the chapters that follow are concerned chiefly with economic inter-nationalization and its relation to the dynamics of modern capitalism.[a] It is thus useful to offer a brief introduction to that concept and its several dimensions.

James Kurth suggests in chapter 15 that the claims of theorists of "trans-national society" and of "internationalization" to be describing new and unique characteristics of the contemporary international system should be treated with a certain skepticism. He points out that transnational organizations and internation-alization "have existed in virtually every era." On the other hand, he goes on to argue that multinational corporations, if not without historical precedent, have in-creased markedly in scale and scope so as to constitute a "new system." If not qualitative change, then quantitative change. And we may be justified in asking at what point "quantity" turns to "quality."

The multinational corporations (MNC) may be the most widely proclaimed— or bemoaned—facet of the new international environment. Three of the chapters that follow (14, 15, and 17) are chiefly preoccupied with their nature, causes, and consequences. But the "new system of MNCs" is itself just one aspect of a larger process of economic internationalization that has reached qualitatively distinctive proportions in the 1970s. We can identify five aspects of economic internationalization.[6]

1. *Larger flows* (movements) between countries—flows of commodities and services, credit and capital, technology and entrepreneurship, and labor
2. *Higher sensitivity* (mobility) of flows between countries
3. *Larger stocks of factors of production* of foreign origin—labor, financial capital, real capital
4. *Internationalization of institutions: political* intergovernmental institutions like the GATT, IMF, EEC, EFTA, LAFTA, OPEC, EACM; *interest group institutions* of firms, employees, trade unions; *market oriented institutions*— multinational corporations, foreign subsidiaries of firms
5. *Internationalization of externalities* of systems of production—waste disposal in air and sea, disturbances of the worldwide ecological system, exploitation of "international commons," such as the oceans and the sea bed

This economic internationalization process reflects a number of underlying factors or causes: technological development biased in favor of communication and transport, increased role of technology as a factor of production, increased skewness in the consumption and production of raw materials, and high income elasticity for differentiated products, the falling costs of directing huge

---

[a]Pierre Hassner's chapter 16 reminds us that the processes of internationalization are broader and more pervasive, extending to social and cultural systems as well.

organizations over large distances, complementarities between managerial skill
and technological inputs, a speedier product cycle, and the rise of regional
trading blocks.[7] Among our authors, Stephen Hymer emphasizes the internal
dynamics of monopoly capitalism and American "imperialism," whereas James
R. Kurth prefers the concept of "hegemony," which he combines with a product cycle and technological change explanation.

Most theorists would probably agree, however, that this postwar internationalization came about largely because of the deliberate policies followed
by governments.[8] American policy makers in particular saw the causes of
World War II as basically economic—the failure to revive the international
economy after World War I and the rise of competitive trading blocks and "beg-
gar your neighbor" protectionist policies. The key to postwar reconstruction
(and to the pursuit of American self-interest) lay in doing away with nationalistic and discriminatory measures such as trade preferences, exchange controls,
quantitative restrictions, competitive currency depreciations, so as to maximize
the growth in the volume of international trade and in the rhythm of domestic
economic growth. American policy in the 1940s and 1950s was then directed
toward building an open system of multilateral trade relations: viz. the patterning of Marshall Plan aid, United States pressure to create the OEEC and support
for the ECSC and EEC—all linked to NATO and the Cold War goal of bloc
security and prosperity.

Consequences of Internationalization at the Level of the Nation-State

If economic internationalization processes have flowed from deliberate
policy choice, how and why have they become problematic? Many explanations
and interpretations are possible and several are discussed in the Chapters that
follow. Perhaps the most common argument is that of the Wizard's Apprentice,
namely that nation-states have unwittingly released forces beyond their power
to control—MNCs, Eurodollars, etc. This can take several forms. Marxists like
Hymer and Alberto Martinelli stress the contradiction between the *internationalization of capital*, which breaks or weakens the ties of the oligopoly capital
sector to any particular state, and the efforts of labor, petty bourgeois, and
sectors of small capital to use the nation-state to defend themselves against
large capital and against the effects of internationalization. The dominant elite
is thus fragmented, and demands for a nationalist or neomercantilist policy may
emerge that can be threatening to the interests of internationalized capital.
Liberal economists express a similar point in terms of a *strain* between the consequences of internationalization and "ambitious" domestic policy goals of
national decision makers.[9] Economic internationalization seems to produce
stiffer competition and a fall in product margins, rapid changes in comparative

advantages, accelerated rates of structural change in domestic economies, an increase in frictional and structural unemployment, more uneven distribution of unemployment within regions, an increase in mergers and in the extent of industrial concentration, a drop in private investment, more and more rapid transmission from one country to another of inflationary pressures. Multinational firms as economic and political "actors" confront all but the most powerful governments with a host of problems that although long familiar to weaker, more dependent or vulnerable developing countries, are now also making themselves felt in advanced industrial countries as well. The catalog is familiar: the economic impact of decisions taken by a firm whose central office is outside the country, direct intervention in policy formation, use of MNCs by home country to exert pressure on host counties, ability of MNCs to avoid monetary and fiscal policies in both home and host countries through bookkeeping manipulations and transfers of funds, impact of currency speculation on short-term instability in balance of payments, repatriation of "value-added" to other countries than host, implications of "inappropriate" patterns of technology transfer (serves needs of MNC rather than host country) and of foreign ownership of natural resources and economic infrastructure.

In these and other ways economic internationalization imposes new problems or demands on the national decision maker. But the impact is deeper yet, for as has become increasingly clear in the international "slumpflation" of 1973–75, governments are not only more vulnerable to inflationary and recessionary impulses originating outside the country, but many of their preferred policy instruments for dealing with such instabilities have been rendered less and less efficacious. Economic internationalization diminishes the usefulness of interest rate and other monetary policies, as of governmental fiscal policies. The impact upon stabilization policies was already evident in the 1960s; for example, the United States tried to fight unemployment in the early 1960s by lowering interest rates, but found that this led to an outflow of capital, and a deterioration of the balance of payments, West Germany tried high interest rates to fight inflation but this drew in financial capital and a set of restrictive monetary policies. As long as the disequilibria that resulted was financed chiefly by a United States deficit, and as long as other countries were prepared to hold growing reserves of dollar assets and to acquiesce in American economic and military policies, the situation was generally acceptable. But by the late 1960s the political situation had changed and the degree of political integration provided by American hegemony was attenuated. This, plus the growing impact of economic integration, made it more and more evident that it was becoming increasingly difficult to manage national economies. Some, like Charles Levinson,[10] argue that the nature of the multinational corporate system has completely transformed the problem of economic management. The giant industrial firm, he argues, is driven by technology and global competition for which it demands ever greater "capital fixes." Such firms must rely on self-financing and hence must raise prices and/or reduce their wage bill in order to assure a flow of capital. They have an investment cycle substantially longer than any national public policy, are international in their operations and can shift funds around to avoid taxation or other legislation, and are simply not responsive to instruments of budgetary control or interest rates or controls on the money supply. The matter is in considerable doubt, as the recent flurry of conferences on world inflation would seem to imply. At the very least it would seem irrefutable that internationalization makes very high demands on the economic adjustment processes of any country. Small, highly centralized and generally consensual societies like Sweden, with a long history of refined and innovative Keynesian demand management, can be expected to fare much better under these circumstances than the United States, in which stabilization policies are much more narrowly conceived and imperfectly executed. Indeed, the United States and worldwide recession of 1974-75 has been attributed by many to American economic mismanagement, and fears are growing in some quarters that the United States may be becoming a danger to itself and to the rest of the world.[11]

Much the same seems to be true of national allocation and distribution policy objectives. Assar Lindbeck has surveyed governmental goals and instruments in these areas and concludes that "the nation state tends to become a less and less efficient unit for decision making, at the same time as they adopt more and more ambitious policy goals."[12]

Of course, economic internationalization also carries many advantages and benefits for nation-states, although these may be unequally distributed between different states and among groups and classes within any one (as between capital and labor, center and periphery, etc.). And it is not clear that the balance of advantages to disadvantages has shifted all that decisively since the late 1960s. Another way of analyzing the increasingly problematic perception of internationalization would stress the dissynchronization between processes of international economic integration and international political integration. As we have seen, the consequences of economic integration of the 1950s and 1960s were in balance acceptable because American hegemony—some would say leadership, others imperialism or exploitation—was generally accepted as, if not legitimate, unavoidable and perhaps even useful. For a variety of reasons this is no longer the case in the 1970s. With the waning of American leadership/hegemony/exploitation (and all three concepts are appropriate depending upon the questions asked), the economic and political instruments and decision rules and structures that governed the system and provided a minimum of coordination and agreed goals began to weaken or collapse. We are thus left with a multifold process of international economic integration combined with a disintegration of political arrangements, which has extended to established regional organizations such as the European Community, as well as to broader relations among the advanced capitalist nations. (We return to this issue below.)

What are the domestic political consequences of these increasingly problematic internationalization phenomena? There is one interesting point of convergence among Marxist and non-Marxist writers. Hymer and Lindbeck, for example, both see a resurgence of the political over the economic and of the national over the international. Lindbeck and many other economists fear a "neomercantilism" that will distort the price mechanism, diminish economic efficiency, distort trade, lead to unwise subsidies of weak firms, concentrate power in bureaucrats and the heads of large firms, and increase international conflict. Hymer looks forward to a return to a "national self-sufficiency" that would break the power of international market capitalism. Hymer and Martinelli both speculate that this might come in the form of an increasingly nationalistic labor movement. "In the new world economy, the state may finally become the instrument of labor rather than capital, i.e., of socialism rather than capitalism, but only if it acts to destroy the world market" (Hymer at Monterosso).

Others, both Marxists and non-Marxists, emphasize the contradictory process whereby internationalization produces a demand for far more coherent national planning, while at the same time diminishing the capabilities of the state to plan. The state then becomes less effective as a guarantor of capital accumulation and of social stability and political legitimacy. Still others point to the possibility of drastic policy errors as economic theories and policy paradigms are rendered lame by the emergence of a truly integrated world economy. The Mundell-Laffer hypothesis[13], for example, argues that the double-digit inflation and subsequent recession were both to a large degree a direct consequence of faulty economic policy that did not adequately take into account the extent to which there is a closed world economy.

> Much of the world inflation has resulted from the breakdown of Bretton Woods, bringing in its train the crisis in confidence in Western institutions and doubts about the appropriateness of free economies in the modern environment. In return for this mess, the U.S. now has an independent monetary policy, which amounts to a "right" to have more unemployment when policy errs on the side of tightness and the "right" to have more inflation when policy errs on the side of looseness.[14]

The solution according to Mundell-Laffer is to go back to a world currency based upon fixed exchange rates, but this would seem to bring us back to the earlier dilemma of the lag of political integration behind economic integration.[15]

Linkages and Interdependencies Among States

In addition to directly altering the internal load/capability ratios of modern states, economic integration is one among a variety of forces that have fundamentally altered the texture of interstate relations. Linkages among states—as among societies and economies—are characterized by more diverse and diffuse interdeterminancies that seem likely to have important consequences for domestic political and economic development, and a rich conceptual vocabulary has been developed to describe them. For a time, the study of interstate, intereconomy, intersociety linkages was dominated by preoccupations with policy experiments in regional integration—first in Europe and then in Latin America, Africa and elsewhere. Concepts of political community formation and political integration proliferated.[16] In the sixties and early seventies, the concern for other patterned aspects of interstate relations has displaced that earlier literature. Pierre Hassner's chapter 16 provides a valuable survey of such concepts: of interdependence, dependencia, penetration, contagion, indirect influence, exploitation, comparative vulnerability, unequal exchange, center-periphery relations, imperialism, asymmetrical vulnerability, etc. He then uses them to explore how military security, political, economic, cultural, and ideological relations among states are being transformed. Hassner points out how much of this literature had made simplistic assumptions about the direction of dependency and vulnerability relationships.

> It is now plain for everyone that the periphery may sometimes
> unite and the centre become divided, that what is center to some
> may be periphery to others, that the dependence of industrial countries on primary products producers may be more stringent than the
> converse.
>   The irony of interdependence is that it has a taste for replacing
> the links we construct by others we do not expect.
>   It is an illusion to believe that the process increases the ability
> of states to manage the evolution of societies, whether their own,
> those of adversaries, or those of allies.

He develops his argument with special reference to relations between Eastern and Western Europe. There Hassner finds a complex picture of "asymmetrical interdependence" involving "incomplete domination" and "imperfect reciprocity" as issue areas become separated from each other (economic from security, trade from cultural-ideological influence, etc.), and as the "universal contradiction" between state and society is intensified (states become more dominant and societies more penetrated). He raises a host of questions for investigation, the importance of which extends well beyond intra-European relations. To what extent can the tensions of societies be held in check by the barriers of the interstate system and of national institutions; to what extent will they succeed in eroding these barriers or in bursting them wide open? What are the relationships between social interpenetration and political domination? Does

"what is lost" go to the domination of an external power or to the reciprocal
interpenetration and integration of comparable units, leading to the creation of
a new unit or a functional network? What is the influence of the military balance
upon the evolution of societies? In a system where the direct use of force seems
excluded, to what extent do its indirect projections along with economic interdependence and sociocultural influence enter the complex equation of dominance
and vulnerability, between and within states, alliances, and organizations? What
are the consequences of detente and cold war, or interpenetration and self-
closure, for the respective legitimacy crises? How should one weigh the erosion
of defense budgets in the West versus the erosion of ideological fervor in the
East? Another set of stress inducing factors flows directly or indirectly from the
interaction of supply scarcities, national allocational decisions, and emerging
patterns of dependence and asymmetrical vulnerability. How will different
national policymakers' efforts to cope with problems arising from critical questions of a scarcity of resources, and to maintain domestic support and stability,
affect the claims they make upon other countries? How will regulatory decisions
that allocate resources domestically then produce further claims from other
nations that further expand the national distributional dilemma? Who will bear
the burden of a rise in costs generated outside the country and how will this be
justified and legitimated? On what grounds can one compare national and international claims to equity? Under what circumstances will supply scarcities and/
or price increases be perceived as unjustified and hence blamed on another
nation?

A New International Political Economy

Pierre Hassner writes that we are

> on the verge of a political economy of international relations which . . .
> must start from the rediscovery of power at the heart of exchange and
> exchange at the heart of power and lead to the unveiling and the study
> of the relations between different forms of dependence and different
> forms of power which are at the heart of international life. Whether
> one starts from economics or from politics, a consensus seems to
> emerge for defining it more and more as the management and manipu-
> lation of interdependence.

What Hassner is calling for is a shift from how internationalization processes affect
politics and policy making in individual countries and the pattern of their relationships with other countries to a concern for their impact upon the world system
itself.

Implied here is the position that important influences upon the pattern of national development, and upon policy options and choices, may originate in features of a world system that cannot be understood simply as an aggregate of nations or a complex of discrete linkages between nations. Walter Salant[17] has made this point with reference to the analysis of contemporary inflation. He argues that an aggregative approach to inflation is likely to understate or neglect the importance of supranational factors such as the role of levels and changes in world monetary reserves or the development of the Euro-currency market and that it may misjudge the origins of inflationary impulses (treating them as autonomous rather than induced). But he also points out that a "supranational" or global approach involves "wrenching outselves out of deeply ingrained habits of thought" and assumes an ability to develop appropriate concepts and analytical tools at this macroglobal level. Such conceptual and methodological advance should be high on our list of priorities for contemporary social science research, for we will not be able to understand the dynamic properties of our internationalized and interdependent global system without them. Nor will be able to manage the crises and conflicts that contemporary developments in the global system seem to portend.

One of the principle conclusions that seems to emerge from the articles in part IV and one that is also reflected in other literature cited, is that we are heading towards an increasingly mercantilist international political economy. By mercantilist is meant

> the priority of national economic and political objectives over considerations of *global* economic efficiency. The mercantilist impulse can take many forms in the contemporary world: the desire for a balance-of-payments surplus; the export of unemployment, inflation, or both; the imposition of import and/or export controls; the expansion of world market shares; and the stimulation of advanced technology.[18]

Advanced capitalist societies are experiencing powerful parochializing trends simultaneously with strong internationalizing forces. When combined with the tendencies identified in the first three parts of this book, these seem likely to lead to a more and more inward-looking or endogenously determined process of policy determination at the national level. This can be symbolized by the massive growth of the positive state, by the extension of planning, and the displacement of the market as an allocative mechanism. This process is further intensified by the pressures that lead governments to resort to incomes policies, and that make inequality and the share of wages in national income once more into an explicit and direct political issue. The result is that the nation-state is expected—by capital, by labor, and by other groups or interests within the polity—to perform more and more functions. The legitimacy crises that flow from this increase in state activity, and in particular from any obvious biasing of that intervention to suit the accumulation and reproduction needs of capital, rather than the needs of other groups or of society as a whole, seems likely to further intensify this preoccupation with the national arena. Growing awareness of the declining capabilities of the state for attaining national stabilization, allocation, and distribution goals may, paradoxically, have the same effect.

It is difficult to find reason for complacency, either in the chapters that follow, or in those that preceded either insofar as concerns the political stability and cohesiveness of an increasingly taxed nation-state, or the quality of inter-state relations, and this does not portend well for a world in which powerful internationalizing and parochializing forces seem to interact in a dialectical and contradictory pattern, in which increasingly complex linkages between states seem to act as a solvent both of established ways of thinking about the inter-relations among policy sectors, and of the ties among state, society, and culture, and in which conflicts of interests rooted in basic shifts in power, resources, and dependency relationships are on the rise. We can imagine a number of possible futures for such a neomercantilist world.

1. *Reversed dependencia* in which raw materials and extractive industry ex-porters manage to force a major redistribution of income and wealth at the expense of the developed, industrial nations
2. *Dominance by international monopoly capital* perhaps in tacit alliance with the dominant home states
3. *Development of international rules, regimes, and institutions* to manage interdependence on the basis of cooperation and a "free partnership by the world's diverse regional communities"[19]
4. *Anarchical conflict, disruption of trading and finance, and a general world economic crisis*

Each of these broad outcomes can be "logically" derived from the present situation, depending upon the assumptions one makes about the nature of capitalism, about the relations between economic intergration and political integration, about the balance of parochializing to internationalizing forces, about supply and resource constraints, about the mechanisms of the inter-national transmission of economic disturbances, about the adaptability of capitalist economies (e.g., to lower rates of growth), about the internal stability and external vulnerability of societies, about the relative balance between what Robert Gilpin calls "malevolent" and "benign" mercantilism, about the avail-ability of international "leadership," and so forth. As it stands we lack the concepts and methods, as well as the empirical findings and theoretical development to do more than speculate.

Among the many foci for research which might be mentioned, the follow-ing seem especially pressing. Can we develop more adequate analytical tools for analyzing the global political economy as an interrelated system? How adequate are existing models such as the economists' LINK model or the multi-level world system model developed by Mihajlo Mesarovic and Eduard Pestel[20], as nonaggregated representations of this system? Are they or can they be made useful for the analysis of the consequences of a pattern of mercantilist policies on that system and the feedback from those effects upon the coherence and stability of those same nation states? Is Hymer's (and Keynes') vision of "national self-sufficiency" viable, and under what conditions and at what costs? What changes in growth and development styles and strategies will be imposed upon advanced capitalist states by supply scarcities and by reversed patterns of dependency, and what will be the domestic political consequences? What will be the consequences of neomercantilist policies for established regional group-ings such as the European Community? What will be the reciprocal interactions among forces inducing economic integration, economic "disintegration," politi-cal integration, political disintegration? Will we see a sequence of economic integration—to a corresponding need for political integration—to mercantilist policies—to economic disintegration—to renewed demand for political integra-tion because the costs are too high?[b] Can an international political economy, which seems to be developing dangerous destablizing dynamics, be stabilized without leadership? How will such leadership be provided if, as Charles Kindleberger argues, the world requires such leadership but suffers from an "underproduction of the public good of stability" because of the "free rider" problem?[21] How can one distinguish between leadership and exploitation? What are the domestic political and economic consequences of an effort to assert leadership at a regional or national level? What are the domestic con-sequences of possible resort to military intervention as a substitute for "leader-ship"? Questions of this order can be fruitfully investigated by careful study of such international issue areas as food, energy, and particularly, inflation. The national politics of inflation control—of economic management more generally, are becoming increasingly conflictual and problematic. Struggles over shares of national income are becoming more overt.[22] Internationalization has at the same time made economies more sensitive to each other, thus heightening policy and automatic transmission effects. Governments have launched a search for new policy instruments to get greater leverage over this conjunction of increased instability, more strident and "objectified" demands, and declining efficacy of established policy. Indexation, including indexation of export prices, floating exchange rates, periodic currency reevaluation or appreciation so as to avoid importing inflation,[c] renewed efforts to gain control over the domestic economy

---

[b]Research done on the history of economic and political integration in the context of the European Community might well be mined for suggestive hypotheses about this and other possible sequences.

[c]Such is the conclusion drawn by Scandinavian economists relative to small, open econ-omies. It is a strategy that has also been successfully followed by West Germany in the 1970s.

through planning and intervention in processes of capital formation and investment decision, etc. The effects of such policies on the functioning of the global
system are unknown, but this will be a prime front upon which to analyze the
interaction among economic and political integration (recall Robert Mundell's
conclusions),[23] competitive efforts to provide the "public good" of leadership,
and the generality of the "free rider problem."

Notes

1. See chapter 14 in this book, and also Robert Gilpin, "The Politics of Transnational Economic Relations," *International Organization* 25 (Summer
   1971).
2. C. Fred Bergsten, *The Future of the International Economic Order: An
   Agenda for Research*, (Lexington, Mass.: D.C. Heath and Company,
   Lexington Books, 1973).
3. Robert Gilpin, "Three Models of the Future," *International Organization*
   29, no. 1 (Winter 1975), p. 38.
4. See for example the winter 1975 special issue of *International Organization*
   on "World Politics and International Economics," edited by C. Fred Bergsten
   and Laurence B. Krause.
5. For a full development of this approach see my "Strategies and Priorities for
   Comparative Research" in Leon Lindberg, ed., *Politics and the Future of
   Industrial Society* (New York: McKay, 1975).
6. Assar Lindbeck, "The National State in an Internationalized World Economy,"
   Institute for International Economic Studies, University of Stockholm, 1973.
7. Ibid.
8. Gilpin, "Politics."
9. Cf. Lindbeck, "National State," passim.
10. Charles Levinson, *Capital, Inflation and the Multinationals* (London: George
    Allen and Unwin, Ltd., 1971).
11. See for example the statement by Leonard Woodcock and Wassily Leontieff,
    "For a National Economic Planning System," *Challenge*, March-April 1975,
    pp. 51-53.
12. Ibid.
13. Jude Wanniski, "The Mundell-Laffer Hypothesis and A New View of the
    World Economy," *The Public Interest*, no. 39 (Spring 1975), pp. 31-52.
14. Ibid., p. 48.
15. On the relationship between economy and political integration and the prob-
    lem of a common currency see the work of Hans O. Schmitt, especially
    "Markets and the Unification of Europe," *World Politics* 20, no. 2 (January
    1968), pp. 228-44; "Integration and Conflict in the World Economy,"
    Journal of Common Market Studies 8, no. 1 (September 1969), pp. 1-18;

and "The National Boundary in Politics and Economics," in Richard L. Merritt, ed., *Communication in International Politics* (Urbana: University of Illinois Press, 1972).

16. For a review of that literature see the various essays in Leon N. Lindberg and Stuart A. Scheingold, eds., *Regional Integration: Theory and Research* (Cambridge, Mass.: Harvard University Press, 1971).

17. Walter S. Salant, "A Supranational Approach to the Analysis of World Inflation," paper prepared for Conference on Global Inflation sponsored by The Brookings Institution, Washington, D.C., November 21-23, 1974.

18. Gilpin, "Three Models of the Future," p. 47.

19. See Mihajlo Mesarovic and Eduard Pestel, *Mankind at the Turning Point* (New York: E.P. Dutton & Co., Inc./ Readers Digest Press, 1974), p. 157.

20. See Mesarovic and Pestel, *Mankind*, and the technical reports therein cited.

21. Charles Kindleberger, "Power in the International Economy: Exploitation, Public Goods, or Free Rides," paper presented at the Conference on 20th Century Capitalism sponsored by the Council for European Studies, Cambridge, Mass., 1974.

22. Charles Maier, "Political Contexts of Inflation," paper originally given at the Council for European Studies Conference on 20th Century Capitalism.

23. See note 13.

14

International Politics and International Economics: A Radical Approach

Stephen Hymer

To be radical, or to be a scientist, is the same thing; it is a question of trying to go to the root of the matter. For Marx, this meant trying to uncover the "economic laws of motion of modern society," that is, first of all, seeing society as an organism in motion constantly changing and developing as it moves from its beginning to its end, and second of all, searching in the economy, i.e., in changing conditions of production and exchange for the underlying basis of this motion.

In this essay, I wish to follow Marx's approach by viewing the present conjuncture of international politics and economics in terms of the long-term growth and spread of capitalist social relations of production to a world level. More concretely, I want to try to relate the current crises in national and international politics to the world market created during the last twenty-five years by the American Empire, firstly by examining Keynes's 1933 warnings of the difficulties and dangers for the development of modern society posed by the world market, and secondly, by using Marx's analysis of the general law of capitalist accumulation, and, in particular, his theory of the reserve army to go deeper into the roots of our present difficulties.

The basic text for this analysis is a provocative statement Marx wrote to Engels in October 1858:

> We cannot deny that bourgeois society has experienced its Sixteenth Century a second time—a Sixteenth Century which will, I hope, sound the death-knell of bourgeois society just as the first one thrust it into existence. The specific task of bourgeois society is the establishment of a world market, at least in outline, and of production based upon this world market. As the world is round, this seems to have been completed by the colonization of California and Australia and the opening

Stephen Hymer was killed in an automobile accident on February 2, 1974. This chapter is the first (and only) draft of an article he prepared in November 1973 for a conference on international politics and international economics sponsored by The Brookings Institution. The draft has been widely circulated elsewhere. This version was prepared for publication by a collective of Hymer's friends who are editing his remaining notes and papers. The collective made no changes in the phrasing or content of the draft version, but provided more complete footnotes and made minor corrections. This chapter has already appeared in Spanish translation in *Cuadernos de economia*, vol. 2, no. 4 (1974). For permission to reprint contact David Gordon or Heidi Hartmann at the New School for Social Research.

up of China and Japan. The difficult question for us is this: on the Continent the revolution is imminent and will immediately assume a socialist character. Is it not bound to be crushed in this little corner, considering that in a far greater territory the movement of bourgeois society is still in the ascendent?[1]

The Beginnings of Industrial Capitalism

Capitalism began as a world market system in the Mercantilist age of the 16th and 17th century when the discovery of America and the rounding of the Cape led to an explosion of maritime commerce and the creation of the first international economy. The epoch-making significance of this great burst of international trade, however, did not lie in the world market itself, but in the transformation of the home market that it unwittingly brought about.

It has been said of Columbus, who died thinking he had discovered a new route to India, that he was a man who, when he set out, did not know where he was going, that when he got there did not know where he was, and that when he returned did not know where he had been. The same irony characterized the Mercantilist system as a whole. The merchants, adventurers, financiers and sovereigns of this age set out on an international quest for gold, spices and new lands, but the really important discoveries were made at home. Specifically, the expansion of foreign trade and the growth of merchants and finance capital resulted, along with other factors, in the disintegration of the traditional non-market domestic economy and the setting free of labour from its pre-capitalist forms of production. This newly-created wage-labour force, when harnessed by industrial capital first into manufacturing and then into modern industry, unleashed an explosion in productivity that provided society with an entirely new material basis for its existence and ushered in the modern world.

Once the force of this great discovery of the value of labour power had been demonstrated by the English industrial revolution, other nations were compelled either to adopt this new mode of production or to be subdued by those countries which did. The mercantilist era had been characterized by active state intervention and acute national rivalry. At first, the new world economy of the nineteenth century took on an internationalistic or a nationalistic guise as it seemed that this age of industrial capital would be dominated by market principles and a government that governed best by governing least.

This was certainly the trend in Britain where the newly-triumphant capitalist class set about (1) to systematically dismantle the state apparatus used by Feudalism and Mercantilism to control production and trade, and (2) to enlarge the extent of the market internally and externally. To some extent this tendency was followed by other nations, but actually a double movement was involved. On the one hand, they too had to dismantle the system of pre-capitalist controls, but at the same time, they had to unify the nation and strengthen the state in order to industrialize.

The first focus of the new industrial state was primitive accumulation, i.e., a conscious political effort to establish the conditions of modern capitalist production by setting free a wage-labour force to work and fostering a national industrial class to organize it. Those countries which did not effect such a transformation of the domestic economy soon fell prey to one imperial power or another and became underdeveloped.

Once industrial capitalism got going, a second task emerged; namely, that of keeping it going by mediating the contradictions it inevitably produced. These contradictions stemmed from two basic interconnected conditions: (1) the anarchic relations between capitalists which produced great waste and resulted in periodic crises, (2) the concentration of people into factories and cities and their growing politicization. With the accumulation of capital, these contradictions intensified and a large and elaborate superstructure was formed to contain them.

Thus we find during the late 19th and early 20th Century that the growth and spread of industrial capitalism was accompanied by a strengthening and not a declining nation state and an intensification of national rivalry rather than its withering away. Internally, the visible hand of the state operated continuously alongside the invisible hand of the market. Internationally, one by one, countries erected national barriers against trade and in the late nineteenth century a scramble began to divide the underdeveloped countries into exclusive spheres of interest and into a new colonial system. The end result of Laissez-Faire, Pax Brittanica and Free Trade was the "welfare state," the First World War, and the complete breakdown of the international economy during the depression.

The World Market Versus National Welfare

It is at this point that our story begins. We find in 1930 a world economy in which:

1) The industrial revolution has more or less spread to Western Europe, America, Russia and Japan, but is far from complete in the sense that to varying degrees large pockets of non-industrial, non-capitalist sectors remain in each country. Although certain beginnings towards industrial capitalism have been made in isolated spots in Latin America, Asia and Africa, the vast majority of the world's population lives outside these enclaves.

2) There is a strong disenchantment with capitalism and internationalism and a belief that the nation state and not the invisible hand will play the dominant role in economic development. (Even the Fascists call themselves National Socialists.) On the other hand, thinking still remains one-dimensionally

capitalist as far as production is concerned since no alternative has emerged to the alienated work process of the capitalist factory. Marx had felt that the working class would organize itself in revolt against the dominance of capital and create a new system of production, but in the 1930's an international revolutionary working class to lead us beyond capitalism still had not emerged.

It is in this context that we turn to Keynes's analysis of the conflict between a world market and national welfare as presented in his 1933 article on "National Self-Sufficiency." In this article Keynes argues that a restoration of the world market would unnecessarily prolong capitalism with its inherent evils and interfere with our progress towards the good society.

Describing himself as a man "who in the last resort prefers anything on earth to what the financial reports are wont to call 'the best opinion of Wall street'", he argues that world peace, prosperity and freedom could best be achieved by emphasizing non-capitalist national self-sufficiency rather than international market capitalism.[2] In stronger language than almost any other economist would dare use, he came to the following conclusion:

> I sympathize, therefore, with those who would minimize, rather than with those who would maximize, economic entanglement among nations. Ideas, knowledge, science, hospitality, travel—these are the things which should of their nature be international. But let goods be homespun whenever it is reasonably and conveniently possible, and above all, let finance be primarily national.[3]

He supports his case with three basic arguments. First, he notes that contrary to the belief of the 19th century free traders, the world market created in the Golden Age of Pax Brittanica did not ensure peace but ended in war and a depression. In his words:

> To begin with the question of peace. We are pacifist today with so much strength of conviction that, if the economic internationalist could win this point, he would soon recapture our support. But it does not now seem obvious that a great concentration of national effort on the capture of foreign trade, that the penetration of a country's economic structure by the resources and the influence of foreign capitalists, and that a close dependence of our own economic life on the fluctuating economic policies of foreign countries are safeguards and assurances of international peace. It is easier, in the light of experience and foresight, to argue quite the contrary. The protection of a country's existing foreign interests, the capture of new markets, the progress of economic imperialism—these are a scarcely avoidable part of a scheme of things which aims at the maximum of international specialization and at the maximum geographical diffusion of capital wherever its seat of ownership.[4]

Second, he deals with the question of economic efficiency. He argues that the spread of modern technology makes it easier to produce locally the basic needs of a community and makes the argument for international specialization and export-oriented growth less compelling.

Third, and I think this is the most important part of his case, he argues that the free trader's economic internationalism assumes the whole world was, or would be, organized on the basis of private competitive capitalism. In contrast, Keynes felt that we had to go beyond capitalism if the fruits of the industrial revolution were to be realized in a humane and rational way. But a world market would prevent experimentation in soci-economic organization and thus inhibit the free and full development of our potential.

Expressing a view that is not very popular today except among socialists, Keynes argues:

> The decadent international but individualistic capitalism, in the hands of which we found ourselves after the war, is not a success. It is not intelligent, it is not beautiful, it is not just, it is not virtuous—and it doesn't deliver the goods. In short, we dislike it, and we are beginning to despise it. . . .
>
> We each have our own fancy. Not believing that we are saved already, we each should like to have a try at working out our own salvation. We do not wish, therefore, to be at the mercy of world forces working out, or trying to work out, some uniform equilibrium according to the ideal principles, if they can be called such, of *laissez-faire* capitalism. . . . We wish—for the time at least and so long as the present transitional, experimental phase endures—to be our own masters, and to be as free as we can make ourselves from the interferences of the outside world.[5]

The Internationalization of Capital

Keynes' view, as expressed in this article, had little effect on the policies which governed the post-Second World War reconstruction and development plans for the world economy. Instead, the best opinion of Wall Street and the City prevailed.

"Let there be no mistake about it," wrote *The Economist* in 1942 in an article on "The American Challenge," "the policy put forward by the American Administration is revolutionary. It is a genuinely new conception of world order."[6] In this way *The Economist*, reflecting the policy discussions taking place in London during the war, welcomed the plan to create a postwar world economy based on international capitalism under American hegemony.

The goal of this plan was "'a new frontier, a frontier of limitless expanse, the frontier of human welfare,'" and "'the instrument will be industrial

capitalism, operating, broadly speaking, under conditions of private enterprise'".[7] Or, as *The Economist* put it, "the idealism of an international New
Deal will have to be implemented by the unrivalled technical achievements of
American business. The New Frontier will then become a reality."[8] Or as
Fortune expressed it with regard to underdeveloped countries, "American
imperialism can afford to complete the work the British started; instead of sales-
men and planters, its representatives can be brains and bulldozers, technicians
and machine tools."[9]

As we now know, this plan was highly successful. The world experienced
a twenty-five year long secular boom in which employment, capital and technology grew rapidly and even the Socialist countries began to be drawn away from
autarky into the whirlpool of the international market.

Ironically, Keynes' theory of State policy, which he himself believed to be
a tool for bringing about the end of capitalism, was used to preserve it. In the
General Theory, Keynes argued that by restoring full employment through
government intervention, we could in a reasonable time destroy capital's
monopoly and free ourselves from its grip. He judged that "it might be comparatively easy to make capital goods so abundant that the marginal efficiency
of capital is zero," and that this peaceful evolution might "be the most sensible
way of gradually getting rid of many of the objectionable features of capitalism."[10] In his view technological change could rather quickly (one or two generations) reduce the rate of profit and thus bring about "the euthanasia of the
rentier, and, consequently, the euthanasia of the cumulative oppressive power
of the capitalists to exploit the scarcity-value of capital."[11] And at the same
time we could save money on management through "a scheme of direct taxation
which allows the intelligence and determination and executive skill of the
financier, the entrepreneur *et hoc genus omne* (who are certainly so fond of
their craft that their labour could be obtained much cheaper than at present),
to be harnessed to the service of the community on reasonable terms of
reward."[12]

Keynes was as far off the mark here as he was in his call for national self-
sufficiency. One generation has already passed. The rate of profit has not
fallen; instead, the state has been harnessed to shore it up and ensure the continued growth of private wealth nationally and internationally. Neither have
managers' salaries been reduced. Rather the techno-structure has gained in
status and income as it has become an even more crucial element in supporting
the expansion of capital and preventing its euthanasia.

Thus, contrary to Marx and Keynes, the world market and the welfare state
have not sounded the death-knell of capitalism. At least not yet. Instead capitalism revived from the interwar crisis and flourished in the quarter century
following the war.

Now, however, there are signs of strain in the system and a wave of reexamination and reconsideration of its basic framework is taking place in the

light of emerging contradictions and crises, national and international. The tightening of the web of interdependence, to use a now popular phrase, seems to be becoming increasingly uncomfortable as we progress into the 1970's. There is a certain unease in many quarters (dramatized by the oil crisis) that we may be too much at the "mercy of world forces" and too little "our own masters." And there are signs of an outbreak of the national rivalry that Keynes thought was scarcely avoidable if we placed too much emphasis on the world market.

I have argued elsewhere[13] that due to the internationalization of capital, competition between national capitalists is becoming less and less a source of rivalry between nations. Using the instrument of direct investment, large corporations are able to penetrate foreign markets and detach their interests from their home markets. At the same time, capitalists from all nations, including underdeveloped countries, are able to diversify their portfolios internationally through the international capital market. Given these tendencies, an international capitalist class is emerging whose interests lie in the world economy as a whole and a system of international private property which allows free movement of capital between countries. The process is contradictory and may break down, but for the present there is a strong tendency for the most powerful segments of the capitalist class increasingly to see their future in the further growth of the world market rather than its curtailment.

In the next section of this essay, I would like to turn to the other side of the coin and examine the interests of labor in the world market. The main theme is that labor will tend to become more nationalistic and possibly more socialistic as the continued growth of the world market undermines its traditional strategy.

Labor and the World Market Stage of Capitalism

"Accumulation of capital is, therefore, increase of the proletariat."[14] This is the key concept in Marx's analysis of the general law of motion of capitalist society. Capitalist competition leads, at one level, to the concentration and centralization of capital in large corporations tied together by a capital market and unified at the political level by the state. At another level, it draws an ever-increasing portion of the population into the wage laboring class, concentrates them into large factories and urban centers and develops in them a group cohesiveness which makes them a political force in opposition to capital. In this way, capitalism, which is based on the competitive wage labor system, creates within itself forms of social organization which are antithetical to competition and the market system and which, in Marx's view, serve as the embryo of a new society beyond capitalism.

The trend towards class consciousness is, however, a long-drawn-out process that proceeds dialectically out of the competition between workers. On the one hand, the continuous expansion of capital and extension of the market unifies wage workers into larger and larger groupings as they strive to eliminate competition between themselves; on the other hand, it also introduces new elements of competition which divide workers into antagonistic groups and inhibit their realizing the latent potential of their unity.

Marx identified two major forces in the development of capitalism (in addition to the ideological superstructure of the corporation and the state) which continually create competition between workers and allow capitalism to reproduce itself on an expanded scale and to survive even its worst crises. First, technological change substitutes machinery for labor: by throwing, or threatening to throw, the worker out of the factory and into the market, it breaks up the cohesiveness of labor organization and reduces workers to individuals or small groups competing with each other instead of cooperating. Secondly, capitalism continuously breaks down pre-capitalist areas—what Marx calls the latent surplus population—thus forming a fresh supply of non-class conscious workers to compete in the labor market.

These two dynamic forces create a stratified labor force which keeps the pretensions of the working class in check. Above the proletariat stands a vast officer class of managers, technicians and bureaucrats to organize it and to overcome its resistance by keeping it divided. Below it is a pool of unemployed, underemployed, and badly-paid strata continuously fed by technological change and the opening up of new hinterlands, which undercut its position and inhibit its development towards class consciousness. This reserve army drives the labor aristocracy to keep on working and keeps it loyal to the capitalist system from fear of falling from its superior position. By the nature of things, these different strata often come from different regions within a country, different racial or ethnic groups, and different age and sex classes. Thus, the competitive cleavages between workers often reflect lines of race, creed, color, age, sex, and national origin, which make working class consciousness more difficult.

The significance of the world market stage of capitalism into which we have now entered is that this competitive process, which both brings labor together and separates it, has not taken on an international dimension. The growth of world trade brings labor of different countries into closer contact and competition; the internationalization of production via the multinational corporate system was a reaction on the part of capital to this fact. American firms, for example, found that the recovery of Europe and the development of labor surplus economies in the Third World, made it possible to produce certain things more cheaply abroad than in the United States; and competitive pressure from emerging non-American capitalists forced them to invest abroad or enter into licensing and management contracts in order to preserve their position and maintain their growth. More generally, the emergence of a unified world commodity market, which in effect is the emergence of a unified world labor market, switched the domain of competition and its accompanying tendencies towards concentration and centralization from the national to the international plane. But this quest for profit, which led capital to shed its national character and escape the narrow confines of the nation state, has also intensified competitive pressure on labor and undermined its traditional organization and strategy. This, I suggest, is bound to bring about a new stage of development of labor organization, and it is here we must search for the root of the matter if we wish to understand our present predicament and the development track we are on.

In short, we must view present developments in terms of the long-term spread of commodity production, based on wage labor, from the local towns of the Middle Ages and the small enclaves of the transition period, to the national market and now the world market. The process of concentration and centralization of capital occurring within this framework led both to the steady growth and development of modern enterprise from the workshop to the factory to the national corporation to the multidivisional corporation and now to the multinational corporation, and to the parallel spread of the financial system from the local to the national and now to the international plane. At the same time, this growth has led to the continuous spread of labor organization in response to the opening up of new sources of competition and the emergence of new contradictions. This took place partly through the spread of the trade union movement to a broader and broader basis, and partly through the joint action of workers of different industries in the struggle over the working day, health, education, social security, unemployment, etc., at the political level. Workers' organization has so far taken place almost entirely within national boundaries through a struggle to obtain civil rights and national laws to protect labor from some of the necessitudes of the competitive labor process. Now internationalization of capital, combined with certain domestic contradictions of the welfare state, has brought the established structure of labor organization to a critical juncture, and it is to this problem that we must now turn.

The Political Role of Labor

From a Marxist perspective, the main theoretical shortcoming of Keynes' analysis is that he paid no attention to the conditions of production and the political role of labor. He viewed the market system, based on greed and selfishness, with considerable disdain and wanted to go beyond the profit motive towards a society managed by a society-oriented elite, operating in a loose framework that combined state planning and large quasi-public operations. He did not believe that either the capitalists or the "boorish proletariat" could or would lead us to this higher form of organization, but felt that the process of capital accumulation and technological progress would achieve this end naturally despite the wrong-headed interferences by capital and labor. Thus, neither in his political nor his economic writings, did he pay attention to class struggle as a moving force in capitalist development.

Ironically, this limited perspective was also in one sense his genius, for in fact during the post-war period, the issue of class struggle was highly subdued and labor did not form a serious challenge to capitalism as a system, but instead cooperated within its framework. This was one of the reasons capitalism grew so rapidly and one of the reasons Keynes' theory of monetary and fiscal policy could work.

In the *General Theory*, Keynes shifted the focus of discussion away from the labor market to the capital market. Classical economists saw unemployment and stagnation as the result of too high a level of wages. (In Marxian terms, too low a rate of surplus value.) Keynes instead postulated an elastic supply of labor at the going wage and sought the breakdown of the system in the contradictions between savers and investors, i.e., the rentier class and the entrepreneurial/managerial class. Keynes' preferred way out of this dilemma seemed to be through an expansion of the state and public consumption at the expense of the rentier class, but the alternative preferred by the capitalist was an expansion of the state to promote the growth of private wealth through the stimulation of private investment and private consumption. It was this path that finally predominated.

This strategy was possible because of specific conditions emerging from the Great Depression and the War which restored the workings of the labor market. In Marxist theory, the functioning of the wage labor market, upon which capitalist expansion depends, is maintained in the first instance through the institutions of the reserve army.

> The industrial reserve army, during the periods of stagnation and average prosperity, weights down the active labour army; during the periods of over-production and paroxysm, it holds its pretensions in check. Relative surplus-population is therefore the pivot upon which the law of demand and supply of labour works. It confines the field of this law within the limits absolutely convenient to the activity of exploitation and to the domination of capital.[15]

In this sense, the long period of large scale unemployment of the Thirties served as a disciplinary action on labor to make it ready, willing and anxious to work again in the postwar period. But action at the political level was needed as well.

> As soon, therefore, as the labourers learn the secret, how it comes to pass that in the same measure as they work more, as they produce more wealth for others, and as the productive power of their labour increases, so in the same measure even their function as a means of the self-expansion of capital becomes more and more precarious for

them; as soon as they discover that the degree of intensity of the competition among themselves depends wholly on the pressure of the relative
surplus-population; as soon as, by trade unions, etc., they try to organize a regular cooperation between the employed and unemployed in
order to destroy or to weaken the ruinous effects of this natural law of
capitalistic production on their class, so soon capital and its sycophant,
political economy, cry out at the infringement of the 'eternal' and so to
say 'sacred' law of supply and demand. Every combination of employed
and unemployed disturbs the 'harmonious' actions of this law. But on
the other hand, as soon as (in the colonies, e.g.) adverse circumstances
prevent the creation of an industrial reserve army and, with it, the absolute dependence of the working class upon the capitalist class, capital,
along with its commonplace Sancho Panza, rebels against the 'sacred'
law of supply and demand and tries to check its inconvenient action by
forcible means and State interference.[16]

The New Deal, the World War and the Cold War made it possible in the
United States to purge the labor movement of its radical elements and create a
system of collective bargaining within the framework of the welfare state. This
system left the basic capitalist institutions of private wealth and wage labor
largely untouched and channeled labor protest into narrowly-defined trade
unionism, which concentrated on selling labor at a more advantageous price
without challenging the prerogatives of management and capital, either inside
the plant or out of it. Trade unions confined their horizons to the interests of
their own membership and instead of unifying all of labor in a class perspective,
maintain cleavages within the best-paid aristocracy of the working class and
between it and the reserve army. The law of supply and demand was thus altered
by the growth of unions, but still kept working within conveniently confined
limits. The history of the European movement was different in content but
similar in effect, that is, the elimination of radical perspectives and the creation
of a framework in which labor was willing to submit to the dictates of capital in
order to obtain economic growth and capitalism's "New Frontier."
    A major factor in making the system work was the existence of a latent sur-
plus-population in the underdeveloped countries and backward sectors of advanced countries which could be broken down to form a constantly flowing surplus
population to work at the bottom of the ladder. In the United States the replacement of southern sharecropping agriculture by modern capitalist methods
created a flow of black labor to the northern cities, just as the "development"
of Puerto Rico led to large-scale immigration into the eastern United States.
Similarly, in Europe modernization of agriculture and the importation of labor
from foreign countries played a major role in creating the labor supply needed
for capitalist expansion. In addition, the advanced countries benefited from cheap
prices for raw materials made possible by the creation of a labor surplus economy
in the underdeveloped countries.

Thus, during this twenty-five year period, labor was able to enjoy prosperity and growth as it concentrated on working harder for steadily increasing standards of living and refrained from challenging the system politically. By and large the major source of rebellion and protest did not come from the established proletariat during the Fifties and Sixties, but from the new strata being incorporated into the wage labor force from their previous position in the latent surplus population. These groups were highly critical of the conditions of capitalist production, as they found themselves caught between the breakdown of the old system and the unfulfilled expectations of the new one. They were acutely aware of the coercive nature of the capitalist work relationship, since, unlike the traditional working class, they were "disadvantaged," i.e., they had not yet internalized the capitalist values of alienated work. And they were also extremely bitter at the inequality of their position and the discriminations they suffered.

These factors, which gave such great force to their reaction, also limited the scope of their challenge to capitalism. Because they were outside production and at odds with the privileged strata, they were relatively powerless to actually transform the capitalist system. Their programs often tended to be backward-looking, harking after a return to older forms of community production, and/or anarchistically radical, seeking to burn, destroy and sabotage the system which oppressed them, rather than to seize it for their own. They were caught in a dilemma. On the one hand, they were antagonistic to capitalism, but on the other hand, they also wanted to get into it and share its benefits and privileges. The result of this dualism was a tendency for their group to split as some entered the labor force and became part of the system, while others fell down into the stagnant part of the reserve army with extremely irregular employment, well below average conditions of life, and into the lowest sediments which dwell in the sphere of pauperism, thus forming an incredible pool of wasted human beings in the slums, ghettos and rural hinterlands of the capitalist economy.

Thus the uneven development of capitalism, accumulating wealth at one pole and misery at the other, was from the political point of view a stabilizing force because it divided the potential opposition to capitalism into conflicting groups. The question is, then, for how long can this go on? In the next section, I examine the pressures on the labor aristocracy which I believe are bringing this phase of capitalist expansion to an end and leading us to a period when class conflict between capital and labor will be a major force in the economy and polity, nationally and internationally.

The Seeds of a New Class Conflict

The success of the "American Challenge" and the "New Frontier", we have argued, rested on a particular set of initial conditions arising out of the great depression and the World War. These wore down the resistance of labor, destroyed its radical wing and made organized labor into a willing participant in a strategy based on strong state action to promote growth and international expansionism. But the very success of the plan has tended to undermine these initial conditions and to lead us to a stage marked by crisis and reorientation of basic strategies.

In the first place, memories of the Thirties and Forties have faded in this period of affluence, while the "New Frontier" has turned out to be less rewarding than it promised. The growth of national income satisfied some of the pent-up needs of previous decades and created new needs which the market system cannot fulfill. The consumer durable revolution provided most families with a car, a television set and a refrigerator, but also resulted in overcrowding, pollution and an energy crisis. The middle class standard of living, towards which the working class aspired, is predicated in large part on only a few people having it. When everybody has a car, the result is not freedom to escape from overcrowded cities into the countryside, but a crowded countryside. Similarly, when everybody has access to higher education, its elite qualities and privileges are destroyed and a college degree no longer means a ticket to the top of the hierarchy, but an upgraded job at the lower level. Thus, many of the promises of capitalistic consumption tend to be illusory, while alienation and exploitation in the work process remain an ever-present reality. Therefore, job dissatisfaction and a decreased motivation to work has increased steadily over the last twenty-five years, and resulted in the productivity crisis causing so much discussion and concern in business circles.

In the second place, the latent surplus population has been steadily drying up, thus exhausting national pools of cheap labor and lessening the competitive pressure on the work force. Moreover, as more and more people from the non-wage sector are drawn into the wage labor force, the locus of their struggle against discrimination, alienation and exploitation shifts from outside to inside, thus infusing the labor movement with new dimensions of protest and militancy. At the same time, the demands for welfare and other support programs by those who are nonincorporated into the wage labor force eat up the surplus and limit the scope for expanding wages.

These two trends have seriously threatened the collective bargaining strategy which dominated the trade union movement over the last twenty-five years. Trade unions can obtain higher wages within capitalist expansion only to the extent that they are matched by increased productivity or passed on to lower strata of the labor force. However, the tightening of the labor market that accompanies capitalist expansion increases the pretensions of the working class, both with regard to wages and relief from work, at the same time that it diminishes the possibility of placing the burden on disadvantaged sectors. Hence, wage demands result in inflation and a crisis in labor organization. (A recent article in *Business Week*, for example, focused on three crises in the union movement: dissatisfaction on the part of consumers concerning the inflationary consequences of wage demands, dissatisfaction on the part of businessmen over the ability of the unions to deliver the intensity of work contracted for, and dissatisfaction on the part of the rank and file over the responsiveness of union leadership to their needs.[17]

These tendencies in the labor market, which are occurring throughout the advanced capitalist world as capital expansions occur (usually called a shift in the Phillips Curve by non-Marxist economists), have led to the widespread adoption of wage and price controls, thus signalling the de facto end, or at least the beginning of the end, of the era of collective bargaining. Trade unions can no longer confine their horizons to the struggle between their membership and its employers, but must bargain politically at the national level over the share of wages in national income. In Marxian terms, the material conditions of trade union consciousness are coming to an end in advanced capitalism since the trade unions can no longer confine themselves to wages, but must deal directly with the problem of the aggregate rate of surplus value which is a class phenomenon. At this point of development, they soon find out that there is very little that can be done about the rate of surplus value within a capitalist framework, since increases in the share of wages cut down on investment and result in unemployment and a slackening of growth. A socialist alternative, under which the working class seizes control of the investment process, could open new possibilities of organizing production and promoting the growth and development of the potential of social labor. Failing this radical break, the working class is a hostage to the capitalist class on whom they depend for capital accumulation and to whom they must provide incentives in the form of profit and accumulation of capital, that is, more work.

Thus, labor organizations must shift their horizons from the industrial to the national level, that is, they must shift from economic to political action. At the same time, the growth of the world market and the internationalization of capital implies they must also shift their horizons to the world level. Once again, they discover how limited their options are if they do not challenge the capitalist system. If, for example, they adopt a protectionist policy, they can lessen the competition from imports, but they cannot insure a high rate of national investment if capitalists can escape their national demands by investing abroad. If they try to control capital flight, they then discover that the size and complexity of multinational corporations and the international financial market provide capitalists with numerous escape valves and that unless they take over the whole system, they can only achieve partial control.

Another strategy is international trade unionism, which can alleviate competition in certain industries but is still partly limited on two accounts. First, organizing workers in developed countries for higher wages at the cost of reduced employment, though it obtains the support of some groups, increases the gap between the small local labor aristocracy and the vast reserve army and creates politcally volatile conditions which have to be brutally suppressed. Second, international trade unionism can only struggle over industry wage and working conditions. But a great part of labor's historical gains have occurred at the political level and are embodied in national social infrastructure in the fields of health, education, welfare, social security, etc. Equalization of this infrastructure to remove competition involves far more political unification than a simple trade unionist strategy can provide.

Therefore, on both counts—the internal reserve army and the external reserve army—labor is in an objective crisis where its old institutions and policies no longer work, and, what amounts to the same thing, so is capitalism. This is what I believe to be the radical view of international economics and international politics at this juncture in history.

The Next Twenty-Five Years

Work in the Marxist framework is a political relationship. In the market, where workers sell their labor in exchange for wages, it seems to be only an economic phenomenon, but this is an illusion. What the workers sell is not labor but labor power, that is, their life activity. How this labor power will be used, its duration and intensity, is not settled by competition but by struggle and force. Hence there arises within the business enterprise a political superstructure whose function is in part to coordinate work and in part to overcome the resistance of workers arising out of the antagonistic social relations of production. Similarly, the stuggle over work leads to the capitalist state whose function in the last instance is to insure the reproduction of the basic structural elements of the work relationship—capital and labor. The rise and spread of the market system is thus closely connected to a political struggle to create and maintain the wage labor force, divided by competition, upon which capitalism rests.

Politics—the getting, keeping and using of power—is mainly a question of uniting your allies and dividing your enemies. Marx's analysis of the general laws of capitalist accumulation is an attempt to uncover the tendencies towards concentration and class consciousness that develop in the two main contending parties as capitalism progresses.

The peculiar feature of capitalism is that it obtained power and in some sense maintains it with an inherently limited degree of class consciousness. Capitalism is a system based on the mutual indifference of its participants, operating in a structure of competition and the pursuit of selfish interests. In economists' terms, it is a highly decentralized system based on private profit maximization and united through the invisible hand of the market, that is, the law of value. The great strength of this system, which differentiates it from all previous modes of production, is that the competition between capitalists and between capital and labor forces a continuous revolution in technology and an epoch-making expansion of material production. But this competitive market nexus is also its chief limit, for it prevents the development of a total view of society commensurate with the increasingly interdependent social division of labor that it is creating. The capitalist state attempts to provide some sort of total view, but is sharply limited by the divisions in capitalist society between capital and labor and between capitalists themselves. As capitalism progresses, this contradiction intensifies. The problems of "externalities," to use economists' language, and "socialization" and "legitimization" become more important as more and more problems arise which cannot be managed by the invisible hand of the market. The world market, created since World War II, has brought things to a critical point. Capital has expanded to global dimensions, but still maintains a consciousness based on narrow private calculation. The structure of the American Empire, which kept some sort of order on this process in the past, is dissolving and a Hobbesian-like struggle of all against all seems to be emerging at the world level. As the anarchy of competition asserts itself, we find ourselves facing numerous crises, with even greater ones looming in the background.

Labor, in contrast to capital, though it too is divided by competition, steadily struggles to eliminate this competition at higher and higher levels until it reaches a world historic perspective far more total than capital and replaces capitalism by socialism. This unification, however, is a long-drawn-out process, requiring a high development of material forces, i.e., a long expansion of capitalist production.

> Competition separates individuals from one another, not only the bourgeois but still more the workers, in spite of the fact that it brings them together. Hence it is a long time before these individuals can unite, apart from the fact that for the purpose of this union—if it is not to be merely local—the necessary means, the great industrial cities and cheap and quick communications have first to be produced by big industry. Hence every organized power standing over against these isolated individuals who live in relationships daily reproducing this isolation, can only be overcome after long struggles. To demand the opposite would be tantamount to demanding that competition should not exist in this definite epoch of history, or that the individuals should banish from their minds relationships over which in their isolation they have no control.[18]

In this paper we have tried to suggest that the world market, by expanding the edge of competition, has created a critical juncture in the labor movement which will force a change in its strategy and structure. During the last twenty-five years, capital has been able to expand and internationalize, first by strengthening and then by eroding the powers of the nation state. During the next twenty-five years we can expect a counter-response by labor and other groups to erode the power of capital. This response will take a political form, i.e., a struggle over state power around the central issue of capitalism and its continuance. Since states are territorial, the locus of the struggle will be largely national, or at least regional, even though the context is international. In the United States, it will probably tend to the formation of some sort of labor party. In Europe, it will probably lead to unification and a closer union between Social Democratic and Communist parties. In the underdeveloped countries, it will lead to an increased role of labor in politics as the new proletariat emerges. And so on.

In this paper we cannot even begin to examine the complexity of the struggle and the numerous paths it can take between the following two extremes:

1. A privileged part of the new working class in the advanced countries joins with capital in a new imperialistic alliance to get higher benefits in return for suppressing blacks, Third World people, foreign workers, women, the aged, etc. I personally think that this extreme is unlikely due to the large numbers and strength of the disadvantaged groups and the enormous brutality it would take to contain them.
2. At the other extreme, we can imagine a socialist consciousness which unites the disparate elements of labor to effect the transition from capitalism to socialism. Since socialism implies that communities obtain control over their own work and consumption, it would probably have to be based on national or regional self-sufficiency, as Keynes suggested; though with a great deal of international cooperation to permit the free flow of ideas, hospitality, etc.

Much research needs to be done on both labor and non-labor political groups before we can sort out the possible sets of intermediate alliances that might emerge, and analyze their implications for the balance between capitalism and socialism, internationalism and nationalism. This paper merely attempts to point to the crucial role of the capital-labor struggle that we can expect in the future. We might end by noting that whatever the outcome—international fascism, socialism, or mixed free enterprise—a great deal of conflict and struggle domestically and internationally is in store for us, especially in the Third World, as the powerful forces unleashed by advanced capitalism come to a head. Our main problem as social scientists and human beings is not only to analyze what is happening, but also to decide which side we want to be on. That is why I spent so much time on Keynes, who asked the right questions, even though he was sharply limited in his answers—because he tried to think history without Marx.

Notes

1. "Marx to Engels in Manchester, London, October 8, 1858," in Karl Marx

and Frederick Engels, *Selected Correspondence* (Moscow: Progress Publishers, 1965), p. 111.

2. John Maynard Keynes, "National Self-Sufficiency," *The Yale Review*, vol. 22 (Summer 1933), p. 766.

3. Ibid., p. 758.

4. Ibid., p. 757.

5. Ibid., pp. 760–62.

6. "The American Challenge," *The Economist*, July 18, 1942, p. 67.

7. Sumner Wells, quoted in "The New Frontier," *The Economist*, June 13, 1942, p. 824.

8. "The New Frontier," p. 825.

9. "An American Proposal," *Fortune*, May 1942, p. 63.

10. John Maynard Keynes, *The General Theory of Employment, Interest and Money* (London: Macmillan & Co., Ltd., 1964), p. 221.

11. Ibid., p. 376.

12. Ibid., pp. 276–377.

13. Stephen Hymer, "The Internationalization of Capital," *Journal of Economic Issues*, vol. 6, no. 1 (1972), pp. 91–111.

14. Karl Marx, *Capital*, 3 vols. (New York: International Publishers, 1967), I:614.

15. Ibid., p. 639.

16. Ibid., p. 640.

17. "Trouble Plagues the House of Labor," *Business Week*, October 28, 1972, pp. 66–76.

18. Karl Marx and Frederick Engels, *Selected Works* (Moscow: Progress Publishers, 1973), I:63.

15 The International Politics of Postindustrial Societies: The Role of the Multinational Corporation
James R. Kurth

Two "Unreal" Portraits

The two most promising, or at least most promoted, notions in political science today are the concept of postindustrial society and the concept of transnational organizations. The first concept is the new wave in the study of comparative politics; the second is the new wave in the study of international politics. Each wave, in its own way and in its own domain, is washing away or at least wearing down the two concepts—modernization and the unitary state— that dominated the analysis of comparative politics and international politics respectively in the 1960s. For political scientists, too, "there is a tide in the affairs of men which, taken at the flood, leads on to fortune."

It might seem natural, then, to combine these two new paradigms and to conclude that the foreign relations of postindustrial societies (or, a less controversial term, advanced industrial societies) are best analyzed with the concept of transnational organizations. But this concept, as we shall see, has some problems.

A Liberal Portrait: Transnational Organizations

The concept of transnational organizations has been developed most systematically by liberal political scientists such as Robert Keohane, Joseph Nye, and Samuel Huntington.[1] They have defined transnational organizations as nongovernmental and quasi-governmental actors that operate across national frontiers, away from close control by national states, but with a major impact upon these states and upon their citizens. Such actors have an obvious and undeniable importance today. But as an analytical device with which to capture the distinctive international aspect of postindustrial societies, however, the concept of transnational organizations is doubly flawed.

First, there is the problem of vagueness. The words "transnational organizations" have a rather misty quality about them; in themselves, they bring no obvious images to mind. The transnational theorists have given as examples of transnational organizations such diverse phenomena as General Motors, the Catholic Church, the Ford Foundation, and even the CIA. But a concept that is so broad in scope risks overlooking the distinctive features of one of the most important kinds, and currently the most debated kind, of transnational organization, that is, the multinational corporation. Thus far, the concept of transnational organizations remains at best ambiguous and at worst vacuous.

Second, there is the problem of newness. The words "transnational organizations" may be new, but the phenomena they describe are not. Transnational political organizations have existed in virtually every era. The Nazi Fifth Columns of the 1930s, the various socialist, communist, and anarchist Internationales from the 1860s to the 1930s, the Masonic revolutionary fraternities in Southern Europe in the early nineteenth century, and the Catholic political orders in Southern Europe in the eighteenth century are only the most significant examples. It would be difficult indeed to demonstrate that transnational political organizations are more important today than they have been in the past. Transnational economic organizations also have existed in virtually every era. The multinational oil corporations were already powerful transnational actors before World War II, as were the great banks of the City of London from the 1870s to the 1930s and the chartered merchant companies in the eighteenth and early nineteenth centuries. Here, however, it is not difficult to show that the scale and scope of one form of transnational organization, the multinational corporation, have greatly increased in the last generation over that in earlier times. Again, there is an advantage in narrowing the analytical focus from transnational organizations to multinational corporations.

A Radical Portrait: American Imperialism

There is, of course, another group of theorists of international politics, who, in the last decade have focused on the multinational corporation. These are the radical economists, such as Harry Magdoff, Paul Sweezy, and Andre Gunder Frank.[2] Their major concept is not transnational organizations but American imperialism. But this concept also has its problems, which are many and familiar.[3] Here we will mention only one, the problem of wrong predictions, which has become especially evident in the last few years.

Consider the major events in international politics that have occurred in the 1970s, at the very time that the theory of American imperialism has become most developed. The list of major events would include the following:

1. The United States detente with the Soviet Union, including the SALT agreements, and with China
2. The United States withdrawal from the Indochinese War in 1973, in spite of the discovery of offshore oil in the South China Sea and in spite of the continuing North Vietnamese threat to the pro-Western regimes in Indochina
3. The international monetary crises of 1971-73, including the devaluation of the dollar and the adoption of flexible exchange rates

4. The international energy crises of 1971-74, including the massive price, tax, and participation concessions made by the multinational oil corporations to the OPEC countires
5. The consequent international economic crisis afflicting almost all advanced industrial countries

None of these major events would have been predicted by the radical theorists of American imperialism. Rather, their analyses of American imperialism would have predicted (and indeed in many cases did predict) the opposite of the events that actually occurred.

It is true that, after the fact, a radical explanation can be constructed that interprets each of these events as in the interest of the American multinational corporations and therefore as the consequence of them. But any theory that can "explain" not only an event but its opposite is seriously flawed. Whereas the concept of transnational organizations is at best ambiguous and at worst vacuous, the concept of American imperialism is at best gross and at worst wrong. The first presents a portrait of multinational corporations that, like a French impressionist painting, is dim; the second presents a portrait that, like a German expressionist painting, is distorted.

This essay is an effort to examine the new system formed by multinational corporations. It is a system centered on the advanced industrial societies. These societies are the home countries for virtually all multinational corporations, and they are the host countries for more than half of total world direct foreign investment. We will consider three aspects of the new multinational corporate system: (1) its contours, (2) its causes, and (3) its consequences.

The Contours of the Multinational Corporate System

A committee of the United Nations Secretariat has calculated that, in 1971, the book value for direct foreign investment undertaken by all investor countries totaled about $165 billion. The value of production from this direct foreign investment was calculated to be about twice the book value or about $330 billion. In contrast, the exports of the investor countries amounted to $312 billion [4]. The new system formed by multinational corporations is very grand indeed.

The most basic way to view the contours of the new system formed by multinational corporations is to examine the aggregate economic statistics for the major investor countries. Table 15-1 presents those investor countries whose stock of direct foreign investment exceeds $1 billion.

The United States accounts for the major share of all direct foreign investment. In 1971 the $86 billion of the United States formed fifty-two percent of the $165 billion for all investor countries. Also, for the United States the value

Table 15-1
Major Investor Countries: Foreign Investment, Foreign Production, and
Exports, 1971 (Millions of Dollars)

Country	Direct Foreign Investment	Estimated Foreign Production	Exports	Foreign Production as Percentage of Exports
United States	86,000	172,000	43,492	395.5
United Kingdom	24,020	48,000	22,367	214.6
France	9,540	19,100	20,420	93.5
West Germany	7,270	14,600	39,040	37.4
Switzerland	6,760	13,500	5,728	235.7
Canada	5,930	11,900	17,582	67.7
Japan	4,480	9,000	24,019	37.5
Netherlands	3,580	7,200	13,927	51.7
Sweden	3,450	6,900	7,465	92.4
Italy	3,350	6,700	15,111	44.3
Belgium	3,250	6,500	12,392	52.4

Source: United Nations, Department of Economic and Social Affairs, *Multinational Corporations in World Development* (New York: 1973), p. 159.

of its production from foreign investment was almost four times the value of its exports from foreign trade, a higher factor than that for any other country. This production value of $172 billion made American investment abroad the fourth largest GNP in the world, after the United States at home, the Soviet Union, and Japan.

The United States and the United Kingdom combined accounted for $110 billion or sixty-seven percent of all direct foreign investment. In years to come the Germans, the Japanese, and the Arabs may loom larger in the community of investor countries. But in the early 1970s foreign direct investment was in large measure a province of, as de Gaulle had put it, the "Anglo-Saxons."

Given the predominance of the United States, a second way to view the contours of the new system formed by multinational corporations is to examine the familiar aggregate statistics of American direct foreign investment, as published each year by the U.S. Department of Commerce. Table 15-2 presents figures for several years, including 1972, a year that is a recent one but also one for which comparisons over time are not yet significantly distorted by inflation.

The overall size of American direct foreign investment is impressive enough; more interesting, however, are two patterns of concentration that appear when we break down the aggregate data: (1) concentration in time and (2) concentration in space.

In regard to time American foreign investment nearly tripled between 1960 and 1972, from $33 billion to $94 billion. In recent years American foreign

Table 15-2
American Direct Foreign Investment (Millions of Dollars)

	1950	1960	1970	1972
All areas	11,788	32,778	78,178	94,031
Developed countries	5,697	19,328	53,145	64,114
Canada	3,579	11,198	22,790	25,784
Europe	1,733	6,681	24,516	30,714
Japan	19	254	1,483	2,222
Australia, New Zealand, and South Africa	366	1,195	4,356	5,393
Underdeveloped countries	5,735	12,032	21,448	25,186
Latin America and other Western Hemisphere (excluding Canada)	4,576	9,271	14,760	16,644
Africa (excluding South Africa)	147	639	2,614	3,086
Middle East	692	1,139	1,617	2,053
Asia and Pacific (excluding Japan, Australia, New Zealand)	320	983	2,457	3,402
International, unallocated	356	1,418	3,586	4,733

Sources: 1950 and 1960 data: U.S. Department of Commerce, *Survey of Current Business*, August 1962, pp. 22-23; 1970 data: *Survey of Current Business*, November 1972, pp. 28-29; 1972 data: *Survey of Current Business*, September 1973, pp. 26-27.

investment has been growing by about ten percent a year, roughly double the growth in GNP for most industrial countries, including the United States. It is this rapid growth, this concentration in time, of American foreign investment that has contributed to the perception that multinational corporations are *new* actors in international politics; in fact, they are more accurately seen as old actors with a new scale and scope.

In regard to space a concentration in developed areas is apparent. A high proportion of American foreign investment is located in developed countries—$64 billion or sixty-eight percent—and a corresponding low proportion is located in underdeveloped countries—$25 billion or twenty-six percent. Canada alone accounts for $26 billion or twenty-eight percent (more than the entire underdeveloped world), and Europe accounts for $31 billion or thirty-three percent.

Since 1950 there has been a much greater expansion of American foreign investment in developed countries than in underdeveloped ones. The investment in developed countries grew from $5.7 billion in 1950 to $64.1 billion in 1972, or by a factor of eleven; the investment in Western Europe grew even faster. Conversely, the investment in underdeveloped countries grew from $5.7 billion in 1950 (the same amount as in developed countries) to $25.1

billion in 1972, or by only a factor of four; the investment in Latin America grew even slower.

At first glance this concentration in particular developed countries might suggest that even if American foreign investment is a major component of foreign economic relations, the investment in underdeveloped countries is not.

Such a conclusion does not logically follow, however. First, much of the American foreign investment in developed countries is dependent upon the petroleum sector, either directly (in the sense that of $64 billion invested in developed countries in 1972, $14 billion or twenty-two percent was in the petroleum industry) or indirectly (in the sense that much of American manufacturing in Western Europe runs on Middle Eastern oil).

Second, as Thomas Weisskopf has pointed out, "although the *value* of U.S. private investment is now much higher in the developed than in the underdeveloped countries, there is much less of a difference in the level of *income* from that investment."[5] Thus, in 1972 total earnings from American investment were $12.4 billion; earnings from developed countries were $6.8 billion or fifty-four percent, while earnings from underdeveloped countries were $5.1 billion or forty-one percent. Indeed, the difference is reversed for the category of "interest, dividends, and branch earnings," which corresponds roughly to earnings repatriated to the United States. In 1972 these totaled $8.0 billion; the amount from developed countries was $3.3 billion or forty-one percent, while the amount from underdeveloped countries was $4.3 billion or fifty-four percent. Phrased differently, for underdeveloped countries in comparison with developed ones, a much higher proportion of earnings is repatriated to the United States rather than reinvested in the host country. The relative weight of earnings from underdeveloped countries, of course, was even heavier in the earlier years.

A third way to view the contours of the new system formed by multinational corporations is to examine how important their foreign operations are to the corporations themselves. In order to get a complete sense of the importance to particular corporations of their foreign investments in particular countries, we should present systematic comparative data for all large corporations, for all host countries, and for several years. Unfortunately, the corporations refuse to make such data available, allegedly because the information would be useful to competitors. It is particularly difficult to get comparative data for investments in particular host countries. However, global data is available and is presented for the twenty-five largest corporations in Table 15-3.

As a very rough summary, American automobile corporations have about one-fourth of their operations and assets abroad; American oil corporations have about one-half of their operations and assets abroad. Some analysts have interpreted these figures to mean that American multinational corporations are so global in their interests that they are no longer vulnerable to pressure from the United States government. I would look at it the other way, however; even after a period of massive expansion abroad, American multinational corporations are heavily dependent upon their operations and assets in the

Table 15-3
Major Multinational Corporations: Foreign Content of Operations and Assets

Company	Nationality	Total Sales (Millions of Dollars) (1971)	Foreign Content as Percentage of					Number of Subsidiary Countries (1971)
			Sales (1970)	Production (1968)	Assets (1968)	Earnings (1970)	Employment (1970)	
General Motors	US	28,264	19	—	15	19	27	21
Standard Oil (N.J.)	US	18,701	50	81	52	52	—	25
Ford Motors	US	16,433	26	36	40	24	48	30
Royal Dutch/Shell Group	Neth.-UK	12,734	79	—	—	—	70	43
General Electric	US	9,429	16	—	15	20	36	32
International Business Machines	US	8,274	39	—	27	50	51	80
Mobil Oil	US	8,243	45	—	46	51	24	62
Chrysler	US	7,999	24	22	31	—	—	26
Texaco	US	7,529	40	65	—	25	—	30
Unilever	Neth.-UK	7,483	80	—	60	—	70	31
International Tel. and Tel. Corp.	US	7,346	42	60	61	35	72	40
Western Electric	US	6,045	—	—	—	—	—	—
Gulf Oil	US	5,940	45	75	38	21	83	61
British Petroleum	UK	5,191	88	—	—	—	—	52
Philips' Gloeilampenfabrieken	Neth.	5,189	45	67	53	—	73	29
Standard Oil of California	US	5,143	45	46	9	43	29	26
Volkswagenwerk	FRG	4,967	69	25	—	—	18	12
United States Steel	US	4,928	54	—	48	62	70	—
Westinghouse Electric	US	4,630	—	—	—	—	—	—
Nippon Steel	Japan	4,088	31	—	16	—	2	5
Standard Oil (Ind.)	US	4,054	—	—	—	—	—	24
Shell Oil (subsidiary of Royal Dutch/Shell).	US	3,892	18	12	12	—	—	20
E.I. duPont deNem.	US	3,848	17	17	—	—	—	—
Siemens	FRG	3,815	39	—	—	—	23	52
ICI (Imperial Chem. Industries)	UK	3,717	35	42	25	—	27	46

Source: United Nations, Department of Economic and Social Affairs, *Multinational Corporations in World Development* (New York: 1973), p. 130.
Note: Percentage figures are for different years in some individual cases.

United States. The United States government retains many potential pressure points with which to influence the corporations.

Finally, we can note again the familiar observation that the largest multinational corporations have an "annual product" (gross annual sales) equal to the "annual product" (gross national product) of the smaller advanced industrial countries. In this sense General Motors is roughly equal in size to Belgium or Switzerland.

The Causes of the Multinational Corporate System

What are the causes of the large expansion in scale and scope of multinational corporations since World War II and especially since about 1960? The explanations that have been offered by various analysts are many; we shall briefly consider three of them.

The American Hegemony Explanation

Most explanations for corporate investment abroad focus on the economic incentives of the corporations themselves. But Robert Gilpin has argued forcefully that the basic framework, the necessary condition, for major American investment abroad was the military and political hegemony of the United States after World War II.[6]

The connection between American military and political hegemony and American corporate expansion is rather obvious for extractive industries in underdeveloped countries. The most dramatic case was the entry of American oil corporations into Iran after the CIA-supported coup in 1953. But the United States government also gave strong diplomatic support to the entry of American oil corporations into Saudi Arabia after World War II.

The connection between American military and political hegemony and American corporate expansion is less obvious for manufacturing industries in Western Europe. However, during the Cold War, the Europeans' need for an American military protectorate precluded any effective resistance to the American corporate presence. And when the Europeans established the Common Market in 1958 they accepted the demand of the United States government that the EEC discriminate only against American exports but not against American investments. This combination of restraint of trade and freedom for capital naturally accentuated American corporate investment in the Common Market countries in the 1960s, in order not to be excluded by the new tariff walls but rather to turn them to advantage. American military and political hegemony also permitted another inducement for American investment abroad:

the overvaluation of the United States dollar from about 1960 until about 1971. This overvaluation made it especially advantageous for American corporations to buy up foreign assets.

Given the American hegemony explanation for American corporate expansion, one might have predicted that a decline in American military hegemony would soon be followed by a shift in the balance of power and in the distribution of rewards between American corporations and host countries, a shift to the advantage of the latter. And this seems to have happened. In regard to the underdeveloped world, the effect of the Indochinese War was to radically reduce the expectation of United States military intervention. To an advocate of the American hegemony theory it would be no accident that, beginning in 1968 with Peru's seizure of a subsidiary of Standard Oil of New Jersey, a wave of expropriations or, more commonly, drastic renegotiations hit American corporations operating in underdeveloped countries. Similarly, in regard to Western Europe the effect of the Soviet-American detente was to radically reduce the need for United States military protection. At about the same time, the United States gave up the overvaluation of the dollar.

The American hegemony explanation can go a long way in explaining American corporate expansion since World War II. It operates only at a highly aggregated level, however. For a clearer sense of why particular industries invest in particular countries at particular times, we must turn to a second explanation.

The Product Cycle Explanation

A second explanation for corporate expansion abroad focuses on the concept of the "product cycle," developed by Raymond Vernon and his colleagues.[7] Although the product cycle concept primarily applies to manufacturing corporations, within this limited scope it is very powerful indeed.

Vernon argues that a corporation goes through a regular cycle in manufacturing and selling its product: (1) production in the home country for sales in the home market (domestic trade); (2) production in the home country for sales in foreign markets (foreign exports); and (3) production in foreign countries for sales in foreign markets (foreign investment). We might add to Vernon that there is yet another phase: (4) production in foreign countries for sales in the home market (foreign imports).

This pattern presumably could apply to any manufacturing corporation. But Vernon argues that, within a given industry, it will normally be an American corporation that will undertake the product innovation and initiate the product cycle. The great size of the American domestic market and the high wages of the American labor force each put a high premium on capital-intensive and mass-produced goods.

The period since World War II was the time when many large American corporations entered on a large-scale into phase 3 of their product cycle (although some corporations already had begun the process before World War II). This was true of the largest American industry, the automobile industry, which in General Motors, Ford, and Chrysler included three of the largest corporations in the world.

The product cycle theory also argues that corporations will tend to invest in those countries whose consumer demand structures are similar to that of the home country. As the economic development of a foreign country brings it close to the consumer demand structure of the home country, the corporation will move in on a large scale. Thus, an American manufacturing corporation normally invested first in Canada, and then in Britain, West Germany, France, and Italy, in roughly that order. In the last decade American corporations have tried to break down the barriers to investment in Japan, and they have undertaken large investments in Spain, Argentina, and Brazil. In the automobile industry it is almost as if the automobile corporations have rolled into a country (or into a region, as in Southern Brazil) as the society rolled over an economic threshold of, say, $1,000 per capita GNP.

Indeed, a product cycle theorist would have a ready explanation for the Nixon Administration's policy of detente with the Soviet Union. It was at just this time that the corporations, which had recently invested heavily in Southern Europe and the more developed parts of Latin America, were searching for the area with the next highest level of economic development, which of course was Eastern Europe and the Soviet Union.

In many cases the American corporations have continued to expand into countries of even lesser economic development, beyond the point where a similar consumer-demand structure has already emerged. In the early 1970s American automobile corporations invested in Malaysia and the Philippines. The usual sequence of foreign investment seems to suggest a pattern in which an American corporation first invests in countries that are closest to the United States in per capita GNP (or perhaps total GNP) and then gradually moves down the development ranking. Alternatively, but relatedly, it might suggest that the corporation first invests in countries that are closest to the United States in cultural terms (the Anglo-Saxon countries) and then gradually moves away on the cultural dimension.

In regard to the automobile industry the product cycle theory may now be obsolete. The recent quadrupling of oil prices and the current excess capacity in the world automobile industry should inhibit additional foreign investment by the automobile corporations. In regard to another large industry, the aerospace industry, the product cycle theory may never get a chance. By itself the theory would predict that American aerospace corporations in the next few years will attempt direct investment in Britain, West Germany, France, Italy, and Japan. Such expansion will probably be aborted, however. Again, the quadrupling of oil prices and the excess capacity of the aerospace industry, added on to the close connection of the aerospace industry with national governments, should inhibit additional foreign investment by the aerospace corporations.

The future operation of the product cycle probably will be most pronounced in the chemical, computer, and advanced communications industries. American corporations in these industries probably will expand their foreign investments in Western Europe, and perhaps in Japan, over the next few years.

The Technological Development Explanation

American hegemony and the product cycle combined still might not explain why many small companies, which had previously been inhibited by the "foreignness" of foreign investment, joined the rush overseas in the 1960s: Here, an accessory, if not a necessary, condition was the development in computer, communications, and aerospace technologies. The computer complexes, communications satellites, and jet airliners of the last fifteen years surely made foreign countries more accessible and foreign branches more manageable. By providing an infrastructure of information, communication, and transportation systems, they greatly encouraged the spread of multinational corporations.

The Consequences of the Multinational Corporate System

The most interesting aspect of multinational corporations concerns their consequences, both for the host countries and for the home countries, such as the United States.

Consequences for the Host Countries

What are the effects of the presence of American or other multinational corporations within a host country, even one that is a large, advanced industrial society? This presence, it has been frequently argued, imposes several actual or potential constraints or distortions, even on such large and advanced countries as Britain, France, and West Germany. The arguments are familiar, and I shall mention them only briefly. Their thrust primarily is against American multinational corporations, but some could be extended to cover multinational corporations based in other countries.

1. National elites are denied the role of directing and profiting from the

most advanced industrial and technological sectors of the national economy. Thus, businessmen, managers, investors, scientists, and technicians are limited to old-established, static industries; what John Kenneth Galbraith calls the technostructure of the new industrial state is stunted.

In actual practice in Western Europe and Japan this argument is rather limited in its scope, that is, to the computer and communications industries. The European and Japanese aerospace industries have their problems, but they are not the result of ownership by American multinational corporations. Thus far, American corporations own only about ten percent of the European aerospace industry. And the European and Japanese automobile corporations are at least as technologically advanced and economically viable as the American ones.

Other arguments have more general validity.

2. National governments increasingly will lose control over their domestic economic policies, that is, monetary, fiscal, and employment policies, as the American corporations alter the sources of credit, taxes, and jobs. The recent international monetary crises, accentuated by the rapid movement of liquid capital by multinational corporations, are only the most dramatic examples.

3. National governments occasionally will have their own foreign policies affected by restrictions the United States government imposes on American corporations abroad. The most obvious (and now rather trivial) example is the Trading with the Enemy Act.

4. In the case of the true multinational corporation within the European Economic Community, the corporation can shift its investment from country to country; the American multinational corporation may come to play off one European nation-state against another, as the American national corporation played off one American state against another a century ago. One likely casualty will be laws to protect the environment.

Further, there is developing a sort of new Internationale, centered in post-industrial America but including businessmen, managers, and technocrats from all the industrial nations. With it is developing a new ideology, and international co-optation is reinforced by a sort of international corporatism, which sees the great corporations as the legates of order and progress in an otherwise anarchic world. The present world order based on nation-states would gradually be replaced, some say, by a world order based in part on multinational corporations dominated by American corporations and in part on international organizations dominated by the United States government. We would see a neomedieval world order on a hypermodern economic base, a preindustrial polity on a postindustrial economy. Thus, great nation-states, like France or Germany, would dissolve once again into a confederation of corporations and communes, as Simca and Opel recapitulate medieval guilds, and Brittany and Bavaria revive. In turn, the local corporations would reunite into new and great multinational ones. And, loosely and remotely presiding over it all like a latter-day Holy Roman Emperor would be the President of the United States. Thus, in the end, it would be said of a modern nation-state what de Gaulle feared for France: "There would doubtless still be French workers, farmers, engineers, professors, officials, Deputies and Ministers. But there would no longer be France."[8]

If the presence of multinational corporations imposes such constraints or distortions on large, advanced industrial countries, then a fortiori it would seem to impose even greater constraints and distortions on small, underdeveloped ones. In addition, underdeveloped countries are prone to military coups while developed countries are not. Thus, in an underdeveloped country, multinational corporations can make alliances with military groups against national political leaders, much like the oil corporations did in Iran in 1953, United Fruit did in Guatemala in 1954, and ITT attempted to do in Chile in 1970. More commonly and less dramatically, in underdeveloped countries, more than in developed ones, multinational corporations can undertake the systematic corruption of national political leaders in order to get their way.

None of this, however, prevented the wave of successful expropriations and renegotiations that the underdeveloped countries imposed upon multinational corporations in extractive industries during the last six years. Indeed, the only case where the corporations were able to effect, or at least to enjoy, a restoration of the *ancien regime* was Chile in 1973. The oil producing states, especially, are hardly examples of "sovereignty at bay." Rather, we have, in the words of M.A. Adelman, "oil companies as OPEC tax collectors."[9]

Consequences for the Home Countries

Most analyses of multinational corporations have focused on their effects upon host countries. This results in the distorted view that the home country, usually the United States, is the happy beneficiary of a costless enterprise. But of the items listed on page 384, numbers 2 and 4 also apply in large measure to the United States. In addition, other arguments about the costs of multinational corporations have been put forward in recent years.

1. Foreign investment drains away capital from the home country that would otherwise be invented in new technologies and then in new industries.[10] Multinational corporations choose to produce the old commodity in new countries rather than new commodities in the old country. For the United States this means that nearly $100 billion was invested abroad rather than at home.[a] In effect American multinational corporations have placed a ceiling on the further technological advancement of the most technologically advanced country. To holders of this argument it is no accident that the United States has produced no major new industry since 1960, that the United States is having

---

[a]But some of this amount consists of profits from foreign operations that have been reinvested abroad.

a productivity crisis, and in turn that this has reinforced a general economic crises. As such, just as British portfolio investment abroad led Britain into an industrial "climacteric" and economic decline almost a century ago, so American direct investment abroad will lead the United States down a similar dismal path in the years to come.[11] (This argument is the converse of the first argument considered under the host countries).

2. Foreign investment drains away capital from the home country that would otherwise be invested in maintaining the old industries and thus in maintaining the base of industrial power. Multinational corporations are "runaway shops"; they export not industrial goods but industrial plants. In this sense multinational corporations accelerate the *post*industrialization of advanced industrial countries.

3. Relatedly, multinational corporations induce a shift in the structure of political forces in the home country; the balance of power between labor and capital shifts to the advantage of the latter.

4. Multinational corporations can become hostages for the foreign policy of the home country. The major examples have been the American and European oil corporations in the Arab states. There also have been less dramatic cases of a host country achieving something in negotiations with multinational corporations, which they could not achieve in direct negotiations with the home country. Canada, for example, got American corporations to recognize a 100-mile pollution-free zone along the coast, when the American government had refused to do so.[12]

The Future of the Multinational Corporation: Four Models

What are the prospects for the future in the relationship between multinational corporations and national states? Here we will consider four models, which in symbolic terms, might be called OPEC, ITT, ICC, and 1931.

OPEC

The original, even classical examples of multinational corporations were the oil corporations and more generally the corporations in extractive industries. Multinational corporations in extractive industries were associated with, and for some analysts seemed to be the cause of, enclave economies, underdeveloped societies, and dependent polities. Such corporations seemed to be the purest cases of multinational corporations as powerful and independent actors in international politics.

The events of the last few years in the international oil industry have demonstrated that this view needs considerable revision. The multinational oil corporations are still doing very well indeed economically; in 1974 most of them recorded exceptionally high profits. But with the massive changes in the structure of oil prices, taxes, and participation that began with the Teheran agreements of 1971,[13] with the oil embargo imposed upon the United States and the Netherlands after the Yom Kippur War of 1973 and the threat of other embargoes in the future, and with some $80 billion in oil revenues in 1974, oil-producing states are the reverse of cases of *dependencia*. As noted above, the oil-producing states are hardly examples of "sovereignty at bay"; rather the oil corporations have become "OPEC tax collectors." Oil corporations are not so much new actors in international politics but rather new *agents* for old states. And if there is still exploitation in the international oil industry, it is not the exploitation of the oil-producing countries by oil corporations, but rather the exploitation of the oil-consuming countries by them both.

Will the OPEC model be generalized to other extractive industries in the future? There are good reasons to think that the *cartel* aspects of OPEC, with the resulting high prices and effective embargoes, cannot be reproduced in other major extractive industries, such as copper and bauxite.[14] However, the *participation* aspects of OPEC, under which the oil-producing states in effect carry out the incremental nationalization of the oil corporations, already have been generalized to major investments in other extractive industries, including copper and bauxite. Such participation arrangements, now often written into the original contract for a new investment and termed "joint ventures" or "fade-out ventures," are a very likely model for future relations between multinational corporations and national states in extractive industries.

Most underdeveloped countries have reached the point where their governments can now acquire without major difficulty the managerial and technical skills needed to operate an extractive industry. The threat of nationalization is thus a real option. Some analysts, however, argue that the bargaining power of host-country governments is much less vis-à-vis manufacturing industries. This suggests another model, one at the opposite extreme from OPEC.

ITT

In years to come there may be cases when manufacturing corporations undertake dramatic and drastic acts to achieve their aims in a host country, perhaps carrying out a plan similar to that of ITT in Chile in 1970. ITT, in collaboration with the CIA, hoped to persuade other American multinational corporations to create, in the words of an ITT memorandum, "economic chaos," in the hope that "a swiftly deteriorating economy (bank runs, factory bankruptcies,

etc.) will touch off a wave of violence, resulting in a military coup."[15] The
ITT-CIA plan included these suggestions:

1.   Banks should not renew credits or should delay in doing so.
2.   Companies should drag their feet in sending money, in making deliveries, in
     shipping spare parts, etc.
3.   Savings and loans companies there are in trouble. If pressure were applied
     they would have to shut their doors, thereby creating stronger pressure.

     In fact, however, other American corporations in Chile thought the plan too
risky for their own interests, and they declined to participate. On October 7,
1970 W.R. Merriam, an ITT vice-president in charge of the corporation's Washington office, wrote to another ITT vice-president, "repeated calls to firms such
as GM, Ford, and banks in California and New York have drawn no offers of
help." Two days later Merriam wrote to John McCone, Director of the CIA from
1961 to 1965 and since then a director of ITT.

> Practically no progress has been made in trying to get American business
> to cooperate in some way so as to bring on economic chaos. GM and
> Ford, for example, say that they have too much inventory on hand in
> Chile to take any chance and that they keep hoping that everything will
> work out all right. Also, the Bank of America had agreed to close its
> doors in Santiago but each day keeps postponing the inevitable. Accord-
> ing to my source, we must continue to keep the pressure on business.

(The "source" to which Merriam referred was "our contact at the McLean
Agency," i.e., the CIA).
     Three years later, however, economic chaos similar to that contemplated in
the 1970 ITT-CIA plan did lead to the military coup that ousted the Allende
regime in September 1973.
     Since GM and Ford, anyway, saw their Chilean properties nationalized by
the Allende regime in 1971 and 1972, they may be less hesitant toward any
future challenge from a Marxist government in the future. And Popular Front
governments led by Marxist parties could well come to power in Portugal,
Spain, Italy, or Greece in the next few years. These countries have a large American presence in their manufacturing sector, they frequently have deficits in their
foreign trade, and they rely upon the frequent roll-over of short-term loans. As
such, they may well be vulnerable to the recapitulation of the Chilean model on
a grander scale.

ICC

A more benign model for manufacturing multinational corporations is also plausible, one that would be a recapitulation on a global scale of a traditional pattern within the United States. The states of the United States a century ago, like the nation-states of the world today, confronted constraints and pressures imposed by the "multistate corporations" of the day, the national corporations. The response, of course, was a series of interstate regulatory commissions, beginning with the Interstate Commerce Commission (ICC) in the 1880s. By analogy and even by analysis one might expect the creation in the next decade of a series of international regulatory commissions to regulate the multinational corporations.

These commissions could be established under the authority of international organizations composed of advanced industrial societies, most probably the European Community or the OECD. The international organizations, and the national governments behind them, could give the new international regulatory commissions the power to issue operating licenses and to assign taxes during times of normal economic activity and to recommend subsidies and to guarantee loans in times of corporate distress. This combination of carrots and an occasional stick could be used to enforce regulations dealing with such matters as standardization of transfer-pricing practices, the true multinationalization of corporate management, the harmonization of corporate plans for worker participation (e.g., co-management) and for worker benefits (e.g., pension plans), and the preservation of the quality of the environment. One could imagine such diverse agencies as an International Communications Commission, an International Energy Commission, an International Pharmaceuticals Commission, an International Securities and Exchange Commission, and a North Atlantic Aviation Administration.

Of course, continuing the analogy one might also expect that not long after the establishment of these agencies close ties would develop between the executives of the multinational corporations and the executives of the international commissions, probably even an interchange of personnel, of "in-and-outers," and once again but now on a global scale "the regulators would be captured by the regulated." But "the symbolic politics of (international) regulation" and "the folklore of (international) capitalism" (to amend phrases about American regulation written long ago by Murray Edelman and Thurmond Arnold) would persuade the mass publics of the advanced industrial countries that their interests were being safeguarded. The new international regulatory commissions would thus dull the edge of any neo-Populist or neo-Progressive movement that would otherwise be directed against those great trusts of our own time, the multinational corporations.

1931

Finally, we can consider what would be the darkest future of all. The quadrupling of oil prices since 1973 has led to the massive transfer of funds from the advanced industrial societies to the oil-producing states, a transfer that may soon reach the rate of $100 billion per year. This rapid and massive disruption of the normal patterns of international trade and finance can in large measure be traced to the supine concessions (which could have been called appeasement or even un-American activities in an earlier day) made by the multinational oil corporations to the OPEC states in 1971-72. And this disruption of international trade and finance could result in the failure of major European banks or the depression of major American, European, and Japanese industries. This in turn could result in a general world economic crisis reminiscent of "the terrible year" of 1931, which saw the famous collapse of the Credit-Anstalt, the driving of Britain off the gold standard, and massive unemployment throughout the industrial world.[16] In the ensuing Great Depression the world stock of foreign direct investment was reduced, and nations turned inward from global economic horizons to regional economic blocks. Finally, the incompetence of the transnational economic organizations of the 1920s, such as the great banks of London and New York, led to the insurgence of the transnational political organizations of the 1930s, such as Nazi, Fascist, and Communist parties.

Is 1931, then, the most likely model for the future of those transnational economic organizations of our own time, the multinational corporations? Probably it is not. But if the multinational corporations and the rest of us should escape such a fate, it will not be because of the role played by that largest complex of multinational corporations in the world, "the heavenly seven" composed of the seven major oil corporations. It will rather be in spite of it.

Future Research by Political Scientists

Given the interests of the citizens of the advanced industrial societies, the best outcome of the four that we have considered would be the ICC model, in spite of its obvious limitations. And within the ICC model there are a variety of potential outcomes, some most favorable to the national state and some most favorable to the multinational corporation. As the American experience with interstate regulatory commissions demonstrates, the distribution of benefits and burdens between state and corporation can vary from one commission to another and, within any one commission, can vary over time.

This suggests a modest role for some political scientists in their future research. One focus of research could be on the issue of regulation. What conditions encourage effective regulation of private corporations by national states? Here, comparisons of the history of different industries within the United States and comparisons between the United States and the West European states would be useful.[17] A second focus of research could be on the issue of harmonization. What conditions encourage effective harmonization of public policies between national states? A fine example of this type of inquiry is a recent paper by Donald Puchala.[18]

The topics of regulation and harmonization, when combined, could suggest new ways of undertaking the international regulation of multinational corporations, and they could suggest the best mixes or least evils among these ways. The end result would be yet another parade of alphabetical agencies, some of them inept and some of them corrupt. But some of them would work to serve the interests of a more general public. And for the next decade or so, that is probably the best that we can get.

Notes

1. Robert O. Keohane and Joseph S. Nye, Jr., eds., *Transnational Relations and World Politics* (Cambridge, Mass: Harvard University Press, 1972); Samuel P. Huntington, "Transnational Organizations and World Politics," *World Politics*, April 1973, pp. 333-68.
2. Harry Magdoff, *The Age of Imperialism* (New York: Monthly Review, 1969); Andre Gunder Frank, *Capitalism and Underdevelopment in Latin America* (New York: Monthly Review, 1967) and *Latin America: Underdevelopment and Revolution* (New York: Monthly Review, 1969). Also see articles in K.T. Fann and Donald C. Hodges, eds., *Readings in U.S. Imperialism* (Boston: Porter Sargent, 1971).
3. Robert W. Tucker, *The Radical Left and American Foreign Policy* (Baltimore: The Johns Hopkins Press, 1971); Benjamin J. Cohen, *The Question of Imperialism* (New York: Basic Books, 1973).
4. United Nations, Department of Economic and Social Affairs, *Multinational Corporations in World Development* (New York: United Nations, 1973), p. 159.
5. Thomas E. Weisskopf, "United States Foreign Private Investment: An Empirical Survey," in Richard C. Edwards, Michael Reich, and Thomas E. Weisskopf, eds., *The Capitalist System* (Englewood Cliffs, N.J.: Prentice-Hall, 1972), p. 431.
6. In a forthcoming book, Robert Gilpin, *U.S. Power and the Multinational Enterprise: The Political Economy of Direct Foreign Investment* (New York: Basic Books, 1975).
7. Raymond Vernon, *Sovereignty at Bay: The Multinational Spread of U.S. Enterprises* (New York: Basic Books, 1971).
8. Roy C. Macridis, ed., *DeGaulle: Implacable Ally* (New York: Harper and Row, 1966), p. 240.
9. See his article, M.A. Adelman, "Is the Oil Shortage Real? Oil Companies as OPEC Tax Collectors," *Foreign Policy*, Winter 1972-73, pp. 69-107.
10. This argument is made systematically by Gilpin, *U.S. Power.*

11. See, in this connection, Charles Kindleberger, "An American Climacteric ?" *Challenge* (January–February 1974), pp. 35–44.

12. Robert O. Keohane and Joseph S. Nye, "World Politics and the International Economic System," in C. Fred Bergsten, ed., *The Future of the International Economic Order: An Agenda for Research*, (Lexington, Mass.: D.C. Heath, 1973), p. 144.

13. On the crucial events of 1971 see M.A. Adelman, "Is the Oil Shortage Real?"

14. See the exchange presented in Stephen D. Krasner, "Oil is the Exception," and C. Fred Bergsten, "The Threat Is Real," *Foreign Policy*, Spring 1974, pp. 68–90.

15. This and the following quotes can be found in: U.S. Congress, Senate, Committee on Foreign Relations, *Multinational Corporations and United States Foreign Policy, Hearings on the International Telephone and Telegraph Company and Chile, 1970–71* (Washington, D.C.: U.S. Government Printing Office, March, April, 1973).

16. For a good account of the last world economic crisis, see Charles P. Kindleberger, *The World in Depression, 1929–1939* (Berkeley: University of California Press, 1973).

17. A beginning in this direction is made by the contributors (only two of them political scientists) in Raymond Vernon, ed., *Big Business and the State: Changing Relations in Western Europe* (Cambridge: Harvard University Press, 1974).

18. Donald J. Puchala, "Domestic Politics and Regional Harmonization in the European Communities," paper presented to the 1974 Convention of the American Political Science Association, September 1974.

16 Dominant States and Vulnerable Societies: The East-West Case

Pierre Hassner

To link or not to link, that is the question.

This chapter deals with a series of links made possible or necessary by a series of gaps. Increasingly, international relations in general and, more particularly, East-West relations that will serve as our main example, are characterized by the incoherence, the contradiction, or at least the lack of coincidence between their various dimensions. Ultimately, these contradictions are best seen in terms of Karl Deutsch's definition of international relations as "the gap between interdependence and control," and of Edward Morse's repeated observation that the movement of modernization increases this gap as the growth in interdependence tends to diminish the ability of governments to control either their domestic or their international environment.[1] In philosophical and historical terms this gap can be seen in terms of the crisis of the nation-state, itself an inevitable consequence of the dialectical separation between state and society that is implicit in the emergence of modern economy and culture. The split between *society*, characterized as a network of groups, activities and relations preoccupied with private life, work and exchange, and the *state*, as a legitimizing symbol, a group of individuals, and a set of institutions, preoccupied with the authoritative integration, organization and direction of the whole, was seen by Rousseau as well as by Hegel as the central problem of modernity. To the extent that the extreme anarcho-liberal solution (of complete absorption of the state by society) and the extreme totalitarian solution (of complete domination of society by the state) are impossible, all modern regimes are dominated in different forms by the dialectic of state and society, of the public and the private. As Zbigniew Brzezinski and Samuel Huntington point out, ideological regimes like the Communist ones start with the primacy of the state but discover the increasing pressures of society that are then seen as threats to the authority of the state as well as to the efficiency of its methods like central planning. Instrumental regimes like Western capitalist ones start with the primacy of society, but increasingly experience a growth in the social and economic role of the state.[2] Here again, this provokes a crisis—both of efficiency and of legitimacy; the state encounters the resistance of what Jürgen Habermas calls "civil privatism"; in trying to contain social conflicts and to mitigate the strains of the economic system it has no reserve of participation and citizenship to draw upon: "Missing legitimations have to be replaced by social rewards such as money, time and security." If the state fails to deliver on these, it may try to "make up for legitimation deficits by means of well aimed manipulation" but the limit to "ideology planning" for an instrumental system is "the structural dissimilarity between areas of administrative action and cultural tradition."[3]

It becomes clear, then, that the crisis, experienced in different ways by authoritarian systems and command economies challenged by demands for individual initiative and satisfaction, and by instrumental systems and liberal economies challenged by the need for state intervention and authority, is both exacerbated and internationalized by the crisis of the nation-state as such. It lies in the increasing gap, discrepancy, or "structural distance" between the dimensions and levels required for fulfilling its various functions. The nation-state does not seem on the verge of collapse. However, as a solution for the gap between state and society, its original conception was of a tight and self-contained unity between authority, community, loyalty, culture, language, defense and, if possible, economy. This is being challenged today by the fact that both the optimal dimensions of units and the scope of the subjective feeling of solidarity or community seem to vary if one looks at the military, at the economic, the political, or the ideological or cultural aspects. Nor is this limited to nation-states as such; under the impact of technology, mass communications, and cultural diffusion, a common fate may encompass provinces, states, regional, and ideological blocs or alliances; that of being powerless here and sovereign there, of overlapping with their rivals and being challenged by their components. This makes for divided loyalties, cross-cutting cleavages, limited sovereignties. And, as I argued in 1967,

> just as with the multiplicity of roles and hierarchies for the individual in a differentiated modern society, this multi-dimensionality, if it is kept within tolerable limits, makes for healthy pluralism and for the relativization of inequalities and conflicts; if the degree of distance is too great, if between the various levels or roles there is not only potential tension but flat opposition, it makes for neurosis, paralysis and disintegration.[4]

Again, both the degree of flexibility of the respective organizations and the degree of linkage between the various dimensions of their mutual relations are essentially relevant to the result.

The problem can be seen at a global level as that of the relations between the interstate system and transnational society and, at the regional level, as that of the relations between the bipolar alliance structure and the evolution of European societies.

The French philosopher Eric Weil, who puts the dialectics of state and society at the center of his system, points out that modern society, being essentially based on technology, is essentially, or potentially, one (even though

ridden with inequalities and frustrations) whereas the states, being essentially
based on authority and legitimacy, are essentially several.[5] Hence, the struggle
of the states to maintain their respective and rival sovereignties in the face of
the pressures and the penetration of the transnational forces of modern technology and contagious social aspirations is the manifestation at the international
level of the dialectical struggle between identity and communication. But the
very forces that challenge the sovereignty of states are, at the same time, being
used by them, albeit in an indirect and uncertain way, in their stuggle against
each other. The classical definition of the modern state as holding the monopoly of the legitimate use of violence, and of international relations as the state
of potential war, are being challenged by the developments of technology (from
nuclear weapons to the vulnerability of modern societies to transnational
terrorism) and of social values (more and more hostile, in the developed world,
to organized violence between states). The state has more and more trouble
keeping its monopoly of force internally and using it effectively externally.[6]
Domestic politics look increasingly like international politics and vice versa;
but in both cases the absence of a consensus on legitimacy combined with the
difficulty in the use of the ultimate sanction of war or revolution make for
the perpetuation of a kind of diffuse anarchy or immobile agitation where shifts
of power are made mainly in a kind of indirect and tentative way rather than
through confrontation—hence the importance of indirect influence, of comparative vulnerabilities, of the manipulation of this very interdependence that
challenges sovereignty and limits the use of force.

Regionally, the problem of Europe has been characterized by a Yugoslav
statesman in terms of the clash between the requirements of scientific progress
and of productive forces and the structure of blocs and societies.[7] Alliances
as well as nation-states are challenged by the aspirations of their members both
to more autonomy and to a greater opening towards the outside world. This,
then, conflicts with the political military structure of the continent, whose
stability is based precisely on the division between nation-states and between
blocs or alliances. Again, the problem is more easily accommodated in the
West and suppressed in the East, but everywhere the coexistence of contradictory structures of communication, conflict, and cooperation (for instance between the economic and the military dimension) does raise the problem of
linkage.

When J. Rosenau first introduced the notion of linkage in 1966 he meant
it as an instrument for dealing with the mutual influence of domestic and
international systems, of distinct domestic societies, and of distinct issue areas
upon each other, in function of various domestic and international environments.
Since then, as he himself acknowledges, the concept of linkage has fallen out of
fashion.[8] He lists alternative attempts at promoting central concepts for theorizing across systems, some of which, like adaptation, integration, interdependence,
or, one might add, transnational politics, have inspired more discussion and

research than that of linkage. But meanwhile the term has sprung up in practical discussions stemming from debates on arms control and negotiating strategies for SALT. Could the nuclear balance and the dialogue leading to its stabilization be separated from the whole of Soviet-American relations or, the causes of the arms race being political and economic as much as strategic, did the dialogue aiming at its limitation and at prevention of nuclear war have to include the whole spectrum of conflicts between the two superpowers, or even within them, between their respective opposing bureaucratic and social forces?

In another form the problem of linkage came to the fore in the relations between the United States and its allies. There, the linkage under discussion was between, on the one hand, the security provided by American troops and, on the other hand, the political solidarity and economic concessions demanded in return.

For a long time the tacit rule of the Atlantic Alliance had been not to operate any explicit linkage, not to mix various problems and various negotiations, but this rule relied on the implicit awareness that there was, in fact, an essential compatibility between the various dimensions that made more superficial divergences tolerable. During the "year of Europe" controversy this tacit understanding that European states would have liked to perpetuate was challenged both by France advocating a complete separation of the various dimensions, and by the United States seeking to link them in a more direct and often explicit and detailed fashion.[9]

But the most spectacular, and at the same time the most difficult and challenging, area in which the problem of direct or indirect linkage between different issues has become a political reality is, of course, East-West relations. The classical example is the Jackson amendment, which links the two ostensibly unrelated areas of trade (more specifically and initially the granting of most-favored-nation treatment) and emigration (more specifically that of Jews from the Soviet Union). In Europe Brandt's *Ostpolitik* involved a certain trade-off, both in terms of immediate bargain and of long-range hopes, between the recognition of Germany's division and a certain easing of its human consequences, as well as between economic advantages for the Soviet Union and an improvement in the security of West Berlin. The Conference of Security and Co-operation in Europe has found its main theme in the West European attempt to establish a link between the recognition of borders (basket I) and an increase in their permeability (basket III). The problem seems to gain both in complexity and in sharpness as we approach a given type of relationship and a given period, namely relations between Western and Communist societies, especially European ones, at a time of detente when ideological, social, and human differences between regimes are both challenged and confirmed by the common interest of these same regimes in entering new strategic, economic, and political relationships.

East-West relations in the developed world—relations between the United States, the Soviet Union, Western Europe, and Eastern Europe—provide a particularly favorable case for studying the increasingly contradictory character of multilateral relations between and across societies and states, alliances and organizations. They should be helpful in bringing back into theory the complexities of the real world. The literature on interdependence or on integration, for instance, has focused mainly either on the horizontal dimension of relations within the capitalist industrialized world or on the vertical dimension of structural dependence between this world and the underdeveloped one. It has not been sufficiently sensitive to what may be called transverse or diagonal relations, which combine features of both similarity and contradiction, reciprocity and inequality, interdependence and multipolarity. These are characteristic of international relations as a whole, but more so in the area where the potentially universal influences of Western society and of Communist organization meet, within the limiting framework of the bipolar nuclear balance and of the resilient multiplicity of nation states.

In the present phase of international relations, within alliances and between them, between East and West, between North and South, between states and societies, we witness a double and contradictory phenomenon. On the one hand, issue areas, dimensions, or levels of reality that hitherto were or seemed to be fused or converging or at least compatible, appear to undergo a growing differentiation and divergence. On the other hand, those same aspects that were either limited or separated, indistinguishable or isolated, seem to be increasingly overlapping and influencing each other.

Both within the hierarchy of power and within relations between units, aspects that traditionally went together—defense and offense, deterrence and influence, military and economic strength, domestic control and external influence, potential war (or implicit threat of war), systems and psychological hostility are increasingly separated, thus leading to paradoxical or ambiguous mixed-motive situations. The separation of the traditionally inseparable leads to the coexistence of the normally incompatible; for instance, economic and technological cooperation between the same superpowers who pursue an arms race with each other or the combination of peaceful coexistence and ideological struggle, of diplomatic detente and domestic hardening. But at the same time the internal evolution of alliances and nations is influencing their external relations more than before.

The same is true of the indirect and mutual influence of relations between societies and between states. Emancipated dimensions no longer can be fitted into neat compartments. Precisely because the international world can no longer be seen under the aspect of two united and mutually hostile blocs, precisely because the coexistence of contradictory relations according to issues and to actors is increasingly obvious and important, the relations between these different dimensions raise questions that are both more complex and more specific.

Politically, the choice is between a globalizing strategy, which tries to link the various contradictory dimensions by balancing them against each other and making them the elements of an implicit or explicit deal where conflicts arising on certain levels are solved thanks to the common interests that persist on others; and a "decoupling" strategy, which tries to separate problems as much as possible and to treat each issue on its own merits in order to prevent, so to speak, the bones of contention from poisoning the areas of agreement.

Theoretically, the first question to ask is whether the dualistic thinking, relying on the confrontation of symmetrically opposed ideal types or models, which has characterized much of the discipline of international realtions, is not counterproductive: the dichotomies of domestic and international politics, of the civil state and the state of nature (or of war), of economics and politics, of low politics and high politics, of cooperation and conflict, of transactions and interactions, of communications and power, of interdependence and inequality, of horizontal and vertical relations, etc., which pervade the literature from Raymond Aron to Johan Galtung, are all legitimate but may all be dangerous if they encourage the illusion that they necessarily either coincide or converge or that the two opposite terms of each dichotomy and the various dichotomies themselves can be kept separate. As Manfred Halpern put it, "We live in an age marked in every society in the world by the continuous breaking of connections, leading to permanent incoherence in all systems by which man has organized his life." This "incoherent, revolutionary change"[10] can be grasped only by a more flexible sociological approach, ready to pay as much attention to mixed forms as to pure ones and to their dialectical contradictions and mutual transformations as to their static juxtaposition.

Along these lines, the present writer has suggested, following the lead of T. Schelling's theory of "incomplete antagonism and imperfect partnership," the need for a theory of what Rousseau called the mixed state, that is, "a theory of the incomplete state of nature and imperfect civil state, of incomplete war and imperfect peace," based precisely on the international consequences of the contradictions between state and society.[11] Similarly, discussions on power and interdependence should lead to a theory of "incomplete domination and imperfect reciprocity."[12] The point is not simply that we live in a world of ambiguity and compromise but that we live in a world of overlapping and contradictory structures and processes, that the processes transform the structures, that even when old structures do not disintegrate or amalgamate, their internal content and their external relations may change to such an extent that they are ultimately affected or superceded by new ones.

A sociology in the tradition of G. Simmel, continued in the United States by Lewis Coser, T. Caplow, and P. Blau, provides perhaps the best conceptualization of the process of *de* and *re* structuralization. Along the lines of P. Blau recent research has shown the mutual relations and transformations of exchange and of power, the element of power in exchange relationships, and the element of exchange in the definition of power. Similarly, the "dialogue of the deaf" between the three prevailing schools in international relations, the classical interstate approach, the liberal-functionalist and the neo-Marxist one, could fruitfully be replaced by focusing on the dialectical relations between *multi-polarity* (the starting point of "international anarchy" or of the classical paradigm), *interdependence* (emphasized by the modernization, communication, and transnational paradigm), and *inequality* (the strong point of the Marxist and "dependencia" schools): The multipolar conflict of states is limited and transformed by the interdependence of societies; but this interdependence, far from being harmonious and symmetrical, is itself the product and the cause of inequalities within and between societies. However, these inequalities are not likely to polarize into one permanent and structural hierarchy; more likely, they give rise to new, changing, and contradictory relations and centers of power. The nature of the relations and of the centers of power, hence the identity of the units and the definition of power and interdependence, are themselves changed in the process that is thus both cyclical and creative. The key lies in the multidimensional character of international relations, their dynamics being provided by the complex—partly complementary, partly con-tradictory—relation between these dimensions themselves.

The discussion on high and low politics, the discussion on the interstate and the transnational paradigms, the discussion on conflict and cooperation, the discussion on power, and the discussion on interdependence, all lead away from dogmatic assertions of static identity, separation or priority, and toward the empirical study of dynamic relations whose structure is mutual but asymmetrical, or multilateral but differentiated, in influence, and whose nature goes from influence through transformation to conversion.

The same goes for the two dichotomies implied in the title of this chapter. Associating the state with domination and society with vulnerability, in par-ticular at the international level, does point to an important contemporary trend in the influence of social and economic evolution upon the exercise of political and military power. Another aspect of the same trend could be indicated by an opposition between the independence of states and the inter-dependence of societies. But it is obviously true that states or political institu-tions have their own vulnerability and societies contain their own structures of domination, just as increasingly independent pressures from social forces can lead to increasingly interdependent reactions of states, for instance, joint action against (or competitive or mutually hostile exploitation of) ethnic rebellions or transnational terrorist groups. Our focus upon the international aspects and implications of the relation between state and society (rather than domestic and international politics) and between dominance and vulnerability (rather than between power and interdependence) has precisely the purpose of show-ing the dialectical character of these relationships: the loss of control and the reassertion—possibly autarchic or regressive—of states confronted with the forces of multinational corporations or of social communication; domination as both a cause of and a reaction to vulnerability; or domination over one actor, area or issue leading to vulnerability towards another, and conversely. For instance, American influence over Israel as perceived by the Arabs leads to West European vulnerability to oil embargos by the Arabs and to increased East European vulnerability to Soviet pressures.

The two associated notions of *indirect influence* and of *comparative vulnerability* seem to be increasingly recognized as a useful point of convergence between the discussions on *power* (part I) and the discussions on *interdependence* (part II). Our contention is that partly for this reason and partly because of the specific characteristics of East-West relations in Europe, they should also be increasingly recognized as the most useful guiding thread for the study of these relations (part III). Finally, the key to the differing vulnerabilities between East and West (particularly their different degrees of vulnerability to the indirect influence of each other) may well be in the differing relationships between state and society in the two types of regions, reflected both in the respective structures of the two alliances, the two economic organizations, etc., and in the structure of the relations between them (part IV).

Power, Influence, Interpenetration

The discussion of power carried on in the early sixties leads from direct coercion to indirect influence, or from military coercion through diplomatic influence to social control, that is, to structural domination, not only or necessarily over a given relationship or, more generally still, over the dominating actor himself and his more general relation with his environment—hence to the management of interdependence understood as comparative vulnerability.

The sociological and behavioral discussion of power started by being centered on the direct interaction of wills. This permitted the identification of power as a relationship (rather than as a possession or a substance) as in the most widely quoted definition of power, by R. Dahl: "A has power over B to the extent that he can get B to do something that B would not otherwise do."[13] But from there attention has gone to the structures that may lie beneath or beyond the clash of conscious wills or the interdependence of calculated decisions, to the framework that may permit, prevent, or absorb them. On the one hand, there is the power of brute force—hence the distinction proposed by J.D. Singer between "fate control and behavior control."[14] At the other extreme the perception of the convergence or divergence of interests can be such that the problem of preferences and calculations does not even arise. An optimistic interpretation will, then, deny the presence of a power or conflict situation, since both sides are satisfied; a critical one will say that it is this situation itself that is manipulated by the dominating side so that the question does not even arise for the dominated. The manipulation may be conscious and identifiable, or the observer may judge that the more powerful side is itself alienated and believes it is associated with the powerless one in a functional relationship based on dependence upon objective realities, whereas, again in the eyes of the beholder, this impersonal dependence and these objective constraints are in fact hiding a relationship of domination.[15] One enters, then, into the area where the clash of global, historical, or ideological interpretations takes over from that of positive observations. What the latter can register is the interaction of wills; but this interaction, in turn, receives its full meaning from its insertion into a broader context whose interpretation calls for other analytical tools.

Increasingly, the key to this broader context seems to lie in the notion of a mutual interdependence network that is at the same time a network of power.[16] Never quite unilateral nor quite symmetrical, it is largely determined by the respective situations and motivations of the two partners. These, usually unequal, are the product of present comparative scarcities but also of past coercion. The question, then, becomes: Who determines, to use Michel Crozier's expression, the terms of trade in a given relation[17] or, in the terms of R. Keohane and J. Nye, who defines the *ceteris paribus* clause "the structure of the payoff matrix."[18]

Johann Galtung identifies the notion of "structural power" or "power that derives from position in a structure" and of "relation power," as opposed to "resource power" or "difference power."[19] Both for structural and for resource power, however, there is no simple identification between inequality, the potential domination it implies, and the effective domination that sometimes results from it and that alone coincides with power as a relationship in the classical sense defined by Dahl. Precisely, Dahl among many others, has called attention to the "influence gap," to the fact that potential power (in Klaus Knorr's terminology, putative power) is not mobilized power (or in Knorr's terms, actualized power).[20] It is wrong, then, to identify inequality necessarily with domination or exploitation. But, of course, this useful qualification must itself be qualified by two other notions—that of *prestige* as credit, or influence capital, which permits the exercise of influence without necessarily mobilizing its potential bases, and that of *anticipated reaction*: Often domination is exercised without the awareness or even against the interests of the dominator, simply because the potentially dominated anticipate (sometimes wrongly) his reaction or his tolerance level. Finally, the passage from resources to domination, or from potential influence to effective influence, implies an *opportunity cost*, in relation either to prestige or to other forms of actualized power. The same goes for resistance that in a certain sense, is less natural than domination or submission. When domination is implicitly or potentially present in a structure defined as functional or as corresponding to the common interest, opposition to it implies a mobilization of power, a polarization of conflicts, the acceptance of risks, the refusal of the advantages of the existing order. Violence has a negative productivity superior to its positive productivity; its distinctive potential, if actualized, implies a cost that must be converted into other forms of power (e.g., through legitimization) if it is going to be converted into positive authority.[21]

The discussion seems, then, to lead to a fairly complete picture of the elements that enter the relationship of domination. Following John C. Harsany, it can be defined by the costs and the risks that the two parties are respectively ready to accept in order to secure the transformation of a given volume of resources into social power according to the various dimensions of the latter (types of action used, types of action obtained, degree of increase in their probability, range of positive or negative reactions, number of concerned individuals or units).[22]

Through the intervention of opportunity costs, the third party and the social and natural environment are introduced at the very heart of the bilateral power relationship. This appears even more clearly if, following Karl Deutsch, one generalizes the idea of a cost-power ratio to the relations of a society with its global environment, through a distinction between gross and net power.

> A concept of net power might define it as a difference—the difference between the amounts of change accepted by the actor. The changes imposed are those imposed by the actor upon his environment including changes imposed on relevant antagonists. The changes accepted are those accepted in the values and in the communications and action systems of the actor.[23]

These can be measured in terms of resources, of attention, of time, and ultimately of steering one's own actions and of mastering one's own fate.

From power as strength or force, through power as coercion or influence, one arrives at power defined in terms of social control, of ability to adapt to evolution and to modify it, this evolution being both domestic and external. This is where the importance of indirect influence appears, particularly at the time of stalemate in the international system and of transnational politics. John Burton has given a central role to the existence of objectives whose realization presupposes or brings about a modification of the environment[24] that leads to a dialectic of expansion and conflict, both domestic and external. Other conceptual tools for analyzing the same reality are the notion of externalities, borrowed from economics, or that used by N. North and N. Choucri, of *lateral pressure*.[25]

From the relation of domination among actors we are led to the interpenetration of societies. Their respective vulnerability to mutual penetration appears clearly linked to the relations of state and society within each of them. Social penetration and political domination can be associated or separated; social, cultural, and economic impact can be translated or not into political influence.

A regime whose stability relies essentially on coercive and ideological control by the state will feel more vulnerable to social and cultural penetration than a pluralistic one, accustomed to a more flexible interplay of various forces originating in society. On the other hand it will be less vulnerable to the usurpation of crucial economic decisions by foreign, national, or multinational powers.

The discussion around the notion of a penetrated system is a case in point. J. Rosenau, who introduced it, defines it as a system

> where non-members of national society participate, directly and authoritatively through actions undertaken in common with the members of the society, either to the allocation of its values or to the mobilization of support for its objectives.[26]

W. Hanrieder has tried to generalize the notion by pointing out that all political systems are penetrated because of social interdependence, of communications, of military penetrability[27], etc. Conversely, a Rumanian theorist asserts that

> it is the will to domination and interference of great powers which makes a national system more and more penetrated, not the development of modern military technology or of economic and psychological pressures.[28]

In fact, the problem is precisely that of the relation between social interpenetration and political domination. Penetrated systems are those that are not only submitted to transnational social constraints or to external influence, but those which lose some of the essential attributes of governmental authority that continue to be exercised but, in part at least, by another power. The indubitable fact that modern conditions deprive some of these attributes and, to a great extent, the notion of sovereignty itself, of much of their meaning, leaves open the question whether what is lost goes to the domination of an external power or to the reciprocal interpenetration and integration or comparable units leading to the creating of a new unit or of a functional network. Since some inequality is present even in the latter case, however, the empirical question becomes: When and to what extent does interdependence make it easier to manipulate and control other societies, through penetration, leverage,[29] or linkage, or does it produce a generalized loss of control and new forms of objective limits to the ability of states to dominate societies whether foreign ones or their own?[30]

This is precisely the point where the various debates that have taken place in the early seventies over the notions of interdependence and dependence may converge with each other and with the discussion on power.

Interdependence, Dependencia, Asymmetrical Interdependence

Until recently two parallel discussions seem to have run their course in full ignorance of each other. The first was a discussion that, using J. Galtung's terminology, one could call horizontal: It was dealing with economic interdependence in general, particularly among industrial nations, without really raising the issue of inequality or asymmetry. It opposed, mainly in the United States, a majority of authors like Richard Cooper, Edward Morse, Oran Young, for whom interdependence was perceived as being on the increase, as transforming the nature of international relations by reducing the freedom of action and the control of states, and, precisely for this reason, as making coordination among them more necessary; and a minority, represented above all by Karl Deutsch and Kenneth Waltz, for whom interdependence had decreased in favor of the possibility of, and propensity towards, withdrawal and self-closure of nation-states.

It seems that a synthesis has been emerging both on the conceptual and on the empirical level. It consists in pointing out that the two sides use different definitions of interdependence. The first group understands it as *sensitivity* (characterized by the intensity of relations or the impossibility of escaping the direct or indirect influence of external events). The second defines it as *vulnerability* (characterized by the "costs of autarchy" or the common interest in maintaining the relationship). The first is concerned with processes, the second with structures. One can exist without the other (in particular, the first may grow while the second diminishes). The empirical task is precisely to study their mutual influence.[31] The second debate can be called vertical since, against the optimist vision of liberal economics and of functionalist sociology, it puts forth an asymmetrical model based on the structural dependence—of the periphery on the center, of underdeveloped countries on developed ones (or rather on capitalism, the role and the function of socialist industrialized countries, especially of the Soviet Union, never being very clear), of raw material producers and multinational corporations. This model, often called by the name of *dependencia*[32] because of its Latin American origin, has been generalized, in particular by Samir Amin[33] at the economic level and by Johan Galtung,[34] in an attempt at a more formalized and multidimensional theory.

Here the evolution has come less from theoretical discussion, which has almost always been characterized by the unending repetition and universal application of the same scheme, than from events, particularly the energy crisis, which have spectacularly demonstrated its static and unilateral character: It is now plain for everyone that the periphery may sometimes unite and the center become divided, that what is center to some may be periphery to others, that the dependence of industrial countries on primary products producers may be more stringent than the converse. As the French economist, B. Lassudrie-Duchêne put it,

> the evolution of scarcity lines is shifting the corresponding rents and today's losers may see their relative situation reversed in the future. The most difficult question of international economics may be how to compensate inequalities which are both inevitable and changing, rather than aggrevating them.[35]

Once one recognizes that these inequalities, both inevitable and changing, may be either cumulative or balanced, one recognizes that they are at the crossroads of objective constraints and of their manipulation, of economics and politics. One is on the verge of a political economy of international relations that, it seems to me, must start from the rediscovery of power at the heart of exchange, of exchange at the heart of power[36] and lead to the unveiling and the study of the relations between different forms of dependence and different forms of power that are at the heart of international life. Whether one starts from economics or from politics, a consensus seems to emerge for defining it more and more as the management and manipulation of interdependence.

The idea of unequal or asymmetrical interdependence, the notion that unilateral dependence and equal and reciprocal interdependence are both the exception is rediscovered today, both in economics and in politics, but, even more, in the study of their combinations. A remarkable book by Albert Hirschman had, in 1945, already pointed out the references to be found among the classics and developed a typology of asymmetrical relations between large and small or weak trading countries, between liberal and centralized economies, between direct economic effects on trade (the *supply effect*) and political effects (the *influence effect*).[37] In their search for a political economy political scientists today turn their attention to those doctrines that, more than liberalism and Marxism, attach a decisive importance to political factors, like the work of Francois Perroux with the concepts of "effet de domination" and "emprise de structure," or of ultra-Keynesians like J. Knapp, with his theoretical justification of neomercantilism,[38] and H.O. Schmitt with his analysis of the cumulative attractions of core areas over peripheries.[39]

At the level of international relations theory, the link between the notion of the exchange rate between different forms of power and that of unequal asymmetric interdependence has been developed in a very systematic and satisfactory fashion by R. Keohane and J. Nye in their chapter (see note 18) of the Bergsten study. Through a series of successive definitions (e.g., of power as deriving from patterns of asymmetrical interdependence), distinctions and subdivisions (between the societal level and policy level of interdependence, between intensity of relations and relative power resources, between sensitivity interdependence and vulnerability interdependence), they finally reach a scheme which tries to integrate military power (defined in terms of military vulnerability or differing costs of conflict) economic power based on vulnerability-interdependence (or differing opportunity costs of system disruption) and economic power based on sensitivity-interdependence (or different sensitivities to system-processes). They try to rank them in terms of effectiveness, of costs, and of areas of contemporary applicability. This scheme, trying to integrate military power, economic power based on "vulnerability—interdependence" and economic power based on "sensitivity — interdependence", provides a common ground not only between the two definitions of interdependence, not only between the two discussions on horizontal interdependence and on vertical dependence, but

also between the two dominant worlds of international relations, that of
diplomatic-strategic action and that of social and economic forces and structures.
This leads the authors quite naturally not only to an important reinterpretation
of the imbalance of power in concert but also to provide the most satisfactory
theoretical interpretation of the political problem of linkage with which we
started this chapter.

East-West Relations: Cooperation and Dependence

We are back to the Jackson amendment. Unfortunately, the dominant
analyses of the links between the economic and political aspects of East-West
relations seem, at least in the West, to be inspired by the spirit of "terrible
simplifiers" who neglect the complexity of asymmetrical interdependence in
favor of either an optimistic and interested belief in the harmony of interests, or
of a pessimistic—whether fatalistic of activist—belief in the inevitability of conflict.

At one extreme, one finds Samuel Pisar, for whom economic cooperation
between the two systems under the leadership of multinational corporations is
the key to every problem, including those of the Third World, which is to expect
joint and "transideological" East-West investments. He never raises the problem
of unequal benefits or of asymmetrical dependence between one side and
another, between liberal economies and centralized societies, between economic
or political great powers and small states. Nor does it occur to him that the
Third World or the smaller countries of Eastern Europe might be submitted to
a co-exploitation that, for all its "transideological" character, may nevertheless
increase their dependence.[40]

At the other extreme one finds a more mixed bag of even stranger bed-
fellows than Occidental Petroleum or Pepsi-Cola and the Soviet government. A
first group is that of the Western cold warriors. They oscillate between two
extreme versions, the first pessimistic or defensive version that trade with the
East, and, even more, industrial coorperation with the Soviet Union, may make
the West dependent upon the latter, in particular for energy resources, and that
pluralist societies may always get a bad bargain (as in the case of the grain deal)
from societies with a state monopoly on trade; the second, optimistic, or
dynamic version, hopes to turn economic relations into a direct political instrument, able to extract far-reaching and not directly related concessions from the
Soviet government, and ultimately, to manage its internal transformation. The
other side is seen as either so powerful and cunning that it will always fool the
West, or so much in need of Western technology that for its sake it will abandon
part of its political authority. An opposite group reaches analogous conclusions
from the other extreme of the political spectrum: Scandinavian or German

peace researchers whose intellectual framework and moral commitment are related to the underdeveloped countries, rightly point out the existence of a North-South dimension in East-West relations, but they push this insight to absurd lengths and draw even more absurd conclusions when they warn Eastern Europeans against economic relations with the West, particularly with Western Europe, which they devoutly seek, by predicting that the structure of their exchanges and the vulnerability of their societies will turn them into satellites of the Brussels metropolis.[41]

The cold warriors forget that the social vulnerability of Communist countries imposes severe limits to their freedom of action in their intercourse with the West—hence both upon their ability to lure it into dangerous dependence and upon their acceptance of political demands or of social trends capable of transforming their system by opening it up. They also forget that, particularly today, both ideologically opposed camps may have a real interest in avoiding each other's economic collapse. The critical peace researchers forget that, rather than (or, at any rate, prior to) being in a position of dominance towards Eastern Europe, Western Europe is in a position of dependence towards the United States and, to some extent, the Soviet Union, not to mention the oil producers. Even more important, the small and middle-sized East European states, before fearing a hypothetical dependence in relations with the Nine, are trying to diminish their very real dependence in relation to the Soviet Union; and the main way, for a small state, to increase its independence is, of course, to diversify its dependencies in order to balance them with each other. About vulnerability they forget that, while real, it is qualitatively different in the case of Communist countries, from that of the Third World ones: Command economies, while not immune to the effects of world-wide trends, are better able to insulate themselves from them even while pursuing trade and cooperation with Western firms; even more important, their political regimes are much better equipped to control the social and cultural fallout of economic contacts, to avoid political penetration, and to practice at least partial and temporary *Abgrenzung* when they feel the contamination level is rising dangerously. Finally, the structure of exchanges can present advantages for Eastern Europe in the present phase of the terms of trade and can, anyway, be transformed, as shown by the case of intra-German trade.

Fortunately, a number of studies are beginning to analyse the complexities of asymmetrical interdependence in East-West relations, particularly in Europe, through a combination of dialectical and empirical approaches. It is interesting to note that two of them are using A.O. Hirschman's concepts in order to apply them in one case to the effects of the asymmetry of regimes on Soviet-American trade,[42] and in the other to the "political economy of Soviet relations with Eastern Europe."[43] Both stress the importance of the "influence effect" for the Soviet Union, in the first case

> by the creation, in the United States, of powerful vested interests . . . ,
> anxious not only to preserve the lucrative trade but also to safeguard
> billions of dollars' worth of loans to the U.S.S.R., interests whose lobby-
> ing could decisively enhance the freedom of manoeuver of Soviet foreign
> policy by restricting that of the American. (p. 292)

in the second case by the political gains derived by the Soviet Union in terms of
control, from Eastern Europe's economic dependence that, according to Paul
Marer, have to be weighed against what has become its net economic cost to
the dominant power (pp. 136-38).

On a broader political and philosophical level, Marshall Shulman has shown
the importance of the partly contradictory, partly complementary principles of
"nonintervention" and "free access" for relations between Western and Eastern
states and societies, and the effects of partial asymmetry for the possibility of
a "Western philosophy of coexistence."[44]

Also in the United States, John Hardt, in an excellent series that, consciously or accidentally, gives an unfortunately too reduced importance to
Western Europe, has compared the relative degrees of dependence that can be
expected from Western investments in Communist economies.[45] In England
Peter Wiles[46] and John Pinder[47] are directly studying the problem of bargaining
power and the links between "market power" diplomacy and society. Wiles
has tried to apply economic paradigms to the conceptualization of cultural relations but conversely is pushing the politicization of economic relations through
the notion of linkage to the extreme in the East-West case; he argues that the
West has no economic advantage to expect from Communist countries and
should make progress in cultural access an essential counterpart in any bargaining and agreement with them. But the most important contribution may be
made by John Pinder. The notion of the "balance of market power," introduced by the latter and Pauline Pinder, is of crucial importance, even beyond
economics, for the analysis of East-West relations and of international relations
in general. In France J.P. Saltiel[48] and G. Sokoloff[49] raise the problem of the
role of multinational corporations and dependence in both systems, through
the means of a comparative analysis that, in the case of Sokoloff, is often inspired by Francois Perroux' concepts. In Germany the pioneering study of
Gerda Zellentin[50] tries to apply functionalist theory to East-West relations in
Europe: While it is marred by an excessive faith in economic determinism it
nevertheless recognizes the role of asymmetry and inequality and avoids an
assumption of convergence. At the other extreme the critical peace researchers,
while dogmatically overstressing the divergence of interests resulting from
these same features and neglecting the possibility of a common interest in
cooperation in spite of, or even because of, asymmetry, have nevertheless raised
important questions and shattered rather decisively the facile rhetoric of optimistic cooperation.[51] Finally, a research project of the German Society for

Peace and Conflict Research, led by Gerda Zellentin, is trying to give an empirical answer to the question of the dynamic relations between rapprochement (or cooperation), Abgrenzung (or distanciation) and peaceful change in Europe.[52]

The Effects of Asymmetry: Some Directions for Research

If one continues, as one should, in the direction of combining economic, political, and social analysis, it should be useful to distinguish three fundamental dimensions of interdependence: the interaction of behavior (or strategic interaction), the interdependence of interests (of which economic interdependence is the prime example), and the interpenetration of societies (in particular in the cultural and ideological areas). This distinction could incorporate and make further use of the various formulations we have encountered. For instance, there is an affinity with Nye and Keohane's scheme: Military power is particularly relevant to strategic interaction; the interdependence of interests coincides with their "vulnerability-interdependence"; and the interpenetration of societies is both a result and a cause of increasing "sensitivity-interdependence." At the same time, however, the notions of vulnerability and of sensitivity can be applied to the relations between actions, between interests and between social structures. Similarly, in all three cases, there is "incomplete domination and imperfect reciprocity," that is, various degrees of heterogeneity, inequality, or asymmetry. Strategic interaction is present in any type of contact between individuals and groups, whether their actions are aimed at each other or influence each other through competition or imitation. But it is particularly relevant to interstate relations, within the threat system, through deterrence and compulsion, escalation and stabilization.[53] Conversely, interpenetration, while present at the interstate level (e.g., through the transgovernmental bureaucratic coalitions currently studied by Keohane, Nye, and many others) is by definition the domain of societies and of their challenges to the authority of states and to the autonomy of the interstate system. Finally, the interdependence of interests applies both to the political interests of states, and to the cultural or ideological interests of social forces and global societies in identity and communication, but above all it is relevant to the economic sphere where, more than anywhere else, state and society meet, interact, and interpenetrate.

Again, this helps one understand East-West attitudes toward various forms of interdependence in terms of differences between regimes. All governments recognize strategic interaction and agree on the necessity of controlling it without neglecting its indirect influence.

Where attitudes differ within East-West relations in Europe is toward economic interdependence and sociocultural interpenetration. It is clear, for instance, that socialist countries have made, in the late sixties and early seventies, a fundamental decision to accept economic interdependence and to try to encourage it. But the extent to which they see in it an instrument for economic advantage (supply effect), or for asymmetrical political manipulation (influence effect) varies from case to case.[a] On the other hand, they all fear the consequences of the same economic interdependence regarding interpenetration.[54] They are reproducing the pattern thus described by James Billington, referring to earlier periods of Russian history:

> The consolidation of autocratic power and centralized control under Ivan the Third and Ivan the Fourth, as later under Stalin, involved an almost schizoid process of extensive *technological borrowing* from the West and simultaneously intensified *ideological isolation* from it (including persecution of "cosmopolitan Jews" and the repopulation of Western-oriented Baltic provinces). The agony of the "Time of Troubles" which followed the early period of expansion produced a crisis within a powerful but primitive Moscow, psychologically unable to accept the logic of a Western-style modernization implied in the educational and reform programs of Boris Godunov, the False Dimitri and Vassily Chuisky alike.[55]

Sakharov's appeal for accepting the political, cultural, and ideological consequences of the necessary scientific and technological modernization and communication with the outside world, as well as the rulers' refusal and their persecution of cosmopolitan dissent coupled with the courting of cosmopolitan investment seem to have deep structural roots as well as pressing immediate causes. This historical continuity seems the best illustration of the relation between three types of phenomena: The first consists of the crises produced by the increase in the asymmetrical interdependence in the relations between states and between organizations; the second consists of the specific crises within these states and these organizations themselves; the third consists of their respective reactions to both types of crises. From domestic conflicts through transnational influences (or vice versa) to international reactions and back, this

---

[a]A fascinating case study in this respect would deal with the negotiations between the Soviet Union, the GDR, the FRG and West Berlin over the construction of power plants in the former two for the supply of the latter two. There seems to be a competition between the GDR and the Soviet Union as to who should be the FRG's partner. It is not clear to what extent it is a competition for "supply" or for "influence." As for the FRG and West Berlin, the question is whether more interdependence with the East means more security through increased common interests or more insecurity through increased vulnerability. It seems that Soviet involvement is regarded more in the first perspective and East German involvement in the second one; on the other hand, influencing the behavior of East Germany is a goal of Ostpolitik, but then the question is raised of the priority between influence through direct contact and indirect influence through the Soviet Union. See, in particular, *Der Spiegel*, Nr 43/1974, pp. 29-30 and Nr 11/1975, pp. 41-44.

is probably the dialectic process (or the feedback loop) that has to be watched most carefully. This is what the Soviet Union does both domestically and internationally. What is most striking in this case is both the power of the state and its distrust of any force, domestic or transnational, that it is not certain to control. It is able to prevent any organized opposition, but it cannot tolerate Solzenytzin. It dominates the European continent and equals or surpasses the United States by its military might, yet it will stall for years on the minutest details of a cultural agreement and will let its pet project—the Conference of Security and Cooperation in Europe—be bogged down in boredom because it will not allow even a modest or symbolic measure of free communication between societies.

The Soviet Union is the best example of a combination of a dominant state and a vulnerable society. In its relations of asymmetrical interdependence with the West, it does its best to maintain these asymmetries where they are in its favor and to wipe them out when they go against it. This application of the principle "what is mine is mine, what is yours is negotiable" is valid within the military balance (American strategic superiority must be cancelled, Soviet regional superiority must be maintained), between the economic and the sociopolitical balances (Soviet economic inferiority must be overcome, Soviet superiority in political control must be maintained), between the two halves of Europe (Soviet political influence in Western Europe must be increased, Western political influence in Eastern Europe must continue to be excluded).

To some extent the Soviet Union is, indeed, allowed to have its cake and eat it too. But these same asymmetries that enable it to score these successes also underline specific weaknesses and vulnerabilities. Soviet political access in the West is infinitely superior to Western political access in the East, but the indirect social and cultural influence carried by Western technology, communication media, or tourists has no symmetrical equivalent in the East-West direction.

The same asymmetry is visible in the nature of the two superpowers' relations with their own allies. In the West the American society is tempted by neoisolationism. The use of force enters in American hegemony over Europe only through this indirect and paradoxical way, through the manipulation by the American government of the risks of domestic disaffection leading to a decrease in military commitment. While the Soviet control over its sphere is based on the threat of intervention, the American one is based on the threat of withdrawal. But American economic, social, and cultural penetration of Europe (whether through multinational corporations or through pop culture) are increasing. In the East the Soviet Union certainly exercises no cultural or social attraction, in particular over Central European countries whose spontaneous interest goes to the West. The same is true for their economic aspirations although the economic crises, by increasing their dependence, and the Soviet efforts at increasing cohesion through integration[56] have given Moscow an increasing leverage over Eastern Europe. But the ultimate cement clearly lies in political commitment and military force: Moscow shows no sign of being tempted by neoisolationism and its ultimate threat over its domain is not that of withdrawal.

To some extent this is due to the fact that the degree of "rank disequilibrium" or incongruence is much greater in the East. While in the West, in spite of the relative decline of American productivity as compared with that of Western Europe, economic and military superiority (and perhaps superiority in social and cultural vitality for good or, more often, for worse) coincide. In the East, in spite of superior Soviet bargaining power in a world of scarcities,[57] the dominant power has a lower standard of living and, in many respects, a lower level of development than most of its allies, but an absolute military superiority that thereby gains in ultimate importance.

Of course, this is reflected in the character of Western and Eastern organizations both in their inner structure and in their mutual influence. To begin with, the very fact that, in the West, one has to distinguish between Atlantic organizations like NATO, wider than Atlantic ones like OECD, and European ones like the European Community, indicates a fundamental asymmetry with the Eastern side. In the West, between a) transnational interdependence (or integration in an economic sense) that spans the whole capitalist world under the predominant influence of multinational corporations, b) Atlantic military, and, to a limited extent, political cooperation under American leadership, and c) European integration between small and middle powers involved in a delicate and shifting balance between Community institutions and intergovernmental bargaining, there are an abundance of rivalries, opposing forces, cross-cutting alignments, and chaotic muddling though. In the East the hierarchical and primarily political character of integration under Soviet leadership protects it from the emergence, not to speak of the institutionalization, of these types of conflicts; but it also deprives it of the cement of societal transnational ties and influences between individuals, groups, and firms. Hence, while the Warsaw Treaty Organization, for instance, is much more effectively integrated than NATO because of the much more direct predominance of the leader, there is no real integration among the command economies of COMECON. On the other hand, in Western Europe, too, the trend seems to go, even in the management of the economic crisis, more towards intergovernmental cooperation than towards supranational integration. In economic relations with the East industrial cooperation seems more and more important as compared with classical trade relations. To that extent the COMECON type of integration, based on the coordination of national plans, may be better equipped and serve as a model for East-West economic relations, just as the EEC was better equipped and, to some extent, was serving as a model for Eastern reforms concerning trade and monetary matters.[58]

Our main conceptual tools (indirect influence, comparative vulnerability, unequal interdependence, and the distinction between state and society) converge here towards the question of the effect of asymmetry on the mutual influence and cooperation of parallel but unequal and differently structured organizations. In other words, starting from the two opposing views of East-West developments, the "Monnetist" one, based on the *interdependence of societies* and on the attraction power of a progressively broadened zone of stability and cooperation, and the "Gaullist" one, based on the *independence of states* and their prior and parallel emancipation from their respective hegemonies, I have tried to link them to two implicit models concerning the indirect influence of the respective evolutions in Western and Eastern organizations upon each other. The first is the model of *contrast*—according to which the strength and unity of one camp produce the weakness and the division of the other, whose weaker members are attracted by the former. The second is the model of symmetry or *imitation*—according to which the trends towards integration or disintegration that occur on one side produce their equivalent in the other.[59]   Karl Kaiser has extended and formalized these models.[60]

But the European experience would seem to show that both models taken as such correspond to existing trends, but that they tend to minimize the influence of asymmetry that, again, would seem to call for a more empirical and at the same time more dialectical analysis. This would, I believe, show the influence of cross-systems contagion, imitation, and influence, and also the differing and sometimes opposite results due to the differing reactions, counter-reactions, or anticipated reactions of the respective organizations.

In East-West relations in Europe the most frequent pattern is one of abortive, incomplete, or arrested imitation and contagion, often followed by contrast that, however, incorporates something of the initial contagion. This is particularly the case when the influence goes from West to East. In the East-West direction the symmetry or mimetism model has tended to apply, albeit to a limited extent: Signs of relaxation or of polycentrism in the East have encouraged polycentrism in the West and slowed down the move to integration. In the West-East direction Western organizational initiatives have been imitated in the East through the creation of organizations (like the COMECON or the WTO) whose content bore no resemblance to that of their Western counterparts. When attempts were made to imitate actual processes or mechanisms, they (whether Rumanian moves towards WTO reform or Khruschev's attempt to introduce some supranationality into COMECON) were usually stopped (by Rumania in the latter case, by the Soviet Union in others) and reversed because of the different structure both of the individual states and of the role of power within the organization itself. The same cyclical process goes on with economic reforms and multilateralization. Things never go far enough for fear of their going too far.

Ultimately, as we have indicated, the key lies in the different structures of authority, both within the two types of organization and within the two types of society that lead to different responses both to external and internal challenges, and, at the most general level, to the crisis of legitimacy that strikes at the heart of modern society and of the international system.

The crisis is general and it involves the whole of relations between state and society. The gravity of the crisis and the nature of the responses differ with the nature of these relations themselves. In both cases existing authorities and structures keep their formal status and the physical means of power but are unable to satisfy either the political and psychological demands for participation and self-expression, or the technological and economic demands for efficiency, which emanate from their followers or subjects. Western professional politicians and Eastern apparatchiks seem equally obsolete and irrelevant to technocrats and to hippies, or, more modestly, to efficiency-oriented managers and to spiritually oriented dissenters, both West and East. Yet, in neither West nor East can the latter replace the former. The persistence of power structures with a declining ability to perform their practical tasks and to attract loyalty and enthusiasm, the double weakness of leaders and challengers, none of which can suppress or replace the other, belongs to the European international system and its two alliances, as well as their various member-states. This situation alone proves the impossibility of isolating the game of states from the turmoil of societies. But most of all, the variety and the interaction of the forms taken by the general trend towards political decline and by the responses of leaders and institutions, of elites and regimes, provides the essential dynamic of the present European system.

When first applying this approach to the European system in 1971-72, I suggested a typology of these possible interactions. In the relations between rebellious or dynamic parts of a society and a system that is basically conservative, a protracted but unstable coexistence can lead to an absorption of the parts by the whole, to the latter's erosion under their influence, or to a mixture of the two processes—that is, to a mutually reinforcing decay. A direct clash can lead to repression or to revolution, or, again, to both and to their mutual frustration in some uncontrollable catastrophe. In relation to the outside world both successful absorption or repression and continuing erosion or a cyclical succession of unsuccessful rebellions and repressions may lead either to expansion or contraction of the system (or of its leaders). Finally, among states or alliances, especially those in a situation of contiguity or of competition, such classical notions as expansion, the stuggle for power and security, or the balance of power must be seen in the light of these domestic and transnational processes and conflicts.

The real race may be less to increase one's comparative power than to decrease one's comparative vulnerability, to manipulate not only an opponent's weakness but one's own, to encourage exported erosion or to control contagious explosions, to modify or maintain not so much territorial borders or even diplomatic alignments as what might be called the balance of will and the balance of expectations.

In Europe we are witnessing such a race as a result of a crisis of leadership and institutions within states and alliances being caught up in the conflict between them, but interacting with rather than superseding it—hence, a situation of "competitive decadence" (to use Leo Labedz' felicitous expression) where, for instance, one side's expansion is helped by another's erosion but may also increase its own need of repression and its own risks of explosion.

At the time my judgment, based on the primacy of society in the West and of the State in the East, was that:

> By and large the pressures of expression, erosion, and contraction seem
> to be more prevalent in the West, the chances and risks of repression,
> expansion and explosion more likely in the East.

This seems to be valid for both types of countries and both alliances. The Western alliance is in perpetual discord but manages somehow to survive, while the Soviet bloc seems to know no middle ground between monolithic unity and the brink of war. So also Western countries seem to have entered a phase of chronic civil unrest but one that, so far, does not seem to go beyond an increase in lawlessness and "expressive violence", while Communist countries (particularly the Soviet Union) are better able to impose law and order but only at the cost of ever more violent explosions (such as that in Poland) and at the risk, one day, of revolution or civil war.

I was, however, aware that:

> Of course, many factors could change this pattern. There are plenty of
> potential flashpoints for explosions in Western Europe, particularly in
> the south because of the rigidities of dictatorial regimes and the tensions
> created by a phase of social and economic transition. In Eastern Europe,
> especially in Kadar's Hungary and, it would seem, even in Gierek's Poland,
> there are potentialities for an evolution which may be called erosion from
> the point of view of bureaucratic rule and ideological orthodoxy, but
> which may be called progress from the point of view of social peace and
> prosperity. So far, this evolution seems to be tolerated by the Soviet
> Union: in spite of the instabilities and of the rigidities which we have em-
> phasized, explosions have their dangers, and economies their constraints.
> The impossibility of an East-West war precludes neither East-West hostility
> nor intervention within the Soviet empire, but it does tend to moderate
> them; the need to maintain party legitimacy does seem to pose insuperable
> barriers to the efforts to modernize and reform Communist economies,
> but such contradictions can be lived with when a consciousness of the
> need for communication and compromise is present. Above all, the out-
> come is likely to be mixed, the emphasis being on cooperation where war
> would be the most dangerous and technological needs most pressing, i.e.,
> in the relations between the Soviet Union and the two Germanies.[61]

Writing at the end of 1974 it seems that these factors of change have developed to the point of challenging the validity of the overall pattern. Under the impact of the economic crisis Western erosion seems to acquire an explosive character. On the other hand, the Soviet Union seems to be able for the time being not only to contain change in its sphere by imposing law and order, but to do this with a substantial degree of flexibility and of skill in providing economic satisfaction that makes explosions between societies and confrontations between the leader and its allies less likely in the foreseeable future. This may change, of course, in particular as the consequences of the energy crisis seem to worsen both Eastern Europe's economic situation and its political dependence upon the Soviet Union, which may one day lead again to explosions. But in a world troubled by crises, revolutions, and war, the Soviet Union and Eastern Europe stand out as a solid and impressive, if uninspired and uninspiring, rock of stability. This, together with its superior military power, may even give the Soviet camp a better chance in the balance of influence between societies (in particular between the two Germanies) where it still seems to lack self-confidence. At a time of social and economic crisis, involving personal anxieties about crime and unemployment, the appeals of security and order are increasingly competitive with those of affluence and freedom.

The mutual influence of developments within Communist and capitalist societies faced by global crisis and of developments in the East-West balance cannot be judged, however, if they are not seen within the more complex framework of the European system. The East-West dimension opposing two social systems, two ideologies, represented by two superpowers, dominating two halves of Europe and of Germany is always present. But, increasingly, it has been seen to coexist with two other dimensions. One opposes the two Europes and the two superpowers, or, as the Chinese would say, the first world of the superpowers and the second world of small and medium developed states. Yet, another dimension opposes the North and the South, a more stable and industrialized center and a more troubled and dependent periphery. Orthodox Communists or cold warriors recognize only the first dimension, the Gaullists and the Chinese only the second, the Nordic peace researchers only the third, the Rumanians use all three according to circumstances.

In this respect all theorists should be Rumanians. Only by recognizing the multiplicity of dimensions can they begin to chart the complexities of inequality and interdependence. In particular, only if one is able to distinguish between the bipolar East-West *system* (both territorial and strategic, frozen, precisely, by the presence of the superpowers and their nuclear weapons), the multipolar level of *states* and the transnational level of *society*,[62] can one see the contrast between the rigidity of the system, the flexible actions and combinations of states, and the evolution and revolutions of societies. This is the particular form that the universal contradiction of state and society is taking in today's Europe: To what extent can the tensions of societies be held in check by the barriers of the interstate system and of national institutions; to what extent will they succeed in eroding these barriers or in bursting them wide open? What is the mutual influence between the military balance and the evolution of societies? To what extent, in a system where the direct use of force seems excluded, does its indirect projection along with economic interdependence and sociocultural influence enter the complex equation of dominance and vulnerability between and within states, alliances and organizations? What are the consequences of detente and cold war, or interpenetration and self-closure, for the respective legitimacy crises?[63] How should one weigh the erosion of defense budgets in the West versus the erosion of ideological fervor in the East?

After 1968 it became clear that the domestic dynamics of societies did no longer in Europe necessarily coincide with the geographic, diplomatic, and military alignments of the respective countries. Czechoslovakia showed that a Communist country could be rapidly evolving towards a kind of social democracy; May 1968 in France that a Western country could enter a revolutionary situation where a leftist alternative and its ulterior control by the Communist party was possible. What would be the consequence for the conflict between the rigidity of the system that has been the basis of Europe's military stability and the domestic evolutions of particular societies that feel constrained by it? In 1968 the system won. But while on the Eastern side the answer has the brutal finality (at least for the foreseeable future) of Soviet military power, in the West the evolution in Greece and in Portugal, in Italy and in France, and, last but not least, in the United States itself, raises the question whether, for the first time since 1947-48, the domestic crises, evolutions, or revolutions of particular societies may not modify the alignment of states and, even, the overall balance and the nature of the security system itself.

These questions cannot be answered here, but they also are not answered in reality, since the whole game of politics in the developed part of the world lies precisely in testing various possible answers. Precisely because force is hard to use positively and directly but always present negatively and potentially, precisely because everyone has both complementary and contradictory interests, the game of politics within and between nations increasingly resembles shadow-boxing in the short run and gambling in the long run. Actors are constantly engaged in mock confrontations whose importance lies less in their immediate stakes than in their symbolic testing of tolerance thresholds. In turn, the tolerance that is being tested has less to do with the actions of others than with the effects of processes which everyone tries to manipulate and to manage precisely because no one can predict or control their course.

Detente in general but in particular the relations of West Germany with the GDR and the Soviet Union (as well as, in another way and another area, the 1973 Paris agreements on Vietnam) are essentially expressing a common interest in the short run and common agreement to transfer conflicting objectives and hopes to a long-range process about which each side gambles that it will be more

advantageous to itself than to the other. Would detente, or, to take a more
precise example, the CSCE, contribute more to liberalize the East or to weaken
the West, give more leeway to small countries or more control to superpowers?
Would the Vietnamese and the German treaties stabilize the division or prepare
the reunification of the respective countries? In each case some answers are more
likely than others but if they had been certain there would have been no agreements.

Just as the arms race with the question of the political impact of a military
meaningless strategic superiority, most negotiations today are gambles upon the
evolution of social processes or psychological attitudes; they consist in buying
not real estate or allies but time, just as, in domestic politics, inflation consists
in provisionally solving short-term conflicts of interest by projecting them into
the future. In each case no one can know whether the process will make the
direct conflicts it replaces irrelevant or whether it will bring them back in an
even more dangerous form at an even less propitious time. The question, "to
link or not to link?" with which we started must, then, necessarily be answered
in a twofold way: It is an illusion to try to isolate issue areas or regions from
the process of interdependent change, but it is no less an illusion to believe that
the process increases the ability of states to manage the evolution of societies,
whether their own, those of adversaries, or those of allies. The irony of interdependence is that it has a taste for replacing the links we construct by others
we do not expect, the dominoes we fear by others that fall in unforeseen directions or that we have set up ourselves. Theory and practice can try to bring more
order and more balance. They cannot, fortunately, perhaps, eliminate the un-
predictability of economic, social, and political evolution that has become the
main theme of international politics.

Notes

1. For instance in Edward Morse, *Foreign Policy and Interdependence in
   Gaullist France* (Princeton: Princeton University Press, 1973), pp. 38-45.
2. Z. Brzezinski and S. Huntington, *Political Power: USA/USSR* (New York:
   Viking Press, 1964), pp. 71-76.
3. J. Habermas, "Legitimation Problems in Late Capitalism," *Social Research*
   40, 4, Winter 1973, pp. 655-59.
4. Cf. Pierre Hassner, "The Nation-State in the Nuclear Age," *Survey*, April
   1968, pp. 18-20.
5. Cf. Eric Weil, *Philosophie politique* (Paris: Vrin, 1956).
6. Pierre Hassner, "Force et Politique auhourd'hui," *Defense Nationale*,
   December 1971, pp. 1794-1809.
7. Cf. *Revue de la politique internationale* (Belgrade), March 20, 1970.
8. See his critical overview: J. Rosenau, "Theorizing across systems: Linkage

Politics Revisited," in J. Wilkenfeld, ed., *Conflict Behavior and Linkage Politics* (New York: David McKay, 1973), pp. 25-59.

9. See London Miller, "American in World Politics: Linkage or Leverage?" *The World Today*, July 1974, p. 269-77. For a more general and more favorable view of the importance of inter-issue linkages for U.S. policy, see N. Keohane and J. Nye, "Power and Interdependence," *Survival*, July-August 1973, pp. 153-65. For the specific issue of tacit and explicit bargaining between the United States and Western Europe, see N. Gilpin, "The Politics of Transnational Economic Relations," in N. Keohane and J. Nye, eds., *Transnational Relations and World Politics* (Cambridge, Mass: Harvard University Press, 1972), p. 398-420, and E. Morse, "Core-Periphery Relations and the Bargaining Structure in NATO," (New Orleans: APSA, 1973), and B. Cohen, "The Revolution in Atlantic Economic Relations: A Bargain Comes Unstuck," in W. Hanrieder, ed., *The United States and Western Europe* (Cambridge, Mass.: Winthrop,1974) pp. 106-34.

10. Manfred Halpern, "A Redefinition of the Revolutionary Situation," *Journal of International Affairs*, 23, 1, 1969, pp. 54-55.

11. Pierre Hassner, "Etats, Systèmes, Sociétés: les contradictions de l'état mixte", Munich: IPSA, 1970, (mimeograph).

12. Pierre Hassner, *L'Interdépendence Inégale: de la domination incomplète a la reciprocité imparfaite*, Paris CERI, Conference on "Les relations inégales entre états: domination et dépendence," February 1971, 41 pp., (mimeograph).

13. R. Dahl, "The Concept of Power," *Behavioral Science*, 2, July 1957, pp. 202-3.

14. J.D. Singer, "Inter-Nation Influence: A Formal Model," *American Political Science Review*, 57, June 1963, p. 420.

15. Besides the Marxist and Marcusian literature, see the concept of "non-decisions" in P. Bachrach and M. Baratz, *Power, Poverty, Theory and Practice* (Oxford: Oxford University Press, 1970), p. 139, and the analysis of relations between exchanges, constraints, and gifts and, within constraints, between those of objects and those of adversaries in F. Perroux, *Economie et Société*, (Paris: P.U.F., 1960), pp. 134-56.

16. Richard M. Emerson, "Power-Dependence Relations," *American Sociological Review*, February 1962, p. 31-41.

17. Michel Crozier, *La Société bloquée* (Paris: Seuil, 1970), pp. 33-34

18. R. Keohane and J. Nye, "World Politics and the International Economic System," C. Fred Bergsten, ed., *The Future of the International Economic Order* (Lexington, Mass.: D.C. Heath and Co., Lexington Books, 1973), p. 124.

19. J. Galtung, *The European Community: A Superpower in the Making*, chap. 3, "On Power in General," p. 36.

20. K. Knorr, *Power and Wealth: The Political Economy of International Power*, (New York: Macmillan, 1973), chap. 1, "Power and Influence," p. 13.

21. See my discussion of the fashionable notion of "structural violence" in Pierre Hassner "On ne badine pas avec la paix," *Revue Francaise de Science Politique,* December 1973.

22. See John C. Harsany, "Measurement of Social Power, Opportunity Costs and the Theory of Two-Person Bargaining Gains," *Behavioral Science,* 7, 1962, pp. 67-80.

23. K. Deutsch, *The Nerves of Government* (Glencoe: The Free Press, 1963), p. 115.

24. John Burton, *Systems, States, Diplomacy and Rules* (Cambridge: Cambridge University Press, 1968), pp. 113-144.

25. See also N. North and N. Choucri, "Population Technology and Resources in the Future International System," in "Change and the Future International System, *Journal of International Affairs,* 25, 2, 1971, p. 231.

26. J. Rosenau, "Pre-theories and Theories of Foreign Policy," in R. Barry Farrell, ed., *Approaches to Comparative and International Politics,* (Evanston: Northwestern University Press, 1966), p. 65.

27. W. Hanrieder, "Compatibility and Consensus: A Proposal for the Conceptual Linkage of External and Internal Dimensions in Foreign Policy," *American Political Science Review,* December 1967.

28. S. Brucan, *A Sociological Theory of Foreign Policy,* Munich: IPSA, September 1970, p. 4.

29. Cf. R. Cottam, *Competitive Interference and 20th Century Diplomacy* (Pittsburgh: Pittsburgh University Press, 1967), ch. 2, "Power in Terms of Leverage," p. 78-117.

30. Cf. K. Deutsch, "The Future of World Politics," *Political Quarterly,* 1966, and Nicholas O. Berry, "The Management of Foreign Penetration," *Orbis,* Summer 1974, pp. 598-614.

31. See all the references in the excellent article on the debate by R. Rosecrance and A. Stein, "Interdependence: Myth or Reality?" *World Politics,* October 1973, pp. 1-28. The distinction and the synthesis are developed by Rosecrance in the article mentioned above and in his book, *International Relations* (New York: McGraw Hill, 1973), pp. 136-49, by R. Tollisson and T. Willett, "International Integration and the Interdependence of Economic Variables," *International Organization* 27, Spring 1973, pp. 255-71, and most important, by Keohane and Nye in "World Politics and the International System," ch. 5, pp. 115-79.

32. Among many others, one useful introduction is J. Cockroft, A. Gunder Frank, and Dale L. Johnson, *Dependence and Underdevelopment—Latin America's Political Economy* (New York: Anchor Books, Doubleday 1972).

33. Cf. his books: Samir Amin, *L'Accumulation à l'échelle mondiale* (Paris: Anthropos, 1970) and *Le Développement Inégal* (Paris: Ed. de Minuit, 1973). On the possibility of generalizing, as he does, from the Latin-American case, see his point of view and the much more cautious one of F.H. Cardoso in *L'Homme et la Société,* 27, Jan.-Feb. 1973.

34. J. Galtung, "A Structural Theory of Imperialism," *Journal of Peace Research,* 2, 1971, pp. 81-83. See my critique in "On ne badine pas avec la paix," where I am trying to point out how Galtung's exclusive insistence on individual acts and collective structures leads to a neglect of dynamic processes, and how his desperate attempt at operationalization leads him to arbitrarily turn one type of inequality into an absolute criterion of dependence and exploitation. Another critique along similar lines is by Karl Deutsch, "Theories of Imperialism and Neocolonialism," in S. Rosen and J. Kurth, *Testing Theories of Economic Imperialism* (Lexington, Mass.: D.C. Heath and Company, Lexington Books, 1974), pp. 24-28. See, for a more empirical and political generalization J. Dominguez, "Mice that do not Roar: Some Aspects of International Politics in the World's Peripheries," *International Organization,* Spring 1971, pp. 175-208.

35. B. Lassudrie-Duchêne, "Deux ripostes à la rareté," *Le Monde,* January 22, 1974, p. 15.

36. Cf. P. Blau, *Exchange and Power in Social Life* (New York: Wiley, 1964), and F. Perroux, *Pouvoir et Economie* (Paris: P.U.F., 1964).

37. A.O. Hirschman, *National Power and the Structure of Foreign Trade* (Los Angeles: University of California Press, 1945), pp. 3-85.

38. J. Knapp, "Economics or Political Economy?" *Lloyds Bank Review,* January 1973, pp. 19-43.

39. Hans O. Schmitt, "Integration and Conflict in the World Economy," *Journal of Common Market Studies,* September 1969, pp. 1-18.

40. Cf. his book, Samuel Pisar, *Coexistence and Commerce* (New York, McGraw-Hill, 1970). The most recent and least serious expression of his theses is in "A la barre de la détente," *Le Monde,* September 14, 1974.

41. This is, in particular, the case of J. Galtung. See his *European Community, A Superpower in the Making,* whose very title sounds ironical today. His most recent analysis is *East-West Security and Cooperation: A Sceptical Contribution* (Oslo: University of Oslo, 1975) para. 9. This is also the tendency of the collective work, U. Albrecht et al., *Durch Kooperation zum Frieden?* (Munchen: Hauser Vg., 1974). See in particular the article by U. Albrecht and U. Rehfeldt on "Conditions of Economic and Technological Exchange Processes in the Co-operation of Eastern and Western Europe," pp. 66-100.

42. Gregory Grossman, "Prospects and Policy for U.S.-Soviet Trade," *The American Economic Review,* May 1974, pp. 289-93. On this same problem of asymmetry, see the excellent collection of articles by R. Vernon, S. Rosenfeld, and T. Sorensen, gathered under the headline "Dilemmas of Detente," in *Foreign Affairs,* 52, 2, January 1974, pp. 249-57.

43. Paul Marer, "Soviet Economic Policy in Eastern Europe," in J. Hardt, ed., *Reorientation and Commercial Relations of the Economies of Eastern Europe,* a compendium of papers submitted to the Joint Economic Committee, U.S. Congress, August 1974, pp. 135-64.

44. Marshall Shulman, "What Does Security Mean Today?" *Foreign Affairs*, July 1971. "For a Western Philosophy of Co-Existence," *Foreign Affairs*, October 1973.

45. John Hardt and G. Holliday, *U.S.-Soviet Commercial Relations: The Interplay of Economics, Technology Transfer and Diplomacy*, prepared for the Subcommittee on National Security Policy and Scientific Developments, Committee on Foreign Affairs, U.S. House of Representatives, June 1973; and J. Hardt, G. Holliday, and Y. Kim, *Western Investment in Communist Economies: A Selected Survey on Economic Interdependence* (Washington D.C., U.S. Government Printing Office, 1974). See also Marer, *Re-orientation and Commercial Relations*.

46. Peter Wiles, *Communist International Economics* (New York: Praeger, 1969), ch. 12 and 16 to 18, and a paper, "On the Principles of Cultural Exchange," presented to The Royal Institute of International Affairs on May 15, 1973.

47. J. Pinder, "Comecon, an East European Common Market?" in J. Lukaszewski, ed., *The People's Democracies After Prague* (Bruges: College d'Europe, 1969), pp. 133-85, and an as yet unpublished study, with Pauline Pinder, "The Balance of Market Power in Europe: A Means of Soviet Influence Over the European Community," G.I.P. mimeograph.

48. J.P. Saltiel, "Le fait multinational et les relations Est-Ouest," *Projet*, November 1972, reproduced in *Problèmes Economiques*, 1320, May 2, 1973, pp. 13-20.

49. G. Sokoloff, "Deux strategies d'intégration internationale: socialisme et capitalisme," in "Inegalités structurelles et commerce exterieur," *Economie Appliquée*, 4, 1971, pp. 559-605.

50. Gerda Zellentin, *Intersystemare Beziehungen in Europa* (Leyden: Sythoff, 1970), 307 pp.

51. Cf. G. Adler-Karlsson, "Problems of East-West Trade—A General Survey," *Economics of Planning*, 7(a), 1967, pp. 119-82. J. Galtung, *Cooperation in Europe* (New York: Humanities Press, 1970), 371 pp.; and U. Albrecht et al., *Durch Kooperation*.

52. Cf. "The Preservation of Peace and the Development of Strategies of Transition in Europe," Special Issue Program Area I, *D.G.F.K. - Information,* 1974; and G. Zellentin, "Perspektiven und Modelle wirtschaftlicher Beziehungen zwischen West und Osteuropa," *Zeitschrift für das gesamte Handelsrecht und Wirtschaftsrecht*, 138, 4 (1974).

53. Cf. E. Morse, *Foreign Policy and Interdependence in Gaullist France* (Princeton, New Jersey: Princeton University Press, 1973), pp. 57-65.

54. Cf. R. Legvold, "The Problem of European Security," *Problems of Communism*, Jan.-Feb. 1974, p. 13-34; and P. Hassner, "Les contradictions de la détente: faux dilemmes et vrais problèms," *Défense Nationale*, June 1974, pp. 27-45.

55. J. Billington, "The Intellectuals" in A. Kassof, ed., *Prospects for Soviet Society*, (London: Pall Mall, 1968).

56. Cf. J. Brown, "Detente and Soviet Policy in Eastern Europe," *Survey*, Summer 1974, pp. 46-58.

57. Marshall Goldmann, "The Soviet Economy in a World of Shortages," *Current History*, October 1974, p. 164.

58. Cf. L. Valsalice, "Integrazioni economiche cooperazione e conferenza europa a Geneva," *Est Ouest* (Trieste), 3, 1973, p. 28. Cf. Henry Schaefer, *Comecon and the Politics of Integration* (New York: Praeger, 1972), and "East-West Economic Relations in Communist Perspective," *RFE Research* 24 May 1973.

59. See "German and European Reunification: Two Problems or One?" *Survey*, Summer 1966; and "L'Europe de l'Est vue de loin," *Revue Francaise de Science Politique*, February 1969, pp. 134-43.

60. Karl Kaiser, "The Interaction of Regional Subsystems—Some Preliminary Notes on Recurrent Patterns and the Role of Superpowers," *World Politics*, 21, 1, October 1968, pp. 84-100.

61. Pierre Hassner, "The New Europe: From Cold War to Hot Peace," *International Journal*, 27, 1, Winter 1971-72, pp. 8-9.

62. See, in particular, Pierre Hassner, "Etats, Systèmes, Sociétiés: les contradictions de l'état mixte," Munich, IPSA: 1970, (mimeograph).

63. Cf. the stimulating paper by A.J. Vidich, "Social Conflict in the Era of Detente: New Roles for Ideologies, Revolutionaries and Youth," New School of Social Research, 40th Anniversary Conference, June 1974, 21 p. (mimeograph).

17

Multinational Corporations, National Economic Policies, and Labor Unions
Alberto Martinelli

The Nationality of Multinational Corporations

In the growing literature on multinational corporations, the study of their impact on state economic policies and on the labor movement has drawn relatively little attention. In the following pages we will summarize some of the theses on the contradictions between nation states and multinational corporations developed in a previous paper[1] and we will then further our analysis by focusing on the relationships between international capital and labor unions.

The existence of companies operating in more than one country traces back to the origins of capitalism. International capital was already a major feature of the world economy in the classical age of imperialism studied by Hobson, Hilferding, Lenin, Bucharin, and Luxemburg. The growth of multinational (or international) corporations has, however, greatly accelerated since World War II as a result of direct overseas investment by companies from the leading capitalist nations—the United States in particular, but also Western Europe and Japan. This growth stemmed, in other words, from the setting up of wholly or partly owned foreign subsidiaries and the acquisition of existing companies in foreign countries. In this sense the shift from the export of goods to the export of the production of goods envisaged by the theorists of imperialism of the early twentieth century has taken place on a massive scale.

Contemporary international corporations not only differ from international capital at the beginning of the century in terms of scale, but also in qualitative terms. In fact, until World War II capital tended to be closely identified with a given nation-state and to be an instrument of, as well as a determinant of, state power politics. Companies whose ownership and managerial structure were binational, such as Royal Dutch Shell and Unilever, were very rare, and, more often, nationally based companies tended to operate within the boundaries of protected trading areas and colonial empires. In the present situation, on the contrary, most giant corporations organize their operating divisions across national frontiers of many countries, both developed and underdeveloped, and in some cases extend the scope of their activities to the socialist countries as well, through the so-called "joint ventures." The relative independence of international companies from the nation-states where they operate, and the size of their budgets, which often exceed the budgets of national governments, have brought some students to argue (1) that multinational corporations

425

are the basic operating units of the international economy and even of the world order and (2) that the nation-state is obsolete and needs to be replaced by other institutional forms, such as international political organizations and/or a single supranational state.

We disagree with these forecasts for two main orders of reasons: First, because while multinational corporations are "multinational" in the sense that they operate across national economic boundaries, they also still maintain a privileged relationship with a given nation-state, in most cases the United States government; in other words, there is a nationality of international capital, as we will try to demonstrate. Second, because a variety of social and political factors are still working toward a national characterization of state functions, including those countries that are not in the top position in the international division of labor. Historical encrustations in social stratification, differences in state apparatuses and institutions in general, cultural differences, widely shared nationalistic tendencies and class contradictions within the dominant "historical bloc" are all factors that contribute to the possibility that nation-states' functions can be superseded by a given metropolitan state or by some kind of rather remote supranational state. This is true for the peripheral, dependent countries, and more so for the other advanced industrial countries where United States based corporations have their subsidiaries. The national specificity of those states does not contradict the condition of dependence in which they may find themselves.

The degree of nationality (or of multinationality) of corporations operating in more than one country can be assessed by putting them on a continuum that is defined in terms of the following set of elements:

1. The distribution of authority in the business organization. Although multinational companies tend to have a multidivisional structure with relevant degrees of operational decentralization, they maintain a hierarchy of roles, where top positions tend to coincide with the control of centers of power, that is, of those factors playing a strategic role in the development of the firm, such as financial means, research, and technological know-how, or organization and information. The control of these factors tends to be concentrated in the same place and in the same top executives. Moreover, it tends to coincide with the location of the main sources of supply of these factors, that is, the location of the main financial centers and of the most advanced research institutions.

2. The nature, size, and value of the plants existing in different countries.

3. The geographical distribution of the labor force employed by the multinational corporation, and especially of the most highly qualified labor force having the highest degree of specialization.

4. The location of the markets both for sales and for those inputs having a strategic value and a high technological content.

Multinational corporations (MNCs) may vary very much along these dimensions. For instance, while General Motors and IBM still have the bulk of their production and sales in the United States, the United States-owned Singer and the Swiss-owned Nestle have substantially greater production and sales outside the parent country. But, even in the latter cases, the final criterion to assess the nationality of a company is the location of its centers of power. Moreover, in spite of the cases in which most of the business of the corporation is scattered in several countries other than the one where the financial centers are located, many of the elements we have mentioned tend to converge in one country. This fact does not mean that MNCs are not quite different from national firms, but rather that their multinational character should not be overstressed. There are a series of reasons for this. First, multinational corporations were not historically the result of transnational mergers of ownership and management (with the usual exceptions, such as the German-Belgian Agfa-Gevaert, and more recently the Italian-British Pirelli-Dunlop), but were rather national firms born and shaped in a national context, which achieved an international dimension through a process of "capital concentration" (in the Marxist sense). Second, the countries where the new technology is produced also have an articulated industrial structure that provides relevant external economies for the setting up of new productive units and an extended and rapidly expanding market, especially for new products. Third, public expenditure, both in infrastructures and in services and such industries as the defense industry, represents an increasing share of the national income and tends to be oriented toward domestic products. And, fourth, although MNCs need the cooperation of the states of all countries where they operate, the extent and systematic character of such cooperation varies greatly from one country to another, and cooperation with a single nation state tends to be decisive. In the final analysis the specific relationship that takes place between each multinational company and a given nation-state is based on the discretionary power of each partner in the achievement of the policy goals of the other; in other words, a contractual relationship of giving and taking takes place, which is influenced by the mutual bargaining power of the two partners. In this situation it is in the interest of both the multinational corporation and the nation-state to establish a privileged relationship that is qualitatively different from that which they have with other nation-states; and it is in the interest of a given country to act as parent state for as many international companies as possible.

From what we have said it is clear that MNCs have a nationality and that nationality tends to be that of a highly developed country, with abundant productive, technological, financial, political, and military resources. A politically and militarily strong state can implement not only the strictly national interests of the firms but also their international interests. The outcome of direct investments is influenced by the political and economic power of the parent state to follow its own capital into foreign countries. Any survey of major MNCs in terms of capital employed, amount of sales, profits, number of employees, and growth rates will show a clear predominance of United States-based corporations, although European and Japanese firms are also present. It is also clear that the foremost importance of complementarity with one nation-state does not mean than MNCs consider the parent state's goals as their own. Their operations are oriented to an overall strategy, aiming at the highest long-term profits of the whole business and not of its single parts, however concentrated they may be in a single country. From this perspective the MNCs aim at strengthening their bargaining power, and their power is certainly greater when there is a certain amount of competition among nation-states. The privileged status of the relationship with the parent country is clearly felt, because of the greater dependence of that state on the MNC. But from this fact one cannot imply either a drive toward a supranational state or a clustering of all MNCs around a unique metropolitan pole, that is, the United States, which then becomes the most powerful capitalist government.

Contradictions Between Nation-States and MNCs

In the relationships between multinational corporations and nation-states it is then necessary to distinguish the links with the parent state from those with the host states. In both cases we have systematic relationships, but the degree of cooperation and conflict is different. In the relationships with the parent state international companies and the state, although limited in their support of each other's power, are basically engaged in cooperation. Whenever they enter into some kind of conflict, that conflict either concerns the mutual attempt by the government and the companies to check and control their partner's power, or it reflects a power struggle among different dominant groups that try to win a greater share of influence and control over the state apparatus. In the latter relationships, on the other hand, a structural contradication takes place that is the source of potential conflicts. Simply stated, the contradiction is that, while multinational corporations cannot renounce the traditional bourgeois state functions that are necessary to create favorable conditions for the viable functioning of a capitalist economy and for their privileged position within it (i.e., fostering consensus and social peace), at the same time those very corporations, through their operations, hinder the performance of state economic policies, such as monetary, fiscal, and employment policies, which are instrumental in achieving those broader social goals.

More specifically, international capital needs the government of the host countries to perform a whole set of social and economic functions. There are not only the traditional state functions, such as defending property rights and guaranteeing the free circulation of factors of production, but there is also the growing role of the state in the process of reproduction of the labor force, in the creation of infrastructures, and, more important than these, in maintaining economic control and social peace in the economy and in the society in general. In other words, the capitalist state has played an important role in integrating the subordinated classes, thus creating favorable conditions for capital to develop. But the state has succeeded in this attempt by achieving some standard economic policy goals, such as full employment, balance of payments equilibrium, inflation control, income redistribution through fiscal policy, and the like. The very operations of MNCs, however, have made some of these economic policies difficult to pursue, thus weakening the legitimacy of the state in peripheral countries and its capability to control social conflict.

As an instance of the way in which MNCs undermine the capacity of national governments to fulfill standard economic goals, let us analyse their control of the terms of trade and of important financial flows. MNCs in many fields have direct control over the terms of trade of different countries. Such control cannot be likened to the control that oligopolistic firms have over the production of their finished products, in that insofar as a multinational corporation is made up of vertically integrated productive units located in different countries, the process through which semifinished products are transferred from one local unit to the next are only accounting items for the firm, but represent imports and exports for the countries involved. Prices for the products can be changed regardless of the fundamental limit that the market puts to the manoeuver of prices; in other words, they can be changed without affecting in the slightest way the quantities that are bought and sold. The changes in these accounting prices affect therefore both the balance of payments and the level of income (with its fiscal and monetary repercussions within a given level of public expenditure) and consequently the pattern of growth of the whole economy.

MNCs also control important financial flows. They realize profits, control sources of financial supply, and decide investments over an area including many countries. The proportioning of these variables, that is, self-financing through undistributed profits, external financing, and investment expenditure, is made for the firm as a whole and not for each national unit. For each country, on the other hand, the difference between internal and external sources of financing located in the country and investment expenditure in the local plant means a difference between import and export of capital. These flows not only affect the balance of payments, but also the money market and probably the structure of the financial system.

Given the contradictions we have analyzed so far, one comes to wonder why mutual cooperation between multinational corporations and nation-states is still the rule. Actually, a complex process of give and take occurs; nation-states are not only hindered by the presence of international concerns within their boundaries, but also gain definite advantages. They absorb new

knowledge and thereby increase the value added of their economy — there are
already instances of joint ventures for patents and trademarks and of joint
setting of data systems, such as that of EEC and the Mexican government.
Nation-states also gain new professional and managerial skills, both through
the training of local skilled labor by international capital and through the
necessity to train their own officials to bargain with multinational management. Industrial restructuring carried on by international companies can also
have positive effects in some cases by introducing higher productivity, better
wages, and better conditions of employment. And finally, these companies
bring investments that may be badly needed to help a sagging national economy.

In other words, the relationship between nation-states and multinational
corporations is an exchange relationship, in which some advantage must accrue
to both partners, including the weaker one. The important point is, however,
that this happens according to a strategy of profit-making on a global scale,
disregarding any coordination of productive forces at the national level.
The strategy of profit maximization for the international firm as a whole
surely involved complex interests in a broad range of different situations and
the firm must mediate among them. But more often than not the strategy of
"good management" of local resources must be sacrificed to the needs of
"rationality" on a world scale. It is true that this happens within the national
boundaries as well, whenever local interests are sacrificed to a firm's national
strategy; in this instance, however, the local interests are more likely to be
felt and taken into account at the national level.

If the disadvantages for the national economies where international firms
have their subsidiaries tend to bypass the advantages of their partnership,
there must be other reasons that explain the continuation and expansion of
such relationships. The most obvious one is the power of international
companies, both their economic power and the political power of their
metropolitan states. But, besides that there is the fact that multinational
interests can be consistent with those of the dominant classes of the host
countries — or at least with the interests of those dominant groups that have
been denationalized.

Effects on Labor in Peripheral Countries

These remarks bring us to relax an assumption that we have maintained
so far. We have assumed that national interests manifest themselves, both in
the ideology and praxis of bourgeois governments, without disaggregating in
terms of conflicting social classes. In particular, we have considered a set of
policy goals and instruments that can be referred to as "Keynesian economic
policy." Such policy fosters the interests and reflects the values of the dominant social groups, although not in a narrow way. In order to enhance the

"hegemonic" position of these groups and to control structural contradictions, such policy pursues collective interests as well, but within a well-defined division of labor and distribution of power in society. In other words, one can say that the goals of national interest are defined and pursued according to the respective power of various social classes and that they reflect to some extent the compromises that are worked out among them. For this reason the impact of multinational corporations on state policies is also differently evaluated by the various classes involved.

In the light of these remarks we will now abandon the postulate of unanimous policy goals vis-à-vis international capital and we will try to specify the general contradictions between multinational corporations and nation-states with regard to class antagonism. Maintaining the basic distinction between the parent country and the peripheral country where a multinational subsidiary operates, and focusing on the basic antagonism between labor and capital, we will discuss two sets of contradictions: (1) between international companies and labor unions of the peripheral country, and (2) between international companies and labor unions of the metropolitan country. This implies that labor unions, like nation-states and contrary to capital, are social entities that tend to be nationally organized. However, since there are international labor organizations, we will briefly review their strategies vis-à-vis the multinational challenge as well, as they appear in recent international congress resolutions and joint actions.

The conflict between national labor and international capital is only one of the social conflicts provoked by the latter. International capital is the source of potential and actual conflict with the "national" segments of the bourgeoisie and a variety of vested interests in the peripheral countries, and with the nationally based sectors of the metropolitan bourgeoisie as well. But, since social conflict with the working class seems to us the most important one, we will limit our discussion to this.

More specifically, we will examine two major types of effects of multinational corporations on labor in the peripheral countries: (1) the impact of foreign takeovers and foreign capital penetration on the labor market and the work organization in the peripheral countries; and (2) the impact of foreign control and internationalization of management on collective bargaining and labor conflict in general and, in particular, on union recognition, resistance to strikes because of production switching, level of bargaining, etc. Then we will discuss the effects of outward investments by multinational companies on the level and type of employment in the metropolitan country.

In the summary paper of the CGIL (Italian General Federation of Labor) at the April 1973 Turin seminar on "Trade Union Action and Multinational Corporations," the major concern was the type of industrial restructuring MNCs bring about.[2] The paper states that

the process of industrial restructuring fostered by multinational

companies without any planning and balanced growth policy implies in
most cases a reduction of employment, an intensification of work exploitation and a distorted use of productive rationalization.

Similarly, the British Trade Union Congress stresses the fact that a takeover by a
multinational corporation clearly means that employment becomes dependent on
the global performance of the company rather than on local performance.[3] More
specifically, this means that there will be a tendency toward increased specialization of the labor force as part of the optimization of the corporation's global resources and that attempts will be made to introduce work patterns in the work
organization and wage system that are different from the local experience.
Examples of this kind may be speed-ups, piece-rate types of wage calculation,
etc.

The major concern is clearly the fear of job losses due to industrial restructuring. Foreign takeovers often take place when the local firm runs up against
difficulties of various kinds—financial, technological, market related, etc.—and
the takeover implies a change in business strategy and structure in order to turn
the adverse tide. But, more important than that, the very fact of entering into
a worldwide operating concern basically transforms the local firm, which orients
its activity according to a general plan. Certain types of production can be
dropped, others added, whole departments and branches can be reshaped, the
whole division of labor within the business organization can be modified. The
shift from local firm to local subsidiary of an international company implies a
reshuffling of roles and statuses and, more often than not, an absolute loss of
jobs and/or a high turnover of workers.

Such consequences can be seen as costs of any process of rationalization of
production. The question is, however, who is going to pay such costs; the gist of
the labor struggles related to any process of industrial restructuring is the attempt
to control to some extent the process and to obtain some guarantee that it does
not follow exclusively the imperative of private profit, but that it takes into
account some notion of public interest. International companies are still less
concerned than national firms with social needs, as we have tried to show. If it
is hard to agree with the statement that "what is good for General Motors is
good for America," it is still harder to believe that what is good for General
Motors is good for Great Britain or any other country where GM has its subsidiaries.

In a process of industrial restructuring by foreign corporations, their degree
of discretionary power is much greater than that of domestic firms because they
can threaten to shift production and divert substantial financial flows to other
countries, whenever favorable conditions are not obtained.

Conversely, trade unions are much weaker, not only because they are constrained by their national character in the competition with international giants,
but also because their capacity for putting pressure on the corporations through

their influence on national agencies and governmental institutions is impaired by the very weakness of the nation state. Unions face—as does the whole country—the dilemma of either losing investments or accepting unfavorable terms of bargaining, a dilemma that sometimes takes the form of "blackmail." For this reason, the British Trade Union Congress, for instance, proposed that before any foreign takeover is sanctioned by the government, the latter should obtain prior guarantees about employment levels, forward manpower planning, skill patterns, retention of research facilities, and retention of British management.[4] And Scalia of the Italian CISL in his paper at the aforementioned Turin Seminar states that trade union struggles both in developed and underdeveloped countries should aim at strengthening the legislative and executive powers of the state in order to control international investments, credit and fiscal behavior, and to guarantee that the activities of international companies are consistent with the needs and plans of national development[5].

The second major type of problem raised by multinational corporations for the labor movement of peripheral countries concerns collective bargaining and industrial relations practices. The data gathered in different countries show that recognition of trade union rights and liberties is more problemmatic in the case of multinational corporations. In a 1967 survey the Trade Union Congress found that foreign-owned firms tended to take a much more systematic anti-trade union line than British firms in the equivalent position[6]. In 1970 the Italian CISL prepared a "black list" of twenty multinational corporations, including Nestlé, Kodak, and Gillette, which in several instances refused to deal with trade unions. But the number of multinational corporations that have refused recognition at one time or another is larger and includes IBM, Caterpillar Tractor, Roberts Arundel, Continental Oil, Goodyear, Firestone, United Fruit Co., DuPont, etc.[7] And, although this is not a behavior specific to such companies, it tends to be more widespread than in national firms.

International companies apply different methods in different countries. Wherever repressive governments exist and laws against strikes are enforced, MNCs find a congenial ground for their operations. Leaving aside the operations of such companies as the International Telegraph and Telephone Company that worked to subvert the legitimate democratic government of Chile, there are several less well-known examples of MNCs' interference in the working of local governments. Just as an example Firestone has been able to change labor laws in Nigeria.

Antitrade union policy is by no means confined to dependent countries, where labor movements are weak, or to reactionary regimes, where government takes a repressive stand against labor rights. Although in subtler ways such policy takes place in developed countries as well. A widespread tactic is that of forming company unions such as the "Workers Representation Committees" in order to break workers' actions. This is the case for instance with Kodak, Dupont, CGE, Union Carbide, where such "unions" sponsored and financed by the management are at work.

In general, however, the behavior of multinational companies varies greatly from one developed country to another. In the case of General Motors, for instance, the tendency to negoitate at company level and to stay outside the industrywide collective bargaining agreements is seen in Great Britain at Vauxhall, but not at the German Opel nor in GM French subsidiaries. Here again the flexibility of the multinational company is an asset in its relationships with different national labor movements, and its strategy aims at dividing the counterpart.

These traits of MNCs should not be overstressed. Corporate strategy toward labor is not significantly different from that of national firms in most cases. What is really important are the objective differences in terms of power to implement such strategy. In this respect MNCs tend to be larger enterprises, more dynamic and aggressive, with higher rates of profit often due to their oligopolistic position on the market. They can afford to pay higher wages wherever they are forced to and can show more elasticity in the bargaining process. Moreover, there are specific traits of MNCs besides the ones related to the processes of concentration and centralization of capital and common to all oligopolistic firms. These specific traits are rooted in the very international dimension of such firms. First of all, MNCs can minimize the financial cost of labor strikes and other slow-down methods by duplicating production and by using excess capacity in their subsidiaries abroad. Actual shifting of production quotas may not be necessary; in fact, the existence of alternative sources of supply allows management to threaten production switching, thus weakening labor actions. One can argue that such action is not so easy: Switching production means switching investments, a process that takes time and runs against national and international regulations. But, as we have pointed out elsewhere, there are a variety of accounting devices for transferring financial flows, which are available to MNCs, such as transfer prices, the use of service charges, and the like. Moreover, the cost of divesting before the whole life cycle of capital equipment is completed is also smaller than expected in most cases. Given the relatively fast turnover of capital goods in the more advanced economies—less than ten years—a substantial shift across the borders can be accomplished in a rather short time; the threat it implies is then not too remote.

Finally, as we have already remarked, MNCs are also less constrained by state interventions, both in the form of arbitrary regulations and of political influences of various kinds. Thus, trade unions can rely less on friendly agencies or groups within the state apparatus in order to check business power.

For all these reasons it seems clear that trade union action to be effective must try to coordinate national strategies in order to operate at the same international level at which MNCs work.

Effects on Labor in Metropolitan Countries

The contradictions between international capital and labor are not limited to the workers of the peripheral countries. In the metropolitan country as well the relationship between MNCs and trade unions give rise to problems that are specific to international capital and transcend the usual patterns of labor conflict. Multinational companies and in particular their outward investment have been under heavy attack from American trade unions in the 1970s. Criticisms of them are to a great extent representative of criticisms by labor in all parent countries.

Although American labor is by no means unified around the issue, both the AFL-CIO and the UAW have taken a militant stand. Among the major labor organizations only the Teamsters do not seem to be concerned about the problem. A possible explanation of this neglect is not so much the conservative political outlook of this union—which brought it to support the Republican party and the Nixon presidency—as the fact that its members are mostly drawn from the service sector of the economy rather than the manufacturing sector, and thus their jobs are less directly threatened by capital outflows.

Both the AFL-CIO and the UAW, on the other hand, are highly critical of United States-based multinational corporations; their analyses lead however to some interesting differences in terms of proposed legislation. Their views on the matter can be exemplified by discussing the statements made by Andrew J. Biemiller, director of the Department of Legislation of the AFL-CIO and by Leonard Woodcock, president of the UAW at the Hearings before the Subcommittee on International Trade of the U.S. Senate Committee on Finance in February-March 1973.[8] Biemiller points out that United States-based MNCs are a major factor in worsening the conditions of the American economy, through the export of American capital, labor, and technology. In his words "the devastating impact" these activities have includes:

1. The shutdown of American production and its reestablishment abroad where foreign markets are served and exports to the U.S. are manufactured
2. The location abroad of facilities for corporate expansion and the production of new products and improved products
3. The export of technology by direct transplant, by licensing, by patent agreement and by other methods, thereby eroding the base on which America's industrial society is built, much of which is paid for by American taxpayers
4. The export of capital to build an industrial base abroad at the expense of U.S. industry, the profits of which are often used to speculate in the world's monetary markets against the U.S. dollar[9]

The major concern is the loss of jobs. Outward direct investment can have several negative implications for domestic employment: Plants can be shut down in favor of overseas production; imports from foreign subsidiaries can take the place of American-made products; and foreign subsidiaries can obtain market quotas previously serviced by an American company on the market where it is located or in third countries. According to the 1970 Commerce Department's

Special Survey on Multinational Companies, in the 298 American firms with foreign affiliates analyzed, while manufacturing jobs rose 7.6 percent, employment in their foreign subsidiaries increased 26.5 percent.[10] Moreover, in major industries at home, such as transportation equipment, electrical equipment, and nonelectrical machinery, where multinationals are a key factor, there have been substantial job losses between 1966 and 1972.

The effects of export technology are not less dramatic, according to AFL-CIO. In the aerospace industry, which is taken by Biemiller as the major example of such a trend, United States-based MNCs have allegedly sold and licensed to foreign firms the production of highly sophisticated products, such as the Thor-Delta launch rocket and missile launch system, the F-5E fighter plane, and various commercial aircraft. Thus, "a massive destruction (is made) to one of America's most advanced industries in terms of technology, highly skilled personnel and national security."[11]   From this analysis the AFL-CIO has drawn a well-defined set of legislative proposals, which have been expressed in the Burke-Hartke bill, introduced in Congress in 1972 and 1973. The bill would impose mandatory quotas on imports, increase taxation on earnings from foreign plants, extend restrictions on capital investment overseas, and require strict labelling of the origins of American brand-name products. The bill is clearly an attack on international capital, which is however waged in protectionist and isolationist terms. MNCs are criticized not so much as the most advanced expression of capitalist development, but as un-American institutions. As Steve Babson has suggested, this position can be seen as an attempt by trade-union leadership to direct rank and file frustrations toward an external enemy, that is, foreign firms and foreign subsidiaries of MNCs that undermine American jobs and markets with their cheap imports. "Nothing would make labor leadership more happy than to be able to attack the corporations not as class enemies, but as un-American, unpatriotic 'fellow travellers' of foreign capitalists."[12]   And a complement of such a nationalist position is likely to be the demand for defense spending to counteract sagging employment.

From the point of view of the working class of peripheral countries, the AFL-CIO attitude is the source of conflicting feelings. While some demands for more regulation of multinational activities are well received, the nationalist flavor and the absence of any commitment to solidarity with foreign labor movements are not encouraging.

The UAW position as expressed in Leonard Woodcock's statement before the Committee on Finance hearings substantially shares the AFL-CIO analysis of many of the effects of capital export on full employment at home, labor productivity, competition, and industrial concentration, trade, etc. But, at the same time, Woodcock concentrates on a set of suggested policies, which ask a regulation of multinational corporations, while trying to avoid protectionist implications. At the first question of the Subcommittee, "What can be done to

improve the competitive position of United States industry in world markets and
to create additional employment in the United States and what contributions
can multinational companies make to this end?" Woodcock replies with a seven-
point program of at least partial answers:

1. Effective full employment policies
2. Elimination of tax incentives that encourage investment in other countries at
    the expense of the United States
3. Establishment of a licensing requirement for foreign investment by United
    States corporations
4. Imposing a penalty tax on United States corporations that refuse to compete
    against foreign-made products
5. Amendment of the GATT agreement to provide for international fair labor
    standards
6. Encouraging use of the dollar overhang to reduce the powers of the MNCs
7. Encouraging technological and product research and development by Ameri-
    can industries.[13]

The major differences between the UAW and the AFL-CIO proposals are:
(a) the refusal by the former to adopt a protectionist position through the enforcement of mandatory quotas for import, (b) the attempt to reduce the negative
effects of MNCs on American labor through full employment policy and research
and development (i.e., a demand for positive state intervention besides its negative
actions); and (c) the attempt to regulate the behavior of MNCs not only at home
but in the peripheral countries as well.

The last point is particularly important. The UAW has suggested a new code
of enforceable international law, parallel to domestic regulation that would
channel private investment into socially desirable areas; it has also suggested an
allocation of funds by international agencies—such as the International Monetary
Fund—for the development of less developed countries. These demands, together
with the request for international fair labor standards, are not simple concessions
to the progressive ideology of the UAW, but are rooted in a different perception
of the costs and benefits of a neoisolationist policy for American labor. A significant part of the UAW membership is employed in industries, such as aircrafts
and agricultural machinery, which are among the most important United States
exports and would be damaged by eventual retaliations by foreign countries.
The UAW strategy, on the one hand, tries to weaken through more regulations
and controls by national and international organizations and, on the other, tries
to coordinate labor struggles in different countries in order to foster a united
labor response.

The AFL-CIO position is only apparently more militant. Actually, in order
to foster its neoprotectionist attitude the AFL-CIO overstresses some consequences of MNCs action, with the result that they are easily argued against by

business representatives. The business view has been expressed in a variety of books, articles, and statements. These writings generally stress the fact that: (a) MNCs are the most competitive sectors of the American economy and a bullwark against the aggressiveness displayed by foreign competitors; (b) they have a significant positive effect on the balance of payments and the balance of trade; and (c) they "help to assure the U.S. economy access, on a commercially viable basis, to vital industrial raw materials, including petroleum and other energy resources."[14] The National Association of Manufacturers points out the same argument and in particular, denies that the technology gap between the United States and the other industrialized nations is narrowing because of technology transfers. Moreover, this association stressed the fact that United States-based MNCs significantly help American exports and employment because of the fact that between 25 percent and 35 percent of total United States exports go to subsidiaries of American corporations.[15]

It is hard to come to definite conclusions about the conflicting evidence presented by American labor and American business on the problem. It is, however, possible to take a stand, by distinguishing various aspects. For instance, while the negative implications for employment of MNCs are rather clear, the charges of exporting relevant technology are not equally convincing. Actually, one of the basic factors of the continuing hegemony of United States-based capital is the control of highly advanced technology; and the contrary evidence provided by the AFL-CIO on the aerospace and electronics industry seems greatly exaggerated in order to justify protectionist demands.

It is also very important to compare the major criticisms advanced by American labor with those put forth by trade unions of the peripheral countries. In particular, one should distinguish between those MNC actions that are resented because they do not favor the national interests of the metropolitan country from those that are fought against because they hinder the position of the working class both of the metropolitan and the peripheral countries. The difference is relevant politically, since stressing the former MNC actions can lead to divisive behavior of the various labor movements, while stressing the latter actions can lead to international coorpoeration and joint labor action. The protectionist suggestions of the AFL-CIO are instances of the first type and the demand for international fair labor standards by the UAW is an instance of the second type.

By the same token the concern with either exporting or expropriating technology is an issue on which an agreement between labor unions of different countries is hard to achieve. Actually, American labor and European trade unions seem to come to contradictory conclusions: While the AFL-CIO complains about the loss of a technological edge because United States-based MNCs sell and license products to foreign firms, British and Canadian trade unions, among others, denounce the weakening of the research and development apparatus of their counties because of increasing multinational control of sensitive industries. In this case parallel legislation rather than coordinated action seems to be the most likely union policy, since research and development problems are a matter of national policy.

Joint actions can, on the other hand, stem from the fear of job losses that is shared by labor both in the metropolitan and in the peripheral countries. In fact, the export of capital from one country to another does not necessarily imply a zero-sum transfer of employment opportunities. A process of industrial restructuring in Italy or Great Britain can imply a reduction of employment levels in these countries, since it is carried on in terms of the global strategy of profit maximization of the MNC, and, at the same time, can eliminate potential employment opportunities in the United States.

More important than the cumulative effects on employment because of runaway plants in some counties and industrial restructuring in some others, however, are the implications for labor conflict in both types of counties. The control of financial flows that can be directed toward a given economy in a way largely independent of the power of the national governments and labor movements gives MNCs the opportunity to apply a strategy of *divide et impera*. As Steve Babson remarks,

> . . . the underlying question is not how many people are actually laid off, but what effect the threat of being laid off has on the balance of power between workers and owners. In this case, the option to move abroad does not have to be exercised by management to achieve its desired effects. All the company has to do is periodically threaten . . . that it might have to move overseas if workers make "unreasonable" demands.[16]

MNCs are more powerful than other capitalist organizations because they have the advantages of operating on an international scale, while continuing to rely on the support of their metropolitan governments and, to a smaller extent, on the national governments of the countries where they have their subsidiaries. Moreover, MNCs are powerful because they face a labor response that is divided and scattered in various countries. Corresponding to their specific strengths, however, are specific weaknesses. MNCs double nature as simultaneously national and international entities can bring about the reaction of host governments and the suspicions of their metropolitan state as well. And their double nature can make them vulnerable to a coordinated action by labor movements of the various countries in which they operate. A fact which the UAW seems more conscious of than the AFL-CIO is that international labor struggles are the most effective way to defend the interests of American workers as well.

The MNCs threat to shift production from one country to another can be counteracted by the counterthreat to strike in all the countries where the firm actually operates or can move. The attempt by a MNC to break the resistance of workers in a given country by increasing production in other firms can be

neutralized or severely weakened by refusing extra-hours work in all its plants.
Fiscal and monetary regulations aiming at curbing MNCs inflationary actions
through currency speculations and the like can be supported by labor movements of different countries. And, finally, even such radical measures as
nationalization of foreign subsidiaries by local governments can be supported
by labor movements of both metropolitan and peripheral countries.[a]

Trade Union Action at the International Level

The last remarks lead us to the final topic of this chapter, that is the trade
union role at the international level in coping with the multinational challenge.
It is in fact clear that a trade union strategy to be effective must achieve a high
degree of coordination among different labor movements and the implementation of fair industrial relations practices in all countries where international
capital operates.

Trade union action at the international level has taken the form in the first
place of bilateral contacts between unions organizing workers in the same multinational company. These contacts may take place within a given international
labor association or directly by the unions concerned. There are several instances
of successful coordination, among which the joint action of the Pirelli-Dunlop
workers, the frequent meetings among Italian and French trade unionists at the
time of the fusion of Fiat and Citroen, the binational workers committees in
such firms as Saint Gobain, Hoechst, Solvay, etc. Examples of coordinated actions
exist also outside the metal and chemical industries, which are traditionally the
most active ones in this respect.

These attempts, however, often run against the obsolete confrontation between the two major world confederations, that is, the International Confederation of Free Trade Unions (ICFTU), which gathers a good part of the trade
union movements of most industrialized countries, and the World Labor Federation, which is Marxist-oriented. These international organizations are still marked
in varying degrees by the cold-war climate during which they were either formed
of reshaped. And, as a by-product of cold-war antagonism, they have been bypassed both by the developments of capital concentration and internationalization and by labor response. The international trade secretariats of the ICFTU,
in particular, are still marked by an obsolete anticommunism and by their original function of dividing the labor movements of such countries as Italy through

---

[a]At the international seminar on "Multinational Corporations and Labor Unions,"
held in Nijmegen in 1973, American labor representatives supported the proposals of
nationalization by European governments on United States-based MNCs European
subsidiaries.

financing trade union splitting along ideological and political lines. The recent attitude of the International Federation of Chemical and General Workers Unions (ICF) toward the action taken by Italian and British workers of Pirelli-Dunlop is clear: Instead of making it the basis for a wider coordination of labor responses against a powerful MNC, the ICF general secretariat has attacked this action and has presented it as a Communist move to undermine the ICFTU's leadership in the chemical industry. A similar attitude has taken the International Metalworkers' Federation (IMF) toward the attempt made by the Italian FLM (the United Metal Workers Federation, which represents Communist, Socialist, Catholic workers all together) together with the Catholic and the Communist French trade unions in the same industry to organize an international trade union conference of the workers in the FIAT group. The IMF has vetoed such action and its Italian partners have been forced to recognize it.

The opposition between the two major types of international labor organizations is rooted in Cold War politics, but is it not justified by the objective interests of the workers represented. Actually, most of the recommendations and the actions taken by either one during several international conferences and meetings are very similar. In its recent conferences, in Turin in 1968 and in London in 1971, the IMF has set up permanent autoworkers' councils for the major companies with the aim of exchanging information and agreeing on bargaining tactics; moreover, it has spelled out a set of objectives including protection of purchasing power and ironing out of wage differentials; trade union rights at shop floor levels on such questions as safety arrangements, work tempo and the like; guaranteed annual wages, shorter hours without loss of pay and longer holidays, etc. And the ICF held similar conferences on coordinated collective bargaining, set up similar councils for unions dealing with the same company as was particularly active in urging the United Nations to lay down a code of conduct for multinational companies, which should include the obligation to abide by all relevant ILO conventions and recommendations, to comply with social legislation and to conform to established national patterns of industrial relations.[17]

The resolutions and suggestions of the World Labor Federation stem from a more radical analysis of the role of international capital, but are not substantially different from those of the International trade secretariats. At the international meeting held in Santiago (Chile) in March 1973, Jorge Godoy, President of the Chilean trade unions summarized the conclusions of the discussion that witnessed the active role of participants from all over the world, by asking that: (1) the defense of labor conditions, labor freedom, work safety, in order to avoid the MNCs taking advantage of differences among countries; (2) the respect for international agreements on union representation rights and collective bargaining and social security; (3) effective ways to control MNCs employment, profits, price policy, union rights; (4) the obligation to reinvest profits in the country where they have been realized and to nationalize MNCs in order to guarantee to each country the right to exploit its own natural resources; (5) full rights to strike, nationally and internationally.[18]

And at the most recent meeting of the World Labor Federation held in Damascus in July 1974 proposals were made to organize a world conference of all trade unions, in order to study the problems and implications for trade unions of international capital and of the economic relations between socialist and capitalist countries. Moreover, while Third World representatives insisted on nationalizing natural resources, Italian and French delegates appeared more concerned with the need to coordinate a strategy against MNCs, to enact an international code of behavior guaranteed by the United Nations and to give E.C.O.S.O.C. the specific task to follow systematically MNCs policy and to coordinate similar research activities at ILO, FAO, UNESCO and other international organizations.

Whereas agreements between the two major labor confederations are hard to achieve in the short run, there is a growing impatience at the national level with obsolete ideological cleavages and cold war attitudes. Bilateral agreements among workers in the same international company and between labor federations of different countries, whatever their political affiliation, are growing. The process of labor unification in Italy, which should cancel the remnants of the cold war consequences and has already taken place in the most militant unions such as the metal workers, the pragmatic attitude of the British trade unions and of the French Catholic union, the changing status of the CGIL (the Italian Marxist union) in the World Labor Federation, are all symptoms that European trade unions are moving in the direction of labor joint action across national boundaries. A closer coordination with some sectors of American labor is also gaining momentum. The rapid expansion and growing aggressiveness of international capital made this coordination an imperative rather than a possible option for labor movements all over the world.

Notes

1. A. Martinelli and E. Somaini, "Multinational Corporations and Nation States," *Kapitalistate*, 1 (1973); A. Martinelli and E. Somaini, "Nation-States and Multinational Corporations" in K. Tudyka, ed., *Multinational Corporations and Labour Unions* (Nijmegen: Verkuitgave Sun, 1973).
2. Ufficio Internazionale CGIL, *Le società multinazionali*, Rome, April 26, 1973 (mimeographed).
3. Trade Union Congress, *Report of a Conference on International Companies*, (London: Congress House, October 21, 1970).
4. Ibid., p. 8.
5. Umberto Scalia, *Il movimento sindacale di fronte alle multinazionali*, Turin, 30-31 March 1973 (mimeographed).

6. Trade Union Congress, *Report of A Conference on International Companies,* p. 8

7. International Confederation of Free Trade Unions (ICFTU), *The Multinational Challenge*, Brussels, September 1971, p. 19.

8. *"Multinational Corporations,"* Hearings before the Subcommittee on International Trade of the Committee on Finance, U.S. Senate, 93rd Cong., sess. 1, February–March 1973.

9. Ibid., p. 333.

10. U.S. Commerce Department, *"Special Survey of U.S. Multinational Companies,"* 1970.

11. *"Multinational Corporations,"* Hearings, p. 337.

12. Steve Babson, The Multinational Corporation and Labor, *The Review of Radical Political Economics*, 5, no. 1 (Spring 1973), p. 30.

13. *"Multinational Corporations,"* Hearings, pp. 277–78.

14. International Economic Policy Association, The Center for Multinational Studies, "The Benefits and Problems of Multinational Corporations," A *Compendium of Papers* submitted to the Subcommittee on International Trade of the Committee on Finance, U.S. Senate, 93rd Cong., sess. 1, February–March 1973, p. 94.

15. National Association of Manufacturers, *"U.S. Stake in World Trade and Investment: the Role of the Multinational Corporation,"* New York, 1972.

16. Steve Babson, Multinational Corporation and Labor, p. 26.

17. ICFTU, *The Multinational Challenge*, pp. 24–27.

18. Author's summary of major points in the reports of the meeting.

About the Contributors

Ike Balbus teaches social and political theory as an associate professor at York College of the City University of New York. He is the author of *The Dialectics of Legal Repression: Black Rebels Before the American Criminal Courts* (1973) and a number of articles on pluralism, elite theory, and Marxism; he is working on the Marxian theory of the capitalist state as well as on a long-term project on work, language, and sexuality in contemporary societies. Professor Balbus received the Ph.D. in political science from the University of Chicago and taught at Princeton University before joining the faculty at the City University of New York.

Manuel Castells received the Ph.D. in sociology from the École des Hautes Études en Sciences Sociales, Paris, where he directs a seminar on urban sociology. He has been a visiting professor at the University of Montreal, the Catholic University of Chile, the Latin American Faculty of Social Sciences (UNESO), and the University of Wisconsin-Madison. Professor Castells has published several books, including *La Question Urbaine* (1972; translated into six languages), *Luttes urbaines* (1973), *Monopolville* (1974), and *La lucha de clases en Chile* (1974). His research concerns urban politics, social movements, sociology of development, and the analysis of the consumption process in advanced capitalist societies. He is a member of the Centre d'Étude des Mouvements Sociaux (E.H.E.S.S. and C.N.R.S., Paris).

Stephen S. Cohen is Associate Professor in the Department of City and Regional Planning at the University of California at Berkeley. He has worked extensively on French politics, economics, and planning; his recent publications in that area include *Modern Capitalist Planning: The French Model* (1969); "The Politics of French Regional Planning" (with George W. Ross) in William Alsonso and John Friedman, eds., *Regional Planning* (1975); and "Evolution des Services et Amenagement du Territoire" (with John Dyckman) Service Régional de l'Equipment de la Région Parisienne (1975).

Murray Edelman is Professor of Political Science at the University of Wisconsin-Madison. Among his publications are *Politics as a Symbolic Action: Mass Arousal and Quiescence* (1971); *The Politics of Wage-Price Decisions: A Four Country Analysis* (coauthored with R.W. Fleming, 1965); and *The Symbolic Uses of Politics* (1964).

Charles Goldfinger is a candidate for the Ph.D. in the Department of City and Regional Planning at the University of California, Berkeley. He is a member of the Young Professionals program at the World Bank.

445

Pierre Hassner is Senior Research Associate at the Fondation Nationale des Sciences Politiques (Centre d'Études des relations internationales), Paris, and Professor of Politics at the Johns Hopkins University in Bologna. He is the author of *Les Diplomaties occidentals: unité et contradictions* (with J. Neuhouse, 1966); *Les alliances sont-elles depassés?* (1966); *Change and Security in Europe* (1968); *Europe in the Age of Negotiation* (1973); chapters on Kant and Hegel in Strauss and Cropsey, eds., *History of Political Philosophy* (1973); and of numerous articles in professional journals.

Stephen Hymer was Professor of Economics at the Graduate Faculty of the New School for Social Research in New York. He was killed in an automobile accident in February 1974. He received the Ph.D. from the Massachusetts Institute of Technology in 1960 and taught at M.I.T., Yale University, the University of Toronto, the University of Ghana, the University of the West Indies, and the University of Chile. Among his publications are "The Multinational Corporation and International Oligopoly: The Non-American Challenge," in Charles P. Kindleberger, ed., *The International Corporation: A Symposium* (1970); "The Internationalization of Capital," *Journal of Economic Issues,* 6, 1 (1972), and numerous other articles in professional journals.

James R. Kurth is Associate Professor of Political Science at Swarthmore College. His recent publications include "A Widening Gyre: The Logic of American Weapons Procurement," *Public Policy* (Summer 1971), and a slightly revised version of the same article in Lee Rainwater, ed., *Social Problems and Public Policy: Inequality and Justice* (1974); "The Political Economy of Weapons Procurement: The Follow-on Imperative," *The American Economic Review, Papers and Proceedings* (May 1972), reprinted in Rendigs Fels, ed., *The Second Crisis of Economic Theory* (1972); "Aerospace Production Lines and American Defense Spending," in Richard G. Head and Ervin J. Rokke, eds., *American Defense Policy III* (1973) and also in Steven Rosen, ed., *Testing the Theory of the Military-Industrial Complex* (1973); and "United States Foreign Policy and Latin American Military Rule," in Philippe C. Schmitter, ed., *Military Rule in Latin America: Functions, Consequences, and Perspectives* (1973).

Theodore J. Lowi is the John L. Senior Professor of American Institutions at Cornell University. He also has served on the faculty of the University of Chicago. Professor Lowi's books include *At the Pleasure of The Mayor* (1964); *Private Life and Public Order* (1968); *The End of Liberalism* (1969); and *The Politics of Disorder* (1971).

Michael Mann received the B.A. and the Ph.D. from Oxford University; he is Senior Lecturer in Sociology at the University of Essex, England. His main publications are "The Social Cohesion of Liberal Democracy," *American Sociological Review* (1970); *Workers on the Move* (1973); and *Consciousness and Action in the Western Working Class* (1973). Professor Mann is working on a general theoretical study of the relationship between economic, ideological, and military power in society.

Peter Marris studied at Cambridge University and has undertaken research in Britain, the United States, and East and West Africa. His work has been largely concerned with patterns of response to change, both personal and societal. Mr. Marris is the author of six books, including *Dilemmas of Social Reform: Poverty and Community Action in the United States* (with Martin Rein, 1974) and *Loss and Change* (1974). For many years he was associated with the Institute of Community Studies, and is currently a senior research officer at the Centre for Environmental Studies in London.

Andrew Martin is a research fellow at the Harvard Center for European Studies, where he is completing a book on the evolution of Swedish Social Democratic economic policy. He has taught at Columbia University, where he did his graduate work, and then at the University of Massachusetts (Amherst) and Boston University. He is the author of *The Politics of Economic Policy in the United States* (1973), and "Labor Movement Parties and Inflation: Contrasting Responses in Britain and Sweden," *Polity,* VII, 4 (1975). His main interest is in the comparative politics of economic policy in the United States and Western Europe.

Alberto Martinelli received the doctoral degree in economics from the Bocconi University of Milan and the Ph.D. in sociology from the University of California at Berkeley. He teaches sociology and is director of the Institute of Sociology at the University of Milan. Professor Martinelli has published books and essays on sociological theory, economic development, and social movements. He is coordinator, with Neil Smelser, of the ISA group on "Economy and Society" and is Italian editor of the review *Kapitalistate.*

Renate Mayntz received the B.A. from Wellesley College and the Ph.D. in sociology from the Free University in Berlin. Before going to the University of Bologna as Professor of Sociology she held chairs at the Free University in Berlin and the Hochschule für Verwaltungswissenschaften in Speyer. She has taught at Columbia University and the New School for Social Research in New York, at the University of Edinburgh, and at FLACSO (Facultad Latino-Americana de Ciencias Sociales) in Santiago. Professor Mayntz is the author of *Soziologie der Organisation* (1963); coauthor (with Niklas Luhmann) of *Personal im Öffenlichen Dienst-Eintritt und Karrieren* (1973); and coauthor (with Fritz W. Scharpf) of *Policy-making in the Federal Bureaucracy* (1975).

Martin Rein is Professor of Urban Studies and Planning at the Massachusetts Institute of Technology. He is the author of *Social Policy* (1974); *Work & Welfare Go Together* (1972); and coauthor (with Peter Marris) of *Dilemmas in Social Reform* (1967). He is involved in a cross-national study of family income with Lee Rainwater and Christopher Jencks. Professor Rein's next book, *The Uses of Social Analysis,* will be published in the fall of 1975.

Robert Solo, educated at Harvard University and Cornell University, is Professor of Economics at Michigan State University. He is the author of forty-six articles in journals of economics, business, philosophy, and law; and of seven books, including *Economic Organizations and Social Systems,* (1967) and *The Political Authority and the Market System,* (1974). Professor Solo has taught at a number of American and French universities and has worked with various federal agencies, the National Planning Association, the OECD, the Economic Development Administration of Puerto Rico, the National Conference Board, and NASA. At Michigan State he has recently instituted a program to train doctoral-level graduates for the organization and planning tasks of positive government.

About the Editors

Leon N. Lindberg is Professor of Political Science at the University of Wisconsin-Madison. He received the Ph.D. from the University of California at Berkeley in 1962. Since then he has taught at the University of Wisconsin, and also has been a research associate at the Center for International Affairs at Harvard University (1964-65 and 1967), a visiting research scholar at the Carnegie Endowment for International Peace, a visiting professor at the Institut Universitaires de Hautes Études Internationales in Geneva (1972-73), and a visiting professor at the University of Geneva in 1975. Among his publications are *Europe's Would-Be Polity* (with S. Scheingold, 1970), *Regional Integration: Theory and Practice* (coeditor and author, 1971), and *Politics and the Future of Industrial Society* (editor and author, forthcoming in 1976). Professor Lindberg's research interests include comparative policy analysis, political economy, and social and political change in advanced capitalist societies. He is Chairman of the Council for European Studies, a member of the Board of Editors of *International Organization* and the Panel of Consultants of *Comparative Political Studies,* and Director of the Center for Comparative Policy Research.

Robert R. Alford is Professor of Sociology and Chairperson of the Board of Studies in Sociology at the University of California at Santa Cruz. He is the author of Party and Society (1963), *Bureaucracy and Participation* (1969), and *Health Care Politics* (1975), and is working on a book-length monograph on paradigms of state-society relations, an outline of which appears in this volume. Professor Alford's future research will focus on comparative studies of the political economy of urban social services.

Colin Crouch is a lecturer in sociology at the London School of Economics and Political Science. He is working on problems of the changing role of the state in industrial relations with Britain and other European societies. With Alessandro Pizzorno and various national research teams, he is involved in an international project on the resurgence of industrial conflict in six European countries. His previous publications include *The Student Revolt* (1970) and various articles on higher education, social policy, social stratification, and industrial relations. He is the author of various pamphlets for the Fabian Society, of which he is Vice-Chairman.

Claus Offe is Professor of Political Science and Sociology at the University of Bielefeld in West Germany. He also has served as a research associate at the West European Studies Center at Harvard University (1970) and as a

449

member of the Max Planck Institute in Starnberg, West Germany (1971-1975).
Among Professor Offe's publications are *Leistungsprinzip und industrielle
Arbeit* (1970), *Strukturprobleme des kapitalistischen Staates* (1972), and
Berufsbildungsreform (1975). He received the Ph.D. from the University of
Frankfurt in 1968.